THE Yale Child Study Center Guide to Understanding Your Child

THE Yale Child Study Center Guide to Understanding Your Child

HEALTHY DEVELOPMENT FROM BIRTH TO ADOLESCENCE

LINDA C. MAYES, M.D.,
AND DONALD J. COHEN, M.D.

WITH

John E. Schowalter, M.D., and Richard H. Granger, M.D.
Yale Child Study Center

J. L. Bell • Editorial Consultant
W. Rodney Torbert • Illustrator

LITTLE,   BROWN   AND   COMPANY
BOSTON   •   NEW   YORK   •   LONDON

Originally published in hardcover by Little, Brown and Company, February 2002
First paperback edition, February 2003

The authors gratefully acknowledge the permission
of the Yale University Press to base much of chapter 34
on *Divorce and Your Child: Practical Suggestions for Parents*,
by Sonja Goldstein, LL.B., and Albert J. Solnit, M.D.,
copyright © 1984 by Yale University.

Library of Congress Cataloging-in-Publication Data
Mayes, Linda C.
The Yale Child Study Center guide to understanding your child : healthy development
from birth to adolescence / Linda C. Mayes, and Donald J. Cohen with John E. Schowalter . . .
[et al.]. — 1st ed.
p.   cm.
Includes index.
ISBN 0-316-95432-2 (hc) / 0-316-79432-5 (pb)
1. Child rearing.   2. Child development.   3. Parent and child.   I. Cohen, Donald J.
II. Yale University. Child Study Center.   III. Title.
HQ769 .M373 2002
649'.1 — dc21   00-039116

10   9   8   7   6   5   4   3   2   1

Q-FF

Book design by Fearn Cutler deVicq
Printed in the United States of America

For Dr. Donald Cohen
Our colleague, mentor, and friend
Dor l'dor
(From generation to generation)
l'chaim
(to life)

Contents

Preface

Every creative endeavor is the result of many events, many interchanges, many people. The development of this book is no different. Its behind-the-scenes story starts with the Yale Child Study Center, where hundreds of faculty and friends have devoted their lives to understanding and caring for children and their families.

Beginning in 1911 under the leadership of Dr. Arnold Gesell, the Child Study Center was the site of some of the earliest work on children's development in the United States. Dr. Gesell built the Center on the twin principles of sponsoring careful observation and study of children and making the most up-to-date findings available to parents in an easily accessible, almost poetic style. His now-classic books describing children's development from infancy to adolescence continue to be translated and read around the world. They are the bases of countless other books for parents.

Dr. Gesell's successor as director of the Center was Dr. Milton Senn, another pediatrician and child psychiatrist. Dr. Senn had a keen interest in the inner lives of children and child psychoanalysis. His enthusiasm and vision attracted many young and talented psychiatrists, pediatricians, psychologists, and educators to the Center, such as Dr. Sally Provence and Dr. Samuel Ritvo. With this expanding and energetic faculty, the Center developed state-of-the-art clinical services for children and their families that included individual psychotherapy and psychoanalysis; consultation to schools, hospitals, and pediatric clinics; and work with child-protection and social-services agencies. In the middle years of the twentieth century, the Center's faculty was working with children in orphanages, establishing therapeutic nurseries, and beginning its highly respected child-care program for the children of Yale faculty and staff and other families in New Haven.

Dr. Albert Solnit succeeded Dr. Senn as director of the Child Study Center. Also trained in pediatrics as well as child psychiatry, Dr. Solnit brought the Center into an even more active role in the greater community. His close friendship with Anna Freud and members of the Yale Law School facilitated a series of creative books considering the best interests of children from broken, neglectful, and abusive homes. The Center's faculty gained a national and international reputation for their advocacy on behalf of the most vulnerable and disadvantaged children.

Equally dedicated to careful, state-of-the-art research on child development, Dr. Solnit recruited Dr. Donald Cohen to the Center. Dr. Cohen devoted his early career to working with children with autism and to understanding other serious problems in early development. Many more well-trained, creative scientists joined the Center during Dr. Solnit's tenure. When Dr. Cohen succeeded Dr. Solnit as director, he continued to build the Center's research programs in developmental neuroscience and early child development, while maintaining its dedication to providing mental-health services to children in the greatest need.

Since its beginning, the Child Study Center's highest priority has been to help parents do their best for their children. Members of the faculty have worked closely with parents through their clinical work and counseling, by writing books and magazine columns, and in seminars and classes. This book is just one result of that commitment.

In addition, the faculty and staff at the Center work closely together and value collaboration. Nearly every new creation from the Center bears the mark of this collective influence and echoes the voices of colleagues past and present. This book certainly does. We feel deep gratitude for our many predecessors, including Dr. Arnold Gesell, Dr. Milton Senn, Dr. Albert Solnit, Dr. Sally Provence and Dr. Samuel Ritvo. *The Yale Child Study Center Guide to Understanding Your Child* could not have been written without the wise counsel and collegial support of all of the Center's faculty. We must also thank the many families who seek our help, and our own families and friends for standing by us as we work. Just as this book is about understanding and supporting your child's development, our colleagues' understanding and support has made it possible for us to nurture this project and bring it to fruition.

We would like to express our appreciation to several other persons who were essential to this book. We are most grateful for the wise counsel of Lisa Adams of the Garamond Agency; this project was possible only with her ever-present support. Thankfully, John Bell was our editorial consultant who skillfully helped us manage all the intricacies of the project, gently reminded us when we strayed into academic prose, and showed us where to clarify — or even to throw away and start over. Rod Torbert's sensitive illustrator's eye visually illuminates our words with the everyday lives of children and their parents; we hope this book brings his artistry to the deserved attention of many. We are also indebted to Phoebe Hoss for graciously sharing her editorial wisdom and for helping us focus and clarify our writing voice. Our appreciation to Diana Grubbs for helping us with the first months of research in the project; to Alicia Grendziszewski for her administrative support; and to Marion Mayes for ably and readily stepping in when we most needed assistance.

Our illustrator, Rod Torbert, would also like to gratefully acknowledge the help of Maureen Adams, Judith Arsenault and her husband, Andrew, David and Robin Broadbent, Joseph Chapline, and all those who served as models for the drawings in this book.

Finally, while the essence of this book is about birth, development, and the beginning of families, it is also about the cycles of life. As we were bringing the project to completion, two members of our authorial team died.

Dr. Richard Granger died early in the spring of 2001. Dick was a much-respected developmental pediatrician who made his career helping families understand their children's development and teaching pediatricians how to understand children's minds as well as their bodies. He was a gifted writer with an ability to make the most complex concepts crystal clear. He wrote his own book for parents and was a fervent advocate for children. We deeply miss our friend and colleague and trust he would feel proud and fulfilled by what we have done together in this book.

Ironically, the final page proofs for this book arrived on October 3, 2001 — the day after Dr. Donald Cohen died following a valiant struggle with cancer. Dr. Cohen was director of the Child Study Center since 1983. Under his leadership, the Center became internationally recognized for its multidisciplinary programs of clinical and basic research, professional education, clinical services, and advocacy for children and families. In addition to his many scholarly achievements, Donald had a remarkable ability to bring colleagues together in the spirit of inquiry and collaboration. His highest value was the importance of mentorship. Many members of the Child Study Center faculty were his students and began their careers under his collegial hand and constant encouragement. In that vein, he brought our authorial team together and was very proud of this newest chapter in the Child Study Center's efforts to reach out to parents and families. Just as we encourage parents and children to do in this book, Donald celebrated life with family and friends. We mourn his life cut short for all he had yet to give, but celebrate his durable presence in our lives and throughout this book.

We want to thank our colleagues from the Yale Medical School and Yale University communities who have contributed their expertise to *The Yale Child Study Center Guide to Understanding Your Child*:

Steven Berkowitz, M.D.
Jon Boone
Joanne Burger, M.D.
Nancy Close, Ph.D.
Phyllis Cohen, Ed.D.
Alice Colonna, M.A.
James Comer, M.D.

Catherine Cox, M.S.W.
Kirsten Dahl, Ph.D.
Robert Evans, M.D.
Barbara Fussiner, M.A.
Norris Haynes, Ph.D.
Saylor Heidemann, M.S.
John Holmberg, M.S.

Carla Horwitz, M.Sc.
Lisa Hunter, Ph.D.
Sharon Lynn Kagan, Ph.D.
Ami Klin, Ph.D.
Daniel S. Lewin, Ph.D.
Paul Lombroso, M.D.
Valerie Maholmes, Ph.D.

Jean Marachi, M.D.

Andrés Martin, M.D.

Gretchen Myhre, educator

Lola Nash, M.A.

Barbara Nordhaus, M.S.W.

Rhea Paul, Ph.D.

Sandra Porter

Kyle D. Pruett, M.D.

Mary Schwab-Stone, M.D.

Dorothy G. Singer, Ed.D.

Jerome L. Singer, Ph.D.

Albert J. Solnit, M.D.

Dorothy Stubbe, M.D.

Flora Vaccarino, Ph.D.

Lawrence Vitulano, Ph.D.

Katherine Walden, M.A.

Morris Wessel, M.D.

Preston Wiles, M.D.

Edward F. Zigler, Ph.D.

Lynne Zimmerman, Ph.D.

THE Yale Child Study Center Guide to Understanding Your Child

Introduction

Child rearing — its joys, its worries, its aims — goes back to the dawn of history. To achieve this vital human task, parents looked then, and in the millenniums since, to tradition as a guide and brought up their children largely to conform to the needs of society. It is only relatively recently — owing to the many advances in science and psychology of the nineteenth century — that parents in Western society have begun to question the traditional approach. Now, rather than seeing children as creatures of society, parents tend to think of each child as an individual with his or her own patterns and processes of development. As a result, parents consider themselves responsible both for fostering their child's development in accordance with his or her personal needs and for helping him or her grow up to function as a productive and responsible member of society.

Ever since the first stirrings of the science of child development in the early twentieth century, books on how parents should rear their children have proliferated. These books, coming from many different points of view, all strive to help parents be more effective by giving them the newest knowledge about children. *The Yale Child Study Center Guide to Understanding Your Child* builds upon that foundation as it seeks not only to help you understand your child and his or her development from before birth to adolescence, but also goes further to explore how you understand yourself as a parent.

Since 1911, the Yale Child Study Center has been at the forefront both of the scientific study of infants and children and of the use of developmental knowledge to provide guidance to parents, educators, and professionals. Research conducted in the Center has helped shape our modern understanding of children and their lives. Today the Yale Child Study Center is a source for creative collaboration among experts in child and adolescent psychiatry, psychology, social work, pediatrics, education, neuroscience, nursing, human genetics, and law. The faculty connects with a wider public through their work with national and international media, government agencies, and public and private child- and family-advocacy organizations.

Our research has been enriched by the diversity of our personal backgrounds and professional fields. Trained as child psychiatrists, pediatricians, psychologists, and child psychoanalysts, we also write as university teachers, as parents and grandparents, and as friends of children. In addition, we have sought the consultation, wisdom, and help of many of our colleagues in the Yale community — pediatricians, teachers, child psychiatrists, and parents. Thus, this book reflects the collective voice of dozens of people who have devoted their working lives to helping children and families.

It also reflects the stories of thousands of parents and children whom we have met in our cumulative years of practice. Some families come to the Center because they have developmental, behavioral, or family troubles; others, to participate in studies of psychological and neurological development or to attend our nursery schools. The Center has worked with thousands of families over the years: today we see the grandchildren of adults who came to the Center during its earliest years.

The stories we have gathered from many families — parents and children from all walks of life who relate in different ways — deeply inform our developmental approach to, and understanding of, parenting and childhood. Through the situations these families encounter — their best and worst moments, joys and worries, triumphs and disappointments — we trace what it means to raise a child and to be a child. Not every story we tell represents a single family; some are combinations of experiences. We combine stories with observation, the practical with the theoretical.

In this book — as at the Center in our responses to parents' questions and concerns — we speak from three perspectives: the most up-to-date knowledge of the science of child development; a child's point of view at particular ages and stages of development; and the parents' expectations and experience of that development.

From the first perspective — the scientific one — we discuss the most basic needs you as a parent must meet: helping babies sleep, finding the most developmentally engaging toys for infants and toddlers, managing aggression, choosing day care and schools, returning to work, caring for a sick child.

In offering information or suggesting ways to think about a difficult situation or handle normal concerns, we also emphasize that knowledge alone is not sufficient. Thus, from the second perspective, you must balance facts with an understanding of your child's feelings. Appreciating how your two-year-old understands feelings and ordinary day-to-day circumstances differently from a five-year-old helps you navigate the rapidly changing development of a young child.

Finally, to balance facts and your child's feelings, you must also be aware of and allow for your own inner life as a parent. This all-important third perspective makes this book unique. For your feelings — how you imagine yourself as a parent, and what you imagine and hope for your children — are as important as what you do or say, if not more so.

This third perspective is also about making room for your child in your mind and in your life. Your child lives within your mind long before you become a parent and long after she has left home and is a parent herself. In these mental portraits of your children, you define yourself as a parent. In your imagination, your children usually exceed your grasp. They join and then continue your business or become doctors, lawyers, farmers, or parents themselves. They are smarter, more beautiful, wiser, and kinder. They avoid your perceived mistakes and overcome your life-defining hardships. Mothers and fathers assign children some of their own interests, dreams, and hopes: to be a novelist, a most valuable player, the president, or a fulfilled adult. You imagine a world in which your children are better adjusted, happier, healthier, and stronger than you know yourselves to be.

Thus, your view of yourself as a parent and your mental portrait of your child shape your parenting style; and that, in turn, influences your child — as, in turn, your child's own personality affects you. As your child grows and develops skills in language, learning, and emotional and social behavior, this interaction will become deeper and more complex, with its own particular pattern. The more you understand and appreciate the process, the more insight, confidence, and wisdom you can bring to your role as a parent.

All three perspectives demand equal attention. It is our aim in this book to help parents combine them, to find a balance among the practical, the factual, and the inner lives of yourself and your child. Only then can you learn to balance your own needs, feelings, and wishes with your child's possibly very different ones.

A child develops through forward leaps, plateaus, even steps backward. As much as you may like to think of yourself and your child as moving ahead all the time, you will often need to pause and even revisit old memories and developmental stages. From time to time, in keeping with this point of view, we may repeat ourselves to remind you that even as development moves forward, familiar themes will pop up again and again.

We have organized this book not according to traditional ages and phases, but along the broad paths of children's development: parental imaginings, pregnancy, and birth; the science of development; the various aspects of development — physical, cognitive, social and emotional; and finally the effects of stress, both minor and major, both ordinary and extraordinary. We begin in part 1 where children begin — with adults imagining what it would be like to be parents. Although, at this stage, you and your spouse are not holding an actual child, you are doing so in your mind's eye. It is at this point that you start to get acquainted with your child and with yourself as a parent. We move from this process to a brief discussion of the many forms of family today, to the way in which you prepare for your baby both psychologically and practically, to pregnancy itself, and then to the moment you bring your newborn infant home. The section closes with a chapter on working with your pediatrician.

In introducing the science of development in part 2, we discuss how your child's physical, cognitive, and emotional development builds upon the basic foundation of genes, brain, and mind.

We take up physical development in part 3: how a child moves, eats, sleeps, and does other things with his or her body. These concerns are often uppermost on a parent's mind when he or she starts caring for an infant, and never disappear. After all, thoughts and feelings come out of physical experiences: one is never separate from one's physical body. In part 4, we address cognitive development, how children learn both before and during school. And in part 5, we look at children's social and emotional development, from feelings and friends to moral development, at home and in the community.

Parts 6 and 7 concern sources of stress in a child's life. The challenges families can expect to face, or events that happen to most children within the regular developmental processes, include separation, the arrival of a new sibling, and having other caregivers in day care or at home. Among the more difficult problems, we address the effect of death, divorce, violence, and mental disturbance. Part 7 closes with the advent of adolescence, not necessarily a problem, but a challenge requiring parents once again to work through both their knowledge of what is going on physically and psychologically in their child, as well as what they imagine, to help him or her become an adult.

As you — mothers and fathers — are the endpoint of countless generations, so your children are the beginning of generations to come. They need your protection as well as your guidance. At the same time, raising children is never an easy endeavor; it is often lonely, rarely predictable, sometimes frightening. Often parents feel overwhelmed with seemingly unanswerable problems and questions. While we do not hesitate to offer clear opinions, we also know that no one model can work for every family. Our hope is that this book will help you to understand the many ways children develop, to learn to observe your child's individual personality, and to reflect on your own development as a parent. Our aim is thereby to empower you both to reconcile your child's individual needs with your own needs as a parent and to work out your own solutions. This is what it means for you to create your own family.

PART I

Preparing to Be a Parent

CHAPTER 1

The Decision to Become a Parent

The decision to become a parent is momentous. It will affect your life more than almost any other decision you will ever make. It will engage you in a lifelong enterprise — shepherding and nurturing one or more human beings from birth to adulthood. And it will affect how you think and feel and change who you are in both your own eyes and those of others. Yet, in making this decision, you probably didn't think of it in this way at all.

Perhaps, for you, it is the "next step," according not only to your own expectations but to those of family, friends, even the culture as a whole. It may be one decision among others that you have made that have shaped your grown-up life: what schools to attend, what kind of work to do, where to make your home, whom to commit yourself to for a long-term relationship or marriage. Or perhaps, overwhelmed by worry, depression, or poverty, or distracted by the pressures of work, you and your partner have found yourselves pregnant without seeing it as a choice.

Maybe, like many couples or single men and women, you wanted a child in order to pass on some legacy from your own lives: the strength of your relationship as a couple, a musical talent you both share, the athletic prowess of one. You want to pass on genes, values, energy. You want to share your expectations of how families and communities look out for one another, along with the traditions and stories of your parents, grandparents, aunts, and uncles. Ultimately, your children will preserve a piece of you in the world, guaranteeing a bit of immortality — as you have for those who came before you.

In these terms, the decision to have a child is the beginning of a venture with enormously high stakes and risks. In a sense, you are gambling with your genes, rolling a pair of biological dice on the chance of extending your family and yourselves. Although gambling may seem a trivial metaphor for an event as serious as having a child, luck operates as powerfully in the one as in the other. As carefully as a couple may plan a pregnancy and watch over the mother's health, no one can be absolutely sure that the baby will

9

be healthy. Nor can anyone predict how a young child will grow and develop, through whatever crises may arise, into an adult; or guarantee that your children will share your talents or strengths — or weaknesses. The choice to have a baby is based on the future you hope for. You decide today because of what you want for yourselves and your children tomorrow. You are propelled forward by your biology and your wishes. Deciding to become a parent is, then, both conscious choice and true leap of faith.

Five Decisions for Parenthood

In the following five stories, a variety of adults — two heterosexual couples, a gay couple, a single woman, grandparents — make this choice through pregnancy, adoption, or both. Common to all five sets of parents is the wish to give something of themselves to their children and also to express through their children an aspect of their own selves as nurturing, caring adults. Common to them as well is the effort and desire to examine all their reasons for deciding to take on the care of a child.

A Planned Pregnancy: Mary and Ethan

Mary awoke with a sense of expectation. The day before, late in the afternoon, she and her husband had rushed from their respective jobs to her obstetrician to find out whether they were pregnant. Mary smiled at how she and Ethan thought of themselves as both pregnant: having a child was something they would do not just as a man and a woman but as a unit. And the doctor's news had been good: their first child was coming in the spring. They had been so relieved, happy, shocked, and worried that, in the rush of feelings, she could not quite remember leaving the doctor's office.

In her mind, Mary tried to reassemble the rest of the evening. They had walked slowly together, and she found herself looking at every woman they passed. Had she been pregnant? Mary wondered. Did she enjoy being a mother? Where are her children now? Mary had seen the image of her own mother in the older woman sitting in the coffee shop, and in the park she had imagined seeing her child. Mary smiled again. In her mind, their child was already in second grade.

Mary and Ethan had spent many a long evening together wondering about their first child. They had each surprised the other with how strong their images were. Ethan seemed always to see in his mind's eye a tall, brown-haired, brown-eyed girl. Mary had realized many months ago that she always imagined a son with brownish-blond hair, quiet but energetic, witty, gentle, and full of life. She always saw him as taller than she, looking down patiently, if not a bit puzzled. Funny how even when she wondered about the baby, he took the shape of an older child. And that thought raised a question: Would she know how to take care of the baby? Ethan seemed to pull resourcefulness from a well deeper than the earth itself. In some ways she had married him because she deeply believed he would be a good father. But could she keep up?

Ethan was awake, too, silently imagining his child to come. He thought back, feeling a little guilty, to his first real girlfriend, and how for several weeks they had played a game of imagining what their children would be like. They had come up with a large family, at least four children, in a big house in the country. He would be quickly successful in his writing, with an immediate bestseller, so he could spend his days at home where they would raise the children together. Ethan smiled at how young and naive they were. Just a few months after they had broken up, he met Mary at a baseball game — in the early spring, he recalled, right around the time of year when their baby would come.

As much as they both wanted children, Ethan and Mary also wanted to establish themselves in their work. He was working his way up in a publishing company, and the demands on his time were extraordinary. Mary, too, was just starting her career in an investment firm. For both, taking time off might mean an irrevocable setback in their dreams for themselves and for their marriage. Ethan had always thought he would be a very involved father, but now he was not sure he could be. As special as this pregnancy was, suddenly their world felt turned inside out and upside down. Yet Ethan knew, and was sure that Mary agreed, that their life before the obstetrician's announcement had felt incomplete. While there were still many uncertainties, somehow they both felt that the baby they were just now beginning to imagine would fill in their lives together.

A Single Mother Adopts: Joyce

Joyce was a successful defense attorney in her late thirties. All of her adult life had been dedicated to the goal of being a well-trained, respected, and competent lawyer. Full of energy and extraordinarily creative, she had worked long hours in volunteer organizations during law school and still managed to be on the law review. She headed a student-run advocacy group for poor families, worked in soup kitchens, and helped poor mothers complete applications for welfare and food stamps. She had even created a volunteer group of law students who served as mentors to one or two local children every year. Joyce had taken on three children and been their mentor all through her law-school years. All three had stayed in touch with her, even fourteen years later.

After law school, Joyce had received many offers to join various law firms. She had picked a prestigious firm that specialized in defending individual rights. The hard work suited Joyce's high energy. She lectured at the law school about advocacy work, supervised students in a clinic that provided pro bono services to poor families, and became involved in many volunteer organizations. Joyce had made partner in her firm when she was thirty-six, and was securely placed in her professional career. Her life was full and rewarding. Many colleagues were sure she was on the track for a judgeship.

Joyce had a circle of close friends, both from the law and from her volunteer work. She had had a number of relationships, but none developed into marriage or a long-term partnership. This was a private loneliness for Joyce. She was sure that eventually she would meet someone with whom she might share a loving, enduring life, but it had not yet happened. Meanwhile, her two younger sisters were married and, in the last four years, had three children between them. Joyce took great joy in being with her two nieces and her nephew. She had always assumed that she too would have a family and be a mother. Her own parents were teachers, a two-career family before the term was fashionable, so she had a model for combining work and family.

But time seemed to be running out. Suddenly Joyce was acutely aware that she was in her late thirties and that if she was going to be a mother, she needed to begin thinking about whether she wanted to keep waiting for the right circumstance or take action on her own. Joyce was not someone who put her faith in chance. Yet she was also not sure she was up to single motherhood. She had the financial resources, but she agonized over whether that was the kind of family she wanted to give a child. Joyce explored many options, including adoption and in vitro fertilization. She wanted very much to have a child that was of her genes, from her body, and to have the experience of being pregnant. But she also realized that she would want to conceive a child with someone she loved, not a donor.

In the end, Joyce chose to bring a baby girl into her home. She tackled the adoption process with the same thoroughness and energy that she applied to other tasks. Her contacts, her status in the community, and her work as a mentor all helped open doors for her. Before long, she was caring for a baby in her home; and after a few months, the public agency responsible for the little girl recommended that Joyce become her legal mother. As Joyce waited for the adoption to be final, she realized her whole image of herself was changing. Joyce loved the law as much as she ever had, and looked forward to telling her daughter about being a lawyer, but now she was expanding her old self-image to include the new reality of being a parent.

Two Gay Men Adopt: Jim and Stan

Jim had been the first to bring up the possibility of their becoming fathers, where Stan was not so sure. But Jim had always been the more decisive of the two. He had announced his homosexuality in high school, having known since the third grade that he felt different from other boys. An only child, Jim remembered how surprised his parents had been. His mother, the town librarian, took many hours to think about her son's homosexuality and tried to see the world through his eyes. Jim's father, a businessman, had been initially angry and embarrassed to be with his son. But the anger and awkwardness wore off, and soon father and son were spending even more time fishing together at their favorite creek. Gradually, they were able to talk with more openness than before.

Stan, on the other hand, had not come out until college, after he and Jim had begun dating regularly. They had met at a seminar. Jim struck Stan as being so comfortable in his own skin — not just with being gay, but with who he was overall. Stan had always been cautious about revealing his homosexuality to others and had not had a serious relationship before Jim. Stan's parents still did not know about Jim, though he had confided in his older sister, Cindy. When Jim and Stan had begun spending time together, they visited Cindy several times. She welcomed them as a couple and enjoyed having them take care of her two-year-old daughter and four-year-old son.

After college, Jim went to law school and Stan began work in journalism. They lived in a community that offered each of them good professional opportunities and where they could imagine settling down. They were amazed their life had worked out as well as it had. They had a close group of friends — gay and straight, men and women, singles and couples. Jim eventually joined a small law firm, and Stan started to work freelance. They bought a home together. As many of their straight friends began to have children, Jim suggested they think about adopting a child.

Jim had talked often with his mother about wanting to have a child. He had even asked his father if he would teach a grandson to fish. Stan, however, was initially unsure, wondering what it would be like for two gay men to raise a child. His mind raced ahead to his having to take the child to school and to explain how he and his partner were the parents. What would they do when their son or daughter started asking them about their sexuality, or when other children teased their child about having gay parents? Was it fair to adopt a child into a household that society did not yet fully embrace? Jim knew all of these issues, but he saw himself and Stan not primarily as two gay men but as two individuals who could give a lot emotionally and materially to a child. Jim also knew that being a father would fulfill a need he felt in himself.

Ultimately, Stan came around, though his misgivings returned each time someone reminded them that their situation was "unusual." He and Jim wondered if they would improve their chances by volunteering to adopt an older child, though they both wanted to care for an infant. Finally, through a private agency, they were put in contact with a pregnant woman who wanted to put her baby up for adoption. They visited her several times, followed her through her pregnancy, and were present at the delivery. By law, only one partner could adopt the baby; legally, he was a single parent. But it was Stan and Jim together who brought their son home and introduced him to his new grandparents, aunt, and cousins.

Adoption and Pregnancy: David and Katherine

Katherine, an artist who taught painting at a local school, had had several successful small shows. David, a contractor, had taken over his family's business of remodeling and restoring historic buildings in Connecticut.

On the side, he had also developed his own small woodworking shop. David always assumed he would be a father and a husband, though he had never thought deeply about it. He had dated through high school and college, but had no serious relationship. Right after college, he had taken a summer trip across the country with his closest friends. They stayed a week in New Mexico — and there David met Katherine, his friend's sister. They seemed to hit it off instantly. She was as different from anyone he had ever met as the desert landscape was from the New England shore. Their courtship began quietly with phone calls and letters and after three years, David and Katherine were married. They came back to Connecticut together, and David started building them a house on the weekends.

Katherine and David had always wanted children, two or three kids at least. David imagined teaching them how to build houses, Katherine wanted to show them how to see the world in terms of color and form. When Katherine had not become pregnant during the first year of their marriage, they were both disappointed but thought that it probably was for the best because they had so much to get used to. (And David was still working on their house.) But by the end of their second year, then their third, they were both worried that something was wrong. They were sure that Katherine had miscarried, perhaps twice, but no pregnancy had seemed to go past a month.

David and Katherine consulted an infertil-ity clinic. Test after test yielded no answers. They tried various medications to induce ovulation, and Katherine had daily shots to increase the chances of her being able to maintain a pregnancy. David's sperm were counted and recounted. Becoming pregnant became the focus of their lives; they could think about little else. Every time they tried a new intervention or medication, they were sure this one would succeed. Several times Katherine was able to carry the pregnancy to around the third month before she went into labor and miscarried. Finally, they decided to stop trying for a while and began to pursue adoption.

Thinking about adoption brought Katherine and David to a whole other set of decisions. Should they pursue a privately arranged adoption so that they might know more about the baby's mother? Should they be open to overseas adoptions, with more uncertainty about the health of the baby? Finally the couple decided to put their faith in an international agency with an excellent reputation. Within a year they had the option to adopt a ten-month-old girl from Russia. David and Katherine flew to Moscow together and spent a few days in the orphanage, getting to know their daughter and working through the administrative red tape.

In the first months after the family's return, little Katerina was quiet, even a little withdrawn. With time, however, she became lively, babbling, and engaging. The agency's caution ensured that she was as healthy as any other baby. Katherine and David were deeply satisfied with being parents. They were even thinking about adopting again to fill out the family they had imagined. But both secretly regretted they had not been able to have their own child. They decided to try again, promising each other this would be the last attempt. They returned to the infertility clinic when Katerina was eighteen months old. In six months, they were pregnant. By the time they both turned thirty-eight, David and Katherine were the parents of a lovely toddler and newborn twins.

Grandparents as Parents: Edith and Steve

Edith and Steve had three children, two girls and a boy. Edith had done most of the child rearing, as they both would acknowledge, while Steve had worked hard in a bank, provided a good house, and helped out on the weekends. But that was what couples of their generation had expected of each other. After their youngest, John, had gone off to college, Edith began to work in an insurance office. In their early sixties, the couple decided to retire at around the same time; they looked forward to enjoying their hobbies, traveling, and being together. Already they were enjoying being grandparents to John's six-year-old son, Joshua, and three-year-old daughter, Katie.

John had come back to the area after his graduation and started work as a teacher in the next town. He had married Helen, another teacher at the same high school. She had always wanted to be a writer, she told

Edith, but went into teaching to support herself and also to have an opportunity to teach others about her craft. Within a year of their marriage, Helen and John were pregnant. Joshua weighed nearly eight pounds and was a husky, active baby who crawled easily toward anyone's open arms. He seemed immediately fond of his grandparents, and Steve and Edith were always willing to take care of their first grandson. Being grandparents brought back many memories of raising John and his sisters, but now Edith felt more experienced. As for Steve, he felt he finally had the time to take pleasure in a baby's spontaneity and playfulness.

Helen and John had decided they would try to have another baby after Joshua turned two. They carefully planned the pregnancy so Helen would deliver in the summer, when they were both off from teaching. Steve and Edith shuffled their travel schedule so they would be around to help with the baby and with Joshua. Katie's delivery went well; she was as petite as her brother was husky, and as quiet and observant as he was bold and vocal.

After that pregnancy, Helen did not bounce back as quickly to her old self. She felt run down and tired. She noticed herself losing weight afterward far more quickly than she had with Joshua. Instead of getting her strength back, however, she seemed to be getting weaker and weaker. Helen began the school year on a reduced schedule, as she had arranged ahead of time so she could spend time with Katie, but still she felt exhausted. She consulted her physician. To the whole family's shock, Helen was found to have lymphoma, a form of blood cell cancer. Her doctors were confident that the disease could be completely cured, but warned her that the treatment would take a number of months and that she would have to take a leave from teaching and have help with her children.

So Edith and Steve came out of their parenting retirement. With even less time to adjust than a mother who suddenly finds herself pregnant, they readied themselves to help their son, grandson, and granddaughter through a trying time. They spent a month helping John fix up an extra room in his house. One or the other of them stayed there with the family to help get the children off to school and preschool, and to take care of Helen after her treatments. With the distress and uncertainty of their mother's illness, the children needed even more attention. And this — with their experience, confidence, and willingness to adjust their own expectations — was something Edith and Steve could provide.

Conclusion — and Beginnings

These five stories illustrate how vital one's wishes, fantasies, doubts, and past experiences are to the decision to be a parent. How well you are aware of them all is a major concern of ours in this book, for they not only determine your decision but will also affect how you behave as a mother or a father. With clear self-understanding, each of these parents is likely to fulfill their dreams of being good parents to the children they have chosen to nurture. Thus, the more completely you understand why you have chosen to become a parent at a particular time, the more clearly you can perceive what you deeply, perhaps even without articulating it, wish for your offspring. We will address this issue at length in chapter 3 as part of the preparation, both psychological and practical, for your baby. In the subsequent chapters of part 1, we will deal with the actual pregnancy, with bringing home the new baby who is the outcome of your decision to become a parent, and, finally, with the professional who will assist you in the momentous task of raising a child.

But first, let's address another aspect of

your decision to become a parent: family. Even before your actual pregnancy — perhaps even before the decision — you have thought about family: the one you came from, the one you and your partner will be making as parents. From time immemorial, families have been a sort of glue binding together human communities and larger societies. Before you add your bit to your own community, you may find it helpful to know something about what families have been, as well as what they can be today.

CHAPTER 2

The Many Faces of Family

What is a family? The answer to this question depends largely on whom you ask. Nearly every four-year-old could answer with certainty, but each child's response would reflect not only his experiences and what he sees around him in his community, but also what he has picked up from the larger culture and what he wishes for. A child growing up in a household with one parent may nevertheless say that a family is a mother, a father, a brother, and a baby. Or she may define a family as when Grandma lives next door and everyone goes there for Thanksgiving. She may include her dog, her doll, or cousins she has heard of but never met. Families are very individual — both in reality and in imagination.

In your mind, a family is ideally what you most need or want it to be: a gathering of people, usually relatives, who share a common understanding and history and among whom you can find comfort, acceptance, stability, solace, and good times. After a long family holiday or reunion, however, adults of-

ten shake their heads and mutter, "You can have too much family," and everyone listening nods in silent agreement. Most people understand that the family they imagine or hope for is never quite the same as the family they have, and some families are very painful to grow up in. Nonetheless, no one really wants to be without a family. A man without a country may be lost, but a person without a family is orphaned in the most basic sense of the word — no home, no parents, no identity. A family is where you start to define the experience of loving other people and sharing your life with them.

As for more formal definitions, the U.S. Census Bureau says that a family is a group of two or more persons related by birth, marriage, or adoption, and residing together. The dictionary defines family as a group of related individuals. A child could list all the people she lives with and say they are her family. But where does that definition leave other relatives to whom she is emotionally attached? How can a child fit in her beloved live-in

babysitter? What about a child being raised by a single parent who sees her other parent regularly, or one being raised by her grandparents, or one being cared for by two people of the same sex, only one of whom is biologically or legally her parent? All of these people have places in children's hearts and roles in their development.

An individual's definition of who is included in a family may well change as he grows and fosters relationships outside his biological family. A single adult is likely to include siblings and older generations of relatives. Newlyweds may consider themselves a family of two and perhaps also a branch of their respective families. Some adults include in their families people to whom they are close and yet not related, people with whom they share a common experience or ideology. When people try to define family, they naturally begin to consider an ideal, yet they also recognize how death, illness, divorce, and other rifts inevitably disrupt that ideal. Perhaps "family" is the conglomeration of all the significant relationships in a person's life. Even that expansive definition, however, leaves out a person's inner portrait of a family. Your mental idea of "family" also includes the kind of family you wish eventually to have. In other words, a family is not only the group you are born into but also the one you see yourself making.

As people move from childhood into adulthood, many look to the future and imagine the family they will help to create. What place will children have in your life? What family model influences your hopes, dreams, and expectations? Are you interested in re-creating the family life you experienced as a child or perhaps the one you thought others had? Can you imagine yourself as a single parent? Is your ideal family a mother and father raising children together or, even more traditionally, an extended family with parents, grandparents, aunts, uncles, and cousins close by? How much has tradition shaped your image of the ideal family? Since ideas about what families should be have changed over time, especially in recent decades, we will briefly relate some historical background before describing some of the family structures people choose today.

The Family Within a Changing Society

Society is a complex tapestry of relationships, a fabric composed of many threads that include shared philosophies, religions, science, politics, laws, and the mass media, all of which affect and are affected by the family. Workplaces, social groups, schools, churches, and other religious groups all offer people opportunities to interact on a regular basis. Yet family relationships are generally the core of a person's daily life. How you perceive and experience these close relationships has a lot to do with your beliefs about the past, your present emotional needs, and your views of the future. It is difficult to pull on one thread of this tapestry — the family — without noticing how it is tied to all the others.

Today's families are taking part in a far-reaching transformation of society that involves redefining people's expectations of, among other things, gender roles and family structures. In many families, men and women share parenting tasks more equally than their own parents did. Families are often more isolated from their extended relatives than in the past, and economic pressures mean that many families are spending less time together or interact in their time together very differently from the way their ancestors did. Adults outside the family, such as nannies and day-care teachers, now have a hand in raising children.

Such changes may be more or less prevalent in your own family and community. They may also be more or less consonant with your ideal family — the one you have imagined since you were young, shaped by your memories of your parents and your expectations for yourself. However, even if you are pleased with many of the ways life is changing and are adjusting to these changes, they may be unsettling and troublesome at first.

Yet however profound these changes seem, society has always been in flux. Philosophies, religious beliefs, popular culture, and economic and political systems all change over time, even though not all at the same rate. Thus the traditional, centuries-old family structure, which was the economic and social center of a person's life, has evolved into the many conceptions of "family" being lived out today.

The Shift of Industrialization

Before the nineteenth century, in most households both men and women provided for their families. Family members worked together on farms or in small household businesses, trading goods and services within their community. While some tasks were traditionally assigned to women and others to men, the responsibilities for family life and economic livelihood were shared. On farms, where most American families lived, men did most of the work raising the cash crop while women tended gardens that fed the family directly. Mothers sewed and knitted garments while fathers made shoes. In enslaved families, men and women usually did the same fieldwork. Some tasks, such as weaving baskets, had no traditional gender assignment, and the whole family worked on them together. These different sex roles were a carry-over from European social structures, in which men held authority over the women and children in their families in accordance with legal, political, and religious traditions. Nonetheless, women had equal economic value in a family, and children also had significant economic value as laborers, as they would until the early 1900s.

With the Industrial Revolution, the American economy moved away from the local exchange of goods and services to large-scale production. With this shift, the majority of households began to depend on wage earners rather than exclusively on self-employment. Some family members had to work outside the home for wages to procure the household staples. Others had to do the further work of maintaining the house and preparing most of those staples for consumption: making the cloth into clothes, the flour into bread. At first, both young men and women worked in factories, away from farm and home. Gradually, men and older children took on the wage-earning jobs, and mothers took on all the domestic tasks, including child rearing, cleaning, food preparation, and laundry. This division of labor changed how husbands and wives viewed themselves. People came to identify masculinity with economic activities and femininity with nurturing care.

As the factory system of production became firmly established, the division of labor within families became more distinct. Working-class married women often stayed home, while men, single women, and older children went off to earn wages. Higher salaries allowed men in the middle and upper classes to free their wives and children from working for money. In these families, men were the sole wage earners, and women and children remained at home. Many women in the upper class, with servants to carry out some or all household and child-rearing jobs, took on public roles as caretakers of society's morality. They led maternal associations, reform societies, and charity organizations. For the most part, these women's work was categorized as traditionally feminine humanitarian aid to other women and children, rather than as activism on social issues of labor conditions and poverty.

In the late 1800s, people began to see the economic sphere as devoid of altruism, a "dog-eat-dog world." Gradually the notion grew that independence and concern for others were mutually exclusive; and that, except for legal contracts, people were obligated to care for others only in private relationships. A husband was to be his family's representative in the world, the provider and protector. A wife was to speak up for moral concerns without asserting independence. The private, nuclear family became a center of middle-class morality and identity, the source of loyalty, obligation, and personal satisfaction. Exhausted from the Civil War, Americans were encouraged by religious and political leaders to invest in rebuilding the family. As Theodore Roosevelt exclaimed in 1911, as long as "the average man and woman are . . . first of all, sound in their home life, and the father and mother of healthy children whom they bring up well — just so far, and no farther, we may count our civilization a success."

This emphasis on family structure was motivated also by the high rate of immigration into the United States around the turn of the nineteenth century. Millions of people were forsaking their homes in Europe to come to America, leaving behind some of their relatives and bringing different images of family with them. Since immigrants tended to be poorer than the average citizen, they were more willing to move in search of work and to share crowded living quarters. This situation produced contradictory complaints that immigrants had no family ties, and that their families were too large; either way, they were not "sound in their home life."

In the following decades, even as immigration was limited by law, migrations within the United States — from farms to nearby cities, from the rural South to the urban North, from the East to the West — produced far-reaching changes. Railroads and then automobiles made it easier for people to move away from their homesteads, though telegrams and telephones also helped extended families to keep in touch. The older and younger generations within many families started to differ about how best to adapt to their new homes, how to socialize children, and what was proper behavior for men and women.

In the early twentieth century, newly enacted laws that regulated work by children, firmly established the public-education system, and granted the vote to women had significant effects on the family. By the 1920s, a majority of American children were no longer in the workforce. They lived in homes where the father was the breadwinner and the mother was the homemaker. Women's work was still seen as less valuable than men's — though anyone who bothered to calculate the cost of hiring a nanny, a maid, a cook, and a laundress might have discovered that a wife's value was on a par with a man's.

Even as popular opinion extolled the virtues of living in a nuclear family, the housing shortages during the Great Depression and immediately after the Second World War caused more generations to live together as extended families. First the Depression and then the war affected women's roles in wage-earning labor. During the 1930s, some families depended on women's income because men were out of work; while in some communities, in order to spread jobs among households, employers refused to hire women whose husbands were working. In the 1940s, during the Second World War, women were urged to join the industrial workforce while men went to the battlefields. And then, as soon as the war ended, the government and employers pressured women to return to their prewar tasks in the home. Not surprisingly, this return coincided with an upsurge in new family members — the famous baby boom. Society was eager to settle down to a new ideal life.

From the Extended Family to the Nuclear Family

In the decade after the Second World War, many people's hopes for better times became reality. Wages rose more than in all other years since the turn of the century, and new laws and court decisions began the long process of making the American dream available to citizens of all ethnic backgrounds. Less competition in the world market contributed to an expansion of new industry, creating more well-paid management and skilled positions. Postwar America produced many people with more money than ever before, with the promise of more to come.

Popular culture romanticized the middle-class nuclear (as opposed to extended) family and encouraged the young to strike out on their own. Many Americans were more than ready to minimize their ties with older generations. The national dream promised both upward mobility and family stability, as long as career men followed the proper track upward through the system from the bottom. For women, personal service to the family was the highest fulfillment. Young wives were to be sexy and glamorous and willing to attend to all domestic needs; the home was their creative environment and source of identity. In those years, a mother was expected to deliver her babies without her husband at hand; he was to wait in another part of the hospital. A wife and mother's role was to offer her husband a home and a growing brood so attractive as to both motivate and demonstrate his success.

Young newlyweds were buying new single-family homes as quickly as they were built. They started families earlier than many of the generations preceding them and typically had fewer children, closer together. The suburbs filled with families who were all at similar stages in life. This community of support and common middle-class experience fostered parents' belief in the American dream that better opportunities were always available to those who worked steadily. In the 1950s, optimism was high, as was confidence in the institutions of government, business, education, and marriage. Consumerism gained a strong foothold; husbands worked hard to afford the newest modern conveniences and thus keep up with everyone else who seemed able to afford them.

But many families in the middle class found it increasingly difficult to maintain both their nuclear structure and their dream of a prosperous lifestyle, and ultimately had to choose between their two ideals. Since the labor force still needed women (newspapers were filled with advertisements for women's jobs — which they listed separately from men's), many married women with children chose to work outside the home.

Modern Families

By the middle of the 1960s, the postwar babies were coming of age and questioning the status quo. They resisted the media's representation of a homogeneous society and responded to the calls for social reform of activists targeting racial discrimination and restraints on political speech. Over the decade, the "younger generation" gained in political power and persuaded the nation to attend to a wide range of social concerns: the lack of affordable housing, inequities in pay, restricted education, sexual double standards, and the persistent needs of families living below the poverty level. In this tumultuous time of the Vietnam War, Watergate, and political unrest, people began to reevaluate accepted concepts of individuality, equality, social values, gender roles, and family structure. Drawn to popular culture and its promotion of individuality and "doing your own thing," young people felt conventional family life to be unrealistic and constraining.

As beneficiaries of a period of great economic expansion, these baby boomers had expectations of a high standard of living. But on entering the employment market, they found fewer high-paying jobs, smaller benefits, and declining wages. The proportion of income that a young couple needed to spend to buy their first home was substantially more than it had been for their parents. At the same time, a shift in women's view of themselves as only wife and mother, combined with the development of new technology such as the birth control pill, allowed them to seek fulfillment for themselves in other roles. Soon there were more American families with two wage earners than with one. Couples had even fewer children, born much later in a marriage. By the 1970s, women with young children were the fastest-growing group of female workers, and as more couples discovered that "traditional" family structures might not be economically viable, family and other societal roles had to become less gender-specific. When both spouses earned wages, the question of how to allocate other family responsibilities was thrown open for discussion and adjustment of traditional roles. Choosing or sharing roles required people to change how they thought and felt about those roles.

Compared with previous decades, the 1980s and 1990s seemed to be characterized by economic extremes. Fewer people came to possess a larger proportion of the nation's wealth. Many people fell deep into poverty and debt, yet the per-capita income rose. Although more women and minorities had moved into new, more lucrative careers by the turn of the twenty-first century, many people felt more pressed for time and more precarious in their achievements. Workplaces had typically been slow to offer families with two wage earners such supports as day-care benefits and flexible work schedules.

Thus we seem to be in transition again. Values, structures, and strategies that once coordinated an individual's personal life with a family's economic life are now largely out of sync. With two parents working more hours, traditional ties to family, school, and community are harder to maintain, and the changing dynamics are often blamed for widespread social problems such as violence, teen pregnancy, broken families, increased work hours, decreased compensation, a decline in altruism, and community decay. Because politicians and the media still promote the traditional nuclear family as an ideal, departures from it can produce feelings of guilt and inadequacy or attract society's condemnation: Should Mom really stay home with the children? Is Dad not being an adequate provider?

But, as history shows, a large society is too complex to allow such simple causal relationships. Furthermore, this is far from the first time that people have criticized the changing American family for not measuring up to American ideals. Our social fabric ripples and stretches and contracts. Families do the best they can to make their current set of variables work. No one family form will work for everyone. Many types of families exist; some types work better for their members than others do, and often those differences depend on the individual people and circumstances involved. Across all the changes in this society, we find one constant: the families who appear to function best for their children are those who have built meaningful, solid networks and commitments beyond their own boundaries. They depend on others and, in turn, help others.

A Multitude of Family Structures

A person's own experiences and memories of family come from a variety of relationships. A child's sense of herself is dependent upon her primary relationships — in large part, her family. All children want to feel valued, known, and accepted for who they are. They also want to know that they will be forgiven for making mistakes. A child's family is made up of the individuals who are ready to satisfy these needs. The family may include his biological parents, or it may not. It may include more than one generation of relatives. It may include others who are related to him not by blood or law, but simply by love and respect. The important variable is the quality of the relationships.

Thus, having looked at the family from the outside in, we now turn to the family from the inside out. In examining a variety of family structures, we will show how each is the result of compromises among everyone in a family, even the youngest members. These family structures include: the nuclear family, the extended family, the single-parent family, the blended family, the foster family, and grandparents and grandparenting.

A Contemporary Nuclear Family

The nuclear family — mother, father, and siblings — is a frequent theme in discussions of family. Typically it is portrayed, as we have said, as a unit hallowed by tradition or biology. Within it, the biological father is the procurer of the resources that ensure physical safety and food for all family members, and the biological mother is chiefly involved with child rearing and home management. Although families frequently do not conform to these biological ties and gender roles, the nuclear family remains an ideal.

In many contemporary families, however, gender is not a primary consideration for family roles. Fathers are more involved in cleaning and child rearing than their fathers were. Dads are adjusting their work schedules to accommodate their children; some work from their homes in order to be available for the daily events and needs of the family. Others find a way to participate in sharing the before- and after-school responsibilities of carpooling and attending kids' activities. In the family life of Justin, Karen, and Nan, for example, the responsibilities of Mommy and Daddy depend on the circumstances of each individual in the family, with a primary focus on the child's changing needs.

Justin and Karen planned thoughtfully for Nan's arrival. They both prepared to take some leave from work after the baby was born. They did not want their child to go into day care until she was at least eighteen months old. After carefully considering everyone's needs, the expectant parents decided that Karen would return to work full time after about four weeks, and Justin would work from home and be available for the baby.

The little girl they named Nan arrived right on time, and Justin and Karen thoroughly enjoyed their first month together, getting to know each other in their new roles. It was difficult for Karen to go back to work the first day, but knowing that Justin would be home with Nan made it much easier. Karen loved her job, her husband, and their child, and juggling the relationships was emotionally draining at times. But her choice to continue her career was important for both her and the family. Justin managed his business from home and found time to work with clients in the evening after Karen got home. He became a great cook, and even took on some of the household maintenance jobs that Karen had done before. This gave Karen more time to play with Nan when she got home.

Much too quickly, Nan reached eighteen months, the age that Karen and Justin had decided would be the earliest they would consider day care. The family began to study day-care centers and scheduling alternatives. (See chapter 29 for our advice on this process.) When Nan reached the age of two, her parents enrolled her part-time in a nursery school. Justin happily continues to provide for Nan's needs during the day, dropping her off at day care, making her breakfast and lunch, and being available if she needs to be picked up early. Karen joins in during the evening, and loves the nightly routine with Nan. With much communication, attention, and consideration of all the needs to be filled, Karen and Justin have found a way to structure their family life. To their parents and grandparents, this form of family might be strange, even unthinkable, because it violates the gender roles they valued. Yet it is a tight nuclear family all the same.

The Extended Family

While the majority of America's families today contain two wage earners, an increasing number are composed of a single parent raising two or more children, sometimes with the help of friends and relatives and sometimes with little help. In either case, child care is a major concern for single parents in their children's infancy and preschool years. When the parent is working outside the home, the caregiver or caregivers he or she chooses share the parental functions of nurturing and socializing the child. For some families, this means bringing other relatives into the home to take on parenting and household responsibilities: a grandparent or another relative from a prior generation, or a sibling of one of the parents. For others, the choices may include unrelated live-in help, such as a nanny or an au pair. (See chapter 29.) Either way, this child can be said to be living in an extended family.

Andy is one such child. At age two he moved east with his parents, his older brother, Dave, and his grandmother. Mom was going to school for two years, Dad found a teaching job, and Dave went to elementary school. That left Andy and Gramma. Andy had never known any other place but his original home, and at his age the change was both exciting and frightening. Gramma, everyone recognized, provided Andy with an important tie to the familiar. They learned about the new community together: the stores, the library, the post office, and their favorite place, the beach. Andy depended upon Gramma to interpret these new places for him. He missed Mom, but he was glad to have Gramma to be with him and answer all his questions.

Gradually Andy became more comfortable with his new environment. Mom, Dad, and Gramma decided it was time for him to spend regular amounts of time with other children of the same age. It took a while before Andy gladly played at day care without Gramma. Sometimes she stayed the whole morning so he wouldn't cry. But eventually he settled into a routine, and he has grown fond of the people at school. It is fine for Andy to stay for the whole day, and when Gramma brings him home, he likes having dinner with his extended family.

In other families, two parents who work full time choose an all-day day care for their child. Ideally the facility cares for the child's needs and nurtures her development so well that, for her, the experience is an extension of family life. The professional caregivers share an important role in reinforcing the child's positive sense of self, nurturing her understanding of the world, and guiding her in forming links with others. In a long-term relationship with people at day care, a child may very well develop "family-like" connections. Surrogate moms, dads, sisters, and brothers are part of her day, helping to teach and reinforce life's early lessons. Parents need to recognize the depth of such ties when they make changes in what has become the child's extended family.

The Single-Parent Family

A variety of circumstances can lead to a single-parent family. For one reason or another, a mother and father may not be interested or willing or able to raise their child together. The child may be a product of an uncommitted relationship, or a single person might adopt a child. One parent in a nuclear family might die. Frequently, however, single-parent families are created when partners separate or spouses divorce. A choice is made, and the child resides with mother or father. (See chapter 34 for information on divorce.) That parent, who usually needs to earn an income in order to keep the child out of poverty, then begins the awesome task of making both work and family life function smoothly.

Spending a day at a full-time job is often enough to exhaust anyone. But for a single parent, work can feel like only the first job of the day; then come errands, after-school activities, mealtime, laundry, bathing. An older child can help out and look after himself to some extent, but an infant or a toddler needs care and supervision all the time, and there is no partner to take turns with. Not only does the working single parent need day care for a young child, but she needs to give that child extra attention to smooth the transition between day care and home (see chapter 31 on separation issues), and then take care of all the evening, nighttime, and early-morning responsibilities.

Marsha is a single parent. After she had Kevin, she went back to work full time at the end of her maternity leave. Kevin's father had moved out of state a couple of months before he was born, and had not called or visited since. Despite Marsha's great job and benefits, her salary did not cover the living expenses and the full-time day care Kevin needed. So for the first few months after Kevin was born, they moved in with Marsha's parents, and Marsha worked while her mother watched Kevin. But this arrangement required a long, grueling commute; and when Marsha's parents developed health problems, she knew she needed a place of her own. After about six months, she and Kevin moved into a new apartment, not as nice as her parents', but affordable. Marsha's commute to work was now shorter, giving her

more time and energy to share with Kevin. He quickly grew to love the day care nearby and the new people in his life. He has been there for two years now, and his attachments to his teacher and friends are strong. Marsha has also formed good relationships with the staff, who regularly make time available to answer parents' questions about children's development and behavior.

Marsha's day is long. She and Kevin get up at 6:30 and begin the routine of dressing, making breakfast and lunch, packing the backpack, writing shopping lists, and driving to day care. Kevin likes his Mommy to stay at the facility for a while, at least long enough to read two stories. And when he is ready to start his day there, the good-bye game begins, with the horn blowing and dramatic waves from the window. After a full day at work, Marsha picks up Kevin. If he isn't too wrung out from the day, they often run an errand or two on the way home, then have dinner, a little playtime, bath, and a story. Then Kevin begins all his avoidance games to prolong his time with Mommy and push back bedtime. (See chapter 13 on getting toddlers to sleep.) By lights-out in Kevin's room, it is usually around 8:30. Marsha ends her day doing housework, unwinding, and planning for tomorrow.

Although Marsha loves Kevin dearly and treasures his presence in her life, more than once she has wished that she could just have all of tomorrow off. Fortunately, Marsha's parents are still a great source of support. When they are able, sometimes as often as once a month, they take their grandson for the weekend. Kevin thrives on his mother's commitment to their life together and on the relationships he has with his day-care providers and grandparents. Previous generations would undoubtedly respond to Marsha's situation with some disapproval: yet in every period of recorded history, unmarried mothers have raised children on their own. And there is no question that Marsha and Kevin constitute a family.

The experience of a single-parent family is very different when it originates in divorce. Families that have always had one parent build daily routines around that fact. But when a family begins with two adults and one leaves, all family members must adjust. Everyone feels stress from the upheaval of routines, as well as from the emotional, psychological, and economic components of the change. Children and parents must redefine their interpersonal relationships — how much emotional support each individual can give and get — as well as their family traditions. The custodial parent may change jobs and work schedule; the family may need to move and change schools. At this time, connections that parents and children enjoy with people outside of what once was a nuclear family can be crucial. Bonds with relatives, friends, and other individuals; religious congregations; and support groups can ease the tensions everyone feels. Together they can create the new family architecture.

The Blended Family

There are many kinds of blended families: those formed from portions of two families by a new marriage, those that have welcomed foster children or adopted children, and single-parent families augmented with a new partner. Each of these scenarios is a unique experience, but all share some elements. Previously unrelated people have chosen to form a family and construct new relationships with each other. The care and nurturing of the children is a major focus of these families.

Stepfamilies are a common experience for children. This sort of blended family faces many challenges in growing and evolving into a healthy, functioning unit. Members must form and strengthen their interpersonal relationships and establish a new family history and culture. When two people without children decide to have a baby and help that child grow, the new parents have time to acclimate to their roles; the child grows up with them, influenced by and influencing their behavior as the family evolves. But a new marriage can produce "instant family." Suddenly each child has another parent, each parent more children; the oldest child may no longer be the oldest, the baby no longer the baby. It takes an average of two years for a stepfamily to become established. The results are often well worth the effort, however, as stepfamilies can offer all the love and support of biologically related families. (For more discussion of how remarriage affects children, see chapter 34.)

Adoptive families are formed when a couple or a single adult commits to care for a child for life. Sometimes one of the parents in an adoptive couple is related to the child by blood, and the other is adopting. An increasingly common form of adoptive family involves two parents of the same sex, one of whom might be the child's biological parent. In "open" adoptions, the children know and may even remain in contact with their birth mothers or parents, further widening the family. Whatever the configuration, bonding with and parenting an adoptive infant can have all the qualities of raising a birth child. Adopting an older child might be better compared with forming a stepfamily: the members must get to know one another's established personalities and expectations and form new ways of doing things together.

The Foster Family

Foster families are usually temporary. While some members may come and go, however, a foster family can also provide some of the most stable relationships in a child's life. Often children who have lived for significant periods in a foster family stay in touch with those "parents" and "siblings," no matter how conditional everyone knew the arrangement would be.

A foster family is formed when state social workers find it necessary to remove a child from his regular home and place him temporarily with an adult, a couple, or an entire family who has agreed to look after him. The foster parents rarely know the duration of their child's placement. Children are removed from their original homes for a variety of reasons: abuse, neglect, or when a parent is sick or otherwise unable to care for them and no other adult relative is immediately available. Sometimes foster parents will re-

ceive a call in the middle of the night asking if they can provide an emergency bed. The children who arrive can range from infants to teenagers. Since, at any age, these children's regular lives have been seriously disrupted, foster parents need to be nurturing, understanding, and protective.

The families who decide to offer homes to foster children have unique relationships with each child and face many challenges that other family types do not. A complicated mix of variables from the past, the present, and the future shapes foster-care relationships. The quality of a child's relationships with the adults who have thus far cared for her largely determines how she forms new ties, and frequently foster children need help in adapting comfortably to their new environment. Since, whenever appropriate, state agencies prefer to reunite a child with her birth family, foster parents and children can find bonding difficult at best. The child may resist close ties to the household members, feeling both loyalty to her family and wariness about losing new loved ones. The foster parent and other family members may be almost as reluctant to bond closely with a child who might soon depart.

Since the state remains the guardian of foster children, responsible for them legally and financially, the child-welfare agency makes the major decisions regarding their lives. Nevertheless, motivated by the love of children and the desire to give them a safer, more secure environment, foster parents can offer a new vision and experience of family life and thus play a vital role in their development.

Before choosing to become a foster parent, you need to consider many factors. Are you flexible enough to care for the next young person who comes through your door? Can you work well under the authority of the child-services agency? If you have other children in your household, are they psychologically able to accept a temporary sibling, someone with different ways of playing and different needs? One factor that ideally should not sway your decision is the money that states provide as living expenses for foster children. Because there normally is a long interview process before a state agency approves a foster family, you will have ample time both to reflect on your strengths and expectations and to prepare to help a child through a difficult time.

Grandparents and Grandparenting

All families have had grandparents at some time. More important than that obvious biological fact, however, is the place of grandparents in the mental life of a family. Even if you only dimly remember your mother or father, those memories affect how you envision the task of being a parent. No matter how nuclear American families have become, grandparents are still part of most people's ideal family image. Grandparents may live in a nearby house or apartment, providing a place where toddlers love to visit and teenagers feel they have a refuge. Or grandparents may live hundreds of miles away but make their home the site of holiday gatherings and thus a focus of family traditions. A visit from Grandpa and Grandma usually feels both new and familiar to children, exciting and comforting at the same time. Near or far, grandparents also provide children with additional adult role models as they grow up.

Just as people feel many different emotions about becoming parents, so grandparents can have a mix of feelings about their role. Some see their grandchildren as a comforting reminder that all that hard work raising their own children has paid off, that their genes and traditions will last. For other people, the arrival of grandchildren is a sobering reminder that life is going by more quickly than they wish. Most of us carry images of grandparents in our minds, often doing the stereotypical activities of cookie baking, fishing, hosting huge family dinners, and so on. But as a grandparent, you need not conform to those pictures. You can love your family in your own way.

Many grandparents help to raise their grandchildren. They may care for an infant daily while both his parents work, or look after youngsters for a weekend. More and more often, grandparents are taking on active parenting roles as divorced or single parents move back home or close by. In some families, grandparents must take over the job of raising children full time because young parents are no longer around or are unable to carry out this responsibility.

Grandparenting is, of course, different from parenting. In some ways, it is easier. You have already helped at least one child through to adulthood. You have a generation of experience behind you. You do not have to learn the same lessons over, or repeat the mistakes you feel you made. In other ways, however, helping to raise children as a grandparent is more difficult. You are not as young as you once were. You may have hoped to be doing something else at this age, not going back to change diapers and check homework. And, if you are taking on these jobs because of what you perceive as a failure in your child's life, you may feel embarrassed or resentful about the whole situation. A mix of feelings is normal. The important thing is to recognize those mixed feelings so that the negative ones do not erupt in some hurtful way. Indeed our central message applies as much to grandparents as parents: what you feel and imagine about the children in your family, and how you see yourself as their grandparent or parent, are vital parts of your family life.

Other potential tensions come with being a grandparent even — or especially — if you are eager for the job. You cannot help but perceive some aspects of your children in your grandchildren, yet you must also get to know each grandchild as a separate, special individual. You may not completely agree with your child's parenting style or with current trends. You may have reservations about your son- or daughter-in-law. Most important, if your children are actively involved in raising their children, you must recognize the boundary between being a grandparent and being a parent. Some older adults find a grandparent's lesser responsibility a relief. In other families, tension can arise over who should make the final decisions about the children.

The Child and the Human Family

So who belongs in a child's family? We have described how the answer to that question has changed over time and differs from home to home. Yet another way to approach this question is to imagine a set of concentric circles with the child at the center. In the next rings are the child's mother and father, then the siblings. In the next circles are the child's grandparents and other relatives, other members of the household, professional caregivers. Then come teachers, neighbors, friends and their families, pediatricians and other health-care providers, police officers who patrol the child's street, grocers who supply the child's food, and the rest of the child's community. Any of these links, even those close central relationships between child and parents, can be broken by the misfortunes of life. Yet when the other connections remain strong, the child will still have a family to depend on. That is why it is important for all these people to be present, supporting a child in a web of love and responsibility.

Some people have come to expect generosity and sharing from their family members, and only from them. They view everyone outside the household as a stranger. Their alienation from the community is directly related to whether the family has tried to maintain give-and-take relationships with others, as well as to how safe or unsafe a neighborhood really is. Other people, in contrast, operate on the belief that family is already synonymous with community. They consistently consider how their behavior and choices affect others and they work to strengthen the interrelationships of daily life. Closeness with distant relatives, friends, and neighbors can be "familial" in the way it nurtures and supports a person's emotional, psychological, and economic needs. Such an attitude allows you to view yourself as part of many families. You have the family you live in and the family you imagine. You and your baby belong in the family you are creating together and in your birth family, your neighborhood, your hometown, the American family, the human family.

CHAPTER 3

Making Room for Your Baby: Mental Images and Practical Realities

However you find yourself expecting a child, whether through pregnancy or through adoption, you are entering into a period of major transition, one of the most profound in life. You will be moving from being a relatively free and independent adult, having in mind only your own needs and desires and possibly those of a partner, to being a parent, a mother or a father. From here on in you will need to concern yourself with and bear full responsibility for the needs and desires of another human being — from birth to adulthood.

To make this transition most effectively, you have to make room for this new being not only in your dwelling and your daily life but in your mind. You have thus two primary tasks: to prepare yourself psychologically and to make a variety of practical arrangements. As you move from psychological to practical and back again, they will intertwine and energize one another. Responding fully to both makes for a healthy parent. In this chapter, we will describe how to prepare both mentally and practically for your baby.

The Psychological Role of Mental Images

When forming a new relationship — whether friend, potential partner, or colleague at work — you probably think of yourself as simply "getting to know" that man or woman. In fact, what "getting to know" means is that you are comparing that person — through daydreaming or imagining — with an image of someone already established in your mind as important in your life: "He has the same eyes as my old boyfriend in high school." "She's so full of energy — a real can-do person like my older sister."

You may also look for ways in which a new person is unlike the people you have known well. Indeed, many people look for an exact opposite trait, taking it as either very attractive or a warning to go slow: "My mother never made a decision, but he's not like her at all. He knows his own mind, and I like that." "She's as stubborn as my father, and that just drives me crazy." If you pay close attention to your own thoughts and feelings as you get to know another person, you may see glimmers of all the people in your past who have contributed to your impressions of him or her. Most of the time, however, you probably are not aware of this process going on in your mind. And you may never understand why you are attracted to one person and want to avoid another entirely.

Another aspect of this process is the common tendency to try to fit a man or woman into a mental template, or portrait, of an ideal friend or partner, selecting those characteristics of the real person that fit that ideal. If a woman can create in her mind a man who feels comfortable, then she can get closer to the actual man; as she comes to know him a bit better, she can adjust that mental portrait to match her new knowledge, feel even more comfortable as a result, get closer to him again, gather more knowledge, and so on. Gradually, if the match continues well, she makes permanent mental room for him, where she thinks about him as an active part of her life.

This mental matching and comparing is part of human nature, built into our genes. It helps to make us social beings who create small groups, families, and neighborhoods, which buffer loneliness, help people find partners, and provide security and comfort. It is a psychological process that helps people build those groups, families, and neighborhoods by easing the formation of their smaller components: relationships between adults and between parents and their children. It is a kind of mental economy, allowing you to sort out the many people whom you

meet and to find those with whom you wish to share a piece of your life — for whom you wish to make mental room. The process goes on throughout life and is most effective when you recognize it in yourself.

Paying attention to your thoughts and feelings as you form new relationships not only enriches your life and underlies the success or failure of those relationships, but is crucial with the new human being who will be your baby. You also need to be aware of the negative feelings as well as the good — of what characteristics you might find difficult to accept, perhaps — because, along with the good feelings, they will determine how you respond to a new person or to your baby. For instance, someone who as a child was acutely sensitive to the fact that his parents lavishly praised his older sister for her good grades and overlooked his efforts to do well may grow up simply to grit his teeth when a peer is promoted or praised instead of himself. Thus, he responds as he did as a child in the face of his sister's success, rather than being aware of his feelings and dismissing them as irrelevant in respect to his peer and being able to judge this person's success on its own merits. Becoming aware of your feelings, both good and bad, allows you to control them for your own benefit and the benefit of your relationships with other adults and, especially, your children.

Through daydreaming, you start to make room for your baby in your mind in five stages, starting even before pregnancy: imagining yourself grown-up, imagining parenthood, imagining your pregnancy, imagining your baby, and, finally, settling on a name for the real child to come.

Imagining Yourself Grown-Up

As a young child, you probably played at being a mother or a father, performing those grown-up tasks you saw your parents doing. You pretended to make dinner in the kitchen, to get ready for work, to clean the house, to set and enforce rules for imaginary children. And as an adolescent you probably also spent long hours dreaming about who you would be when you grew up: maybe out on your own, living in the big city in your big apartment; or having your own house, farm, business, company. Or, like many young people, you may have dreamed about being able to go wherever you wanted, whenever you felt ready and with whomever you chose — solitary master and captain of your own life. This image probably survives in the common adult dream of having your own job where you can make your own money and all your own decisions, fully and deliciously independent. And also, like other young people, you may have imagined having a family someday, perhaps even soon — fantasies that seemed perfectly compatible with your dreams about moving away from home as a carefree, independent adult. By allowing you to practice in your mind a major step you are thinking of taking, such daydreams help you to prepare for them.

Fortunately or not, life on your own never quite turns out as you dreamed in the security of childhood and adolescence. People are never as independent or carefree as they have imagined they would be. A job brings regular working hours, bills, and income taxes. Being the complete master of your own destiny can be lonely, and most people seek to bring others into their lives, perhaps even a close partner. When two people develop a more committed relationship to each other, their daydreams and lives take yet another turn. Now each is accommodating another person's needs and wishes; each is sharing his or her days, weeks, and years with another soul. And each must adjust his or her early daydream of being independent to the new one of keeping a partner to love.

If all goes well, people weave each other into their daydreams. As two individuals become a couple, they may imagine together how they will spend the years ahead: traveling, working, balancing each other's likes and dislikes. Just as a young person daydreams about leaving home, a couple may daydream about making a home. And these images may include having children: what they will look like, what kind of parent each partner will be, how the children will have the best of both parents. These daydreams take up some of the same mental space that each person once employed to imagine being a couple together forever.

Indeed, the chances are that your partnership, long-term relationship, or marriage is not quite as you imagined when you entered into it. Some things are probably far better than you anticipated; others, not so ideal. You may have to live in a small apartment or with relatives as you start your married life together. Or you both may work long hours and rarely see one another. Or work may take you far from the extended family of one or both of you, compounding the difficulty of adjusting to one another with having to separate from home. Each discovers quirks about the other that are endearing or irritating, preferences that are compatible or totally alien.

As a result of the discrepancies between daydreams and reality, you are continually adjusting your imagined life to your real one. Once again, unconsciously as well as consciously, you daydream — both to prepare yourself for disappointments you do not want to put into the glaring light of words, and to play with exciting possibilities, however distant these may be in reality. Imagination helps you both to adjust and to change your real life. For example, even if partners do not have the extra money to take a longed-for trip together, they may conjure up the place they would like to visit by reading books and watching television programs about that place. Or one partner might prepare the other's favorite food from that place for a special surprise dinner at home. And sometimes imagining children is a way to re-model your anticipation of life as a couple — to bring the two of you closer again when life's day-to-day realities have proven too stressful.

Imagining Parenthood

The more completely you understand why you are becoming a parent at a particular time, the more clearly you can perceive what you deeply, even unconsciously, wish for yourself and your offspring. Take time, then, to reflect on what you hoped starting a family would be like. You may be surprised to recognize many motivations you were not previously aware of. You may want to bear children to feel creative or productive. You may hope that someone will always be there to love you. The idea of being a mother may make you feel more like a woman; or of being a father, like a man. As you look deep within yourself, you may realize that you want children to bring your spouse closer or to ease the lonely feelings you have when he or she is away. Children may bring purpose to an adult's seemingly empty or undirected life: a child represents that person's best work and finest hour. Becoming a parent may fulfill what you think (or know) your parents wished for you or for themselves. You may yourself want to have children so that your parents can see them. You may feel pressure from society or cultural traditions to carry on a family line. Or you may seek to repair some secret disappointment, to fill in a loss or an absence, or to fulfill long-held aspirations and convictions. You cannot help but bring such deep intentions and needs to your parenting.

None of these reasons is unusual or wrong. They are all perfectly human. Each reason hints at expectations that parents have for their children, expectations they may or may not be aware of. That a mother sees her child as proof of her own creativity and value is healthy and expected; but that mother may also be profoundly disappointed, sad, and angry if her child proves to have developmental or behavioral problems. A father who always imagined coaching his son in football may be hurt when the boy prefers swimming instead, and may not enjoy seeing how good a swimmer he is.

Only when you are aware of your wishes, both fulfilled and failed, can you acknowledge and overcome any disappointment or frustration, as you must do for the sake of your child. As much as you may try to hide your feelings from your children, they will sense them and feel that they need to help you to fulfill your expectations — perhaps even before they feel able to fulfill their own. Children who come to feel incapable of making their parents happy are likely not to develop normally. Thus, the more you pay attention to your innermost wishes, doubts, and beliefs, the more self-observant you will be as a parent and the more open you will be to the realities of your children.

Imagining being a parent is different from imagining pregnancy or your children, though people usually imagine all of these at the same time. A woman might find that imagining future children pushes her closer to imagining herself as a mother. She envisions the satisfaction of holding her baby, teaching a son to play baseball, watching a daughter excel in school, and decides — often without even seeing this as a decision — that she will definitely become a parent. The image of her children carries the day. The opposite is

sometimes true, too. Another woman imagines holding a helpless baby who is completely dependent upon her, and lets her worries make the choice: Could I ever be so reckless as to let myself be responsible for a little one's needs?

In reality, you can never fully imagine or anticipate all of the adjustments you will need and want to make as a parent, just as you can never imagine or understand all your reasons for choosing to be one. You never fully anticipate how children will change both your individual lives and your life as a couple. Your mental picture of how you will feel when you first see your new baby never quite matches reality. Nor can you grasp ahead of time how your children will preoccupy your mind. Many parents are sure they will both return to work in six weeks and in their usual, competent, highly organized ways take care of their baby, their jobs, and each other. Others, on the other hand, are certain that at least one of them will want to stay home with their baby and not return to work until the child is well into school. You can never fully imagine how love, worry, disappointment, even anger may overwhelm you when your new life as a parent bumps into your mental image of that life.

Imagining Pregnancy

Biologically, of course, pregnancy begins with fertilization. But in a woman's or a man's mental world, it begins in imagination and in daydreams. How you think about or imagine being pregnant even before you actually are is as much a part of your well-being during the months of pregnancy as is your physical health.

Not only does pregnancy significantly change a woman's body, but it also changes her state of mind and her partner's. The more we learn about the human body, the more evidence there is that these changes in mental perspective are based in part on biology and genes. They are an essential part of pregnancy and also prepare the way for you to be able to care for your children. Thus, pregnancy is both a physical and a psychological state.

Both men and women spend time imagining pregnancy. A man may think about becoming a father, the sexual intimacy, his potency or virility, as well as how he will care for his pregnant partner. He may imagine how he will feel when others see his partner

pregnant and know that he is fathering a baby. He wonders how healthy or vigorous his sperm is. He imagines how he will manage the delivery: Will I be present? How will I handle the waiting? Will I be cool and supportive? Will the baby be healthy? How well will I be able to provide for my partner and our new baby?

A woman imagines how pregnancy will change her body, how for nine months she will have the biological responsibility to provide a nurturing, safe world for her baby, how she will feel when the baby begins to move. She, too, worries about her potency: How healthy are my eggs? Will I be able to carry the baby to full term? Am I strong enough for the labor and delivery? How good will my milk be? Will my partner and I know what our baby needs, are we up to the task of parenting, will I match my own ideal of the good mother? She wonders, too, whether she is taking enough care of herself: Am I worrying too much? Did that argument I had last week overstress my baby? A part of imagining your pregnancy also involves all the real measures that you believe you are or are not taking to ensure your baby's health. You try to get more sleep because you imagine this is good for the baby (as well as for you). You avoid a particular food that you have always enjoyed but aren't sure the baby needs. To protect your baby from stress, you walk away from an argument you might otherwise have faced head-on.

During the early months of pregnancy, a woman's fantasies about her pregnancy are as important as her physical health because they shape how she begins to think about her child. How much a mother planned and wanted her pregnancy versus how surprised, even distressed, she was also affects how she feels about the baby growing within her and how she anticipates delivery and bringing the baby home. If a couple were not quite planning on becoming pregnant at a particular time, they may look toward the delivery date with a sense of worried resignation. Or a woman who has waited for many years to become pregnant may feel anxious over every change in her body and sit vigilantly waiting for her baby's every movement. A couple's thoughts and feelings about their pregnancy endure long after their baby has arrived. These feelings shape their plans for future pregnancies and color the stories they pass on to their children about when they were growing inside Mommy and about the day they were born.

The imagined pregnancy has become an even more important starting place in our society because more and more often pregnancies are not traditional. Couples have more control over when they can become pregnant, and often choose to put off becoming parents for some years. Ovulation, a basic biological event for women that typically occurs every month until menopause, also becomes a regular psychological event, particularly for a woman hoping to become pregnant. She may count down to those days when she is most likely to become pregnant, and surround that time with fantasies and wishes for a baby. To a woman nearing menopause and still waiting for a child, every monthly ovulation may feel like a soon-to-close window of opportunity.

Other methods of becoming a parent also affect the imagined pregnancy. Now, with alternative means of conception, infertile couples, single women, or gay couples who have long desired to become parents can have children on their own. In addition, the process of planning and waiting to adopt a child has many of the psychological characteristics of a pregnancy, even without the physical changes for the mother. Finally, when a pregnancy ends prematurely, either as a miscarriage or in premature birth, a couple's psychological pregnancy may not end at the same time. They may continue for months to imagine the baby who would have been born, and to think about their future together as if they would soon be holding that child.

Imagining Your Baby

Creating a mental portrait of your baby is a crucial step in your transition from imagining being a parent to becoming one. Usually mothers and fathers begin creating such a portrait of their future child's personality and physical characteristics during pregnancy: "She'll look just like my sister," or "He'll be much less demanding than his brother was." When couples become pregnant, they often use details from the pregnancy to fill out their imagined portrait: "He kicks all the time — he's going to be a really active boy." "He likes Sinatra records, just like me. He always stops moving when I play Sinatra." Adoptive parents also have the same powerful need to create a space in their minds for the child they expect to love. In their imaginings, they, too, link and compare their adoptive child to members of their respective families, even though they know they cannot be linked genetically. When you actually meet your baby (as we discuss in chapter 5), whether at delivery or at an adoption agency, he or she overlaps with your imagined baby, and you begin the process of reconciling the two — or not.

Your mental portrait of a child is always a mixture of positive and negative — traits you like and those you dislike, even hate. As hard as it may be to acknowledge, it is nonetheless human nature for you to have both loving and angry feelings toward the people close to you, even your children. These angry or hateful feelings may be related to your thoughts about other people or to aspects of being a parent that have disappointed you. Parents do not always realize why they feel so angry or disappointed with their child or their baby. Although they most often see their child's behavior or shortcomings as the cause of their distress, usually the negative feelings arise as much, or more, from their own mental lives. Such negative feelings can contribute to many forms of child abuse; but merely having these negative feelings does not make anyone either an abusive or a bad parent.

Thus, as pregnancy progresses and the arrival of your baby nears, take every opportunity to reflect on your thoughts, feelings, worries, and daydreams. The greater your awareness of your inner life, the more available you will be to your child and to his or her inner self.

What's in a Name?

The names you pick for your children inevitably reflect your hopes and fantasies about them. Conversations about possible names can be cherished memories for the expectant father and mother but also lead to disagreement. For some couples, picking a child's name is a long, deliberate process that starts early in their pregnancy. For others, who may have put off the task because it seemed so daunting, the name comes as a sudden inspiration in the exhausted hours after delivery.

Today a new mother and father often choose not just first and middle names, but also their baby's family name. Will the child carry her father's surname, her mother's, or some combination? What does this choice say about the family's commitment to equality and practicality? Couples may spend late evenings or early mornings coming up with given names for their infant, testing how each possibility sounds with the family name. What would be possible nicknames? How well would a name fit an infant, a toddler, a first-grader, a senior in high school? What might the child's peers make of it? What will the child himself think about the choice?

There is, of course, deep meaning in every name, meaning that extends well beyond the definitions offered in baby books that explain that Thomas was an Aramaic word for "twin," for instance. The more important meanings in a name are those the parents bring to it. Does a name match their image of themselves — creative, conservative, eccentric, dignified, novel, traditional? Does the name convey toughness and strength, intelligence and perception, even a touch of whimsy?

Names may derive great significance from family traditions. Some cultures urge parents to name their children after honored relatives. A baby may thus be the fourth in a line of Davids, or every generation of a clan may have a woman named Sarah. Parents may also choose a name that appears in both their families, or take a first name from one side of the family and a middle or last name from the other. If you think your uncle Lee was a man of great integrity and generosity, you might wish to preserve a bit of that legacy by naming your son or daughter Lee. Calling a boy "Junior" naturally implies that he will share more than his name with his father.

Children's names also signal how their families regard the larger culture. Every period has names that seem old-fashioned and others that seem fashionable. Many families choose unusual names without a precedent, or spell a common name in a new way, to signal how their family stands out. Others choose names that reflect, intentionally or not, immersion in the larger culture; in recent years the most popular choice for Asian American boys has been the Irish name Kevin. A name may also honor a childhood or current hero; in the months that followed Charles Lindbergh's 1927 flight across the Atlantic, many more American infants were named Charles than had been before.

Finally, contained in each child's name are the parents' intimations of personality:

"Ethan reminds me of a quiet, thoughtful man, and that is who I'd like our son to be." "We can call her Jennifer after your great-aunt, but at home she's going to be plain 'Jenny.'" As with everything else parents imagine about their children, however, these images may need to change when the babies come along. A "Jo-Jo" can turn out so solemn, even in his crib, that no one calls him anything but Joseph. An infant's casual family nickname may stick with her throughout life. Growing children may insist on being called something different. Nonetheless, with whatever name you choose for your child, you are creating an identity for him or her in your family, community, and culture. You are putting a name to the space you are creating in your mind for the person you are getting to know but have yet to meet face-to-face.

The Practical Realities

Now to move out of your head into the practical realities that you will be more and more concerned with as pregnancy progresses. We deal with them in conjunction with the psychological tasks of imagining parenthood and making room for your baby because, as we have said, the two go hand in hand. Both are essential to the transition to parenthood. Musing over your mental images of your child-to-be and imagining how you'll be as a mother or father make it easier to do the practical tasks, enrich the whole experience, and just make it more enjoyable. And the practical tasks feed your mental images. This interaction will continue even after you are a parent, as will be evident throughout this book.

Although the practical tasks of preparing for a baby vary from family to family, three are universal: analyzing your resources, choosing a pediatrician, and getting help. Planning for these together with your partner is not only prudent but fun.

Your Resources: Time, Money, Space

Before having a baby, you first need to examine your resources in respect to time, money, and space. When you think about time, consider questions like these:

- How much time will you have to get used to being a parent and having a new baby in your home? If you are working, what is your employer's attitude toward parental leave? What kinds of benefits are available to you?
- Is this a good time for you and your partner to become parents? For example, if you are in the middle of an intense training program, how will you manage the added demands of a baby? Will your partner be able to slow down his career while you finish your training? Will you be able to manage an eight- to ten-hour workday and have the energy to take care of your baby?
- Are you settled in your location, or do you anticipate moving in the next year, right before or after the baby is born?

Life's stresses are cumulative. As positive an experience as having a new baby may be,

finding yourself suddenly finishing school, moving, taking a new job, or looking for a new house at the same time that you are pregnant or about to deliver is stressful (even if you pride yourself on handling anything that comes your way). When too much is going on, a parent cannot think clearly about anything, much less how to care for a baby. In making this transition, timing is everything.

In regard to money:

- Have you considered the additional financial costs that having a baby will entail? Coverage for prenatal care, the delivery, and visits to the pediatrician are basic. But what is your health coverage for postpartum and well-child care?
- Have you added the costs of bringing your baby home to your budget: setting up a room with furniture, buying clothes, diapers, food, toys, and a car seat for that first trip home? There are also the possible costs of child care, either in your home or at a center. (See chapter 29.)

For some fortunate couples, these costs are not a burden; but for many other young couples and single parents, even the most basic costs of adding to their family increase their monthly debt. Anxiety about finances can cloud the transition to parenthood and can seriously disrupt a couple's relationship.

As for space, consider: Where will the baby sleep? Will he have a room of his own? Will he sleep in your room? Will you and your partner make something special for your baby — a crib, quilt, toy? Or can you prepare the baby's room together? Late in their pregnancy, many parents find themselves urgently engaged in making a physical space for the baby. Like birds building their nest, they begin to paint a room, pick out furniture or move it down from the attic, and stockpile clothes, diapers, and blankets.

These practical tasks also enhance your awareness of the baby you are both imagining. Even in your choice of furniture, colors for the room, and clothes for the baby, you are giving substance to your mental image of the baby and also to the role you expect to play as a parent. One parent-to-be may be very invested in the baby's comfort, taking special care to see that the crib is well padded and cozy; while the other will want to be sure that the baby is surrounded by beautiful, stimulating things for her to see.

Choosing a Pediatrician

Almost nothing does more to authenticate imagining parenthood and your baby as finding out about and then consulting a pediatrician, the medical doctor who will one day help you care for your child. The physiological and psychological aspects of a child's development are almost completely intertwined for the first year of life, and remain linked (although to a decreasing extent) over the preschool period. A baby's physical health at twelve months, for example, affects her ability to walk, which in turn affects her social development. A pediatrician is trained specifically to deal with all such aspects of a child's life.

Upon graduating from medical school, pediatricians undergo a minimum of three years of training in a children's hospital or inpatient and outpatient children's unit in a general hospital. They rotate through services representing all areas of a child's life, from newborn nurseries and intensive care units to adolescent wards and clinics. In their training, pediatricians see the broad spectrum of children's diseases, injuries, and psychosocial situations. No other group of primary-care professionals has training that is anywhere near so intensive or extensive. For this reason, pediatricians are usually the primary caretakers of choice for children through adolescence.

If you choose your pediatrician before your child is born, you have one less thing to do in the busy days afterward. In some parts of the country, choice of pediatricians may not be an issue because there is only one doctor or group of doctors with that specialty. Some health plans will also limit your choice. Often health plans ask the families they insure to choose a "primary physician," and unify all your care and records at one site. That doctor coordinates your medical care through prescriptions, referrals to other doctors, and admissions to the hospital. Adults usually designate a general practitioner or internal medicine specialist as their primary caregiver, rather than a specialist in a particular area of medicine. But while that choice may well be right for you, it is probably not the best choice for your young children. Fortunately, many plans allow families to designate different primary physicians for different members of the family.

Almost as soon as people know that you are expecting your first child, they will probably begin recommending pediatricians to you. Opinions will come from relatives, neighbors, schools, obstetricians, local hospitals. Almost anyone you ask is likely to have a suggestion. Even the most restrictive health plan is likely to present a list of local possibilities. How to choose? Begin by asking the people who give you recommendations what they like and admire about each physician, so that you will have some idea whether the referrers have thought about the subject or are just reacting automatically to your news with a name they know. Consider also whether their reasons for recommending their doctor matter to you. A family who suffers from allergies, for instance, may have chosen their pediatrician because he specializes in treating that set of problems, but that does not mean he would be the best doctor for your child.

If you have strong feelings about which hospital you would like your child to be in if he becomes seriously ill, find out in advance whether a pediatrician can admit children into that hospital and care for them there. You can phone a doctor's office and ask what local hospital or hospitals she is affiliated with. If any of the hospitals in your area is connected to a medical school, you might also find out whether a pediatrician has a teaching appointment in the school as well as in the hospital. In most areas only the most highly esteemed practitioners have such appointments.

Another measure of quality is whether a doctor has passed the National Pediatric Board examination that certifies competent specialists. Once upon a time, older practitioners in the field did not bother to acquire such a credential, but now almost everyone who is eligible by training knows that it is essential for practice. A pediatrician cannot be a member of the American Academy of Pediatrics (AAP) without having passed the boards. When you visit a doctor's office, look on the wall for a certificate announcing that she is a Diplomate of the American Board of Pediatrics. Or ask the doctor or her staff directly. Don't feel intimidated by a white coat (if this physician happens to wear one).

Probably the best way to choose a pediatrician is to narrow your list down to a few candidates and then make appointments to meet with each one face-to-face. When you make these appointments, make it clear that you are still looking. It is not fair to ask all these doctors to set aside time for a full appointment and prenatal interview if you have not yet made up your mind. Learn what you can from your visit, and respect each doctor's desire to serve his or her patients (and earn a living).

Here are some common questions to ask:

- Where did the doctor study medicine? At what hospitals did he train? Why did he choose pediatrics as a specialty? How long has he been in practice? The goal here is not to identify which doctor's medical school was rated best in recent magazines, but to get to know each candidate and all that he brings to his practice. If you plan to stay in the area and have several children, you could be seeing this pediatrician for two decades, so you might prefer a young doctor over an established one who plans to retire in a few years.

- Does the doctor have any particular subspecialties or interests? Many pediatricians do not, preferring to see a wide variety of children. Others build up their knowledge in one area, such as allergies or autism or sports injuries, while continuing to see other patients.

- If the doctor is part of a group, might any of the pediatricians in that group see your child when you make an appointment for a regular checkup, or do you always get the physician of your choice?

- If the doctor is in a group, can you meet the other pediatricians and get a quick sense of what they are like?

- Who sees the doctor's patients when she is not available? A pediatrician should not just go away and leave you to fend for yourself; she should make specific arrangements with one or more other pediatricians to see urgent cases. In this situation, a pediatrician who is part of a group often has an advantage.

- What specialists does the pediatrician use when he thinks more specialized care is called for? It will certainly be important to you in a crisis to know that the specialist he will recommend is not just any surgeon or cardiologist, but one trained specifically in the surgery or the heart problems of children.

- Is the office convenient to your home? Do the visiting hours fit your schedule? Some doctors have weekend and evening appointments for families who cannot visit any other time.

- Does the doctor reserve a block of longer appointments for families who have special problems they want to discuss?

- Last, but far from least, does the doctor show interest in your child's whole life and not just his physical health? A good pediatrician wants to know about developmental landmarks, behavior, friends, schools and how a child is performing in them, and how you and your extended families are all getting along. This quality may be difficult to judge when your baby is not even born yet, but one gauge is whether the doctor asks about you, your families, and your plans for parenthood. Another way to approach this topic is to ask the pediatrician how she tracks children's development, how she recommends helping them get ready for school, and other open-ended questions.

Both parents should attend these sessions to select a pediatrician. Just as important as the answers to your questions is how you respond to each pediatrician as a person. You need to know that your doctor and his office environment will suit your style. A physician may be the most highly esteemed in the community, but you can still find him a cold fish. You will want to feel that your child's doctor has some empathy with her and with you. Would you be comfortable putting questions to this doctor and not worry about feeling dumb or being laughed at? If you feel afraid that you might mistreat or hurt your child, is this doctor someone you could go to for help? You should also feel comfortable with the doctor's reception or business staff; you may be seeing a lot of them. It is not a good sign if a pediatrician is rushed and hurries you through a conversation you have scheduled: she may not manage time well, meaning that you and your child would spend long periods in her waiting room.

Nowadays most thoughtful pediatricians begin their formal relationship with a new patient by conducting a prenatal interview. This conversation gives a doctor a sense of your family and background; how the pregnancy is going physically and psychologically for both mother and father; what expectations, hopes, and plans you both have for the coming infant; what kind of feeding program you are planning; what kind of help you will have in the first days and weeks; your plans about going back to work; and so on. If you have questions or concerns about immunizations, this is a good time to bring them up. Some pediatricians will have made all of this a part of that first interview, and others will require another visit. In either case this session is an important first step in the relationship between you and your pediatrician, and you should expect her to charge for it. (For more about working with your pediatrician, see chapter 6.)

Getting Help

Consider now, before your baby arrives, whether you will need help and, if so, how to get it. Who will be there to support you as you care for your new baby, whether you are a single parent or a couple? Who will help you to keep your baby safe? How will you get time to yourself — a night out, a day off? All parents need to take care of themselves physically and psychologically so as, over the long run, to be better able to take care of their children. In our society, both parents are often separated from their extended families, so grandparents, uncles, and aunts may not be close enough to help you in this. Do you have friends you can rely upon? Have you thought about child care? Of course, in each of these areas, there are many individual issues and needs. Planning for them will bring actual parenthood a bit closer to reality.

Your Own Reality

Becoming a parent will not only change your view of yourself but alter every other relationship in your life. A new parent moves to a different psychological orbit. Sometimes he makes his child the center of all of his feelings and activities; even when he does not, he is always aware that he now has a new role. For many couples, the greatest strain in the transition to parenthood will not be the various material stresses — space, time, and money — but rather the change in the balance of their relationship. Both of you will have to focus on the baby rather than on one another; and one partner may feel left out or neglected in the shift. You will need to reorient yourselves to one another at the same time as you begin to think of yourselves as parents. No longer will you be able to decide spontaneously to go out for the evening or run away for the weekend. You will have a baby to think about. No longer will you be able to stay up with friends till all hours. The baby will need a schedule and sleep — and so will you.

Whether you are a single parent or a couple, your friendships will change, especially with friends who have not yet made the same transition. No matter how hard you may resist, much of your conversation will be about being a parent. Your child will, more often than not, be the center of your life and uppermost in your mind. Things that seemed extremely important before you became a parent will melt away. This is a very common reaction, which seems even to have a biological basis. It will take thoughtful attention to help old friends make the transition with you and include them in your new life — if they want to be included.

Extended families also change, and this can be rough going. Relatives may have a hard time catching up. Parents or older siblings may still see you as the baby in the family, even though that baby now has a baby himself. They will want to be sure you do this right since you are, in their minds, still young and inexperienced. Extended families are indeed a repository of valuable information about how to raise children, but the urge of every generation to make this transition in its own style can cause tension. New mothers may draw closer to their own mothers or pull further away, depending on whether the older generation accepts the younger one's maturation. Older siblings who have already mastered this parenting thing may want to tell their younger brother all about how to do it. Grandparents who used to dote on you may turn their full attention to their new great-grandchild. It can take years for some families to let their children become parents in their own right. Just as you need to reflect upon your new identity, so the members of your family need to adjust their own mental portraits of you. Even in the first weeks and months of your pregnancy, your relationships and your sense of your own role and priorities will begin to change. It is then that your transition to the reality of parenthood begins.

CHAPTER 4

The Course of Pregnancy

The image of the expectant mother is a powerful icon across cultures. The pregnant body with its full, rounded abdomen, full breasts, and flushed cheeks represents continuity across the generations as well as hope, nurturing, goodness, abundance, and even the essence of being a woman. Since prehistoric times, pregnancy has symbolized fertility and good fortune. It also gives a woman a different status in every society, as people gather around to protect her and watch over her health. In some cultures, fertility and pregnancy even make a woman more powerful, as she joins the privileged state of Motherhood.

Many societies also take it upon themselves to monitor, even intervene in, a pregnant woman's behavior and her physical health. During no other time in a woman's life do strangers approach her asking such personal questions as, "How far along are you?" or "You really shouldn't be drinking that wine, should you?" These unsolicited personal comments can make a pregnant woman realize that this most personal, life-changing event is also a most public one. She may feel that she has shouldered a responsibility not only to her baby and the baby's father but to her extended family, community, and culture as well. And it may well be that this is society's way of preparing her for those responsibilities.

Each expectant mother has her own feelings about the changes in her body. You may feel deep satisfaction and pride as you become more and more evidently pregnant. Even the inevitable swelling of your feet, the discomfort of so much added weight pulling on your back, and the baby's kicks in the middle of the night do not diminish your contentment with your pregnancy. Or perhaps your body changes are not particularly satisfying or comforting, but a necessary step, even a burden, before having a child. Women who take neither pleasure nor pride in their pregnancy perceive the questions of colleagues, the concern of family and friends, or the uninvited friendliness of strangers as intrusive. Both maternal responses are normal.

Some of these feelings will, inevitably, become woven into a mother's view of her baby. Thus, she might later tell her child, "I was so happy to be pregnant — I loved every month, even finding clothes I could wear as you got bigger and bigger. I felt like my body was your first home and I wanted to take care of it for you." Or, "Those last months I was miserable. Those hot, humid weeks of August — I thought you'd never come! By the middle of the day, my clothes were soaked through. My feet were so swollen, I couldn't wear my shoes and had to prop my legs up. I just kept wishing you would hurry up. But when you were born, I was so glad to see you!"

Of course, as a mother's body changes, her baby is changing as well. Women often imagine these internal changes as much as they notice the external evidences of their pregnancy. Even before a mother notices "quickening," or the first movements of the baby around the fourth or fifth month of pregnancy, she already has all kinds of fantasies and thoughts about the person growing inside her.

A baby's development in the mother's uterus has three well-defined developmental stages with clear time boundaries. We shall discuss these in some detail before going on to address the well-being of your fetus and the delivery of your baby. In this chapter we shall also speak about the premature baby and about adoption.

The Stages of a Baby's Development

Understanding the process and timing of pregnancy will help you to deal with both its physical and psychological aspects. The more you know about the biological aspects of pregnancy, the more you feel confident about taking care of yourself physically. Your confidence in turn encourages and supports your reflecting upon your thoughts and feelings about your pregnancy.

The length of a human pregnancy is calculated in lunar months of twenty-eight days each. Human pregnancy typically lasts ten lunar months, or 280 days, when the time is counted (as is customary) from the first day of the mother's last menstrual period. More accurately pregnancies are about 266 days long, as fertilization does not usually occur until ovulation, twelve to fourteen days after that last menstrual period.

The three stages in the development of a baby in pregnancy are: the fertilized ovum, the first trimester, and the fetal stage.

Fertilization

Fertilization is a complex, choreographed process. When a woman ovulates, an egg is ejected from one of the two ovaries into the space between the ovary and one of her two Fallopian tubes. Tiny, delicate fronds on the end of the tube contract or wave rhythmically to move the egg into its opening. Once in the tube, the egg begins to move toward the uterus, but fertilization usually occurs before it arrives there, when it meets a sperm. These sperm swim into the uterus from the vagina and up the Fallopian tubes. A man usually ejaculates as many as 20 million sperm cells; but once one sperm successfully penetrates the outer covering of the egg and fertilization occurs, the egg becomes impenetrable to other sperm.

After fertilization, the egg is carried the rest of the way to the uterus by the rhythmic contractions and currents in the Fallopian tubes. The journey requires between five and nine days; by the time it reaches the uterus, what started out as a single fertilized egg cell is about 125 cells. They are still in a microscopic ball, hardly larger than the ovum was at the time of fertilization. Sometimes the fertilized egg does not move successfully into the uterus and continues to grow in the Fallopian tube, resulting in what is called an "ectopic pregnancy," a dangerous situation for the mother. Even after a fertilized egg, or zygote, makes it to the uterus, it still needs to implant itself firmly into the womb's muscular wall and begin to grow. When the fertilized egg fails to attach to the uterus, it will be carried off during the woman's next period. Many pregnancies end at this stage, with the parents none the wiser.

This initial stage takes about two weeks. Up to this point, a woman may note a missed menstrual period or the first twinges of morning sickness. Her desire or anxiety over a possible pregnancy will heighten her sensitivity to these changes in her body.

The First Trimester

The second stage of development stretches from the second to the eighth week of pregnancy. During this stage (also called the first trimester), your baby takes form. At the beginning, the embryo already contains cells differentiating themselves into skin, nerves, and bone. A recognizable human form emerges from the microscopic zygote: a body with a recognizable head and the rudiments of eyes, ears, and nose. Bud-shaped arms and legs are in place by the end of the eighth week, and a very simple heart starts to beat. By the end of the first trimester, the embryo is on average two inches long and weighs about two-thirds of an ounce. Embryos develop from head to tail and from inside to outside: that is, the brain and internal organs appear first, and the head develops before arms and legs or fingers and toes. This pattern of development is remarkably consistent across species.

This second stage is very sensitive. Various events may affect the course of the embryo's development. Viral illnesses, certain prescription and nonprescription drugs, and alcohol each have the potential to influence dramatically the development of nearly all the baby's organ systems during this stage. The baby's physical appearance may also be affected. It is in these first eight weeks that the baby's brain begins to form, especially the neurons that will be the building blocks of all mental activity for the rest of his life. (For the continuation of the brain's development, see chapter 9.)

The Fetal Stage

The third stage of a baby's development, the fetal stage, begins in the eighth week and lasts until birth, covering the second and third trimesters of pregnancy. All the baby's organ systems, including the brain, are clearly defined and grow in size during this time. By the end of the tenth week or third month of pregnancy, the head of the fetus is one-third of its entire length. The fetus begins simple sucking behavior. By the end of the fourth month, the fetus is around six inches, the bones have begun to form, all organs are clearly formed, and the baby is starting to move. By the end of the sixth month, the mother can feel the baby moving just by putting her hand on her abdomen (though the baby has been moving since the third month). You can now hear a clear heartbeat. The baby can open and close its eyes and weighs close to twenty ounces. Babies born at this premature point may be able to survive in a modern intensive-care nursery.

During those last few weeks in a pregnancy, when the mother is aware of gaining much more weight and size, the baby is growing rapidly. It is also storing up the reserves it will need for delivery and the first weeks of life. After the seventh month, the fetus grows from about fifteen inches long to twenty inches at the end of pregnancy, and from about two and a half pounds to, on average, seven and a half pounds. In the last half of the twentieth century, babies generally increased in birth weight, a change that reflects the overall better health of mothers, better nutrition, and more widespread prenatal care.

Before turning to your final preparations to meet your baby and for your delivery, we need to address the health of the developing baby.

Fetal Well-Being and Prenatal Care

Good prenatal care is vital for every expectant mother — not only for your health and the health of your baby but to help you find out about and prepare yourself to deal with any adverse factors such as birth defects.

Even in this age of advanced medical care, many women do not get adequate prenatal care or nutrition during the last months of their pregnancy. A mother must eat enough to allow her child to develop fully in the womb. Severe maternal malnutrition delays fetal growth, as we know from the twentieth century's famines and food shortages during wars. Infants who are shorter and weigh less at birth than normally nourished infants of the same age (as measured from conception) are referred to as "small for gestational age" (SGA) or "intrauterine growth retarded" (IUGR). Usually, we say an infant is SGA if his birth weight is 90 percent or less than what would be expected for an infant the same gestational age from the same culture or ethnic background.

When a mother is malnourished during pregnancy, several mechanisms are called into play to protect her infant's brain. Developing infants first slow down in weight gain, then in bone or linear growth, and last of all in brain growth. A baby born with a reduced head size as well as reduced weight and length has been severely malnourished. Other factors, including smoking and alcohol, also slow normal fetal growth in the third trimester by interfering with how the placenta provides nutrients to the baby. Infants born SGA may catch up in their physical growth in late infancy and early toddlerhood, but some evidence suggests that characteristic intellectual and behavioral difficulties may persist through childhood.

Pregnancy increases a mother's nutritional and energy requirements as much as 10 to 15 percent. Protein is most essential for adequate fetal brain growth. A pregnant woman's body also makes protein at greatly increased rates so as to form a placenta and enlarge her uterus as her baby grows. In other words, the body begins to manufacture more materials to construct the architecture of the pregnant body. A pregnant mother also stores more fat to accommodate her increased energy needs, and burns fewer carbohydrates so as to have more sugar or glucose available for her fetus. Pregnant women need more minerals (including calcium, iron, magnesium, and zinc) and vitamins (including D, E, and B_6); they have a particular need for the vitamin folic acid. These requirements may be as much as a quarter to a half more than a woman needs before pregnancy.

Parental Age at Conception

Your and your partner's age can affect the physical well-being of your baby. A woman over age forty is about forty times more likely to have a child with Down syndrome (produced by an extra chromosome) than is one in her twenties. For an older mother, smoking or general health problems are even more likely to cause problems for her infant. Similarly, for men over fifty-five, the probability of fathering a child with Down syndrome rises 20 to 30 percent. Other deformities in chromosomes also become more common with advancing parental age. On the other hand, improved prenatal care and new technologies such as amniocentesis often make it possible to determine the presence of any chromosomal abnormalities or other defects early in a pregnancy (as we discuss later in this section). These techniques have encouraged more couples to become pregnant later, and the number of pregnancies among women in the middle to late thirties has increased dramatically in the last two decades.

Birth Defects

Two kinds of agents can cause birth defects: teratogens and mutagens. Teratogens include events such as the mother's illness during pregnancy; substances such as a drug, including alcohol and cocaine; and any of various chemical pollutants that affect the developing embryo or fetus directly. Many of the teratogens we now know about were not recognized as such until they affected a significant number of pregnancies. Thalidomide, a drug once prescribed for morning sickness in Europe (but not legally in the United States), turned out to be one of these.

The effects of a teratogen may not be evident immediately after birth, but can appear later when a baby requires more complex brain functions or other metabolic activities. Some teratogens are expressed as late as adulthood: for example, the link between a mother's exposure to diethylstilbestrol (DES) and late-onset vaginal cancer in her adult daughters. Teratogens also do not necessarily produce only physical malformation. So-called behavioral teratogens, such as cocaine and alcohol, affect the brain and can impair psychological functioning.

The effect of a teratogen depends on the timing of the mother's exposure (how early in pregnancy, especially the first trimester), on the amount of the exposure, and even on genetic factors. The genes of some parents may determine their vulnerability to the effects of certain teratogens, such as alcohol. Stress and malnutrition during a pregnancy may render a fetus more susceptible to the effects of teratogens. Stress itself may even have some teratogenic effects. Many cultures identify specific foods as dangerous (even if they don't call them teratogens) and prohibit certain actions, such as walking past a graveyard. A pregnant woman may still hear warnings about these dangers.

In contrast to teratogens, mutagens cause changes in genetic material; thus, the effect of mutagens on the development of a fetus can be passed from one generation to another. Deafness caused by a mutated gene may affect successive generations, whereas deafness caused by a mother's exposure to a viral infection during pregnancy will not do so. Nuclear radiation is a well-known mutagen whose damage to exposed genes may be passed on to future generations. Therefore, if you think you may be pregnant, avoid having X rays and do not work with radioactive materials.

Ultrasound and Amniocentesis

Parents-to-be tend to be convinced either that their baby is healthy, or that something is terribly wrong with their pregnancy. Every physician should respect and take seriously these feelings, especially when the parents' anxiety persists. Through modern technology, including ultrasound imaging and amniocentesis, physicians can both monitor a fetus and also give you a chance to see your baby in the womb long before delivery.

Ultrasound (sometimes called a sonogram) uses sound waves to create an image of the fetus. Because sound travels at different speeds through water or solids, it creates patterns based on the density of the material it passes through. Ultrasound is among the least harmful and least invasive techniques for examining a fetus. It is used to check how a baby is growing and whether there are any obvious birth defects. It is also a good method for estimating how far along a pregnancy is, for seeing how the baby is positioned in the uterus, and for identifying multiple fetuses.

Ultrasound images also make it possible for you to see movement, including prenatal behavior such as thumb sucking. Ultrasound images may sometimes let you know the sex of your baby without amniocentesis and chromosomal analysis, though determining a baby's sex from an ultrasound depends on getting good images of the genitalia, which in turn requires the baby to "cooperate" by being in a convenient position. Using ultrasound, physicians can examine bone structure and get a more precise age of the fetus by determining the size and development of body structures such as arms and legs.

Amniocentesis is the technique of extracting a sample of fetal cells from the womb for chromosomal analysis. Ultrasound is always used with amniocentesis to guide the physician in sampling the amniotic fluid without harming the baby. But since the information from sonograms does not derive from fetal cells, it is not as extensive or as accurate as that from amniocentesis. In "amnio" a needle is inserted through the mother's abdomen and uterus into the amniotic fluid surrounding the fetus. The fluid contains fetal cells, which technicians examine for such problems as extra or missing chromosomes. The sex and blood type of the baby can also be determined from an amniocentesis. Chemical compounds such as alpha-fetoprotein (AFP) are also assessed in amniotic fluid; an elevated AFP may indicate a problem with the development of the baby's nervous system (so-called neural tube defects). Amniocentesis involves a slight risk of infection and miscarriage (usually in fewer than 1 percent of women) and is not usually performed until the fifteenth to seventeenth week of pregnancy.

Coming to Delivery

Just as in the earlier aspects of pregnancy, the last few weeks are a mix of the psychological and the practical — each now, though, building in intensity.

Preparing to Meet Your Baby

Since the latter half of the twentieth century, technology has allowed parents to build up bits of "real" information about their baby long before delivery. Ultrasounds and other tests during pregnancy can not only let you know very early whether to expect a boy or a girl, twins or triplets, a healthy baby or one with possible problems; but can also allow you to see your baby's video in real time, receive a blurry black-and-white Polaroid of her curled in the womb, and listen to her heart beating vigorously and in stereo.

These blurry pictures may answer some of the pressing mysteries of your pregnancy, such as your baby's gender and whether she is healthy, but they also affect you psychologically. Parents often carry around ultrasound images as if they were a baby's first professional portraits. They can heighten your sense of having a real baby and may thus increase or allay your worries. As tangible symbols of the new baby to come, they also may make expectant mothers and fathers more eager to get things ready for him or her.

As the baby gains weight in these last two to three months of pregnancy, mothers increasingly turn their thoughts inward. The outside world, while ever-present, seems more at a distance, as if you were viewing it through a misty lens. This inward turning is not constant. It may — especially in the late stage of pregnancy — feel stronger during quiet moments early in the morning or late at night, but recede during the day in response to the demands of work and other children. Through this natural reverie, a woman's mind is preparing her for the enormous attention her newborn will require. This increasingly preoccupied state also happens to fathers, as they find themselves thinking more and more about their baby and the changes ahead in their lives. Many parents say that, even when they try to distract themselves, they cannot get their minds off the coming baby. Nearly every thought, every line of conversation leads back to the pregnancy, the baby, the upcoming delivery.

At the same time, of course, during the last weeks of pregnancy, parents are also actively preparing for their baby — buying supplies, a car seat, a crib — packing a few things in wait for the delivery and lining up people to help care for their newborn. (See pages 42–48.) Research has shown that the preoccupied mental state and the baby-related activity of parents-to-be are as much biological as psychological: both are set in motion, at least in part, by changes in the neurochemistry of the brain. Thus, the human species has evolved in remarkable ways to ensure that a mother and a father will be ready, psychologically and physically, to care for their infants.

As these preparations in thought and action make the idea of the baby about to be born more vivid, they allow you to begin to form an attachment with him or her well before that moment. In this psychologically vital, necessary stage, you are expanding the place in your minds and in your physical lives for the baby that your imagination started to form months ago. By now, you are likely to be very conscious of your mental portrait of your baby and even of what kind of personality she or he will have.

During these last few weeks, you communicate with your baby more and more. Your efforts to make contact reflect both the increasingly clear picture you have of the baby in your mind's eye and the baby's increasing responsiveness and activity. You may intuit that he prefers certain kinds of music. You may talk to him more often. You may recognize the baby's own rhythms — noticing when he is quiet and still and when he is more active. Sometimes these cycles reflect your own moods and cycles, and sometimes the baby already seems to have a mind of her own — awake and kicking vigorously at four in the morning, as if to announce her presence. If there are other children in the family, they may begin to hang around more, wanting to lay an ear on their mother's abdomen to listen for the baby or to feel the movements.

They, too, want to let their new sibling know they are there, waiting and curious.

Giving Birth

In American society, labor and delivery tend to be considered medical procedures. Most births occur in a hospital, with doctors and other medical personnel focused on the safety of the mother and her newborn. In this setting, technology is readily at hand to affect the course of labor, intervene at the first indication of difficulty, and even perform a cesarean section if the labor moves too slowly or the baby seems in distress. But the medicalization of birth is an invention of the twentieth century and industrialized society. In the past, and still in many places, births occurred most often at home or in special huts or rooms set aside for labor and delivery. Older women who were experienced with birthing babies attended the delivery. Around 1900, infant and maternal mortality rates were high: more than 10 percent of all newborns died during delivery and mothers commonly died from blood loss and infection as well.

Some couples choose to take advantage of modern obstetric technology, especially if they are worried about pain and possible complications. Others prefer to give birth in their home, or in a specialized clinic or hospital unit. People can have divided opinions on whether to arrange for an obstetrician or a midwife, or to bring in a doula (a woman trained to advise and support a mother through the birth and postpartum period). They may place great value on various details of the birth, from not having a cesarean section to arranging for the event to be videotaped. Much as you may want and prepare for a certain type of delivery, you should recognize that the baby and circumstances will not necessarily cooperate with your plans.

Labor and delivery vary according to the individual. The story of those hours, brief or drawn out, becomes a part of the baby's oral history and the attributes parents assign to their child: "It took you nearly a day to be born. The doctors even had to help you push your way out of my body." Or, "You were so ready to meet us you were born in just an hour. You came out all red and crying and already letting everyone know you wanted to be heard." Or, "Even when you were born, you hurt me. You were such a big, strong baby, I couldn't handle you even then." These stories have a way of enduring for years, becoming part of how you define yourself and your children.

The mechanism that causes labor to begin is complex and still largely mysterious. The legendary Greek physician Hippocrates thought that labor begins when the baby is too large for the uterus. As the baby grows, he wrote, there simply is not enough nourishment; so he stretches his arms and legs in agitation, ruptures the membranes, and pushes his way out (head first because the head is so much larger and heavier than the rest of the body). These ideas persisted into the eighteenth century. Even now parents use such images in their stories: "He got so big that he just had to get out." "He was so active, he almost crawled out himself!"

Nonetheless, labor proceeds in stages from the first contractions and rupture of the amniotic sac to the final stage of full cervical dilatation when the baby's head is visible in the birth canal. These final moments between full cervical dilatation and the baby's birth may last from minutes to hours. Although pictures and video cameras now capture these moments with more fidelity than parental memories, your mental images are still the strongest and most enduring.

When the baby is born, parents usually feel a sudden rush of anticipation mixed with relief and fatigue. They (and their friends and relatives) usually want to know the answers to many questions: Is the baby healthy? Is she physically all right? What does he look like? How big is she? How is the mother? It is at this moment that you begin to bring your imagined and real baby together in your mind.

The Premature Baby

Some babies are born prematurely or with conditions that require immediate treatment. An intensive-care nursery is a difficult environment in which to begin to know your baby. The monitors needed to track the infants' breathing and heartbeats make a lot of noise. The nursery is very warm because preterm babies, who are not able to control their own body temperature, lose heat quickly. And it is brightly lit, often for twenty-four hours a day, so the staff may watch the babies closely.

Until recently, premature or sick infants were kept in incubators or isolettes with a minimum of human contact. This isolation was thought to be necessary to protect their delicate systems from infection. Studies now show, however, that preterm infants do better medically and gain weight more quickly when they are held, caressed, and touched. Researchers also notice benefits when parents and medical staff talk to babies and provide them with visual and auditory stimulation, such as mobiles and music or a recording of their parents' voices. Furthermore, by holding and touching and being physically close to their preterm infant, parents can begin to adjust their interrupted vision of a healthy, full-term baby to their child as she or he is. This mental melding of imagined and real baby is especially critical when a baby is premature or sick as a newborn.

Prematurity is defined as birth after thirty-six or fewer weeks — that is, four or more weeks short of the forty weeks of a full-term pregnancy. In the United States, approximately 10 percent of infants are born prematurely, but proportionately more preterm babies are born to young, poor women who have received little to no prenatal care and may be malnourished or have other health problems. Similarly, in underdeveloped countries with less prenatal care available, rates of prematurity are considerably higher.

Not only does prematurity interrupt the natural pace of parents' mental and physical planning for their new baby, but (depending on how premature the baby is) they may also be faced with a seriously ill infant whose chances for survival are moderate or slim.

Additionally, the complex technology needed to care for the many possible complications in the baby's condition can be frightening and confusing. Finally, they have to live with the uncertainty of whether their baby will develop healthily and normally after leaving the hospital.

Parents' worries and fears about a preterm baby often endure for years, even when she has grown up to be a healthy, vigorous teenager. When a baby's health and survival was threatened early on, many parents remain on the alert for danger. Every later illness, however minor, reminds them of that early, serious time, and they work ever harder to protect and shelter their child. Although their child's vulnerability and frailty may be much more in their minds than in reality, this overcautious behavior may unintentionally convey their fears to her. She may, in turn, come to accept her parents' view of herself as weak and fragile and begin to behave as if their attributions were true.

Today the developmental prospects for infants born premature are more optimistic than ever. Even as late as the 1960s, a preterm baby weighing between four and a half and five pounds was about six times more likely to die in the nursery than a full-term six- to seven-pound baby. Now more than 90 percent of preterm infants weighing between two and a half and three and a half pounds survive, and the majority of these infants develop normally.

The outlook for smaller infants is less optimistic. Chances of survival decrease 10 to 15 percent for every 100 grams less than 1000 grams (a little over two pounds) of weight at birth. And over half of those infants who live and leave the nursery have physical and mental disabilities, including lower intelligence, learning disabilities, and motor delays. Even in the smallest weight group, however, not all preterm infants have developmental problems. The fewer medical complications the babies have after delivery, the less likely they are to have long-term developmental complications. (For what to expect when you bring a preterm baby home, see pages 71–72.)

Pregnancy after a Long Wait: Adoption

Many couples cannot become pregnant naturally. Usually they discover this only after trying, often quite hard, for several years. Being a parent is so much part of some people's images of themselves that the long effort can be extremely frustrating, and the news confirming infertility a major shock. The reasons for infertility vary, and often the search to find out the reason for one couple's difficulty is arduous and expensive. Today a remarkable collection of technologies not only allows a better understanding of infertility but also provides many options for achieving a pregnancy that would otherwise be impossible. A couple must usually make a series of attempts, each one physically and psychologically difficult, before the mother carries a successful conception to a full-term pregnancy. Infertility can be a source of considerable stress and sadness for many couples. One partner may blame the other; they may separate as the fertile individual tries to find another partner with whom to fulfill the need to have a child. If the couple keeps trying together, the long process of finding a cause for the failures to have a child increases the "value" of the resulting pregnancy.

Due either to infertility or to choice, many couples today reach their late thirties or early forties before finding themselves pregnant. Such parents, knowing that at their ages they have fewer chances for conceiving, are especially vigilant about any sign of possible complication. Throughout their pregnancy, they are as preoccupied as more normally pregnant parents are in the latter part of the third trimester. Like the very premature infant who survives the intensive-care nursery, a baby born after a long-awaited pregnancy is carefully protected and watched over. And as in that case, the parents' heightened vigilance and worry affect how they imagine the infant and child to come.

Parents seek to adopt a child for many reasons. Some adopt an orphaned child of relatives or friends; others, a child born into less fortunate circumstances. Gay couples may adopt children, so also may a single adult wishing to be a parent. When a pregnant mother has agreed to put her child up for adoption, the adoptive parents sometimes follow her pregnancy as they might their own, their preoccupation and preparation for the baby similarly intensifying as the due date nears. Indeed, most people adopting children have a "psychological pregnancy" as, waiting months or years to learn about an available child, they, too, imagine what their child will be like.

The older an adoptive child is, the more established his personality. This child and his new parents will all have to adjust their habits, desires, and expectations to accommodate each other. Parents adopting an older child may go through a long period of adjustment as a child with a more established personality works to fit in with his new family and his new parents work to know him. These efforts are just as important as pregnancy in preparing people to become parents. All parents, biological or adoptive, need to spend time to make a welcoming space in their minds, in their lives, and in their family for a new child.

CHAPTER 5

Bringing Your Baby Home

The big day is finally here: the day you bring home that new person you've been anticipating so keenly, your new baby. You have put him in his crib where he's sleeping quietly, or he is in his mother's or father's arms being fed by breast or bottle. Perhaps your parents are with you, and they and you are focused on the baby, watching every movement, smiling at the tiniest of sounds, and admiring his perfection. In these first days, time stands still — these are special moments that you will long remember.

The last few days — the hours leading up to delivery, the labor, anxious moments of wondering if everything about your baby will be all right — are probably a blur in your mind. Mother and child were probably, as for most normal births today, in the hospital only a day or two. Thus, you are likely feeling exhausted but not sleepy; dazed but extraordinarily vigilant. If your baby was born prematurely or had health problems, you may have had to wait longer than average to bring him home. Or you may have brought your

child home after the tense ordeal of adoption or after years of trying to conceive.

Whatever the circumstances of your baby's advent into your life, you are now alone at home with her. For months, she has been growing in her mother's body and has been the chief focus of your imaginings. Now she is out in the world, breathing, sucking, real. Now she is separate from you, yet intimately of you. Your first hours and days with her are very special as you begin to get to know her — as you learn both to recognize her separateness and uniqueness and at the same time to appreciate how much she needs you.

There is no standard way for mothers and fathers to achieve this psychological transition, but however you have defined and created your family, all parents need to make it. Before birth you began to imagine your baby, to prepare psychological room for him, just as you prepared his actual physical room. That preparation enters a new phase when you bring your baby home and start the process of adjustment. The more you are aware of this process, the more expansive and flexible you will be as you incorporate your child into your life as a family.

Getting to Know All about Your Baby

After the rush of the delivery and the congratulations of friends and relations, your first hours alone with your child can feel timeless. In the quiet of your own home, you can look at her closely, perhaps more closely than you did in the hospital or just after the delivery. You can explore every inch of her body, looking at and touching her soft skin, smelling her softness, listening to her breathe. Whom does she look like? Are those her father's eyes? Can you see your mother's hands or nose? Where did all that black hair come from? Many parents experience highly positive and possessive thoughts: "Isn't he strong?" "Look how he nestles his head right on my shoulder!" "Watch how intently he studies me!"

In these first days after birth, you make your baby yours psychologically, focusing all your attention on him: feeding and caring for him, falling in love with him, learning what his cries mean, adjusting the mental portrait you have been composing of him these many months to the real baby in your arms. As we have said, the preoccupation you experience as an expectant parent is an adaptive biological mechanism — from an early period in human history when newborns were at greater risk from predators, accidents, and illness than they are in the United States today. That automatic increase in attentiveness will stay with you in the first months after your baby's birth. Thus, the biology and psychology of parenting intertwine to create the best environment in which your baby can survive, grow, and thrive.

The Misleading Issue of Bonding

For nearly three-quarters of the twentieth century, it was standard practice in American hospitals to separate mothers from their newborn infants. The babies were kept in sterile nurseries and brought to their mothers' rooms only for feeding; and even then, the nurses took many precautions to protect the newborns' health. But around the 1960s, researchers observing how animal mothers connect with and care for their newborns found that there was a critical, narrow window of time during which a newborn mammal becomes connected to its mother. If, for example, a mother dog and her newborn pup are separated from one another in the hours after birth, the mother would not only fail to care adequately for the pup, but she might even completely ignore it. Investigators studying these animal mother-infant pairs hypothesized that, during this brief period, mothers bond exclusively to their young and that such bonding is stimulated by close physical contact between them. Each baby animal's smell, cry, and touch provides critical bits of information to its mother. Her response to these signals ensures the mutual relationship we call bonding.

Starting in the late 1960s, pediatricians

Marshall Klaus and John Kennell asked whether there is a similar sensitive period during which human mothers become attached to their infants. If so, was the standard practice in hospital nurseries actually working against the emergence of healthy mother-infant relationships? Klaus and Kennell's studies were among the first to consider whether newborns who spend more time with their mothers in the first days and weeks after delivery fare better than those who do not. They measured the infants' growth and performance on early neurodevelopmental assessments and evaluated the quality of mother-child interactions. Among the mothers they studied — many of them poor single women who had not been enthusiastic about becoming parents — there was a notable improvement if mothers and babies spent more time together just after birth. Klaus and Kennell's work changed hospital practice across the country. Newborns began to spend far more time, if not all their time, near their mothers.

While it is good that parents and children now have the chance to interact more fully, these early and subsequent studies do not provide solid proof that human families have only a brief time to establish adequate relations. Infants are receptive to care from the many adults around them for a far longer period than early descriptions of the bonding process allowed for. And, when they are healthy, newborns have ways to engage the interest and care of those adults. The term "bonding" is thus not really appropriate for human infants because it implies that if mothers (or fathers) do not spend an intense,

sustained amount of time with their newborns in the days after birth, as animals do, there will be serious and long-lasting consequences. "Bonding" also implies that a strong connection will quickly and naturally, almost magnetically, form between parents and child.

In fact, attachments between parents and their children deepen over time, varying in immediacy and passion with the individual personalities involved. The biological mechanisms by which parents become hypervigilant about their newborns only sets the stage for their developing an enduring relationship with their baby. There is no solid evidence that an infant who does not spend the first hours after birth with his mother and father develops more slowly or has a less stable relationship with them. Even parents who are unable, because of their own or the baby's illness, to spend time with their infant right away nonetheless do develop a deep, caring relationship with him. Many factors influence your baby's attachment to you, including your fantasies about him, how you and your partner each were parented, whether either of you are depressed or stressed, and the amount of support you have from other people around you. The attachment between you and your new infant takes shape in the first months after your baby is born, and will constantly be remodeled and refined throughout her development.

Falling in Love Again

Falling in love with a man or a woman is a state of mind like no other, except perhaps falling in love with your baby. When you fall in love, you just cannot get the other person out of your mind. Everything, even the tiniest extraneous detail, seems to contain his or her essence and presence.

Furthermore, when you fall in love, everything about the other person is, at least for a time, near perfect. Mannerisms you would have thought silly, even irritating, at an earlier moment now become endearing or arousing. The way a loved one laughs or smiles, or tosses his head or swings her arms, the person's habitual expressions and even often-repeated jokes: all these come across as signs that no one could be more ideally suited to you. Surely the two of you are meant to be together.

Ideally, parents feel much the same about their baby. Mothers and fathers alike describe spending hours upon hours studying their new baby. You can lose track of time as you gaze lovingly, even longingly, at your child. You fill up rolls of film with pictures of the baby (particularly the firstborn) in every pose, every mood, every time of day. Like an impressionist painter trying to capture the slightest change in light, you try to secure in words, pictures, actions, and moments of reverie the unique qualities of this new person who is your child. It is neither accident nor self-centeredness that leads you to talk nearly constantly about your baby: again, you are psychologically and biologically compelled to have him in mind.

Often parents report that, in the initial weeks of getting to know their child, they feel as if they have become different: "Where has

my mind got to?" They wonder whether they have lost their usual level-headedness and good sense: "Is my memory slipping?" Both mothers and fathers can find themselves thinking about the baby as much as half to three-quarters of their waking hours. Even when you go back to work, your thoughts are with the baby. Tiny things are powerful reminders: a whiff of powder, the giggle of a child in a park outside your office window, a pregnant woman walking down the sidewalk, or a businessman rushing to catch a plane with a brightly wrapped toy alongside his briefcase. In the middle of an important meeting, you may drift off suddenly as you relive the feel of your baby in your arms early that morning. These thoughts can also be negative: you may not be able to banish worries about your baby even if everything seems fine. At such moments, you may worry that you are becoming unnaturally obsessed. But these persistent parental thoughts, even when your baby is not actually present, are part of getting to know her and refining the mental space you are making for her.

As you study your child, a realization dawns: there can be no child more perfect. Every other baby pales in comparison. "Who can doubt that this baby belongs to us?" you think. "Who else can appreciate his perfection as much as we do?" Each toe and finger has been shaped sublimely; your baby's every yawn, stretch, and hiccough are clear signals of how well tuned his body is. His hair gleams like threads of gold or shines as black as fine onyx. All parents feel these convictions to some degree. Even when their baby is clearly not perfect, when there are visible problems or a frightening illness, many parents find something in her that makes her more perfect than any other child: maybe an unusual fighting spirit in the face of illness, or the perfection in one hand even if the other is not quite right, or the lusty cry in a weak body.

The fact that you believe your baby is perfect tells you many things about yourself. Perhaps first and foremost, it shows how hard your mind is working at preparing you to be a parent. Someone so special, so rare and perfect, deserves your greatest attention and care. You know that you must do all you can to preserve this unique gift.

At the same time, when you believe your baby is perfect, you are also granting that you, too, must be special. Much as you may sometimes deny your competitive spirit, you cannot help but take pride in the belief that you have exceeded even your own parents in producing a perfect baby. He reflects the best in you (and in all the people in your and your partner's families before you). He even seems to improve on that heritage: you may breathe a quiet sigh of relief when your baby does not exhibit those features you like least about yourself or your partner. In valuing your baby so highly, you reassure yourself that the best of you will endure — your child is your piece of immortality.

A new parent's intense preoccupation probably lasts for about six months. As your baby becomes gradually more vocal, more mobile, and better able to let the world know what she needs, it is not so urgent for you to stay so close physically and mentally. When she gets a few months older, you will spend less time wondering and watching. Your apparent forgetfulness will disappear, and your memory will return to normal. Nevertheless, you are really never quite the same again. Now that you have made room for her in your mind, she is rooted there and will always be in your thoughts, on the edge of consciousness at least. Even two decades later, on college graduation day, you will still see your child as a tiny infant, as she was at your first intimate meeting with her.

Interpreting Your Baby's Cries

One of the first things you learn in getting to know your baby is that he has his own voice. It is as unique as his fingerprints, and you can distinguish it from the cries of other babies, though not as immediately as your newborn's smell. You may at first feel helpless when your baby cries and cries and you are unable to soothe him and have no idea what he wants. Crying is, however, not simply the global automatic response it may at first seem, but your baby's way of transmitting information, just as your own adult tone of voice can convey a variety of messages. Research has shown that a baby's cries are acoustically different, particularly in terms of both pitch, and moment-to-moment changes in pitch, depending on whether she is feeling hungry, sleepy, or in pain. The cry of a hungry baby usually differs from that of a tired one. Over time you will learn to recognize when your crying baby is tired, hungry, or just fussy. (For more on a child's development of communication skills, see chapter 17 on language.)

You react to your child's crying, as you do to all types of infant behavior, according to your own assumptions and state of mind. While no one likes to hear a baby cry, some parents find the sound to be very unpleasant, even aversive. Others start to feel anxious or helpless around a crying infant; the child may sense that anxiety as his parents try to soothe him. Many parents interpret every cry as a communication of need, and their response can vary: they may feel proud of being able to help, eager to give the baby attention right away, or frightened by the baby's extreme dependency. You and your baby will thus develop a distinct communication pattern that both reflects and shapes your individual psychologies.

Certain cries are generally perceived as particularly unpleasant and therefore harder on parents. Crying that is very high-pitched or that does not vary in pitch is extremely hard to bear. Studies show that adults, on hearing recordings of such cries, almost always believe the infants are sicker, more vulnerable, and in greater need of help than babies with lower or modulated cries. In fact, because of damage to certain parts of the brain during development, infants with some types of neurological difficulty or genetic disorder have high-pitched, nonvarying cries. Severe malnutrition also produces a distinctive cry — long, shrill, faint, and without regular rhythm. Since an individual infant's cries are widely variable, these characteristics can also occur in children who do not have genetic or nervous system disorders or other known problems.

Are You Who I Imagined You'd Be?

You probably have had the experience of meeting someone you have heard about for a long time, perhaps years, and about whom you have formed impressions, maybe even a specific mental image. While your first real meeting may seem like a reunion with an old friend, you may be surprised by the mismatch between your mental image and the real person in front of you and have to make an effort to adjust the two.

Meeting your new baby is very much like that. For months, you have been building up a mental portrait of your child. Well before his birth, you have plotted a course for him, assigning him many of your personal hopes and dreams, while at the same time worrying that some black-sheep gene might unexpectedly crop up. You also have a mental picture of your baby's looks: skin like dark cocoa; blond hair and blue eyes; curly hair, a quick smile, thin and tall. You imagine special talents and skills: sure catcher, good dancer, musician, explorer, solid citizen, great leader. You may even imagine your children as parents themselves and, decades in the future, as grandparents.

Parents have, for example, fairly set expectations for how active or complacent their baby will be. Some of these beliefs are based on how much the baby moves around during pregnancy; others, merely on hope. Even when parents have learned to know one child, they still will have in mind an image of her sibling-to-be, who will be more or less vocal than her sister, or less demanding, or more active.

It may be that sometimes these images are borne out in how your baby looks and acts as a toddler, preschooler, or adolescent. But the important thing is that your image of your baby is likely to reflect the mix of how you were raised, how you would like to be as a parent, what you like most and least about yourself, and your aspirations. You naturally see your baby — at least early on — as an extension of yourself: born of your and your partner's genes, your body, and your culture. But your baby is an individual. He is not at all a replica of you, your partner, or any ideal either of you might have. It is crucial, in the early stages of getting to know your baby, to adjust what you thought your baby would

look and be like to who he or she really is (so far). One of the most common and essential first adjustments involves the baby's sex. While amniocentesis or ultrasound may have let you know your baby's gender before she was born, that doesn't do away with the need to make this adjustment — it just changes the timing by which it occurs.

Accepting your baby's gender is one of the primary tasks in making room for him or her in your mind. Sometimes one parent imagines a boy; the other, a girl. Right away, one parent will have to change his or her image of the child. Humans have been hoping primarily for girls or for boys for centuries, based on everything from dowry traditions to simply wanting "one of each." Nearly every culture has folk charms and traditions for determining the sex of the child a mother is carrying. But after all those centuries, families are still surprised. Henry VIII divorced one wife, beheaded another, and broke with the Roman Catholic Church because he wanted a male heir. Most parents these days are more enlightened and embrace both sons and daughters.

Parents have to make other adjustments, too. You match the baby in your head to the baby in your arms: a long, thin infant up against a short, compact one; curly black hair meeting wispy blond locks; blissful sleep in the first hours compared to alert looking around. These adjustments continue silently for days, months, even years. You will be aware of some of them; others are beyond conscious thought. They are all, however, part of the process of making this baby yours. Sometimes parents are reminded of their expectations when a grandparent says, "First red-haired baby on our side of the family in years," or when visitors wonder, "Who does he look more like, his mother or father?" A newborn baby is something of a blank screen in whom all adults see what they want to see. You see a history of your two families and, at the same time, a new story unfolding. You would like to think you know how that tale will play out; but as soon as you meet your baby, even if she is healthy and all went well with the delivery, uncertainties arise.

Clouds in the Sky: Ordinary Doubts and Worries

Any change brings uncertainty into life, and a child brings a great deal. Becoming a parent does not guarantee that all will work out well. The path ahead is not clear: How will the baby develop? What kind of person will he be? Will we as parents do the right things at the right time? Will we be there for her? All parents worry about their baby, and your worries will be partly rational and realistic, partly irrational, and even disturbing. You may feel surprised, and perhaps a little guilty, to recognize you are worrying even as you gaze, enthralled at your new baby. Do not reproach yourself. These are completely natural thoughts. Recognizing and accepting them will help you deal with your worries realistically.

A parent's thoughts about a new baby can be disturbing, even frightening. You may find yourself worrying about how she could be injured, sick, or harmed in some way, even how you yourself might accidentally hurt her. These thoughts, though painful to recognize and acknowledge in yourself, are common. They, too, reflect how vigilant you have become both to outside threats and to your own missteps. Warning yourself about bad things that can happen to your baby keeps you on the alert. While it may be easier to recognize your concern that other people — whether spouse, grandparents, or friends — might not take good care of the baby or, even worse, might neglect or harm her, normally parents also worry about their own capacities as mothers and fathers.

Worries about your baby may also break the spell of perfection. As we have mentioned, real physical impairment or illness can intrude on those first weeks when you are prepared to see your baby as perfect. Similarly, you may worry that what you have passed on to your child is *not* the best of either of you. "Is my mother's gloominess cropping up in her grandson?" you may wonder when your baby won't stop crying. Worry about what you might have passed on in your genes is just as natural as the conviction that you are giving the best of yourself to your child; the two feelings may exist side by side. Sometimes, however, parents' doubts about how they are caring for their child, and whether they will be able to meet all the challenges they anticipate, preoccupy them so insistently as to interfere with their ability to care for their newborn. This may happen even when parents don't feel depressed or blue. When these worries interfere with a parent's ability to care for a newborn, the family may find it helpful to consult their pediatrician. Also, anticipating failure and disappointment is a common strain in the first months of getting to know a newborn. These feelings are as essential as rejoicing in your baby's apparent perfection. After all, a newborn makes enormous demands of parents, and it is natural to recognize this and feel worried.

Regrets, such as "If only I didn't have to take care of this baby, I could do such and such," are real and normal. Every parent probably experiences them, with more or less intensity. Even as you are caught up in the wondrous intimacy and love of your new baby, you also regret and mourn what you imagine you have lost and the real changes that have happened. You are no longer free to go out as a couple whenever or for as long as you wish. Sex may not seem the same. You cannot sleep as continuously or as late as before. Your time is divided between more than spouse and career; now you must serve another, completely dependent individual. There will be many times when a father cannot stay late for an important meeting because he must get to the day care to pick up the baby. Or a mother will be too tired after an evening caring for her infant to finish an important proposal. At times you may even, in frustration, fleetingly blame the baby for upsetting your familiar ways of doing things and for making it difficult to live by an orderly plan.

Tensions and compromises are a necessary part of the contemporary blending of careers and parenting, as we discuss in chapter 28. These demands play out in very real ways from day to day, often starting before the child's birth. They also affect parents who already have children, though perhaps less intensely. Even the compromises that you have not yet had to make, those you only imagine, color your outlook. Trying to resolve the inevitable tension between what you have given up and what you have gained in becoming a parent is part of the psychological task of making room for your baby in her first months.

Recognizing and pausing to reflect on your worries is as essential as rejoicing in your baby's perfection and daydreaming about his future. Indeed, appreciating these doubts will help make it possible for you to accept a critical aspect of being a parent: you can actually predict almost nothing about who your child will become or what will happen to all of you in the months and years after his birth.

Baby Blues and Postpartum Depression

After delivery, most mothers experience "mood swings," feeling elated one minute, tearful and distraught the next. In your happiest periods, everything is perfect, moments seem to last forever, your baby is the most lovely human in the world. In distraught and sad moments, life is an overwhelming burden, there is never enough time, and you feel alone and unable to stop worrying. After giving birth, many mothers feel mildly depressed. They find it difficult to concentrate, and often cannot sleep even though they feel exhausted and their baby is comfortably napping. As many as eight out of ten mothers experience these "baby blues" in some degree. Such feelings are normal and usually disappear between one to two weeks after delivery.

Some new mothers, however, suffer much longer and more severe symptoms of depression, even panic and anxiety. They may experience crippling and persistent worries about their baby, about their own or their spouse's health, and about the possibility of bad things happening to the family. They may find themselves repeatedly doing such tasks as checking the baby, making sure the stove or the iron is off, washing the baby's clothes over and over — actions that feel absolutely necessary yet don't resolve the anxiety. A new mother might sometimes experience more serious symptoms, such as a loss of interest or pleasure in the usual details of her life; decreased energy and motivation; a loss of appetite or serious overeating and weight gain; difficulty falling asleep and staying asleep (especially early in the morning) or sleeping more than usual; increased crying and tearfulness; hopeless or guilty feelings; restlessness, irritability, or anxiety; worries about death and about harming the baby. These severe and prolonged symptoms are signs of what is called "postpartum depression." Although about one in ten mothers experience the problem, it was not even recognized until relatively recently. Doctors now see postpartum depression as a true depression, different from the "baby blues," and offer treatment that can include medication and psychotherapy.

It is not clear why some women experience a severe and prolonged depression after having a baby. Many obstetricians and psychiatrists believe the cause lies in the rapid changes in hormones that occur with pregnancy and delivery. A few other factors also seem to play a role. A mother who feels very stressed during pregnancy, has few supports around her, or feels less connected with her partner (when a couple has marital difficulties, for instance) is more likely to be depressed after giving birth. Also at greater risk are women who have had previous difficulties with depression and anxiety not associated with pregnancy. Obstetricians, pediatricians, and internists are usually aware of the potential for depression and can help with the proper referrals.

Although many new mothers now know about the possibility of postpartum depression, the full impact of this condition is difficult to anticipate. A postpartum depression may begin as soon as twenty-four hours after delivery or not appear until months later. Like all forms of depression, the condition weakens a person's will to get help; and when the onset of depressive symptoms is slow, a mother may attribute her increasing fatigue and worry to the stress of taking care of the baby and her other responsibilities, not to the experience of pregnancy and delivery. If untreated, postpartum depression can last for months, maybe even into the second year after the infant's birth. After this kind of depression, mothers seem more susceptible to subsequent depressions, both after later pregnancies and even between them. Therefore, a new mother, her partner, and her family should be alert for the symptoms of post-partum depression and take steps to alleviate them rather than suffer through them.

Bringing Home a Premature Baby

Bringing home a baby who was born prematurely can evoke mixed emotions. You may feel especially joyful after weeks of waiting but awash in worries about your preemie's health. (See pages 58–59.) Once you and your baby are home, you may still feel — as other parents do — anticipation laced with uncertainty. Even as your baby sleeps quietly in her own crib, you cannot forget the hospital nursery, with its nurses and doctors, the monitors tracking her beating heart. Though your child may be huge in comparison to her birth weight, she may still seem very small and fragile.

As with other babies' homecomings, many friends and relatives will want to see you and your baby. While it can feel good to have supportive people around, some of those people are certain to comment on the baby's size and how delicate he is. You will hear a hundred variations of the question, "Is he all right now?" Someone with a cough may visit and feel hurt when you ask her not to touch the baby. Another may tell you stories about all the preterm babies he knew who left the hospital too early or got sick after a couple of days at home. You will hear more advice than you ever thought possible. Meanwhile, if you have older children, they may still be worried about the arrival of a new sibling and also need a lot of your attention. In addition, because you delivered long be-fore you expected, the baby's room and other arrangements may not be ready. In sum, bringing a premature baby home is usually an unsettling experience, even if his stay in the hospital was smooth.

There are many books about the physical aspects of taking care of preterm infants — how to feed them, help them stay warm, and know what to watch out for in terms of infection. Parents should also expect preemies to behave differently in some ways. Preterm infants spend less time looking around in the bright, alert fashion of other newborns and they tire more easily. You thus need to adjust your expectations and seize the moments, however brief, when your baby is ready to play.

Some pediatricians are particularly interested in helping parents take care of a preterm baby after she leaves the nursery. These doctors can be excellent resources; and if you do not already have a pediatrician, you should ask your obstetrician to recommend one for your family's situation. If you are already working with one, ask him directly about his interest and comfort in taking care of preterm infants.

As we have stressed throughout the book, your memories, wishes, expectations, and worries powerfully influence how you feel about bringing your baby home. Fear for the future, mourning the loss of your hopes to have a completely healthy child, even misplaced guilt about having delivered ahead of schedule — any of these emotional responses is normal. Most likely, they will fade as your child's individual personality, strengths, and needs become apparent — as real, immediate concerns and pleasures take precedence over what you imagine or fear. Nevertheless, those emotions and memories will not disappear.

Nearly all preemie parents find themselves thinking about their child's first days for many years after. Watching his sixteen-year-old football player score a touchdown with ease and grace, a father suddenly remembers him as a one-pound infant hooked to a respirator and protected in an incubator. Recalling how a grown child looked and felt as a newborn is common for all parents. For parents of preterm babies, the emotions involved — both anxiety and relief — can be more intense.

Other Problems

Although an infant who is born needing medical care or with a permanent disability hits parents' expectations hard, her mother and father will, as we have said, spot special qualities that help make up for any disappointment. Still, these parents will need to make more adjustments than average. A fragile baby needs even more than usual care, which may cause her parents to worry even more about their own capacities. They may wonder if their child inherited her problems from one of them, even when the condition does not have clear genetic links. Sometimes a newborn needs so much care in the hospital that it prevents her parents from easily getting to know her as a person; intensive-care units now try to let parents hold their infants daily, at least for short times. In such difficult circumstances, you must keep in mind that your child is much more than her medical record, and exert yourself to discover her individual personality behind the condition or the hospital apparatus or the genes.

The parents' circumstances can also alter the usual adjustment to a new baby. So far in this chapter, we have looked at the process primarily as it occurs in the average family: a husband and wife, raising a child they have conceived together. But, as we discussed in chapter 2, people choose to be parents in different ways, and babies grow up in many different kinds of families, each with its own delights and tensions. These differences also affect how parents adjust to new children.

Single parents, usually mothers, face an extra challenge. A single mother has good reason to worry about her ability to undertake the eighteen-year, twenty-four-hour-a-day project of caring and providing for a child or children on her own. Her child may, moreover, remind her of the absent father and his genetic legacy; and her response to this thought naturally will depend on how she feels about that man. Or a single mother with a baby boy, or a single father with a baby girl, may look down the road and worry if she or he will be able to help a child of the opposite sex through adolescence. Such concerns are natural, but far less crucial than the next feeding.

New parents with children from previous relationships are not the only members of the family who must adjust to a newborn's arrival. A mother who has had children with a previous husband may see her new baby as the embodiment and consummation of her new marriage, a prize she and her new husband, as well as her other children and his, can all share. Her stepchildren may, however, resent the new arrival for changing their lives even more. (For more on being a stepparent, see chapter 34.)

Some couples travel a longer road than others before bringing their baby home. Parents who have had difficulty conceiving (perhaps finally resorting to technological assistance) or those who have chosen to adopt have focused for a longer period on how much they want a child and on their vision of one. These parents may take longer than usual to adjust to the child who does arrive. On the other hand, after a long wait, they are likely to feel especially happy about their new baby.

Parents who adopt older children have usually met them over a period of months. This allows the adjustment to take place gradually and makes clear that the child is a separate individual from the start, and that all the family members have to get to know one another. A disadvantage of some foreign adoption programs is that parents and children have little time to become acquainted and to adjust their expectations before they officially become a family.

Finally, in some forms of parenthood, a new baby has genetic links to one parent but not the other. The child may have been conceived with a donated egg or sperm, and perhaps even carried to term by a woman who will not raise him. Such couples may know their baby's other biological parent, or not; that person may remain part of the baby's life, or not. Naturally, all these factors can affect how the custodial parents view their child when they bring her home. Will she be closer to her father because she senses some genetic link to him? Is that crying a hint of something ominous we don't know about our donor? A parent with no genetic link to his child may be eager to influence her upbringing in order to affirm himself as her parent. As we emphasize often in this book, nurturing is just as important as biology to a child's development and ultimate personality. Both custodial parents are real parents.

"What Have We Gotten Ourselves Into?"

However easy it is to understand parental obligation in the abstract, you don't truly appreciate it until you two are actually alone with your baby. Then a new reality sweeps over you: You're it. This baby is completely dependent on you to live. No chain of command, no possibility of going back on your decision to become parents. At your job you may think you have hefty responsibilities and that you carry them out well. But in your heart, you know that if you stopped showing up, someone else would eventually do your work, maybe not as well, but it would get done. Having a baby is different. Many first-time parents comment about how, on bringing their baby home, they feel responsibility flooding them, almost overwhelming them. And parenting is a responsibility, possibly the most important job that anyone can ever have.

It is also a most unpredictable job. You

may have thought you had everything planned for bringing the baby home. You have a car seat, the latest crib. Your mother and mother-in-law are ready to come in separate, brief shifts to help you in the next couple of weeks. You've stocked up on diapers, posted the pediatrician's telephone number in a prominent place, and prepared a comfortable chair so the baby can be cuddled in his mother's arms to be fed. Both you and your spouse have made arrangements with your employers: one of you will take off a week; the other, six weeks. That seemed like a very long parental leave when you planned it; suddenly it is whizzing by. (For more about work outside the home, see chapter 28.)

You both thought that whole days at home would seem endless — that, since babies sleep most of the day (see chapter 13), you could use his naps to catch up on thank-you letters to friends for their shower gifts or to do some other task that once would have been easy to fit into your routine. But a baby sleeps and wakes and eats according to his own schedule, and tends to make his parents adopt — or, at least, adapt to — it. What may seem endless is how you barely get through one cycle of feeding, diapering, and napping before your baby is ready to start all over. Soon you may find that all three of you crash together. And all your efforts to adjust to your baby — to make room for him in your life — can lead to mood swings and irritability. Your baby may seem the calmest member of your family!

Parents who have brought an earlier newborn home remember some of what to expect, but they usually have other people to care for now. A younger child who seemed so mature as you approached delivery suddenly acts like a baby again. She wants her bottle back; he wants to curl up very close to his parents; one may even wish to breast-feed again. These siblings are as much on edge as you are. They, too, are adjusting to the baby. The new "big brother" may have looked forward to playing with a sibling, but this little sister can't do anything yet! And she takes so much of Mommy and Daddy's attention. Many times grandparents and parents plan special activities for the older children to help them feel that they are not losing out in the new family situation. (For more on sibling relationships, see chapter 30.)

As exhausted and dazed as you may feel in these first days at home, you have also accomplished a great deal. You have made a physical and psychological place in your family for this new person. You have embraced, even with a little dread, all of the unknowns that come with being a new parent and getting to know your new baby. You will continually try to see what's around the corner for your baby, and try to sweep the way clear for her. Over the next months, she will change nearly every day — it will be hard to keep up with. She will get stronger, become more sociable, more curious, soon talk to you when you talk to her. Soon you will find yourself wanting to slow things down because she is growing so fast. As your baby grows, so will the mental room you have begun for her expand.

And as your child's personality takes

shape over time — through the years of toddlerhood, preschool, and school — the three of you will grow together. In the rest of this book, we will describe what to expect in those years up until adolescence: first, the basics of child development; then, specific motor, cognitive, and social and emotional development; and finally, what is involved in and how to meet the small and large crises of family life. Before launching into this, however, let us speak further about the professional on whom you can call for help with your child throughout this process: your pediatrician.

CHAPTER 6

Partners:
You and Your Pediatrician

Y ou've chosen your pediatrician. She is kind, thoughtful, well trained, on the staff of the right hospital and the faculty of the medical school, has some evening and some Saturday office hours, has excellent backup coverage that comes mostly from people right in her own office, and uses all the best pediatric specialists in town as helpers. Or, if you haven't found such a paragon, you at least have a doctor with whom you are comfortable. And you have probably already begun to forge a partnership during your face-to-face prenatal interview and in the hospital after the delivery. (See pages 44–47.)

We speak of a partnership to emphasize that you not only have a choice in your child's medical care but should actively participate in it. This means that you meet with your pediatrician not only for an authoritative diagnosis and recommendation but also that you work closely with him or her, asking questions and bringing information you have gathered yourself. Thus, you and your pediatrician decide together, as equal partners, about how best to keep your child healthy.

Pediatrics is a relatively recent specialty in medicine. Odd as it may seem to us now, childhood was not recognized as a distinct stage of life until 1800. Before then and throughout that century, physicians treated children much as they treated adults, only lowering the dose of a medicine (which probably did not work well anyway) for a child. By

1900, advances in anatomy, physiology, pharmacology, the treatment of infectious diseases, and genetics showed that growth and development in the first twenty years of life make a child very different from a mature adult. Pediatrics first became the specialty that dealt with all aspects of a child's physical growth and development; more recently, many pediatricians have developed a special expertise in young children's psychological development. As you prepare for a long-term partnership with your pediatrician, you need to understand the basics of pediatric care and to have some guidelines for working together during your child's different developmental phases.

Well-Baby Care

As we discussed in chapter 4, it is a good idea to interview and select a pediatrician before your child is born. After that meeting, the next time you see the pediatrician will almost certainly be in the hospital after delivery. He will examine your baby in the nursery or at your bedside, depending on the hospital setup. If he examines her in front of you, he can demonstrate newborn reflexes and other normal behaviors so that they will not worry you later. (See pages 142–144 for more on a newborn's reflexes.) If there are problems, he will certainly discuss them with you, explain options for managing them, and consult with you about what to do next. For instance, he might reassure you that the little white bumps on your newborn's face are a common skin condition called milia, which disappears

naturally. Or he might discuss how to deal with jaundice, another common and occasionally more serious problem for newborns. If things are fine, the pediatrician will talk about feeding, particularly breast-feeding, along with other aspects of infant care. He also will explain the state-mandated screening tests for certain genetic diseases and make arrangements with you to begin your child's well-baby care.

The American Academy of Pediatrics (AAP) has established a standard regimen of visits for well-baby examinations and immunizations following a baby's birth. Although some HMOs or other managed-care plans have established their own schedules (usually with fewer visits), most pediatricians follow the AAP plan for providing optimal care. If the doctor you want to work with does not do so, rule her out only if she cannot demonstrate that she has reasons other than an HMO payment schedule for how often she sees her young patients.

According to the AAP, you should take your baby to the pediatrician for his first checkup by the time he is one month old. Most parents like to do this after being home with their newborn for a week or so; this allows them to learn more about their baby's temperament and habits and to identify the "real world" questions they want to ask. A standard well-baby exam includes:

- measuring the infant's height, weight, and head circumference.
- assessing his vision and hearing by, for instance, checking whether his eyes follow

a penlight or he turns his head in response to noises.

- conducting an overall physical examination or, after the first couple of appointments, examining the features and functions that are unusual, may bear watching, or might have changed.
- judging his general development and behavior in comparison with most other babies of the same age.
- most important, talking with you about your child's history and what you might expect before the next visit.

You should meet with your pediatrician when your baby reaches the ages of two months, four months, six months, nine months, and a full year. During some of these visits, the doctor will provide immunizations or conduct tests for common medical problems. The guidelines for which vaccines and tests to administer at what times vary according to the child's circumstances.

The AAP recommends that you continue to take your child for regular medical examinations at fifteen months, eighteen months, and two years old, and then every year until she turns eight. After that, an appointment every two years is appropriate. The doctor will perform most of the same assessments as before: recording the child's height and weight, tracking her physical and behavioral development. After the first year, it is rarely necessary to continue measuring a child's head, but blood-pressure tests are recommended starting at the three-year mark. Sometimes formal, objective hearing and vi-

sion tests will replace the doctor's subjective appraisal. Within certain periods, the doctor will also want to perform more immunizations and screenings. In addition, when a child is three years old, the AAP recommends that doctors refer their young patients to a dentist.

Pay attention to the way your pediatrician manages well-baby visits. Recent studies have shown that, after the first visit or two, objective data from routine physical examinations add little to a doctor's knowledge of a child (unless there is some intermittent illness or clearly aberrant set of symptoms). It is a much more effective use of visit time if your pediatrician talks to you about how your baby is doing and any concerns you might have. He should ask both specific and open-ended questions that will give you an opportunity to voice any worries and give him a chance to sense whether you and the baby are thriving. Most pediatricians will also talk directly to both infants and older children during the exam, in part to remind you how important it is for you to talk with your child. At some point in the exam, the doctor will listen both to your child's own description of how she is feeling and to your observations, and should make clear to her that her input matters. The information gained from this sort of give-and-take is much more useful to the physician than data obtained strictly from physical examination and measurements. If your pediatrician does not manage visits that way, you may want to steer her in that direction or find another pediatrician who does.

One of the most important things the pediatrician can offer parents in these conversations is a preview of changes or developments that are likely to take place before the next visit. This advance notice can help you prepare for changes and, indeed, facilitate them. It also prevents you from worrying about behaviors that are likely to be perfectly normal. Your well-baby visits will be much more helpful if you come prepared for them. Think about your concerns and questions in advance and write them down to bring with you. Many doctors' offices are stocked with handouts — brochures, booklets, manuals — on different subjects. Take advantage of them, but remember that, however helpful they may be, they cannot replace the personalized give-and-take among pediatrician, parents, and child that arises from informed and thoughtful interviewing.

Have You Had All Your Shots?

Making sure that your child is protected against common fatal bacteria and viruses is one of your most important responsibilities as a parent. The AAP, along with other organizations, issues detailed guidelines about which vaccines have been proven safe and effective against powerful illnesses and when children should have each one. This schedule changes every year or so as vaccines improve and doctors recognize new threats to health. The following are the 2001 AAP guidelines:

- Soon after birth   Hep B (hepatitis B vaccine; this requires three doses, and their timing varies according to the outcome of tests for whether the mother has been exposed to this virus)
- 2 months   DTaP (diphtheria, tetanus, acellular pertussis)
  Hib (*Hemophilus influenzae* type b)
  IPV (inactivated polio vaccine)
  Rv (rotavirus — after consultation between doctor and parents)
  possibly Hep B
- 4 months   DTaP
  Hib
  IPV
  Rv (after consultation between doctor and parents)
- 6 months   DTaP
  Hib
  Rv (after consultation between doctor and parents)
- 12–15 months   Hib
  IPV or OPV (oral polio vaccine)

MMR (measles, mumps, rubella)
Var (varicella — the chicken pox virus)
possibly Hep B
- 15–18 months   DTaP
- 4–6 years   DTaP
IPV or OPV
MMR
- 11–12 years   Td (tetanus, diphtheria)
Hep B
MMR and/or Var (if the child missed doses earlier at the ideal times)

Although a discussion of each of these vaccines and the illnesses they are designed to prevent is beyond the scope of this book, we do need to address family attitudes toward getting these immunizations. Vaccines, which are among the most influential and effective discoveries since the nineteenth century, have saved countless children from crippling disease and early death. Yet thousands of youngsters in this country are still not immunized when they should be.

Some parents put off having their young children vaccinated because they are busy doing other things or feel they cannot afford the doctor's appointment. Parents who dislike going to a medical office or clinic for themselves may be especially quick to find an excuse not to take their child to one. Since most schools require children to have up-to-date immunization records before they can enroll, you will have to go to the pediatrician eventually. While you wait, your child is at risk for the diseases these vaccinations protect against, and some of these diseases can be fatal. Your child may also miss the

ideal time to be immunized against certain viruses. Since pediatricians are prepared to administer most vaccines during one of your regular visits, you should keep up that schedule of appointments and lose no time having your child immunized.

Children often dislike getting shots, even more than adults do. In some cases, a child's fear of a needle may make him so anxious that he asks not to see his doctor or even becomes ill at the prospect. Distress about shots might reflect your child's overall anxiety about seeing the pediatrician; a medical appointment, where one bares one's body to a stranger's scrutiny, can make many people feel vulnerable.

If you have bad memories of hypodermic needles yourself, you might be reluctant to subject your child to them. Keep in mind that not all immunizations are shots: some are administered orally, and even those that do require a hypodermic are well worth the slight pain. Rather than skip the shot, put your energies into keeping good records of the vaccinations your children have had so they can avoid unnecessary inoculations later. Help your child to be brave, promise a treat after the appointment, and rejoice in your power to protect her from many once-common and virulent diseases.

Your Child's Health Problems

Naturally, your child will have health problems. Sometimes, he will obviously need medical care to deal with an injury, a high fever, a persistent pain. And even though modern immunizations have greatly reduced the frequency and severity of childhood illnesses, there are many common infections — ranging from serious diseases to the aptly named common cold — for which there is still no protection. Your pediatrician should talk with you about signs of illness that you should pay attention to, such as your baby's temperature, specific symptoms, or changes in behavior, and give you guidelines for when those signs warrant a call to her.

If your child's symptoms neither match the doctor's guidelines nor seem serious to you, it is all right to wait until the pediatrician's office opens before you call. In fact, your doctor will probably appreciate your waiting. If, however, your child's symptoms meet your pediatrician's guidelines, call him at any time of day or night. He will probably ask you a few questions to get a clear idea of your baby's condition and to help you decide what to do. You might think your child's symptoms are too minor to make a special trip, especially with his annual appointment just a few weeks away, but problems like fever and

dehydration can harm children much more quickly and severely than they affect adults. Phone your pediatrician's office and explain the situation.

Doctors can advise many courses of action, based on what they hear about your baby's symptoms and on what they know about him already. Your pediatrician may prescribe some medicine, such as ear drops, cough medicine, or antifever drugs, over the telephone to relieve his symptoms. She may want you to do certain procedures at home, like running the shower to create steam, or giving the baby a tepid bath, or offering him clear liquids to drink. She may think the problem warrants attention quickly, or she may be able to move up your regular appointment so she can treat the immediate problem and discuss your child's overall health in the same visit.

If your doctor decides that she or another doctor should see your child, she is likely to ask you to come to her office (if you called during office hours) so she and her staff can examine the child and perform any necessary tests. If the office is closed, she may suggest that you go to the local emergency room where special staff are on call to provide the same level of care. House calls are rarely part of health care today. They are an inefficient use of the physician's time and, because so many decisions now depend on laboratory tests not available at home, usually produce equivocal or unsatisfactory results. If your child is sick enough to require hospitalization, your pediatrician will certainly want to visit and maintain regular contact. Whether she can actually manage and control the treatment depends on the rules of the hospital involved. (For helping your child deal with serious illness, see chapter 32.)

Along with helping you to manage your child's physical health, pediatricians can also help with chronic problems or developmental and behavioral issues that arise as your child grows up. Indeed, according to research on the issues parents most often bring to pediatricians, developmental concerns are far and away the most common. Well-trained and interested pediatricians can help you with your questions about what to expect at different developmental phases, help you find and evaluate infant stimulation and preschool education programs, and put you in touch with the best psychological and child-psychiatry services, should that be necessary. Because your pediatrician understands the interaction between physical and psychological health, she can also interpret and integrate any information you receive from other subspecialists you may consult.

Avoid the situation pediatricians call, "Oh, by the way, Doctor . . ." A parent who has come to the office for a "routine" well-child visit waits until the session is almost over and then, with her hand on the doorknob on the way out, says, "Oh, by the way, Doctor, Johnny has been wetting the bed." Or, "Mabel has been thrown out of nursery school for fighting." Or, "My husband and I are getting divorced." Or whatever. Since these problems, although rarely life threatening, can interfere with normal social and intellectual development, they are as important as any other area of child health care. You should be able to trust your doctor enough not only to ask about them but to do so in a way that allows time to talk about them.

An experienced pediatrician will set aside some periods during the week for longer appointments just to deal with nonurgent but important concerns. He will ask you and your spouse to make an appointment for one of those times, usually without your child at first. During that meeting, he can take a careful history of the problem and think through with you what might be done. Several more visits and further examinations of your child may be necessary before all the ramifications of the problem become clear enough for you to make a decision. A good pediatrician will make as much of an effort to know you and your partner as individuals, as a couple, and as a family as she does to know your child. Some busy practices or insecure pediatricians do not set aside time for such discussions and, therefore, cannot really offer you a lot of help with your concerns. If this is true of a doctor you are working with, consider interviewing other physicians to find one who has more time for your questions and concerns.

As Adolescence Approaches

By the time a child nears or reaches puberty, he has developed his own relationship with his pediatrician. Your doctor will meet with you at some point during your regular visits, but everyone should understand that the discussions between doctor and young patient are confidential. They should be shared with you only if, in the doctor's opinion, it is dangerous to your child to maintain that confidentiality. Some parents may resent this shift, seeing the doctor as coming between them and their child and accelerating the breaking away that occurs in adolescence. Others may worry about what their teenage child may come to talk about behind those closed doors. Will it be . . . sex?

Your child is not necessarily telling his doctor anything he does not also tell you, but it is important for him to feel comfortable doing that if he feels he has to. Many children, especially adolescents, feel uncomfortable discussing some subjects with Mom and Dad. An emerging adult also needs to test some ideas and feelings outside the family. It is a tribute to you if he chooses as an advisor someone you originally selected as trustworthy. Talking with one's doctor is an adult task: be proud that your child is able to do it.

As a related issue, some adolescents become greatly embarrassed about being examined by a pediatrician of the other sex. Doctors and nurses are professionals who deal with many undressed bodies and many private concerns every working day. That fact may not comfort a self-conscious teenager, however; and if this anxiety is preventing him from obtaining adequate medical care, speak to your pediatrician about the problem. The doctor may be able to recommend a colleague — sometimes even someone within the same

group practice — who could make your child more comfortable. Or you might agree that this is the time for your adolescent to start seeing a doctor who specializes in adults — perhaps a gynecologist for young women or an internal medicine specialist for young men. There are even doctors who specialize in adolescent medicine. While teens are in many ways still children, and would benefit from the extra knowledge and training of a pediatrician, they should not feel embarrassed or intimidated about their health needs.

Making the Partnership Work

Ideally your partnership with your pediatrician should last from birth throughout the years of childhood. These guidelines will help you make that ideal a reality.

- Although no one likes to wait a long time in a doctor's waiting room, be realistic about your pediatrician's time. Each appointment can bring up problems your pediatrician could not anticipate, and emergencies can arise at any time. Morning appointments are probably better if you cannot wait, because there is less time for the doctor to get backed up. Only if your doctor seems consistently unable to stick to her schedule should you look around for another pediatrician. On the other hand, once you make an appointment for your child, you have a responsibility to keep it. If you cannot, phone the doctor's office as soon as possible.

- You also have a responsibility — both to your pediatrician and to yourself — to diligently follow the treatment you two decide on. If you have concerns about what the doctor suggests, such as the cost of medicines or the difficulty of an exercise program, bring them up immediately. There may be ways around those problems.

- You and your children need to be truthful about their history, symptoms, and how closely you have followed the treatment prescribed by your doctor. If you do not tell the whole truth (even when the truth may be uncomfortable), you will only confuse the situation.

- Facilitate the payment of your bills. At one time, we could have simply written, "Pay your bills," but nowadays medical costs are often handled by insurance companies, with families paying only a portion of the total. As a consequence, both pediatricians and parents can face a lot of paperwork. Supply your pediatrician's office staff with all the forms and authorizations they need.

- If you are uncomfortable with your doctor or his way of doing things, describe your concerns to him. If he cannot or will not change, you may need to find a new pediatrician. Do not take this step lightly, however, or go shopping for a doctor who will give you particular advice. Your children will benefit from a long-term relationship with a physician who treats each patient individually.

The relationship between pediatrician and child can be compromised when a family is forced to choose a new doctor. This may happen when the family moves out of town; today it more commonly — and most unfortunately — occurs when a parent's employer transfers its coverage from one managed-care program to another, and in the process the list of participating pediatricians is changed. We can only hope that this intrusion into the doctor-patient relationship will soon become a thing of the past.

When you cannot avoid switching pediatricians, there are a few things to think about. First, arrange to transfer all the records of each child's immunizations, surgeries, and other treatments to the new physician. The most useful thing you can do is to try to have your former pediatrician convey at least some of his special knowledge of your family to the new doctor; in this way your new pediatrician can gain some sense of your child's personality, what sorts of concerns you usually bring to your pediatrician, and the other nuances that make a relationship personal. While your partnership with your new doctor may not immediately be as comfortable as your relationship with your first doctor, starting it off on a solid basis gives it a good chance of becoming both supportive and rewarding.

PART II

The Basics of Child Development

CHAPTER 7

Understanding Your Child's Development

A two-year-old is different from a young adult. And both are different from newborns. "Of course," you may reply, "of course, children don't look or behave or think like adults. Of course, something turns babies physically and mentally into grown-ups." And when you chide a friend or colleague for being "childish," you are implicitly acknowledging the process whereby an unruly child changes into a mature adult capable of accepting responsibilities and behaving appropriately. Even as you secretly hope that your child will grow to be like (or unlike) you or your partner, you are accepting the process — perhaps mysterious, not entirely predictable, even a bit frightening — by which the infant in your arms will someday be a young worker, a graduate, even a parent. This is the process we have come to call "child development."

Most people today probably understand that a child's body, behavior, and mind mature according to various biological and genetic programs. Research has also found that just as an engine needs fuel, a child needs to have certain experiences for these programs to run properly. But experience is just part of the picture; clearly, children do not become adults through their experiences alone. The process isn't something you can orchestrate: you cannot teach your four-year-old to think and behave completely like an adult, or stop a twelve-year-old from becoming an adolescent. These important changes occur according to a timetable that is influenced, but not controlled, by outside events. Development thus involves a complex interplay of genes, other biological factors, and experience.

Developing the Idea of Human Development

Until late in the eighteenth century, children in Western society were viewed as essentially small, untutored adults. Every characteristic of an adult was thought to be present, however indistinctly, from birth. What separated the child from the adult was mostly size and knowledge. Though children legally remained minors until they were twenty-one or so, most nonetheless made an early entrance into the working world. Children on farms worked alongside their parents; others went to work when they were as young as five. Many of the first slaves in this country were poor children swept off the streets of English seaports without the approval, or even knowledge, of their families and transported to the colonies to serve as indentured servants. In short, until relatively recently, children were thought to function like adults in small bodies, to think like adults who lacked sufficient experience and teaching, and to behave like adults without the benefits of socialization into their communities and cultures.

In the late nineteenth century, scientific research into prenatal development began to change that view. Careful study of fetuses revealed for the first time that their physical development occurs in stages, with forms and organs emerging gradually. The fetus is not, in fact, a fully shaped little human who simply gets bigger. These findings were followed in the early twentieth century by the discovery that after birth, hormones in the body produce a series of physical changes, including growth and puberty.

This notion of gradual, lifelong physical development set the stage for the idea that humans also undergo a *psychological* development that defines and shapes one's abilities. The concept of emerging abilities was applied to mental and behavioral development by the early 1920s, when psychologists, teachers, and physicians began to map out the stages of mental growth.

By the middle of the twentieth century, the basic foundations of child development were widely accepted, and scholars turned their attention to the ways in which a child's thinking differs from an adult's view of the world. The Swiss psychologist Jean Piaget (1896–1980) made the radical proposal that children's approaches to their surroundings appear illogical only if one assumes that their minds function as adults' do. Based on his research, he concluded that children make sense of their world using a series of thought processes that have their own logic — thought processes that appear in a regular order, each characteristic of a particular age. (See pages 90–91.) In mapping out children's progression through these different ways of knowing about the world, Piaget provided a new window on how children learn and how their minds develop a variety of capabilities for learning and understanding.

As the Second World War spread across Europe, clinicians who were caring for war orphans applied a similar developmental approach to understanding children's emotional development. Anna Freud, among others, discovered that just as children have their own order and logic for understanding the inanimate world, they also have a standard progression in their capacity to understand their emotional world. The emotional skills required to understand their own feelings and the feelings of others, to cope with disappointment and sadness, and to care for their own bodies and needs emerge over the course of early childhood. (See chapters 21–22 for more on emotional development.) Researchers trying to understand the emotional life of children also called attention to the importance of a child's emerging ability to play imaginatively. They recognized that far from being "child's play," imaginative play is an important way station in a child's ability to try out, practice, and master various emotions and experiences. (See chapter 16.)

The years since have provided much more scientific evidence to support this modern view of child development. In this view, children travel, both chronologically and developmentally, across a complex web of developmental pathways in different sequences and at different paces. This passage is influenced by a variety of factors.

Nature or Nurture — or Both?

The discovery that a child's mental, motor, and emotional skills unfold along a more or less regular timeline made scientists think, at first, that all development proceeded in ordered stages regulated by a biological clock. In this view, while children might vary in how early or late they reach a stage, the majority, pushed along by their biology, ultimately move through each stage on a path to adulthood. Researchers later revised this "maturational theory of development" by suggesting that a child's experiences shape how quickly he approaches each developmental stage and how well he masters what is most important during that stage. For example, children who grow up with little language stimulation may be slower both to begin using language and to learn the language skills they will need for subsequent stages of development.

The contrast between these different approaches to development is captured in the debate between nature and nurture: How much does biology contribute to children's maturation? How much do experiences? The pendulum has swung from a mid-twentieth-century preference for nurture — in which almost every aspect of a person's behavior is ascribed to his early childhood experiences (most especially, critics have written, to how he was treated by his mother) — to the more current preference for discovering biochemical or genetic roots for a range of behaviors and conditions. Some scientists even claim that a child's genes influence her future behavior and health more powerfully than her experiences do.

Most of us, however, see a mix of causes. Contemporary theories of development do not make either nature or nurture primary. Each is seen to influence the other. The most current understanding of child development embraces the idea of gene-environment interaction. Genes provide the individual blueprint for a child: blue eyes, brown hair, tall or short, athletic or musical or both. But genes are not simply set in motion in the fetus or newborn, playing out like a movie from beginning to end: experience plays a vital role in much of a child's development.

Particular experiences may be critical for some genes to turn on (that is, become active and express their genetic code) and allow capacities to develop. For example, for the full connections to the visual centers of the brain to develop, the eye must be stimulated by light. And movement and muscle stimulation are required for muscles to grow. Good nutrition or language stimulation enrich the expression of genes into a person's full potential. An event early in development may continue to influence many later events, including the later expression of genes. Thus, if a young child experiences serious illness, malnutrition, or overwhelming stress, those long-past events may delay the onset of puberty when she reaches her teens.

Your baby's brain and body are genetically set to respond to his environment, and genes provide the structure for the gradual, timed unfolding of the central nervous system in fetal and postnatal life. But your child's experiences, provided at first by you as you love and care for him, "switch on" critical processes in his central nervous system that prepare him to make use of the attention that caring adults provide. The earliest interactions between your baby's genetically timed biological systems and her environment have an effect on *both* her brain and her behavior, a topic we will cover at greater length in chapters 8 and 9.

The Main Stages of Cognitive Development

Jean Piaget was one of the first scholars to study systematically how children learn. Over the course of his career, he developed several new scientific fields, including developmental psychology and cognitive theory. Although Piaget started his career as a zoologist, studying mollusks, he later moved to Paris to study logic and abnormal psychology. Working with Alfred Binet, a pioneering researcher on intelligence and the codeveloper of an important standard IQ test (for more on this test, see pages 282–283), Piaget studied the way young children approach intelligence

tests, and wanted to find out whether there are patterns to the mistakes they commonly make.

Piaget concluded that children (and adults) learn in a two-step process. Upon encountering something new, a child first considers how it is similar to what he already knows. By this method, he fits new experiences into the picture of the world that he has in his mind. Piaget called this step, whereby one notes how a new thing is similar to familiar things, assimilation.

Eventually, however, a child encounters phenomena, people, or objects that she cannot fit into her worldview, or realizes that her initial assumption that something is familiar proves not to be the case. For instance, a preschooler may decide that she can play with the ball she found in the sandbox because it is a toy like those she has at home. But as soon as a bigger child comes to take his ball back, she realizes that something was wrong with that conclusion. Faced with this discrepancy, she takes the next step in learning: she changes her thinking to *accommodate* reality. Children and adults follow these two steps continually throughout their lives and, in doing so, gradually fill out and refine their knowledge of how the world really works.

Based on many years of observing how children of different ages conceive of physical reality, numbers, and morality, Piaget posited that there are four main stages of cognitive development:

- The sensorimotor stage lasts on average from birth to about age two. In this stage, a baby learns through his movements and senses, especially hearing, sight, and feeling with his hands and mouth. He identifies the boundary between his body and the rest of the world, and learns which basic sensations and feelings are connected with which events around him. Early on, babies can identify simple goals and work toward them. Toward the end of this stage, babies grasp what Piaget called "object permanence": the knowledge that an object is still around even when he cannot see it. A baby in his first year will not look for a toy if something blocks his sight of it. After eighteen months or so, not only does he know the toy is still there, but he also loves playing with this new knowledge.

- The preoperational stage generally lasts from two to seven years old. Young children in this stage start to work with symbols, using words, letters, numbers, and toys to represent concepts. They begin to use simple rules, classifications, and logic to organize their picture of the world, although these rules are often simplistic. For example, children of this age commonly assume that a tall glass must contain more milk than a short, wide glass, and that books spread all over the floor must be more numerous than books shelved together. They still have some difficulty seeing another person's point of view.

- The concrete operational stage lasts from seven to eleven years of age, on average. In these years, children's logical abilities grow much more powerful, especially when they tackle concrete or hands-on challenges. They understand how to think backward from their goal in order to figure out how to do what they want to do. Among the more difficult concepts that children grasp in these years is how time works, how "more" can mean different things in different situations, and how two people can view the same event from different perspectives.

- The formal operational stage starts around age eleven and lasts through adulthood. Preteens and young adolescents are finally able to master many types of abstract thinking: hypothetical situations; analyses that involve multiple points of view and sets of values; complex mathematical, linguistic, or scientific functions. This capacity leads them to think more about social issues, justice and fairness, and their own place in society.

While subsequent generations of child developmentalists have augmented and revised Piaget's ideas, we still rely on many of his observations and insights about children and particularly on his ideas that children of different ages simply understand the world differently — not because they know less but because their minds function differently.

Principles for Understanding Development

As you observe and participate in the process of your child's development, keep in mind the following principles: at any one landmark, there is a great deal of revision and adaptation; each child is unique and does not necessarily develop at the same pace as any other; and a child's progress is, in part, a process of maintaining harmony and synchrony among what is happening in various areas of development.

Revision and Adaptation

When we talk about development, we do not mean simply that a child is always growing bigger, stronger, smarter, more articulate, and more agile and adding new skills on top of others. Certainly, if all goes well, this does happen. But central to the development of any skill or competence are the linked processes of revision and adaptation. In the first process, a child revises functions, skills, even behaviors as necessary. New skills borrow from old ones, and your child will weave old skills into new capabilities, so that what was once a skill unto itself is no longer as distinct or recognizable. For example, a newborn's sucking reflex is subsumed into the many other skills of biting, chewing, and sipping that a child needs to eat. (See chapter 12 for more about feeding.)

The skills a child develops first are not necessarily just primitive versions of his later skills. In some cases, infants actually lose early capacities as they develop. Infants are born, for instance, with the ability to recognize many more sounds than appear in any single language, but each infant gradually comes to distinguish only those sounds her family uses to communicate. (See chapter 17.)

Babies give up crawling for walking, but once they become competent walkers, they are never again so competent at crawling. A baby can still crawl, but he is less facile and less likely to choose that form of locomotion over walking no matter how competent a crawler he was. The muscle actions a child uses for crawling are programmed in the brain; as those actions adapt to walking, the brain program is revised. A new skill has emerged and replaced an old one. Development is thus like remodeling an old home. Vestiges of the old are woven into the new; eighteenth-century beams hold up a twenty-first-century roof.

Development also means that some abilities and even behaviors are more prominent at ages when a child most needs them to adapt to his environment, and are more obscure at later ages. Newborns are "prewired" to pay attention to special kinds of information — those bits and pieces of data about the adults who take care of them. An infant is especially alert to the rhythms of speech, to the contours and boundaries of a face, and to the smells of her mother and father. (See chapter 15 on early perception.) These special capacities are present from the first hours of life, even before experience brings them out. As your baby grows, however, her sensory radar for details that signal the presence of important adults become woven into more complex abilities. These include being able to play such games as peekaboo, to remember you when you are not present, and ultimately to imagine happy moments, such as your surprise on finding daffodils in the pocket of your coat on your birthday. The infant's basic attentiveness to smells, sounds, and touch thus becomes a small part of a more complicated repertoire. A new set of abilities has emerged and incorporated the earlier, basic ones.

You have probably sometimes had the sensation of reliving something you remember deeply from your infancy — perhaps a smell in the air, snatches of a song, an old, worn, soft toy or blanket. You cannot quite call up a specific incident or story, but you feel a wave of emotions: comfort, longing, even sadness. These moments most often happen with tiny bits of sensation — seeing, hearing, smelling, touching. They may well be the vestiges of your earliest abilities to perceive especially well those bits of the world most connected to your parents.

Adaptation is another key aspect of children's development. At each stage of development, children acquire, practice, and master skills that are most useful to them at that time. For example, after children learn to walk and run, they can go greater distances from their parents. Developing language in the same months gives a youngster a way to stay in touch: she can call out to Daddy in the backyard as she walks away to look at a neighbor's kitten. At the same time, children of this age are more emotionally sensitive to separations. They practice games of hide-and-seek, coming and going. (See chapter 31 on helping children deal with separation.) Each of these developmental phases and

skills is adaptive to the child's current overarching concern: how to stay safe and protected even as she moves physically apart from her parents. As she masters those tasks, she can "move on" to the next challenge: caring for her own body, dressing and feeding herself, telling stories about what she did when her parents were not there to watch. As she gets older, hide-and-seek becomes a game to play with her friends. Then it becomes a "baby game" she no longer plays, even as she uses the same skills to locate the outfit she plans to wear the next day. What is adaptive at one developmental phase may be less appropriate or less necessary at another.

Variability Among Children

The second principle underlying the idea of development is that every child is different. None follows a map precisely, nor does every area of development adhere to the same timetable. One child may walk earlier than another or use words a few months later. A child may "skip" crawling and instead stand and walk with support. He may be precocious in his language development but slow to learn how to dress himself or to tolerate frustration.

Not only is there great variability in how and when individual children achieve developmental milestones, but there are also variations in how each child moves up and down these "developmental ladders." Often a gain in one area is matched by a loss or slowing in another. For example, a child learning to walk independently may for a few weeks add no new words to his vocabulary. Newly gained skills such as language are sensitive to stress, and a toddler who has just learned to talk when she develops pneumonia or loses her beloved nanny may stop talking for days or weeks. Or a young child who has mastered going to the toilet on his own may begin wetting himself again when his family moves to a new home some distance from his beloved grandparents.

Children simultaneously proceed along several paths of development, not just one. Generally, experts recognize the areas of physical, cognitive (learning), social, and emotional development, but there are many variations even within these categories. Abilities from different areas are often interrelated, as walking and talking are; sometimes it is difficult to proceed along one pathway without having developed certain skills in another area. Yet each child moves along the various developmental roads at his own pace. This principle of variability explains how a bright student can also be socially immature — mental and social skills are different. A child who can remember dozens of sports statistics can forget to send her grandmother a thank-you letter, and a young bodybuilder may seem unable to lift a laundry basket up the stairs.

In sum, development is not always linear, stable, or consistent. Gains may be paralleled by temporary losses, and children may leapfrog over one milestone to reach another. Maps of how babies grow up into young adults are usually on target for the whole population of babies, but do not necessarily predict the route your special, individual child will take. Developing in different areas at different times is part of what makes each child unique.

Harmony and Progress

Finally, typical development involves both harmony and integration, and normal elaboration and progress: that is, how evenly matched is a child's development in various areas of competence? Are his motor skills, say, far more advanced than his language skills, or are both progressing at a more or less similar pace?

When psychiatrists and other experts assess a child's development, these two principles help them determine whether a particular behavior — or lack of it — is relatively normal or seriously discrepant. During an assessment, pediatricians and child psychiatrists try to evaluate a child's overall functioning: How integrated and coherent is her mental functioning — the ways in which she shows her needs for food, care, and affection? What is the balance between her loving and assertive natures; between her intellectual and emotional expression; between her ability to be independent and her need and ability to accept care? We like to see a certain wholeness and evenness of progress across all these areas. Ideally, a child should be at about the same level in language and thinking, in social relations, in self-esteem, and in motor skills. A child with this kind of evenness and integration seems, even at the age of twelve months, to have her own personality. Children with some areas of great precocity or remarkable delay — an uneven or mixed profile of development — may be at more risk for emotional problems. Unusual patterns raise the question about what may be interfering with the process of integration. Children who are living in stressful conditions or have had long illnesses may sometimes show unusual patterns of development.

Since children differ enormously in their normal rate of development and in their development in individual areas, such as motor skills and emotional independence, standard tables of development are only rough guides. Nevertheless, all parents compare their children with other boys and girls in the sandbox, the playgroup, and day care. If your child is falling noticeably behind in one or more areas, your worry is natural, and you should speak to your pediatrician. He or she may arrange for you to consult a child psychiatrist or psychologist skilled in conducting developmental assessments.

Charting Development and Pinpointing Difficulties

A healthy baby is born ready to become quiet when comforted, to search the world with his eyes and ears, to enjoy a good feeding, to make his needs known through lusty crying, and to show his contentment with sweet smiles. These inborn, biologically based behavioral capacities prepare the child to learn and relate socially. When all the innate systems are functioning well, your baby is quickly able to establish a special rapport with you and to regulate his sleep, appetite, and arousal. The care you give him, along with his other early experiences, quickly shape these core competencies.

Some basic skills that appear to be inborn actually reflect the interplay between a child's biological preparedness and a nurturing environment. For example, children are born with the mental apparatus to scan objects visually and to pick out certain shapes; but they learn what is important to pay attention to, and develop more sustained attention skills, as their parents engage them by talking, looking at things, and sharing one another's focus of attention. Babies who do not experience such quiet and sustained play and interaction may later seem to have an inborn problem with attention — even a disorder, such as attention deficit hyperactivity disorder (ADHD).

Similarly, children are born ready to babble and to communicate, but they learn to be fluent, creative speakers, with good vocabularies and expressive skills, first by hearing a lot of language around them and then by being engaged in communication by their families. The poor speech of an infant who spends hours in front of the television, and is rarely engaged in long baby-talk conversation, may seem to have biological causes. (See chapter 17.) But children are born prewired to learn, and what and how they learn depends, to a great degree, on the intimate social world into which they are born.

Each child also has a distinctive "character," even from the first weeks of life. Some babies are angelic, while others are annoyingly assertive. Some take to nursing without thinking, and others need days or even a week or two to get the knack of breast or nipple. Some of these individual temperamental styles remain with a child over months and years; they become his personality. Yet a baby's temperament also changes with development. A calm baby may become irritable as he faces a new challenge and feels frustrated; he may settle down once his new skills, such as toilet training or eating on his own, are well established. The aspects of a child's personality that become reinforced depend, to a considerable extent, on how her style of behaving elicits affection or annoyance in her parents. If you enjoy activity and energy, a quiet baby may be too boring; but if you are a quiet, contemplative parent who enjoys orderliness and calm, a high-strung child may prove an overwhelming ordeal. As a child perceives his behavior being reciprocated or rebuffed, he adapts it accordingly. A mismatch between the styles of parent and baby — where one persistently rebuffs the other — can seriously confuse the baby and give rise to emotional and behavioral problems.

Lines of Development

During the first years of your child's life, you can chart the unfolding of her competencies along normal lines of development. These include the pathways from being fed to feeding herself; from being bathed to washing herself; from babbling to speaking in phrases and sentences; from biting to controlling her anger; from urinating and defecating spontaneously to being able to hold back long enough to use the toilet like an adult. Emotionally, a healthy child journeys from needing approval all the time to feeling inner pride in her own achievements. She moves from acting to please her parents, to doing things right because she does not like to feel ashamed, and to doing the right thing because she has developed standards of her own and wants to avoid feeling guilty for not performing up to them.

At each phase, children confront developmental tasks or challenges. These arise both from within as part of the push of maturation and from the world outside through interaction with parents and other caregivers. In the first months of life, a child's developmental tasks involve regulating her basic physical needs — eating, defecating, sleeping — and synchronizing her patterns and rhythms with yours. The child who handles these demands feels secure and comfortable most of the time, and enjoys being held, soothed, played with, and fed. At age two, his challenges involve navigating the world more on his own, out of Mom's arms and Dad's sight. These tasks may be more demanding when the child is also in day care. Then he needs to modify his needs for the sake of the other children; to deal with their stimulation, aggression, and intrusions; and to adjust to the changing style of his caregivers.

A toddler's tasks in emotional development may include using her new, possibly scary, imaginative skills to deal with the birth of a sibling; being assertive enough to get what she needs without becoming a danger to others; and taking pride in her body and her gender. The emotional tasks that come with childhood and adolescence center around a child's increasing responsibilities, autonomy, and styles for expressing and satisfying needs (hunger, care for his own body, affection), showing and accepting love, and dealing with his own anger and the anger of others.

Development along these pathways continues throughout life. A child may wish for the impossible — to become as strong as Dad or as rich as a star baseball player — with little regard for the realities of time, power, hard work, and the rights of others. With maturation, there is increasing harmony between ambitions, abilities, and values. These three sectors of life become balanced: as your child gets older, he will learn to wish and to work for things that are within reach and consistent with his sense of right and wrong. The aspect of your child's social development that starts at age two, when she moves from playing on her own to having fun when other children are playing nearby, evolves into the pleasure in having a best friend at age eleven and then the satisfaction of intimate partnership in young adulthood. For navigating through society, children move from primary dependence on parents, to reliance on peers, and then to reliance on their own personal skills.

When Development Does Not Seem Normal

All children go through slow or difficult periods, even occasionally regress. Nevertheless, a child who exhibits a symptom of mental distress or physical impairment can worry parents and grandparents. Is this a normal symptom like the occasional squeak a fine piece of equipment gives off? Or is it a sign that something is seriously awry? One way of assessing a child's symptoms is to consider the tasks he is facing, how stressful these are, and how well he is coping with the anxiety that is part of that challenge.

Toddlers typically say a loud "No!" to almost any request, but should preschoolers do the same? If children vary in their development and learn physical skills at different ages and different levels of proficiency, when should you be concerned about, say, your child's clumsiness? Patterns of normal development provide a framework for answering such questions. A child's variations from those so-called normal patterns can be especially useful in evaluating mental health, where trouble is often less obvious than a physical problem. (See chapter 33.)

When assessing a child who seems troubled, professionals consider his strengths as well as his difficulties. He may be having a terrible problem in one area — with his temper, for example — but is he doing well in other ways? Most important, how is his overall adaptation? In addition to his problematic temper, is he, in general, moving ahead in his social skills or communication or self-care? Only when a problem interferes with the forward momentum of development does it become a major focal point for clinical evaluation and help. A child's symptoms are especially worrisome when something seems to be impeding integration and harmony; when progress is very uneven or very delayed; or when he is falling behind in adapting to life at home, in school, and in the community. Clinical understanding of a child focuses not only on a single behavior or symptom — such as slowness to walk, overactivity, or a tic — but on the full picture of the child as a whole person.

Children who are successfully meeting the tasks of emotional development can love wholeheartedly and work hard. They take pride in their achievements, enjoy becoming more competent, and accept disappointments and losses without becoming sour. They fight fair and shake hands at the end of a battle. When they fall off the horse, they get right back on or decide to try a different challenge. None of this is easy. Each task of development helps your child acquire new emotional, intellectual, and motor skills. At the same time, each can overchallenge a particular child and become a nodal point for emotional and behavioral problems. By thinking about your child's developmental situation — the challenges that he unconsciously and consciously experiences at a particular moment in your particular family — you may get a clue to the emergence of a particular symptom or problem.

Successful Development

If all goes well in pregnancy, human babies come into the world biologically ready for many environments — hence the wide range of cultures and family structures with which our species has populated and developed the globe's continents. With every child growing and developing at his or her own pace, siblings may develop very differently from one another: one may talk early, while another is slow to use even single words. Children may respond quite differently to the same parenting styles. Whatever their individual differences may be, you should aim to provide your children with consistent, predictable care.

An infant's innate, all-purpose readiness quickly adapts to her particular world through the predictable and confident caring activities of her parents. When you and other adults care for your children, you and they do much more than just feed, or bathe, or comfort. You are helping your child's brain develop (see chapter 9), shaping her temperament and personality (see chapter 21), and teaching her how to function in the world as you know it.

A crying three-month-old turns toward the sound of her father's voice, quiets, looks intently, slowly smiles, and begins to coo. Her father can smile back and take this moment of alert attention to tell his baby a story about her grandfather, sing her a song, or just hold her close. In thousands of such moments of being held, fed, protected, and consoled, babies connect the sight, sounds, feeling, and warmth of their parents' presence with the experience of being distressed and then comforted, overwhelmed and then calmly attentive. Through these basic acts of caring, your baby will build up emotional portraits of you and your partner that link experience and feeling and, at the same time, cause connections between brain regions to form and refine. When all goes well, these emotional portraits are of protective, loving, listening parents to whom your child can always turn — at first, in reality; later, in memory and imagination.

These experiences of a child's first years of life — at home, in out-of-home child care, in the community — lay down the patterns for all future development. These experiences need not be painless and flawless. Indeed, they cannot be. But predictable, stable, nurturing care by you and other adults — nannies, friends, daycare teachers, and relatives — interacts with your baby's biological readiness to push her development forward and teach her to care for herself and, ultimately, for her own children. By being loved, stimulated, talked with, comforted, and attended to, children learn both to enjoy the pleasure of being competent and successful and to tolerate disappointment and failure without sinking into despair. Such fortunate children will see the world as basically safe and secure. They will feel valued and effective, trust themselves and others, and be able to use their intellectual, social, emotional, and physical potential to its limits. This is successful development.

CHAPTER 8

Genetics and Your Child's Development

You hear a great deal about genes these days. "The newspaper says they've found a genetic test for sickle-cell anemia. Pretty soon they'll know the gene for *everything*." "My aunt died when she was only thirty-seven, so I asked my doctor to test Cecily to see if she has the same gene." "Bobby never cleans his room. I just don't think he was born with the cleanliness gene."

Of course, people have recognized for millenniums that physical traits like hair color, nose shape, and height are passed down in families. And many folks are inclined to believe that some aspects of personality (especially a "noble" character — as defined mostly by nobles) can be passed down as well. At the same time, however, parents in every generation have been surprised at how their children turn out: the daughter who is the only family member with pretty red hair, for instance, or the son who exhibits a very different temperament from his parents. Such surprises reflect the complexity and variability of human biological inheritance via genes.

Many parents still believe that "blood runs true," that predilections for behavior and other psychological traits are passed down in families. When you say, "He's got his father's sense of humor," or, "She has her mother's temper," you are invoking genetic explanations for behavior. In this chapter, we aim to give you some basic understanding of how genes and experience work together to shape and direct your children's development. (See also chapter 9 on brain development.)

What Are Genes?

Genes are chemicals that act as blueprints for the way the human body develops and functions. Each gene contains a set of instructions for building one of the thousands of proteins that the human body needs. Together, your genes not only define your possibilities and limitations at conception, but they also keep your body and brain functioning throughout life. Each gene is a specific segment of a long molecule of deoxyribonucleic acid, or DNA — a chemical that functions like a large database of recipes for all the proteins the human body needs. (See "Mapping Genes," page 108.)

A DNA molecule is not like a water molecule, which is always made up of two hydrogen ions and one oxygen ion: H_2O. Rather, the term DNA refers to a family of molecules that all share the same basic ingredients and structure: two long strands twisting around each other in the shape called a double helix. The strands are made up of chemical building blocks called bases. Like a rung on a ladder, each base on one of the strands bridges to a corresponding base on the other strand.

All DNA is made up of only four different types of chemical base: adenine, thymine, cytosine, and guanine. Adenine (A) in one strand always pairs with thymine (T) in the other, and guanine (G) always pairs with cytosine (C). The order in which the bases occur determines a gene, in the way letters combine to make a word. Thus, one sequence of bases might spell out GACCTC-TAG. (This segment would always be paired with CTGGAGATC on the other strand.) It takes an average of 3,000 bases in proper sequence to make one gene. Many of the sequences along the DNA strands seem to have no function, but simply connect one gene to the next.

Every cell in the human body contains molecules of DNA called chromosomes. Each of these molecules contains 50 million to 250 million chemical bases. Different types of chromosomes are distinguished from each other by size and appearance. (Other species of animals, plants, yeast, and even bacteria have different numbers and sizes of chromosomes, but they all depend on DNA in the same way.) In the core, or nucleus, of nearly every human cell (the exceptions are the sperm and egg cells) are two sets of twenty-three chromosomes: one set inherited from a person's mother and one from his or her father. Each set is made up of twenty-two autosomes carrying various genetic information, and one X or Y chromosome (named for its shape), which determines sex. A female inherits an X chromosome from each of her parents, while a male gets an X from his mother and a Y from his father. The two sets of chromosomes combine to make forty-six molecules of DNA — more than 3 billion chemical bases — in every ordinary human cell. Unlike these, each sperm and egg cell carries a single set of twenty-three chromosomes, selected from both the maternal and the paternal lines. Thus, when an egg and a sperm combine, a new and unique set of forty-six chromosomes results.

According to the latest research, a human being has at least 30,000 genes strung together on any one human chromosome like beads on a necklace. Every gene is made of thousands of the four chemical bases just mentioned. Although every cell in the body contains the same chromosomes, cells turn on only the genes they need at a given moment or phase of development, and keep all the others turned off. Each gene contains instructions for how a cell manufactures a specific chemical, usually a protein. That protein in turn initiates a specific action inside the body. Some genes, which carry messages for basic proteins used throughout the body, are active in many types of cell. Other genes carry messages for proteins unique to a particular kind of cell, such as a nerve cell in the brain or a bone cell. Researchers estimate that at least half of a human's genes are devoted exclusively to brain growth, development, and maintenance. Indeed, much of human evolutionary development has been devoted to building up genetic codes that support complicated brains and elaborate psychological functions, such as language and abstract thinking.

Some genes are active for only a short time. For example, genes important in fetal development shut down completely after birth. One gene makes the oxygen-carrying protein hemoglobin for the fetus, but a completely different gene makes hemoglobin for the adult. Genes controlling change in cartilage and growth at the ends of bones are at work throughout childhood and early adolescence, but shut off when a child reaches the height for which his genes have programmed him.

Some genes actually switch other genes on and off. Some of these "regulating genes" are exclusive to humans, while some are shared with all other mammals and some just with other primates. Those abilities that all mammals share (such as vision) are likely to have similar regulatory genes, but uniquely human abilities (such as language) have unique regulatory genes. Some genes are on at all times to maintain the basic life

of a cell (such as the genes involved in making material for cell walls). Other genes are responsive to environmental changes and turn on and off accordingly. Some regulatory genes actually "wait" for certain experiences before they switch on; if those experiences do not occur, these genes and the genes they regulate never go into action. The DNA segments that control how the human brain processes vision are one example of such experience-dependent genes: if a baby's eyes do not start sending signals to the brain early in life, those genes never get switched on and never build the connections in the brain that would allow that baby to see. We refer to the process by which a gene's message affects body functions by saying that the gene is being "expressed." By some estimates, only one percent of genes in a cell are being expressed at any given time.

How Genes Work

The process by which a gene creates a protein is called "decoding." This decoding process starts with copying the gene; the original sequence of DNA in the chromosome is not used in the actual protein making because that might mar it. To make a copy, the two DNA strands are taken apart or unzipped, and the particular gene is duplicated base by base into a new molecule called "messenger RNA." This messenger moves from the nucleus into the body of the cell to a manufacturing center (called a "ribosome"). There the messenger copy of the gene provides the instructions for assembling the protein from its building blocks, which are "amino acids."

The proteins that result from this decoding process are the means by which genes determine how your body grows and develops, how efficiently your brain works, your physical characteristics, even aspects of your personality. Single, relatively simple genes are the basis of such inherited traits as eye or hair color. But many proteins must come together for a complex function such as height. Some of the genes that are involved may be close to one another on the same chromosome; others may be on different chromosomes. Further complicating matters, the environment affects when many genes turn on and how they interact. Thus, while you might inherit a probability for a particular height, the environment often determines whether you actually grow to that height. The same is true for your genetic susceptibility to a disease. The environmental influence on personality and how it reflects biological makeup seems even stronger, as we will discuss. Calling the total of your genetic inheritance your "genotype," and the product of that inheritance (as affected by the environment) your "phenotype," we say that the genotype is expressed as a phenotype.

Genes also control all of your day-to-day bodily functions: how you process food, how you respond physically to infections or injuries, how you maintain the same body temperature even as your surroundings change, how you go from waking to sleeping with all the bodily repair and maintenance that goes on during sleep. Health and development depend on the ongoing manufacture, maintenance, and interplay of thousands of proteins in the proper organs. Many people assume that genes "get one going" — they determine who one is — and then the body operates like a machine that has left the genetic assembly line. But in truth, the decoding of genes and assembling of proteins is a continuous process throughout one's life, from the moment of conception to old age and death.

Genetic Errors, Heredity, and Disease

In such an intricate, complex system, errors occur. These mistakes in genetic function are called mutations. A single base in the DNA may be changed, left out, or added, as in a misspelled word: CGATTCAGT becomes CGATTCATG, reversing the last two chemicals. Sometimes whole segments of DNA are repeated erroneously or cut out completely. Whether a mutation is serious or harmless depends on how it changes the message for a particular protein and, once the message is read, on how much that protein changes. The effect of a mutation also depends on how vital the protein coded by that gene is for normal development. Some mutations are apparently silent, affecting neither the structure of the protein nor its function. Other mutations result in a completely altered protein that may be less functional, totally disabled, or never produced. In sickle-cell anemia, for example, the hemoglobin that carries oxygen in the blood is flawed. It functions reasonably well in ordinary circumstances, but if a person demands more from his hemoglobin (by going to a higher altitude, for example, where his blood would need to carry more oxygen to his organs), the protein does not function.

Mutations can be inherited from one or both parents or acquired after conception. Hereditary mutations, passed from parents, are present in the DNA of every cell of a child's body; every time a cell divides or multiplies, that mutation is copied. Acquired mutations that develop during a person's lifetime, however, can be limited to individual cells and the copies of those particular cells. Environmental toxins, such as radiation or chemical pollution, can produce acquired mutations. More often, these mutations happen during the normal process by which a cell makes a copy of itself and divides into two. In this replication process, where a cell must copy billions of DNA bases, it is easy for mistakes to crop up. Since cells divide often, acquired mutations happen frequently throughout the body. Fortunately, cells usually have the capacity to recognize errors and repair them before replicating again. These repair mechanisms can fail, however, and become overwhelmed or less efficient over time. When this begins to happen, mistakes accumulate. Certain kinds of tumor may be the result of acquired mutations in cells with faulty repair mechanisms.

Genes also come in a number of variant forms called "alleles," which can be passed on within families. For instance, there are several alleles of the genes responsible for making eyes, and different alleles produce

different shades of brown, blue, or hazel. While there are average or "normal" alleles that occur in most people or most individuals in an ethnic group, other alleles neither occur so often nor are passed on so easily. Because genes come in pairs, with one copy from each parent, a person can have two different alleles of the same gene. In the simplest situation, a dominant allele from one parent prevails over the other; the genetic code of the dominant allele is the one that is expressed. A recessive allele is expressed only if the other allele of the pair is somehow not functional — or also happens to be recessive. If the other allele is dominant, the recessive allele will not be expressed. A person with an unexpressed recessive allele is nevertheless a "carrier"; she can pass on the allele to her children, giving that variant gene another chance of being expressed.

In this simple situation of parents' dominant and recessive alleles, you can easily work out the mathematical probabilities of what your children might inherit. If both parents have two dominant alleles for a particular trait, such as brown eyes, your children will have a 100 percent chance of having brown eyes. If only one parent has that dominant allele, each child in the family will have a 50 percent chance of inheriting it. Genetic surprises are usually the result of recessive alleles. If two parents each carry one normal and one recessive allele, neither exhibits the physical trait linked with the variant gene. But each of their children has a one-in-four chance of getting two recessive alleles and thus the trait, a one-in-four chance of inheriting two normal alleles, and a two-in-four chance of receiving one recessive allele and thus becoming a carrier without showing the trait. Blond hair is a common example of a recessive allele that can pop up in families. More worrisome recessive alleles include the genes for cystic fibrosis, Tay-Sachs disease, and sickle-cell anemia.

Few diseases or physical traits and functions, however, follow such simple inheritance patterns. Many factors influence how genes are expressed. Even a dominant allele does not always produce a disease or other trait. For example, not all individuals with some cancer-susceptibility genes develop that particular cancer; only a percentage do. (The probability that a given allele will produce a trait is called its "penetrance.") Some traits require that specific alleles or mutations occur in two or more genes at once. Conversely, mutations in several different genes can lead to the same trait, as appears to be the case with some forms of Alzheimer's disease. Finally, through a little-understood process called "imprinting," either the gene from the mother or the gene from the father may be more active in a given pair of genes. Such complexity is particularly important when we try to apply genetics to behavioral and psychological development.

Genes and Behavior

Scientists agree that genes contribute significantly to human psychology. But psychological traits and disorders are complex. Their inheritance within a family does not follow the traditional dominant/recessive patterns we have described. Even when we see evidence that some conditions or predilections are inheritable, we rarely know the exact location of the gene (or genes) that determine them. Environmental variables, such as a mother's illness or stress during pregnancy or an early birth, contribute to the genetic expression of behavior and psychological traits. Illnesses during early childhood, poor nutrition, and serious injury may also influence a person's psychological characteristics. Also, more than likely, multiple genes influence behavior and psychology, and these genes may have to be expressed together or in different combinations during development for particular traits to emerge. It is also clear that one's experiences, including how a child is parented and what happens during childhood, shape personality, behavior, and how one's brain works.

Being predisposed to a particular trait does not mean you are predestined to have it. Every gene has a range of expression, within which it can be fully or partially expressed, depending on a person's experiences. A child of very tall parents and grandparents may not reach his full genetically endowed height if he is chronically ill or malnourished during childhood. Similarly, a person with the genes for particular psychological traits may develop those to a lesser or greater extent because of her upbringing.

The expression of genes may shape how you experience your world. When certain genes are being expressed, as in puberty, you are more receptive to certain experiences or to seeing the world in a different way. Also, both experience and environment shape how much and when genes are expressed. Nowhere is the collaboration between genes and experience more noticeable than in the development of the brain, as we discuss in the next chapter.

Although we are a long way yet from understanding fully the genetics of behavior and personality, there are some common methods for studying the relative contributions of genes and environment to personality and to such serious psychiatric problems as depression. One such method involves twins. The underlying genetics are straightforward. Identical twins share the same genes at concep-

tion. They are known as monozygotic, or MZ, twins. These twin births result when an already fertilized egg divides into two identical embryos very early in the gestation. If a trait is completely determined by genes, then MZ twins should always share it. In contrast, "fraternal" or dizygotic (DZ) twins arrive when a mother ovulates two eggs at once, and both are fertilized. Like single births, these fetuses receive different sets of chromosomes from each parent. They share only half of their genetic material on average and should be no more alike than siblings born as singletons. If a trait is dominant, then dizygotic twins should be only 50 percent likely to share it, while monozygotic twins should be 100 percent likely. As we said, the mathematics of most psychological traits are not simple. Even identical twins may develop very differently if, starting before birth, they receive different amounts of blood from the placenta during gestation and thus weigh significantly different at birth. Nevertheless, researchers conclude that, when MZ twins share a trait more often than DZ twins (a phenomenon termed "higher concordance rates"), the trait has some genetic basis.

The study of MZ and DZ twins raised in different families who adopted one or both has had interesting results. This approach begins with the assumption that the environments in which separated twins grew up were significantly different, and thus that any unusual similarities they show are likely to be results of their genotypes. With the cooperation of such twins, researchers have explored the genetic basis for personality, intelligence, and such psychological problems as autism. While the answers are far from clear and neat, there are striking psychological and physical similarities in personality, sensitivity to stress and anxiety, and even vulnerability to depression among MZ twins reared apart.

Another approach to the study of the genetics of psychology and behavior involves multiple generations of one family. Recent advances in pinpointing genes make this approach even more exciting. So-called linkage analysis is enabling researchers to better understand the connections between generations: genes that are linked very close together on a chain of DNA are usually inherited together. We now have identified small but recognizable variations in about 1 percent of genes. These differences (called "markers"), unlike some mutations, do not usually cause diseases (though they may cause small variations in the protein they code for), but they are passed along among family members. Linkage studies make use of a characteristic of genes during early gestation. As egg and sperm cells divide in the earliest stages of the embryo, pairs of the maternal and paternal chromosomes sometimes break and exchange places with one another (a process called "cross-over" or "recombination"). Markers that are very close to one another are less likely to be separated during a recombination than are markers that are far apart. Among the 30,000 total human genes, there will usually be about 1,000 recognizable markers. This means that there will be enough variations on

a chromosome from any one person to make it distinct from that of any other person. By examining the DNA from one person's parents and other relatives, we can usually tell which side of the family passed on each particular variation.

Markers are most useful when linked to a gene related to a disease or an important trait. The inheritance of the marker can be used to track the transmission of a particular complex disease (such as depression) within a family. With DNA samples from a family member with the disease and from other relatives who may share markers, we can trace the lineage of that characteristic. We can also possibly (depending on the markers) come closer to identifying where on a chromosome the gene for that disease or trait is located. By looking for markers that are consistently inherited by people with the trait and not found in relatives without it, scientists can narrow down the likely address of the gene.

These techniques are enabling researchers to make enormous progress in understanding the genetics of behavior and development. But since similar behavior may reflect different motivations and mental conditions, we still must define more and more precise phenotypes of the behavior, traits, or psychiatric disorder in question to better understand the depth of their genetic roots. Nonetheless, there is real evidence for a genetic basis for some early reading disabilities; for forms of depression and anxiety; and for behavior that includes tics, obsessions, and compulsions. There also seems to be a moderate genetic contribution to how vulnerable people are to feeling stressed and overwhelmed or to suffering long-lasting psychological effects from serious trauma. The evidence for these links is far less clear for problems with attention and activity.

Genetic Testing

Many families consider the option of genetic testing at one time or another. You may have been concerned about whether your baby had a serious disease while you were still pregnant, and asked your doctor to order tests on a sample of your amniotic fluid. (For more about prenatal testing and amniocentesis, see chapter 4.) If a relative in your extended family has a child with a serious genetic disease, such as cystic fibrosis, you may have decided to see whether your cells carried that particular gene, too. Such carrier testing can help parents know whether they

---

MAPPING GENES

In 1990, the Human Genome Project set out on the extraordinary task of tracking down and identifying every chemical base in the 30,000 genes then thought to be in one person's body, as well as marking the spaces between genes on the long chain of the chromosomes. This extensive study, originally projected to take fifteen years, was completed in 2000. As an achievement, the human genome — or a complete map of all the genes in a human body — ranks with the astronauts' moon landing in 1969. Geneticists expect that a full map of all the human genes will produce major changes in the practice of medicine as well as revolutionize studies of child development and child psychiatric disorders.

Just as geographic maps take different forms to show streets, topography, and political boundaries, maps of human genes come in three different types. First, genome maps provide detailed "street addresses" for the order of genes and the individual chemical bases within them, as well as other landmarks such as the material between genes that makes up the rest of a chromosome. A second kind of map uses the markers for linkage analysis (see page 107) to assign a gene to a region on the chromosome. As more markers are identified, linkage maps will become more and more detailed.

Finally, to learn the gene's exact location on the chromosome, scientists use physical maps. To make a physical map, a chromosome is broken into small pieces of DNA. Each piece may be several genes together or a part of a single gene. The pieces are copied in the laboratory and lined up to reflect their order on the original chromosome. Through this technique, the researchers gather chemical information about the exact bases at each location, as in GACTCTACGTT. . . . When a genetic linkage map indicates that a gene seems to be in a particular region of the chromosome, the physical map of that region supplies information about the exact chemical base arrangement.

Searching through the body's 30,000 genes and identifying the one associated with a specific trait or disease takes a long time. In the case of Huntington's disease, a fatal neurological disorder developing in adulthood (the disease that afflicted the folksinger Woody Guthrie), it took ten years to move from findings in the linkage markers to the exact identification of the gene.

might pass on a potentially harmful recessive allele to their children. Sometimes a child is unusually slow to develop or has specific developmental delays in language, motor, or other skills; your pediatrician might recommend genetic testing to see whether there were any recognizable genetic causes for these difficulties. And in some cases, genetic tests can be used to look for possible predisposition to a disease.

Other types of genetic analysis are becoming common. DNA tests are increasingly being used to identify individuals accused of serious crimes or to exonerate them after years in prison. With more and more sophisticated techniques, we can perform DNA analysis on very small samples of blood, hair, or other body tissues; sometimes we can obtain DNA from preserved samples of these tissues. There are increasingly accurate, genetically based paternity tests to identify an individual's likely parentage or ancestry. Even the field of evolutionary biology has been changed by DNA analysis, as scientists make educated guesses about how often mutations occur and estimate when different species split off from a common ancestor. DNA analysis will probably become even more common, widely available, and technically powerful in the next few years.

The most widespread use of genetic testing is in newborn screening. Each year in the United States, all infants born in a hospital (the majority of newborns) have blood samples taken to look for abnormal or missing gene products. There are several types of genetic testing. One type examines a picture of all the baby's chromosomes to see whether there are forty-six and whether they look physically normal. Sometimes an extra chromosome occurs, as is the case in Down syndrome. Or a piece of a chromosome can be shortened or broken off, and sometimes a molecule appears malformed. Particular diseases are known to be linked with other chromosome patterns. Another form of newborn testing looks for genetic problems by checking for the effects of a gene on the body rather than for the gene itself. One example is the phenylketonuria (PKU) test for elevated levels of an amino acid that builds up when a newborn's body is missing a particular gene.

More specific forms of genetic testing look for the presence of a particular mutation or allele. Once a gene has been linked to a significant disease or trait and studied in detail, lengths of single-stranded DNA (called "DNA probes") that match the chemical bases of the known gene (A to T, G to C) can be used to determine whether that gene is present. The probe is tagged with a radioactive atom and mixed with the DNA being tested. If the probe binds to an area of that DNA, the gene "lights up" on an X-ray film. If the probe does not find a place to link or bind, the gene in question is not present.

As sophisticated as current genetic testing is, however, it still cannot answer every question about inheritance or genetic traits. For one thing, many of the genes researchers hope to identify are very large and contain thousands of chemical bases. Searching through the long stretch of DNA to identify them is difficult and takes years. Second, a single gene can have many mutations and may appear slightly different in different people. Not all of these mutations will be important, but they can befuddle a DNA probe. For example, the gene linked to cystic fibrosis has over three hundred different mutations, some of which seem not to be linked with any symptoms. Thus, a positive test for a gene does not guarantee that the disease is imminent, while a negative test does not always rule it out. Furthermore, many genetic tests, especially those that are meant to determine the likelihood of cancer, deal with probability rather than certainty. One person with the gene may develop the disease while another will remain healthy, and no one knows why. The gene may respond to the commands of other genes not yet identified, or may be switched on by an environmental factor such as sunlight or stress.

If you are thinking about genetic testing, consider how it may reverberate throughout your family. Unlike other medical tests, a genetic test reveals information not only about you and your children but also about your relatives. Genetic tests can, for example, reveal long-held family secrets about paternity or adoption. If genetic analysis indicates that your developing fetus has a particular condition, you will be faced with the difficult decision of whether to go ahead and have that child. Genetic tests may increase a family's worry about future pregnancies or about the future health of a child even as he or she seems completely healthy in the present. The most promising area of research for genetic testing is the effort to identify children who

are at risk for developing a particular disease later in life — so-called predictive gene testing. Tests are available now for two to three dozen diseases; as more genes are studied and linked to conditions, more predictive gene tests will become available. You must usually ask your doctor to perform such tests. They are not routine, both because they are so new and because other important variables determine whether it is ethical to screen all babies for a particular condition. One of those variables is whether the disease can be passed on to the public; inherited diseases obviously cannot. Another issue is whether doctors can treat the condition they detect. Nearly all states screen babies for PKU because recognizing that genetic disorder in a child's first week allows parents to begin the special diet that wards off mental retardation, cerebral palsy, and other severe problems. If the timing of such treatment were not so important, the PKU test would not be required.

Usually parents request special genetic testing of a child only when they have reason to suspect she has a higher-than-average chance of carrying a particular gene. One such reason might be that several relatives have developed the same inherited disease. Again, the results of these tests can bring up many questions for parents. The knowledge that your child has a big chance of becoming seriously ill might affect how you or other relatives perceive and treat her. It may also affect how she perceives herself and behaves as she grows older. She may seem more precious or more fragile — even though her health is not necessarily any different from other children's. Remember that these tests usually deal in probability. How probable or serious must a disease be for it to be worth worrying about? There is no clear answer to that question. Each family's response will be different.

The science of genetics is rapidly advancing: changes happen in weeks and months rather than in years. The important information for parents, however, will remain the same: genes are integral to your child's individual endowment as a human being. They shape your child's brain and how her brain responds to the outside world. But in spite of the enormous significance of genes, the environment you provide for your child is crucial to how and when your child's genes are expressed. Genes are as dynamic as behavioral and psychological development. Our most current thinking about child development allows for a cooperative, interactive relationship between genes and experience.

CHAPTER 9

The Developing Brain

Your two-year-old looks across the back-yard and sees the neighbor's puppy. "Dog! Me see dog!" he says gleefully. He glances up at you, smiles, jumps off the bottom step of the porch, and runs across the yard. Just as he approaches the puppy, he slows down, looks at it carefully, and then looks back to you. You nod encouragingly. He stoops to pet the puppy, laughs and giggles, rolls on the ground with the puppy tumbling on top.

In this brief moment, thousands of cells in your child's brain have responded. Perception, language, intention, expressing wishes and emotions, jumping, running, interpreting social signals, gently touching, exploring: these are all complex behaviors that require connections among many areas of the brain and among many specific cells in those areas. But such complex linkages are not confined to a two-year-old's brain. Thousands of brain cells also respond when you comfort your crying three-month-old or play peekaboo with your nine-month-old. Some brain cells are actually turned on or activated by these experiences; at other times, connections between brain cells are strengthened and new connections are formed.

Usually, when you watch your children play or you parent in a particular way, you do not think of brain development and surely not of individual cells in the brain. Still, you will sometimes wonder how a particular decision you made, a particular event, or even a phase of development has influenced your child's personality, moods, and behavior. In that, you are implicitly asking the deepest of questions: How do environment and experience shape the brain, and vice versa? How does what happens in the brain work out in your child's (and your own) behavior? Is it all nature, or is your nurturing at all responsible?

Nature and Nurture Intertwined

The human brain is not fully formed at birth. Research has revealed that it develops from conception according to a finely tuned timetable that is set up and regulated by an individual's genes. In fact, almost a third of one's entire genetic endowment affects how the brain matures and functions. Genes "switch on" brain construction and reconstruction projects, and the start or end of these projects can in turn switch on other genes that regulate further construction and the remodeling we spoke of in the last chapter. Thus, a baby has an all-purpose readiness to receive the world in his first hours, weeks, months, and years — a readiness that is channeled and shaped by the specific experiences his world offers him. These experiences decisively affect both the actual architecture of the baby's brain and how fully she will develop capacities that will be with her throughout her life.

Clearly, we can no longer think about nature or nurture as separate, independent forces. Rather, they are continuously intertwined and interactive influences. Nurturing activates certain genes and biological processes in a baby and child; and nature's endowments allow that baby and child to receive, interpret, and metabolize experiences. The experiences your children have not only affect the general direction of their development, but actually influence how the circuitry in their brains is put together.

Understanding current knowledge about brain development may not change your behavior at 2:00 A.M. when your baby is crying and can't fall asleep. But it does illuminate why development is rapid in early childhood, why adolescence seems to drastically change the sixth-grader you thought you knew every inch of, and why even as an adult your early

memories seem so enduring and lively. The early brain development described in the next few pages underlies much of the childhood development traced in the rest of this book. Here are the key points:

- Brain development, like all development, hinges on the interplay between a child's genes and biology and the affection, stimulation, and teaching she receives from her caregivers.
- The human brain develops and changes throughout life, but for many aspects of early development, timing is crucial. There are prime times for acquiring certain kinds of knowledge, skills, and capacities.
- The human brain is specially constructed to benefit from and make optimal use of consistent and loving care in the first years of life. Early experiences have a long-lasting and decisive impact on the architecture of the brain. That nurturing influences how children develop and shapes their abilities to learn, regulate emotions, and care for and be with other adults.
- Conversely, negative experiences or the absence of appropriate care may cause serious, enduring harm to early brain development.

The Birth of the Brain

The brain is an extremely complex organ. It not only monitors all body functions and activity, but it receives and processes all the information a person's sensory organs receive from the outside world. Since it would be inefficient for the brain to receive separate bits of information and act on them one by one in isolation, the brain has evolved to be able not only to receive but to store and adapt information. The human brain can thus process more possibilities than could be realized in any one lifetime.

The brain has billions of cells to carry out its functions. Of these, the nerve cells are the control centers. Nerve cells, or "neurons," are tied or wired to each other by as many as a thousand links apiece, in the form of connecting, or "glial," cells. These connections link not only neighboring neurons, but also different regions of the brain. The coupling of a sensory experience and a memory, or an emotion and a decision to do something, occurs because the neurons in one specific region of the brain are connected to neurons in another region. The connections are not random but follow a blueprint coded in a person's genes.

A baby's nervous system develops in a series of ordered steps, also coded genetically. This development starts in the womb, reaches critical phases in the first two to three years after a baby is born, and continues throughout life. New connections in the brain are continually being formed, and old ones continually remodeled. The gradual unfolding of the brain is a remarkable process. In the first weeks of a mother's pregnancy, a group of cells called mother (or progenitor) cells begin to divide. Some of the cells from

those divisions do not themselves divide but instead become neurons or glial cells. The timing of this process depends in part on the baby's genes and in part on signals from other developing cells.

Early in brain development and throughout life, neurons communicate with one another in two ways: through the connecting cells, much like the wires of an electric circuit, and also through chemicals called neurotransmitters that carry instructions to various cells. The neurotransmitters are made very early in brain development. Before nerve cells are ever physically connected to one another, these messenger chemicals convey many messages. On the surface of all cells in the brain (and throughout the body) are special receiving stations, or "receptors," that are ready to read particular chemicals. When a cell receives a specific chemical message or signal, it initiates the appropriate series of events. Before describing what happens when chemical signals initiate such processes in neurons and other cells, and how this relates to genes switching on programs or abilities, we will turn to the beginnings of the brain itself.

The Brain's Building Blocks

A child's brain starts to form during the mother's pregnancy. Between the sixth and seventeenth weeks of pregnancy, the child's complement of neurons is formed from the progenitor, or mother, cells. Until very recently, scientists thought that the neurons formed during fetal life were all that would ever develop. New studies have shown, however, that the brain does retain the ability to generate new neurons, at least in response to injury, even late in life. During fetal development, each neuron is "born" with a precise identity and job to do; the chemicals that it will use to communicate have already been determined. First, these nerve cells must migrate from the clump in which they have formed to their proper place, also predetermined, in the brain. A particular set of regulating genes cues these neurons not to divide again and to migrate instead; the genes then turn off quickly so as not to send the same message to too many other cells. Neurons begin their migration by "climbing up" paths laid by specialized connecting cells. These "guide" cells appear early in pregnancy; their only purpose is to guide the neurons to their intended homes. Some nerve cells form the thinking regions of the brain, called the cortex, while others make up the regions involved in emotion and memory. Once they are in place, the neurons still need the final weeks of pregnancy to mature and connect with other neurons.

Various environmental experiences can harm the orderly, timed development of the brain. Certain events can alter the appearance of the guide cells and the timing of the nerve cells' migration, so the neurons do not make it to their intended destination. For example, if a mother drinks too much alcohol during pregnancy, takes certain prescription and nonprescription drugs, or contracts a virus such as rubella, these events can dis-

rupt the orderly unfolding of brain development in the developing fetus. Some effects early in pregnancy are so severe that the fetus cannot continue to grow and the pregnancy ends in a miscarriage.

On the other hand, the human brain has some built-in resiliency. The fetal brain creates about 200 billion neurons, roughly twice as many as a child will have at birth and far more than it actually needs to accomplish any given function. This safety margin makes room during every pregnancy for some migrations to fail. Nerve cells that don't make it to their programmed spot in the brain, or are damaged along the way, are genetically programmed to self-destruct. These cells are cleaned up and discarded throughout fetal development and through the first months of infancy. Of all the organs in the human body, only the brain is formed by creating more cells than will ultimately survive.

Wiring the System: Connecting Neurons

In speaking of the brain as "wired," we refer to the connections among neurons and among the different regions of the brain. This process begins in fetal brain development. After neurons reach their targeted homes in the developing brain, they begin to make growth factors. These growth factors communicate with other neurons and encourage neighboring cells to link up in a group. Neurons that cannot respond to the growth factors will be eliminated. The neurons also develop extensions (called axons) to reach other neurons and the connecting cells. The axons and smaller branching fibers called dendrites make it easy for the mature neuron to connect to many other neurons. The neurons also become more receptive to neurotransmitters carrying messages from distant parts of the brain and body. Late pregnancy and the first two to three years of life see the most rapid formation of such connections in the brain.

At birth, many of the neurons in the newborn's brain are still not connected into the crucial networks of cells. The formation of connections, or "synapses," between and among neurons continues through the preschool and school years. Indeed, the increased brain activity of very young children tells us that toddlers and preschoolers are genetically primed for learning and for taking in the world. In the first decade, your child's brain is extremely active and forms trillions of connections. Axons hook up to the dendrites of other neurons; neurotransmitters facilitate the passage of messages across the many connections. One neuron may be connected to over 15,000 other neurons in a complicated network of neural pathways. Particularly in the first three years, the connections among neurons and regions of the brain increase nearly exponentially. By the age of two, a toddler's brain is as active as that of an adult. The three-year-old's brain is superdense with connections and nearly two and a half times as active as that of a college-age adult. During this period of intense activity, the brain produces far more synapses than it will eventu-

ally need. This high level of brain activity begins to decline only with puberty, when mature, refined networks of neural connections can afford to be less active because they can process signals more efficiently.

Your new baby's brain is ready to process many different experiences from many types of environment, and the surroundings and events she experiences help to determine where and how many connections are formed in it. The network of neurons thus quickly adapts to your particular environment. For example, if a child grows up in a setting where adaptation depends on hunting, her experiences will enhance those brain connections that support specific perceptual and physical skills. In contrast, when a child grows up in a crowded city, his experiences likely will enhance connections that filter excessive stimulation and enable him to attend and learn.

The most important elements in the child's environment are her parents, family members, and other caring adults to whom she begins to form attachments. As your child interacts with her environment — taking in your tone of voice or a new caregiver's face, processing and storing that information — signals race along neural pathways and may activate new connections and new pathways. Enhanced connectivity among neurons is crucial to efficient processing and storage of information. The connections and neural networks formed early in childhood stay with the child throughout life.

Neural connections that are activated many times by repeated experiences tend to become permanent, but connections that are not used often or at all tend to be pruned away — a true "use it or lose it" process. As this process of elimination proceeds throughout childhood, the superdense connectivity of the preschooler's brain is refined and remodeled into a more efficient network. The density of synapses remains high throughout the first decade and then gradually declines. The pruning picks up pace in the second decade of life, though not at the same rate in every area of the brain. In those areas that control basic body processes such as breathing or heart rate, few changes in connectivity occur. But in the cerebral cortex where the basic rational actions of conscious life (thinking, planning, remembering) occur, connections are dramatically remodeled. At some moments, thirty to forty synapses may be eliminated every second — suggesting that in peak periods of development, the brain is responding quickly to conditions that promote or impede learning.

By the time a child reaches late adolescence, about half of the synapses in his brain have been eliminated. From this point on, the absolute number of connections will usually remain relatively constant throughout life, though in certain networks the density of connections may increase or decrease depending on use and activation. Throughout life, the brain actively produces connections among neurons and actively eliminates them as well.

Thinking efficiently depends on using not all of your brain, but only as much as you need to complete a task. Research on the electrochemical activity in different areas of the brain during different tasks demonstrates that adults' brain activity increases when they address difficult tasks. But if the task is familiar or easy, there is little or no detectable increase in brain activity, and thought comes easily. When there are efficient links among neurons and brain regions, signals travel easily, and processing information requires little increase in energy or activity.

The Timing of Development

Some basic environmental experiences are absolutely necessary for the brain to develop fully: that is, the brain needs to be stimulated at a particular, or critical, time for particular interconnections between neurons and brain regions to form and mature.

Critical Periods

For some regions of the brain, if the essential stimulation does not take place during a particular time (called a critical period), that region's function is lost and cannot be regained. For example, as a newborn begins to see, connections form between neurons in the area of his brain responsible for vision. His eyes do not really see yet; they simply transmit information to those neurons, which must make the necessary connections — that is, learn to process that stimulus into an image. Were the baby continuously blindfolded or unable to see because of, for example, congenital cataracts on his eyes, the area of his brain responsible for vision would never develop properly; if this happens, a child will remain blind even if surgeons later remove the cataracts.

As a baby begins to recognize patterns, such as familiar faces, new connections between neurons will form. The connections not essential for the task at hand are lost or pruned, while the most essential or efficient connections are made stronger, especially in those areas of the brain important for memory and for learning. Similar remodeling and forming new connections must happen with every new skill. And there are thousands of these moments in the first two to three years of life — crawling, walking, first words, first sentence, reaching out and pointing, holding a spoon, recognizing familiar relatives, and appreciating strangers.

The task of putting the brain together in the first years of life and adapting it to the baby's particular world is monumental. The critical periods form a kind of "list of priorities" for development, a plan for building a brain. The construction plan indicates that it is best, for example, for infants to see well before they tackle the task of recognizing faces and expressions. If certain brain functions or activities do not turn on according to the timetable, the pruning process starts to remove the unused cells. It is then, as we have said, much more difficult, if not impossible, for the nervous system to construct what it needs for these functions later.

While alternative functions that can handle at least part of the needed function may develop, these are never quite the same as the original ability. For example, a child who is blind from birth often develops a heightened perception of sound or touch. These abilities are alternatives to vision and serve some of the function that vision would by orienting the child and providing information about her immediate surroundings. But touch and hearing can never become vision, and they do not fully make up for that original loss. They become prosthetics for an ability that the child cannot regain. As children grow older, the pruning process slows down, and such extensive prolonged remodeling does not occur in their later development or in the adult brain.

The Stimulus of Stimulation

Since pruning is designed to give the baby a brain best suited to the environment in which he finds himself in the first months and years of life, an enriched environment during infancy is of prime importance. In the most basic way, impoverished environments diminish the number of connections between neurons and regions of the brain, and rich and stimulating environments increase the connections. Both conditions affect later development. This is why an enriched environment during infancy may significantly influence later development.

Stimulation does not mean you play Mozart recordings in the nursery twenty-four hours a day to turn your newborn into a musician. The stimulation infants need includes not only learning but also all sorts of sensory experience and an emotional bond with her caregivers. A child's capacity to control her emotions hinges to a significant degree on neural networks shaped by her early experiences with important adults. A strong, consistent, loving relationship between parent and child is expressed in many psychological and behavioral ways, but also biologically in the development of the child's ability to withstand, and even learn from, the ordinary stresses of daily life.

There is no single "right" way to provide properly stimulating environments for babies. Warm, consistent, responsive parenting can take many forms and be given by many individuals besides parents. There is probably a wide safety margin for what defines too much or too little stimulation for optimal brain development. Surely a few days of less-than-usual stimulation, when you have the flu or when someone other than the usual caregiver cares for your baby, will not crucially diminish the connections in his brain. And there is a limit to how much stimulation babies can take in and how much is best for optimal development. Babies, like adults, need "down time" to process all they have experienced in the last few hours. Too much stimulation is, for babies and children (and parents), likely not to activate but to overwhelm. In response, your baby will shut down for a time, unable to take much in. On the other hand, the brain is genetically programmed to help your baby and young child seek out more stimulation when she is ready to receive it.

The amount of stimulation your baby can tolerate will change as he grows. A raucous family gathering might overwhelm a three-month-old because her brain is not mature enough to handle all that stimulation. She cries inconsolably or goes to sleep. But that gathering of familiar and not-so-familiar relatives laughing and talking may well not faze her twelve-month-old cousin, who has recently begun to walk. His brain has matured to the stage where he can absorb relatively complex information for relatively long periods of time with more people and more sources of stimulation. Thus, he has a more refined capacity to discriminate differences and familiarities in the people around him and can also, with his new mobility, seek out the people who seem more interesting, safe, or familiar. In essence, he is able to control, or ration, the stimulation in his environment.

Sights and Sounds: Toys for the Newborn

A newborn baby is not up to manipulating many playthings. She does not have control over her body and is still sorting out her sensations of the world around her. Simply hearing and seeing interesting things is all she needs to amuse herself and to stimulate her quickly developing brain. The most interesting sounds for a newborn are her parents' voices. (See pages 230–234.) And the most interesting sights are her parents' faces: talking, smiling, and laughing. In your baby's first two months, spend as much time as you can with her, introducing her to yourself and to the world.

When you cannot be with your newborn, there are other ways to provide enjoyable stimulation. Newborns have good hearing, and recordings of music or singing delight them. Their sight is not so keen: they see best about a foot in front of their faces. It is easier for them to pick out objects that move slowly or appear in bright, contrasting colors, especially yellow against dark blue, violet, or black. Many companies sell music-box mobiles that dangle interesting objects in the breezes beside a newborn's crib.

You can also make your own mobile with colored paper, ribbons, and aluminum foil. Remember that a newborn cannot yet hold his head straight and so cannot watch a mobile directly overhead. Research shows that most new babies look to their right. Keep those generalities in mind as you position your mobile or other stimulating objects, but also notice what your newborn seems to prefer.

At around three months, infants develop control over their own limbs. They uncurl, they wave their arms and legs in the air, they roll from front to back, and they hold their head straight. Two of their favorite playthings at this age are their own hands. In preparation for manipulating objects, they grip and ungrip their hands, grab one with the other, wiggle their fingers, and feel their faces. They reach for toys that catch their eyes, often needing several tries to grasp them. These are the first steps to hand-eye coordination, one of the earliest skills in motor development. Some of the best toys for this period are those that produce a noise when the baby hits or shakes them: some are electronic, others are old-fashioned rattles. They should make sound easily, however, because young infants do not have a lot of strength, skill, or patience. Soft, squeezable toys are also good for tiny hands to explore.

A little dexterity can be a dangerous thing: a three-month-old may reach just far enough to get into trouble, and soon — sooner than you might think — she will be mobile. If objects are hanging or posted near your newborn's crib, move them well out of her reach now. A three-month-old's vision and head control have improved enough that he can now enjoy watching a mobile turn overhead. A string of toys dangling across crib, playpen, or seat is a safety hazard, however; an infant might strangle on the cord. It is often useful, however, to tie individual playthings to the bar of a stroller or the side of a high chair. When you sit an infant of this age at a table full of toys, she will immediately reach for her favorites. And, because she does not yet have fine motor control (see pages 147–150), she will almost as quickly knock or drop them onto the ground. (This is different from the game of intentionally dropping things, which comes later.) She will need your help in retrieving her toys, and the strings mean that you won't have to bend as far or retrace your steps to find what she has dropped.

Day-to-Day Help for Your Child's Brain

Most parents wonder about the best toys to provide for their children: Which playthings are both enjoyable and educational and, of course, safe? Some parents take this concern a bit too far and buy any item touted as educational, even for their newborn. Of course, you want your children to have "the best," but it is wise not to try to make children into "the best" according to a particular standard. Toys do help children learn and practice new skills, but getting the most out of these skills depends on the other, interconnected strands of development. A single toy or set of toys cannot make a child more mature. Give yours a toy that is developmentally appropriate for him rather than one ahead of his skills. Furthermore, especially for infants, no toy can substitute for meaningful and stimulating interaction with parents. (See "Sights and Sounds: Toys for the Newborn," page 120.)

However remote from the world of tiny brain cells your day-to-day activities with your child — giving a bath, buttering toast, singing a bedtime song — may seem, they involve interconnecting neurons. In any activity, however brief, your child's brain cells are forming new connections and strengthening old ones, pruning unconnected neurons, and exchanging a wash of neurotransmitters with each other and with other cells in the body.

There are many things you can do to optimize your child's brain development. Some are basic; others take more planning. Some are routine, and some are fun. They all start with attitude. Work to develop a warm, caring relationship with your child. Express delight in who he is, and help him feel safe and secure. Each child is unique. From birth, children have different temperaments (see chapter 21) and grow physically and mentally at different rates. Accept your child's pace and individuality and hold on to the belief that every child can succeed in his own way. Respond to your child's cues and clues. Notice her rhythm and moods, how these change through the day, over the week and month. Remember that both of you have good and bad days, weeks, and months. Try to understand what your child is feeling, what she is telling you in both words and actions, and what she is trying to do.

All of the functions we will discuss later in this book — including language, perception and motor abilities, and emotional understanding and control — depend on a healthy brain. The following tips provide a good base for those areas of development; you will find much more advice in later chapters.

- Ensure your child's health, safety, and good nutrition first with regular prenatal care for yourself, and then with regular pediatric visits and immunizations for your baby. (See chapter 6.)
- Take care of yourself mentally and physically — when you're not well, you're not available for your child. Plus, your baby

worries about you just as you worry about him.

- Establish routines. Only when you are sure about what is probably going to happen can you enjoy the unexpected and take pleasure in changing plans. Young children, who are still trying to figure out what they can and cannot count on, are slaves to routine. They seek out familiar events and take enormous comfort in their presence. Create routines and rituals for special times during the day, such as meals, naps, and bedtime. Be as predictable as possible.

- Hold and touch your children. Play with them, following their lead. Children are good playwrights — they script, direct, cast, and act — so join their games. (See chapter 16.)

- Talk, read, and sing to your children. Become the narrator or play-by-play announcer of your and your child's day. Surround her with language and maintain an ongoing conversation with her even before she can answer back with words. (For more discussion on language development, see chapter 17.) Tell your child what you are doing and comment on what he is doing. Sing to him (even if you think you can't carry a tune), play music, make up stories or tell him real ones, and read books.

- Ask your preschooler what happens next in a story; get her involved in her own imagination. (See chapter 18 for more advice about reading to your child.) Play word games. Ask questions that need more than a yes or a no answer, as in "What do you think about this?" or "What would happen if . . . ?" Ask her to imagine what just has occurred in the past or will occur in the future.

- Talk to children about what they seem to be feeling. Teach them words for those feelings. (See chapters 21–22.) When necessary, make it clear that you do not like the way your child is behaving, but that you understand his feeling and you love him always. Explain the rules and consequences of misbehaving so that your child learns the "why" behind the "I say so." Tell her what you want her to do, not just what not to do. And show her how her behavior affects others. (For more on moral development, see chapter 27.)

- Encourage safe exploration and play. "Nothing ventured, nothing gained" truly applies to children's exploration and play. The child who feels it is risky to explore will not push back the limits of his own knowledge. Give children many opportunities to explore, to test things — and be prepared to step in if they are at risk of hurting themselves. Also, safety-proof the places where your child plays. Use a car seat, a bicycle helmet, and other protective devices to guard against serious injury.

- Help your child explore relationships with others as well. Arrange for her to spend time with other children of her own age and other ages. Help her learn to negotiate with others and to solve inevitable conflicts, scuffles, and disappointments while maintaining and strengthening her friendships.

- Limit television: as exciting as it sometimes is, and as wonderfully mesmerizing as it can be when you need to fix dinner or have a moment's peace, only a minority of programs encourage children's imagination, and too many leave them no time to exercise that imagination. Have set times for television and videos, and make sure your children are watching and learning what you want them to.

To help your child get the most from the amazing brain he was born with, do all you can to nurture him — to enhance and broaden his experiences and help him develop a healthy curiosity about himself and the world around him.

CHAPTER 10

Your Child's Unfolding Mind

Your brain is the physical organ in your skull. It is composed of millions of nerve cells, has a particular squishy texture, and weighs a certain amount. Your mind is, on the other hand, the weightless, invisible product of that brain and those cells as they interact with your body and your world, both inner and outer. Your mind is your *experience*, how — consciously or unconsciously — you organize the signals that are continuously streaming into your brain and act in response to them. While your mind has no physical reality, in many ways it *is* your reality: through it, you receive a variety of data both from the outside world we all share in and observe, and from the inside world of emotions, fantasies, and wishes that is unique to you. Through your mind, you imagine ways to deal with those data and try to delve into the minds of other people. For you — or anyone — to be a fully functioning, comfortable human being, your mind must perform all these tasks.

As children's brains develop, so their minds unfold along three interwoven strands: physical, cognitive, and social-emotional. Thus, for example, a child's ability to ride a bicycle depends on mental skills that include her practiced sense of balance, her memory that persistence can pay off, and her capacity to interpret her parents' directions. In turn, a young bicyclist's ability to go farther and faster makes her think about her world in new ways. And, although we treat them separately, the cognitive mind that learns, reasons, and makes choices is not really separate from the feeling and imagining mind. As we have said before and will again, feeling and imagining are central to how parents and children behave, to what they do and say, and to how they learn and make decisions.

Emotions and imagination play roles in everything you do, starting with the way your mind translates all of your experiences into memories. Emotions also color how you communicate with others; they fill in what words cannot express easily, if at all. The old adage "A picture is worth a thousand words" hints at how much information people convey by facial expression and body language. You are constantly attending to the ways other people respond to you and express themselves. You can choose (or learn) not to act upon these observations; you can even ignore another person's feelings. Nevertheless, emotions remain a vital currency in every interchange between two adults, between parents and children, between a child and his peers, and even in your solitary discussions with yourself. (See chapter 21 for more on emotional development.)

The same is true for the mind's ability to imagine and fantasize. If you did not imagine yourself performing different jobs, making the varsity team, going out with that special girl or boy, or winning medals with the speech club, you might never take the chance to try any of those challenges. You spend long hours thinking about your beloved partner (or your child), and use these reveries to ease lonely moments when you are not with these people. As we said in chapter 3, you imagine your children long before they are born, and always view them through the mental picture of who you want them to be. You can use your imagining mind to work out your problems or to escape from them. Or to travel to places you cannot go. Or to let you become stronger, brighter, handsomer, more articulate — all those traits or accomplishments that you cannot quite achieve in real life.

A feeling and imagining mind is the vehicle for all of these healthy, regular activities.

Without it, you would be as stalled as if you had no hands, legs, or senses. Your feeling and imagining mind also influences how you see the world and all the people in it and how you experience every situation in your life. Depending on what is commonly called your "frame of mind," a sunset may seem to you brilliant in its play of colors or sad, even frightening, as you face another lonely night with a sick baby. Another person's smile of greeting may appear to be just a casual convention or an exciting sign of mutual attraction. Your mind thus shapes the meaning of each experience in your life. Indeed, according to some philosophies, it is so difficult to separate one's existence from one's mental picture of it that one might as well treat every experience as if it occurs only in the mind.

In this chapter, we discuss four important aspects of the unfolding of your child's mind — from his ability to interpret from others' behavior what they are thinking and feeling, to comprehending that sometimes those interpretations and beliefs are wrong, to recognizing the difference between what is real and what is imagined, and, finally, to appreciating that every person around him has a separate and uniquely individual mind. The adult mind that gives shape and meaning to your experience is a long way from the mind of your infant, who sees the world entirely through her caregivers' actions toward her. Yet it is exactly because you interpret her behaviors as expressive that she is able to start to develop her own mind and her unique inner world.

UNDERSTANDING AUTISM

As we have said, babies are born with a special orientation toward people, human faces (especially moving ones), human voices, and human touch being the most appealing stimuli. This orientation puts them on the road to developing increasingly sophisticated ways of interacting with people.

In 1943, Leo Kanner, a pioneer in child psychiatry, described a group of children who he thought had been born without this natural attraction to people; instead, they preferred looking at and touching inanimate objects. Kanner called this condition "autism," from the Greek word for "self," as these children appeared to live in "a world of their own." They took little interest in others, even their parents and siblings. These children's failure to interact with people disrupted many aspects of their development, including their language and communication skills, their play, and their imagination.

For about twenty-five years after Kanner's work was published, psychologists held the grossly misguided belief that bad parenting caused autism — specifically, that of "refrigerator parents" who did not respond to a child's emotional needs. In the mid-1970s, scientific studies began to show that autism occurs in all societies and cultures, that it is a congenital disorder of the brain, and that it is, at times, associated with known genetic disorders such as Fragile X syndrome. Nowadays, autism is seen as a family of "disorders of socialization." Children with autism share profound deficits in social interaction, but the degree to which each child is affected differs. On one end of the range is total isolation: the child spends hours on end in a corner playing with a block puzzle, for example. On the other end, children may seek out people too much and in an insensitive manner: the adolescent, for example, who keeps on asking peers or adults the same inappropriate questions.

Children with autism also exhibit profound disabilities in language and communication, and the severity of these difficulties varies as well. Some children with autism never talk. Some parrot or echo what they hear exactly as they hear it. Other autistic children have good vocabulary and command of language, but their communication skills are severely impaired because they speak mechanically (without inflecting the voice) or cannot maintain a conversation (speaking too little or too much, not allowing for the give-and-take of normal social interaction).

Autistic children may also dis-

Social Interpretation

You probably take for granted that you can sometimes guess what another person is thinking. This ability requires no psychic powers but simply confidence that everybody shares certain experiences and customs. Since you are continuously observing other people's behavior and remarks, and judging from them what each one feels and believes and desires, you are, in other words, always making assumptions about what is going on in someone else's mind. And the closer you are to a person, the more assumptions you probably make about her. When your infant is crying, you assume she is sad or needs something. When she is laughing, you think she is happy. When she goes to her toy box, you assume she wants to play. When she points to the orange-juice container, you assume she is thirsty. If the child brings her pillow to the couch and curls up with her

play bizarre actions: repetitive and purposeless movement (flapping hands, twirling, rocking), "ritualistic behaviors" such as flicking an object in the air, difficulties with minor changes in the environment, unusual sensitivity (to light, sounds, or pain), and attachment to such odd objects as a piece of string. Some injure themselves repeatedly. About 70 percent to 80 percent of children with autism also have mental retardation. Nevertheless, some are bright individuals who simply have profound social and communication disabilities. A small minority of mentally retarded children with autism have so-called savant skills; despite their intellectual disability, they excel in one unusual skill such as drawing, music, calendar calculation (knowing the day of the week on which a given date falls), or memorizing trivial information like lists of telephone numbers.

Although we know autism is a disorder of the brain, we as yet have no definite knowledge of what causes it. Research implicates some areas of the brain involved in understanding social stimuli, such as the limbic system. There seems to be a genetic contribution: identical twins are usually both affected; the likelihood of a child with autism having a sibling with a similar condition may be as high as one in ten; and an autistic child often has several other relatives who show difficulties in social and communication skills. Because autism is one of the most researched disorders of childhood, and because of formidable advances in genetics and brain research, our understanding of the condition is likely to improve markedly in the coming years.

The treatment of autism is primarily educational: helping children maximize the language and learning abilities they do have. In most cases, an autistic child needs intensive and structured schooling, often individually or in a small group. Research has shown that early and intense educational interventions may considerably alter the course of the disorder. Nevertheless, no treatment has been shown to *cure* children with autism, and many aspects of the condition are thought to be lifelong. Medical treatments are of limited value, although drugs may help decrease some severely debilitating aspects of the condition such as self-injury, self-stimulation, or anxiety. Although there is periodic publicity about a new "cure" for the disorder, so far only educational treatment has been shown to substantially benefit children with autism.

blanket in the middle of the afternoon, you assume she is tired — or, you might realize with a start, she could be sick!

Often there are two or more possible explanations for a person's behavior. If a friend does not call when he said he would, for instance, you may either worry that something has happened to him, or resent that he does not care about your relationship. If a teenager slams a door, you may quickly assume she is angry — but when you later step through that same door and feel a draft blowing, you realize the door may have shut much more forcefully than she intended. Which explanation, if any, do you act on? Which makes the deeper impression on your memory? Your frame of mind at the moment may influence the assumptions you make about your daughter.

You do this kind of mental work every moment of the day. On the whole, despite the pitfall of assuming too much, you seldom err crucially in judging what other people think and feel. You rarely even think about the process — you just do it. You judge what you cannot see in accordance with visible and audible behavior. This evaluation happens in your imagining and feeling mind, informed by your thinking, cognitive mind. Experience tells you that children go to their toy boxes when they want to play. Experience tells you that a child who lies down in the middle of the day may have a fever, and that even if that possibility is small, the outcome would be serious enough to warrant further investigation. Your social conventions have taught you not to slam doors and to follow through on what you promise, so something must be wrong if a person violates these conventions.

Fortunately, your mind can also revise its initial assumptions when you gather further information. When a six-year-old boy in the city playground does not return your daughter's toy truck even though she has politely (as you have taught) asked him to do so, you might assume the new boy is behaving badly — until you remember overhearing his conversation with his caregiver and recall that he was not speaking English. Your interpretation of the boy's behavior completely changes and your own response shifts too. Rather than lecture the boy, you show your daughter how to communicate her request with gestures instead of words.

Interpreting other people's thinking and feeling minds from their behavior and words is part of being human: it is how we all get along in our social society. Indeed, your brain and senses, and thus your mind, are "con-structed" for gathering and judging such information. When something in a person's brain interferes with this mental process, the result is autism (see pages 126–127) or a related disorder. Social interpretation is thus a developmental skill that a young child needs to achieve. Over time, he learns that many events go on in his mind — thinking, feeling, worrying, learning, remembering, wishing, dreaming — and that all of these are unique to him. He also learns that other people's behavior gives clues to what is going on in their minds. In imaginary play, children practice these "mind-behavior" questions: they practice the mental language of living in a social world that can be as confusing as it is comforting. Such rehearsals are an important step toward the adult's ability to participate in full and deep loving relationships with friends, partners, and ultimately one's own children. (For more on play, see chapter 16.)

A child develops an imagining and feeling mind through thousands upon thousands of moments in the company of his parents. Your imagining and feeling mind and the behavior that reflects it tutor your child from his first hours. When your baby coos and smiles in response to your rubbing his head, you may say, "What a handsome boy you are!" or, "Oh, is that what you're thinking?" or even, "Tell me more." You pretend to have a conversation — adding meaning to coos, pausing at appropriate moments, even playing both roles in the dialogue. Your feeling and imagining mind is providing a foundation for emotional understanding. Though your baby is not yet able to join in the verbal play, he experiences your pleasure, your admiration, and your responsiveness. There is no proper way for parents to provide this lesson: if all goes well, it just happens. Each mother and father has her or his individual style. Some are more expressive; others more subdued. But whatever your style is in these moments, you are using your imagining and feeling mind.

Your child also experiences the way you observe his gestures and attribute intention to them. In other words, he experiences how you "read" his mind to infer what he wants to do or convey. Of course, this does not always happen perfectly. It might take several guesses before you realize what your one-year-old means by "da" or "ba." Research shows that the more you are able to consider what your child might be *thinking,* rather than reacting simply to what your child is *doing,* the more you convey to him the importance of understanding other persons' minds. Similarly, parents who are able to consider their children's feelings, beliefs, and even wishes produce children who both are better at this same task when they get older, and feel more secure in their personal relationships with other children and adults.

Interpreting a child's true thoughts is not always straightforward: parent and child get to know each other intimately over time, just as spouses do. Consider a fifteen-month-old sitting at the dinner table, happily crinkling up a piece of red wrapping paper. Her father comments, "Isn't that shiny paper fun?" When he leaves the table for a moment to get something, the paper falls to the floor. When he returns, the baby starts to point urgently toward her red juice cup. In the instant when the father sees his daughter pointing, he has two choices. He can read from how she points to the cup that she wants juice. Or he can see that she is pointing to something red like the paper she had been so happy with: so she wants him to bring the paper back! Either response conveys a message about trying to fulfill another person's desires.

Imagine that the father takes the cup into the kitchen for juice. At best, bringing back juice might distract the child from the lost paper, but juice is not what she was really thinking about before. If the father sees the shiny red paper on the floor and retrieves it, his daughter probably smiles and returns happily to crumpling the paper, having learned that her father can figure out what she wants. A single gesture can thus have many possible meanings, some obvious and some more connected to an individual moment between a parent and a child.

Or, consider a three-year-old who has had a wonderful visit from his grandmother. She read him stories, they baked cookies, and they took a long walk along the edge of a pond. Then, in the afternoon, Grandma left. At supper, when the boy's mother tells him to stop playing with his food, he begins to cry. His mother waits a moment and then leans over and hugs her son, saying quietly, "I know you miss your grandmother — you had a really good time today. You'll get to see her again next week." In this moment, the mother interprets her son's tears to refer not just to her reprimand but more deeply to his sadness at missing his grandmother. Parents who spend a lot of time with their children usually develop an intimate sense of what different gestures and sounds and emotional displays mean. At such moments throughout each day, your young children experience your successful interpretation of their feelings. They learn that this is something people do for each other.

As your child moves into his second year, his ability to communicate a range of thoughts and feelings expands, but you still need to do some interpreting and filling in. An eighteen-month-old may look at a yellow flower, look back to you to get your attention, and then look again at the flower, pointing, even saying "da" or "lello." That, too, is the early imagining and feeling mind in action. Your toddler is curious about the flower, wants to interest you as well, and, most important, wants to share this moment with you. She expects, from many earlier and similar moments, that you will join in this experience. Maybe you will smile and laugh at her energy, maybe you will comment on the color or the word, maybe you will kneel and look at the flower on her eye level. You may even add to the moment by asking her whether she can find other yellow flowers, or sniff the flower and invite her to do the same. You may tell a little story about how you planted these seeds in the

ground not long ago, and remind her that she helped by pouring water. You might also play a game wondering, "Who made that flower?" You might ask whether your toddler's treasured teddy bear would like to see the flower, too. All of these responses come from your feeling and imagining mind.

This interaction may last no more than a minute or two. Still, many developmentally remarkable interactions are packed into this brief time. Your child's looking at an object, looking to you, pointing and looking back is something child developmentalists call "joint attention." Your adding to the moment by asking her to find other yellow flowers, showing her about the scent, or telling a story is called "scaffolding." By taking your toddler's simple act and giving it more meaning, you provide a "scaffold," or structure, for your child to add to. In your action, you convey, "Yes, I know from your pointing that you're

thinking about the yellow flower and you want me to be interested in it with you. I'll tell you what *I'm* thinking about that flower, tell you something about you and me together, and help you learn both about flowers and about our sharing experiences with each other." You do not have to explain how this stimulates your child's imagining and feeling mind: and, indeed, a toddler will not understand it explicitly anyway. The lesson is contained in what you do. You also stimulate her own curiosity by showing her that you are interested in her mind and in her sharing her mental world with you. (See also "Human Curiosity," pages 132–133.)

Such behavior comes naturally to parents. The simple, common activities occurring in hundreds of brief moments every day are the stuff of learning: making breakfast, getting dressed, bathing, brushing teeth, making the bed, playing in rain puddles, making cookies, buying groceries, doing the wash, cleaning the car, folding the laundry, brushing the dog, taking out the trash, recycling the papers, picking up sticks in the yard, sweeping the garage, going to the cleaners. At first, your mind supplies most of the action and content: you put words to your child's behavior. But she is joining in, too. When she turns to you and points to the flower, she is saying, "Let's explore and understand this world together."

Working Through Misinterpretations

Part of understanding another person's mind is realizing that sometimes you both make incorrect assumptions and act inappropriately because of them. As we have said, people often make quick assumptions about others' motives from their behavior and a few surrounding clues. You are doing this in your mind even when your assumptions don't require any action. For example, if you were walking down the street and saw a man stop, turn, and run into a bakery, you might well assume that the smells drifting out the bakery's door had caught his interest, especially if they had caught yours. But perhaps this man remembered that he owed the baker money from their last card game, or urgently needed to use a phone, or had finally decided to ask the store manager out on a date. With experience you come to realize that sometimes people make decisions based on incorrect or false beliefs. For example, if the same man tries the door of the bakery before the shop opens, you may assume he does not know the bakery's hours or the correct time — or that he's trying to break in. In the latter instance, you might act on your assumption and call the police, only to find out later that the man had been expecting someone to meet him early in the store.

You are also continuously making assumptions about your child's actions. One afternoon, after you've just finished baking the cake cooling on the kitchen table, you see, out of the corner of your eye, your child walking quietly into the kitchen. You call out, "You know you can't have any cake before supper." You assume he had smelled the warm cake, even seen you baking it, and was about to have a taste. But he may have been getting some

HUMAN CURIOSITY

The trait of being curious has a mixed reputation. Sayings like "Curiosity killed the cat" and "Some things are better left alone" imply that children can be too curious for their own good. On the other hand, curiosity is what motivates a child or adult to keep learning about their world. Curiosity can help a person spot potential dangers and opportunities and find new solutions to old problems and mysteries. Society tends to value inquisitive people, though we may view them as eccentric; we often believe they see life in a special way and know a bit more than most of us.

There is some evidence that curiosity is a natural drive: scientists observe animals exploring their surroundings even when they are well fed and protected and have all their other needs satisfied. As Albert Einstein once said, "Curiosity has its own reason for existing."

Even infants in their cribs display curiosity. When faced with an unfamiliar sensation, such as a new sight or sound, they usually pay careful attention to it until it is no longer new. When researchers design experiments so that these new sensations appear when the babies do something, such as move their heads in a particular way, the infants usually discover that trigger and repeat the action so they can experience the sensation again. If the researchers change what triggers the sensation, infants will try other actions to make it happen, exploring and seeking novelty at the same time — two aspects of being curious.

If all goes well in development, toddlers are even more curious than infants. To them the whole world is a vast undiscovered continent to explore. Their new mobility brings more places and things within their reach; their new language skills open up another way of learning about their surroundings. They are full of questions about all they see, feel, hear, touch, and taste. Toddlers ask questions that we adults rarely if ever dream of (though we probably once did): Who makes thunder? Why does Daddy wear a tie? Why do birds build nests in trees? How do planes fly? What makes big tomatoes from little tomato seeds? Does poking on the keys

juice or even looking for his crayons that he had left in the kitchen the night before.

Realizing that people sometimes act or make decisions based on incorrect beliefs or feelings is an important step in a young child's social development. With this understanding comes the knowledge that other people may not see the world quite as she does, and that individuals behave differently because of their different states of mind. This distinction is not easy for young children to make. Imagine three-year-olds watching their cousin Sam put his favorite chocolates in a kitchen drawer and leave the room. Then they watch as Sam's friend comes into the kitchen and moves the chocolates to the refrigerator. When Sam returns, where will he look for his chocolates? If you ask the three-year-olds this question, they usually will point to the refrigerator. Since they know the chocolates are there, Sam just *can't* believe anything else! In other words, they won't let Sam have a false belief and look in the incorrect place for his chocolates.

Four- and five-year-olds begin to understand how other people's states of mind can

hurt the computer? Underneath your child's endless questions is a driving curiosity about her own body and how it works, about what makes girls and boys different, about where babies come from, about why she looks different from Mommy and Daddy, and about when she will grow up.

Events and circumstances can, however, interfere with a young child's curiosity. (See also "The Child Who Cannot Play," pages 222–223.) To explore the world, a child must first be capable of sustained attention. He must not be overly anxious and worried. A child who has spent much of his first years in the hospital, or has experienced parental illness or death, is often less curious. There is already too much in his day-to-day life that is stressful and frightening for him to consider other mysteries. When parents fight or are in the middle of divorce, toddlers often show diminished curiosity. While, paradoxically, these situations may stimulate many questions, young children often seem to sense that they cannot discuss with any comfort or freedom what is stressing their families. To wonder openly about his world and himself, a child needs both mental space free of worries and fears, and mental time not crowded with the rigors of moving from one home to another or racing to scheduled activities. Likewise, school-age children and adolescents are effectively curious about their world when they are rested, relatively free of stress, and enjoying enough time to be reflective and observant.

Encourage and nourish curiosity in your young child both by responding to her questions and by wondering aloud with her about things you see. Why is there time between the lightning and the thunder? What makes rainbows? Why does your next-door neighbor put those sticks in his garden? As your inquiries encourage your child to wonder with you and to observe her world, you demonstrate the value of asking questions and thinking about people and events beyond what you can see on the surface. Children who are more curious are able to use their intelligence more fully, can be more creative and flexible in their thinking and learning, and are more imaginative as older children and adults.

differ from their own. They understand that Sam will look for his chocolates in the kitchen drawer where he last saw them. They realize that people can be led astray by incomplete knowledge, false beliefs, or misinterpretations. This discovery helps them to master many simple but essential transactions that are a casual part of social life. A child thus learns that when a friend does not return her telephone call, the reason may be that he has not yet received the message. When a school-age child's aunt Maria gives him a present that is appropriate for a younger child, he can understand that she has a false image of how grown-up he is but is still trying to show her love. Eventually older children can imagine that one person can have different states of mind, and may have more than one reason for a particular behavior and thus try to reserve judgment until they learn more. Accepting the possibility of false belief is basic to a child's recognition of the individuality of different people's minds.

Another aspect of mental life that you as an adult take for granted is being able to change your mind consciously. You believe things today that you once did not know or disagreed with. You can muse on how you came to change your mind: Why exactly did you dislike broccoli, and what in the world could you have seen in that girl? Knowing that you have changed your mind is essential to social relationships as well as to emotional and cognitive growth. But young children do not yet understand that concept. Thus, you can go to an ice cream store with your three-year-old after he has been asking for chocolate ice cream all day, and find that, once in the store, he orders strawberry. If you remind him that he told you he wanted chocolate, he will probably say with great certainty, "No, I always wanted strawberry!" He is not being stubborn or willful; he just does not grasp the notion of a changeable mind. He knows that he wants strawberry and believes that what is true *now* about his feelings, wishes, or memories always has been (and always will be) true.

By the time children enter kindergarten, they are beginning to grasp the idea of changing one's mind, but it is not fully in place. You cannot actually talk to a child about what she once thought or wanted until she is around six or seven. This is also about the age that children can start to look back on when they were "babies," recognizing that they no longer think, act, or believe things the same way.

Let's Pretend: The Imagining Mind

Late in their second year, young children start using their imaginations to investigate behavior they see in others. Your toddler's toy bear may join her at the breakfast table and, shyly at first, nibble on toast with jam. Although the bear may become quite sticky in this game, letting a toy pretend to do a real behavior is an important step in the development of an imagining mind. Your response will depend on your own tolerance for messes and sticky plush toys at the breakfast table. You may address the real situation, urging your daughter, "Finish your toast, and *then* you can play with Bear." Or you may join in the play briefly, wondering whether Bear prefers orange marmalade or strawberry jam. Or, you can strike a middle ground, commenting, "It's nice to have Bear join us for breakfast, but girls eat first in this house." There are many variations on a theme, and rarely only one correct or appropriate response. When you are trying to get out the door to catch your car pool and get to work for that eight o'clock meeting, bears and jam don't mix well. You may have to wait until supper to play bears and peas instead.

The important thing about such a moment is how your child's actions reflect her imagining and feeling mind. Your daughter is beginning to pretend, to act out behavior she is pretty sure is impossible, but enjoys playing with. This is very early pretending, sustained for just a brief moment. Indeed, she is not always certain that the game truly is pretend. She may insist tearfully, "Bear *really* is hungry! Bear really *needs* to eat breakfast!" Not until she is four will she be certain that all this is a game of pretending and even be able to joke with you about Bear being "really,

really hungry." (See chapter 16 for more discussion of imaginative play.)

The ability to pretend is itself a big achievement. It begins when a fourteen-month-old "drinks" from an empty cup and smiles, or puts on Daddy's glasses and laughs. It comes into full flower when a three-and-a-half-year-old walks through the house claiming to be a big huge dinosaur who needs egg-salad sandwiches to take on a dinosaur picnic. Between drinking from an empty cup and playing *Tyrannosaurus rex* are many steps that establish the foundation for imagining — for thinking about and playing with things that are not actually visible or present. Being able to pretend not only gives your child the capacity to experiment with different roles and experiences, but it also signals a big step in his mental development. With it, he gains the ability to let one thing stand for something else — what we call, in technical terms, the ability to understand and create a "representation."

Representations are all around you. A photograph is a representation of a real person or place. A letter of the alphabet stands for one or more sounds. A play is a complex representation of people's lives. In all cases, you expect the symbols to conform to what you know about the real things. You are surprised, sometimes disappointed, when a photograph is distorted or faked, a letter is silent, or characters in a story do not act the way you expect human beings to behave. The ability to represent — to have one thing, person, or experience stand for another — is a critical developmental step. It underpins all mental life.

One of the most important uses of representation is in systems that people share, such as spoken and written language. For everyone who speaks English, the word "apple" stands for a real fruit. The word "mother," indicating one's own mother or mothers in general, brings to mind a whole group of qualities. Those qualities may belong to a particular mother (she smelled sweet, baked me cookies, had a lovely laugh or a quick temper) or to mothers in general (they take care of babies, are understanding, always make things better). When you talk, without even thinking you depend on other people's ability to use a shared set of representations. They understand what you mean by your spoken words and references, as well as your gestures and tones and facial expressions. Without this representative ability, a person might as well be in a foreign country trying to understand what the native speakers are saying to each other.

Very young children acquire this mental ability in steps. The first step seems simple: understanding that everyone can use one thing to stand for another. A picture of a person stands for that person but is not alive. A toy car stands for a real car but does not have to be the same size. This is an important concept for children and, in the very beginning, a hard one. In their first year, infants are interested in pictures: your baby will find pictures of people especially captivating. But she does not clearly match a picture to a person. This ability does not emerge until the second year; and even then, toddlers are not always certain about the match between symbol and reality. They may wonder why they cannot eat the toy apple. Adults often explain the difference: "This is a pretend apple, not a real apple."

Gradually, children acquire the ability to hold more and more complex representations in their minds. They learn to use something other than a toy car, such as a block, to stand for a real car. Then they create stories and more elaborate pretend games, making a box into a spaceship and a bowl into a magic helmet. They recognize their own pretending as well as the pretend play of their friends. During their early preschool years, children begin to understand differences between mental and physical events: your child starts to appreciate that another person viewing an event from a different position may not see the same thing he sees. Very young children seem to believe that if they cover their eyes and cannot see a person, that person cannot see them either; but a preschooler knows that if she wants to hide from her brother under a blanket, she has to cover her whole body and lie still. Preschool children also begin to recognize that people feel happy or sad depending on whether they get what they want — happy to receive the last piece of chocolate cake, sad when ice cream slips off a cone on a hot day.

In their second and third year, children also begin to view people differently from objects. Your child sees that other people are very like him. People move and act at will, and sometimes respond to his requests and communications, while even his favorite toys do not respond so promptly, though he can

make believe they do. During this time, children also begin to develop a capacity for empathy. They recognize that a person is hurt or sad. They try to offer comfort or ask, "What's wrong?" They thus start to experience other people not just as doers but also as experiencers — as individuals who react to the world with feelings as well as actions.

Discovering Her Own Inner World

By their fourth birthday, children make another significant step in mental development. A preschooler begins to fathom that other people have beliefs about the world around him that may be different from his own beliefs. Every person, therefore, has their own, unique thoughts — even Daddy and Mommy! Four- and five-year-olds can understand that their thoughts, feelings, wishes, and beliefs are private unless they tell other people. At this age, your child recognizes that someone might believe something and might act on that belief even though another person knows it is wrong. He can appreciate the story of Sam and the misplaced chocolates and will know that Sam will look where he last believed the chocolates to be. Four- and five-year-olds begin to appreciate deception and illusion. Your child can play tricks, such as hiding or moving an object, knowing that people will look for it where they last knew it to be. She begins to be able to tease and joke, expecting that others will recognize that she is playing.

Throughout the school years, your child's understanding of what is going on in his thinking and imagining mind becomes more elaborate. He comprehends memory, concepts of time, and how thoughts and beliefs can change. He recognizes thinking as an activity people do to solve problems and understand one another. He knows that people think and imagine even when they are not pretending — that a person can create and enjoy a full imaginary life parallel to real life. These developments in a child's awareness of thinking, believing, wishing, imagining, and remembering are all part of her unfolding physical, cognitive, and social-emotional world and her own personal inner mental world. That world, unique to every child, forms the center of her individuality.

PART III

Mastering the Body's Basic Functions

CHAPTER 11

Your Baby's Motor Development

Infants, toddlers, and preschoolers grow rapidly. As their bodies grow, they also learn how to move around and explore their world. Physical development in the early years of life is more than just learning to walk. It's also about your baby's learning to feed himself, establish regular, predictable sleeping habits, master toileting, and become curious about his own body and gender. Thus, in part 3, we discuss the basic functions of your child's body: motor development, feeding the whole child, sleeping habits, and sexuality and gender.

There are two main divisions of motor development: gross and fine. Gross motor development refers to the actions of the larger muscles of the body — those that control the major movements of the trunk and extremities. Fine motor development involves the actions of the muscles that control smaller and more pinpointed movements, particularly those of the hands and fingers. The earliest progress occurs in the gross motor realm. We include toilet training as a part of motor development, since your child's ability

to manage his own bowel and bladder require some coordinated voluntary motor skills.

While some aspects of physical development move along more or less on a timeline, you also play an important role in shaping your child's pleasure in his body and delight

in his many new physical achievements. When you care for your child's body by bathing and dressing him, you help his physical development by reassuring him that you not only understand his rapidly growing and changing body but are not afraid of it. For very young children, their bodily skills are both exciting and frightening. Sometimes a child learns to walk before she is fully able to understand that you are in the other room she has just toddled away from. In this chapter, we discuss how children learn to control their bodies.

Gross Motor Skills

Children generally learn how to sit up, crawl, walk, and otherwise control their bodies in a regular sequence: that is, from head to toe or, in technical language, in a cephalo-caudad direction. The order of these developments never changes, but the exact timing differs from child to child. There is a fairly broad range of normal variability, and you should not try to match your child's landmarks to some standardized list. If you cannot control your anxiety about whether your baby is late learning to roll over or run or achieve some other ability, consult your pediatrician before you decide that something is wrong.

Your Newborn's Motor Skills

The normal newborn infant has a limited repertoire of motor skills, of which a fair number are reflexive rather than voluntary. She can turn her head but not lift it. She can wave her arms in the air, but not purposefully and not across the line down the center of her chest. She can kick her feet and legs, but those limbs cannot support her weight. A newborn cannot balance himself in a sitting position or support his trunk against gravity. Since he does not have voluntary control of the muscular sphincters in his bladder and bowel, he urinates and defecates spontaneously and involuntarily when those organs are full.

There are two major reasons for this limited vocabulary of movement. The first is the immaturity of the muscles themselves. Like almost everything else in the newborn's body, the muscles and most of their attachments are formed and intact, but they are far from finished in terms of strength and function. The young infant's other major limitation is that the central nervous system does not have complete control of those muscles. Much of that system is not yet organized well enough to generate and transmit the commands needed to make the muscles perform in their adult fashion. The wiring is not fully formed. As nerves develop, they acquire a protective sheath called myelin, which functions somewhat like the insulation around electrical wires. Just as insulation allows electricians to create integrated but separate circuits, myelin improves the performance of nerves and smoothes the way they stimulate particular muscle groups. Furthermore, in a newborn's body, many of the nerves that grow out from the lower levels of the spinal canal have not even reached their destination in the muscles of the legs and the sphincters of elimination. Even if those muscles were in full adult shape, the infant would still not be able to walk or control his bowels or bladder. So your baby's gains in motor coordination reflect nerve growth and increasing nerve insulation through the myelin.

Much of a newborn baby's major activity is prompted by the startle response or reflex. Sudden noises or changes in position make a baby thrust both arms and legs outward and then gather them toward himself — almost as though trying to hold onto something so as not to fall. This physical reaction usually fades after the first two months of life. Another easily seen newborn reflex is called "palmar grasping": when a small object (a parent's finger, for example) is pressed into an infant's palm, her hand will close tightly around it and grip for an indefinite period. This response lasts until she is about six months old. Similarly, touching the soles of a baby's feet may cause her toes to fan upward in the newborn period and then to curl downward for most of the rest of her first year. These reflexes are a holdover from earlier evolutionary epochs in human development when parents needed an infant to grip automatically when they moved or sensed danger.

Newborns have other innate physical reflexes that have obviously developed to help them obtain food. Even in the womb, a baby-to-be is sucking, usually on her thumb. After birth, as soon as a nipple or baby bottle or anything similar touches the roof of her mouth, her sucking reflex kicks in. Also helpful for infants' feeding is what is termed the "rooting reflex": when something strokes a newborn's cheek or lips, he turns toward that stimulation. This helps him locate what

touched his face and, if it was a nipple, to start sucking in the right place. Some infants develop the skill of coordinating their breathing, sucking, and swallowing more easily than others do; after all, that combination was not required in the womb. (For more discussion of feeding, see chapter 12.) A newborn will also instinctively protect herself by trying to shake off a corner of a sheet or pillow that has fallen over her face, or by turning her head away from an object headed straight toward her (while ignoring an object moving slightly to one side or the other).

Other reflexes are less easily explained by the baby's needs. For instance, when the head of a newborn lying flat on her back is turned gently to one side, her arm on that side often becomes straighter. The arm on her other side curls toward her body, producing what may look like the pose of a very small fencer. Babies do not always exhibit this "tonic neck reflex," especially when they are distracted or upset, and the response disappears when they are around six months old. You can see another of a newborn's reflexes by holding your one-month-old baby under the arms (supporting his head carefully) and dangling his feet on a firm surface. He will probably react by moving one leg in front of the other, as if trying to walk. These are not, however, precocious "first steps," since a newborn's leg muscles and coordination are not nearly powerful enough to walk, even with an adult's help. This stepping is a reflex and lasts only about two months. Later in your baby's first year, you can see him make the same sort of steps as you hold him;

that action is voluntary and truly is the start of learning to walk. Indeed, after the first several weeks of life, almost all of a child's major motor activities — even seeking her mother's breast and sucking — are voluntary.

An infant's first intentional actions are holding up his head and keeping it from wobbling and, then, lifting his head up from a prone (face-down) position. After his facial muscles develop, he can smile. Next, the arm muscles begin to have more discriminate function, which lets him reach for an object after fixing on it with his gaze. He suddenly becomes able to move his extremities across the midline of the body — this allows him to reach with either hand and to transfer objects from one hand to the other. At this point, it becomes possible for you to pull your infant from a supine to a sitting position while the muscles of her upper trunk provide some balance as you do so. Soon enough, parents want to help their child to stand. Initially, your infant can support weight on her legs but cannot move them; at first her legs can't do any more than provide rigid support. Before she walks, your infant recapitulates all these steps on her own; rolling over, working into a sitting position, crawling to some piece of furniture, and using it for support as she pulls herself up onto her feet.

Steps to the First Steps: Crawling, Walking, and Other Voluntary Movements

By the end of her first three months, your baby has probably learned several basic, voluntary movements. When you lay her down on her stomach, she can lift her head and push her chest off the surface, supporting the weight with her arms. When you lay her on her back, she can kick or straighten her legs. It takes another three months or so before she is able to roll from her stomach to her back, or vice versa — whichever seems more interesting. By about seven months, most babies can remain seated by themselves, no longer needing the support of a parent or a snug chair to keep from slumping over (though at first they rely on their hands for balance). Also, infants of this age can for the first time support their whole weight on their legs, though they are still far from balancing by themselves.

In the second half of their first year, infants master several new physical skills. Children vary in motor development not only in timing but also in the way they may seem to achieve certain skills. Crawling is a good example of this individual variability. Most children get up on their hands and knees and move them alternately — the right arm with the left leg, and then the reverse. But some children will begin by pulling themselves with their arms alone. Others will get into a sideways, half-sitting position and hitch along on their bottoms, using their arms to pull and one leg to push simultaneously. Sometimes children will skip crawling altogether and move directly to taking steps. These are all normal variants. Each leads just as well as the others to the next steps of major motor progress.

Crawling is exciting for a child, since it opens up much more of the world to explore.

A baby of this age is gradually becoming more independent: usually he can get into a sitting position without anyone's help, and from a seated position, he can turn around to crawl or lie down on his stomach. It is also during these months that a child learns to pull herself up to her feet and move while leaning on an object. At one year, most babies can stand briefly and walk two or three steps without help; the timing of this achievement varies according to a child's interests, environment, and sense of encouragement. Toward the end of the first year, your infant has begun walking and has become a toddler.

Few events in children's lives are more eagerly awaited than their first steps. Parents exult in this accomplishment and firmly remember it. An important landmark in motor development, unaided walking also marks a watershed in the relationship between parents and child. As an infant develops that skill, he becomes physically independent of his parents. He can go where he wishes on his own. To the whole family, this is both liberating and frightening. Your child revels in his newfound freedom but is still psychologically dependent enough to react with fear if he suddenly finds himself out of his parents' sight. Mother and father heave a sigh of relief that their child has managed this major achievement and no longer needs to be carried; they also worry about injuries and safety and how to protect their new toddler without constricting him. In addition, for parents the baby's first step is a foreboding of all the stages of separation and liberation yet to come. (For more on the challenge of separa-

tion, see chapter 31.) Although your baby will not remember how she learned to walk, you will: it is usually a momentous day.

As with so many other aspects of a child's development, the speed and ease with which she acquires motor skills depends on her genetic endowment, her overall health, and her interaction with parents and other caregivers. Crucial to mastering this skill is the motivation parents provide by responding happily and excitedly at each of the stages leading to it. The importance of motivation is evident in families with many children, where a new baby may well learn to stand and walk later than average. Why go to all that trouble when so many siblings will carry you or fetch what you want? Who is bold enough to try standing up for the first time inside a bustling mob? But when those children do take their first steps, there are many loving relatives around to applaud, and that approval and excitement will encourage them to try more. Whether living in a large family or with a single parent, a child depends on his caregivers' approval to risk those first steps.

Learning to walk opens up a much bigger world for children: they can move farther, reach higher, and escape faster. There are still some important skills, however, a one-year-old cannot master. She does not remember what happened the last time she pushed the reset button on Mommy's computer, nor can she predict what will happen the next time she pushes it. Her spirit of adventure may be stronger than her ability to climb a steep flight of stairs. Therefore, although your one-year-old is making great progress in walking and in other skills, she still needs someone to watch over her closely. (See "Making Your House Safe" below.)

By the age of two, most children have passed through the stages of walking (or toddling) easily, walking while first dragging and then carrying their toys, running, and balancing on tiptoe. They can probably even kick something big and not too heavy, such as a balloon, out of their way. Many challenges remain, however: getting up onto chairs and sofas without help, walking up and down stairs, and bending over consistently without

tumbling over. The coming year is also the time when most children learn to jump, climb, and pedal a tricycle. Mobility remains a great motivation for learning new skills.

At four, the average child can both hop and balance for a few seconds on one foot. She can move backward and forward easily. In the backyard, she can kick a stationary ball straight and throw a smaller ball overhand as well as underhand. Nevertheless, she is still a long way from being ready to play outfield: she probably has trouble catching either ball and must wait for it to bounce first. Already

MAKING YOUR HOUSE SAFE

The best way to avoid feeling anxious about your crawling child when she starts moving around and exploring is to make your house safe for her. Install gates across stairways, windows, and overhangs. You may also be more comfortable if you fence off your kitchen, workshop, and computer reset button so that your infant can play near those areas without an adult watching. Put childproof latches on cabinets and drawers. Store knives and other sharp tools where children cannot reach. Unload guns and lock them away securely; even safer, do not keep guns in the house at all. Be as protective of your child as you are of your fine china and glassware (and move those out of your child's reach, too).

Many parents like to let their children play with metal pots and pans from the kitchen cabinets. Playing with these is just as effective for developing fine motor skills as are expensive toys (few of which are also useful for cooking!). Do not, however, let your child open these cabinets on his own; teach him to wait for you to open them. Otherwise, he might feel free to investigate what lies inside many other cabinets as well.

Household poisons are especially troublesome because infants and toddlers often explore new things by putting them in their mouths. Go through your bathroom and kitchen to remove potentially hazardous substances you don't need, such as old prescription drugs or old paint. Move other toxic substances out of reach: drain and oven cleaners, furniture polish, alcohol, aspirin, pesticides, and so on. Do not overlook paint thinner, antifreeze (some types of which taste sweet), bleach, and other poisonous substances in your workshop or garage. Poinsettia leaves, castor beans, and a few other household plants are also toxic, so check your greenery.

Take these safety steps well before your child is moving around on her own. Today's crawler becomes tomorrow's walker overnight. You will have enough trouble keeping up with her without also trying to make your house hazard-free on the fly.

mobile, the child's prime motives for learning new activities are independence and play. Knowing how to hop, skip, and jump, a five-year-old will turn his attention to mastering the swing set, the seesaw, and all the different ways to hang from the jungle gym. By that age a child should be able to dress and undress on his own, use silverware (starting with spoon and fork), and go to the bathroom by himself most of the time, though for social reasons he may still ask a parent to accompany him.

To a large extent, walking completes the major part of gross motor development. Children will continue to refine those skills as they learn to run and jump, hop and skip, climb, ride a bicycle, throw and kick a ball, perhaps try out gymnastics or juggling, and do much more. These are important new achievements, but their significance pales next to that original moment of walking itself. From that time on, much of the baby's progress occurs in fine motor development.

Fine Motor Skills

Children also acquire fine motor skills in a generally predictable sequence, but vary in how quickly they proceed from one skill to the next. Some of this variation is due to temperament, some to how each child's environment motivates and rewards the attainment of certain skills, and some to genetic endowment. A baby still being breast-fed will not be as interested in learning to use a spoon as one who sees that *spoon* as the key to all his food. A child who never watches her family members writing or drawing will not associate using a crayon and pencil with pleasure. And a child will learn to write letters, even rudimentary ones, if he has been exposed to letters and the stories they tell through sharing books with parents. (See chapter 18 for more benefits of reading with your children.) It is not always possible, however, to accelerate a child's fine motor skills with a stimulating environment because a little body needs first to become physically capable of each task.

As we noted earlier in this chapter, a newborn's hands reflexively grasp an object pressed on her palms. If the object is a rattle or bell that makes a noise, she can shake it with pleasure. She can also bring her hands to her mouth, obviously a preparation for feeding herself. But it is nearly impossible for your newborn to seize an object, even one hanging in the air; until about four months, the best she can manage is to swipe at something. By the age of six months, an infant can usually reach for an object with the nearest hand rather than with both. Once he has the item in his grasp, he can move it from one hand to the other. When gathering up an object, however, he must still rake it toward his body, instead of picking it up with fingers and thumb.

Even as a child is learning to crawl before he can walk, his fine motor skills are also beginning and consolidating. When infants first reach for objects intentionally, they grasp them in a whole fist with the thumb playing little part. Or, a baby will reach for an object on a tray or table in front of her and try to rake the object toward her by moving her whole hand and lower arm. Soon this grasp gives way to a pincerlike movement of thumb and forefinger. Eventually your baby's whole hand becomes more supple and its movements more intricate and delicate, and she grasps things with all her fingers.

As motor development progresses, your infant is, of course, becoming more and more skilled in other areas as well: language development, social interactions. The developments in all these areas blend into each other, allowing her to accomplish more complex, interwoven activities. An infant's ability to feed himself develops because of his increasing comfort with eating and being fed, his expanding familiarity with different kinds of food, and his desire to please you, as well as because of his increasing skill in manipulating his hands and fingers.

At twelve months, a typical baby is not only getting up onto her feet but also finding new uses for her hands. She can poke or point with her index fingers, lift things by grasping them between finger and thumb, and let go of objects voluntarily. A one-year-old enjoys banging blocks and other things

---

RESOURCES FOR EXPLORING: TOYS FOR SIX TO TWELVE MONTHS

In the second half of his first year, a baby can usually sit up and use his hands to inspect anything within reach. When he starts to move on his own, he has a whole new way of exploring, and the whole world is his playground. Unfortunately for you, everything in that world is fair game: magazines on the coffee table, a tasty piece of yarn on the carpet, whatever might be inside the cupboard under the sink. Since your infant is getting better at grabbing things and is able to move ever more quickly but does not understand the word *no*, an adult has to watch him whenever he plays. Playing with your baby has many positive benefits beyond safety, of course: you can share new discoveries, show him how to use certain objects, and let him see your pleasure as he acquires a new skill.

At this age, one of your baby's most popular tools for exploring the world is her mouth. Hand-eye coordination is really hand-eye-mouth coordination. It is easy for a baby to control her mouth, and putting things in it can provide many kinds of stimulation: of temperature, taste, texture, shape. (Tradition holds that children start mouthing objects while they grow their first teeth, but research has shown that the habit does not depend on teething.) Moving objects to their mouths is indeed a skill children must learn in order to feed themselves, but many things in the world are not safe to suck on. You cannot defeat this habit; you simply have to be watchful. Choose rattles, wooden blocks, and other playthings that are made of nontoxic materials, interesting to the touch, and too large to go entirely into the mouth.

In the early part of the second year, children start to explore how things appear and disappear. Now your child will deliberately drop a toy off her high chair: "All gone!" she proclaims in delight by the time she is two. This is not mischief: she is simply fascinated at being able to make something vanish. Likewise, children enjoy moving objects in and out of a paper bag, a cardboard box, or a plastic container. The objects themselves need not be expensive playthings: blocks, plastic bracelets, spray-can lids, small boxes,

together, and moving items in and out of containers one by one. He may also try to mimic writing with a crayon or pencil on paper (or the wall), but this is normal imitative play rather than a real attempt to communicate through letters.

In their second year, children start to enjoy creating things with their hands: they scribble, pound on clay, and build towers of blocks. They can fit round shapes into round holes and enjoy forming patterns. Most toddlers need more months of practice, however, to put other shapes — squares, triangles, and

so on — into matching holes; this challenge requires not simply identifying the proper hole but orienting the shape to fit through it. At this age, you may begin to see signs that your child favors one hand over the other for tasks that require particular deftness. Slightly more than 10 percent of children will write more easily with the left hand, and it is useful to recognize left-handedness early so your child does not lose time trying to match the dominant style. Left-handed writers do not necessarily perform all other tasks with the left hand, but if you observe your child using

spoons, and many other common items work just as well, as long as they are durable and provide a variety of textures. You can play a finding game with any object by covering most of it with a cloth and letting your baby uncover, and discover, the whole thing. You can also take advantage of your baby's interest in vanishing acts by putting most of her toys away at night, and bringing out different playthings each day or week: each reappearance will be a delightful rediscovery. Often a toy that its owner initially ignores becomes a favorite when it returns.

Babies in their second six months are gaining a greater capacity for understanding routine. If you have not already started to read to your child regularly, this is the time to do so. (See chapter 18.) This is also the time to set aside a playtime, when the two of you play with toys together (as well as regular mealtime, nap time, bath time, and so on). Model some play activities: stack some blocks and knock them down, play patty-cake with the bear, bang on a toy drum. These should not be challenges or tests, just inspiration for your child to play in the way that most appeals to him.

Infants of this age delight in banging on things: aluminum pie plates, plastic containers, and (once again) wooden blocks. Tambourines or bells on a string have similar appeal; just make sure that these instruments have no small pieces that might come off in play. Such play is more than an exercise in making noise; it is the first step in learning to use tools, in applying one object to another to make something exciting happen. The noise is an infant's incentive to improve her fine motor skills.

Sometimes placing a familiar, appealing toy just out of an infant's reach gives him the motivation to scoot toward it and eventually to crawl. After about eight months, when a baby is probably crawling easily, she might enjoy pushing and chasing after a ball. Before a child develops that skill, however, a ball that rolls quickly out of reach will mainly be frustrating. It is best not to put a child in one of the wheeled "baby walkers"; they have been involved in too many accidents and do not really help babies exercise the muscles and develop the balance they need to walk on their own. Let your baby's own interest in exploring, and your enthusiasm, lead her to take her first steps.

his left hand to throw, eat, hammer, cut with scissors, work hand puppets, and turn keys or knobs or lids, the odds are that he will be a lefty when writing and drawing as well.

Encouraged by her parents and by what she sees she can accomplish, a three-year-old can demonstrate many fine motor skills. He can usually turn the pages of a book, grasping only one leaf at a time. He can unscrew lids on jars, though screwing them back on properly is still a challenge. He can also turn doorknobs, dead-bolt locks, and other latches that are familiar and within reach. At this age, an average preschooler is ready to hold a crayon in the position for writing, as opposed to holding it in a fist, and can make lines that go more or less where he wants them: straight up and down, side to side, or in a circle. After another year, a child can draw circles and squares and accurately copy squares that you draw, but copying triangles and other shapes may take another year. An average four-year-old can also draw very simple people and copy big letters — if you show her how. Within another year, she should be drawing people and writing letters that you can recognize. She also learns to handle tools like scissors and to brush her teeth and hair. By the time a child turns five years old, she has probably mastered all the motor control and skills that she needs to enter school.

Toilet Training

Controlling one's bladder and bowels is a motor skill as important socially as learning to walk. Helping children achieve this ability seems to frustrate American parents more than any other task, judging by the large number of books and articles on the subject, and the many gadgets and medications on the market. There are any number of reasons for this difficulty. From your child's standpoint, attaining continence is as natural a developmental achievement as crawling or walking, but learning to use modern plumbing is not. Differences in temperament can certainly complicate this parent-child interaction; some children are more malleable from birth, and some are much more stubborn or oppositional. Parents are often confused both about exactly when their child is ready for this step, and about how to help. Many families accept a historical pattern as inevitable ("All the boys in our family wet the bed until they were thirteen"), which can interfere with parents' natural inclinations to move ahead. But, oddly enough, ours is almost the only country in which toilet training is so difficult. Properly understood and approached, it does not have to be.

The first and most important principle is that toilet training must be a form of training: it is an educational process, *not* a disciplinary one. Your role is to teach and enable, not to coerce. Your goal is for your child to control the sphincter muscles in his bladder and bowel so that they remain closed most of the time but open without difficulty when he is in the appropriate place to discharge their contents. To approach this as a control issue is to guarantee losing: control will always rest entirely with your child. It involves, after all, *his* sphincters, *his* pee, *his* poop. He has to decide to accomplish this feat. He needs a reason to do so. Failure to understand this basic truth is at the root of many training failures, which in turn develop into malfunctions such as wetting or soiling one's pants or the bed.

It is nearly as important for parents to be able to recognize when their individual child is physically ready for toilet training. As we have said over and over, although the timeline for developmental steps is essentially linear, the actual timing of each step is not. The process of "innervation," where the nerves that control the muscles for walking and elimination become fully attached to their eventual working sites, occurs slowly and symmetrically through your child's first year. Her ability to take unsupported steps is an indication that the nerves are fully connected in her legs and, by implication, in the sphincter muscles of her bowel and bladder as well. Walking is, thus, the first point at which the child is physically able to become toilet trained. Since some perfectly normal children walk as early as nine or ten months, and others not until they are fourteen or fifteen months old, this enormous spread — almost half a toddler's age — gives you a rough measure of when your child is ready for toilet training. Nonetheless, since it is hard for a child to focus on two major developmental leaps at the same time, you would probably be wise to wait until the child has been walking steadily for two or three months before beginning the next process.

It is also helpful if your child has some regular pattern of elimination or some warning behavior that alerts you to his need for toileting. Some children will pull at their diapers, some will cry in a recognizable way, some will always defecate after a certain meal, and so on. Being able to recognize these signs will allow you to exert maximum effort, such as putting the child on the potty, at the most effective times. Without these early warning signals, you will have to pick the times most convenient to you and try to introduce a pattern into your child's day. Once you have started this, anticipate that your child may make some alterations in the schedule to accord with his own body rhythms.

Just because a child is physiologically ready for toileting does not mean that she is psychologically ready. Some children show clear discomfort when they are wet or soiled and want to be changed as quickly as possible: these toddlers are often easily trained. But other children never show discomfort and sit around in soiled diapers without complaint. In that case, you may have to rely on your sense of smell to know that your child needs to be changed. Other motivating factors come into play, especially as children become a little older. Many want to achieve training once they realize their parents see it as a maturing step. They come to value giving up diapers for pullups or regular underwear and more grown-up clothes. Innately, most children really want to progress; in fact, lack of that desire is often a sign of problems in a child's psychosocial development. But this thrust to mature is not equally strong at all times. It may wax and wane, particularly when some external event in the family or environment is stressful for the child and makes him feel out of control. Some children even regress, at least temporarily, to an earlier developmental stage under such stresses as illness in a parent or the birth of a sibling. If these pressures exist in the child's life at a given moment, that may not be the time to introduce the new challenge of toilet training.

All of these conditions — walking, a pattern of signals, and a child's wish to mature — are likely to coalesce somewhere between eighteen and twenty-four months at the earliest. But parents also need to believe that training at this time is truly possible and, we might add, desirable. Your child may well be ambivalent about the value of this socially civilizing step, but you should not be. Despite what some pediatricians and diaper companies have stated on television recently, it really is not okay for normal children to be five or six years old and not toilet trained. One of the strongest incentives for children to learn to control their elimination is their desire to please their parents. This motive

BED-WETTING

Most toddlers and preschoolers wet their beds on occasion. But according to surveys, about 10 percent of American seven-year-olds, or 5 million youngsters, still urinate in their sleep at age seven, some three or more times a week. Most of these children are boys. The problem seems to disappear as children grow older, and less than 1 percent of eighteen-year-olds still wet their beds.

Bed-wetting is not a problem of discipline. It may make sense to punish a child who deliberately urinates in his bed, but to punish him for what he did while asleep makes no sense at all. You may ask an older child to share responsibility for cleaning up: changing pajamas, remaking the bed, helping with laundry the next day. But you must not punish or humiliate him. Those actions can produce lasting shame and resentment, but they cannot solve the problem.

Help your child reduce the likelihood that she will urinate in her sleep by encouraging her to urinate regularly before going to bed. She should also avoid caffeine in both food and drinks. If your child has a history of allergies, try changing her diet. If bed-wetting suddenly returns or becomes a serious, ongoing problem, consult with your pediatrician. She can check for infection as a possible cause and perhaps prescribe medication. Also, alarms that sense the first drops of moisture and wake the child in time to get up and go to the bathroom often help condition her body to end the problem in a month or two. Praise your child when she follows the steps of treatment carefully, not just when she achieves complete success.

Bed-wetting can be very embarrassing for school-age children because they are so concerned about their standing among their peers. Encourage your child to talk to you about his emotions and fears, and correct any false ideas he has picked up. If you remember wetting the bed yourself, do not hesitate to share memories about how you felt. A child who worries about wetting his bed might be especially anxious about sleepovers and may even get sick beforehand. Work out a preemptive solution, such as providing him with his own sleeping bag to take along and extra pajamas.

can only come into play if you make it clear to the child that you confidently expect and will be pleased by his achievement.

Assuming that all is otherwise well in the child's life, you may start the training by suggesting to the child that he can, and may want to, begin to take charge of the functions of elimination himself. Do this in a friendly, positive manner, showing that you approve of his doing this but do not insist on it. Show the potty or other apparatus you have chosen, and explain it to your child, letting it become part of the household scenery for a few days before he tries to use it. If the child protests violently, back off for a while and then introduce the subject again. Some parents (and some children) prefer a separate potty chair standing next to the regular toilet. This chair is sized for the child, sits on the floor so the child can get on it himself, and removes the fear of falling that some children have. If you want your child to use the regular toilet, you should select a training seat that has both arms and a footrest. Both of these make the child feel more secure and give him something to push against when the need arises. (Imagine how you would feel trying to have a bowel movement with your feet hanging in midair!)

It is probably not helpful or useful for parents to try to explain urination or defecation by example. Adult anatomies are different enough from a child's to make the demonstration almost impossible to understand. Besides, many parents find themselves too uncomfortable even to try, and their embarrassment further complicates the message the child receives. Your message should be: using the toilet is something you are old enough and big enough to do, and both you and I will be pleased when you do it.

It is highly unlikely that your child will perform the first time and continue to do so uninterruptedly forever. Rather, success will at first be intermittent. (See "Bed-Wetting," page 152.) You may need to work out the best times for putting her on the potty or toilet over a few days. At these times, you should praise with moderate enthusiasm. Standing on your head and doing cartwheels is neither necessary nor useful. Defecation should not be that important to you, nor should your child have any reason to think it is.

A large study undertaken a decade ago found that 95 percent of normal children tutored by this method were fully trained by three and a half years. And 80 percent of these became dry at night within one month of becoming dry in the daytime. If your child is not toilet trained by this time, you should discuss the issue with your pediatrician and ask her assistance and advice. She can reassure you or discover that your child is that extremely rare case where some physical problem is interfering with the training process. In any event, the important message is that your approach be low-key but positive, assuring but not coercive, helpful but not controlling.

Encouraging Your Child's Motor Development

Normal motor development assumes two important factors: a child with an intact neuromuscular apparatus and an environment that facilitates each of his steps along the way. Obviously certain inherited or acquired injuries or paralyses can interfere with, or even make impossible, certain stages of development. A child with cerebral palsy, for example, may have difficulty learning to walk and need help to learn alternative ways to get around safely. In some cases, serious diseases can set back or delay parts of the developmental profile, especially if they occur at critical moments when the child is making incremental progress. For example, after getting sick, many children who have only recently become toilet trained may revert to wetting or soiling for a time. Fortunately, patience and specific remedial help by parents, under the supervision of qualified physical or occupational therapists, can often go a long way to overcome such reverses.

While development is programmed into the human newborn and driven by a powerful, innate thrust toward maturity, your child's development can, as we have said, be enhanced or endangered by the environment. Nothing is more important to young children than the approval of their parents. Nothing is more harmful than parents who fail to encourage or facilitate their child's progress. For example, if you take no notice of your child's first attempts to crawl, you are hardly encouraging her to keep on. On the other hand, parents can also slow their children's progress by doing too much for them: if you never let your child out of your arms, he is obviously not going to be motivated to sit up in order to see you.

You must also guard against letting your own anxieties cause your child to be fearful of trying new activities. Do not hover over your child at each corner when she starts to crawl around the house. Also, a child learning to stand or walk or climb or run or ride a bicycle will inevitably fall sometime. And you should certainly try to provide an environment in which those falls will not be seriously harmful. (See "Making Your House Safe," page 146.) But, since no parent can protect his or her children against all the painful eventualities in life, you can help your child to learn to handle the big obstacles better by giving him a chance to try getting over the smaller ones.

To enhance your child's development, do not just respond to new motor skills, but actively stimulate them. Provide age- and level-appropriate playthings and opportunities for your child to move along in skills and competence. Materials that the child can manipulate and experiment with are essential. As we have said, the latest and most expensive developmental toy is not a requirement. Many kitchen utensils offer just as much chance for your baby to develop hand skills as the gaudiest plastic assemblage from your local toy store. (See "Resources for Exploring: Toys for Six to Twelve Months," pages 148–149; and "Toys in the Second Year," page 155.)

Once again, we emphasize that every child is different. There are no strict deadlines by which a child has to display certain skills. Every child develops in his or her own way, and a baby who is a month behind the

TOYS IN THE SECOND YEAR

Since one-year-old children are developing their gross motor skills, toys that exercise their whole bodies and limbs are better than those that require fine manipulation. Thus, a scooter is more appropriate than a picture puzzle. Wooden blocks will probably be less frustrating than the plastic blocks that interlock. A child of this age will also probably develop a close attachment to a particular stuffed animal or other love object. By providing a small island of stability in his life, this item helps him overcome his anxieties about separation. Naturally, you should take care that this toy is not left behind on any of the many journeys it will take.

Making noise is important to a young toddler, and she has the energy to dance almost endlessly to music. As an outgrowth of the disappearing game that younger babies like, toddlers also enjoy making their music stop suddenly. Your child might enjoy carrying around one of the rugged tape recorders designed especially for young children. Though a one-year-old does not have the finger strength and dexterity to operate such a machine's buttons on her own, she will want to grow into that task.

At this stage, a child can use toys to pretend. He can tuck his bear into bed. He can wear a pie tin as a hat and eat invisible food from his cap. All these games are forms of imitating what he has seen adults do. One popular toy for such play is a ring of large plastic keys. Children, seeing their parents' keys, want to play with the shiny, jingly things themselves; giving them their own ring of keys ensures that yours will not so easily disappear. Your toddler might enjoy imitating a grown-up by pushing a baby carriage or using a wagon, vacuum cleaner, lawn mower, or telephone. The best toy telephones are not the expensive, heavy models that talk in the voices of TV characters; there are simple models that are light enough for a toddler to carry around and have the advantage of letting your child's imagination create the conversation. You do not want a toy that plays by itself. Even the latest "interactive" toys designed to prompt responses from children do not encourage as much creativity as when the child steers the conversation with another human being.

For a very young child, bathtime toys are mainly useful for giving you a way to keep her amused and not crying while you bathe her. For a young toddler, however, the act of bathing is an-other opportunity to explore how things work. This is when rubber ducks, boats, dolls that will not be damaged or waterlogged, and other bath toys become fun. Also useful are ordinary cups, sieves, and funnels for pouring water, and sponges and squirt bottles to squeeze. Use only one or two items in the water at a time.

After your toddler stops chewing on everything, you can introduce her to crayons, clay, and other art supplies. Until she learns where not to color or to stuff the clay, however, you should always watch the artist at work. Thick nontoxic crayons that are flat on at least one side are the best sort for young preschoolers. Thin, round crayons are likely to frustrate her by breaking or rolling away. When two young children are using the same set of crayons, expect some squabbles over popular colors, such as red. Most important, do not expect or encourage toddlers to produce art in the "right" way. They will be more interested in pounding on the clay than in making recognizable shapes. They are not ready to color inside the lines or to form letters. As they approach the age of three, toddlers are still exploring the simple process of making a mark on the objects around them — a necessary step to expressing themselves more clearly. (For more on creativity, see chapter 16.)

average in learning to crawl or matching shapes to holes may be ahead in other areas. The pleasure a child takes in each type of activity depends in large part on the pleasure he sees in your responses. The basic requirements for enhancing your child's motor development are these: safeguard the environment, provide appropriate materials with which the child can develop new skills, and ensure suitable places in which to use them. Help your child to learn about these materials by demonstrating their use, and let your child know how pleased you are with his or her achievements.

CHAPTER 12

Feeding and Eating: Food for the Whole Child

The first time you feed your baby, just a few hours after her birth, is simultaneously wonderful and terrifying. Elated and exhausted, you contemplate the tiny being in your arms, feeling you have entered a different world. You have, most likely, already decided whether to breast-feed. (See "The Benefits of Breast Milk," page 158.) And your baby's response as you offer breast or bottle may well create in you an enduring impression of him or her: "He took to my breast immediately, and I felt so terrifically useful and maternal." "She wasn't able to suck at first, and I stood by my wife, both of us feeling so helpless." "He didn't like my milk — he has always been picky." "She has been a good eater from that very first hour in the delivery room." "I thought she would pull my breast off — she always wants more, more, more."

Feeding is important not just physically but also psychologically. For infants and children, as for adults, eating is a social as well as a nutritional event. And as crucial as it is developmentally for babies, it is equally impor-

tant for parents. Of all the duties you have as a parent, feeding your child pierces most deeply into the fantasies and beliefs that first arose during pregnancy about what it means to provide for a child. A mother often perceives how fully her baby grows inside her womb as a measure of the health of her body and even as a gauge of her success as a woman and mother. For fathers, the growth of the baby represents the strength of their genes and their potency.

Family myths and cultural superstitions often involve the foods of pregnancy — people really do think you are what you eat. You will hear that your baby's favorites will mirror what his mother was most fond of, that certain foods are better for his growth and brain development, or that whatever a mother eats, drinks, and inhales during pregnancy also goes to her baby. And it is commonly believed that the baby's intake in those months influences, perhaps unalterably, his development and personality. (For more about the influence of fetal exposures to toxic substances, see pages 53–54.)

THE BENEFITS OF BREAST MILK

We believe that for most families, breast-feeding is preferable to giving formula to a new baby. On both a psychological and emotional level, the face-to-face closeness of feeding fills the baby's need for warmth, cuddling, and interaction with her caregivers.

Physiologically, breast milk is clearly the easiest food for an infant to digest. It is also unmatched in its capacity to help protect an infant against certain diseases in the critical early weeks of life. Breast milk contains immune globulins with antibodies the mother's body has developed in response to her past infections or immunizations. These antibodies are especially prevalent in the colostrum (the rich, creamlike milk of the first few days), but appear in all breast milk for the first few weeks after delivery. Your baby absorbs them through her intestinal wall, and they remain in her body for several months. By the time they gradually disappear, the infant's own early active antibodies are ready to take over and provide permanent protection.

These advantages notwithstanding, parents can have good reasons for choosing to feed their children formula, either instead of or alongside breast milk. Your decisions about feeding must fit your family's individual needs. A mother who is infected with HIV should not breast-feed because she might pass the virus to her baby. If a mother is not available for feedings throughout the day and night, or if she has difficulty producing all the milk her baby wants, formula is a good and nutritionally sound alternative or supplement. Holding an infant close during bottle-feeding can provide you and your baby a sensory experience that is much like breast-feeding.

Breast pumps provide parents who choose to breast-feed with a number of advantages. A mother can express extra milk when it is most convenient or comfortable for her and refrigerate it for a baby to drink (warmed up) later. A father can take his turn at feedings with bottles of breast milk, thus allowing the baby to enjoy familiar fare, the baby and father to experience these intimate moments, and the mother perhaps to sleep a little longer.

Food for the Senses

What your newborn needs from his feedings goes well beyond his basic physical demand for food to grow. In fact, mealtimes limited to that end alone would seriously restrict your baby's emotional diet. At feeding times, which are the major opportunities for a newborn and his mother and father to be close to each other, all of your baby's senses come into play. Thus, in interacting with you, he is imbibing not just milk but all the other things he needs: comfort, caring, and physical and social stimulation.

Your newborn cannot yet take in stimuli from her body and so depends on you to come to her. Of all of her developing senses, hearing is the one that reaches farthest into the world. From your voice and the other sounds that fill the space around her, your baby learns to recognize your presence and begins to sense the range of human emotions. Vision brings in the closer world; most newborns' eyes focus exactly at the distance of a parent's face when Mommy or Daddy holds them in their arms. Smell and taste, the oldest of the senses, are highly adapted to allow a baby to recognize her mother's milk — the essence of early feeding and eating. But touch brings the most early information: the softness of a blanket, the warmth of a parent's lips, the roughness of a washcloth, the tickle of fingers lightly touching her tummy or the soles of her feet. In each of these moments, a baby's skin is her most communicative sensory organ, especially in helping her feel the security or the harshness of the surrounding world.

During feedings, your baby's intake should include pleasant sights and sounds (the parent's smile and soothing voice) and agreeable touch (the warmth and comfort of a grown-up's body), as well as the familiar smell and taste of milk. Hold your baby close during his feedings; do not leave him in the crib with a bottle propped beside him. By nourishing all of your baby's senses as you feed him, you not only fill his stomach and relieve the discomfort of hunger, you also help him to begin to feel his environment as safe and agreeable.

An infant's earliest memories, formed well before she has the capacity for words or even pictures to express them, are set in such feeding experiences. And as these experiences are reinforced by hundreds of mealtimes, your baby will begin to anticipate the satisfaction and security they bring. He will come to associate a feeding with feeling satisfied, well cared for, and close to his parents. His fussing will quiet at the sound of his mother's voice or, in later months, when he hears the sounds of food being prepared. The power of such early memories is extraordinary. In later years, when your child is distressed, even snippets of a melody you sang repetitively while feeding or the hint of your favorite soap or perfume can comfort him.

These early sensory memories are deeply woven in childhood and often reawaken in adults when they become parents. When you pick up your newborn for the first time, hold him close, watch his contented sucking, and feel his body slowly mold to your own, the powerful traces of your similar experience as an infant shape and color your response to your own child. You may recognize that timeless feeling when you hold your infant and have the sense not only that you have been in such a close relationship before but that you know your baby very well: he or she is you. The more nurtured you were as an infant and young child, the more available you will be to nurture your own infant. On the other hand, the more you experienced your own parents as less available to you, the more vulnerable you are to feeling sad and less available to your infant. (See pages 69–71.)

Mothers who are breast-feeding for the first time may be surprised and even disturbed that nursing their babies can be physically pleasurable. If you worry that such a sensual response to your child is not natural and make the nursing experience abrupt and "businesslike," you will diminish the closeness and warmth you can share with your baby. In fact, early breast-feeding often in-

volves shared pleasure. It is one way that nature encourages breast-feeding. And it is sexual in that this shared pleasure is critical to the foundation of a child's sexuality. Breast-feeding conveys your comfort and delight in your baby's body and in the way it interacts with yours. If your baby learns that bodily sensations are sources of enjoyment and comfort, especially when shared with another loving person, he is making the first step toward a healthy sense of sexuality. (See chapter 14.) Most nursing mothers soon become used to the novel sensations of breast-feeding and are able, with their infant, to relax into a comfortable and pleasant routine.

Feeding Your Baby Right

Food is a real — as well as fantasized — glue that holds families and communities together. The secret recipes that parents use to comfort and cure are woven into a family's legacy. For children and adults alike, eating provides the most basic experience of need and satisfaction: of feeling drained and then being cared for. You eat when you are sad or worried, when there is good news to celebrate or loss to mourn, relationships to forge or loved ones to bid farewell to.

Parents often worry about how they will know when their new baby is hungry, or how much he wants to eat, or whether what they offer will be good enough. Will your child grow as he should, not too much or too little? Food becomes even more important the more you worry about it. Parents attach considerable meaning to the energy and strength with which a baby eats, to her weight gains and losses, and to even the slightest hints of liking or disliking her mother's milk. Inevitably there will be times when your infant will spit up, turn away from the bottle or breast, or cry inconsolably even when you offer food. Such reactions may trigger your deepest worries about not being able to provide basic nutrition or your deepest fears about being rejected. When you feel hurt and insecure at these moments, remind yourself of the wonderful sense of success and competence you have felt the many times when your baby has gazed steadily into your face as he ate and how he then fell peacefully asleep in your arms.

You probably have a mental image of what an "ideal" baby looks like — lean, long, compact, or chubby. Indeed, different cultures and even different individuals within a family accept certain ideal pictures of what a healthy, well-fed, well-cared-for baby should look like. Your own notions are influenced by your family, your memories of siblings and cousins, the advice of your pediatrician and other experts, and the prevailing cultural beliefs about infant health. Advertising and television set their own "standards" for what babies should look like, standards that themselves have shifted over time. The chubby, round-faced Gerber baby of the 1950s slowly changed to the leaner but still smiling Gerber baby of the 1990s — perhaps reflecting America's increasing emphasis on lower-fat diets and leaner and fitter adult body images.

Knowing when and how to feed your baby takes more than doing what comes naturally (despite the assurances of many parents, friends, and relatives). It really requires learning by trial and error. Ideally, you should offer food at a time of your baby's choosing rather than yours. Most babies will be clear about being hungry, and you will maximize the effectiveness and pleasantness of the feeding experience if you respond to her signals. Babies, like adults, have their own rhythms and ways of recognizing and signaling their needs, and it takes time for you and your baby to learn each other's habits and idiosyncrasies. At birth, and for much of your baby's infancy, you bear the responsibility for understanding his cues. You will gradually come to understand the different meanings of your baby's cries and fussing and the daily rhythms she prefers.

Realizing that a newborn is hungry — either from his crying, his agitated movement, or the time of day — carries different weight for different parents. Your response will depend, in part, on your own state of hunger, fatigue, and worry. (For more about how parents learn to recognize their baby's different cries, see pages 65–66.) For some parents, a baby's hunger is a matter of urgency: they want him never fully to experience that need. They may well see their baby's hunger as their own failing: "If I had only fed him earlier, he wouldn't be crying now." For other parents, however, signs of hunger signal that, while fulfilling a basic need of their baby's, they can have a good time with him. Most reactions fall between these two extremes.

Remember that hunger, like many other states and feelings we discuss throughout this book, is inevitable for all human beings. No one can completely eliminate this sensation from an infant's life. What matters is that you regularly satisfy your baby's need for food and, in so doing, help her experience the world as fulfilling and protective. When she can reliably depend upon your care, hunger can provide a way for your infant to begin to learn the most basic steps in caring for herself: the pleasure of being well fed but not too full, as well as of being socially intimate while being physically satisfied. While she will build upon these lessons as she moves into toddlerhood, she begins to learn them in her first days home from the hospital.

Feeding Problems

Several factors can interfere with a mutually satisfactory feeding. Mothers and fathers who were not well or satisfactorily fed by *their* parents may have a difficult time making the feeding experience happy for their children. They may misinterpret their infant's cries or other signals and try to impose a rigid schedule on him. Or they may depend upon some fixed plan to determine the amount of food their baby needs, rather than pay attention to when she indicates she is full. Above all, parents who have uncomfortable memories are often made uneasy by the intimate sensory experience of feeding and satisfying their baby's needs.

Sometimes a baby suddenly seems less interested in his mother's milk. The simplest and most common explanation is that something the mother ate — garlic, fish — has made her milk less enjoyable for him. (Or perhaps she has *stopped* eating something that gave her milk the taste her baby has come to love.) You can handle this problem by making simple changes in your diet. Other babies seem frequently to spit up what they take in, a problem that distresses all parents but particularly a mother who is breastfeeding. Is her breast milk bad? Is the baby rejecting the very essence of her body? Repeated spitting up often causes parents to try other formulas and then to bring their child to the pediatrician.

More troubling is when a baby's acute illness, or certain neurological or muscular problems, cause him to be uncomfortable at feeding times. In these circumstances, feeding can become a truly disagreeable experience for parent and infant alike, and parent and child can suffer lifelong difficulties that go beyond food. Consult your pediatrician, who may in turn suggest that you consult a child psychiatrist.

There are many reasons for a baby's failure to eat comfortably and fully and thus to grow well despite his parents' best efforts. When babies are born very early or have had many medical problems in the nursery, they are often fussier and harder to feed. These babies are sometimes weaker and do not suck strongly. They also need to eat more often — taking smaller quantities at more frequent intervals. Similarly, babies who were born prematurely, or who did not grow adequately during the pregnancy, may be more irritable and not suck well. For parents already facing the challenges of prematurity, mysterious feeding problems can be frightening, frustrating, and demoralizing. (See also "Physical Problems That Interfere with Feeding," page 163.)

In her child's second six months, a nursing mother might feel him start to bite her nipple as he sucks. In this stage of life, a baby is exploring the boundaries between his body and other bodies, and experimenting with effecting change in his world. From a baby's point of view, biting Mommy may be just as much fun as sucking. He is sure to get a quick reaction from her! Your experience as his mother is, of course, very different. You may feel hurt, attacked, or even pushed away. When he bites during nursing, however, your baby is trying a new and interesting (to him) way to get even closer. You should realize that your baby is not angry with you or purposefully trying to hurt you. Of course, you do not

PHYSICAL PROBLEMS THAT INTERFERE WITH FEEDING

Although every baby spits up sometimes, you should be concerned if your baby does not seem able to keep most of her food down. One of the most commonly diagnosed reasons for vomiting in infants used to be pyloric stenosis. The symptom of this problem is that the vomitus actually shoots like a projectile some distance out of the baby's mouth. Pyloric stenosis is caused by a thick muscular band that develops around the outlet of the stomach, seriously delaying the organ's emptying time. A pediatrician or surgeon can actually feel the thickening at the stomach's lower end. A fairly minor operation to cut this band relieves the problem almost immediately.

In recent years, for no clear reason, pyloric stenosis has become less common, and the major cause of problematic vomiting in infants is now gastroesophageal reflux (GER). GER is the antithesis of pyloric stenosis: it is caused by loose musculature at the upper end of the stomach which allows milk to slide back up the esophagus and ooze out of a baby's mouth. The vomiting in this case is never projectile. For some babies, switching to a thicker formula is helpful, making it more difficult for the mixture to flow back up the esophagus. For other infants, propping up the head of the crib makes it more difficult for the milk to flow backward. For a number of babies, however, a surgery called "fundal plication," in which the muscles at the upper end of the stomach are tightened so that milk cannot flow back out, is the remedy of choice for GER.

One of the most mysterious and serious eating disorders in infancy is known as "failure to thrive" (FTT). In FTT, the infant clearly cuts back on his caloric intake and either fails to gain weight or actually loses it. Although the infant may show no other sign of illness and may even be reasonably active, his progress as measured on infant growth charts falls off the standard curve and ends up well below the normal parameters for both height and weight. The problem becomes increasingly dangerous if the growth of the child's head also falls below the normal range.

Two types of this disorder are generally described: organic and nonorganic. In the former, doctors can attribute the problem to some physical defect in the infant's digestive system, such as a hole or a stricture in the stomach or intestinal wall which prevents his body from absorbing major nutritional elements. Nonorganic failure to thrive (NFTT) is much more difficult to diagnose and to treat. Although NFTT has been ascribed to serious psychological difficulties between parents and children, this does not always seem to be the case. Both these conditions require a pediatrician's attention. Fortunately, they are rare.

have to put up with being bitten either. You can firmly but gently stop your baby by removing your nipple and saying, "No." Although the infant may not yet understand the word, he does understand his mother's tone and the action. A baby usually learns fairly quickly that nursing will not continue if he bites, and nursing is still what he most wants.

When Your Baby No Longer Lives by Milk Alone

Although families display many differences in feeding habits related to culture, geography, and ethnic and other traditions, most modern child-health experts agree that infants do not need or profit from solid foods before the age of six months. Infants thrive and gain weight at optimal rates on breast milk or formula alone throughout this time period. Breast milk and formula are easy for the baby's immature stomach and intestines to digest, and newborns prefer to suck rather than to chew and swallow. Indeed, a breast-feeding baby may learn to open her gullet and let the jets of breast milk shoot right down her esophagus without her even having to swallow. At this age, other foods are difficult for an infant to absorb; even though she may swallow solids, she derives relatively little nutritional benefit from them. When babies do start to eat solids, most experts suggest that they begin with cereal, especially rice cereal. Because rice cereal is one of the most digestible and least allergenic of foods, it gives you and your child the best chance of a smooth transition to solids. After cereals, strained fruits and vegetables are the next step. Of course, fruits are sweet, and many children prefer them to vegetables, but any given infant's food preferences are totally unpredictable. As your infant nears one year of age, you can introduce forms of meat and poultry. Although prepared infant foods are easy to buy, blenders and food processors make it easier and cheaper for you to fix your own strained foods for your infant if you prefer.

Introducing solid foods brings a whole new set of opportunities and problems to mealtimes. Now your baby needs to learn new skills: to accept a spoon into her mouth, to develop new tastes, and to swallow semisolids. For parents, semisolid foods are a mixed blessing. Many enjoy introducing their child to foods that they themselves like (or, at least, are closer to what they like); but others, particularly nursing mothers, can feel left behind when their baby opts for strained peaches over breast milk.

The transition to solid foods brings other changes. A father can become as active as a mother in feeding their infant. No longer lolling in your arms, your infant usually eats in a high chair or other seat and you are farther away and sitting opposite rather than gazing down. Utensils are used, new colors and tastes appear, and some of the closeness of the early situation is dissipated. Your baby has much more opportunity to look around and be distracted by siblings, pets, and intrusive noises, such as the telephone or television.

Your baby also has more opportunities to interfere with, or even abort, the feeding process. Indeed, the shift to solid foods heralds the beginning of your baby's independence and separate likes and dislikes. He can push the dish off the table, dodge the spoon, and play with the food. Often control becomes an issue as the baby tries to block, steer, and even hold the spoon or refuses to open her mouth as it approaches. Many parents find such behavior disruptive and almost delinquent — especially if your good gray suit is suddenly dripping with applesauce, rice cereal, or strained carrots. You may question where your sweet infant has gone, be tempted to return the gesture, or even wonder why you decided to have children in the first place. Conflict over feeding is an even more poignant problem for a parent who is reprising old battles from his own childhood. As we say in regard to other such conflicts, you can never win them. A wise parent faced with dogged opposition withdraws quickly. Once the battle is well engaged, you will have no graceful retreat.

When children enter their second year, their newfound mobility — crawling, walking, and running — gives them some independence from their parents. Their world has changed vastly, and this can be a scary time for everyone. If you are used to your infant's closeness and total dependency, you may mourn that loss when you see your toddler running ahead of you; or you may rejoice that finally you have a "real" person in the house, someone who can do a few things without needing help. As exuberantly as she may run forth into the relative unknown, she needs to have some assurance that her parent is close by if there is danger. A toddler's eagerness to push the limits of her world is constantly balanced by her returning to safe and familiar ground.

The same pattern holds in regard to foods and eating. A toddler may suddenly reject a much-loved food and take a new one in its place. He may go through relatively long periods where he wants only one or two foods or a very few flavors and consistencies, morning and night. In one family, three-year-old Debbie said that she wanted only mashed potatoes. Used to her whims, on the first night her parents simply suggested that she would enjoy her peas and bread as well, and cleared them away when she did not. But when Debbie asked for mashed potatoes at lunch the next day, and then again at dinner, her mother became worried. Debbie's father came up with a solution: "If you don't eat at least half your carrots, you won't get dessert." For Debbie, this seemed like a fair bargain, and she happily ate her mashed potatoes.

The following night was the family's weekly pizza dinner, and Debbie asked for mashed potatoes. Her older brother helpfully suggested that he could eat her pizza for her. Debbie's parents admonished him for encouraging what they saw as an unhealthy eating habit. As the week went on without a change, they became more concerned. Debbie's mother found herself making more mashed potatoes than usual, figuring that if she could not make her toddler eat balanced meals, she could at least be sure she ate enough. Finally, pizza night rolled around again. And this time Debbie said, "I want mushrooms on mine." (It took another two weeks before her mother was able to serve the last of the leftover mashed potatoes to the family.) A "problem" like Debbie's should not be a big worry for parents. Insistence on particular foods usually lasts no more than two weeks, and as long as the food of the moment is available, your child will neither starve nor become seriously malnourished.

Toddlers and preschool-age children often establish and insist on certain routines in their eating: the bread on one's sandwich must be just the right consistency with the crust cut off, another's ice cream must be melted just right. They get very upset if adults offer new choices or variations on a theme. This same insistence on consistency is usually evident in other parts of the two- or three-year-old's day — the bedtime routine, the favorite sweater, and the familiar stuffed toy. Routines and rituals, as maddening or insignificant as they may seem to you at times, serve an important function. They reassure a young child about the constancy and stability both of his world and of the people closest to him. In some ways, they are the young child's way of providing himself with a safe anchorage as he ventures out into new seas. Since food and the ritual of eating are central to a child's life, so they are to these routines as well.

Along with their new mobility, toddlers can begin to get their own food — to take crackers or cookies or to open the refrigerator or a cabinet and point to what they want. By the time your child is two or three years old, you may find it helpful to have a special cabinet, box, or shelf where you keep snacks that your toddler can get for himself. The downside is that younger children also tend to eat whatever they find, from the dry food for the dog to some unidentifiable tidbit from floor or table. Some children like to find out about a new object by putting it in their mouth. Before your children become mobile, go through your house and check that dangerous substances — foods, drinks, poisons — are safely locked away. (For more advice on this important preventive step, see page 146.)

For the toddler and preschooler, mealtime continues to be a social affair even if it is not as intimate as it once was. When your child joins you and older siblings at the table — though they may make dinner a raucous and sometimes chaotic time — you convey the message that food brings everyone together for a shared time. Even if a two-year-old spends only a few minutes sitting with the rest of the family at the supper table, that is a valuable lesson. If your family eats "on the run" — sometimes literally not even sitting down — you forfeit a valuable opportunity for you and your children to spend time together.

For young children, as for infants, mealtimes should signify more than nutrition. Your child's interaction with you and other caregivers fuels her social, language, and cognitive development. There is ample evidence that a child's facility with language, informational discourse, social graces, and many other skills comes in large part from what he sees and hears around the dinner table. The family meal is, among many other things, a structured situation where children quickly learn about rules and limits to their behavior and can eavesdrop openly on adult conversation. When you enhance dinnertime by directing amicable conversation, questions, and information at your sons and daughters, they develop more mature language and other skills that prepare them for further interaction in school and, later, in the adult world. When mealtime is hasty, tense, or uncomfortable because parents are continually angry or agitated, children lose the maturational and emotional benefits of the time together.

As your toddler becomes four and five years old, he expects to participate in the general mealtime conversation. Showing an interest in what matters to him by speaking of it at the dinner table will enhance his feelings of self-worth and competence. While the old adage that "children should be seen but not heard" may have produced quiet mealtimes, the children who obeyed sometimes grew up to be insecure adults. Children should not dominate family conversations, but they should be interested and valued participants. Fortunately, just as a school-age child's conversation grows more sophisticated, so does her capacity to learn dinnertime etiquette. You can and should educate your children about how to behave in a restaurant, how to respond politely to being served foods they don't know or don't like, and when *not* to tell the grossest joke in the world.

What Did You Bring for Lunch Today?

In the early school years, children are exposed to many media images of food and eating. Some children will ask for a cereal "that's been on TV" or for the most heavily advertised candy in the supermarket. It is up to you to make your family's shopping lists, but you might allow your child to buy such extras with his allowance so as to judge for himself what these foods are worth. (See "Buy Me That!" page 366.) A more troubling idea that some children, especially preteen girls, pick up from the larger culture is anxiety about their weight. Talking about diets and "watching what they eat" are thus ways that girls can become more like the slender young women they see on television, in print, and often in their families. Serious eating disorders are rare among preteens, but experts feel that excessive concern about body weight at a young age, especially as a mirror of self-worth, may lead to such potentially life-threatening eating disorders as anorexia or bulimia. (See chapter 33, pages 483–485.)

When children enter school, lunchtime brings the most notable change in their eating habits. From this point on, what the crowd in the cafeteria thinks of eating may carry more weight than family traditions do.

Foods that a child's classmates do not recognize may become a source of embarrassment; in some communities, buying one's school lunch is more "grown-up" than bringing food from home. For religious, ethical, or health-related reasons, you may choose not to feed your children pork, beef, or meat of any kind. But that rule may not matter to them at school since, in some lunchrooms, trading in food is as ferocious as that in the Chicago commodity exchange. Be sure to teach your children the importance of any dietary restrictions that affect their health: sugar, if they have diabetes; peanuts and other foods, if they have severe allergies; and so on. Otherwise, recognize that school-age children will be exploring new eating habits with their peers just as they explore other parts of their widening world.

CHAPTER 13

Sleep: Helping Your Child Through the Night

For parents and children alike, sleep is much needed and welcome. At the same time, it is mysterious and frightening. Sleep can bring restful dreams and bodily rejuvenation — "meat for the hungry, drink for the thirsty," as Cervantes wrote in *Don Quixote*. Or sleep can elude and torment you, coming only in restless, nightmare-laden bursts. For infants and young children, sleep is also a scary time — often the first time — when they feel separated from the comfort of their parents.

A child's sleep poses many questions for parents as well. In the first days after you bring your newborn home, you may spend hours watching her sleep or, at least, checking intermittently to be sure she is still breathing. You may see your baby smile fleetingly during sleep. Is she dreaming? About you? Folklore held those smiles to be signs of the angels, messages from ancestors looking out for a baby. These same tales hinted that during a baby's sleep, the angels might lure her to go with them. Today we have other explanations, but there is still a great deal to learn about sleep.

Almost all that we know about sleeping and its importance has been learned within the past sixty years. Yet the purpose of sleep is far from understood. Indeed, it seems better to say "purposes," for sleep serves many functions in the course of each night and in the course of one's life span. Before early adolescence, when sleep states and patterns first become comparable to those of adulthood, children's sleep patterns go through many changes. These parallel and play an important role in their physical, neurological, mental, and emotional development. In this chapter, we outline the complexities of sleep in children and its development across early childhood.

We also describe some of the problems in sleeping that parents and children experience. Too much or too little sleep, frequent wakings, and difficulty falling asleep may be signs of underlying physical or emotional problems. At the same time, struggles around bedtime are part of normal development. By understanding the range of healthy and normal sleep in newborns and young children, you may be able to avoid or ameliorate conflict with your child. Thus, we begin with a modern definition of sleep and what happens in the brain and body, and then move to a basic concern of all parents: how to help your infant or child go to sleep and stay asleep.

What Is Sleep?

Before the sleep research that began in the mid-twentieth century, many ancient ideas about sleep remained common. These held that sleep is either a suspension of wakefulness, "a disturber of the 'natural' waking state," or a point midway between death and consciousness. Sleep is, in fact, made up of a wide range of states of consciousness. Many important events occur during this time.

By observing humans and animals, scientists have identified and named several broad categories of sleep that, in addition to healthy conscious states, make up the range of a human being's mental functioning. They have also found that across the twenty-four-hour day, one's sleep and waking states follow a relatively stable cycle, maintained by a clocklike center within the brain. Most important for understanding young children's sleep, we know that newborns progress through certain stages during a sleeping period, while older children and adults share another pattern.

Sleep States in Your Newborn

Many parents talk about watching their baby sleep in the first days to weeks after they bring her home. You may find yourself checking on your baby several times a night to see if she is sleeping and if she is breathing. (See "Sudden Infant Death Syndrome," page 177.) This checking is normal. It is part of your inevitable preoccupation with your baby's comfort and well-being that we spoke about in the first section of the book. It is also part of your getting to know your baby and your own wish to have him with you all the time, even during the quiet time of sleep. As you watch your baby during these moments of nighttime reverie, you will see him during different sleep stages.

A newborn spends as much as twenty hours a day sleeping, but not all those hours involve the same type of sleep. Both fetuses and very young infants go through stages of active sleep, quiet sleep, and a transitional stage called indeterminate sleep. Up to three months of age, a newborn's sleep is divided equally between active and quiet sleep, with a very small portion of time spent in indeterminate sleep. They suck, smile, grimace, and move their arms and legs significantly more often during active sleep than in the other two stages. A newborn is not likely to dream as much as an adult because her brain is just starting to process images and memories, but we really do not know how she experiences sleep. (For more on the development of the brain, see chapter 9.)

REM Sleep

By approximately six months of age, the active sleep, quiet sleep, and indeterminate sleep stages have developed into new phases of sleep that will remain (in varying proportions) with your child throughout life. These phases have been studied extensively in adults. The first is rapid eye movement (REM) sleep. True to its name, when babies (or adults) are in REM sleep, you can see their eyeballs shifting back and forth under their eyelids. This type of sleep develops out of the newborn's active sleep. An infant continues to be physically active in this stage, frequently moving parts of his body, smiling and grimacing, and breathing quickly and unevenly.

In contrast, older children and adults exhibit a profound loss of muscle tone during REM sleep. The bursts of eye movement beneath closed lids are often associated with twitches of the face, hands, and feet, but there is little other activity. In fact, REM sleep was originally called "paradoxical sleep" because researchers observed that, while an adult sleeper's brain is as active in this phase as when one is awake, one's body enters a state of near paralysis. Among other physical and mental changes that occur during REM, the body loses its ability to regulate body temperature. As a result, sweating and shivering — both indications that a person's built-in temperature control mechanisms are working — do not occur. Both males and females may experience sexual arousal during REM. Heart and breathing rates are irregular.

In both babies and adults, REM sleep defines a very active time in the nervous system. The brain is replenishing itself neurochemically. During this time, it processes and stores all of the day's events and learning. Researchers have found that individuals deprived of REM sleep for long periods are unable to learn, to perform usual tasks, or to remember or recognize familiar people. The amount of REM sleep that you need declines with age. Infants, who have much to process, spend at least half of their sleeping time in this state. For sleepers aged ten to sixty-five years, REM sleep accounts for only about a quarter of sleep time.

In adults, REM sleep is associated with dreaming. People wakened from REM sleep are relatively alert and oriented, and readily recall their dreams. Often they report that noise and light from the environment are woven into those dreams, but in distorted ways. Rain on the roof may appear in a dream as the tide on a beach, or a dog barking to go out in the morning sounds like wolves howling in a forest. Most dream images have little or nothing to do with the sleeper's immediate surroundings.

The long narrative dreams that occur during REM sleep have captured human interest for millenniums. Their content is infinitely varied. They are sometimes pleasurable, at others mundane and tiresome. Disturbingly realistic nightmares can jolt a person awake with a scream. Dreams are thought to occur in real time, but their logic and the flow of time may or may not be realistic. Sigmund Freud suggested that unconscious wishes and desires are disguised and woven into the content and structure of dreams; careful analysis, he wrote, can decode dreams to expose underlying conflicts and suppressed memories of the past. Some scientists propose that dreams are just a random jumble of thoughts and sensations, and it is the waking mind that tries to assemble them into something meaningful.

There are many and varied theories of why dreams are useful to humans. Dreaming may play an important role in facilitating long-term storage of the information and behavior that one takes in or experiences each day. Dreaming may also be a by-product of other biological processes; producing dream content by stimulating all the regions of the brain may be necessary to maintain the functioning of the billions of brain cells suppressed during non-REM sleep.

Non-REM Sleep

Non-REM (NREM) sleep is a regular or deep sleep marked by slow, even breathing and few body or facial movements. By the age of two, approximately 70 percent of a child's nighttime sleep periods are composed of NREM sleep. This form of sleep is further divided into four stages. The first two stages seem to grow out of a newborn's indeterminate sleep, while quiet sleep is the precursor to stage-3 and stage-4 NREM.

Stage-1 NREM is a transitional relaxed state that you enter when you first fall asleep. Your body becomes physically relaxed, and your heart and breathing rates slow. The electrical activity in your brain calms down, dampening consciousness and making you less aware of your environment. Simple thoughts and dreams occur during this state, and sometimes vivid images (called "hypnogogic hallucinations"). As the body relaxes, it occasionally jumps, jerks, or twitches; sometimes these movements give you the sensation of falling.

Stage-2 NREM makes up most of nighttime sleep after early childhood. During this stage, heart and breathing rates and brain activity slow further. Two characteristic types of brain waves appear during stage 2, generated from centers deep in the brain. These are thought to block out a person's sensing of sounds, lights, and other stimuli in the environment, and to quiet internal thought processes, particularly those sleep-disturbing ruminations over what you have to do tomorrow.

Stage-3 and stage-4 NREM are characterized by even deeper physical relaxation and very slow brain activity. During waking hours, your brain shows fast and random activity as hundreds of regions coordinate your thoughts and sensory experiences from the world around you. When you are in stage-4 sleep, these same higher centers of the brain send out slow, rhythmic, coordinated brain waves. During stage 4, information is blocked from coming into very deep brain centers, and the slow rhythmic brain waves from the high-level brain centers wash out all but the simplest thoughts. In contrast to REM sleep, in stage-4 sleep you can shiver and sweat to control your body temperature.

It is extremely difficult to waken young children from stage-4 sleep. Older children and adults awakened from stage 4 are groggy and disoriented, which is not the case when adults are awakened during a REM cycle. Nevertheless, adults in stage-4 sleep are responsive to specific signals, such as someone calling their name, a baby crying, and shouts of "Fire!" This selective responsiveness has obvious benefits for keeping you and your children safe.

REM and NREM Cycles

Adults experience the stages of NREM and REM sleep in a regular cycle: you quickly move from stage-1 to stage-4 NREM sleep, and then back up to a brief period of REM sleep. Then your sleep becomes deeper, usually reaching stage 4 again before returning to REM sleep. Throughout a typical night, an adult might cycle four or five times through this pattern. The average cycle takes ninety minutes, but the shifts slow as the night goes on, so that a sleeper spends increasingly longer periods in the REM stage and in stage-2 NREM. In addition, after the first three hours, a sleeping adult does not necessarily enter stage-4 NREM again. Often a long period of REM sleep finishes the night — this period is probably the source of any dreams you remember when you awake.

Researchers are still testing different theories about what roles REM and NREM sleep play in the development of the brain. REM may, for instance, help a child to learn patterns of behavior before they emerge into his repertoire of activities. It has also been proposed that REM exercises the portions of an infant's brain that are not yet functionally active during a time of day when the baby receives minimal input from the environment.

The Organization of Sleep States

Thus, sleep is not simply inertness, but a complicated behavioral state during which body and mind cycle through periods of activity and inactivity. Many mechanisms control sleep and its various stages. These in-clude the release of hormones, the buildup and breakdown of chemicals in the body and brain, the use of energy resources, and several clocklike centers in the brain. We are far from understanding the purposes of all these stages, but we do know that sleep and many other body functions are organized around biological clocks and rhythmic patterns — most prominently human circadian and ultradian rhythms.

Circadian Rhythms

Circadian rhythms are the patterns of sleep and waking that recur over daylong cycles. Many of these various clocks in the brain that turn body functions on and off at various times of day are controlled by a central master clock located deep in the brain, near the vision-processing area. It takes its cues from daylight to keep the other clocks in your brain functioning on schedule and plays a critical role in controlling sleep and wake cycles. Your brain needs the external stimulus because, while an earth day is twenty-four hours long, a human being's natural sleep/wake cycle is about twenty-five hours. Light helps to reset your internal clocks so that you are not driven to fall asleep an hour later every day.

An external clock does not guide a newborn's sleeping and eating patterns, as new parents quickly learn. But there is evidence of rudimentary organization of sleep periods as early as the fourth week of life. By the end of an infant's third month, a combination of light, feeding schedules, and other factors have begun to regulate his internal clock. His sleep periods lengthen, and he sleeps primarily during the night. After six months, a baby settles into sleeping increasingly longer during the night. We will say more about this welcome development when we discuss how to help babies set more regular patterns of sleep.

Ultradian Rhythms

A different set of internal clocks controls the regular alternating cycles of REM and NREM sleep stages, or "ultradian rhythms," and far less is known about these than about circadian rhythms. The ultradian-rhythm clock grows most actively in the first six months of life. Up to approximately three months, infants enter sleep in the active/REM sleep stage. During a fifty- to sixty-minute period, they cycle through active/REM sleep into quiet/NREM sleep. Then they return to active/REM sleep, and the cycle repeats for the duration of their sleep period. By the age of two years, the REM/NREM cycle has extended to seventy-five minutes. By five years of age, a child's typical cycle approaches that of adults, which is approximately ninety minutes.

During these first months, the length of time before a child enters her first REM period after falling asleep also changes. By six months, infants enter most of their sleep periods through NREM sleep, and descend rapidly from stage 1 to stage 4. The longest period of stage 4 occurs early in sleep and is followed by a very brief REM period. Stage-4 NREM periods become shorter and shorter over the night as REM periods lengthen. By five years of age, a child's patterns of moving through the night between REM and NREM are similar to an adult's.

In both adults and children, the transitions between sleep stages are associated with lapses in sleep of varying degrees. Sleep specialists define an "arousal" as a lightening of sleep, such as a shift from a deeper to a lighter stage accompanied by a body movement, a sigh, or a whimper. In contrast, an "awakening" is an actual break in sleep. The break may be so brief that the sleeper does not recall it, or a child may cry out or even come to get a parent. Infants between one and two months of age tend to wake up often from active/REM sleep. From six months of age and on, there are generally five or more full awakenings during each night, and many more partial arousals. Some young children and infants signal virtually every awakening; others, unbeknown to their parents, lie quietly cooing or playing for long periods and return to sleep on their own.

Developing Good Sleep Habits

Although there are average sleep patterns for different age groups, there are also big differences among individuals of any age. Some children sleep long and some short, some lightly and some deeply. They can be more or less sensitive to schedule and environmental changes. Some people cannot sleep in a hotel room, while others can and will sleep anywhere. There are "owls," folks who prefer to go to bed in the wee hours of the morning; and there are "larks," who like to bed down and rise early. Since the tremen-

By three months of age, a baby's sleep periods lengthen to between four and five hours, the longest usually starting during the night. The total sleep time in a day decreases to between fourteen and fifteen hours. At three months, an infant begins to adhere to a light/dark schedule, with more regular cycling of REM and NREM. Around four months, a baby often has two clearly defined napping periods in midmorning and in late afternoon. At around the same age, we see a gradual decrease in the amount of REM sleep and an increase in the amount of stage-4 NREM during naps.

The fourth month is a critical period for the development of good sleep habits. It is around this time that children's circadian clocks become linked to cues in the world around them: whether it is light or dark, busy or quiet. Infants who spend this period in the well-lit environment of a hospital intensive-care unit often have a difficult time adjusting to the usual night/day pattern of home. Associating bedtime rituals with falling asleep has a powerful affect on infants, as well as older children and even adults. A baby's feeding schedule can either help or interfere with the onset and continuity of his sleep. Depending on family habits, he may come to associate going to sleep with being held, rocking, nursing, lying down in bed with his parents, or being laid down in his crib.

Six months is an important milestone in the development of children's sleep/wake cycles. Their longest continuous sleep period lengthens to about six hours and occurs during the night. Six-month-olds tend to take

dous variation among individuals makes it hard to diagnose sleep problems, our aim here is to help your whole family get enough rest together, not to make a child (or an adult) conform to a particular sleep profile.

Sleep Patterns at Different Ages

From one to six months, babies sleep sixteen to eighteen hours a day. Not all at once, of course — they alternate between periods of sleep and wakefulness that each last for three to four hours. Although some newborns stay asleep during most of their (fortunate) parents' regular sleeping hours, there is generally little or no regularity to a baby's sleep and waking states. Their active/REM and quiet/NREM sleep periods tend to be evenly distributed throughout the day and night.

two extended daytime naps, each lasting three hours or more. Their average total sleep time is around fourteen hours per day. After the six-month landmark, babies show less change in the overall organization of sleep states and schedules. Any shifts that occur from then until adulthood are gradual. As the duration of their daytime naps slowly decreases, there is a slight increase in how long they sleep at night. Sometime in their second year, most children give up their morning nap, and five-year-olds usually drop their daily afternoon nap as well.

The sleep of children between the ages of two and twelve tends to be ideal. They feel a powerful drive to sleep ten to fourteen hours a day, and there is generally less time between going to bed and falling asleep, as well as fewer conflicts about bedtime. The quality of the different stages of sleep is high, and the transitions between them tend not to be disruptive. While sleep problems related to stress and trauma do develop in children of this age group, sleep is rarely again as good.

A whole new set of challenges occurs during adolescence. Until the age of eighteen, adolescents still need eight to ten hours of sleep, cycling through the normal sleep stages. Their vast physical changes, maturing identities, and social and school pressures, however, all help to erode sleep quality. As a result, teenagers tend to be sleep deprived. Furthermore, along with the physical changes that occur during puberty, there is evidence of a shift in the speed and rhythm of their main circadian clock. While the effect varies from child to child, the clock does slow down:

thus, teens tend to go to bed later and sleep in later. Unfortunately, as students get older, school traditionally starts earlier. Some school districts have experimented with later school days, hoping to improve attendance and performance. Be aware of the pressures of adolescence and the shift in circadian rhythm. Help your teenage child maintain a regular schedule of sleeping and waking — it is just as important in these years as in infancy.

Adjusting Your Own Sleep Habits to Your Baby's

Each newborn sleeps exactly the amount that her body and individual makeup require. As parents, you can provide comfortable conditions for your baby to sleep soundly and undisturbed, but you cannot make her sleep more or less. Very young infants have a remarkable ability to fall asleep when they need to, wherever they are — in a park, in a crowded family gathering, or even in the middle of playing with Mom or Dad. Similarly, they usually wake up due not to events around them but to internal factors: feeling hungry or cold, passing a bowel movement, or being jerked awake by the twitches that accompany REM. Your main task is to keep your baby comfortable while she sleeps.

Babies make the transition from wakefulness to sleep gradually, drifting quietly in and out of sleep or napping. Sometimes a breast-feeding baby looks so relaxed — eyes shut, breathing closely, hands open and at his side or lightly resting on his mother's arms — that only another short burst of sucking makes you realize he is not really sound asleep.

It is the newborn's parents, therefore, who define when he is fully asleep or awake. The infant does not necessarily need those lines drawn, but they help his parents a great deal. When your baby is asleep, you usually wrap him gently and place him in his crib or other usual sleeping place. When he is awake, you have him close beside you. These actions structure the parent's day. It would be very hard to live by a baby's schedule and patterns — falling asleep whenever and wherever you need to, unbound by activities, light, or time of day. In the long run, however, the early structure you provide will help your infant to define her own sleep needs and cycles. As she learns to associate sleep with her crib, bassinet, or even car seat, she starts to establish more rhythmic sleep patterns.

Waiting for your newborn to establish these patterns can be wearing, especially if she is getting you up six or seven times each night. You, too, need sleep so that you will have both the energy to provide your child with lively interaction during the day and the good spirits to communicate your affection for her. To grab as much rest as you can get,

SUDDEN INFANT DEATH SYNDROME

Sudden infant death syndrome (SIDS), or crib death, is what we have come to call the unexplained death of a healthy baby as he sleeps. About 4,000 children die of SIDS every year in the United States. This is a small percentage of all infants born here, but each case is a heartbreak. Fortunately, researchers have identified several ways to reduce this risk to your child:

• Put your baby to sleep on her back, not her stomach. Full-term babies who go to sleep on their stomachs are fifteen times more likely to die of SIDS. For premature babies, sleeping on the stomach multiplies the risk of crib death by a factor of 49. There are exceptions to this rule: such conditions as gastroesophageal reflux (see page 163) and certain breathing ailments mean some infants are better off lying on their stomachs.

• Give your baby a smoke-free home. Infants who live with smokers are more likely both to die of SIDS and to contract colds and other illnesses. Not smoking also improves your own health, of course.

• Put your baby to sleep on a firm mattress, not a soft pillow, sheepskin, waterbed, or big stuffed toy. One possible explanation of SIDS is that a pocket is formed between a sleeping infant's face and the soft bedding so that, by breathing in the air just breathed out, the baby gradually is deprived of oxygen.

• Avoid overheating your baby. Keep her room at a temperature that feels comfortable to you.

These steps will make your child's small risk of SIDS even smaller. Checking your baby every hour to see if he is still lying on his back does not lower his risk enough to be worth the trouble. Nor should you worry about your infant's lying stomach-down when he is awake; in fact, wriggling around on his tummy is beneficial exercise. As a young child learns to associate lying back in his crib with going to sleep, he makes this position part of his healthy sleep habits.

try going to bed thirty to sixty minutes earlier than you did before you had your baby, or even just after you put her down for the night. Take naps on weekends. Although you may thus have fewer hours to clean the house or read, house and books will stay around. Also, since young infants often wake up at night to nurse, try feeding your baby regularly in the day and again just before you go to sleep, so that she will sleep longer or even through the night. Or, if you and your spouse take each night feeding in turns, you each may have fewer cries to respond to.

Bedtime Rituals for the Newborn

Part of your job in the first months is to help your baby tune into a basic night/day rhythm: that is, to sleep during the night and stay awake for more of the daytime hours. Babies vary in how fast they adapt to this pattern: some do not for many months, others do quite quickly. A few practical steps may help your baby make the night/day adjustment. Establish a special ritual for nighttime. Behave differently when your baby lies down for a nap in the day and when she is going to sleep at night. Bathing, putting on pajamas or other night clothes, a routine of singing and holding and rocking, even an evening feeding in the baby's room or close to her crib — all these activities can differentiate evening sleep from a nap. See that her room is dark (with only a night-light). You can also wrap the baby more securely or swaddle her.

Like a newborn, the four- to six-month-old baby still sleeps as much as he needs to.

An infant of this age has, however, usually undergone a dramatic shift in his patterns of daytime napping and the length of his sustained nighttime sleep. A baby who wakes up early in the morning during this age may go back to sleep for a few more hours after a quick feeding, or he may be content to come into bed with Mom and Dad as they grab a few more hours of sleep. As children get older, they are more likely to be able to entertain themselves awhile in their crib if they wake up before the rest of the family. (Often infants pass this time by playing with different voice sounds; see page 233.)

Most babies four to six months old are awake for a particular part of every day. For many, this time is late afternoon, just as things may get busier in the home: older children coming home from school, parents arriving from work, supper preparations beginning. This is a good time for your baby to be habitually awake: there are many opportunities for social interaction with people other than the adult who has been home with him for the rest of the day. Being very alert with a lot of attention late in the day may also help her enjoy more sustained sleep periods at night. Also at this time, however, she is more likely to be fussy and inconsolable, and you may have less energy for her.

Keeping Themselves Up: Six to Twelve Months

By the time babies reach the middle of their first year, many have established a night/day sleeping pattern. It is common for infants of this age to sleep ten to twelve hours a night. Even though they concentrate more sleep during the dark hours, however, these babies still do not sleep straight through the night. Most six- to twelve-month-olds wake up from once to half a dozen times. They spend about half the day napping in two or three stretches, usually in midmorning and midafternoon. Thus, these infants' alert times tend to be early in the morning as the rest of their family is up and about, around noon (lunchtime), and in the afternoon as the family may gather. Babies of this age no longer automatically fall asleep after eating; indeed, they may be more ready to play after mealtimes.

By the latter half of their first year, babies are also much more susceptible to disruptions in sleep because of noise around them, family tensions, or their own worries. A nine-month-old baby is keenly aware of strangers, of the comings and goings of his parents, and of a need to be close. Disturbances in sleep that reflect separation distress — a reluctance to let go of Mom and Dad for the night — begin in this period.

By the age of six to twelve months, your baby has much more control over his own states of sleep and wakefulness. In other words, he can keep himself awake. He does not necessarily fall asleep even if he needs to; indeed, he can become so overtired and upset from fatigue that, paradoxically, he cannot go to sleep. Resistance to being put to bed and difficulty going to sleep is the most common problem for parents during this age; and no child or family is entirely immune

from it. Crying and repeated wakings may keep parents at the crib for hours until they become sleep deprived themselves.

Sometimes this trouble appears after an obvious disruption in routine, such as a vacation or an illness. Even apparently minor things such as rearranging nursery furniture, buying a new crib, or changing the baby's room can be upsetting enough to make going to sleep more difficult. But this trouble may also begin as a baby more clearly, actively, and vocally expresses his attachment to his parents. In short, difficulties going to bed in the latter half of the first year are a result of the baby's close and warm relationship with his parents. He does not want to let them go even in exchange for much-needed rest. (Babies who readily go to sleep at this age can be just as attached to their parents as fussy babies are, but may be blessed with a greater sense of security.)

The sleep habits and rituals that you share with your child starting at six months and lasting to five years of age are very important. From birth, but particularly during the latter half of the first year, your child develops an attachment to you that provides the foundation for emotional, intellectual, motor, and even physical development. Sleep is generally the first area in which your child experiences losing you for an extended period. Even if you never let an infant fall asleep alone, he will most likely awaken alone in a dark room. He may even have had a bad dream. Your role is to be available for support and to establish rituals, limits, and good habits. Some problems correct themselves with time; others require minor changes such as a shift in feeding schedule or the introduction of a transitional object, such as a blanket or a stuffed animal. Severe difficulties may require the intervention of a professional, such as your pediatrician or a child developmentalist. If you establish healthy patterns and rituals during the first year, however, later steps toward independence will be likely to proceed with greater ease.

The main goal of bedtime rituals now is to make your baby's transition to sleep feel less like a time of loss and more like a time when you are nearby whenever he needs you. Establish a bedtime routine that does not suddenly move your baby from a warm, family-filled room to a cooler, darker spot down the hall separated from everyone. (See "The Co-Sleeping Controversy" below.) Provide some winding-down time and a few familiar rituals. These might include stories in the kitchen or living room, a few songs or nursery rhymes as you carry him off to bed or a bath, a familiar routine with one or more stuffed animals (for example, "Goodnight, bear. Goodnight, doggie. Goodnight, lamb."). Leave a light on and the door slightly open so that he can hear you and other family members.

THE CO-SLEEPING CONTROVERSY

Families in Western cultures usually prefer that their six- to twelve-month-old babies learn to sleep on their own. For most of human history, however, parents did not enjoy enough living space to make that choice: a baby slept beside her parents' bed in a cradle, or directly beside them in the "family bed" or hammock. Many modern couples, especially those in apartments and small houses, still keep their newborn's crib in their bedroom. Eventually, however, families tend to move the baby into his own room. And in many cases the question arises:

What if your child wants to come back to share your bed?

Such requests for "co-sleeping" produce a mixture of feelings in parents. Some enjoy being physically close to their children, especially when they start to nurse less often. They worry that a child sleeping alone will feel unloved and, therefore, insecure. Others prefer to keep their privacy, or fear that they will roll over and crush the baby. And some parents worry that sharing their bed might distort their child's psychosexual development. To balance these concerns, here are some useful principles that might aid your response to your child.

First, the issue of where parents and child sleep is up to you and your child. Grandparents, friends, and well-meaning child-development experts are not really involved; do not let their disapproval overrule your decision. No formula works for every family because children have different biological needs for closeness. By the same principle, your family's choice is not just about what the child wants: adults have every right to be comfortable in their own bed. And it is their bed, not the "family bed." Mommy and Daddy have usually been sleeping in that bed a long time, after all, and the children have their own beds.

Second, your decision should be guided by two goals: the short-term goal of allowing every member of the family to enjoy ad-

You might do some tasks close to his room for a few minutes, such as getting clothes ready for the next morning or straightening up toys. (For more information on handling young children's separation issues, see chapter 31.)

Getting Toddlers into Their Beds

Separation remains your child's primary concern about sleeping even after she has been a toddler for some time. Even by late in the second year, over half of all children fuss about going to bed. Some may protest every night, others when they are especially tired or stressed. By the time children reach age two, their bedtime rituals are more elaborate, more fixed, and sometimes more tiring for parents. Many a toddler has to hear the same story told in the same way each night. Such rituals provide a comforting stability. Going off to sleep may mean giving up good times with parents and others who get to stay up, but if everything else about bedtime stays the same, then surely Mom and Dad will be there just the same in the morning.

While toddlers may carry their need for consistency to an extreme, they are just expressing a lifelong human need. People tolerate change best when some things remain comfortably the same. Nonetheless, your toddler's insistence on a fixed routine can be

equate sleep and the long-term one of helping your child become independent. Sleep comes most easily if no one in the family is tense, angry, or fearful. Lessons in independence and being polite to Mommy and Daddy are important, but toddlers are unlikely to learn those at night when they feel alone and terrified. It is confusing and unsettling for your child when you teach him that his parents will not comfort him at certain times, or that expressing fear or wanting affection are weaknesses. You do not, however, want your morning interactions with your child to be harmed by resentment because you could not enjoy private time with your spouse.

Third, it is important to see both sides of the argument regarding communal sleeping habits in other cultures. In our Western culture, we value independence, individuality, and autonomy; these qualities seem necessary to succeed in the postindustrial age. We do not live in a society that prizes subsuming the individual's identity to that of the group. Many people might argue about whether this is a good thing, but this emphasis on independence has been a central cultural value for Americans for a very long time. Allowing your children to feel secure in their own beds — eventually coming to feel loved enough to be able to soothe themselves — helps them develop a sense of individuality and autonomy.

Although we tell you here how to make toddlers comfortable going to sleep on their own by reassuring them that Daddy and Mommy are still nearby, you and your partner may decide otherwise. If you feel that allowing your toddler to sleep with you is the best course, do not feel troubled by that choice. When the child becomes a little older, the wish to share the parents' bed is motivated not simply by anxiety about separation or darkness, but by hopes to be close to one parent or the other. (See chapter 14 on the early development of sexuality and gender.) Almost all preschoolers resist going to bed and wake up several times in the night, and there is no clear evidence that "co-sleeping" changes these patterns.

exhausting. Many parents will do almost anything to avoid an upheaval around bedtime. You may let your child come back downstairs and join the family around the television (in hopes that she will fall asleep on the couch). You wearily carry your sobbing two-year-old into your bed even after you have decided not to have her sleep with you.

There is an ongoing debate among child developmentalists about the impact of letting children cry alone in their rooms until they go to sleep, rather than responding to the requests and protests that are part of most toddlers' going to bed. There is no one right path. As for most of these issues, you have to find the approach that best fits your own style and sense of comfort.

Here are some middle-of-the-road approaches that may be helpful. You wish to balance the toddler's fear about being left alone and her wish to continue being with you. Do not imply "Toughen up!" Bedtime is neither solitary confinement nor exile. Nor should you let your child decide when he wants to go to bed: toddlers are just as able as adults are to ignore every physical signal telling them that they need to rest. You want to convey to your child that there is a time for bed, that there is nothing to be afraid of tonight, and that you will, of course, be at his side when he needs you. As you leave his room with a last "Goodnight," wait to see whether his final protest turns into full-blown crying. If it does, go back and reassure him briefly: "It really is all right — but now it's time to say goodnight. See you in the morning." Pat him gently, and leave again.

You may need to do this many times (and it may take as long as a week or two for the child to begin to respond to this approach). Each time you return, do not linger, be as matter-of-fact as you can, and convey the message that although you will come, the day is over and nighttime is not for play or a long time together.

If your toddler cries, it is probably best not to let too much time elapse before going to comfort him. Advocates of letting a child "cry it out" rely on conditioning and associative learning: the child learns that no one is going to come to his side no matter how much he cries and that the experience of crying alone is unpleasant. But, again, you may not want to imply to your child that, at certain times of the day, you will not respond to any distress. Also, children (and adults) do not learn well when they really are upset and afraid. You want to build a trusting — not a fear-conditioned — response: "Times might be scary, but Mommy and Daddy are there if I really need them."

What you say to your toddler in these moments is not as important as your own state of mind when you say it. If you're going back and forth to your two-year-old's room as you put the finishing (or starting) touches on a report due in your office the next day, you may not be in the most patient or accepting frame of mind. Or if you feel terribly guilty about leaving your child crying in his room, you will probably respond more quickly, your tone will not be matter-of-fact, and your child will surely sense your trepidation. It often helps to share bedtime routines with your spouse, a grandparent, a nanny, or even your adolescent son or daughter. Not only is their support helpful to you, but your child also learns to rely on several different people, not just one.

Also, as we have stressed many times before, your own feelings about leaving your toddler (or your baby) in her crib alone for the night influence how you react to her insistent crying or frequent trips to your room. For all parents, having a young child reawakens memories and feelings from their own childhood. Perhaps you too were afraid to sleep by yourself; perhaps you are struggling to separate yourself from your own parents even now, as you try to define your style of parenting. Whatever your individual story, it is important to remember that your child's struggles around nighttime separation will reawaken those same old worries and memories in you and color how you respond to your child. They will influence how consistent or wavering you are, how much you stick to a routine or try to adjust each night to her wishes and feelings.

When a child seemingly cannot stay in a bed by himself, an alternative strategy that makes many parents more comfortable is sitting quietly beside their child's crib as she falls asleep. After she is sleeping, they gradually leave — first moving into the hall just outside her bedroom, then a little farther away. Increasing your distance *gradually* is the key (and the most difficult aspect of this approach if you feel pressed for time). A child waking up after you have left (as children invariably do) and finding you are not close by has her fears in some ways confirmed. It may also take several weeks for this technique to affect your child's bedtime patterns.

Here are a few more practical hints to help your baby go to bed:

- The best place for sleeping is a quiet, comfortable, and dark environment, but use a small night-light for your child's comfort. Try to keep the room's temperature even and matched to what seems to be your baby's preference.
- Too much physical exercise or mental stimulation within two hours of bedtime can increase the amount of time it takes anyone — adult or child — to fall asleep.
- Sleeping on a full or an empty stomach causes discomfort and can disrupt sleep.
- Drinking too much liquid shortly before bedtime results in multiple bathroom trips or wet diapers, both of which can prevent good sleep.

Keeping Toddlers in Their Beds

Going to sleep is only half the challenge: most toddlers wake up at least once during the night, and many several times. Toddlers wake up for many reasons, but not because they have learned a "bad habit" or are trying to manipulate you. Both children and adults arouse several times during the night; toddlers may arouse more often to full wakefulness because of worry about being alone. Sometimes a young child stirs, sees nothing disturbing or hears his parents nearby, and falls right back to sleep. Other children need to check in with their parents on every awakening. Even a familiar room may seem scary at night.

Taking account of these facts may help diminish night wakings for your child or, at least, help him go back to sleep on his own:

- Rooms really do look different in the dark of night, shadows have funny shapes, a stack of books suddenly looks like an animal, or a doll leaning against the wall seems to have moved. A night-light chases out the scary shadows.
- As a child goes to sleep, his body temperature falls. While your toddler may be active and very warm when she goes to bed and refuses any covers, she will likely wake up later feeling cooler. Spreading a light blanket over her when you go to bed may help.
- Outside sounds, such as the television in the den or a dog barking, may disrupt sleep. You may need to think of some ways to soundproof your baby's room or find a better location for his bed.
- Remember that your own pattern of checking on your child has an influence on his sleep. Parents can unwittingly turn a light sleep arousal into full awakening as they quietly tiptoe to their baby's door to look in.

Nightmares and Night Terrors

Since the sleep of school-age children is usually deep and regular, disruptions in that pattern are particularly meaningful. Both children and adults can "lose sleep" after a traumatic or scary event: a fire, a divorce, crime in the neighborhood. If your older child is having such a problem, he may benefit from talking about what is on his mind with you or a professional counselor. (See chapter 33.) To make sleep easy again, consider turning his night-light back on or providing another symbolic reminder that you are nearby and caring. Reinforce bedtime routines to encourage your child to sleep on a regular schedule.

Most children will at some point wake up frightened by a dream. They may be crying inconsolably as if something terrible and irreparable has happened. In these instances, go as quickly as possible to offer comfort; nothing escalates fear as much as being left alone with it. You may need to spend much more time calming your child during these moments than during a normal waking — fifteen minutes to half an hour is not uncommon. Do not be surprised to see more of these episodes when your child is between the ages of eight and ten. Nightmares may be a manifestation of the child's daytime anxieties, but in themselves they are fortunately not dangerous.

"Night terrors" are more troubling: a child sits up from a deep sleep screaming in terror, eyes wide, perhaps not fully awake. Unlike nightmares, the child is unable to recount a dream or other reason for her fear. By morning she may not even remember the episode. This problem seems to be biological, not psychological; some pediatricians attribute it to apnea, a disruption in the child's normal breathing during sleep. Night terrors are hazardous when they cause a child to jump out of bed suddenly. Even more than nightmares, these terrors require parents to take time to calm and reassure their young child. Fortunately, episodes tend to occur during the first three hours of sleep, when parents are often awake, and they tend to decrease markedly after the age of seven.

Almost every family must deal with bedwetting at some point, but usually at irregular and infrequent intervals after their child's early years. Good toilet training at a young age usually prevents this from becoming a regular problem. (See pages 150–153.) Sleepwalking is a much less common problem, appearing most often in children between the ages of ten and fourteen. People once thought sleepwalkers were acting out their dreams, but we now know that they are coming out of deep NREM sleep and not dreaming at all. Fortunately, this unconscious habit usually goes away by itself. Make your child's environment safe, without sharp objects on the floor or corners to stumble into. Block staircases and secure windows. Sleepwalking is often the result of disruptions in your child's sleep/wake cycle, so helping him return to a regular schedule can alleviate the problem and ensure his enjoyment of regular, healthy sleep.

Sleep is life sustaining and developmentally essential. Books for parents from earlier in this century discussed sleep as one of the basic "habits" of childhood along with eating, toilet training, and daily personal hygiene routines — the implication being that it is important to form good sleeping habits early to ensure healthy, adapted development. Sleep habits develop through the relationship between you and your child; his sleep patterns are a reflection of your own attitudes toward sleep and your own efforts to help him feel secure in the inevitable separation that sleeping in his own bed brings. Because sleep and dreaming go together and because sleep is a temporary, daily separation from the waking world, it is also a habit layered with mystery and feelings. Good and bad things come to mind when we sleep, and no matter how much you try to help your child with his sleep habits, these feelings of mystery and even a little uncertainty inevitably creep in. Remember, too, that no matter how stable and secure your child's sleep habits, they can always be disrupted by stress, illness, or times of great developmental change such as adolescence. As with so many other aspects of parenting, the more you are aware of your own feelings about sleep, the more you will be able to help your child with his.

CHAPTER 14

Sexuality and Gender: How Children Come to Know Their Bodies

The initial biological processes that determine sex and set the stage for sexuality occur when your baby is in the womb. But during fetal development and in infancy, there is little difference between the sexes beyond physical architecture. Young boys and girls have similar amounts of male and female sex hormones in their bodies. Sex-hormone production increases and becomes more gender-specific only between the ages of five and eight years.

"Gender" is a complex psychological construction. It includes many different thoughts and fantasies about what it means to be male or female. Some of these thoughts and fantasies are conscious; others unconscious. One's sense of one's own gender, whether as a child or as an adult, incorporates thoughts and fantasies about what it means to be a member of the other sex, if only to solidify one's own sense of identity. In this chapter, we discuss how children begin to understand their sexual body and to develop their gender identity.

Your Child's Sexuality

An infant eagerly snuggles up to her mother's breast for milk and affection. For the third night in a row, a preschooler comes to his parents' bedroom with anxious eyes and asks to sleep in their bed. A mother and father joke about how much time their sixth-grader, Cindy, spends on the phone, and then hear from her younger sibling that Cindy is chatting with a classmate named Kyle — and that the word on the school playground is, "Cindy and Kyle are going out." All these familial moments reflect, in different ways, the development of sexuality in children before adolescence.

Although what we call the sexuality of children is in significant ways markedly different from the sexuality of adults, there is continuity in the basic characteristics of the two. Sexuality involves sensations on and in the body that are emotionally rich and linked to personal fantasies. It evolves from the sensuality of the small baby to the toddler's exploration of her own body to the young child's intense desire for a specific person. After a period of relative calm or "latency," during which sexuality never really goes away completely, it reawakens in puberty, heralding adolescence.

Discovering and Exploring Bodies in Infancy

The seeds of sexuality are planted before birth and bloom in infancy as a baby explores his mother's face and body with his eyes and hands during nursing and play. The nursing experience itself is full of sensual feelings. During his first six months, a baby is unable to make much distinction between the pleasurable sensations his mother provides. He does not yet fully understand the boundary between his body and his caregiver's body. The baby just knows he enjoys sucking in the milk and making his tummy full. His whole body feels good during this experience, but especially pleasurable are the sensations centering on his mouth, sucking (even biting) on the nipples, being held, and touching his caregiver. Mothers usually feel intense pleasure themselves during the intimate, sensual nursing experience.

As a baby gains increasing control over her body during the second half of her first year, she also begins to realize that her mother is providing the pleasurable sensations associated with nursing. Thus, she makes a connection in her mind between pleasurable bodily sensations, sensuality, and the importance of another person. At this

age, a baby is able to suck vigorously, to stroke her mother's face and to look at it or away from it, and to touch the bottle or breast while nursing. Around this time, she also becomes able to bite. These behaviors are all simple ways of exploring her mother's body as well as creating new sensations inside her own. (For more on the important interaction between mother and baby during feeding, see chapter 12.)

During your child's second year, his increasing motor control gives him more opportunities for finding pleasure. He can move himself where he wants to go. He can control his fingers, hands, and arms. He can grab objects and put them in his mouth. Just as your toddler sees a whole new outside world to explore, he typically also begins to explore his body. He is curious about the new sensations he can create in his mouth, ears, toes, and other body parts. He can put all sorts of objects in his mouth to discover whether they are smooth or rough, soft or hard, good tasting or bad tasting. He puts his fingers and toes into various places to see what they feel like, what new sensations they give him. Creating so many sensations for himself is very exciting.

At this time, many children begin to explore their genitals as well. The discovery of the difference between touching one's genitals and touching one's mouth is momentous. Some parents, feeling uncomfortable about this new and (for their baby) exciting bodily touching, become concerned that it is masturbation and think it should be stopped. It is really not masturbation at this age, however. A baby is not focused on touching her genitals as a source of sexual pleasure in the same way that an older child or an adult might be. Her curiosity is a further development of her understanding of her own body. This exploration helps a child develop an image of her own body, how it works, and how it is put together. The discoveries the child makes during these explorations contribute significantly to her later ability to feel comfortable with her body and to explore her own sexuality as a teenager and adult.

Once a toddler can get himself where he wants to go, he is also able to follow Daddy and Mommy to see what their bodies are like. Most toddlers exhibit a heightened curiosity about the bodies of their parents and other caregivers. Some express an active interest in exploring these people's bodies, not only touching faces but wanting to touch breast or penis. They can be quite ingenious in finding ways to learn more, often following people into the bathroom and watching them shower or bathe. A mom or dad may feel, "I never have any privacy!" and respond as if their toddler were spying on them. The intensity of your toddler's curiosity about other people's bodies can be at times amusing and at other times embarrassing. And toddlers, of course, can be imperious about what they will or will not do.

It is hard for many parents to locate a comfortable balance between keeping their toddler out of private spaces and letting him know that his curiosity is natural and acceptable. Certainly a toddler quickly figures out just how comfortable each parent is with her intense wish to see, touch, and explore the body of someone she loves. Some parents feel that the way to convey a comfortable and natural attitude toward the body is to relinquish all their privacy. They do not prohibit their child from seeing them in the bathroom or from exploring Mom's or Dad's body as much she wishes. But with this approach you avoid teaching your child a valuable and necessary lesson. While you need not be prudish about your child's touching your body, he does need help to understand that each person's body is private, and that everyone — parents, siblings, friends — has a right to have some control over that privacy.

When your young toddler is very eager to observe or touch your body, the wisest response is probably amused tolerance and acceptance of his curiosity, rather than shock or horror. Using language that feels natural to you and appropriate for your child, explain the value of privacy in a mutual way: "People don't always like other people to look at them without any clothes on or to touch them. If someone doesn't want to be looked at or touched, then you should respect their wishes about themselves just as you would want them to do with you. You can show them you love them in other ways." Your toddler will gradually learn that, although his interest in the bodies of others is natural and not naughty, some things are off-limits. (See also "Awkward Moments for Parents," pages 192–193.) He also needs to learn that some touching and exploration is acceptable, but other kinds may not be — especially if the other person says no. Gradually a growing child will come to recognize that bodies (including his own) are sources of pleasure and delight, but that nobody, including himself, necessarily wants their body or space to be invaded. At the same time, as he gradually begins to feel that he has control over his own body, he will develop a sense of physical integrity. He will also understand that he has the right to decide when to let others view or touch his body.

Intense Curiosity in Ages Three to Six

By the end of their third year, children have developed an inner image of their bodies: the orifices and protrusions, the soft places and rough places, the "inside" places and "outside" places. Although a three-year-old may not yet be fully toilet trained, she has much greater control over all aspects of her body, including her urethra-genital area and her sphincter. (For toilet training, see chapter 11.) She has had countless, pleasurable, intimate experiences of being fed, held, dressed, cuddled, and soothed by beloved caregivers. She has a distinct sense of what makes her body feel good, of what is exciting, and of what does not feel so good. She also knows that she can create good feelings with and in her own body. She is aware that her body is separate from others, but that everyone's body functions in similar ways. All of these experiences have contributed to her fundamental conviction that she has an intact body over which she has control. Because, however, many of her bodily experiences have involved another person, she also believes

passionately that people she loves and trusts can be sources of bodily pleasure.

By this age, one also knows whether one is a boy or a girl and that people are divided between male and female. Children can categorize people by sex, although their categories are often idiosyncratic and unstable, as in, "She's a girl because she has frilly socks." This knowledge, however, is not the same thing as a sense of gender, which is a more complex psychological conception. By the age of three, children are very curious about the differences among people's bodies — not just male and female, but big and little, strong and weak, powerful and powerless.

Much of your child's imaginative play is stimulated by his attempts to arrive at some satisfactory conclusion to the various questions raised by these differences: If I am little, am I helpless? Could I be big and powerful by wishing it were so? Will I ever get to be big? What would I do if I were as big and powerful as my parents? The family is the laboratory in which he can investigate these mysteries. They have an added urgency for him, because by age three a child is cognizant of the limitations imposed on him by reality: that is, that he *is* little and relatively powerless, and that he cannot magically make himself powerful. The small child wants very much to join his big, strong, attractive parents as an equal.

With her growing imagination, a three-year-old can grasp that her beloved parents share a relationship from which she is sometimes excluded. No matter how loved a child feels, no matter how much parental attention she gets, she can recognize that her parents have interests beyond her. For the small child, this realization is a great blow. She would like to be not just "best beloved" but also "only beloved." Sometimes she wants her father's exclusive, exciting attention and fears her mother as a rival; at other times she wishes to be her mother's only love and experiences her father as an intruder. These feelings may be stronger or more confused when a child has only one parent, one who is attempting to carry on a social life. A boyfriend or girlfriend seems like an intruder who could disrupt the exclusive relationship the child once enjoyed (or thinks she enjoyed).

Between the ages of three and six, a child struggles with these powerfully jealous and possessive wishes. He is also fearful at times that he will become unlovable if his parents

learn about his competitive feelings. His wish for an exclusive relationship with a beloved parent has many components: the hope to be big and powerful like that parent, the desire to be the most admired, or the resentment of the parents' relationship. Central to these wishes are fantasies about the exciting activities the parents engage in when he is absent. Preoccupied as the young child is with his own body, with what it can do and what pleasures and excitement he can experience with it, he assumes that his parents must be doing exciting, sexual things, too.

Since your child's fantasies develop in response to what he finds exciting, they may not correspond closely to what adults think of as sexual activity. For the child, however, these fantasies are as meaningful as adult sexual intercourse is for his parents. Some children imagine adult sexuality to be very aggressive, with one person in power and the other helpless. Others imagine their parents' sexual relationship as focused on making exciting explosions and messes. Still other children imagine it as similar to nursing, with one person feeding the other. Whatever form a child's fantasy takes, however, for this child at this point in time, that is what being sexual is all about.

Preschoolers' heightened interest in their own sexuality and awareness of their parents' exclusive relationships can propel them once again into the parental bedroom. They may accomplish this intrusion through waking at night because of nightmares and the wish to be comforted or simply by walking into the bedroom. Although it is important to reassure your child that she and Mommy and Daddy are all okay, it is equally important to help her understand that her job is to sleep in her own bed, in her own bedroom. This can at times be a daunting task. Some children are particularly persistent in coming into their parents' bedroom, and it can be hard for parents to be firm when they are exhausted and worried about having to get up in the morning. (For discussion on whether to allow toddlers into the parental bed, see pages 180–181.)

Your three- to six-year-old's wish to share the parental bed does not mean what it did to your toddler. For the preschooler, permission to join her parents stimulates the fantasy that she *can* be an equal partner to the parent she desires. At the very least, the child has succeeded in keeping her rival from "winning." Although these fantasies are exciting and at times pleasurable, they also make a child anxious, because she knows she is still small and would be beaten in any real contest. She thus experiences her momentary "victory" (gaining the parental bed) as a source of danger. The child feels more helpless in the face of this internal danger and less able to be "big." She can become increasingly uncertain about whether her parents would *really* love her if they knew what was going on inside her head. In other words, the triumph carries with it a tremendous price: it endangers the child's sense of autonomy, independence, and adequacy.

During the preschool years, children's genital sensations are more focused. As children begin to recognize that their genitals can give them a lot of pleasurable excitement, their masturbation often becomes more intense. During the early part of this period, many children engage in public masturbation, often to the point of embarrassing their parents. A little boy, for instance, may walk around regularly with one hand clutched over his fly. Unlike the toddler's genital exploration, a preschooler's masturbation appears intentional, and fantasies frequently accompany the activity. Now is a good time to help your child to understand that her sexual activity is (like her parents') not something she can do anywhere or in front of other people, that it is private to herself.

The years between three and six are exciting for both parent and child. The youngster now has many capabilities: linguistic, motor, social, and emotional. She becomes able to draw representationally, to construct all sorts of complicated structures, and to play imaginatively. She is interested in other children as friends and can make some compromises in order to sustain a friendship. The inner world of the preschool child is dominated by momentous questions: How can I feel big and adequate when in reality I am small? How can I love and be loved without becoming so jealous that I destroy my other important relationships? How can I manage the exciting curiosity about Mommy and Daddy's activities and privileges without feeling overwhelmed or overstimulated? How can I feel like a good person when sometimes I wish I could do terrible things to the people I love?

These inner dilemmas are not always fueled by the child's heightened sense of his own sexuality, but frequently that sexuality gives the conflicts their intensity and force. Parents often feel confused, pulled in one direction and then another. You can feel quite disturbed to be confronted with your small child's emotional intensity, whether the issue is who is in control, who is big, who is right, or who can be the best beloved. It is hard not to let yourself be pulled into the maelstrom of the child's inner struggles. A parent cannot always remain above the fray. Nourish your sense of humor in order to maintain some distance. Try to remember that your child's fierce opposition to you reflects his or her own intense inner struggles.

Engendering Gender

The concept "core gender identity" is sometimes used to refer to a child's fundamental conviction that he or she is either male or female. This conviction usually corresponds to the child's actual anatomy. Because this is a psychological construction,

---

AWKWARD MOMENTS FOR PARENTS

Preschoolers' fascination with their sexual feelings, bodies, and internal sensations heightens their curiosity about many associated questions: Where do babies come from? Why do some people have penises and some people vaginas? What do Mom and Dad do together when they are alone? Some children are comfortable asking these questions of their parents or other relatives. For others, these are private scientific investigations. If your child is a questioner, keep in mind that the question you think he is asking may not be the one he has in mind. For example,

when a child asks, "Where do babies come from?" his interest may be quite specific: from a special place inside the mother or from the grocery store? Be sure, therefore, you understand what your child is actually curious about. Then answer only what he is asking; do not go on and give an answer worthy of the encyclopedia. It is important to give the child what you believe is a truthful answer, but also a simple one within his grasp.

Because preschoolers are so curious about what goes on between their parents, your child may well surprise you while you are in the middle of making love. What is best to do in such a moment? Try to break off lovemaking calmly, cover your bodies, and ask the child to leave the

room. If it is your toddler who has come into your room as a result of his problems with sleeping (see chapter 13), you may want to take him back to bed as you have been doing routinely on other evenings. However hard, it is important both to strive for calmness and to avoid being either frightened or angry. Parents often worry that their children will be traumatized by witnessing the sexual act — and under certain circumstances, a child can be. If, however, you carry on as we recommend, your child is not likely to be unduly upset. In fact, she will probably be much less upset than you!

Talk to your child — as you take him back to bed after he has interrupted you during sex, or the next day — calmly and reas-

however, some children's core gender identity may not correspond closely to their anatomy. The concept "gender role" is sometimes used to refer to an individual's ideas and fantasies about what is appropriate behavior for each sex. The construction of gender is influenced by the child's experiences with his parents, by their transmission to him of the values their culture holds about what it is to be a man or a woman, and by the child's own experiences with his body and fantasies about his bodily experiences.

Your child gradually acquires a sense of gender between the age of eighteen months and approximately six years. By the end of this period, he understands that he cannot be both sexes and that his body has its limitations, an important one being anatomy. Ideally, the child has developed a fundamental sense that his body is not only a source of pleasure and delight but is also appropriate for him.

During the years when children are most active in imaginative play, they often dress up in the clothes of the other sex. Given fashions today, this behavior is usually apparent or troubling to parents only when a boy tries on his mother's dress or makeup. Such be-

suringly about what he saw. Say you know that he is probably very curious. Offer a simple explanation, along the lines of, "Since Mommy and Daddy love each other very much, sometimes they want to be very close to each other and hug each other." Help your child to understand that this is a private activity, just as you know that some of his activities are private, and that that is why you closed your bedroom door. If you have not yet done so you can use this as an opportunity to give some clear guidelines for privacy: a closed door means "private," and anyone should knock before entering; your child can call if there is a real emergency, and so on.

Just as children can surprise their parents in sexual activity, so parents can catch their young children experimenting. In the preschool period, many children engage in sex play together. This behavior is stimulated both by their intense curiosity about other people's bodies and by their own heightened genital sensations. In general, you should not be concerned by it. If you become aware that sex play is taking place, it is appropriate to interrupt and help the children find other activities to do. Sometimes this can be another occasion to remind the child that sex is a private activity and that other people's bodies are private. There are some circumstances when it is appropriate for a parent to do more:

• The child appears overwhelmed by the experience.

• The other child is significantly older.

• Coercion is involved — either force or threats.

• Your child strongly resists your attempts to distract him.

• The sex play appears to be compulsive: that is, he seems to need to play this way, especially when he is worried or stressed.

In such situations, you might consider consulting with your pediatrician or a mental health specialist to see whether there is some emotional disturbance behind your child's sex play.

havior is almost always part of a preschooler's normal role-playing games, not a sign of true gender confusion. (For more on play, see chapter 16.)

To instill accurate and healthy thoughts about both genders, avoid answering children's questions about anatomical differences by saying that one sex lacks something the other has. Thus, rather than saying, "Girls don't have a penis," say, "Girls have a vagina instead of a penis." Children should not feel incomplete sexually; they should feel comfortable with the sex they are.

Concern about a Child's Gender Identity

You should become concerned about your child's gender identity if she either insists that she does not want to be the sex she is or claims she is not, in fact, that sex; and if this wish is persistent, rigid, and pervasive, ultimately determining what the child will regularly wear and with whom and with what she will play. Not only are children who have a gender identity disorder dissatisfied with the identity they have, but their view of the gender they wish to be is usually rigid and stereotypical. A girl wishing she were a boy, for example, will insist that girls have to have long hair (which she hates), can never play sports (which she enjoys), always have to give in during arguments, are crybabies, and so on. A boy wishing to be a girl usually wants to be stereotypically "feminine": long curly hair, always wanting to wear dresses, and so on. Children exhibiting such gender identity confusion are usually suffering from multiple

uncertainties about who they are. This situation indicates a need for counseling.

Solidifying Gender Roles in the School Years

As a child approaches six years of age, she gradually develops the ability to recognize and tolerate the limits imposed by reality. She knows she is not helpless, or even powerless, though she is small. She knows she is loved deeply, even if she cannot have the exclusive relationship with one parent that she desires. She feels she is "good enough" and "big enough" to tackle the larger questions posed by the wider worlds of school and friendships. She knows she can experience deep pleasure within her body, but does not have to feel overwhelmed by these exciting sensations. She feels in control of her body and of the feelings she experiences within it. These inner achievements prepare her for entry into the school years.

By the end of the preschool period, gender identity has become consolidated and, though not fully conscious, appears for most children to correspond to their bodies' anatomy. Thus, a boy has a firm sense of what it is to be a boy, as a girl does about being a girl. Because this knowledge is such a new achievement, frequently the child insists on a rigid dichotomy: "Boys *can't* wear pink; only girls can." "Girls *don't* play sports; the boys do." To begin with, as we have said, the gender "rules" are usually those of the wider culture, transmitted into the home by parents and television. Later, the opinions of schoolmates strongly influence these notions, as they do everything else in the child's life. It is common to hear boys complain, "All girls are stupid," or girls state, "Boys are yucky and mean." Often girls will refuse to have anything to do with boys, and vice versa. At times, it seems as if all grade-school children have a positive aversion to the other sex.

Sometimes your young grade-school-age child's rigid distinctions between the sexes contradict what you believe and want to teach. Generally, however, he is not as rigid as his statements imply. It may be that he has to hold on to strict dichotomies as a way of reassuring himself that he is what he is, that he cannot change, and that this is a good thing. He wants to resist being pulled back into the maelstrom of sexuality. Careful observation of children in classrooms reveals that the lines between the sexes are not really as sharp as children maintain. Many children manage to sustain a friendship with a member of the other sex in spite of peer pressure — especially if their other friends do not tease them into thinking of the relationship as sexually charged (as in saying, "Sam is Carrie's boyfriend!"). If your child makes statements that you consider sexist, you can point out to him that in real life people are more complicated and can do all sorts of things. People's behavior depends more on their particular training, talents, and interests and less on their sex.

The passage from preschool to "big kids' school" is a significant step for all children, and one that is made possible, in part, by a calming down of their sexual feelings. These feelings do not disappear, but the impulses seem to carry less urgency, and students are more able to turn their attention to academic concerns. Although curiosity about sexual matters continues, the child's interest in sex usually lessens in the grade-school years. This "breathing space" both is created by your child's increased cognitive capabilities and drives her acquisition of academic skills. Enjoy it while it lasts.

The Approach of Puberty

By fifth grade, many children begin to experience a marked hormonal upsurge that foreshadows the onset of puberty two years later. Even though these children may not yet appear to exhibit the physical characteristics that show puberty is on its way, they feel the hormones' effects internally. They begin to feel moody and irritable and are confused by these new and unpredictable swings in their emotions. At this age, preteens show an increased interest in the current styles in clothing, hairdos, and music. As boys and girls become interested in each other once again, many experiment with "going out." The term means the boy and girl have agreed to say this, but not much more. Elementary-school couples may talk on the telephone or walk around the playground together, but rarely is the relationship more than a somewhat charged and exciting friendship.

Parents frequently worry that these signs mean their child is about to leap precociously into adolescence. Usually you can understand all this behavior as your child's attempt to "try on" being a teenager, to imagine what the impending transitions will bring. Still, it can be very hard to know how seriously to take such apparently adolescent behavior. By monitoring these early attempts at friendship with the other sex — neither forbidding them as too grown-up nor treating the still grade-school child as if he had already achieved adolescence — you reassure your children.

As the hormonal push increases, children begin to develop the secondary sex characteristics (growth spurt, body hair, breast buds, and penile growth) that forecast the onset of puberty within the next eighteen months or so. On average, girls enter this stage one or two years before boys. For most children, this change coincides with the junior high school or middle school years, the ages between eleven and thirteen. As their bodies radically and visibly transform themselves, many children are both excited and confused. And there is much secret observation of one another, silent speculation, and impassioned conversation. Generally, children do not share the confusions and excitements of this phase with their parents, but turn instead to peers for information and reassurance. Most children (as well as their parents) closely watch their bodily changes, seeking some certainty about when puberty actually will begin.

Girls are more anxious about puberty than boys. Many girls worry a lot about the onset of menses, their first period. They are particularly frightened that this event is something over which they will have no control, and that they will find themselves hu-

miliated and ashamed. During this phase, girls tend to turn to their girlfriends for understanding and information about what constitutes critical "signs." When Mom tries to be reassuring or to give some more specific information, most girls tend to turn away emotionally.

Boys focus more on the changing size of their penis and the exciting but uncontrollable sensations it can stimulate. Like girls, boys turn to their peers for reassurance and information, frequently presenting an uninterested or "cool" front to their parents. Since a boy also wants to look cool in front of his peers, however, he often has to maneuver delicately to find out how much other boys know without revealing how little he knows himself. In the process, children of both sexes are likely to hear a great deal of misinformation.

Boys and girls both long for the old comforting, reassuring relationship with their parents and fear that this will pull them "backward," turning them into helpless little children again. Since they are already struggling with feelings of being out of control, helpless to predict what is going to happen and when, these longings for the parent of their earlier childhood feel particularly dangerous. Thus, much of your prepubescent child's defiance is particularly fierce.

As the parent of a prepubescent child, you may feel you are entering an alien universe. Familiar rules seem not to apply. The one dominant message seems to be that whatever you are doing at any moment is wrong. Many parents, unfortunately, accept this message as being the full story and back off, giving up any effort to maintain order or rules. It is a mistake, however, to cut back on supervision and to monitor your child less than you did when he was younger. If you pull back at this point, you appear to him to be saying, "Okay, if you don't need me, I don't need you! Anyway, now that you are almost a teen, you're on your own." In fact, children of this age need, in many ways, *more* attention, *more* supervision, and *more* parental availability. At a time when their universe is shaky, parents offer the one firm, constant point of guidance.

Children in this stage have an intense interest in the other sex. They eagerly anticipate school dances, even if the girls all dance with each other and the boys throw food around. Children attend more to personal grooming and to how attractive they may seem to others. As many children become painfully concerned with whether they are "popular," they imagine that the so-called popular kids are having a much easier time of it. Both boys and girls also have intense same-sex friendships, often dominated by excited speculation about who likes whom, who's "going with" whom, who "dumped" whom. Parents and teachers often feel like ancient observers, shut out from a child's most important social experiences.

Some children attempt to bypass the confusion, anxieties, and vulnerabilities of this phase by forming a premature sexual relationship. Such children hope that it will give them the sense of security, confidence, and peer acceptance for which they desperately long. Those children, particularly girls, who jump into precocious sexuality, however, tend to feel worse about themselves afterward. The sexual relationship exacerbates their sense of being out of control — especially if they have the added burden of feeling they have been taken advantage of. Children who engage in precocious sexual activity often cover up their unhappiness and shame with a flamboyant bravado, as if to flaunt to their peers that *they* aren't confused and vulnerable, that *they* are successful adolescents. This behavior should worry a parent. Although prohibitions alone may have little effect, your taking a firm stance about what is acceptable, and why, can in fact reassure your child.

In the year following the onset of puberty, most children begin to settle down. They are not the youngsters they once were, although most parents can see traces of those earlier ages — as well as catch glimpses of the young women and men to come. Before taking up this passage again in chapter 36, we need now to backtrack and cover the learning child and then the social child.

PART IV

Cognitive Development: The Learning Child

CHAPTER 15

How Your Baby Learns: From First Perceptions of the World to Making Sense of It

A newborn slowly opens her eyes and looks straight into her father's face. For moments suspended in time, the two study each other. She follows his face as he moves from side to side; she seems to look right into his eyes as if memorizing this instant. He is amazed at how intently she watches him and how much she seems to be taking in. Her eyes look so much like his, but the way her mouth turns into a little "o" as she breathes is the perfect image of her mother. He has never before realized how a newborn baby tunes into the world or how quickly he and his daughter would seem to know one another. Will she really remember this moment of theirs together?

What do babies know when they are born? How much do they understand? How quickly do they learn? For centuries, adults caring for infants have puzzled over the mystery of babies, hoped for their safe and healthy development, tried to understand how they learn about the world. Although the study of cognitive development in infants has progressed most dramatically since the early 1960s, the question of how babies learn is old. In the fifth century B.C., the Greek historian Herodotus described what might have been the first study of language development in children. An Egyptian king supposedly ordered twin baby brothers to be kept away from anyone except each other. He allowed no one to talk around the brothers so that he could observe what language the babies would speak naturally: if they spoke Egyptian, the king would be sure that his people were the most ancient of all races. The brothers did indeed speak, but in a language no one had heard. Court scholars reasoned that the twins' special language must come from a civilization even older than Egypt's — a finding that may have had an immediate and fatal effect on their careers!

At the beginning of the twentieth century, many professionals thought that babies were born into the world completely helpless and unable to interpret any information they sensed. Scholars thought that newborns were essentially blind, felt no pain, and did not distinguish tastes or smells — that they

LEARNING IN THE WOMB

People often think of life in the womb as dark, quiet, and still. While it is true that no light penetrates that far into a mother's body, the uterus offers many other types of stimulation. Think of being completely underwater in your bathtub, hearing the swish and echo of water in your ears. Then imagine that you share your tub with gushing hoses, the equivalent of the placental blood vessels and umbilical cord that keep a baby alive. Finally, imagine that your bathtub is connected with several other pumping machines, that your tub can move around, and that a whole world of sounds is just outside. That is the sensory environment in which a fetus actually develops.

Despite this racket, babies-to-be spend most of each day in a sleeplike state (though research shows that in the third trimester they can be startled by loud noises). For physical stimulation, fetuses often tug and squeeze on the umbilical cord and occasionally kick (as all mothers learn), but they spend much of the time sucking on their thumbs.

Do babies start learning even before they are born? Are their brains absorbing and processing information while they are still in their mothers' wombs? Mothers and fathers commonly sense that their newborn already knows their voices, their favorite music, and their activity schedule. And early evidence suggests this parental instinct is correct.

Investigators of prenatal learning knew that what a fetus hears most is the mother's heartbeat, voice, and stomach noises, and wondered whether the newborn baby might prefer to hear these sounds, too. In a series of creative studies, where newborns could keep a tape recorder playing by sucking on a nipple, they sucked harder in response to recordings of their own mother's voice and similar intrauterine sounds. In related studies, researchers asked mothers to read a particular children's book aloud twice a day during the last six weeks of pregnancy. After birth, the newborns sucked harder on the nipple so as to hear recordings of their mother reading that familiar text, but not when they heard recordings of their mother reading another book. Similar research has shown that a baby is more likely to recognize her father's voice if he talked to her while she was in the womb.

Does this mean that playing opera for a fetus will improve the baby's ability to learn? Or that hearing recordings of people speaking French will accelerate his recognition of that language? There is no solid evidence to suggest those benefits, though there are many devices on the market that promise them. Recognizing the typical vocal tones and cadence of a mother and father is a task that a baby's brain seems set up to do early. You do not need to buy a "womb phone" or some other device to communicate with your baby-to-be. Just speak normally about what makes you happy. Similarly, mothers can enjoy music with their fetus and, in the last trimester, may even feel their baby move in rhythm with that music. Do not, however, choose recordings for their supposed educational effects.

Far more research needs to be done before we will know what kinds of prenatal experiences benefit newborns the most. There is no conclusive evidence that specific types of stimulation during pregnancy make infants smarter or quicker to learn. On the other hand, you and your baby are surely getting to know one another during your pregnancy. That process can naturally include talking to your baby, reading aloud, singing, or communicating in whatever ways you find most meaningful.

were empty vessels ready to be shaped and molded by the world into which they were born. Child health experts held unwaveringly to the ideas that newborns and very young infants grew and learned only from their environment, and that the environment was far more powerful than endowment. So strong was the confidence that adults could shape a baby's life course that John B. Watson, a leading child psychologist, proclaimed in his 1925 book *Behaviorism,* "Give me a dozen healthy infants, well-formed, and my own specified world to bring them up in, and I'll guarantee to take any one at random and train him to become any type of specialist I might select — doctor, lawyer, artist, merchant-chief, and yes, even, beggarman and thief."

All we have learned in the last few decades about infants, genetics, and how experience and biology shape one another has overturned these convictions. (For details on how nurture and nature intertwine in brain development, see chapter 9.) We now know that infants come into the world as active learners capable of paying attention to what interests them. They recognize faces, sounds and voices, smells, and touch. Within a few weeks, they can remember very simple events and can recognize and respond to familiar people. Far from being passive blank slates, babies are actively engaged with their world from their first moments after birth and even before. (See "Learning in the Womb," page 202.) Newborns come into the world equipped to make some basic distinctions among shapes, smells, and sounds. Each

baby is preprogrammed genetically to try to engage adults' attention and to react to their care — the first step of learning. From this a child goes on to describe and exercise his imagination, to learn language, and to go to school — all of which we cover here in part 4. In this chapter, we discuss the ways in which your baby or young child both perceives and makes sense of the world of social interaction, of the people who provide the most influential experiences in his first years, if not throughout his life.

How Your Baby Senses the World

Your baby's perceptions include all the ways in which he gains a quick, immediate awareness of what is happening around him. Immediacy is a key quality in perception for people of all ages — information comes through your senses most of the time without your being aware of it. You see, hear, smell, taste, and touch your environment nearly every waking second. You know where your body is in relation to the rest of the world through the sense called "proprioception": this tells you whether you are still or moving, how close your hands are to your head or your legs, and (when combined with your sense of balance) whether you are in danger of falling down. Yet you hardly ever have to think about any of these powers of perception.

Think about them now. Take a moment to tune in to all your senses. Feel how much information flows into your brain each sec-

ond — temperature, light and darkness, background and foreground sound, the bend of your spine, the clothes resting on your skin, this page beneath your fingers. Overwhelming, isn't it? Stimuli come from the world close beside you (where you are sitting and the few feet in each direction) and from great distances (the sunlight on your window, the sounds of wind and traffic outside). Over many years, you have learned to sort out stimuli, to focus on those that are most important to you.

As an adult, you can also change what you sense by walking into another room, going outside, or telling the kids to quiet down. You can use the perceptions that you have stored to re-create hearing, seeing, tasting, and feeling in your imagination. By combining bits of past perceptions, you can create new imaginary experiences when you read a book or listen to a story: thus, you fill in the experiences of, say, "a dark and stormy night in Denmark"

or "huddling with a lover during a blinding snowstorm" with sensory information you have stored in your mind.

Your newborn does not have the power to move around and change her immediate sensory world. Nor, at least in the very beginning, does she remember or anticipate experiences. Newborns and very young infants live in a completely immediate sensory world, which they learn about at first totally through their senses. As a baby comes to know how her mother and father smell, look, and sound, she learns how those sights, smells, and sounds are linked to her feelings of being hungry and then satisfied, cold and then warm. Linking sensations with experiences is one way the baby begins to connect meanings with what she perceives. Most important, this is how she comes to have special feelings for her parents and other caring adults.

Newborns enter the world especially ready for social interaction. Their sensory systems are pretuned to the sound of human voices, the shape of human faces, and maternal smells. Your newborn's readiness to interact with you pulls you into that game very early. In a way, a baby brings out the parents in a couple, getting each of you to supply exactly the sort of experiences that his central nervous and sensory systems are most ready to receive.

"Can't Take My Eyes Off of You"

If all goes well, from the first hours after birth, an infant is visually alert and learning about the world through her eyes. For nearly all of us, a baby's gaze is captivating. Just for the reward of a moment's look from a baby, adults will behave in all manner of ways they probably would not otherwise — blowing bubbles, making exaggerated faces, saying short phrases like "pretty baby" over and over in a high, slow voice.

Instinctively, it seems, you look into a baby's eyes for clues to his feelings, intentions, and interest — just as you look into other adults' eyes. Indeed, in some cultures it is said that "the eyes are the windows to the soul," or that someone with an "evil eye" can control other people's lives just by looking at them. Parents often interpret their newborn's glances as having great significance: "You could see it in his eyes — he loves me." "Her eyes lit up when her grandmother walked into the room." "Maybe he's sick — he doesn't look at me the same way this morning." Parents think of an alert, highly sociable baby as having "bright eyes." "Weak eyes" sometimes seem to mark the very tiny or sick baby in the premature nursery.

Vision, including the brain system that controls how information from the eyes is processed and stored, is the most carefully studied of all the sensory systems in newborns and infants. The visual abilities of a newborn are even more developed than popular beliefs claim. Furthermore, these abilities are especially adapted to social interaction. For newborns and very young infants, a human face commands far more attention than does any other stimulus. Even cartoons of faces, or circles with two dots for eyes and a line for a mouth, are interesting to babies. If a baby is shown a cartoon face on which the eyes and nose are switched from their normal positions along with an unaltered cartoon face, she will look longer and more often at the drawing that is closer to reality.

From birth, babies scan faces carefully, but over the first months, a baby's pattern of visual scanning changes. Researchers tracing infants' eye movements have found that a newborn is most captivated by borders — the outer edges of the face or the edge of the hair against the forehead. By two months, infants look far more intently at specific features — eyes, nose, and mouth — but focus most intently on eyes. Around this time, many parents report that their baby suddenly seems different, more interested in them, more involved in the world, maybe even more like a real person. This feeling seems to reflect the baby's newfound ability to look directly at her parents' eyes, not just at their faces. Once infants can take in the specific features of a face, they can begin to recognize familiar people just by their faces. (Until then, infants recognize their parents through a combination of sights, smells, sounds, and other clues.) Babies at four to five months can also distinguish different emotional expressions — a smile and a frown, an angry face and a bored face.

Hanging on Your Every Word

Learning to listen is a different sort of challenge. When you look at something, you take in many characteristics simultaneously — size, color, shape, distance away from you. When you hear, information tends to come bit by bit, or sequentially. For parents and infants together, sound is one of the most important elements in play and in expressions of love. Hearing lets an infant feel comfortable even at a distance from her caregivers; their voices in another room assure her that they are nearby even if she cannot see them. Hearing also conveys feelings, but sometimes the shadings of an emotion are harder to pick out in the speech you hear than in the faces you see.

While you can turn to a sound and refocus your eyes, concentrating on a particular sound out of all those coming into your ears is a task for the brain to sort through. Infants seem able to exert the effort to turn toward a sound selectively and have an innate ability to pick out specific sounds. Newborns will turn toward the sound of a human voice in preference to a nonhuman sound of the same pitch and volume. It even seems that early in life the brain starts to process speech sounds in a special area apart from other sounds, a fact that lends further weight to the idea that newborns come pretuned to social information. Newborns are particularly open to the higher-pitched frequency of the female voice; adults intuitively speak in this tone when they address a baby. Within a few weeks of life, an infant is even able to pick out his own mother's recorded voice from among tape recordings of strangers. Such back-and-forth communication is the earliest step toward learning language. (We trace the full development of language in chapter 17.)

Music is a particular sort of sound — rhythmic, melodic, and patterned — that appeals to both babies and adults. Singing, whistling, humming, and playing musical instruments all stir powerful feelings in people.

When you make music, you encourage listeners to join in your rhythm. Furthermore, the brain tends to link musical sounds to emotional experiences. A grandmother humming as she cooks, the jazz playing softly as a father writes, or a mother's quiet lullaby remain etched in the mind from early childhood.

From the first days of life, babies start to combine what they hear with how they move. As with their other forms of interaction with the world, this behavior appears most naturally with a newborn's caregivers. Infants seem to coordinate their movements with the rate and rhythm of their parents' speech. When films of parents doing such basic daily activities as diapering or bathing their babies are played back to those babies at slow speeds, the infants appear to move in synchrony with the speed and the rise and fall of their parents' distorted speech. It is almost as if the baby is trying to use movement to join in with his parents' talking and singing.

I've Grown Accustomed to Your Smell

Smell is an ancient sense. The area of the brain that receives and stores information on smell (the "olfactory cortex") is one of the oldest regions. It develops early in gestation and is similar in structure to the same area in other mammals. The olfactory cortex is close to and extensively connected to areas involved in memory recall and emotional experience. Thus, smells can trigger nearly instantaneous associations to memories and feelings, to longing, comfort, fear, uneasiness, joy. The hint of a familiar perfume reminds you of past loves, of parents and grandparents. Chocolate cakes in the oven may make you feel warm and loved, evergreen trees and kerosene can always mean summer camp, and the sharp smell of rubbing alcohol might immediately take you back to a pediatrician's office.

Newborns show preferences for certain odors and turn away from others. Even one- and two-day-old infants are able to recognize their mothers' smell. Using two pads soaked with women's breast milk, researchers found that a one-day-old baby will turn toward the pad containing his mother's milk. (Mothers can also reliably pick out the aroma of their own infant as they sniff cotton shirts worn by different babies.) While other mammals rely on smell even more than humans do to locate and recognize their infants, this sense may still play a very important role in building the relationship between mother and baby in their earliest hours together.

Coordinating the Senses

Imagine how distressed you would feel if you turned to a familiar face and heard someone else's voice come out of it. Your reaction at such a mismatch reflects how closely the brain links various sensory experiences. When you walk down the hall and change direction to avoid a chair, you are linking vision with your sense proprioception we mentioned earlier. When you hear a voice and pick out the speaker's picture, you are coordinating hearing and vision. Or, when you can quickly feel out an object in the dark that you saw in the light, you are linking touch and vision. Even newborns have this complex

and multilayered linkage among the senses, or "cross-modal" perception. An eight-hour-old infant is able to watch an adult and copy simple facial movements, thus using vision and proprioception. By one month of age, an infant can pick out by sight a pacifier that she has previously not seen but only felt in her mouth.

Cross-modal perception is extremely important for learning and for social interaction at all ages. Adults take conversational cues from other people's tones and look to see if their faces express the same emotion. If there is a match, they respond directly to the emotion; if words and expression do not match, they naturally feel less comfortable or start to watch closely for further clues.

Even by his first birthday, your infant is developing the same useful ability: he is both looking at and listening to his parents. During this first year, he becomes more skilled and efficient at tying together all the information he receives through different senses. By around eight months, infants can match up the words they hear at a particular speed with the film showing the corresponding mouth movements. They can also pick out the right facial expression for the emotion being expressed on a sound track, matching an angry expression with an angry voice or a smiling face with a happy voice.

Learning How Your Baby Makes Sense of the World

For every human being, from newborn to senior citizen, learning requires at least three steps: paying attention to and recognizing new information, processing mental images by sorting and grouping them, and creating memories. These steps allow infants and adults alike to progress from receiving sensory input to being able to act on it. As with all mental skills, the ease with which a child accomplishes each step depends on both biological factors and the stimulation that her environment, most especially the interaction with family members, provides.

Tuning In and Forming Mental Images

As the first step in learning, an infant needs to pay attention to, or focus on, something or someone. This is a matter of selection, and it is an effort for an infant to filter out the other stimuli he is getting from his senses. If sleepy or worried, he most likely will not be able to accomplish even this first step.

Paying attention actually involves several smaller steps. Once a child or an adult has selected something to examine, he needs to pay attention long enough to see, hear, feel, or smell the essence of that thing. This is called "sustained attention." Different areas of the brain are important and active in each of these steps of attending, and each depends greatly on the preceding one. Your child cannot study something carefully before she has picked out what she wants to study. And she cannot pick out something before she has actually slowed down and tuned in to the world around her.

As a baby or a young child studies some-thing for a sustained period of time, he forms a mental image of what he is studying. This image may be visual, or it may be made up of the sound, feel, or smell of the object or action. Forming that mental image or making a notation in the brain ("encoding") is the second step of learning.

In a very important part of this encoding, the baby compares the information she is currently taking in with what she has previously encoded. If she already has a mental record of the thing before her, she can give it less attention than she needs to give something new. "Been there, done that" is the most powerful method for learning about the world; you benefit from quickly sorting out the new from the familiar. This use of memory is both efficient and protective. Imagine how overwhelming life would be if every time you walked into your home, you had to look around carefully as if seeing the place for the first time. You could never catch up, never quite "learn" anything. Fortunately, the comparison of what you are sensing with what you have sensed before occurs in a split second and unconsciously. If you already have the object in your memory, you move on. If not, you pause, though you will rarely, if ever, be aware of this process.

Sorting the World: Primary Colors and Shades

Even before you actually commit something to memory, you place what you are seeing, hearing, feeling, or tasting into categories. These "mental files" are another essential part of the process of taking in information. Like home or office filing systems, your mental categories need to be fairly efficient and quickly accessible. If you have a recipe collection, you probably do not sort dishes by the number of ingredients or the date on which you first tasted each. More likely, you arrange your recipes by types of food (breads, main dishes, desserts) and possibly by main ingredients (fish, noodles, broccoli). Similar guidelines work for how you categorize things in your mental files.

Just as in your home and office, from time to time you change or reorder your filing system. You learn better "rules," or you learn so much about a topic that you need a much more complex and subdivided system. You might start out planning to be a parent, for instance, by thinking in broad categories — infancy, grade school, high school, and college — but pretty soon you realize that each grouping covers a bit too much ground, and you divide them up further.

Children go through the same process. A two-year-old who learns that doggies have four legs and a tail may start putting every quadruped with a tail into her mental file for "doggie." But as soon as she sees a lot of animals (and hears a few corrections from her parents), she learns that filing system is not very helpful. By the age of four years, most children have developed many mental categories: real animals and stuffed animals, wild animals and tame animals, cats and dogs, lions, tigers, and bears.

Remember, too, that you also cross-reference your filing systems: your recipe collection may contain dishes to make with zucchini, entrées that take less than an hour, or foods that were popular at the last potluck. You could have four, five, or more levels of cross-indexing, depending on how deep you want to get into a system. Those cross-references allow you to pick out different items depending on which factor is most important to you at the moment. Adolescents learn to sort classmates not just by sex but also by who is in a relationship at the moment. For young children, animals may be mean or nice, soft or squishy, long before they are doggie or non-doggie. Thus, not only does your child refine mental categories as she grows and learns, but she continues to tailor them to fit in each period in her life.

Even before words, babies are finding categories for their experiences. Though not expressed verbally, these categories are available in an infant's mind as ways to sort the world. We can only guess at what they are. There is good evidence that even one-month-old babies can distinguish between sweet tastes and pungent tastes, for instance; but those sensory distinctions do not appear to be the main categories in their mental filing systems. Rather, infants probably start grouping memories by emotions rather than perceptions: "things that make me cry," rather than "loud things" and "sharp things." At the very least, some of a person's earliest memories seem to be powerful linkages of basic senses and emotions: the smell of a burning woodstove on a cool fall afternoon may trigger the feeling of closeness to a distantly remembered grandparent.

As a baby has more experiences, she may

start to file feeling hungry with the sensation of being fed to comfortable, sleepy fullness. She may group cold with being wrapped up in a soft blanket and held tight. And she will associate both of these experiences with the grouping of sights, sounds, and smells that she has come to know as her mother or father. Thus, as an infant gets older, the people in his life become more than the conglomeration of their particular sensory qualities; their identity includes the consequences of their behavior as well.

Memory

Remembering — pulling memories out of a person's mental filing system — is basic to all learning and to all human relationships. Yet to say you "remember" something covers a lot of ground. Everyone has had the experience of recognizing someone's face but being completely unable to recall that person's name. Sometimes the opposite happens: seeing someone whom you have not thought about in years lets loose a flood of vivid memories. You might recall the tune of a song but not the words, the words but not the title, the title but not the singer — or hearing three notes might bring you back to exactly where you were standing and exactly how you were feeling when you first heard that song.

These are examples of different kinds of memory. "Recognition" memory makes experiences resurface when you encounter someone or something familiar. Recalling something without a concrete reminder, however, is a more complex process. Another kind of memory involves knowing how to do

something even if you cannot recall the steps of learning that skill. Walking, riding a bicycle, and playing a musical instrument are common examples. While you surely learned each of these skills step by step, each remains as the memory of an entire process that cannot be broken down into the components that led to it. (For how memory also depends on healthy sleep, see chapter 13.)

Parents have many questions about their infants' early memory abilities, including the one with which we began this chapter: What is a baby thinking? When you first look in your newborn's eyes, you may wonder whether she will recall that moment. Will she even recognize you tomorrow? How long do babies retain a memory? How much experience with something do they need before they remember it? Later, parents ponder whether their growing child will retain the family stories or last week's spelling lessons. For that matter, will he remember where he left his shoes? On the other hand, as your children grow, you may sometimes worry that they will recall events you would rather protect them from.

Analyzing infants' powers of recall is difficult because they do not form memories using words. Nevertheless, we know that eight- to twelve-week-old infants are very active learners. They demonstrate recognition memory for persons and repeated events. They smile and become excited in anticipation of a familiar routine: a three-month-old may begin to smile at the very beginning of a nightly bubble-blowing game with his father or at the first sounds of his regular bedtime lullaby. As infants become older, they require much less time to remember a picture they have seen before. Five- to six-month-olds can recognize a brightly colored pattern after looking at it for only a few seconds.

How long can an infant remember something she has encountered only once or twice? At four weeks, newborns seem to remember particular speech sounds or phrases for up to two days. The three-month-old has a much better memory and can recognize a picture up to a week later. By six months, a baby typically recognizes photographs of faces for two weeks. Infants seem to use the same memory strategies that adults use. You depend a lot on surroundings: you can easily recognize a person you have not seen in a while if she appears where you are used to seeing her, but she can seem like a stranger if you see her in a very different setting. Infants rely on the same types of clues. If you show a baby in a crib a brightly tinted mobile, his ability to quickly and accurately recognize the same mobile a week later will be affected by changes in his environment, such as changing the color of his sheets or the bumper guard around his crib.

Learning Styles: It Takes All Kinds

Newborns immediately demonstrate differences in their styles of learning, in their curiosity about new people and things, and in their energy for seeking out novel experiences. An individual style of approaching the world appears within a baby's first hours. Some newborns seem almost always ready to look at, finger, or listen to something new.

They gaze with seemingly bottomless interest at every new face and appear to gobble up the world with long, intent looks. When this same child is older, he runs toward a new toy and immediately explores it from all sides. In contrast, other babies are quieter, more reticent, perhaps even cautious in their approach to new things. As newborns, they look briefly and quickly glance away. When they are older, they may stand back and watch a new toy from afar before they approach. Slowly, as they grow more at ease, they poke gently and peer more closely. Most babies seem to learn in a mixture of these two styles, sometimes with energetic abandon, at other times with discriminate care. (For more on such differences in temperament, see pages 302–304.)

These different styles of learning are not particularly related to speed of learning. Many adults associate excited reactions and intent gazes with intelligence and a good memory, but shyer babies who take more time to explore new things usually learn just as much about them. The learning styles are important, however, in how parents come to play and interact with their babies.

Helping Your Baby Learn

Today you hear everywhere that parents should read to their babies, play music for them, give them interesting pictures and objects to look at, provide toys and surroundings with varied textures, and even seek out playthings that pose problems for the infants to solve. You may have been told that the more such sensory and intellectual stimulation you provide, the brighter your child will be — and the more likely to become a successful adult. This wisdom would have parents believe that if they engage in constant intellectual nurturing and make themselves always available and extremely attentive, they can create a "superbaby."

The idea that you can stimulate your baby to be smarter is based on findings about infants in severely deprived environments — where, for instance, a child is kept in a crib day after day with little adult contact other than feeding. Such newborns usually do suffer delayed development, but researchers have found that these delays can be overcome when the children receive attentive nurturing and an extra dose of sensory stimulation. But it is a mistake to reason from that good news that *all* babies benefit from so much extra attention. Nevertheless, many toys, magazines, and other products are sold on the basis of that idea, and parents are deluged with information about how to help their infants learn faster and develop to their full potential. (See "Sights and Sounds: Toys for the Newborn," page 120.) Even in your child's first year, some authors say, you can make her a quicker, more eager learner. This puts unrealistic pressure on mothers and fathers to stimulate their baby continually and to provide as many learning experiences as early in life as possible.

The most basic ingredient for healthy learning in infants is a warm, reliable, protective relationship with their parents. Babies learn best when they feel well cared for and know that their parents will be there to take care of them. Probably the single most important activity you can do to help your baby learn, and to make the world seem enticing to him, is to talk. Long before he can respond with words, telling your baby about all that is going on around him puts words to experiences and feelings. Many studies have shown that babies whose parents have used every opportunity to talk to them are more active and curious explorers in their second year and also begin to use words earlier. (For a longer discussion of talking to children in their first year, see pages 230–234.)

On the other hand, there is no solid evidence that *extra* stimulation makes a baby raised in normal, loving circumstances more competent. In fact, a deeper question is whether babies can be *too* stimulated. More is not necessarily better. Infants, like older children and adults, need downtime. When babies are asked to be alert for hours on end, they often withdraw by going to sleep, looking away, and becoming more irritable and harder to take care of.

What, therefore, is the best amount of stimulation for your child? The most important measure is how much you enjoy the activities you share. When you are emotionally involved in your play, and not feeling bored or dutiful or anxious, your infant will be more involved, too. Playing with your baby in ways that you both enjoy is the best way to stimulate her senses and her thinking. Therefore, if you like listening to Mozart, by all means play Mozart as you rock your infant. But if you prefer to sing along with Ray Charles, there's no need to choose Mozart instead. The games, books, and other products that keep you and your child interested are more useful than those "recommended by experts" for children in general.

As you get to know your infant, as you play together, you will learn the clues that tell you she is overstimulated or tired — that she has had enough for now. All babies (and adults) have their own thresholds for stimulation. Some of us need more quiet, while others can play for hours. Indeed, one's pattern of seeking stimulation and novelty may be a characteristic that persists through infancy into adulthood. Thus, there is no one correct way to stimulate your baby. Find what works for you and your baby, and remember that all babies have limits as well as needs.

The learning your baby does in his first year sets the stage for the next important developmental milestones. Talking and reading to him introduces him to language and communication. Exploring the colors, sounds, and textures of his world is his earliest play and the foundation of the curiosity that will serve him well in school. In your daily care of and love for your baby, you begin to build her confidence and provide her with the security that will stand her well as she starts to learn about the world around her.

CHAPTER 16

Child's Play: Child's Work

Six-year-old Douglas's glasses and quiet demeanor made him look serious and studious, old beyond his years. But when he sat down with his collection of plastic dinosaurs and building blocks, it was as if Indiana Jones had come to life. Douglas was both playwright and actor in a drama that spanned centuries, defied gravity and natural history, and earned the admiration of his parents and teachers. So vivid and carefully crafted was his play that everyone wondered whether Douglas was headed toward a career as a writer.

Janice, on the other hand, seemed to have great trouble playing. When the children in her nursery school invited her to join them on the fire truck (actually the big couch) or to dress up like their teachers, this five-year-old shook her head and sat aside, clutching her favorite doll. The nursery-school teachers became concerned. Obviously, Janice was well developed in many areas: she was speaking well, even reading one or two simple books on her own. But her discomfort in the imaginary games that engrossed her classmates

hinted at trouble. Indeed, the teachers knew that Janice's family was going through great trauma: her mother was in treatment for cancer, and when the little girl's father picked her up each day, he always seemed frazzled and depressed. Apparently, with that sort of confusion at home, Janice did not feel safe about throwing herself into pretending. And yet her teachers thought that imaginary play was just the sort of activity in which she might be able to sort out what was going on at home.

We feel that healthy child development is closely linked to a full, vigorous imagination and imaginative play, as in the case of Douglas. This has not always been an accepted point of view. Not so long ago, fantasy was discouraged, imaginary play and even fairy tales were thought to be harmful, and having an imaginary friend was considered a serious sign that a child had a poor sense of reality. Daydreaming took up too much time, allowing a child to ignore the practicalities and realities of life. Children who daydream, experts said, must be unhappy and unable to accept themselves and their life's circumstances. This conviction was even used, up to the early part of this century, to justify putting children to work. And from time to time today, these old admonitions about time wasted on idle play and dreaming still crop up in advice to parents and even in curriculum for young children. Nonetheless, it is now generally accepted that imagination and imaginary play are vital and should be nourished as both the earliest expression of creative thinking and the practice ground for a child's emerging social and cognitive skills.

What Is Play?

Play, broadly defined, covers many activities. There is the rough-and-tumble of children running, jumping, chasing, and wrestling with one another, which is amazingly universal across most cultures and even across different species. The young of many animals engage in forms of rough-and-tumble play, which seems particularly useful for teaching children and pups alike how to cooperate and interact with one another. There are verbal forms of play that are uniquely human, in which children play with sounds and words, even inventing their own language and rhymes. Manipulating and exploring toys and other objects (rocks, leaves, shells, worms) is a form of play in which, through trial and error — looking, feeling, tasting, listening — young children learn. Babies enjoy peekaboo, hide-and-seek, and the ever-popular game of dropping things off their high chairs onto the floor — all ways to explore how things seem to disappear and reappear.

Pretend play begins around age two, or just before children are able to let a real object stand for either another object or something imaginary. When your toddler begins to brush her doll's hair, it is the very beginning of her ability to pretend. She is using a toy (a doll) with a real object (a brush) to represent what you do for her. When she starts to feed the doll with a spoon, smacking her lips loudly and blowing on the spoon to cool the soup, she is going one step farther: she is "representing" imaginary food. And when she offers that food to another doll or an adult, the full ability to pretend — to represent her mental world through play — is in flower.

Children's pretend play varies remarkably in quality, content, intensity, and degree of engagement with other children and adults. In part, a child's developmental maturity defines the type of play she is capable of. Very young children under three years of age often play alone with a toy or other object. They may roll a truck around, making authentic truck sounds, even providing appropriate warning beeps as they back up. But they make no special effort to invite others to join their play. Even if they allow a cherished adult to join them, they are not interested in other children's help. In "parallel play," which is also characteristic of children three years of age and younger, two or more children play by themselves but close to each other. They may even use similar toys, such as a bucket and sand, but they are not playing with one another. They are simply in close proximity. If both children want the same bucket, you will soon discover that they have not yet learned to share and cooperate.

Children three to four years old begin to engage one another. They do share toys, pass them back and forth, even talk about the same activity and follow one another. Their play is still not completely cooperative, however. A preschooler who has no real companion nearby may evoke an imaginary friend as a playmate. (See pages 346–347 for more about imaginary friends.) When children are around four years old, they begin to engage one another in games in which they share a goal and a story. They assign roles, direct action, even carry stories and games from day to day. This is the blossoming of play, both in its imaginative qualities and in the cooperation that children now manage almost without thinking about it.

The ability to pretend requires the ability to symbolize — to let one thing stand for another, just as a picture of a car stands for a real car. The ability to translate from a symbol to its meaning is a critical part of human life and communication. You know that an octagonal red sign or a blinking red light means, "Stop your car and look for traffic before moving ahead." Lighted exit signs tell you where to look for a door even if you cannot read the word "exit." Hand gestures can communicate, "Follow me," "Look at that," "Good job," or "Stop immediately." When your child begins to create symbols or representations, she can enter a more complex and layered world of social communication, where imaginative play flourishes.

A child learns to use symbols in several different levels, or stages. In the earliest, a baby picks up a spoon and touches it to the edge of a bowl. She thus shows she understands this object's use (the action a spoon is associated with), even when she is not using it for that action. A later variant on this stage starts when a child "eats" from an empty spoon and looks with a smile to her father as she nibbles. Similarly, a toddler can act out sleep, closing his eyes for a few seconds before looking to see whether Daddy is watching. This is early evidence for game playing: these children are pretending in ways related to themselves. One toddler communicates through smiles and giggles that she knows (or is at least pretty sure) that her parents also

FILLING THE TOY BOX: WHAT IS THE PROPER TOY?

The toy business is a billion-dollar industry. You will hear that you must have this set of blocks to accelerate your toddlers' learning, or that type of dress-up set because children cannot pretend without it, or this video game because, well, because all the other kids at school have it. If sometimes you are unable to avoid giving your child the faddish toy of the moment, mix it in with more tried-and-true and diverse play materials.

And keep in mind this general principle: the more a toy encourages children to use their own imagination, the better (and, probably, the cheaper). Blocks, Legos, and construction sets are all examples of toys that let children build and create what they see in their mind's eye (as well as what they see on the boxes). Crayons, markers, clay, and construction paper are also materials that encourage children to use their own imagination.

When your child is ready to pretend, your task as a parent is twofold. First and foremost, be prepared to be an enthusiastic audience. Second, provide the three types of playthings she needs to inspire her imagination:

- Start with miniature or play versions of common objects like telephones, movie cameras, cash registers, stethoscopes, dining sets, plastic food, and so on. These do not need to be expensive, battery-powered devices that really work: your child's imagination will be all the power she needs. Most children like cars, trucks, and other vehicles, both the little kind they roll with their hands and the larger bikes they push or pedal. All these toys are made for just this sort of pretending. (On the issue of toy guns, see page 228.)

- Supply some costumes. Hats are most exciting and easy to take on and off as roles change. Children also appreciate clothing that older members of the family have outgrown or worn out, and it helps if you can pin or hem the legs and sleeves so your child does not trip over them. Shoes and costume jewelry, the gaudier the better, are always useful for dress up. Children also enjoy playing with makeup and face paint, though obviously you will want to supervise these explorations closely.

- Equally important are such raw materials as big cardboard boxes, egg cartons, plastic containers, and pads of paper. Parents sometimes joke that children enjoy the box a toy comes in more than the toy itself, and often they do. Children turn boxes into everything from TV sets to tombstones as they enact the dramas of their day.

know that there really isn't food on the spoon, while the other shows that he really isn't asleep. One action represents another. A preschooler who pretends to feed a doll, put it to bed, and read it a story shows that she is capable of a more complicated level of pretense. Her parents can build on this skill. They can join in reading the story, be sure the doll is tucked in, wonder whether it is having good dreams or will wake up and want a glass of water. By adding to the game, you join your child in this new type of communication.

When children begin turning one representation into another, such as by turning a cup into a spaceship or a stick into a tooth-brush, their pretend abilities have become even more sophisticated and consequently open up more avenues for expression. Parents, indeed all adults, may have a hard time playing with children who are at this level of pretend. You may want to be more basic or concrete than your child and inclined to say things like, "Oh, that's a cup, but I guess it can be a spaceship," or, "Be careful with that stick! It might be dirty." Of course, you need to be sure children are safe during their pretend play. But if your child is capable of this level of pretend, she is probably clear about what the real object is and does not need to be reminded all the time. Talking about things as they are rather than as what they might be is a natural behavior for you as an adult, who has, in many ways, set aside your ability to imagine impossibilities in order to cope with day-to-day realities. But if you keep reminding children of the difference between real and pretend, they sometimes stop their play as if they have gotten the message that the adults important to them find their play disturbing, or at the least, not an appropriate, safe activity. While returning to imaginary playing with your children may take some getting used to, enjoy the invitation. Let yourself, in entering into your child's play, suspend the reality of bills, school, promotions, and getting older.

Imaginary Play

Children's cognitive ability to let one thing stand for another, and to enjoy different levels of pretend and enter whole scenes and stories, is a part of the necessary cognitive foundation, or scaffolding, for a remarkable developmental phase. Between about three to seven years, if all goes well, children are master dramatists. They are completely engaged in their imaginary world and in playing out their thoughts, fears, and wishes, even beliefs. In some ways, a five-year-old with a highly developed ability to play and pretend is like a reflective, introspective adult: where the adult puts thoughts and fantasies into words, the five-year-old puts them into play and action.

For those of us most concerned with how children feel and what goes on in their inner worlds, the capacity for imaginary play opens a window into how a child's mind is taking shape. What a child "means" in her play is more important than all the mental or cognitive feats that make play possible. It's like stock car racing: no matter how well honed the engine of each car may be, the race goes to the driver who can visualize his car on the track, feel how it is performing, and imagine the possibilities for using that engine. A child's ability to represent, to pretend that a bottle is a boat or a spaceship, is the engine that drives her play. To make fullest use of the possibilities of play, she revs it up. The more she is able to drive her imaginary car, the better she will know what she can do in her imagination and how far it can take her.

In play, children practice development. In their imaginary games, they test out and master various developmental challenges. When children play school or waiter or doctor, or try on their parents' professions for size, they are

JOSH'S ACCIDENT

Four-and-a-half-year-old Josh was very active and imaginative. Even at three, he had pretended to be many things: cowboy, pilot, firefighter, builder. He liked to climb the sturdy maple tree in his backyard, which had several low, heavy branches. The older and stronger Josh got, the more he moved up the tree. One afternoon, he missed his footing and fell about two feet to the ground, breaking his arm. Josh's mother, who had been working in the garden when this accident happened, quickly bundled him up to go to the local hospital. Before they could get into the car, however, Josh insisted that his mother bring his favorite cap with the space shuttle patch on the front and one of his tiny toy airplanes. Josh, though pretty scared in the emergency room, pretended to be cool. He said he was a pilot whose plane had crashed, but he had managed to fly the plane to a good landing spot so that the machine was not too badly hurt. The emergency room doctor worked efficiently, taking an X ray and showing it to Josh, assigning him small tasks to "help" in preparing his cast.

When Josh and his mother got home, he stood for a few minutes staring quietly at the tree. He stayed quiet all night, ate little supper, and insisted on going to sleep with his cap on and his plane collection close by. For several days afterward, Josh brought out some old stuffed animals, including his favorite, well-worn tiger, and made them characters in a drama full of falling from rooftops, crashing planes, rescues, and recoveries. He was at once doctor and injured, frightened and scared, invincible and vulnerable. His old tiger had every leg wrapped with white paper and tape and was in the "hospital" for weeks. Sometimes firefighters were standing ready to catch the falling characters; other times, they let them crash to the ground. Through these days, Josh wore his cap, barely looked at his cast, and was reluctant for anyone to touch his arm or comment on it. Gradually, he started to move his fingers and even went back to the tree and climbed one-handed onto the lowest limb. Finally, one evening at supper Josh asked his dad to draw a plane on his cast, maybe even two planes, two jets! As his dad drew on the cast, Josh asked for the first time, "How long will I have to wear it?"

In his play, Josh had worked to master many feelings — his fright, his worry about whether his arm would work again, his surprise that he fell. Josh's mind was working on very serious matters even though his worries arose from his imagination as much as from the real event of the fall and his broken arm. Only after working through his worries was he ready to face the reality. Young children see themselves as invincible, and at the same time worry terrifically about scratches, cuts, and bruises. A small injury is a bigger injury to their sense of invulnerability and being all-powerful in a world that is nonetheless much bigger than they are. Josh had to work out many questions: Was he injured because he was bad? Did he do wrong by climbing a little higher in the tree than his parents had said he could? What if his mother had not been close? Did those X rays take a picture of his thoughts and feelings as well as of his bones? Would he ever grow big like his father? Who would protect him when he climbed the tree again? What would his arm look like when the cast came off? Josh couldn't put these worries into words; some he was probably not even aware of in his own private thoughts. But he was able to put them into the words and actions of his play.

using play to understand these situations and experiences in much the same way — only more actively, visibly, and often far more elaborately — as you daydream for many an hour about a new job, your home, or a love relationship.

By repeatedly telling the story of a major change in their life, such as the birth of a new sibling or of some traumatic event, children adapt to and learn from those real-life experiences. In play, children can also try out solutions and options that would never be tolerated or even possible in their real home. They can return their new baby brother to the hospital, leave him for dwarfs or witches to find, even feed him to wolves. In these ways, they can both express their dismay at having to share their parents with a new baby and play with their fantasies for solutions. In his play, your child does not necessarily directly reflect what has happened to him. He can tell a real story or, like any good fiction writer who uses scraps of his own experience to tell an imaginary story, weave bits and pieces of real events into whatever larger story makes sense to him at that moment.

In giving children a venue for practicing new learning and social skills and an outlet for expressing worries, play is also a safe way for them to try to understand the world around them. (See "Josh's Accident," page 219.) Through their games, children try to figure out where babies come from, what happens when grown-ups go to work, why mothers have to go to hospitals to bring home a new brother or sister, what happens when grandparents get sick, if children are really

old when they go to school, what being married is all about, how cars run, and where the dinosaurs went.

Sometimes what is going on in a child's mind can totally surprise adults. Five-year-old Victor was playing with a new student teacher at his nursery school. Victor got the teacher to join him in a game of cars and weight lifting. He told the attentive adult about his special strength and bravery and invited the young man to admire how high he could lift a toy car. Then Victor said that his mother's Honda was badly hurt. He became sober for a moment and started to ride the toy car back and forth with vigorous race-car sound effects. Gradually, over a few minutes, the student teacher heard the story of how Victor's mother had been in a car accident: the car was hit; Victor's sister, Cassie, was in a car seat; Victor was in the backseat. His mother was scratched a little, but Victor was very brave: he helped out, and everybody was all right except the badly damaged Honda. The teacher listened sympathetically, making the right statements about how scary all of this must have been, how brave Victor was. To all of this the boy nodded seriously and whispered, "Yep." Soon he changed the subject back and invited his teacher to join in a vigorous game of who could lift the blocks higher.

For all the world, Victor's play seemed to tell a story of a dramatic and scary event — just the sort that a preschooler would work out in play. And just like an adult trying to avoid thinking about something painful, Victor changed the subject when he had approached his limit of being able to think about it. When the student teacher next saw Victor's mother, he said how sorry he was to hear about her car accident and glad that she and Victor's sister were all right. Victor's mother looked puzzled: there had been no car accident. Victor did not have a sister named Cassie, or any sister at all. The entire story came from the little boy's imagination.

Victor was not intentionally lying or trying to fool his teacher. In fact, children of this age are still hazy about how and why people say false things. Rather, in their stories and dramatic play, preschoolers assume roles that are uppermost in mind at the moment. To a child this age, the line between reality and pretend is fluid enough to allow him to step into an event that is, for a time, real and lively. Possibly Victor heard another child talk about a car accident, or saw one on television or while driving with his parents. His story may serve as an effective way for him to proclaim his own bravery and strength as he tried to make sense of how scared and how powerless he often felt in general. He may have created this story to talk about other feelings he needed to think about in play, even how to deal with this young man who had come into his nursery school.

At some point in their early school years, children move away from acting out imaginary play and begin to tell stories as a way to express their fantasies. Their imagination does not fade, but they begin to rely more on daydreams, structured imaginary games, and written narratives to express their innermost thoughts and feelings. It is as if once children

understand the world of private thoughts and daydreams, they do not need to express so much through action. They become able to think privately and reflect on their fantasies and inner concerns. Your child's imagination continues to be active as she grows up, and the more imaginative preschoolers go on to be imaginative school-age and adolescent children. A vigorous, wide-ranging imagination in early childhood is one likely hallmark of a creative teenager or adult.

Creativity

Creativity and imagination are not one and the same, though they share some common ground. Imagination is literally the process of forming images in one's mind, both the old and familiar images you bring up to comfort yourself and new scenes and objects no one has seen before. Only the latter are usually considered creative.

Psychologists and social scientists have tried to define both creativity and what makes a creative individual. While there are many definitions, there is some consistency among them. Most agree that creativity involves forming new combinations out of familiar materials or ideas, combinations that provide a new way either of seeing or achieving a goal. These combinations may bring together very diverse materials or ideas, such as applying an engineer's point of view to sculpting or computer programming to music. Sometimes the composite that results is so significantly new and different as to change a field completely. Thus, when the psychologist Jean Piaget asked how children know what they know and tried to understand children's learning processes in and of themselves, he applied a philosopher's perspective to the study of child development. Before Piaget, psychologists simply accepted that because children's minds were immature, they did not see the world as adults did. Piaget's work made clear that, if one accepts a different way of thinking and viewing the world, children's "errors" are not errors at all. His novel perspective opened so many new lines of inquiry that it completely changed how teachers and child developmentalists view what children say and do. (For more on Piaget, see pages 90–91.)

Another characteristic of creativity may be the ability to think flexibly and spot several potential solutions to a given problem. Creative thinkers see many sides to a situation and employ so-called "divergent thinking" (as opposed to "convergent thinking," which aims for a single, correct solution). Many adult creative thinkers are seemingly more imaginative than their peers as young children.

In one of the various tests for divergent thinking, children are asked to list as many uses as they can for a brick. Both the number and the diversity of responses matter, especially the ability to cut across typical or standard responses. Besides suggesting bricks for building, for example, a child might say they can be used as paperweights, decorations, bug squashers, foot warmers, conversation pieces, anchors, charitable gifts. There is a clear parallel to a child's flexibility in how he or she uses play materials: whether a cup is more than a cup but also a boat, a hat, a spaceship, a house, a cave, a hiding place, and so on. Although some children are naturally more flexible in their play than others, you can support and encourage your children's attempts at creative approaches to play materials by accepting and even being curious about the cardboard box that is a castle or the old stick that is a magic saber.

The Child Who Cannot Play

Pretend play is as necessary for a child's healthy psychological development as are learning to read and the other basic school tasks, and it also actually helps children to learn and to adapt socially. It is, therefore, significant when a child cannot or does not play. Autism is one condition that cuts a child off from being able to use play to make sense of the world. (See pages 126–127.) But there are many children who, although they have all the necessary cognitive scaffolding and have mastered the representational or symbolic skills, still do not play imaginatively. Sometimes the minds of these children are overwhelmed by chaotic or stressful events in their lives.

To understand such a child, think of how you respond to times of extreme stress. You probably do not daydream much or at all; you may not even dream much at night. In order to play and dream, you need some space and time. When worries and stress are high, you (and your brain) automatically go into a vigilant mode, as if you were afraid and responding to danger. (For more on this response to fear, see chapter 22.) This extreme alertness cuts off your ability to use imagination and daydreaming as ways of problem solving, managing emotions, and relaxing. The same is true for young children who cannot play: their external reality crowds in on them mentally and emotionally, depriving them almost literally of the room to learn to read their own thoughts and feelings. Because their external lives are so rushed and stressed, their time to daydream, imagine, and reflect upon their mental world is foreshortened. In this tragic situation, children who are caught in the middle of a divorce, or whose parents are fighting constantly or are depressed, or who are growing up in unsafe neighborhoods with little sense of security, often cannot play. Sometimes children who have anxious personalities are also unable to play well. They feel their anxieties so intensely that they seem paralyzed, unable to talk in their play or to free themselves of their worries. If your child is otherwise developing normally but is not able to play, counseling may be necessary. Psychotherapy or some other intervention can help children become sufficiently free of their worries to find once again the mental space and time to play imaginatively. (See chapter 33 on children's mental health.)

Allowing Space and Time for Your Child's Play

You can be the producer but not the director of your child's drama. In other words, while you should provide the space, time, tools, and occasionally the companion or audience necessary for games, young children supply the imagination. In fact, directing your child's play does not give her the full opportunity to choose the topics she will explore or the directions her stories will take. Too much intervention, teaching, or structure, or too little time to play, robs very young children of the freedom they need to follow their natural bent.

Toddler's Play

Toddlers, as we have said, are naturally curious. They are scientists, explorers, inventors, engineers, and artists all combined. Space for toddlers to play in need not be elaborate. They do not even need a separate room, especially if they are still working on separating from their parents. (See chapter 31.) But your toddler does need a space where he can be as messy as he wants or needs to be. A corner of your kitchen close to you is sometimes preferable to a room of his own, where he is alone. Toddlers also do not need a roomful of elaborate new toys. They can spend hours exploring boxes, pots, and pans, and connecting blocks. A boxful of scraps of cloth, jars, smaller boxes, or cardboard tubes will allow for a lot of exploring and combining.

Indeed, simple toys often go a long way with toddlers who are interested in patterns and enjoy sorting things by shape, color, size, and other attributes. Children of this age are very detail-oriented. When they receive a set of toys, they will study each piece individually before starting to play with them together. Their fine motor skills are improving, so this is the time to try a set of building blocks that snap together. Simple and durable puzzles, of the sort in which children put a boat-shaped piece into a boat-shaped hole, are another way to exercise these instincts. Every successful restoration of the original pattern will be a triumph.

At this age, you should not put much effort into making playtime educational. It is equally important for older toddlers (as well as preschoolers) to have the chance to play with toys that stimulate their imaginations. Even though a child of two does not have the language skills to create sophisticated stories, she usually enjoys walking little plastic people through their daily life in a little plastic house. And her ability to invent new games means that even playing in a sandbox can be a mental workout as valuable as reviewing her numbers.

Since very young toddlers are just beginning to learn how to explore and combine objects, including toys, some simple help from you can get your child going in interesting and exciting ways. For example, showing her how toy cars can roll in and out of a box ("the garage") opens up the endlessly interesting game of in and out, filling and emptying. You may also want to try to follow your child's lead or set the stage for a game without necessarily playing all the parts: "Here's the car. What else can we do with the car?" On other occasions, you may want to expand a bit on your toddler's play by showing her other things she can do with the things she's playing with. Remember that toddlers have a short attention span: they do not play the same game more than a few minutes at a time and can casually abandon what a moment ago entirely engrossed them.

The line between real and pretend is still hazy for your toddler. Stuffed animals can talk, demanding to stay up late or taking the blame for trouble. When a battery-operated toy talks and moves, however stiffly, she suspects that it is somehow alive. Seeing the same monster or animal on television in even more animated form can confirm her suspicion. But as she grows, she gradually comes to distinguish between real people and animated objects, though she still enjoys pretending and wants you to play along. This discovery tends to parallel your child's even more important realization that other people think and see things differently from the way she thinks and sees them. (See chapter 10, "Your Child's Unfolding Mind.")

Two-year-olds may spend a fair amount of time on their own with their toys, but they also want to be sure their parents are generally in visual range and definitely within earshot. Your toddler may be comfortable if you are reading, cooking, even writing close by. From time to time, he will check in and even invite your help and companionship. Very young children also often need physical help with opening a jar, retrieving a toy, moving a chair. You may want to put a request into words: "Oh, the car rolled under the cabinet, didn't it? You need me to help you get it out." The aim of this speech is not to get a two-year-old to speak in such a complete sentence, but to let him get used to hearing how his desires can be expressed in words. Similarly, you can comment on his play without taking over or directing it: "You found your shovel. Are you digging in the sand?" This gives a child the verbal frame on which to hang and expand her actions. (See chapter 17 for more on language development.)

Another quality of older toddlers' play to keep in mind is that they do not easily share or cooperate. When they pedal around on their tricycles, they will not take turns. When two- to three-year-olds play in the sandbox, each should have his own bucket and a shovel. Gradually they will get better at playing together, starting in pairs and then small groups. (See chapter 24 on friendships.)

The Imaginary Play of Older Children

The space needs of preschool (three to four years) and early school-aged (five to six years) children are different from those of a toddler. After a child turns three, it is usually not necessary to show her how to play anymore. At any moment she may be riding a pretend horse or rolling a ball or being a Mommy. Indeed, a preschooler can turn almost anything into a game, even cleaning up her blocks in time for supper. Older children can also be by themselves more and do not need to check in quite as much with their parents. While they may want Mom and Dad to admire their creation or their game, they spend longer periods playing either with other children or on their own. Older children also may need a space where they can keep a set of toys — a toy army or a dollhouse or a little town — arranged in a particular way for several days. They may come back to this setting, repeating or continuing

the same story like the director of a movie serial. Therefore, if a child at this age does not have his own room, he still needs a place out of the house's traffic flow to set up his toy set. And even when a young child has her own room, she may choose to play in another part of the house because it feels more comfortable or it better serves the needs of the story uppermost on her agenda.

When children of different ages are playing in close proximity, parents should encourage each to respect the other's space. A younger child is likely to grab something belonging to an older child, or begin to explore and mess up things that the older child wants only to himself. The older child's wish to keep all his toys set up as he left them may conflict both with the younger child's wish to be a part of the game and with her lack of fine motor control. If the elder somewhat resents his sibling simply for having arrived in the house, this small conflict can quickly escalate into a screeching turf war. On the other hand, some children can reach remarkable compromises to respect each other's priorities. One group of youngsters was observed running around with a smaller boy roaring happily in their midst. "We're playing cowboys and Indians," a little girl explained. And what role did the small boy have in their game? "He's the dinosaur."

Just as young children need space for their imaginary games, they also need time. If they have a heavy schedule of directed activities — from day care to dance class to swimming lessons and back home for dinner and bed — children do not have enough time for planning and playing. Children need sufficient time just to play and learn how to entertain themselves and explore on their own, whether they are writing a short story or a poem, painting a picture, working on some other project, or just daydreaming.

A common time-drain for young children is television. The moving images can mesmerize them for hours on end. Some people worry that television shows stifle children's creativity by encouraging them to play in only one way, that is, re-creating the stories they see. But parents can usually observe their children either making up new stories for TV characters or using the stories they see as springboards for new games. The real problem arises when children spend so much of their day watching television that they have little time left for playing their own games. Limiting the number of hours your children sit in front of the television and talking to them about what they see are more important and more practical than keeping television out of their lives altogether.

Children like to play actively outdoors starting at about age three. Slides, a jungle gym, a soft spot to jump onto (either a mattress or a sandpit) are all popular. The equipment should be flexible enough to keep up with a child's physical and intellectual abilities. A two-year-old, who does not have the coordination to pump himself on a swing, will need you to push. Many four-year-olds not only can swing themselves higher and higher, but also wonder what it would be like to jump off at the height of their arc. A jungle gym that has several ways to play — a ladder,

a slide, a pole, a hanging bar, and so on — will get more use than a simpler platform.

At age three, your child also begins to use art supplies to express himself. He sets out to draw Mommy and Daddy, though you may not immediately recognize the resulting squiggles. This interest and ability is due in part to a three-year-old's increased fine motor skills and in part to his increased ability to imagine and plan. As preparation for school, children should be taught certain basic skills: how to hold a crayon or thick pencil, how to cut paper with child's scissors, and how to paste one scrap onto another. The art your child actually produces should still be up to her.

In the year before kindergarten, children come to value patterns and rules enough to play simple board and card games. However, they do not like losing (not that anyone does) and it is often more fun to play simple games like Concentration, in which you have the shared goal of finding every pair of cards, rather than to compete openly. When a child is ready to play against you "for real," she will let you know. Do not assume that simply because your child is advanced enough to read the rules to a board game, she is also sophisticated enough to understand those rules and their strategic implications. Board games test many skills. Since there are a wide variety to choose from, you can select an appropriate challenge for every developmental level.

Preschoolers sometimes invite parents to join in their imaginary play in a particular role. Remember that your young child may still be sorting out how much you know and

If your child has an invisible friend or playmate, or projects distinct personalities onto his toys, he may enjoy having you play along with this game. How comfortable you feel may depend on your energy level, willingness to join in an obvious fiction, and your suspicion that your child is trying to get away with something (such as blaming trouble on his unseen companion). It is best to view the invisible friend as another story your child is telling as he works through the mysteries of his life. Imaginary friends tend to disappear by early school age, as pretending wanes as the primary mode of play.

may assume that you know exactly how he wants you to play. When you are handed a cape or a hat, it is wise to ask, "Who should I be?" or "What would you like me to do?" In this way you encourage your child to direct you and to help you follow his lead by verbalizing the scene or story in his head. Imaginary play is not always a story in logical chapters: it may hop from scene to scene, without any plot, rising or falling action, or logical conclusion. A child may suddenly end a particular play sequence because it seemed too scary or worrisome at the time. Or she may simply have gotten bored with it. Follow her lead. Finally, remember that your child's play is not necessarily telling a "true" story about her life. A game about a mean teacher does not mean that her day-care provider yelled at her today; it may be your child's way of preparing herself for the scary jump to kindergarten or simply enjoying being in charge of other children.

After they enter school, children often stop being actors and start being directors. Instead of dressing up as doctors, princesses, and space fighters, they tell their stories through little toy people and animals. Many school-age children spend most of their time manipulating what we might call "miniature worlds." These may take the form of little cars traveling between a racetrack and a garage, a fully furnished doll's house, a plastic street lined with tiny shops, or a space station complete with blinking lights and aliens. Children's growing awareness of sex roles may well influence the type of miniature world they choose, but whether the little people are labeled "dolls" or "action figures," the form and benefits of playing with them are much the same.

Play is your child's work. Indeed, perhaps

THE TUG-OF-WAR OVER TOY GUNS

Parents often debate how strictly they should forbid their children to play with toy guns. There are, indeed, many sides to this issue. You may choose never to give your child such a toy. But would you prevent her from buying one with her own money or bringing it home as a gift? Does your prohibition extend to plastic soldiers, sci-fi laser pistols, antique toy cannons, or video games that involve shooting? Are toy guns that shoot nothing but are designed to resemble real weapons better or worse than huge water squirters?

You may choose not to provide your child with any toy gun, but that will not prevent her from ever playing at shooting. Children do not need toy guns for that game; cardboard tubes, sticks, and their fingers work just as well. And children are likely to come across toy guns at their friends' houses or other places.

Most important, you should recognize that toy guns do not produce aggression in children. A desire to play with them is an expression of the aggressive or angry feelings children already have and are learning to deal with. Nevertheless, you are right in thinking that to give a child such a toy sends a message about what you consider to be a legitimate way of playing and acting. If you shoot recreationally yourself, you probably have even more reason to ensure that your children do not view guns as toys in any way. And with so much concern about guns today, you may want to stress that your child's toy gun is just that, a toy like a toy car.

we should apply the phrase "child's play" not to things easy, or frivolous, but to the most difficult and challenging tasks humans engage in: solving problems of all kinds and honing and concentrating one's social and cognitive abilities. In play, your child has an opportunity to think about and work through day-to-day dilemmas like leaving you to go to day care or going to the doctor. Children who enjoy the mental and physical space and time to play imaginatively learn more quickly, are often more socially skilled, and are more likely to continue to be creative and curious for the rest of their lives.

CHAPTER 17

First Words and Beyond: How Children Discover Language

A single mother, worried that her thirteen-month-old son was saying nothing more complex than "Da da da . . . ," sought advice from a specialist. Since children normally speak their first words when they are between nine and eighteen months old, she was told that her baby was well within that range. It's fun to imagine how a single father would respond to "Da da da": "You said, 'Daddy!' Yes, I heard you — you said, 'Daddy!' " But the "da da da" sound is in both cases as likely to be meaningless "vocal play" as an attempt to say, "Daddy." Hence, this father would be just as unrealistic as the mother in assessing his child's language skills. The big difference is that the father's enthusiastic response would encourage the baby to try more sounds, where the mother's wouldn't. This is a good example of how parents shape their children's language development.

Communication is, by definition, a two-way process. What you say to your baby, how you listen, and how your baby sees you respond all influence language development. This process starts well before a child's first word. Nearly from birth, your child sends messages — in glances, in sounds, in facial expressions and behavior. Parents usually sense this: "I think she looks up when she hears us come into the apartment." "I was feeling down, and he almost seemed to understand." "If she doesn't like something, boy, does she let us know it!" These observations are scientifically sound: many basic language skills seem to be rooted in innate capabilities.

An infant's instincts are matched by his parents' attempts to stimulate his ability to communicate. Most parents are highly pleased when their child develops a facility with language. "I'm so glad Rebecca and I can finally talk!" a mother might say of her three-year-old. "My oldest said something really clever yesterday," a father might tell friends at work. Parents around the world seem to speak to their infants in similar ways that stimulate more, as well as more sophisticated, speech.

As language and communication skills build rapidly and steadily in the first three to five years of life, they draw children and parents closer together, at least until adolescents begin to test their improved skills in argumentation. In this chapter, we will discuss the earliest communication through babies' sounds, the toddler's discovery of names and love for labeling the world, and the preschool child's construction of sentences and simple stories.

The First Year: Communication Without Speaking

Even before infants start talking, they engage in a great deal of communication. They take in information about their environment and express, as best they can, their needs and pleasures. Far from being a blank slate on which adults chalk the rudiments of language, an infant acts to rivet adults' attention and elicit positive responses. This makes evolutionary sense: being able to attract an adult's attention, maintain a social relationship, and evoke caring helps an infant survive. Otherwise, a baby would be merely a helpless, noisy, and rather unproductive member of society.

As every parent knows, a newborn's principal form of vocal behavior is crying. (See also pages 65–66.) Crying is mostly involuntary, a response to some distress the child feels. Although effective at making adults take notice, it is limited in what it communicates. Parents, especially those who hear a lot of crying, may be unaware of the other ways their newborns are sending messages. Infants seem to begin life with a natural preference for linguistic interaction: in other words, they want to communicate. Furthermore, newborns seem to have a common set of behaviors that cue adults to interact with them. These behaviors are so widespread and appear so soon after birth that they seem to be innately programmed.

The Sound Foundation of Language

From the first days of life, infants prefer to hear sounds in the same frequency range as human voices; and within that range, they prefer speech to other rhythmic and musical sounds. (See "Motherese, a Common Language," page 231.) When your newborn hears a voice, he looks for its source, his face registers pleasure when he finds it, and he becomes quiet and still until the voice ceases; he does not do the same when he hears other sounds. A three-day-old infant can distinguish her own mother's voice from the voices of other women.

Newborns are also attracted to human faces. They will always choose to look at a face instead of any interesting but nonhuman object, and typically their own face registers pleasure at the sight of a human face. Conveniently, parents interpret this behavior as a sign of an infant's willingness to interact, and they provide more stimuli — talking, touching, and making faces in response — to keep up the "conversation." The newborn infant thus appears to be biologically organized both to tune into human communication and to attract language input.

Naturally, you wonder how much of what you say to your newborn is really getting through. Research has shown that babies as young as four weeks old have surprising capacities for processing ingredients of language. (See also chapter 15.) One interesting study used pacifiers hooked to tape recorders set to play human speech. When infants from one to four months were pleased by the sound from a tape recorder, they naturally sucked faster on their pacifiers, a reaction that caused the tape recorder to produce more of the same sound. When the babies became tired of a sound, they slowed down their sucking. At that point, researchers could switch the recording. If the infants heard a different sound, they started sucking faster again. If they perceived no difference, their sucking stayed slow. Thus, researchers could tell whether these infants could discriminate one bit of speech from another. By this method, we know that most babies early in their lives can hear the difference between *pa* and *ba,* for example, but have a somewhat harder time with *za* and *sa.*

One remarkable finding is that young in-

MOTHERESE, A COMMON LANGUAGE

How do you talk to a baby? If you're like most adults, you slip into the conversation style we have come to call "motherese." Parents who speak motherese, both mothers and fathers, address their babies in a higher pitch than they use with older children and other adults. They speak more slowly, with shorter sentences. They exaggerate the ups and downs in their intonation to create a singsong quality. The results — quick earfuls of high, varied sounds — seem to match what infants most easily process. Babies prefer to listen to motherese — even if spoken by a stranger — over normal adult speech.

Furthermore, though Ameri-cans seem to speak motherese with more pronounced ups and downs, parents around the world use a rising inflection to catch their baby's attention and a falling inflection to soothe her. Mothers who speak Chinese, in which tonal ups and downs help determine a word's meaning, sometimes break those rules in order to speak motherese. Even deaf mothers communicating to their deaf infants in sign language make their gestures slower and broader; deaf six-month-olds seem to prefer videotapes of such motherese to ordinary signing.

Baby talk is a form of motherese: "Baby has a tum-tum. Toot widdo baby tum-tum." Variations of this speech also appear in many cultures. There does not seem to be a biological justification for it; newborns cannot understand baby talk any better than regular speech. Nevertheless, this harmless form of motherese seems to have an important function in making parents feel closer to their infants.

Parents continue to speak a form of motherese past a child's first birthday. They still use exaggerated intonations, but start to emphasize the real words for things the child can see. They pause between words and keep their sentences focused on the immediate surroundings and activity. As toddlers grow older and more sophisticated in their speech, parents move ahead as well, consistently speaking in the style of a child about six months ahead of their own. Thus, at each stage in a young child's life, parents naturally seem to communicate in the way that best encourages new language skills.

fants can distinguish between bits of speech that sound the same to their parents. For instance, Thai uses consonants that are not used in English; an English speaker would have no need to differentiate between them. When playing these sounds for babies from English-speaking families, however, researchers discovered that newborns heard the differences. Since these children could not have picked up the distinction from their environment, they must have been born with the ability to discriminate between certain sounds. Further research showed that children usually lose this "multilingual" ability by age one year. Older babies who hear nothing but Chinese do not respond to *re, ra,* and *ri* as different because those sounds are not used in Chinese. We can thus conclude that infants are born with the ability to make certain predetermined distinctions between sounds and with an all-purpose linguistic readiness; but as they get older, they retain only those sounds that help them sort out what they hear in their families.

Young babies pick up other clues necessary for normal spoken language. An infant as young as two months often takes turns in vocal interactions with his mother, staying quiet while she talks and making noise after she pauses. In another test, researchers showed eighteen-week-old infants pictures of the same woman articulating two different sounds, *a* and *i*. They played one of these sounds through a speaker located exactly between the two pictures. The babies looked significantly longer at the picture showing the mouth position that matched the vowel they were hearing, and thus showed that they were combining visual and aural information. Around seven months, babies seem to become attuned to the auditory clues that adults insert into sentences to tell listeners how phrases fit together, and prefer looking toward the voice of someone reading sentences with normal pauses rather than with irregular phrasing.

How to Stimulate Language in Your Baby

Being naturally prepared to learn language is, of course, not the same thing as actually learning it. "Wild children," who grow up without meaningful adult interaction, have consistently developed little or no language abilities, even after they are discovered and given intense remedial training. On the other hand, children in a bilingual environment usually have an easier time learning a second language than adults do and are less likely to speak it with an accent. A child's early years thus seem to be a critical period for learning language, and early interaction with parents is the seed of most communication skills.

The "conversation" between parents and their children starts early. As early as four weeks after birth, a wide-awake baby looks intently at an adult face and makes sounds, sometimes imitating her parents' intonation. (See "Baby Sounds: What Does 'Goo Goo' Mean?" page 233.) By three months, infants vocalize more with their mothers than with other adults. As your baby grows older, however, the human face holds less fascination.

BABY SOUNDS: WHAT DOES "GOO GOO" MEAN?

From cooing to babbling to baby talk, infants learn to produce meaningful sounds from their mouths through a series of discoveries. For their first eight weeks of life, newborns can make only a narrow range of sounds. Their mouths are small, their tongues large, and their throats not yet developed to shape air into syllables. The sounds they do make are natural outbursts. When a newborn cries, burps, or sneezes, she is not trying to communicate — she is simply letting out an instinctive reaction to feeling hungry, gassy, or stuffy. Often, especially at first, parents respond to these noises as if the infant meant something by them. That attention may be an important way that newborns learn they can use sound to communicate.

Between the ages of two months and five months, a baby's head and neck grow, allowing him to produce more sounds. Two particular forms of noise, both pleasing, appear in this period. The first is a baby's laugh, usually a response to a pleasantly predictable interaction, such as playing peekaboo with Mommy or seeing Daddy ready to tickle. The other pleasant noise is cooing, a sign of comfort. At this age an infant is simply making the easiest sound he can. As he leans back, his tongue is naturally pulled against the roof of his mouth, the first step in producing the consonant we hear as "g" or "k." Since the easiest vowel for infants is "oo," this gives us the classic "goo goo" sound. Again, parents usually respond enthusiastically to hearing these syllables, encouraging the child to try more.

From about four to eight months, infants are in the stage of "vocal play." They begin to pronounce different simple syllables: "ga," "boo," "nuh." After six months of age, they often babble strings of the same syllable: "bababa." Their growing mouths allow them to try out a wider range of consonants, most commonly *b, p, t, d, m,* and *n,* produced in the front of the mouth. Babies making these sounds do not attach meanings to them. They are simply playing with the muscular and aural process of making noises. Unlike cooing, infants do not emit these sounds principally to respond to or attract attention from adults; in fact, they often wait until they are alone before they start babbling.

It is significant that, until this stage, deaf babies vocalize in much the same way that hearing babies do. As vocal play begins, deaf babies try out a smaller range of consonants. They cannot hear the interesting results of their efforts, so their repertoires shrink further over the next year as hearing babies add more sounds. Babies raised by parents who use sign language to communicate, however, have been found to "babble" in sign language, trying out simple hand movements the way hearing babies play with syllables.

Around the twelve-month mark, many infants start to reuse the same sounds consistently. For instance, a baby might always make the *m* sound when reaching for a toy or a bottle, indicating that he wants it. These are not words, since no one else uses the same sounds in the same ways. They are "protowords," the last step before that monumental first word.

Along with their first two or three words, infants begin trying a more sophisticated type of babbling. They string together different sounds, instead of repeating one: "bata," "aga," "bap." More consonants, including *s, f,* and *v,* appear around twelve months. During a child's second year, words and babble usually coexist, with the latter gradually falling away as she realizes which sounds provoke the best responses from her parents.

He looks at you when he wants to interact, but looks away when he feels tired or overstimulated. This reaction seems to push parents into modifying their behavior in order to keep their child's attention: they stretch their faces into exaggerated expressions, talk more, and vary the intonations of their voices more. In turn, your three-month-old responds by making sounds of her own. In this period, a mother often spends time trying to elicit more sound from her infant. She pauses after every statement, repeats words, and adds intonations that turn her sentences into questions that beg a response.

As we discuss in chapter 10, a baby develops intentions at about eight months. She starts by following a parent's gaze to a particular object and eventually can direct her parents' eyes by looking at objects in the same way. Also at this age, she points at what she wants. Between eight and ten months, although still communicating mostly through gestures and not words, she begins to realize that language is a wonderful way to get her parents to fulfill her intentions. She may even develop her own symbolic vocabulary, waving her arms excitedly up and down to represent a favorite toy kangaroo, for example (and also imitating her parents' playful demonstration of how a kangaroo hops).

As their child develops these capabilities, parents often believe their infant understands more than he really does. While you can make a baby as young as six months stop what she is doing by saying "no" in a clear, sharp voice, saying "yes" or any other word in the same tone probably has the same effect. Not until about eighteen months do most children understand a prohibition, and they do not really begin to understand words out of their usual context until about eight months of age. When a mother says, "Look at the ball. Get the ball. Bring Mommy the ball," to her infant, she might interpret her son's looking, crawling to the ball, and holding it out as an indication that he understands those sentences. More likely, even if he is as old as a year, he is simply following his mother's gaze, crawling to the ball that grabbed his attention, and then responding to his mother's outstretched hand.

As soon as their baby reveals that she wants to communicate, parents start asking for more. They no longer interpret every sound or gesture as part of the conversation. Usually a one-year-old infant's parents demonstrate what they hope she will say by speaking the proper words aloud. Even when a couple can guess what their older infant wants, they may instinctively withhold that response until she expresses herself through language. Parents thus shape their infant's skills and desires into language.

The Second Year: Words and More Words

The second year is a remarkable time for your child's language development. Her eagerly awaited first words foreshadow her grasping the idea that objects have names and that other people understand those names. She can ask for a "cracker" or "juice" just by using the name. Her next step is to put words together into short phrases and sentences. Even the phrase "my bear" is the beginning of a sentence and a story. It says there is a toy called a bear that your toddler declares belongs to her.

First Words

The average child says her first word and takes her first step around the time of her first birthday. A one-year-old's vocabulary is small: she may understand fifty words but speak only three. Those three words most likely refer to objects she plays with, such as *shoe,* and activities she regularly does, such as saying *bye-bye.* A few more abstract words commonly appear, but they usually also have quite concrete meanings for a young child: "No," "Here," "Fun!" As we discussed in chapter 7, a twelve-month-old baby is not yet sure that an object still exists when it disappears from her sight. For that reason, even if she knows the name for an object her parents ask her to find, she may not be able to respond if she cannot see it.

Over the course of their second year, infants expand their spoken vocabulary. This growth comes in fits and starts. The first fifty words build up slowly, and often children seem to plateau around this point. They may even drop some of the words they have learned. Children's word acquisition is also channeled by the types of sound they can easily make. It is easier for them to come out with a new word that begins with a sound they already use; thus, a child who knows *bat* will pick up *ball* quicker than *glove.* And children under two realize that their most powerful vocal communications are still nonverbal. In other words, if your child does not want to do something, he may well scream instead of trying to state his feelings.

By eighteen months, the average child uses between 50 and 150 words. According to one study, a vocabulary spurt follows for about three out of four children. A two-year-old probably uses over 300 words and understands up to 1,000. (A child using fewer than 50 words at this age is at risk of having a chronic linguistic handicap.) Toddlers also send more messages than they did a year before: on average they communicate five times a minute instead of once. The words that two-year-olds speak are usually more complex, with two consonant sounds together and two or more syllables (as in "Grandma"). Most of a toddler's new words are nouns and are usually things she can act on. Thus, since a two-year-old can take off her shoes but needs help with her shirt, she usually learns the word *shoe* first.

Only about 70 percent of a two-year-old's words sound correct by an adult standard. And the meanings infants attach to their words may differ from the dictionary meaning. For instance, they may call every four-legged animal a "cat," even those that have horns and give milk. Two-year-olds often know the names of several colors, but have not sorted them out. If you ask, "What color is the ball?" your toddler will usually name a color, but not always the right one. Such mistakes in the second year may be part of a strategy to feel out the meaning of a word: a child observes adults' reactions so he can refine his understanding.

Creating Sentences

The next process in a child's language development is the creation of sentences. At first, their messages are single words. These can be as meaningful as a sentence — "Up!" for "Please pick me up because I'm tired of walking" — but easier for little mouths to get out. The next stage in sentence forming, around eighteen months, is to string two or three words into telegraphic messages: "Want cookie," "More cookie," "Two cookie!" By the end of that second year, a child's sentences can be three or four words long, but still telegraphic: "Mommy ball" might have grown into "Mommy throw ball." Again, the child's meaning is clear even if grammatical elements are missing.

A typical toddler's sentences reflect her interests and limitations. Because two-year-old children do not have a real understanding of time, they do not express ideas about what will happen soon or what happened yesterday. If you ask, "When did you eat lunch?" your toddler may well answer "Yes" or "Hot dog!" because the word *when* means little to her. Two-year-olds usually understand the concept of a question, but express one with a rising intonation — "Doggie mad?" — instead of shifting the words grammatically. They also know the word "no," but use it as an all-purpose negative: "No go bed," "Mommy no

bye-bye." Interestingly, though different languages have different ways to form a negative, toddlers in all cultures start by attaching a one-syllable word like "no" to their sentences.

Infants aged twelve to eighteen months usually talk about what is right in front of them, and rarely add information that an adult observer cannot perceive. They have a hard time carrying on a conversation past two or three exchanges, especially if they did not start the topic. By the age of two, however, children are more sophisticated about how they use language. They give their parents new information. They start asking for the names of things — "Whazzat?" And they realize that different words can express the same idea: "I thirsty," "Want juice."

In vocabulary, toddlers probably understand three times as many words as they use. In sentence structure, however, the gap between understanding and use is much narrower. A two-year-old's brain can process only so many sentence elements at a time, whether she is speaking or listening. Parents sometimes believe otherwise because children in their second year are good at picking up clues from context. For instance, a father might tell his twenty-month-old daughter, "It's time to put on your jacket." The little girl recognizes *jacket*, sees her father at the front door, and recalls that when they go out Papa wants her to wear a jacket. Away from that context, her father could have said the same words without getting through at all.

Parents respond to their toddlers' new communication abilities by further modifying their own conversational style. Their sentences are still short and simple, but usually grammatical — often more grammatical, in fact, than their speech to other adults, probably because they speak more slowly and carefully to a toddler. Research shows that stimulating a dialogue with children is one of the most effective ways to help them increase their language skills. Seeming to understand this, most parents ask many questions that focus on what the child is doing: "Do you have a ball? Where will you take the ball?" They echo a child's statement exactly, often prompting her to repeat it: "Dolly sleep." "Dolly sleep?" the parent asks. "Dolly sleep!" the child might declare. Parents can also expand what a baby says into a complete and grammatical sentence, encouraging the child to do the same. Thus, a little boy might say, "Juice gone." His father replies, "Yes, your juice is all gone, so now we will wash the cup." The boy might reply, "Juice all gone," adding a word to his original sentence, or might echo, "Wash cup," adding a related idea. Even if he remains silent, he has heard how his message can grow. This sort of interaction comes fairly naturally to most parents and very naturally to most toddlers.

While two-year-olds rely on parents to structure a conversation, they can manage their own response more easily. They know that a one-second pause, especially at the end of a phrase, indicates that it is their turn to speak. They are better at sticking to a topic, though in this case "better" means only that about half their statements are responses to what they last heard. If an adult does not understand a one-year-old and asks, "What?" the conversation is likely to break down, but a toddler may repeat herself, sometimes simplifying or correcting her sentence so that her listener understands.

A two-year-old has also learned to speak differently to different people. He might, for instance, talk to babies in a high-pitched voice as adults do, and address his parents differently from other people. A child this age, however, also assumes that adults know everything; he has learned to distinguish his own mind from others. (See pages 131–134.) Thus some of his remarks will not contain enough information for another person to understand. A two-year-old might hold up a sticker and tell a parent's friend, "I got this from Shirley," without explaining who Shirley is.

The Third Year: Building on Words

Researchers have found that English-speaking two-year-olds amass grammatical building blocks in a fairly regular sequence. First, they grasp how to turn *walk* into *walking* to express something happening right now. They learn that adding the *s* or *z* sound to nouns can make them multiply (*books*) or possess other things (*Daddy's*). Next come simple prepositions — *in* and *on*. English speakers start using articles — *a, an, the* — relatively late. (In contrast, children learning Spanish often master the equivalent *el, la, los,* and *las* early, perhaps because those Spanish articles stand out more in everyday speech.)

Two-year-olds also acquire a larger vocabulary of words that connect or compare the things they see. They are likely to understand many spatial terms: *in, through, next to.* They understand some simple adjectives, usually starting with *big* and *little.* They nail down two or three colors. Most can ask questions beginning with *what* and *where,* and some know *who* and *how* as well. While one-year-olds use "no" as an all-purpose negative, toddlers learn how to use *can't* and *don't,* often before they use *can* and *do.* Two-year-olds are also likely to start using pronouns, especially to refer to themselves.

A growing vocabulary allows two-year-olds to produce more elaborate noun phrases. You may hear your toddler using words to modify nouns, as in "my hat" or "red hat." At three years old, children can even try two modifiers together: "my red hat." After age three, they also learn to use these phrases within a sentence, usually at the end: "I put on my red hat." (They are less likely to use complex noun phrases at the start of a sentence: "My red hat is dirty.")

A similar process turns toddlers' verbs into more powerful communicators. Rather than simply putting the simplest form of a verb into a sentence — "Mommy wash duck!" — they start to use helping verbs. At first, these are nongrammatical forms like *gonna, wanna, gotta.* Toward a child's third birthday, however, she will begin to use *can, will,* and other grammatical helping verbs. Three-year-olds also learn the past tense of irregular verbs, such as *came, went,* and *saw.* When the past tense sounds more like the present tense, as in *wash* and *washed,* a young child is likely to miss hearing the difference. (The use of future and past tenses reflects another discovery of the three-year-old: the passage of time.)

It is rare for toddlers to ask someone to clarify a statement they do not understand. Instead, they interpret sentences that contain unfamiliar words or phrases by guessing at the most likely meaning. Thus, a two-year-old who does not know the word *beneath* will probably translate "Put the cup beneath the table" into "Put the cup *on* the table" because the latter action is more common. When asked to act out an improbable sentence such as "The dog is feeding Daddy," a toddler is likely to portray Daddy feeding the dog.

Parents' natural interactive strategies develop along with their children's abilities. Both an eighteen-month-old and a two-year-old might exclaim, "Girl dolly!" when they see another child's toy. The younger child's mother is likely to expand that brief utterance into a sentence: "Yes, that girl has a dolly." The mother of a two-year-old typically responds in a similar way but also asks for a response: "Yes, that girl has a dolly. Is it bigger than your dolly?" Neither mother explicitly corrects her child's statement, but the second one implicitly asks for more. She models a back-and-forth conversation and cues her older child about what to say next. (For parents' explicit teaching of language, see "What's the Magic Word?" page 241.)

In their third year, children still often drop unstressed syllables from words ("nana" for *banana*) or substitute an easy consonant for a harder one ("doddie" for *doggie,* "sair" for *chair*). It takes time for them to learn how to run consonants together, as at the start of "play"; by age two, a child usually has a few such words in his vocabulary, but combining more consonants, as in "scrape," can take another year or two. Similarly, by age two, a child is probably using some multisyllabic words, but most, even favorites like "spaghetti," remain challenging. The most common pronunciation difficulties involve the late-developing consonant sounds: *l, r, th,* and *s.*

Parents who thought their two-year-old's baby talk was cute often start to worry if the same child is still mispronouncing words as his third or fourth birthday approaches. The child is probably aware of the proper way to say a word; his challenge is to find the right combination of moves in his mouth to make that sound. Imitating a child's pronunciation annoys him, both because he dislikes being teased and because he wants grown-ups to pronounce words correctly. One boy who had trouble with the sound *r* responded to such mimicry by complaining, "Not 'wabbits' — *wabbits!*" You will be glad to know that only about 5 percent of children enter school with a pronunciation problem, and when they do, it is usually confined to only one or two sounds.

In their third year, children learn the many different ways they can use language. They are no longer simply expressing immediate needs or trying to stimulate a response from their parents. They are also conveying new information, talking about the past, stating their intentions, and even pretending. (See also chapter 16 on play.)

The Preschool Years: Discovering and Applying the Rules of Language

By the middle of her fourth year, your child can express herself much more like an adult and much less like a telegraph machine skipping a few letters. This is the time when your child begins to explore the rules of language — how to indicate more than one dog, show his ownership of a toy truck but not of the toy shovel, put two thoughts together, and convey that something is already past or an event is still to come.

Preschoolers' vocabularies are growing fast. Some researchers have estimated that preschoolers pick up new words at a rate of nine a day! They tend to expect each of those new words to have a unique meaning. When preschoolers learn a synonym for a word they already know, they often try to assign a different meaning to it: "An automobile must be a big car," for instance.

Among their new words are some expressing relationships in time: *before, after, since, until,* and so on. They can ask questions with *why, how,* and *when* and answer such questions correctly though it still helps them to see the person or the object a question concerns. Four-year-olds have also added more adjectives to their vocabulary; with pairs of adjectives, as in *thick* and *thin,* they usually first learn the word that denotes the larger measure. Preschoolers also start to use *more* and *less,* though at first they might mix these up, using both to mean "a different amount." By age five, children have mastered comparative and superlative adjectives: *tall, taller, tallest.*

Preschoolers also amass a larger repertoire of helping verbs: *could, must, might, were.* They rarely use two at a time, however, as in "I *could have* finished that." Three-year-olds probably grasp *can't, don't, isn't, won't,* and other simple negative helping verbs. By age four, however, children are using *wasn't,*

wouldn't, couldn't, and *shouldn't.* At the same time, they are learning negative noun forms such as *nobody, no one,* and *nothing*; it is common for children to combine two negatives, as in "I didn't do nothing." Preschoolers start to use helping verbs to form grammatical questions: "Can I play now?" More challenging questions involving negatives or demanding more than a yes/no answer can cause them to misplace the helping verb: "Why I can't have ice cream?"

In constructing sentences, four-year-olds begin using clauses, not simply adjectives, to modify their nouns. They usually start working on the objects of their sentences: "I liked the monkey that swung on a rope," but not "The monkey that swung on a rope was funny." Preschoolers also start building compound sentences: "I want corn *because* it tastes better than lima beans." However, a sentence like "Before we eat dinner, you should wash your face," can confound a young child because the action she should do first comes second. She could more easily understand, "Wash your face before we eat dinner."

In their preschool years, children start to spot patterns in how words change for different meanings. They hear, for instance, how adding *-er* sometimes turns a verb into the person who does that act: *teach, teacher.* It also indicates more: *big, bigger.* They realize that adding *-ed* to a verb means the action took place in the past. Often that realization confuses children about the verbs that do not follow the regular rules. Though they may well have been using *came, went, saw,* and others correctly before, they now try to use the *-ed* form for all past tenses: "I falled down and hurted my knee." Preschoolers thus run up against a fact that both frustrates and fascinates linguists: no natural language follows a completely consistent set of rules.

Because children over the age of three grasp simple patterns of sentence structure, they do much better at understanding what adults say to them. At this age, they hear the difference between "The dog is feeding

WHAT'S THE MAGIC WORD?

One of the few aspects of language that parents explicitly teach their children is how to speak politely. You have many reasons to do so: etiquette skills help your children navigate life; you like to be treated respectfully yourself, and in American culture, teaching children manners is a parental responsibility; and a rude child reflects badly on you. But parents also learn to be realistic. Your one-year-old's first word will not be *please*. You must match your demands for politeness to what a child is capable of at different ages.

Even a toddler can pick up the fact that "Cookie please" is more likely to achieve the result she desires than "Gimme cookie!" Research has found that two-year-olds use *please* most when the person listening is bigger, unfamiliar, or holding something they want. Sometimes children at this age phrase their requests in the form of statements of need

instead of desire: "I can't reach," "I'm tired." When asked to make their requests more politely, two-year-olds often just add the word *please* or put a little whine in their voices. They are trying, but still need your guidance about what people expect of grown-up children.

Three- and four-year-olds move beyond the mere word *please*. With more helping verbs at their command, they can express their wishes in a variety of ways: "Can I have peas?" "Would you cook peas?" Children this age also know how to hint broadly: "Don't forget to pack juice." They realize that they may sometimes have to explain their requests: "Get the towel. I can't reach it." And by age five, preschoolers can embed a request in statements that merely hint at their desire: "Mommy, that cake you made smells really good. You make the best cake in the whole world!"

Try as a parent might, however, there are ways most preschoolers will never be polite. They are not subtle about gaining your attention when you are focused on another task or person.

Nor do they have many persuasive skills. They still see the world exclusively through their own eyes, and have trouble recognizing how someone else's interests could be affected by their own. Consider two siblings who want to stay up late to watch a rocket launch on television. Trying his hardest to be persuasive, the four-year-old says, "I *need* to see the rocket." A seven-year-old might present the same request by addressing what is important to her parents: "I have to do a science report next week, and maybe I'll write about the rocket."

You may think that seven-year-old's request is manipulative, and it is. But so is the four-year-old's statement; he is just less effective. The seven-year-old is more persuasive because she has made the leap to considering what other people value. Your next task in encouraging moral development is to help your child understand that politeness involves more than saying the right thing when he wants something. (See chapter 27.)

Daddy" and "Daddy is feeding the dog," and are no longer guided by the most likely scenario. As with past tenses, however, preschoolers tend to overgeneralize the rules they know. Having learned that a subject usually comes first in a sentence, a child may well understand a statement like, "The dog is being fed by Daddy" as meaning — however improbably — that a dog is feeding her father. Children do not usually grasp the passive voice until they are seven.

Preschoolers can explore a single topic at greater length than before. They have also come to understand that words in one sentence refer to a previous sentence. Thus, a four-year-old can say, "I have an uncle named John. He rides a bicycle. Aunt Annie does, too." In this sequence, "he" refers back to Uncle John and "does" to riding a bicycle. A younger child would not have been able to put those sentences together. If your toddler says, "I went to Grandma's for dinner," and you ask, "Where did you go?" he probably has to repeat the whole sentence. A four-year-old can usually pick out the specific fact you asked for: "To Grandma's."

Most important, in the preschool period, children begin to use language for a much wider range of functions: reasoning, solving problems, making friends, narrating events, and playing imagination games. Toddlers use language simply as a system for mapping what they see and do, most especially in communication with their parents and other caregivers. For preschoolers, it is an instrument of thought: their cognitive and language skills become closely entwined. Language also grows into their primary tool in building and maintaining social relationships. (See chapter 24 on friends.)

Because preschoolers are becoming more sophisticated about how people use language, parents can introduce new concepts in etiquette. For instance, you might teach your child that she has an "outside voice" for calling across a playground and a quieter "inside voice" for speaking to you at home or in a store. She may even have an extra-quiet "library voice," which shows she is trying not to bother the people around her, as in a museum, a church, or a theater. As they prepare to go to school, many children benefit from hearing that teachers will expect to use particular styles of conversation in class. In families who speak two or more languages, children learn fairly quickly when each is most effective; if they will use one in school, they need to know that. (See chapter 19.)

Amid all these discoveries, preschool children also learn they can use language to explore language itself. This "metalinguistic awareness" takes many forms. A little girl might come up with new words just for fun: "This place is 'snakey' because it has snakes." A four-year-old boy may insist, while playing a game, that his playmates use particular words because he knows that language can create a new reality: "You're the baby, so you call me 'Daddy.'" Preschoolers start to be interested in rhymes as they realize that words similar in one way (sound) can be distinct in another (meaning). And, as we will discuss in the next chapter, during this period, children discover one of the most powerful things that can be done with words: they are not only spoken, hence fleeting, but can be written down, hence saved.

CHAPTER 18

Sharing Books with Your Child

Until the early part of the nineteenth century, only the privileged — wealthy families, professionals, clerics — had formal education and were literate. Books were not widely available, and information was conveyed by stories, speeches, or newspapers read aloud by a literate member of the community or family member. Family and community stories were preserved by an oral instead of a written tradition, and storytellers were prized for their accumulated wisdom and historical memory. With the turn-of-the-century's accessible public education and more widely available printed material, not only were more people literate, but reading also became a practical way of conveying information: the printed word preserved traditions and stories. While storytellers brought a community together, books made it possible for information and stories to go far beyond the physical bounds of any one community. Many communities could be linked and information could travel faster through the printed word. Public libraries made books and printed material even more widely available. Thus, anyone, whether rich or poor, could have access to the same information.

Reading brings adults and children together in a different way from storytelling: as children learn to read, they can bring information and new stories to their parents. They can read along with their parents and learn about traditions and stories outside of their immediate ones. Reading is an ability that carries enormous practical advantages, even in our increasingly electronic world. In fact, the primary means of learning the skills required for nearly every technology is still the written word. The spreading and promoting of ideas increasingly depends on a person's talent at writing, and the ability to widely and easily read is crucial to developing that talent. Families who read together demonstrate to their children that books are a primary — and lifelong — source of both learning and pleasure. In this chapter we discuss the importance of reading aloud to your child and ways to encourage your child to read on his own.

Reading Aloud to Your Child

"In the long winter evenings," reminisced Kenneth Grahame, author of *The Wind in the Willows,* "we had the picture books out on the floor, and sprawled over them with elbows deep in the hearth-rug." The short-story master Eudora Welty recalled her mother this way: "She'd read to me in the big bedroom in the mornings, when we were in her rocker together, which ticked in rhythm as we rocked, as though we had a cricket accompanying the story." And the novelist and screenwriter Sherman Alexie has testified clearly to the connection between family relationships and reading: "My father loved books, and since I loved my father with an aching devotion, I decided to love books as well. I can remember picking up my father's books before I could read. The words themselves were mostly foreign, but I still remember the exact moment when I first understood, with a sudden clarity, the purpose of a paragraph."

Many more of the world's greatest storytellers have described being read to as children. You may have your own memories of intimate moments around bedtime, on the couch, or with the whole family at the supper table reading and telling stories. Stories implicitly involve at least two people: the person telling the story and the audience of one or more who listen to it. A story is a social act and, therefore, a potential act of love. Many cultures have preserved their history only through telling stories from generation to generation. Even today, the stories you tell or read to your children are a major part of what defines your family for them. (For more on the family culture, see chapter 26.)

Even if books are crucial to your life as an adult and you already want to encourage your child's interest in reading, you should be aware of how it will foster her development for you to tell stories and read aloud to her in the years before she can read to herself. First, the ritual of reading aloud to your child implies that reading is a skill that you value highly. Second, reading, as another mode of communication between parent and child, produces another dimension of reality that also encourages discussion and imagining. When you read, you can ask, "And what does the doggie say?" or "Wonder why doggies like to run so much?" Or questions that make a somewhat older child actively think about the world: "What would you do if you were this boy?" "Do you think *Tyrannosaurus rex* could swim?"

In a sense, through reading aloud, parent and child together create what many developmentalists call a "shared space." In contrast to other areas in daily life, this is the all-important one of make believe and imagination, as we discussed in chapter 16. Within this space, you and your child can develop a shared language that is both unique to the two of you and to your family and is laden with associations to the stories you have read and told together. "Here comes that curious monkey again." "Are your ears growing so big you can fly like . . . ?" Often parents choose books they remember from their own childhood, thus creating a family tradition.

Reading aloud to children thus juxtaposes two vivid experiences: the one the book itself relates and that of the parent and child reading it together. You can enhance both experiences by asking your child questions: What happens in the story? What does the character want? Who is he, who could he be? What does he know? These should not be "teaching exercises" to see whether your child really understands the story; rather, these questions should arise naturally. If your child resists answering or tries to change the subject, back off. He may be so caught up in the story that he just wants to find out what comes next. A child gradually comes to believe "I can be" just like that brave boy in the story, or is comforted to find that she and a character share difficult feelings, like Jo's anger in *Little Women*. Children can also make value judgments: "I don't like that man." "Jessie shouldn't have done that!" By exploring such issues with your child, you help her to create a sense of herself. Reading also gives a child the feeling that she "knows" something special, something she has learned with you or, as she comes to read herself, on her own.

Parents and children who share reading aloud come also to share not only similar frames of reference, memories, and mental associations, but also values. Thus, as your child gets older, you can use stories and books to convey the values you would like him to think about and absorb from you. And stories that are not about a child's immediate world can provide a psychologically safe way of addressing personal choices and fears. Through stories, you can encourage a child to imagine what else might have happened: What could the boy have done besides run away? Could the father have done something else besides stealing to get the food his family needed? Through fiction, children can witness emotions and traumatic situations that they may one day face in real life but that you hope to put off as long as possible: the death of a pet or a beloved person, the upheaval of war, the temptation of risky behavior. But stories need not be fictional; you may read a biography or true account to your child, especially if you enjoy this type of reading. The essence of reading aloud is putting feeling into words, letting your child sit close and listen to information conveyed verbally, and encouraging him to bring his own feelings and responses to the experience.

Finally, stories are themselves a sort of metaphor — a tale of something that usually did not happen but might have, at least within some version of reality. A child naturally identifies with characters his own age or a little older (the age he aspires to be). At the same time, he knows that he is *not* the child in the story; with thought he can identify ways in which he is different. Reviewing the stories he hears thus helps a child to play with the differences between "me" and "other people," between "real" and "pretend." One day your son may tell you, "I'm not Donnie. I'm the grumpy camel!" and, the next day, say, "That camel shouldn't be so grumpy all the time!" Stories even let young children try on some grown-up roles through identification with animal characters. A fictional bear like Winnie the Pooh can live in his own house like an adult, but his emotions and intellect are often those of a child. Young readers can thus imagine how they would live on their own without the frightening thought that they might really have to. By exploring fiction, at first with you through reading aloud and later through their own reading, children learn that in books they can find answers to many vital questions, learn new things, and think through events that bother them.

Why Read to a Child Who Cannot Yet Speak?

We recommend that you start reading to your children within a few weeks of birth.

Reading stories to infants serves many purposes. At its simplest level, it provides an intimate time together, with child and parent sitting still and close. A ritual of reading, most often after dinner or before sleeping, gives parent and child a regular quiet, relaxed time. Reading books aloud is a task both parents can share equally: while a father cannot breast-feed, he can have the intimacy of holding his new baby in his arms as he reads a story. Reading aloud with children is also one of the best ways to bring an older sibling and a new baby together, with the former sitting close beside while her parent holds the baby and reads. The older sibling has the pleasure of understanding that she knows what is happening in the book while her baby brother is really "out of it." But her baby brother still benefits from listening. Words read aloud convey emotions and the rhythm of language. Even if a baby cannot understand their content, books bring baby and parent together.

Yet another benefit of reading to infants is that it establishes the routine of reading aloud, which continues as your children grow up. This social moment between you and your child is as developmentally important as the story you are reading. Particularly for babies, what is important in reading is the emotional experience: being together with a parent, hearing your voice, watching your face, seeing your changing facial expressions. You can even read the sports page aloud to your one-month-old in your arms. Victories and defeats, batting averages read with feeling — those can begin to define the space for reading together.

Nursery rhymes and songs are especially good for babies because they have rhythm, often repeating sounds and even phrases in regular fashion, and the simple verses encourage you to play with your voice in a way that is particularly appropriate for infants. Nursery rhymes and lullabies are also part of a family's heritage, sometimes passed down for generations. Their playfulness is appropriate for very young children, who are themselves playing with language and babbling nonsensical words.

Everyone, whether trained or not, has a reading voice. This voice usually exaggerates the feelings conveyed in a story, pauses at dramatic moments, and signals breaks through changes in volume and tone. Sometimes, if you are really into the story, you change your voice to suit particular characters. What parent has not tried to sound like a gruff bear grumbling about a cold bowl of porridge? Infants sometimes react with wide eyes the first time they hear such voices, but your closeness reassures them that this is just another way people communicate. Some parents feel self-conscious about reading expressively for a variety of reasons: reading difficulties, painful memories of having to read aloud in school, embarrassment about acting silly. But there is no better time to growl than when you are reading *Goldilocks and the Three Bears,* and no better audience to appreciate your efforts than your child. Self-consciousness is actually another reason to start reading aloud while your child is still an infant; by the time she starts to under-

stand your words, you will be a practiced reader!

A Different Sort of Language

Is it necessary to read from a book, you may ask, to gain all these benefits? After all, a parent can make up a story, or tell one from memory, and enjoy closeness with her child while introducing him to language. Indeed, many children like nothing better than to hear stories about their own parents or other relatives as children, recalled on the spot. And you can gain many of reading's benefits from improvising a story, or adding each day to a story that you and your child begin together. This is a good exercise for families, especially with imaginative children. Parents and children can also, and indeed should, watch television shows or videos together and discuss the characters, action, and issues the stories raise. But neither of these experiences has the same benefits as reading aloud from storybooks. The difference is not simply that when reading a book, unlike watching a video, you control the pace of the storytelling: it has to do with the language of written stories and the way young minds learn to process that language.

A written story always flows differently from a spoken story, no matter how skilled the storyteller. Written text contains the "he said" and "she said" tags as conventions to mark a conversation; these are not available, and not needed, when a person hears two different voices conversing. Even newspaper accounts of that final game in the World Series sound different from the plays as called by the announcers, with the pauses, excitement, and ignorance about the outcome. When you talk with another person, you convey a great deal of information nonverbally through facial expressions, hand gestures, and other physical cues. Your listeners follow your incomplete sentences, shifts of tense or reference, or even topic changes because you give many signals beyond your words — gestures, alterations in tone or body position. The writer of a story must, through marks on a page, convey all of these signals clearly enough to give a reader the feeling of listening to a particular conversation even if, in fact, the author may have invented it. Listening to written text thus gives children of all ages experience with language of different forms and rhythm. Preschoolers who have heard a great deal of reading aloud are more likely to speak in complex sentence structures than children who learn language only from conversations. In our work with many children over the years, those who are early readers and who come to school with a beginning understanding of reading are clearly those who have been read to.

Through stories read aloud, children expand their vocabulary and their sense of the variety of language. Many stories for children are filled with dialects and other ways of speaking that may be new to a child's ears. Even stories about real figures or places expand a child's worlds imaginatively. A child in the Midwest farmlands may never have an opportunity to go to Nepal or see more than a few facts and photos of Mount Everest on the Internet and television. But reading accounts of climbing that mountain brings forth in words the experience of the cold, the loneliness, the uncertainty, and the final success. Similarly, through reading, children can imagine what it was like to live in 1642, to be enslaved in Rome, even to be a teacher meeting a new class of students.

Indeed, by reading aloud to children, you provide another means of learning about language: how words are pronounced and how a group of words together convey a scene, a feeling, or an experience. You also show how language can shift from the concrete to the metaphorical. "Snow hanging heavy in the moonlight" describes a combination of ideas and perceptions that rarely if ever appears in everyday communication. Such language encourages curiosity in a child: How can a flake of snow "hang heavy"? Why does falling snow look heavier in moonlight? How does such a phrase evoke more emotion than a straightforward description of snow accumulation? Such metaphors as "hard rain" and "feeling blue" appear in everyday spoken language, but a story usually links more images and brings forth more associations. Language thus builds on what developmentalists call "cross-modal perception," or experiencing something from one mode of sensation, such as hearing, in another mode, such as touch or vision. Listening to a story read aloud is itself a cross-modal experience. It arouses a child's imagination so that, through her ears alone, she is able to feel chilly winds, watch horses thunder across plains, taste delicious feasts.

The Timing and Technique of Reading Aloud

You can read to your child at any time when the mood strikes either of you. For most young children, about fifteen minutes a day is an ideal amount of listening time. Whenever and wherever you pick, the time and place should be reasonably free of distractions — no phone close by, little chance that an incoming fax or a crying sibling will interrupt you. Reading at bedtime has many advantages: it both allows you and your child to wind down at the day's end and can become a sort of ritual to help children of certain ages overcome nighttime separation anxiety. (See pages 449–452.) Many families set aside a special place in the house for reading together: a comfortable rug by the fireplace, the couch by the window looking out on the garden, the back porch, or even the kitchen table cleared of the supper dishes. Everyone should be comfortable — children and parents together — and not rushed. If you are trying to get the story over with so you can get on to a more pressing task, the experience loses some of its closeness and relaxing satis-

CHILDREN AND COMPUTERS

One responsibility that no previous generation of parents has faced is that of preparing children to work effectively in a computerized world. Applying certain principles of child development to this realm can make the choices easier. For instance, we know that toddlers are interested in doing things with their parents. The most enjoyable software for this age group, therefore, is the type dubbed "lapware," designed for parents and children to explore together. Let your child set the pace. Adapted to a youngster's lack of fine motor skills (See chapter 11), these programs often produce results when your child pushes any key. She can also point to the screen while you click the mouse. As with books, if the program holds some interest for you as well as for your child, you will be more emotional in your interaction, and she will get more out of it. If you are not eager to spend time this way, choose a more exciting activity to do with your child. There will be plenty of other opportunities for her to play with computers.

Educational software for older children should continue to match their level of development. At ages two to four, children work on motor and cognitive skills. With proper software they can practice distinguishing colors and shapes, naming objects, combining images and letters, and producing a tangible product that you can stick on your refrigerator door. In early elementary school, children learn how to read, write, and master mathematics, so their software should provide opportunities to practice these skills. If a program works just like a set of flash cards, however, there is little value in the extra expense; software should do something unique. Older students must develop their research skills, and a child should explore an electronic encyclopedia before trying to gather information from the Internet. While many software developers use games to motivate players to learn, many others claim their programs are educational when they are simply entertainment. As with toys and books, take care that your software

faction. On the other hand, such pressure is inevitable for everyone at one time or another. As with many other things about parenting, if you can share reading aloud with your spouse, a grandparent, or even an older child, it becomes less of a programmed moment that you "have to squeeze in."

What you read to your children will vary according to their ages and your own tastes. Through the public library, you can experiment with different books for your child. If you do not like a particular nursery rhyme or book, you will neither enjoy reading it nor be able to "get into" it and will thus diminish the value of the experience for your child. Therefore, pick something you enjoy reading. For babies, as we have already mentioned, you can read a nursery rhyme or the newspaper, whatever you enjoy. The experience of being together is what counts.

As your child nears the middle of her second year, you can begin to read the simplest picture books. Stories that repeat a given scene or refrain over and over are particularly attractive to a toddler: "And the cow says . . . And the duck says . . ." The rhythm of recurring scenes, like those in *Goodnight Moon*, conveys a reassuring constancy about the

---

choices match your child's interests and learning style.

Children become interested in video games fairly quickly, and there is a broad range to choose from. Some are violent, some are sweet. Some reward players for quick finger reactions; others, for remembering a sequence of moves; still others, for figuring out puzzles or spotting the best solutions to complex problems. As with many desires of middle-grade students, the games that they most want are those popular among their friends. These are not necessarily what you would choose. Fortunately, there are many sources of information about individual games, including the boxes the games are sold in, magazine reviews, and Internet sites.

Some observers see girls losing interest in computers in the fifth or sixth grade, around the time their average interest in mathematics and science also drops. Girls of this age may be starting to spend more time reading and socializing, or heeding cultural messages that say technical things are for boys — a consideration that does not, however, seem to keep girls away from telephone technology. One response to this trend is software designed especially for girls, from programs linked to popular dolls to original adventure games that emphasize relationships and choices rather than quick shooting and slashing. The best software for a daughter speaks to her individual interests, not to a general image of girls.

Most of today's children are growing up along with computer technology. Just as you as an adult did not have to adjust your thinking to accommodate pencils, cars, and television in your lives, so the next generation will view computing as both ordinary and essential. Unfortunately, a personal computer and software library are beyond many families' means. Since the children from these families often go to schools that have fewer and less-advanced technical resources, it is much harder for them to develop the familiarity they will need as adults. Libraries often have public terminals, however, and by signing up to use these, you and your children can enjoy exploring computers together.

world — the same reassurance a child seeks in her bedtime ritual. Thus, a child often insists on hearing the same story night after night. That is one reason to pick stories you enjoy telling: you may well have to repeat the experience. Do not be surprised, however, if your child fastens on a book that is not your particular favorite. You and she are different people with different tastes. You can suggest that you will read the book of your choice *and* your child's favorite, but this is probably the best compromise you can achieve.

By three years of age, children are ready for stories about imaginary events, rather than just about lives like their own. Books that tell a story with pictures and only a small amount of text are best for your preschooler because he can participate with you in telling the story as he looks at the pictures. Again, with familiar stories it is often useful to ask your child, "What's happening here?" or "Where's he going this time?" Play "I spy" as you turn the pages of richly illustrated picture books: "Can you see a doggie on this page?" "Can you see something red on this page?" This game does not require books with hidden pictures — those are challenges for older children (and adults). Nor should you turn this game into a test for your child. "I spy" is simply a pleasurable way for you both to explore a favorite book. Researchers listening to parents read to their older toddlers estimate that the family spends only half of their time reading from the pages; the other half is filled with conversation about the book.

Children entering kindergarten and the first grade are able to sit through and enjoy stories that rely on pictures more than on words. They are developing the ability to imagine and create their own mental images to illustrate the tales or bridge the gap between drawings. (See chapter 16 for more on imagination.) Their memory has also become more powerful, and they can delay the gratification of hearing how a story turns out. Children of this age are ready to hear you tell a story in short chapters, reading one each night. The earliest "chapter books" are really collections of short stories involving the same characters; each installment is satisfying in itself, and the child can anticipate the return of a familiar cast the next night. Chapter books for slightly older readers have stories that continue from one chapter to the next, building suspense. During the day, you and your child can talk about what might happen in the next installment. The story, and your pleasure in reading together, thus acquires a continuity from day to day. (Do not be surprised if one day your child cannot stand the waiting and reads ahead on her own.)

There are many benefits to continuing to read aloud to your children even after they start reading by themselves. Not only does it help to pass the time on long car trips, but it also preserves the same sense of family closeness that you both enjoyed when they were younger. Reading books together demonstrates your continued interest both in what your children are learning and in reading itself. Some children may resist continuing the ritual if they become increasingly busy or view reading aloud as "baby stuff." In this case, you can move to books with rawer excitement for older kids or consider other ways to share time and literature together: your family could set aside an evening each week to read plays, share letters from friends and relatives, or play games like Trivial Pursuit that encourage children to gather knowledge. You and your child can also pick a book that interests you both and read separate copies, talking about it as you go along. There are many ways to make reading a close link between the two of you.

Helping Children to Read on Their Own

For many parents, hearing their child read a story from beginning to end for the first time is as exciting as watching him take his first step. And many adults can still remember the plot of the first book they read through as children. With this feat, a new world opens up for the child, and a special role passes for his parents: no longer will all his stories come through you. Although some children make the breakthrough of learning to read before kindergarten, most know only the letters of the alphabet when they enter school, and a few have not even achieved that beginning skill. (See "Being an Advocate for Your Learning-Disabled Child," pages 291–294.) Teaching children to read is primarily their teachers' responsibility. Your main task in instilling literacy is to make it easy for your children to read. You should, therefore, select reading material that matches your children's developmental levels and interests, ensure that each child has the time and space to read at home, and set an example whenever possible by making books part of your life as well. Teachers assign books; parents have the opportunity to show that reading is a pleasure even when it is not required. That means that you focus on reading for enjoyment and on what your child is doing right, not on how she can improve.

Start early by providing your infant with one or two books made of hefty cardboard or cloth, durable and perhaps washable. Let her play with these as she plays with any other toy: manipulating them with her fingers and mouth, dragging them around. The point is not to have her reading before she turns two: the best you should hope for is that she sometimes imitates how you turn the pages of regular books. The value of such toys is in showing young children that books are part of everyday life, and that some books belong to them alone. You can also give your growing baby old magazines to play with, letting him turn pages and see the new pictures on each one. Unlike books, magazine pages can be freely scribbled on and torn; just be careful that your child does not try to swallow any scraps.

As we said earlier, toddlers love to hear their parents read from books that play with sounds. When a young child hears a simple, well-conceived text over and over, she starts to connect what is on each page with the sounds she hears. Point to the words and pictures as you read to reinforce this knowledge. Give your child some simple "vocabulary" books that show one word and object at a time, as well as storybooks. For durability and ease of page turning, "board books" with colorful cardboard pages are good choices for toddlers. There are really two kinds on the market these days: very simple texts that match word and object or describe part of a young child's life, such as bath time, and popular picture books that have been reprinted in the board-book format. You may recognize the latter titles from your own childhood: many classics have now been issued in this style. The problem with such board books, unfortunately, is that their text and subject matter remain more appropriate for slightly older children. Your child may well grow into them quickly, but help him to make that jump by providing some simpler books.

In the preschool period, children like to put things in order. The alphabet is therefore an appealing plaything. Provide it in the form of alphabet blocks, felt toys, and (after your toddler stops putting everything in her mouth) colorful refrigerator magnets. Show a child how to draw the first letter of her name, and hang that initial on her bedroom door. Make letters part of your family's daily life with cookie cutters and alphabet soup. Keep crayons and paper handy, not just for drawing but for "writing." Meanwhile, keep reading picture books together. When you come to a page with a big letter in either the text or the illustration, ask your child if she can spot that letter. Again, this should feel like a game, not a test.

The preschool years are also the time to introduce your children to the public library, if you have not done so already. Take them to storytelling hour and other events. As soon as a child is eligible, help him to sign up for his own library card; most youngsters are proud of using their own cards, though you will still need to make sure all the books get back on time. Make each visit to the library as exciting as one to the video store: What will we read next? In fact, even a small public library probably has a larger selection of books than a video store has movies. Best of all, there are no fees.

In either a library or a bookstore, a child should feel that he is participating in choosing the books. At first he is probably satisfied just holding the titles you pick out, but even then, describe the reason behind each selection: "This book is about a horse. You liked seeing the horse at the fair, didn't you?" Preschoolers can discuss their likes and dislikes. At some point you will disagree: your child will set her heart on a particular title that you think is too old, too young, or not up to the quality you would like. In a library it is easy to compromise: "You can pick that book, but I'm going to pick this book, and at home we'll read both." Even in bookstores, some parents make a rule of buying one inexpensive book of the child's choosing and one they pick, rather than trying to agree on a single title. Only if a particular book or genre really bothers you should you try to limit your child's reading.

By creating a home that values books and makes letters a pleasant part of daily life, you help your child want to read. Many parents find that, once their child is familiar with a story, they can pause two or three words before the end of a sentence and let her fill in the rest. This cooperation brings preschoolers into the storytelling by drawing on their natural desire for consistency. In another game, you can substitute a silly word for a word your child knows belongs in the story: "The cowboy put on his hat and jumped onto his *banana* —" "No, Daddy! That's a horse!" Such techniques are both more fun and more effective than halting the flow of the story for a reading lesson ("See, that spells 'horse.' H is for 'horse.' . . ."). By filling in the right words, your child is not necessarily reading in the sense of recognizing a word by sight outside its familiar context; she is, however, demonstrating her knowledge that there are words on that page and that reading is the process of getting them right.

The First R: Reading in School

Learning to read in school is a different experience from learning to read at home. The child is now in a large group, with less individual attention and adjustment for his own interests, skills, and emotional state. Schools provide systematic teaching aimed at instilling systematic reading skills. For most children, they are successful. Typical first-graders can read only about 100 words, though their spoken vocabularies include around 6,000. Three years later, children can usually read 100 words each minute, recognize 3,000 words at a glance, and apply over 100 rules for sounding out the words they do not know. And if all continues to go well, by age fifteen students should recognize 100,000 words quickly and read more than 200 words a minute.

In recent years, much attention has been paid to methods of teaching reading, especially "whole language" versus "phonics." The whole-language approach focuses on literature and meaning through immersion in a written language. In this model, a child learns the sound/symbol system through exposure to several types of written materials. On the other hand, the phonetic approach focuses on giving students the skills they need to "crack the code." Students receive direct instruction on the relationship between letters and their sounds and are taught how to blend sounds sequentially to make words.

Although the dispute has become politicized, almost every reading teacher agrees that the best lesson plan combines several techniques. Children do benefit from learning pronunciation guidelines. Unfortunately, English is a large and inconsistent language, with so many phonics rules (well over one hundred) and so many exceptions to them (about one in every three words) that trying to learn them all can leave students discouraged or bored. Preserving and extending children's early love of reading is why whole-language lessons emphasize literature and self-expression. Sticking to either method exclusively, however, seems to work for only a fraction of students. Even worse, having to shift abruptly after changing grades or schools can leave children confused about what their teachers expect. That is why a good mix of methods is best. The most important factor in learning to read is the amount of time a student spends with books in school and at home. Once again, you can help by ensuring that reading remains a pleasurable part of your child's daily life.

As your child becomes more proficient with books, encourage him to read simple, familiar stories aloud to you and his younger siblings. Your goal in these moments is not to review word recognition, pronunciation, or elocution, but to give your child the pleasure of mastery: now *he* is telling the story he loves. When he comes across a word that he does not recognize but is in his spoken vocabulary, encourage him to sound it out. When he meets a completely unfamiliar word, however, read and explain it. At home it should be acceptable for a young reader to make mistakes; reading in that environment will give him practice and confidence for reading at school. If your child refuses to read aloud and insists that you tell the story alone, offer to trade pages: "I'll read one page to you, and then you read one page to me." If all else fails, play dirty: read up to a book's

most exciting part and say you're too tired to go on. Your child will probably insist on finishing the story for you.

A picture book for a beginning reader should have enough text that your child becomes immersed in each page and doesn't flip quickly to the next. On the other hand, if a child stumbles or needs help five times while reading one page, she is not yet ready to handle that book on her own. Beyond those criteria, a "good book" for your child is one that appeals to her interests and tastes. Most kids enjoy stories about children like themselves (and a little bit older) or about childlike animals. Toddlers prefer tales about lives much like their own, but young readers are often ready to explore more fantastic situations and settings: outer space, the high seas, fairyland. Humor grabs almost every child. Familiar characters from television have great appeal, and you would be smarter to harness this fondness to get your children reading than to avoid all such books. If a child still resists reading on his own, do not assume you need better books. Look around for what else could make reading enticing. One little boy learned to read in order to follow his favorite sports teams in the newspaper. Another wanted to play board games on an equal basis with his older siblings.

Some parents are so eager to help their children read that they invest in educational aids, tools, and software in addition to books. The value of these devices varies, and none can substitute for your encouragement. Rather than buy flash cards to teach new words, make your own. Choose words that you know will appeal to your child: the names and species of her stuffed animals, items around the house, landmarks in her neighborhood, objects appearing in her favorite picture books. If your child does not see pigs regularly, a card with the word "pig" on it is going to be much less meaningful than a card that says "Daddy." If you have a card that says "poop," that may well be the first word your child learns. As children grow older, provide the family with a good dictionary and make a point of looking up new words. Computers with educational software and multimedia encyclopedias are useful, but they work best when you and your child enjoy them together, at least occasionally. Otherwise, these can become expensive substitutes for television or a video game system.

Watching television in itself seems to do little harm to children's reading ability. The problem is too much television: four hours or more per day. This amount of passive viewing cuts into other things children can be doing, such as their reading and their physical and imaginative play. Limit the amount of television your children consume: make them choose the programs that mean the most to them. Fill your other hours together with books and conversation.

When you have more than one child, make sure each has his own supply of books, perhaps in addition to children's books that are part of the family library. Each child should feel pride in his own small library and how it reflects his preferences. A younger child will want to catch up to her older sibling's reading level, but at the same time will want to differentiate herself. It is better that she do this by adopting her own reading interests than by deciding she will be different by not reading at all.

Most children become proficient readers after the fourth grade. Over the next few years their parents have a hard time keeping up with all the books these youngsters consume. But it is still important to stay involved in your child's reading selections. Ask what he enjoys about the latest book. What is most interesting or most exciting? What are the heroes like? What happens to them? Listen to your child's recommendations about good stories, and read reviews in the magazines and newspapers. Or read and discuss with your child some of the excellent children's books being published today. (Even one on a subject that wouldn't ordinarily appeal to you will likely be a quick read.)

The Fourth-Grade Slump

Reading teachers see a significant shift around the fourth grade: while most of their students continue to progress at a fast pace, many others — one in every three or four — slow down. They do not become illiterate or stop learning new words, nor are they necessarily suffering from reading disabilities. (See chapter 20.) Rather, these students simply become less interested in reading, and the trend continues as they grow older. According to one National Assessment of Educational Progress survey, about half of American fourth-graders reported reading for pleasure, but only one-quarter of twelfth-graders did. Not only does this large minority fall behind their peers as adolescence progresses, but they also often fail to gain an important new set of reading skills. Kids in elementary school tend to read at only one speed, taking in all the information uncritically: if it's in a book, it must be true. In high school, they learn to sort out which passages to focus on and which to zip over, reading quickly. They also learn to approach books critically: Which novel is better? What historical account should I believe?

Researchers have come up with many explanations for the slump that begins around fourth grade. The reading material itself becomes more challenging. For the first time, students face texts with vocabulary and sentence structure more demanding than those in an average conversation. Books have fewer pictures and less familiar subjects, which can excite some students but intimidate others. Teaching methods also change. Lessons focus on writing, not reading. In-class assignments tend to require silence and faster mental processing of the words. Homework gives students more to read for school, and thus less time to devote to reading of their own choice. Children in the late elementary grades also have many demands on their time as they become more active socially and try new hobbies. All of these changes probably diminish some children's pleasure in reading. In addition, the fact that around this time both parents and teachers tend to stop reading aloud to children may devalue books in some youngsters' eyes.

Boys seem to suffer the fourth-grade slump more than girls do. One reason may be that boys feel social pressure not to read widely, or at all. They are often reluctant to be seen reading a book with a girl as the main character, while most girls remain open to stories about boys. Boys are also less interested in certain genres, especially historical fiction (unless it involves battles) and romance. Sometimes they shift their reading to nonfiction, science fiction, and other socially popular forms. Many boys choose other interests, however, putting their energy into computers, movies, or sports.

Do what you can to keep reading fun for all your children. If one does not seem to have the patience for long stories, subscribe to a magazine on a topic she enjoys: music, cars, electronics. For children who enjoy sports, there is an especially wide variety of material to read — not just newspaper stories and magazines, but how-to books, biographies, serious and comic histories, and novels set on playing fields. If all else fails, the *Guinness Book of World Records* appeals to nearly every schoolchild's interest in the strange and the systematic. Even comic books are valuable if they keep a child interested in reading. Steer your child toward the best "graphic novels" that combine verbal and visual artistry to create rounded characters and complex stories and are not simply excuses to portray violence. The sort of literature a young person wants to read is usually less important than the quality of the literature within the book.

Most important, continue to make reading a visible part of your home life. We have already described how some families maintain the ritual of reading aloud together and how parents can read and discuss the books their children enjoy. But your own choice of activity is equally important. If your child never sees you reading for profit or pleasure, he will get the message that books are not necessarily part of adult life. Consider reading in one of your family rooms, instead of in your bedroom, and encourage your children to do the same. Similarly, let your child see you writing letters, reports, e-mails, and other documents, either on paper or on a computer. If doing your "homework" in view of the family requires turning off the TV or the stereo, consider that an extra benefit.

Preserving a Reading Tradition

In present-day American society, people seem to have less time for long stories that

CAN A CHILD READ TOO MUCH?

You can have too much of a good thing — even of reading, and a child can read too much. It is not that too much reading harms vision. Even reading under the covers with a flashlight is an encouraging sign of your child's enthusiasm for books, not a cause for major worry. A school-age child may be reading too much when that activity cuts into other crucial developmental tasks: building social bonds, gaining physical skills and keeping fit, engaging with the real world.

Encourage your avid reader to extend her bookish interests into action. A child who likes science fiction may be lured into building model rockets or volunteering at a science museum. Or a teen who devours long novels might also enjoy helping to put on a play. You can also encourage your children to write their own stories, dramatize favorite tales in videos, or create role-playing games around well-known characters for their friends to share.

Another common concern is when children read a lot, but not the sort of material that their parents admire. Whether your child chooses horror stories or comic books or simply a narrow slice of literature, you may often wonder whether she is fulfilling her intellectual potential. In this situation, try to avoid conflict, and do not forbid your child to read certain books or genres (though you can certainly choose not to buy them). Concentrate on trying to add to your child's mix of reading material rather than to subtract from it.

At some point, for instance, almost every young reader discovers the pleasures of series books, including well-written novels such as C. S. Lewis's "Chronicles of Narnia" books, formulaic tales such as the Nancy Drew mysteries, or the recently popular Harry Potter series. Reading a series gives a child a sense of accomplishment: "I read all five books," or all fourteen, or all forty-three; and the familiar characters are comforting. But the school-age child can also develop another sort of reading mastery: a critical eye that discerns which titles are better than others. Thus, encourage your child to make critical judgments about which books exhibit the best writing and storytelling. Ask him whether he can tell easily how some books are going to come out, or whether every chapter ends with a cliff-hanger. Spotting these qualities, which are more common in formula-driven series, helps your child develop his literary judgment. Then it is up to him what he reads next.

unfold over time. Information moves quickly and often arrives in short, staccato bits conveyed from an impersonal organization electronically via television, video, and the Internet to individuals who are on the receiving end of an electronic device. Thus, children mostly learn news, facts, and stories through the mass media, rather than through the intimate, face-to-face communication of the family. Increasingly, too, children take in news, facts, and stories on their own. Seldom are parents close by to provide explanations and frameworks and to encourage them to react to — to think about — what they have just heard and seen. Many people nostalgically insist that radio was better than television because listeners had to fill in all those important details they could not see — facial expressions, colors of clothes, how deep the snow, how blinding the rain. More important, perhaps, were the discussions that surrounded the ritual of listening to the family radio: what show to tune in, what was coming up, what might happen next week.

Regardless of whether or not radio afforded advantages over other means of conveying information, the nostalgia for it is really a longing for a medium that brings people and families together and encourages imagination. As we have emphasized, this is the social and developmental value of reading — an activity that parents and children can share and whose benefits are lifelong. While quantities of information will continue to pour in electronically to American homes, it is unlikely that reading, as a basic skill taught early in school, will disappear. Helping your child learn the value of the many ways of communicating through the written word will facilitate his ability to understand the difference between quick and simplistic information exchange and complex stories and conversations. As he appreciates reading as a means to bring people together, he will also appreciate the written word as a means to expand and deepen thought. Communicating through reading to your child even when he is a baby will also go a long way toward helping her be ready for school, the developmental phase we turn to in our next two chapters.

CHAPTER **19**

Off to School:
What You Can Expect

"Tom's first day of kindergarten was just a mess of contradictions," his mother said. "For both him and me. I woke up, all jittery, and I couldn't tell if I was excited or anxious. I had to fix Tom his favorite breakfast, pack his lunch, wake him up, and make sure he was dressed right without all his hair sticking up. And all the while, I was sure I'd have to be reassuring him that he'd have a fine day. I went to Tom's bedroom, half wishing I could just let my little angel sleep, and he opens the door. My regular sleepyhead was fully dressed, backpack and all! And he asks me, 'Is the school bus here yet?'

"'It will be here soon,' I said. 'Let's eat breakfast first!' I watched him run downstairs, all the while thinking: Wasn't it just last year that Tom went down these stairs backward, one step at a time? It seems like last week that he — 'Where's breakfast, Mommy?' Tom calls. The next hour seemed to pass in a blaze. Before I knew it, I was walking and Tom was *running* toward the bus stop at the end of the street. The big yellow bus rounded the corner. Suddenly I feel little fingers clamp onto my hand. 'I don't want to go to kindergarten,' Tom pleads. My heart is aching as I start that reassuring speech I had planned. The bus pulls to a stop. We spot two familiar little faces from Tom's day care peering out. And before I can kiss my baby good-bye, he's on the bus. 'Bye, Mommy!'"

You, too, may find yourself torn between happiness and sadness as your child disappears into the school bus or classroom for the first time. Like you, your child will be experiencing excitement and anxiety, delight and dread, courage and fear. In fact, these contrasting feelings will remain with both of you in varying degrees all along the path toward independence that he begins to follow on that first day of school. This challenging journey requires many new cognitive, social, and emotional skills. And for what could be the first time, you will not be the only person teaching your child all those skills: she will learn them from her teachers and peers.

Starting school is a big step for every child and every parent. It is a crucial developmental transition that lays a foundation for adulthood. Many adult measures of success — profession, financial security, opportunities for promotion — depend in some part on how well your child masters the tasks of formal education. In this chapter and the one that follows, we review how you can help your children enjoy a successful journey through school.

Starting School

For most children, starting formal school means kindergarten or, for a few, the first grade. Nursery school and other programs, however educational their activities may be, are really preparation for elementary school. (See pages 424–425 for advice on preschools.) Remember that your child will be ready for formal education only when he or she has developed adequately both socially and physically, as well as cognitively. (See also pages 265–266.) While you can encourage your child to read at age three, or help her prepare to spend most of the day away from your family, you cannot hurry overall development.

You can, of course, do much to make learning easier for your child. You can choose the most appropriate school for her and provide emotional support as she makes the transition to her new tasks. Throughout your child's school years, show interest in what she is learning to help her value her education. Also, see that she attends school regularly and on time and provide suitable conditions for her to complete her homework. As a parent, you are not expected to

know everything about the science or math or language skills that your child studies; teaching methods change, and people forget a lot of material if they have no cause to use it. But by spending time with your child as she studies, enabling and encouraging her to discover answers, you build her academic self-esteem and respect for her own ability to learn.

Choosing a School

Parents start thinking about which schools would be best for their child well before he is ready to attend — perhaps even before they become parents, as they discuss where to buy a house. Most parents start by looking at public school systems; some consider local private schools if they can afford one. Scholarships and some government school-choice programs are designed to make private schools available to more children, but the price of tuition still limits most families' options. Fortunately, the majority of American public schools provide a good education for a broad population of students.

Once you have identified all the possible schools in your area, choosing one can still be difficult. The decision involves several factors: size, philosophy, coeducation, specialty classes, and curriculum. Thinking about all of these factors at once may feel overwhelming. You will anxiously wonder if you are making the right choice. You will worry about what will happen if your child dislikes the school you choose. You may even wish that he would just take the choice on himself; he's four years old already, he should shoulder some responsibilities! This anxiety is perfectly normal and an important part of your decision-making process. As long as the worries don't debilitate you, they can provide you with the energy to investigate and choose the right school.

First, identify which qualities in a school are relevant to you. For example, if you know you do not want to send your child to a private school, you can eliminate cost as a factor in your decision. Then ask yourself what you want in a school for your child. What do you want your child's school to value? What do you want to know about its teaching philosophy? Are children grouped by ability within grades or classes? What are the educators most proud of? What about mainstreaming policies for handicapped students, art and music classes, fund-raising expectations, athletic facilities and competitions, and much more? Once you know the questions you want to ask, schedule visits to each potential school. Visits are crucial, both to answer your questions and to make a decision you will feel good about. Even if you already know which school you will send your child to, visit it in the year before he is due to start: with what you learn on this visit, you can help your child feel more secure in his new environment.

Before visiting a school, do your homework. Look into its size, local reputation, state ranking, special programs, and other details you can find at your library. Consider how far away it is from your home, and think about how your child will get to school each day. Will he ride the bus, or will you need to arrange your schedule to take him there and pick him up? Bring your list of questions to ask the principal and teachers. Ask as many as you can. There are no stupid questions when it comes to choosing the right school for your child.

During your visit, observe children in classrooms, in the lunchroom, and on the playground. Watch how they interact with each other and with adults. Do they seem eager and involved without running wild? Look at the hallways: Are they decorated with children's artwork, awards, or banners about school pride? Are they clean and well maintained? Do the teachers seem tired at the start of the day instead of at the end? These observations will help you determine whether your child will fit into a particular school environment. You do not need to take your child on these visits. Indeed, her presence could keep you too occupied to ask all your questions, and you might read too much into her reaction to the strange environment. Instead, pay attention to your own feelings during each visit. Trust your instincts. If you feel anxious or unwelcome, that school is probably not the right one for your child.

During your research and visiting period, talk to parents of current students at all the schools that interest you. Find out what they like and don't like about those schools. Ask about their perceptions of the teachers' strengths and weaknesses. Ask questions that you were reluctant to ask or forgot about during the school visit, or that were not answered to your satisfaction. Conversations with parents of current students will give you

HOMESCHOOLING

Homeschooling a child is a tremendous responsibility. Many parents who consider homeschooling decide against it either because they want their children to have the traditional school experience or because they do not feel they have the time or training to be teachers. If you do decide to homeschool your child, understand the responsibility you are shouldering. You must make your household budget stretch to provide educational materials and opportunities for your child. You have responsibility for him every minute of the day. You will have to get someone else to do the errands you might have done when he was at school or fit them around your schooling obligations. You may designate some hours at home as "school time" and some as "family time," but many homeschoolers say this approach undercuts the learning-all-the-time potential of homeschooling. Also, your new role as educator will inevitably muddy your relationship as a parent to your children. In addition, you must adhere to the rules that govern homeschoolers in your state and city. Since society has a responsibility to ensure that its young citizens all have access to education, homeschooling parents must usually demonstrate to a local authority that they have an educational program, that their children are progressing, and so on.

Learn as much as you can about homeschooling before you embark on it. Books, magazines, and the Internet contain useful information, but the most helpful advice usually comes from other parents who have tried it. Also, examine the reasons behind your interest in keeping your children at home to be sure you are choosing for their needs and not for your own. If you are unhappy with the public school system and other local options, are you acting out of some general principle or fear, or because your individual child has responded poorly to her classes? Families should choose homeschooling only for sound educational reasons. Are you trying to soothe your child's separation anxiety or perhaps some worry of your own about losing control? In either case, staying home could hamper that child from developing the independence she needs. As your children grow older, allow them to participate in the decisions about where and what they will learn.

Children need to have playmates from outside their own family, church, and immediate neighborhood to exercise the skill of getting to know people from a variety of backgrounds and with different outlooks, expectations, and ways of doing things. This is a skill everyone needs to succeed in the greater society. If your child is homeschooled, you need to make an effort to create broad social opportunities. Fortunately, most communities provide a rich selection of activities that bring children together outside school. Museums, youth groups, athletic leagues, summer camps, and many other organizations have programs open to every child or to every child whose family can pay their fees. In some areas, homeschooled children can participate in such extracurricular school activities as orchestras and sports teams; in others, these groups are reserved for enrolled students. If you provide your homeschooled child with opportunities to develop both socially and intellectually, there is no reason to fear that she will become introverted or have other social problems as an adult.

It is always possible for a homeschooled child to become a "school drop-in," entering or returning to formal education. If you make that choice, you might need to help him catch up with his new classmates in certain subjects. Returning to school will certainly require your child to adjust to a new way of learning and spending the day.

tremendous insight into a school's culture and philosophy. They will also help you realize that you are not alone in your anxiety about which school to choose.

When making this choice, remember there are no perfect schools. Nor is the school considered "best" according to your neighbor, parents of alumni, or your state's ranking necessarily the best for your child. In fact, even if your older child is thoroughly enjoying a particular school, it still may not be the best choice for his younger sibling. Look for the school that is the closest match for your child's individual needs. Once you have visited schools, talked with parents, and identified what characteristics are most important to you, you will be ready to choose a school. Or you may find that no school meets your child's needs and decide to teach him at home. (See "Homeschooling," page 264.)

Ready or Not

After you have decided where to send your child to school, the next question is whether she is ready to attend. Determining school readiness is difficult and requires careful consideration. Even children who are used to spending their whole day in child-care programs will have to make significant adjustments when they enter kindergarten. (For more on day care, see chapter 29.) Although they have learned how to deal with separation from their parents and how to play with other children in a large group, their kindergarten teacher will expect them to behave even more maturely.

As you think about when to send your child to school, consider several factors. Think about both your child's chronological age and her developmental age. Her chronological age is straightforward, determined by her birth date. Developmental age is how old she acts, a more complex combination of cognitive, social, and language development.

Developmental age is not a measure of a child's intelligence. A child who is developmentally young for her age may have superior intelligence, but not yet the social skills, self-control, or attention span necessary for kindergarten. For some children, chronological and developmental age may be equivalent. Others may be older or younger chronologically than their behavior would indicate. Schools typically determine which children are eligible for kindergarten based on chronological age: if a child will turn five before a certain cutoff date, he can go. This is easiest and is more clear-cut than any other yardstick. But educators are the first to say that developmental age is also important. Just because your child is old enough for kindergarten does not mean he is mature enough to enjoy it. This situation is especially common for children whose birthdays put them near the cutoff date.

Kindergarten-ready children are expected to have a basic set of capacities that allow them to build new skills in the structured environment of the classroom. For example, a kindergarten-ready child should be able to follow simple directions, attend to a teacher's presentation, express her needs and concerns understandably, share materials with other children, and play in groups. Assess your child's developmental age and readiness for kindergarten by comparing her cognitive, motor, attention, social, and language skills with those of other children who are entering school. Talk to your family's child-care providers and observe your child during playdates with friends or on visits to the playground. Watch and listen to how she interacts with adults she does not know. Can they understand her speech? Does she listen to others and not interrupt in order to say whatever she wants? If your child has not yet developed all these skills, that does not necessarily mean she is not ready for school. Rather, it indicates that you might benefit from a further, professional assessment of her kindergarten readiness.

There are other, outside resources that you can use to assess your child's readiness. Your child's preschool teacher can be extremely helpful in finding them. For example, many school districts offer kindergarten screenings to help parents determine their child's readiness. For difficult cases, psychological assessment may be useful. Regardless of what resources you enlist, do not underestimate the value of your own intuition. You know your child well, and you are the best judge of when he is ready to start school.

Helping Your Child Adjust to School

Just because your child is ready to start kindergarten does not mean he will make the transition smoothly. Expect some difficulties as he adjusts to school, and be prepared to be patient, supportive, and willing to seek assistance if you or your child needs it.

Perhaps the most common difficulty facing a child starting school is separation anxiety. (For more on this emotional experience, see chapter 31.) For many children, kindergarten is their first extended separation from their family. Just as you feel some anxiety about separating from your child at this time, he will naturally worry about what will happen to Mommy and Daddy when he is in school. Even if your child has been going to day care for a year or more, kindergarten nevertheless requires him to adjust to a new adult caregiver, a new site, new peers, and new routines. Usually children feel sad about separating from the adult or adults who have been looking after them. (See chapter 31 for more on children's feelings for their professional caregivers.)

Separation anxiety is different for different children. For some, this distress fades after the first week of school. For others, it persists over time or recurs after a further change or a stressful experience. If your child's separation anxiety remains constant for more than four weeks and she is not responding to your efforts to ease her anxiety, you may want to consult your pediatrician or a mental health professional. First and foremost, be patient. Talk to your child about her worries and reassure her. Think of ways to ease the separation. For example, you might walk your child to her classroom door rather than just dropping her off at the school entrance. Taping a photograph of the family inside her lunch box will provide a loving reminder to help her through the day. Give her something of yours to keep while you are apart that can provide the same comfort. Remember that being able to function away from one's family is a necessary developmental task — one that you yourself once achieved.

As you help your child through this transition, be careful not to do things that inadvertently support his separation anxiety. Do not, for example, become a full-time volunteer in your child's classroom simply because you hate to see him cry every time you drop him off. Being a classroom helper is valuable (see pages 278–280), but be sure you are volunteering for the sake of the whole class. If you aren't, you shortchange the class and yourself, and your child will still not have learned to deal with separation.

THE TEACHER'S PERSPECTIVE

September is a special time for parents and children as the new school year begins. And each September is wonderful for teachers, too, as they meet a room of new faces for the first time. Knowing both what it has meant and how long it has taken to get to know your own child, you have some idea of how a teacher feels at the prospect of having to get to know, and teach, not only your child but twenty, or even thirty, more. Even with their training, their years of experience, and the authority that comes with having the biggest desk in the room, teachers find this a daunting task. Fortunately, most teachers have gone into the profession because they truly love working with children.

In each class day, a teacher typically works from an educational plan. Yet as she leads the class, she is also constantly asking herself questions: "Are Davey and Albert listening and learning? Is that group of Emily, Rachel, and Tysha the best combination? Is this project helping the whole class learn to work together? Do they need more time on it? Or should I spend less time on it tomorrow in order to catch up on other subjects? How can I give special help to Justin? And why is Maria absent again?" These questions allow a teacher to adjust to particular students' needs within the course she has laid out for her students.

Typically, a school principal assigns each student to a particular class in a school before the year begins. A teacher has some resources to help him understand each of his students: the school records, memories of other teachers, health files. But two sources of information are more important than any other: first, observation of each child during the first days of school and over the year, as the teacher adapts his teaching methods to a child's individual learning style and as the child learns new skills; and second, regular parent-teacher conferences. In these vitally important meetings, you can speak up about your child's strengths and any concerns you may have about her, while the teacher shares with you his observations, worries, and pride. Together you can come up with ways to facilitate and reinforce your child's learning at home and at school.

Some teachers are at work from before the classroom doors open at 8:00 A.M. or so until mid- to late afternoon. They may also have evening hours for doing their own work or for meeting with parents. For most of that time, a teacher has primary and often sole responsibility for about two dozen children. It is no wonder, then, that teachers appreciate all the help parents can offer. (See chapter 20.)

First Grades: Beginning Elementary School

Parents often ask their child, "What did you do today at kindergarten?" The usual answer is, "I played." When, you may wonder, do the lessons start? Keep in mind, however, that the major goal of kindergarten is to prepare students for years of intensive instruction in the basic academic skills of reading, writing, and arithmetic. And the playthings and games in a kindergarten classroom are mostly designed for that preparation. In addition to the readiness skills we noted, children entering first grade must have learned to follow complex directions, sit at a table or desk for extended periods, complete tasks independently, and inhibit their impulsive behavior. They also should have developed these preacademic skills:

- visual motor skills, such as cutting a simple design with scissors, drawing simple shapes and figures, and printing crude but recognizable letters with a pencil
- prereading skills, such as knowing the letters in the alphabet and that those letters have sounds associated with them
- math skills, such as counting, grouping, and identifying simple patterns

Note the simplicity of these requirements: a child has to know, for example, not the sounds associated with each letter, but only that there is such an association.

Schools work on predictable schedules: the days start and end at regular hours. Students learn when recess and lunch will come, and on what days they go to the gym. Teachers have lesson plans that carry them through the entire year, with the rhythm determined by holidays, extended vacations, and standardized exams. (See pages 282–285 for more on such tests.) Such scheduling is necessary for schools both to keep track of hundreds of children and to teach them what they need to know. But the highly structured school day also helps to reassure young children about their adventure away from home. They can look forward to what will happen from day to day, what their teacher will expect of them. They gain confidence that adults are helping them to look after themselves.

In first, second, and third grades, children will learn the basic skills of reading, writing, and mathematics. Although they will also likely have some introduction to science, social studies, and the arts and literature, getting a firm foundation in the "three Rs" is essential for your child's future academic success. Kindergarten through third grade are the years in which your child will acquire the fundamental academic and social skills necessary to be a citizen in the community of learners that a school provides. Because children's development varies so much at this young age, some kindergartners are not ready to enter first grade after only one year of preparation. Many schools deal with this variability by providing "K-1" classes, where children work on both kindergarten and first-grade tasks. If your child's teacher suggests that your child might benefit from an additional kindergarten year, do not interpret this as a sign of failure or slow learning. As with readiness for kindergarten itself, intelligence and social skills are both involved. If you do not understand the teacher's thinking, ask for input from other school staff such as the principal or the school psychologist. Remember that it is less disruptive for a child to pause now rather than later.

Reading and Other Types of Literacy

Educators quip that "in the first three years of school, children learn to read; after that, they read to learn." Reading is the focus of most instruction in the first two or three years of elementary school. Literacy, the capacity to understand written and other forms of symbolic communication, is the cornerstone of education. Arithmetic, for instance, depends on understanding the symbols for numbers and functions, a process much like reading letters. For this reason, literacy is the yardstick that parents, students, and teachers use most often to measure success. "When will my child learn to read?" and "Why isn't my child reading yet?" are questions that many, if not most, parents ask about their six-, seven-, and eight-year-old children. Children pick up on this concern, trying hard to read the books in the classroom and comparing their progress with their friends'.

Many skills and abilities go into making one a reader. Since reading is a language skill, one must start with a fundamental grasp of the purposes and methods of verbal communication. Reading then requires "cracking a code" — learning the association between sounds and symbols. A competent reader can both decode words from their letters and abstract the essential message from a written passage using lots of strategies, not just one. Think, for example, about what you do when you come to an unfamiliar word in a magazine or a book. You probably try to sound it out syllable by syllable, looking for roots you recognize from other words or languages. You also probably try to deduce the word's meaning from its context in the paragraph you are reading. Both skills are essential for reading and part of most teachers' methods. Experts agree that, whatever the specific approach teachers use, children need direct instruction on all kinds of reading strategies. (For much more on reading, see chapter 18.)

How can you help your child learn to read? Two things are most important. First, as we said earlier, read to your child. Children whose parents read to them regularly from a very young age have more success in learning to read on their own than children whose parents do not do this. Second, support your child's school progress and adjustment by being involved with his teacher and his school. Parental involvement is also crucial to a student's success, as we discuss in chapter 20.

What should you do if your child seems to have trouble learning to read? First, keep in mind that children vary tremendously in when they become readers. A few students begin first grade with solid reading skills. Others need a couple of years of formal instruction before their independent reading skills emerge. There is usually no correlation between when a child learns to read and that child's intelligence. Researchers have shown, for example, that children who learn to read on their own before the age of five are not more intelligent than their peers.

Do not become a tutor for your child. Trying to teach school skills to your child can create tension or confusion since your methods are likely to be different from those of your child's teacher. Most important, your child should feel confident that his parents love him, regardless of his skills — a feeling you are likely to undermine if you constantly pressure him about his lessons. If you are concerned about your child's progress in school, request a conference with your child's teacher, and ask that the reading specialist or the school psychologist attend. All schools can provide additional instruction in reading for children who need it.

Writing, mathematics, and learning to observe the world are other essential components of your child's elementary-school education. The pace at which children develop writing skills varies from child to child, just as reading does. Writing requires the visual motor skill of letter and word formation, the ability to memorize spellings, and the capacity to put thoughts into words. From drawing individual letters in print (and later in cursive), young school-age children progress to copying one-word labels, then to writing short sentences, and finally to composing a series of sentences about a particular topic. Some teachers instruct students to write down their stories and thoughts with-out regard to spelling at first. While the early results of this "invented spelling" approach may startle you, do not worry: your child's spelling will catch up to her other skills.

Mathematics involves learning basic addition and subtraction facts, as well as logic and reasoning. Becoming literate in the world of numbers requires both memorizing facts (the times table, for instance) and comprehending the rules that underlie those facts. To help children approach mathematical concepts from as many directions as possible, teachers often use small playthings called "manipulatives": blocks, pegs, balances, little items to count, and so on. Your child's math lessons might therefore look very different from those you remember from your childhood. Fortunately, 2 + 2 still equals 4. Teachers often have children apply their budding mathematical and writing knowledge to observations of plants, animals, and simple experiments in the classroom — the beginning of science education.

Many states mandate physical education, and sometimes teachers are happy to let children burn off their tremendous energy running around the schoolyard. Recently, programs for younger children are providing fewer recess periods for playing outside and more academic instruction. The change in emphasis reflects both advances in understanding of how much young children are capable of learning in formal academic settings and concerns about teacher liability as they supervise children's unstructured outside play. In the higher grades, children have structured athletics or gym class; as they learn to compete and cooperate in different games, they develop both gross motor skills (See chapter 11) and social skills. They exercise their fine motor skills in art class and other school activities, where they write, cut, paste, paint, and sew. Many schools offer lessons in music, art, and computers, and these classes can be a great source of joy to students as they discover new talents in themselves.

Homework

Invariably parents ask how they should handle homework. In the first two or three years of your child's schooling, you should view take-home assignments as an opportunity to watch your child at work. In these grades, homework problems are usually the

same sort that children do in class. The assignments give them additional practice at those skills and a chance to develop good habits, like reading for pleasure. You can support your child's work by providing a structured time and place to do assignments and by being available as a resource. Often it is helpful to be near your child but involved in another activity. If your young children's personalities mesh well, you can have them do their homework together at the dining table. Some schools ask parents to check their children's homework, but this does not mean doing it over for them. Homework should be your child's responsibility. If you are getting into a struggle with your child over when to do homework, whether it is too hard, and how much to complete, ask your child's teacher for advice. You should also speak up if you think your child is receiving too much or too little homework.

Extracurricular activities are another sort of outside-of-school work for kids. As your child progresses through elementary school, you will need to make choices about such activities as sports teams, scouts, and music lessons. Encouraging outside interests and friendships is an important part of supporting your child's development, but children should also have unstructured free time in which they can play, imagine, explore, and just do "nothing." (See chapter 25 for more advice on activities in the school years.)

Grades, Retention, and Acceleration

One of the big differences between an all-day child-care program and elementary school is that at school your child's work is formally evaluated. For the first time, she can see quite clearly that she spelled only eight of twelve words correctly or that her arithmetic test rates a B. Young school-age children's feelings of competence and value are closely linked to how they think their teacher views them. They are also very sensitive to what they perceive as competition, and very conscious of social comparisons. You should therefore be ready to praise your child when she works hard (even if she does not earn top marks) and comfort her when she feels disappointed. Again, reassure your child that, even though you are especially proud when she does well in school, you are proud of her always.

Be sure you understand the evaluation system at your child's school. Many schools use traditional letter or number grades; others use adjectives like "below average" or "superior." Especially in the elementary grades, schools may report on both academic topics and a long list of skills and behaviors children should be learning — the famous "plays well with others," for instance. By middle school, most end-of-year grades concern academic performance alone. Some teachers try to distinguish results from effort, both to encourage students who tried as hard as they could and to prod those with superior potential who did not try hard. Occasionally schools change the methods by which they measure students' achievement. If you notice a sudden change in your child's grades, this may be a reason.

Remember that grades are only one way

teachers tell you and your child how he is performing in school. Indeed, in an effort to get beyond inflexible letters and numbers, some schools are having their children assemble portfolios of their best work in every subject. At the very least, pay attention to written comments on your child's tests and report cards, other messages from his teacher, and everything you hear in parent-teacher conferences. These will give you a much better idea of how he is developing than his grades alone. In addition, be aware of your gut reaction to a B+ or a C. Some parents have painful memories of their own evaluations from school. Others view their children's grades as measurements of their own success as mothers and fathers. Your response should focus on helping your child obtain the best marks he can.

At the end of every school year, the question arises whether a child is ready to advance to the next grade. Many parents dislike facing the possibility of retention (or being "left back" or "held back") because they, like many educators and children, view repeating a grade as a sign of failure or limited ability. This is a serious misconception. Retention should be seen as an opportunity to make a correction for a child whose development in all areas does not match his classmates. As we have said, young children's rate of development varies a lot, and it is common for a teacher to recommend adjustments in the first year or two of elementary school.

Retention should not be aimed at remediating specific skill deficits. A student who is keeping up with his classmates in other academic areas and in his social development should not be retained simply because, for example, he has not mastered the first-grade math curriculum. Children who need specific skill remediation or special education should be given additional services. (See pages 285–294.) Some school systems have summer courses for students who need intensive help to catch up or stay even with their classmates.

After early elementary school, retention is infrequent. As children grow older and their peer relationships become more important, staying with their friends matters even more than before. If a child must repeat a grade, it is usually best for her to do so in the first year in a particular school, such as seventh grade in a junior high; then she can bond with classmates along with the other newly arrived children, instead of trying to fit herself into an established web of relationships. Retention is slightly more common when a family moves to a different school district or enrolls their child in a private school where there is a significantly different curriculum. And occasionally it is recommended when a child has been ill and missed many lessons.

Acceleration, or skipping a grade, is also an infrequent event. Before deciding to move your child ahead, you and his teachers should consider his development in all areas. If he has particularly advanced skills in certain fields, a special lesson plan in the regular classroom or an after-school enrichment program is often better than placing him in a class with students who are more developed physically and socially. Remember to consider your child's feelings and overall welfare. As proud as you should be that your child is doing work two grades above his level, he would not necessarily benefit from skipping a grade.

The "Middle Grades" and Middle School

After one or two years, parents and children adjust to elementary school. You know the routine. You know what the teachers expect of you. Don't get too comfortable! Things change as a child enters the later elementary and middle-school grades (4–8). Educators' expectations for these classes are different in terms of learning content, discipline, and peer relations. Knowing these expectations will help you and your child make a smooth transition.

Beginning around the fourth grade, your child is expected to use the basic reading, writing, and arithmetic skills acquired in early elementary school to gain more knowledge in specific content areas, such as science and history. Although teachers continue to teach basic skills, they emphasize using these skills to advance knowledge rather than simply acquiring and refining each one.

As your child moves from fourth to eighth grade, schoolwork becomes increasingly complex and abstract. In reading, lesson plans stress comprehension, not just recognizing or sounding out the words. (See pages 257–259 on reading and the fourth-grade slump.) In writing, a child's style, grammar, and punctuation become more significant. Reports are longer. Tests lengthen and start to include short essays. (For more on tests and the anxiety they can produce, see pages 282–285.) In math, being able to explain how you got the correct answer is as important as putting that answer down on paper. In science, lessons no longer involve mere observations but require experiments and problem solving. Homework consists of larger projects that require independent planning. The assignments are often quite different from the work your child is doing in class; children in these grades must often spend several hours each week toiling at their desks.

Depending on the way your district is organized, your child may change schools when she enters middle school (fifth grade) or junior high school (seventh grade). Moving from a familiar elementary school to a new school can be stressful. Many American children spend more years at their elementary school than they spend at any other educational institution (unless, perhaps, they go to graduate school).

The move to middle school can be daunting for other reasons. Middle schools are typically bigger and are organized differently from elementary schools. For example, students have lockers and homerooms instead of staying in one classroom for most of the day. They change classes every period and are responsible for sticking to a schedule. Furthermore, the move to middle school occurs just as most children are entering puberty, and that brings its own stresses and confusion. If you arrange to visit the new school with your child and discuss some of the differences she will encounter there, you can make the transition easier for both of you.

Children are often grouped by ability in their middle-school classes. Decades ago it was common, even in early elementary school, to group students according to skill level. Today most educators recognize individual differences in children and prefer heterogeneous groupings of elementary-school students. In these mixed-class settings, a second grader with advanced reading skills can work on a chapter book, while an emergent reader may be reading a book with controlled vocabulary; these same children might then work together on a task where their skills are equal, such as building a bridge from drinking straws. In middle or junior high school, many districts begin ability grouping so as to offer advanced classes for some students and slower-paced instruction for others. In high school, grouping can be based on both ability and academic goals, as students decide to pursue opportunities for college preparation or for technical training. Although these assignments can affect a child's self-image and may collide with parental aspirations, students do seem to learn better when they do not feel that they are either falling behind or rushing ahead of their classmates.

As your child moves through school, she learns important social lessons: making and breaking friendships, fitting in, and responding to peer pressure. In later elementary school and middle school, her peers will become more important and more influential. That peer group becomes the constant when students start changing classrooms and working with many teachers during the day.

Children of this age begin to become preoccupied with the difference between boys and girls. (See below.) Your child's social development during this period will be marked by successes and setbacks as she struggles to form her identity. You may notice that he or she is suddenly intensely focused on his or her looks or on looking a certain way, and you will certainly have to contend with the desire for the latest fashion fads. You may have to address the more serious topic of how to resist peer pressure to use drugs and alcohol. You can enhance your child's ability to cope with these social dilemmas during later elementary and middle school by steadily supporting and reassuring her about her intrinsic value as a person and by openly discussing the risks of drug and alcohol abuse. (See also chapter 24 on friendships.)

As teachers' expectations increase, their tolerance for classroom misbehavior decreases. They know that no one can absorb or

GENDER DIFFERENCES IN SCHOOL

A great deal of work has been done in the 1990s about the different experiences of girls and boys in the same classes. Researchers have noticed, for instance, how young boys are usually the first to raise their hand or shout out answers. In response, many teachers now make a conscious effort to involve girls in class discussions. Less has been said about how this pattern of typical behavior affects boys, especially those who are less quick or exuberant about speaking in front of the group. Teachers, measuring participation against what they have come to expect from each sex, might see a quiet boy as contributing less than he should while an equally quiet girl appears typical. Perhaps as a result, girls receive higher grades on average in school, while boys score higher on standardized tests that reward quick responses.

Another gender-based problem arises from the traditional assignment of certain subjects to one gender or the other. Introductory shop, cooking, and sewing classes are now open to both sexes and, indeed, are mandatory for all students in many schools. But mathematics, science, and computers continue to be thought of as "for boys." Tests show girls and boys scoring about equally in math and science in the early elementary grades, and thus indicate that they share the same potential. But social pressures and expectations seem to steer older girls away from challenging science and math classes. By the later grades, girls are scoring much lower in these subjects than their male peers. Although schools today are encouraging girls who express interest in math and science, parents, teachers, and students themselves still unconsciously lower their expectations for those who do not express such interest and let them avoid such classes or not work up to the level they are capable of.

In terms of discipline, girls are less likely to be involved in violent acts. As a result, their misbehavior can go unnoticed, while teachers, administrators, and parents struggle to deal with the more overt acts of boys. A quietly troubled child of either sex may need as much help as a disruptive child whom you cannot ignore.

do serious work when some children are running, yelling, or otherwise disrupting the class. If your child tends to be rowdy, he may suffer his first detention or suspension during grades four through eight. An occasional incident is not, however, a cause for alarm. Remember how you were as a child, and help your child think up better ways to handle similar situations in the future. If your child misbehaves more seriously, or repeatedly, or in conjunction with a noticeable drop in his academic work, you should certainly confer with his teacher and perhaps the school's principal. Helping your child succeed in school requires that you work closely not only with him but also with his school and his teachers. In the next chapter, we will discuss some basic guidelines for developing that partnership.

CHAPTER 20

Working with Your Child's School: Challenges and Opportunities

When your child goes to school, you go back to school. Not that you are a student again, of course, but you become part of the community that defines and supports each school. Your own memories of school, good and bad, resurface and affect the way you feel about your child's experiences and your comfort with his teachers and his classroom. In a sense, your child's school is your school, too. Not only do you pay for its services with your taxes and tuition, but you also share responsibility as a citizen for making our American educational system work for every child.

Involvement is crucial, too, because tailoring education to a student's unique characteristics, talents, and vulnerabilities requires feedback and support from you and your child's other caregivers, who know your child best. Parental involvement in schooling is crucial for several reasons. It helps to improve the overall school climate, linking that institution with the community around it. It helps teachers understand their students better and leads to positive educational reforms. Research has also found that parental involvement supports students' learning and achievement.

Teachers, however much they try to provide the maximum benefit to each of their students, have limited time in any school day and must spread their attention fairly among all the children in a class. You will be the first to know how your child's individual needs are changing. Some children may require extra help and support at the preschool and early elementary years and then blossom into thriving, competent students. Others may sail along without difficulty until middle school requires a change in course. A child whose parents are connected with her school in meaningful ways, however, often develops stronger conceptions of her academic abilities, and thus enjoys a better learning outcome. When you work alongside your child's teachers and principal, she will feel as though all the people most important to her are united and devoted to supporting her learning.

Building a Bridge Between Home and School

Even though most parents would agree that they play an important role in supporting their children's learning, they usually don't have a clear idea of how to go about bridging home and school. You can start building a collaborative relationship with your child's teacher with the basics: attending parent-teacher conferences, monitoring your child's homework and school progress, and supporting school events in which he participates. With that foundation, you can take part, as necessary, in decisions about your child's classroom placement, including any special educational interventions. You can also inquire about the implications of any special testing for your child and discuss your child's teacher's approach to discipline.

A variety of factors may make this collaboration difficult to achieve. Time, for one, is a major constraint for working parents. You may feel too busy to become involved in a school — that's what we pay teachers for, isn't it? Or you may have negative attitudes about school because you feel as if you are pitted against the teachers or because you remember bad experiences from your own school years. You may not agree with or trust the system's discipline, opportunities, bureaucracy, or values. Families who are adjusting to life in a new culture or struggling against crime and poverty also have less energy to put toward their children's schools. Most often, however, parents simply do not understand how to navigate through the educational culture. A school is a world unto itself, a little society with its own rules, customs, and even language.

Teachers and other school personnel may inadvertently create barriers to collaboration. They too are busy. And they too may recall bad experiences with parents. (A teacher who meets parents only when they are upset or making demands is naturally wary of them.) Some teachers just miss the best way to engage an individual parent. One mother of a seven-year-old recalls: "Every day when I would pick up my son, the teacher

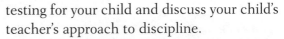

would report to me all the trouble he had gotten into during the day. I began to dread walking into the school. One day I asked the teacher whether my son had done anything *good*. Of course he had; she just hadn't realized that hearing about those things was just as important to me." Fortunately, most teachers are trained to communicate with parents and are eager to do so.

Cultural issues also influence teachers' abilities to communicate with parents. Teachers today often are specially educated about cross-cultural differences. Nonetheless, they may have so many students in a class as to be unaware of all the cultures they represent. For example, in some cultures, parents teach children to show respect by not making eye contact with adults; but in American society, we are trained to consider such behavior as evasive, rude, or shy. A teacher who is unaware of such important cultural differences may tell a parent that their child has a significant problem and inadvertently confuse and even alienate parents.

Start to build a positive relationship with the people at your child's school as soon as she enters kindergarten — or even before, during your first visit. Don't wait for a conflict to arise before introducing yourself. At the start of each school year, let your child's new teacher know that you are eager to be a helpful partner. A friendly tone and a casual and open approach will go a long way to establish trust. If you want to observe a teacher in the classroom, avoid giving the impression that you are there to "keep an eye" on him. While

it makes sense to alert a teacher to your child's learning style, likes, and dislikes, do not present these as demands for special treatment. By your words and your actions, be a resource, not another challenge the teacher must deal with.

Parents often get to know only their child's teacher and perhaps the principal. It is valuable to know all the adults who interact with your child and to understand how they work together to support students' learning and development. Make time to meet other faculty, staff, and parents during the school day or at after-school programs. This will give you a sense of the school's climate and of the opportunities it provides you and your child.

Finally, find out what expectations the school has of you as a parent. Educators rely on parents to make a school more effective for all students, not just for their own children. There are regularly scheduled opportunities for you to interact with teachers and staff: at back-to-school nights, parent-teacher conferences, and appointments to discuss report cards. These are important and useful; attend them whenever you can. Many schools also encourage parents to participate in other activities, such as providing refreshments for assemblies or ceremonies, coaching, or chaperoning field trips and after-school activities. Some school districts rely on parents' fund-raising activities to supplement their budgets. Get a copy of the activities calendar for your child's school and familiarize yourself with the important dates. Being involved is a great way to meet other parents, get to know teachers, and share with your child some of his school experience.

Seek out volunteer opportunities that match your interests and schedule. Do not feel guilty if you cannot give large amounts of time; the quality of your involvement is much more important than the quantity. You can occasionally accompany classes on a field trip or talk with them about your job. If you have particular skills — model building, cooking, or gardening, for instance — your child's teacher might come up with a stimulating project in which you could lead a class or a group of interested students. You can send in stories, pictures, artifacts, and foods that reflect your family's ethnic and cultural background.

Sometimes parents become regular presences at their child's school: they welcome visitors to the building, serve as mentors for students, volunteer in the library or cafeteria, and assist teachers in grading quizzes and preparing materials. In a few schools, parents are official members of the planning and management team, helping to form policies and representing all the parents in the community. Your participation may also vary over time: a child in the early elementary grades may be delighted to see her father at the school library every week, while a young adolescent may feel embarrassed by his presence.

Some public schools even become community centers, serving needs that go well beyond the classroom: computer lessons, health campaigns, and programs that assist parents with family and developmental issues and with interactions involving various social service agencies. The key to such success is an organized program that does not depend on the initiative of any one teacher or parent. Instead, parents and school personnel organize themselves into a team or group of teams with the goal of improving learning environments at home and school. Schools are much better off if they can call on the resources of the entire community rather than being dependent on a single person who might leave the job or get burned out.

The results of positive parent involvement in schools are obvious. Fewer serious problems arise because parents and teachers are able to anticipate difficulties and prevent things from getting out of hand. Solutions are easier to identify when schools have more knowledge and resources. And even when a problem does come up — as eventually one will — the atmosphere of cooperation makes it easier for educators and parents to handle it together. In the rest of this chapter, we discuss three important areas where the parent/school partnership can produce excellent results for all: discipline, standardized testing, and helping children who need extra attention — that is, those with learning disabilities or other special needs and those who are gifted and talented.

Discipline in School

Discipline is integral to education: students develop discipline in themselves as part of the learning process, and schools use disciplinary systems to ensure a climate for learning. In the early elementary grades, a teacher usually handles disruptions in her own classroom. As we have said, in the late-elementary and middle-school grades, consequences for poor behavior can become more serious and may involve detention after school or suspension from school. Since school policies vary, make sure that you and your child are aware of the rules at your school. If you disagree with a regulation, voice your concerns *before* your child gets in trouble; otherwise, your complaint may come across as "sour grapes." If your child is assigned detention or suspended, find out as much as you can about the precipitating event. Give him a chance to explain his side of the story. But do not challenge or undercut the school's decision to discipline unless you are certain that it is wrong.

Your reaction to your child's misbehavior at school will have much to do with whether it happens again. After all, your child expects to have a new set of teachers the next year who may not know about her misbehavior this year, but her parents will still be watching over her as she moves from one teacher to the next. If you ignore an infraction or, worse, criticize your child for being caught rather than for her misdeed, you send a message that good conduct is irrelevant. Do not shift the focus to your own embarrassment. Rather, explain to your child that breaking rules reflects badly on her. Link behavior at school with consequences at home. Suspension from school will not be a strong deterrent to future misbehavior if it just means that she can spend some lazy days at home.

At the same time, do not punish her as if she had not also been punished at school; the total consequence of a child's misbehavior should be fair and in proportion to the misdeed. (See chapter 27 for more advice on instilling discipline.)

The same children who misbehave often suffer academic difficulties. It can be difficult to say which problem is the root of the other. A child who feels frustrated, confused, and incompetent at school is more likely to act out in disruptive or destructive ways. And students who are looking to rebel or to fit in with certain crowds have a social reason to let their grades slide. Yet there are students who break rules and still do well in their classes and — at least in the upper grades — many students who struggle academically but have no unusual discipline problems. Ongoing misbehavior demands a response both in and out of school. It alienates a student from his school and is a serious threat to his intellectual and social development. If your child is repeatedly being disciplined at school, consult with teachers and school administrators. If his infractions involve fighting, destroying property, or other violent acts, such consultation is especially important since these could be signs of deeper psychological trouble. (See chapter 33.)

Let your child know early on that you value his appropriate behavior in school. Tell him how proud you are when he behaves well and shows growth both in and out of class. Demonstrate your interest in events at school, and let him know that you are in touch with his teachers because you want both to help him learn and to know what is going on in his class. When all the adults in a child's life pool their collective wisdom and collaborate, they produce a seamless web of authority. In this ideal situation, parents back up teachers, teachers help parents, and students learn that they can rely on all of you.

Standardized Testing

America is a nation obsessed with measuring, comparing, testing, and rating. Just look at all the "Top Ten Lists" and the scored questionnaires and tests in magazines (including ones on parenting). Educators use

THE INS AND OUTS OF INTELLIGENCE TESTING

Intelligence testing seems like a much bigger deal than standard pencil-and-paper tests, and in a way it is. Good intelligence tests are administered one-on-one by a trained professional. A school may suggest this extra effort to find out whether a student's current classes are serving her well; the results may indicate that she has an untapped ability to learn and would benefit from a different form of teaching. On the other hand, schools and parents should not use intelligence tests alone to determine the course of a child's education.

The best-known intelligence assessments are the Stanford-Binet and Wechsler tests. Both have versions designed for very young children, school-age children, and adults. The questions are progressively more difficult at each level. For instance, the Stanford-Binet test challenges preschoolers to copy shapes on a piece of paper, older children to repeat series of numbers backward, and young adults to explain the difference between pairs of abstract terms. Other tasks that children at different ages might be asked to do include:

- building a tower with blocks

- pointing to a picture of something you drink from

- adding two or more numbers

- stating what is missing from a picture

- reproducing a given pattern with colored blocks

- assembling a jigsaw puzzle

- arranging pictures to tell a story

- explaining the meaning of a saying

Since these tests can take the larger part of a day, some youngsters become tired, bored, or frustrated. The testers, however, are trained in techniques to keep children motivated throughout each session.

The result of each test is a series of numerical scores grouped around the number 100, which for convenience researchers long ago defined as average. The Stanford-Binet test provides scores in three types of reasoning — verbal, quantitative, and abstract/ visual — and in short-term memory. The Wechsler intelligence scale produces a verbal score and a performance score on nonverbal tasks. Both combine their numbers to create a composite score called the intelligence quotient, or IQ.

Remember that a child's IQ score is a *relative* measurement. It comes from comparing his performance on the test with the average for all children his age. More than two-thirds of all people fall within fifteen points of 100.

tests frequently to measure student progress, screen for difficulties, diagnose and repair academic problems, and measure the effectiveness of their curricula. Like any scientific measurement, these data are most reliable when they are grouped — to compare one student body against another, for instance.

Nevertheless, tests are also useful in determining an individual student's aptitudes, strengths, and areas where she needs further work. As with grades and many other aspects of school, understand your own feelings about these exams. Do tests make you feel queasy? Do you see them as a way to show

---

Fewer than 3 percent have IQs either above 130 or below 70 — the point psychologists use to define minor mental retardation.

All children continue to learn, regardless of their IQ. A child whose score is 95 is learning in the average range, as is a child whose score is 105. Both will be able to answer the test questions faster and more accurately when they are a year older. Their IQ scores will probably remain about the same, however, because their peers are learning more, too. Outside circumstances, such as stress, may make a child's result vary from one testing to another, but most people's IQ scores stay within a relatively narrow range. Since the biggest variation between tests in different years comes when a child is very young, the performance of infants and toddlers on learning and attention tests does not reliably predict their IQ at age six or above.

In the 1980s and 1990s, Howard Gardner and other theorists suggested that there are several other types of intelligence, including emotional facility and spatial skills. (Some of these qualities are measured by the Stanford-Binet and Wechsler tests, but no IQ test has yet been proven to assess them all.) More important in this research than redefining intelligence is the fact that it highlights the other qualities that contribute to a child's success in life: drive, resilience, creativity, physical health, and so on. One-on-one nurturing in infancy, good nutrition, and good schooling are important for a child's entire well-being and not just for the fact that they have all been shown to increase intelligence scores.

Another concern about IQ tests is cultural bias. Schoolchildren have to understand the language that the tester is using and have some basic cultural knowledge, such as the days of the week. Intelligence itself is somewhat culturally defined: our society values people who are articulate, solve problems, and get along with others. Nonetheless, researchers have recognized the limitations of assuming that a small segment of our society defines the norm. The Stanford-Binet and Wechsler tests are periodically revised to ensure that the norm they assume is reasonably representative of the whole society.

Rather than wonder how to help your child score well on an IQ test, try hard instead to ensure that her score is an *accurate* measure of her intelligence. People who feel anxious about being tested usually do not perform well. Such anxiety can result from recent events, worry about how others will react to the test results, or feeling that the testing process itself is strange or hostile. Help your child relax. Let her know it's all right to answer some questions wrong, that each test is meant to challenge, and, again, assure her that you will still love her whatever the result.

off your knowledge? Or do your feelings fall somewhere in between?

During your child's school career, he will take a number of standardized tests, some of which will be administered to his class and others to all the classes in his grade or to all the students in his school. Some are called ability or aptitude tests; others are achievement or mastery tests. Some states mandate that students must pass certain examinations to graduate or avoid summer school. A few communities view the standard test for college admission, either the SAT (Scholastic Assessment Test) or the ACT (American College Testing Assessment), as sufficiently critical to include systematic course preparation for them.

Know about each test your child takes, what it measures, how often students have to take it, and whether your child's scores meet the district or state standard. When your child participates in a standardized exam administered by the school, you should receive a letter that tells you about the nature of the test and about your child's performance. It should give you enough information to interpret the test scores, but if you do not understand any aspect of the testing, contact your child's guidance counselor or principal for an explanation. (Families themselves schedule and pay for the SAT and the ACT, and official information about the tests should come from the administering organizations. Nevertheless, a school counselor can probably answer questions about these exams.)

Most children very much want to please their parents by doing well in school. And parents certainly want their children to perform well on standardized tests, but take care how you communicate to your child your attitude toward her performance on exams. Too much enthusiasm can often make a child feel pressured and anxious as the tests approach and can cause some students to perform less well. Some parents have difficulty hiding their disappointment when their child does not do well. They may encourage her to work harder next time or promise to give her things if she improves. While she will probably try to improve, her efforts may only heighten her anxiety and thus make it harder for her to do better. A few children feel so much stress that they can barely perform at all or even become ill just before an exam.

To help your child perform to the best of his ability on important tests, create a relaxed environment in which to do schoolwork, study for finals, and prepare for standardized exams. If he appears to be overly anxious about tests, reassure him of your unconditional love and support. Make sure he gets plenty of rest and a good breakfast before he sits down for the tests so he will be able to concentrate. After the test, let him know once again how much you love him and demonstrate your pride in his efforts to do well. Both will go a long way toward helping him build a positive academic self-concept.

In addition to group-administered exams, some children will be evaluated with individual tests. These may assess intelligence, academic achievement, learning styles, visual motor development, language, and social and emotional functioning. There is no need to study for such tests, and children should not feel that they are under pressure to "pass." (See "The Ins and Outs of Intelligence Testing," pages 282–283.) Individual testing is usually reserved for children who are not making adequate progress in some area. If you feel that this is true for your child, you may always ask that he be tested. If you have your child tested privately, you can ask that his teachers (or other specialists at his school) evaluate the findings. The results of these assessments may be used to design a new way of teaching for that child, as we discuss in the next section.

Special Education and Learning Disabilities

Since the 1970s, federal law has required public school systems to make education available to all children in each district, including children with special needs and disabilities. Furthermore, the law mandates that schools provide that education in the least restrictive environment, that the lessons be appropriate and designed to educate, and that any related services a child needs be provided at no cost to the family. School districts are required to provide special education to children from age three until either their high-school graduation or age twenty-one, whichever comes first. Among the conditions that make a child eligible for special education services are speech and language disabilities, learning disabilities, autism, severe emotional disturbance, mental retardation,

traumatic brain injury, visual impairments, hearing impairments, orthopedic disabilities, and other health impairments.

Some parents know from the time their child is born or shortly afterward that she will need special education. Most children with Down syndrome, for instance, benefit from special classes or from extra help in regular classrooms. For many other families, however, there are no clear signs that a child will need special services or adjustments in her educational program until after she starts school. Sometimes parents become concerned about their child's progress in a difficult area or her general reluctance to go to classes. Often a teacher is the first to raise the possibility of a learning disability, reporting that a child does not seem to be working up to his potential or is consistently falling behind the other students. Either the parents or the school may start to develop a plan to meet a child's special educational needs.

It is important to identify learning difficulties early because their effects often build as children move on to more challenging work. Ongoing difficulties in learning are additive, meaning they may spread to other areas that have not been previously troublesome. A child who has trouble reading will probably have trouble learning other subjects that depend on reading, such as science and history, and may become so anxious about school that she has trouble with mathematics as well. A child may express or mask her frustration about learning through disruptive classroom behavior. Her continued misbehavior in school and difficulty mastering the material are often signs of either emotional problems or a learning disability, and distinguishing among these possibilities requires the school to initiate an evaluation with a psychologist or other mental health/educational professional. In this section, we aim to explain what it means to be learning disabled and to provide some guidance for families who have a child who is diagnosed as having a learning disability. Even if your child does not have such difficulties, it is likely that there will be one or two children in her classroom who do; your child may come to you with questions about why these children are different or why her teacher seems to work with them differently.

What Learning Disabilities Are and Are Not

A child who has a learning disability simply has more difficulty than her peers learning the basic skills in school. This difficulty cannot be ascribed to a lack of ability: the child's teacher and parents can see her talents and potential in other areas. Nor does a severe social or emotional problem explain her problems in learning. In fact, that lack of obvious cause partly defines a learning disability — that is, problems with learning that no other factor can account for. A more mathematical definition is based on test scores: for a learning disability to be diagnosed, there must be a significant difference between a child's tested cognitive (or intellectual) level and his tested educational-achievement level. Thus, a child can have intelligence scores or abilities in the gifted range and still be learning disabled. Or he can be at an average or below-average cognitive level but not test at the same level in educational achievement.

Learning disabilities vary in severity and probably arise from a conjunction of several factors. The difficulty of explaining them is just one of the many ways they are frustrating. Some experts seek to relate learning disabilities to certain underlying neuropsychological processes. That is, they identify learning disabilities as innate handicaps that interfere with a child's abilities to store, process, or produce information. (See chapter 9 for a discussion of these functions in the developing brain.) This interference can create a gap between a student's true capacity and her day-to-day performance.

Learning disabilities can appear in reading, writing, mathematics, or in some combination. The most common learning disability involves reading. It was once called "dyslexia," a word whose Greek roots denote problems with reading. No longer is the term used to mean that one "sees things backward" — a diagnosis given because children with reading disabilities sometimes confuse similar letters, such as "b" and "d," and words, such as "was" and "saw." But every reader confuses the order of letters or numbers sometime and has to depend on the rhyme, "*I* before *E* except after *C*, or when sounded like *ay*, as in *neighbor* or *weigh*." And to read, all young children have to figure out how letters change according to their orientation: even though a cup is still a cup when it is upside down, a "b" can become a "d" or a "p" or a "q" by being turned upside down or over. Today rather than simply "seeing things backward," children with reading and spelling disabilities are seen as having more than the usual trouble remembering letter sequences and orientations.

Consider the three mental functions learning to read involves: storing, processing, and producing. You must store each letter's name and what it looks like. Then you must also store the sound(s) associated with each letter and the rules that indicate which sound is appropriate in certain situations. Think about reading the word "cider" letter by letter:

c   The first letter is a word that sounds like "see." The letter itself has two sounds: like a "k" in "cat," "cow," and "cub"; and like an "s" in "city," "cent," and "cycle." (It can even sound like "ch," as in "cello.")

i   The second letter, which is pronounced "eye," denotes that sound in some words, such as "mine," but a totally different sound in other words, such as "kid."

d   At least this letter has only one sound, but it is not "dee." A child has to remember that "d" stands only for the sound at the front of the syllable "dee."

e   Like "i" and the other vowels, "e" symbolizes at least two sounds. In this word, however, it actually sounds like "u."

r   The "e" and "r" sound differently together from when they are separate.

Finally, after sorting through all these letter and sound combinations, the child must remember the other name for "apple juice." Most students learn this kind of letter-sound

association either by some sort of linguistic osmosis or through a few good lessons from the teacher. For the reading-disabled student, each step is a separate lesson and often requires memory aids with lots of drill and practice.

You might spot some signs of a possible reading disability at home. One example is a child's inability to listen to a story for long. Children who don't enjoy listening may have trouble reading aloud: they may need lots of help decoding and sounding out words, guess at or skip words, or be very reluctant to read to you. Students who read aloud *too* steadily, not noticing errors or failing to change their tone of voice in accordance with the story, may not be processing the meaning of the words they speak. Most children stop moving their lips a few months after they learn to read, especially if you encourage them to do so; children with reading problems are more likely to be struggling to decode words and thus continue to move their lips. Such problems usually show up early and stick with a reader. They may be hard to perceive at first, and many children find strategies to mask or get around their early problems. The greater challenges in late elementary school, however, tend to make reading difficulties more obvious and more troubling. (See chapter 19 for more on the shift in school expectations and chapter 18 for the corresponding shift in reading habits.)

A learning disability is not like appendicitis, which can not only hurt but also be treated with antibiotics. A learning disability does not get cured. It is a neurological condition that is part of the brain from birth. This is more significant than a "learning difference." Everyone has a different learning style, and every child with a learning disability has strengths in other areas. But 10 to 15 percent of all learners have more than a learning difference; they need a special kind of education and will need to be taught different strategies for learning, ones they will rely on all their lives. Remember that a learning disability is a school-based problem with school-based solutions. With special educational help, a learning-disabled student can learn basic skills and acquire strategies for more advanced work. It is the school's responsibility to determine which procedures will be successful and make them available to, and effective for, the students who need them.

Some learning-disabled students may need special education throughout their school careers. Others may move on to junior high and high school needing only classroom modifications and course selections calibrated to match their strengths and weaknesses. For instance, a student may tape her teachers' lectures rather than, or in addition to, taking notes. She may be drawn to drama as a way to express herself if writing is difficult. Many learning-disabled students go on to higher education — college, technical school, or graduate or professional school. Nothing about a learning disability in and of itself limits a child's eventual career choice or potential for success.

Once there is a serious diagnosis of a learning disability in a child, his parents usually find themselves in a confusing maze of educational assessments and services. In order to best help your child, you need to understand what that diagnosis means to you. If you value your child's academic performance highly, you might resist or resent it for seeming at first to limit his opportunities. Remember, however, that the purpose of diagnosing learning disabilities and providing special teaching is to help each student learn all he can. Most families are pleased to hear that there is an explanation for their child's academic difficulties.

There is a hereditary factor in some learning disabilities, and this can complicate a parent's response. In other words, if your child has a learning disability, you, your spouse, or another relative may have a similar problem, perhaps unrecognized. In this instance, you may be especially glad that your child can receive help that you never had, or that you can share with her strategies that got you through school, or support her with special sympathy. On the other hand, you may find yourself reliving your own difficulties, reacting emotionally or repeating criticism you heard from your teachers and parents. Recognizing these responses will help you and your child through the practical difficulties of dealing with the disability.

Getting Special Education Services for Your Child

Getting special school services for your child requires that you both actively collaborate with your child's teacher and other school staff and administrators and learn as much as you can about how schools and school systems work. When a student is having trouble with some aspect of learning, the school typically brings together a team to share impressions and thoughts on how to help her. This team includes you, her teacher, and perhaps other school personnel: a reading specialist, speech and language pathologist, psychologist, and/or principal. Together you develop a plan to make accommodations in your child's classroom. Such interventions might include extra small-group instruction in the problem area, increased home-school coordination, or a simple behavior-management system. Often these changes are enough to help your child make developmental progress.

If your child continues to have difficulties, however, you or the school staff may ask to convene a more formal meeting to determine whether she needs an Individual Educational Plan (IEP), or special education. The team that assembles for this meeting has different names in different states. Sometimes it is called a Planning and Placement team (PPT), sometimes an IEP team, and sometimes a Child Study team. Whatever the name, it is a meeting of the relevant school personnel — usually the classroom teacher, the principal, the school psychologist, and a special education teacher — and the child's parents. If the PPT works well, it really is a *team*. The members work together to determine what makes sense for your individual child. Some parents are intimidated by the PPT because there are so many "experts." Remember, however, that parents are also experts; no one has spent more time

with your child, and no one knows your child better than you do. You are always the most important member of the team, and you have special rights in that meeting.

As a first step, the team usually recommends a comprehensive evaluation of your child by the school psychologist. This is almost always one of the best ways to determine your child's strengths and weaknesses. The testing should be timely and comprehensive. After the evaluation is completed, the PPT will reconvene, and the psychologist will present the results to the group. The assessment may include a classification of "learning disabled." At this point, many parents say, "I don't want my child labeled like that — that label will follow him the rest of his life." But a student cannot receive special educational services without a "label." The teachers who provide the extra help know better than anyone that each child is much more than a label: they get to know their students very well and learn their unique abilities as well as their disabilities. But the government and schools need a way to designate the students who most need that help. Remember that this is a school-based label, not a measure of intelligence or potential. It means that a student's academic skills are not at the same level as his intellectual skills and that he might benefit from special educational interventions.

The range of interventions that might be part of your child's IEP includes special tutoring, counseling, occupational therapy, physical therapy, speech and language therapy, or placement in a special classroom or school. Most educators and parents work very hard to provide an appropriate program in the child's local school, but school districts also support private-school placements for children whose disabilities are so unusual as to require highly specialized services. The school's tentative IEP must spell out the specific goals of the plan and (if your child will remain in her regular classroom) how the teacher will modify your child's lessons, how

GIFTED AND TALENTED STUDENTS

School districts are required to identify not only students with learning disabilities, but also the talented and gifted. Although the districts have no legal mandate to provide the latter with special services, many schools do provide them, especially if they feel a child is being ill served by regular instruction. In some cases, it is up to the parents to decide what to do.

Students may be identified as gifted and talented because of either superior intellectual and academic achievement, especially as shown on standardized tests, or some special artistic or creative ability. Schools vary in the procedures they use to identify such students. Typically, teacher ratings are combined with information from tests. Formally identifying a talented and gifted student requires the school to convene a Individual Educational Plan (IEP) meeting, with the same structure and requirements for special education plans. The interventions in a gifted student's IEP may include special assignments in the classroom, after-school programs, or even recommendations for specialized private schools (which the parents would have to pay for). Acceleration to a higher grade makes sense only when a child has developed socially enough to be a good match for her new classmates. (See pages 271–273.)

Every mother and father would like to think that his or her child is "gifted and talented." And, of course, every child does have unique gifts and talents. This label simply designates students who a school thinks will benefit from education beyond what a classroom regularly provides. As with learning disabilities, the concept does not necessarily reflect a child's intelligence or future. Do not push for your child to be labeled as "gifted and talented" simply for the glory of it.

much time she will spend each week in special education, and the personnel responsible for carrying out further steps. Once approved, this plan will be in place for the entire next school year unless you or a teacher requests a new PPT.

Listen carefully to the details when the school personnel present their plan. If there is anything that you do not understand, ask questions. If you think anything has been left out, point it out. At the very end of the PPT, you will be asked to sign the IEP to indicate your approval. If you totally disagree with the plan, you should not sign it. Not signing will not, however, change your child's situation. If there are just a few points in the IEP that worry you, make sure that your concerns are recorded in the PPT minutes, and sign the IEP so that your child's program can begin. The school must abide by a signed IEP until the next PPT, which is usually in one year. If dissatisfied with a child's program, however, the parents or the teacher can request a new PPT to revise the IEP at any time. As a final step before beginning the IEP, it is often helpful for teachers, parents, and the student to meet together so that everyone hears about the new expectations.

Being an Advocate for Your Learning-Disabled Child

A parent of a student with learning disabilities has two roles: as an education advocate and as a supporter. Before dealing with the latter, we will deal with the role of advocate. At first, most parents find this to be the most daunting. It requires talking about your child's vulnerabilities with a group of professionals, some of whom you may not know well. It requires knowledge about educational methods and about rules and regulations. It requires becoming familiar with the specialized terms of the field, such as IEP and PPT (every profession has its jargon). Nevertheless, over time many parents find that being supportive is the tougher and more important of their two jobs.

As your child's education advocate, you must monitor from afar. In the first place, "special education" means different education, not just the same lessons from the regular classroom presented in a kinder or louder voice. Most likely your child will be either one-on-one or in a small group with a tutor who is specifically trained to teach children with learning disabilities and who will use different methods and materials from those found in the regular classroom. Good teaching of learning-disabled students is both diagnostic and prescriptive. The tutor begins with the child's test profile and determines what methods have worked for other students with similar profiles. She then fine-tunes her instruction based on each student's daily performance. Your child will probably not progress dramatically. The gains will arrive slowly and usually in spurts. Be ready to celebrate the good times and keep up your child's spirits in the slower ones.

As a learning-disabled student progresses through the grades, tutorial assistance often switches from instruction in the basic skills of reading or math to help with study skills and strategies. The child may need to have texts read to him or listen to books on tape so as to be able to participate in class discussions. He may need instructions in using a word processor to complete written assignments or in using a calculator to solve arithmetic problems. A more efficient note-taking system may be necessary so that he has thorough review sheets to study for exams. Some students may also need classroom modifications, such as shortened assignments, extended test-taking times, or even a scribe to take class notes and complete written exams that the student dictates.

Advocating for your learning-disabled child also requires that you learn about the services available in your community. Try not to despair or let yourself become overwhelmed. There are many resources and supports for parents whose children have special needs. Almost every category of special need has a national organization with local chapters that sponsor parent support groups. Every state has a department of education with a special education resource center and staff to assist you in your searches. Every state also has a federally funded parent advocacy center that can help you to secure resources. If you disagree with a PPT's decision, you always have a right to appeal that decision, and a professional from the state advocacy office can attend meetings with you.

Supporting Your Learning-Disabled Child at Home

Support your learning-disabled child as you would support any child trying to learn. Every student who has problems in school worries to some degree about his level of intelligence. These worries probably start before the PPT, even before the teacher might suspect a problem, as the child struggles with his earliest lessons. Students see the pecking order in their class. They know who is reading library books with few or no pictures, who can remember "8 times 7" without a pause, and which students always put a hand up when the teacher asks a question. All of this affects a slower child's self-esteem — as can your disappointment about progress and grades before you recognize the problem behind them. Sometimes talking with a therapist can help a learning-disabled child recognize his self-worth and his own strengths.

Learning-disabled children also need their parents' help in recognizing their strengths and weaknesses. Be honest about these qualities. If you do not address your child's weaknesses, she will not believe what you have to say about her strengths. When you speak to your child, give concrete examples of both, as in: "I know learning how to read is really tough for you. It's like a secret code, and other kids can figure out and remember the code almost instantly and you have to work especially hard to break it. That's why you're working with Ms. Kinder. But I know you're really smart, too. Last night you almost had me blocked in checkers. That's because you can see patterns that are really hard to see. You knew where I was going to move almost before I did." To identify your child's strengths, consider things that she did earlier than the average child or that she does surprisingly well for someone her age. Think about what her siblings and friends rely on her to do: coming up with ideas for games, playing basketball, building models.

When you read aloud to your child, choose books on his intellectual level and not his reading level. This maintains his interest and pleasure in reading and protects his self-esteem — he is not stuck in "baby books" all the time. Reading more advanced stories aloud will also be more fun for you: you can discuss why Stuart Little wants to sail across the lake, instead of how to sound out "green eggs and ham." Starting in the early grades, you might find out from your child's teachers what topics his class will cover soon, and then read about them at home to give your child a preview of them. But do this only in ways that both you and your child enjoy. Learning is hard enough for him without having to deal with a bored parent at the same time. For older students with reading problems, there are books that speak to the interests and emotions of adolescents while using simple vocabulary and sentence structure. Since these books are usually published by educational publishers, they may be hard to find in bookstores: ask the school's reading specialist for recommendations.

You will probably feel tempted to focus on the areas where your child seems to need the most work. Do not turn everything into a lesson. Birthday and holiday gifts should match your child's strengths — no workbooks from the grocery store, no flash cards, no computer games that review addition and sub-

traction. If your child has difficulty reading long books, look instead for videos with sophisticated stories that she will find interesting. Choose chessboards for the game player, floor hockey for the athlete, and arts and crafts supplies for the artist. At the supper table ask, "What did you do in school today?" and not just "What did you read today?"

Remember that you are your child's parent, not his teacher. With homework (which is really schoolwork brought home), your role is to provide your child with quiet time, free of distractions, and space. If the student can work alone in his room, that is best; if not, a quiet seat at the kitchen table is a good second choice. Other family members should not be watching television or talking on the phone in the same room. Be available to answer an occasional question, but if the homework is too difficult for your child to complete independently, do not do it for him. Contact the school about the problem. Meet with your child's teachers and tutors to plan alternative assignments and strategies.

As your learning-disabled child grows older, she must learn two related lessons. First, a learning disability does not excuse her from fulfilling her potential in all areas, whether her abilities are above or below average. Some may need modified assignments, but they do not need to be excused from those assignments. Teachers are almost always open to modifications that a student presents honestly and in ways that make clear she is not trying to avoid learning and working hard. An English or a social studies teacher will usually accommodate a student who explains that she is a very slow reader and wants to know the assigned books ahead of time so as to read on the weekends and holidays. A teacher will also usually honor a student's request for extra time for tests.

A child who has overcome learning disabilities in areas that were difficult for her is better able to recognize her strengths and to know what she wishes to do when she is an adult. She is also able to overcome the inevitable difficulties that arise from trying new things. By developing appropriate learning strategies and maintaining her self-esteem, your learning-disabled child will be able successfully to develop skills in whatever field she chooses.

Throughout the last few chapters, your child has gradually been moving into the larger world beyond your immediate family. In this process, you have been both learning with him and becoming better acquainted with his personality. You have watched his motor, cognitive, and language skills emerge and helped him enter into the larger community of adults who will watch over his growth with you. The bigger that community, the more both you and your child will learn in the next phases of development as she deepens her sense of self-identity, moving ahead in school, extending her circle of friends, broadening her interests and hobbies. The world is beckoning, and she is growing up to meet it. As she does, she will be building on the foundation you have so carefully nurtured during her infancy, preschool, and early school years.

PART V

Emotional Development: The Social Child

Chapter 21

Your Child's Inner World of Feelings

The word *emotion* comes from the Latin for "to move out, to stir up, excite," and an emotion is a strong feeling that, in response to some external excitement, springs up and registers in the brain without any purposeful mental effort. It is emotions — love and hate, joy and sorrow, reverence and scorn, happiness and pride, anxiety and anger, guilt and shame, jealousy and sympathy, silliness and fear — that stir or activate a person. From the moment you are born to the moment you die, your emotions are what make you a social person. They cause you to move toward or move away from other people and arouse you to action, either toward others or toward yourself. Emotions are the essence of your humanity. The ability to trust your feelings and to reflect upon them is laid down in the earliest years of life.

Emotions are a universal language. Across all cultures, people share the basic emotions of happiness or anger, surprise or sadness, and their faces reflect them in much the same way. There is always some combination of mouth movement (upturned or not, teeth showing or not), muscles tightening in the brow, and eyebrow movement. For example, a tightly closed mouth with eyebrows lowered and brow muscles tensed expresses anger, while bared teeth and clenched mouth signal rage. Even infants can distinguish these basic emotional expressions and, well within their first six months, can match tone of voice to facial expression.

Recognizing emotions in others is the first and most basic step in how people interact with one another emotionally. But recognizing that a face is happy, angry, or sad is just the beginning. How do more complex memories and states of mind affect a person's interpretation of a specific emotion? If a man smiles warmly, for instance, you would probably recognize his expression as a smile and agree that smiling goes along with a positive or happy emotion. Yet someone else might interpret his expression differently. One person might respond: "Oh, he likes me a lot." Another: "What a happy person! I wonder what good thing happened to him." Or a third: "Why is he laughing at me? What's wrong?"

Emotional life involves not only being able to recognize what emotions look like in other people but also knowing how they feel to you — in your gut, head, muscles, and skin. You know the physical sensations: the headache, the jumpiness, the churning stomach of anxiety; the heaviness of sadness; the "walking on air" of happiness. While you share these basic sensations with other people, your own experience also affects your feelings, allowing you to attribute meaning to them.

Feelings can be unruly, causing you to burst out in excitement or anger or joy, sometimes to hurt or overwhelm or startle others — even yourself. And feelings can be ambiguous: anger can be either destructive or constructive, while happiness can be excessive, making you oblivious of others' needs. You can express your feelings forcefully or dramatically or hide them behind a face of stone or a smile. You can bury unpleasant feelings so completely that you don't even know what they are. It is far better, however, to recognize your feelings, whatever they are. Only then can you understand what has caused them and thus respond to them effectively. Indeed, only then can you appre-

ATTACHMENT THEORY

One of the basic concepts in the study of child development is attachment theory: that is, a child forms a special attachment with his parents in his first months and years, and these attachments stay with him through life. Research verified this intuitive notion and expanded on it.

Attachment theory actually came out of studies of animals. While studying the crucial bonds between animal mothers and their young, John Bowlby, a British psychoanalyst, found that not just any mother sheep can care for a particular lamb. There is something unique in each ewe-lamb pair. Pondering a similar connection in human infants and young children, Bowlby theorized that the earliest relationships between parent and child lead to "internal working models," templates on which the child builds her expectations of care and her patterns of relating to others. In most cases, that special parent-child relationship is strong and healthy; in some, it is less so. But whatever their quality, a young child's earliest relationships with adults shape her unique patterns of attachment.

Some of Bowlby's students, such as Mary Ainsworth, applied his ideas to mothers and babies in different cultures and observed common "attachment patterns" between adults and children. These patterns are most evident at times of separation, because in the parents' absence, an infant has to depend on his memories of them for comfort and security. A child's behavior upon his parents' return provides clues to the stability and nature of his attachment. A "securely attached" child is less visibly upset by his parents' leaving and greets them happily on their return, often inviting them to join into what he was doing while they were gone. An "anxiously attached" child is worried, even tearful, upon separation, and clings to his parents when they return. These children need reassurance and comfort, and take time to recover. Other children

ciate how they are affected by both the social world you live in and by your own sense of yourself.

Recognizing, learning, understanding: these words belong to the cognitive self, since the feeling self and the cognitive self cannot really be separated. The two are intimate companions: as the feeling self surges with emotion — in delicious happiness, say, or harsh anger — the cognitive self tries to manage, or channel, that emotion in the most positive way. It takes mental effort to figure out what has given rise to your anger and to find a way to act out of it constructively, doing the least harm. Similarly, only by employing cognitive skills can you understand and try to ameliorate the feelings of other people whom your happy behavior may distress. Indeed, being a responsible, feeling person involves learning to express your emotional self effectively, choosing what feelings to share and with whom and reconciling your own feelings with those of others.

Feelings and emotions can draw people together or pull them apart. But by mastering their emotions, different kinds of people live in peace in their families and in society. The social child is one who learns both to know and manage his or her emotions — the hard and difficult ones as well as the good and

anxiously avoid their feelings about being left alone and behave as if separation does not matter. They do not even acknowledge their parents' return and may even avoid contact for a while. Lastly, there are children so anxious and so unable to trust their parents to return that they become distraught and uncontrollable at separation or reunion.

These broad patterns of attachment behavior do not, of course, capture a child's full range of feelings and expectations, and an individual child's behavior can vary according to circumstance. Nevertheless, these groupings have proven useful in further research. For instance, parents and children tend to have matching patterns of attachment; a parent who describes his own childhood memories in ways that reflect a securely attached relationship will be more likely to have children who are themselves securely attached. Perhaps even more interesting is the finding that in many ways an infant's patterns of attachment continue to characterize his social relationships through kindergarten and early school age. Securely attached children tend to be confident in most social relationships, while insecurely attached children tend to have more difficulties on average.

The important message of attachment theory is that the qualities of one's earliest relationships endure. Throughout your life, the way you build relationships and see other people will be based on the template formed by the special connections of early childhood. While you will not consciously seek out people who are like the adults who cared for you, you may suddenly realize that your partner has a lot in common with your beloved grandfather, or that you are simultaneously drawn to and resentful of your boss, much as you were of your mother. Thus, your infant memories of being cared for by important adults not only are active parts of your internal psychological makeup but also influence your choices of friends, colleagues, mentors, and partners.

positive ones — and to develop them in friendships, in school relationships, as a member of a family with its culture and traditions, and finally as a moral person. In this section, we will discuss all these aspects of the social development of children.

STUDYING INFANT TEMPERAMENT

The physicians Stella Chess and Alexander Thomas published the first studies of infant temperament in the late 1960s. In careful observations of two- and three-month-old infants, they asked parents to describe their baby's behavior in everyday situations, such as being bathed or having a diaper changed. The researchers then followed these children into early adolescence. From their interviews with parents, they found that immediately after birth, newborns have different characteristic ways of responding to their environment and expressing themselves, and that these differences sometimes persist through childhood. The behavioral traits clustered in nine different, easily observable areas:

- level of motor activity

- whether infants respond to new situations by withdrawing or approaching

- how adaptable babies are to change

- sensitivity to such stimulation as sound, light, and touch

- attention span

- how persistently infants stick to tasks

- how easily they can be distracted from tasks

- general mood

- rhythmicity, or the regularity and predictability of their sleeping and eating behaviors

The different behaviors that infants display in these nine categories sort into three patterns or types that clearly capture parents' experiences with their babies. "Difficult" infants withdraw from unfamiliar situations, adapt slowly to change, are intense (and negative) in their emotions, and lack predictable feeding, sleeping, or toileting behaviors. "Easy" babies are the opposite: consistent in sleeping and feeding habits, curious and easily interested in novel situations, quickly and readily adaptable to change, and generally emotionally positive and low-key. The "slow-to-warm-up" babies initially withdraw from new situations and are slow to adapt to change; they are not as emotionally irritable as "difficult" infants, but their moods are more often emotionally negative than easy babies. (These temperaments have nothing to do with level of intelligence, physical ability, or tendency to illness.)

Drawing upon these original descriptions of temperamental patterns, developmentalists have devised other ways to capture individual differences in temperament. One method combines some of Thomas and Chess's nine characteristics into three — emotional behavior, sociability, and activity — that encapsulate how infants approach their external world and how well they regulate their emotional states. Emotional behavior describes how easily an infant becomes aroused, excited, or even irritated in situations that are stimulating or frustrating. Sociability refers to an infant's tendency to approach or avoid people. Activity is a measure of his usual energy and tempo in day-to-day play.

Emotions in Infancy

When you and your partner welcome your newborn child into your life and she responds according to her own personality, you also bring her into the social world. Throughout the various stages of childhood, you build on this first loving relationship to help your child discover and deal with her emotional self, both at home and in the world.

First Feelings: Your Newborn's Emotions

The act of birth thrusts a newborn baby into a completely new sensory environment. His early growth and development is a process of adapting: physically, cognitively, and emotionally. Although babies do, indeed, progress similarly over all, each child responds in his own way and time to the sensual aspects of his surroundings. Physical stimuli — bright lights, sharp sounds, changes in temperature, the textures of fabrics, a variety of smells and tastes — can be overwhelming for a newborn. Her body is also newly functioning: coughs and sneezes, lungs inflating and deflating with air, a mouth that sucks, a throat that swallows, the sensation of being empty or full, the movement of excretion. Many of the physical experiences you take for granted and are only seldom aware of feel, to your baby, like a sort of chaos of sensation, which she is as yet unable to sort out or make sense of.

Your newborn's emotions are rooted in these most basic body sensations. Happiness is being warm, full, and alert. It is being held comfortably and hearing someone singing a soothing melody. Unhappiness, in contrast, comes from being hungry, tired, cold, uncomfortable, startled by a loud noise, or alone with no one responding. A very young infant's emotions receive their meaning both from those physical experiences and from her parents' responses. She comes to associate feeling cold and hungry with unhappiness, in part because those sensations feel unpleasant and then are relieved and in part because of your response to her at the time. "Poor baby, you're so hungry [sleepy, cold]. Mommy will help you right now — you'll feel so much better." Hearing such talk helps a baby build up a repertoire of meanings, good and bad, for her physical feelings.

As your infant gradually becomes used to the sensations of the outside world in his first months, you become aware of his tolerances and preferences. (For more on parents' adjustment, see chapter 5.) Your baby's random and unpredictable behaviors start to fade. Digestion usually becomes more stable, and you can realistically gauge how much he is feeding. (See chapter 12.) Although his sleep habits will change further (see chapter 13), they will develop a certain consistency that will allow you to recognize and pay closer attention to atypical events. The differences in your baby's cries become more easily recognizable. You will come to know which type of comforting to offer first: a bottle, a diaper, or a song and a hug. In all these responses you strengthen the meanings your baby gives to his sensations, thus validating his emotions and encouraging him to attend to them as you do.

Temperament and Personality

An adult's particular mode of behavior and reaction is usually referred to as his or her "personality." Your personality includes all of the abilities, habits, and preferences that you have developed through your experience and learning and that make you different from other people. Since babies have little experience in life, however, we use the term "temperament" for the typical way an infant responds emotionally and behaviorally to her environment. Temperament probably has a genetic basis for the most part, while personality emerges through the interaction between one's endowment and one's environment. Temperament may be thought of as the inherited personality traits — normal activity level or dominant mood, for instance — that become evident even in early childhood.

The most basic characteristic of temperament may be an infant's reaction to a new situation or challenge — in other words, the excitability of her central nervous system. Adults certainly vary in the degree to which stimulation excites them: that is, in terms of increases in heart rate, brain activity, sweating, and even motor behavior. Among infants, differences in physiological responsiveness seem to be mirrored in behavioral patterns. The ones who tend to avoid the unfamiliar, to act hesitantly, and to be easily overwhelmed also tend to cry more easily, to be less active,

and to show less curiosity. This trait, called "inhibition" by some researchers, seems to characterize infants through early childhood and may be the most consistent or stable of the early temperament characteristics.

Parents generally believe in the stability and predictability of their child's personality. "He's been hyper since the day he was born," you might say, or, "She was a sensitive baby, and that's been true all along." But how much does temperament really tell about later personality? In long-term studies of the original methods for classifying temperament (with nine categories of behavior and three patterns or types), those babies characterized early on as "difficult" were indeed more likely in late childhood to have behavioral and psychological problems that required professional attention. Infants characterized as shy or inhibited in terms of their reactions to strangers and situations were likely still to be timid, hesitant, and anxious by early school age; conversely, those who were curious and interested in novelty were more likely to be spontaneous and outgoing by school age.

However, early temperament does not reliably predict later personality. For one thing, different patterns of temperament elicit different patterns of behavior and response from parents, and experience is what shapes temperament into personality. A difficult infant, with unpredictable moods and slow adaptation to change, is more stressful and tiring for parents than the adaptive, easy baby and needs (and elicits) a different style of parenting. She requires more predictable, consistent, steady responses from her parents, and they should be flexible and creative if she responds poorly or irritably to their caring. Since mothers and fathers bring their own personalities and beliefs to their parenting, some parents will feel anxious or guilty about their difficult baby, others will find him a challenge, and still others may feel inclined to give up and pull away. Different caregiving patterns may reinforce or mitigate the tendencies that make a baby "difficult." So your baby's temperament is shaping your behavior even as you are helping his personality to emerge.

Furthermore, the relationship between temperament and later personality is affected by a child's wider social environment. The value a culture ascribes to independence, exuberance, and curiosity shapes how people outside the family evaluate and respond to a young child's behavior. In the United States, we tend to encourage these traits, but they have not always been rewarded in all children. Some societies find independence and curiosity to be alarming, and parents in those cultures would tend to encourage more cautious behavior. Thus, despite its biological basis, a child's temperament changes constantly as a result of interactions between a child, her parents, and her experiences with the wider world. The difficult, irritable toddler actually may develop into a graceful, charming, flexible adolescent, while the easygoing baby may be anxious, depressed, and withdrawn as a teenager.

In discussions of temperament, we often use the concept "goodness of fit" to describe how well a baby's temperament matches with the demands and needs of his parents and his culture. Different children in the same family may fit in quite differently. When there is consistency between parents' styles and expectations and their baby's temperament, the fit is good. But when, for example, parents expected a quiet baby who would be easy to understand and care for but have, instead, an irritable, moody infant who does not respond predictably, the fit is less than adequate and may be fraught with difficulty. A difficult temperament does not always lead to a poor fit, however, and an easy temperament is not a guarantee of a good fit. Thus, even so-called easy infants may nonetheless have troubles later in life owing to an unsatisfactory interaction between experience and endowment.

If your newborn's temperament doesn't seem to match well with yours or your spouse's, remember that temperament is a big part of what makes your child special. Consider also how your own personality, perceptions, and preferences shape your responses to your child's temperament. If you are calm and quiet, you may find it more difficult to adjust to a baby with a difficult temperament. On the other hand, if you are more energetic and demonstrative, a quiet, "slow-to-warm-up" baby may feel frustrating. Remember also that every family must adjust at some point, in some ways, to a new family member's personality. The more you try to appreciate your child's own personality and individuality, the more you will be able to create a comfortable emotional blend within your family.

Socialization in Infancy

Your baby comes into the world ready for the stimulation of social exchange. As he becomes used to life outside the womb, notice how attentive he is to his immediate surroundings. A newborn's eyes are capable of seeing objects at many distances, but in the first months his eye muscles are best suited for viewing objects that are eight to ten inches away from his face. This distance is just right for him to study you as you hold him and talk to him. His favorite sights are faces, and he listens intently as you speak to him. Though he still does not know one person from another, he does notice social interaction, expressions, intonation, and attention. (See chapter 17 for more on language.)

In time, as you hold him, a smile will spread across his face. This expression is a bid for a social response. When you greet his smile with a smile in return, there is pleasure all around. (In fact, even before babies smile in response to what they see, adults interpret their expression as an invitation to interact.) After many such moments of sharing smiles, your infant can draw his own individual meaning from the experience.

Social interaction of all kinds, from feeding to diapering to cuddling, leads a child to feel emotionally attached to the adults in her life. By three months or so, your baby can distinguish the adults who are special to her from other people. Week by week, her preferences for companionship become clearer. She will become most attached to the person who has invested the most time in keeping her company, playing with her, talking to her — and, we hope, cuddling her, smiling at her, and loving her. Through this early love, your baby learns your own individual way of expressing love and other emotions. Early loving companionship forges a passionate bond between you and your child. Typically this first bond connects mother and child, but the connection is not about biology and physical care: it is about loving and nurturing. It is not that a baby can have only one attachment or only one special person. For example, a baby who, from birth, has had the good fortune to have two parents equally available to nurture and care for him with the spirit he will one day know as love will respond to each of them, one at a time.

It is in this first relationship that your baby experiences frustration, sadness, and anger — both his own and yours. However much you might like to think that your earliest relationship with your baby is filled with only positive emotions — with happiness and joy — love is actually a mixture of affection, disappointment, anger, frustration, and other intense feelings. Babies become attached to and ultimately love not only parents who treat them lovingly and well, but also parents who are depressed, angry, even neglectful. Babies experience all of these sentiments in their relationships with their parents, and it is normal that they do. In a baby's first love relationship, he learns about himself, other people, and the world. This experience is the foundation for his learning about emotions and how to cope with them.

Your baby will spend much of his time over these first few months of life getting to know you. You become the interpreter of his world. You provide meaning for many of his feelings and physically felt emotions. And just as he will look to you for special attention, he will offer you the opportunity to feel special, unique, and beloved.

You and your baby get to know each other by learning to recognize each other's emotional states and expressions. A large body of observational research clearly demonstrates that in the first weeks of life babies can produce the expressions that commonly reflect certain basic emotional states: smiling, scowling, and looking away. These are your clues to how your baby is feeling. As you learn about her feelings from her emotional expressions, so she will learn from yours. Infants as young as five months respond appropriately to different faces, especially if variations in tone of voice accompany the facial expressions. Your child attends to you with interest and happiness when you show that you are interested in and happy with her. If you are sad and less expressive vocally, your child will look at you less often. And if you are angry, your child may become very still and quiet. In a similar fashion, your child's emotional states promote reactions in you. This emotional dialogue between you and your infant will continue and will become more complicated as her cognitive abilities develop.

Your baby's devotion to you and his loving feelings will remain a prime feature of his life for some time. In his second six months he can certainly include others in his love, but no one else will be as special as his parents are. He may want you to be in sight every waking moment. If you are not, he may experience separation anxiety: uneasiness and even tears. (See chapter 31.) If you leave the room, your infant is aware of your absence but cannot keep your image in his mind or have confidence in your return. As far as he is concerned, you could be gone forever. For some infants this experience is more acute than for others. Sometime during the next twelve months, your child will learn, through continual experience, that things do not cease to exist just because he can no longer see them. And he will understand that, though you may leave his presence, you will return.

As your baby becomes accustomed to daily patterns, she begins to build up expectations. When a familiar routine takes an unexpected twist, she may become distressed and lose confidence, at least temporarily, in her understanding of how things go together. She becomes afraid and bursts into tears. You have always been there before when she woke from her afternoon nap — why is Grandma here today? She may know and love Grandma, but she was expecting to see you. Thus, she is responding not to Grandma's presence, but to the change in routine. Any unexpected alteration in your established pattern can prompt this kind of fearful reaction from your infant.

Brand-new people or places can also produce fear. Your baby's coping skills are tuned to a fairly small circle of experience. He can, at first, be overwhelmed by new places and activities. Although he may become fond of them when he is older and more mature, they may bring tears now. You may need to mellow first-time exposures to rides on swings, party noisemakers, meeting the neighbor's dog, and other such experiences, or even delay them until you think your child is ready. As in many other aspects of temperament (see also pages 302–304), children differ in their tolerance of intense and novel experiences.

You are, as we have said earlier, the interpreter of the world for your infant. You let her know not only what you think is safe, but also which things are good or bad, which activities are fun or not fun. In time, she will come to absorb these attitudes as her own. In her first year, your baby develops the capacity to read meanings from facial expressions. While exploring new toys or new spaces, he deliberately watches your reactions, and your emotional response can encourage or discourage him. By the time he is nine months old, he will notice when you respond to a new situation and will treat your emotional reaction as a guide to how to react himself. If Mommy's face shows disapproval or unease, an infant will hesitate; if Mommy looks calm, baby can play. As she voyages out into a wider world, you are her rudder.

During his first year of life, your baby develops in extraordinary ways, growing from a tiny newcomer into a toddler with strong desires and preferences that he can clearly demonstrate. Through his attentiveness to faces and the loving care of a few special people, he forms his first love attachment. This bond arises out of an emotional dialogue that relies on expressiveness, responsiveness, and sharing feelings with one another. Just as you have learned that he can feel fear, helplessness, anger, and frustration, he, in turn, has become skilled at reading the emotional reactions in your face and voice, and can tell whether he can safely proceed with his explorations. Although a one-year-old has usually discovered that people and things do not cease to exist if they are out of sight, he has yet to see you as being separate from him. Gaining an understanding of his own individuality is part of the next step in your child's emotional development.

Unsteady Balance: Your Toddler's Emotional Life

As your child becomes a toddler, major developments are in store for all. She starts walking and talking and playing in ways that can make her seem older than her years. But wait just a moment! Her emotional balance is delicate, and a small snag in whatever she is doing can upset it.

"Right here, right now!" is a good motto for toddlers beginning their second year. At this age your child is an explorer. He wants to see and touch everything he can get his little hands on. He is never bored. Once he has thoroughly explored his surroundings, he will happily go on to see what might happen if he squeezes this, turns that over, puts one thing inside another, and so on. His playtime could be endless and that would be fine with him — if only he did not eventually get tired and cranky, a feeling he can neither anticipate nor understand.

His inquisitiveness also carries over to people. Up until about thirteen months or so, your child is most likely to be confused or upset when he sees someone in distress; he is unlikely to understand the other person's emotions. As a toddler, he might begin to intervene. He may try to comfort someone who is crying. He will bring them something, make suggestions about what to do, express some sort of sympathy, or seek help from a third party. He is beginning to both appreciate that emotions have causes and identify the conditions or actions that make people happy or sad. He is also beginning to recognize that other people's feelings are separate from his own: he can be happy while another person is sad.

Your toddler is also occasionally going to explore the relationship between events and emotions by deliberately provoking a reaction from you. Wanting to know what will happen, he may treat you like a play object — squeezing, pinching, pushing over. His curiosity is innocent and natural. Unable, as yet, to distinguish right from wrong, he cannot understand the consequences of his actions or recall how he felt when something similar happened to him. He needs help to learn from his experiences. You will often have to repeat the same instructions to a young child over and over again.

Try to keep in mind that your toddler's cognitive abilities are not fully formed. Though she may use a variety of words, she does not understand many subtleties. Her memory for some details and past events is selective and short. Since she has no capacity for forethought, she cannot anticipate the results of her behavior. Since she acts on what she is feeling "right here, right now," she can be impulsive. These constantly changing feelings are both hard for you to keep up with and sometimes difficult for your child to deal with.

As your toddler seeks exploration and experience, she is also beginning to understand not only that she is separate from you but that she has likes and dislikes different from yours. Now she is pushed and pulled from within: both wanting autonomy and feeling scared and wanting your protection and emotional support. Toddlerhood can thus be a time of rebellion, interspersed with frequent desires to nest in the safe comfort of Mommy and Daddy's arms. Your child may be joyous one minute and weeping inconsolably or flinging a toy across a room the next, making you feel as if you were on a roller coaster.

At some point, your toddler's exploratory play begins to include activities that help him discover similarities and differences in what he sees and experiences. By learning to classify and group things in the visible world, he is laying the foundation for forming mental concepts: things that are red, things that are for eating, things that make me happy. Your child's understanding of his environment takes a pretty big leap at this time. As he learns to conceptualize attributes, he can see that he is part of a bigger world and that things in that world are interconnected, orderly, and predictable. This discovery is one reason that toddlerhood is such an exciting and critical time. Everywhere your child looks there is wonder. The simplest things delight him — or worry and frighten him. But as his view of the world widens, so does his ability to understand it. Gathering information everywhere, he is on a mission to understand his social as well as physical world.

At the same time, your toddler is deepening her investigations into other people's emotions and their causes. And as she moves away from being your shadow and toward independence, her confidence in what she knows increases. Her flare for drama lets you know when she is pleased as well as when she is discontented. And as your toddler's cognitive skills become increasingly sophisticated, she gradually develops into a young child.

Trying on Emotions: Early Childhood

As your child enters his third year or so, his playtime will take on some new qualities. He now knows his own desires and beliefs and can identify them for you. His imitative play begins to transform into pure imaginative play (see chapter 16) and his capacity for complex thought is increasing. He can, for example, hold an object in mind and think about it even when it is not present. With this ability, your child is able to enter into

new and important learning realms. At some point he will be able to imagine a fictional situation and identify it as such: "I'm pretending I'm a pirate!" He will also be able to devise imaginary psychological states, such as having particular desires, beliefs, and emotions, and to project them onto playthings: "Dolly's scared of me 'cause I'm a pirate!"

Understanding another person's emotions means that a child must be able to imagine them. In her play, a child can pretend to want something another person wants. She will examine that person's situation, imagining what might happen if her own desire is satisfied or if it is frustrated. As she does so, she will anticipate the emotion that will arise in that person at either outcome and then attribute it to him or her: "You're the bad guy, and you're angry that I'm coming to the rescue again." Through this kind of pretend play, which can go on for hours, a child begins to be able to explain and predict other people's behavior and emotions in real life: "Ooooh, your mom's gonna be mad!"

Imagination is powerful. At times, as your child immerses himself in different realms, he may hesitate on the edge of his understanding of the moment. He may need to check with you or his playmates: "This is just pretend, right?" Sometimes the play can become too intense, and he becomes really afraid of the monster or the bad guy chasing him. If you acknowledge that your child's feelings at that moment are real and help him recognize what he is feeling, you make it easier for him to sort out the reality of the sit-

SELF-ESTEEM AND WHY IT MATTERS

To have self-esteem is to have a sense of inner pride in yourself as a feeling, effective person. This sense does not rest simply on outward success or competence; indeed it may not reflect them at all. Some of the brightest, most successful and attractive individuals feel inadequate. Despite an outward appearance of self-assurance, privately they are convinced that they do not deserve their success and good fortune, and they are waiting to be found out as deficient and fake. Although their anxieties may have fueled their urge to achieve, they cannot truly judge or enjoy their success. This basic lack of self-esteem can cause emotional turmoil and interfere with a person's relationships with others.

Your child's self-image, or how she feels about herself, has its roots in infancy and early childhood. It is based on your actions and words and on those of the other adults who care for her, including teachers, nannies, grandparents, aunts, and uncles. When you tell your baby how much you love her, how handsome, fast, quick, curious, or strong she is, you are beginning to build her self-image and, hence, her self-esteem. Similarly, if you note only a child's misbehavior or comment only on what she cannot do well, you mold her image of herself as a failure and lower her self-esteem. Young children, moreover, sense their parents' doubts and anxieties. Thus, parents who worry excessively that their child may not be able to throw a ball well enough to play Little League or may never do as well in school as her older brother also erode her self-esteem.

You reinforce your child's self-esteem when you let him know that you value him as an individual, whatever his strengths and weaknesses. He may not run fast enough to make the track team, but you love and respect him for trying. She may have trouble reading, but you trust her judgment and admire her sense of humor. Do not, of course, teach your child to accept lowered standards or smother him with empty praise. Rather, help him to value himself for what he does well, to know his limits, and to accept what he cannot do as well as others.

As children get older, they naturally compare themselves with their peers. That urge is especially strong in adolescence, when children, buffeted by physical changes in their bodies and new questions of identity outside the family, often lose their good feeling about themselves. (See chapter 36.) With this loss of self-esteem, they tend to follow the judgment of other people, rather than their own. (See chapter 27 on developing internal moral standards.) But, in respect to peer and other outside pressure, self-esteem can be a child's internal compass — in terms both of moral values and of goals and desires. A child who feels good about himself believes that it is important to do what gives him satisfaction. And, if you have helped your child develop a moral grounding, he will be most satisfied when he behaves well.

Children who feel strong, competent, secure, and adaptable and who understand themselves are far more able than those who don't to weather the ups and downs of life. They are also better able to take pleasure in others' successes. These feelings are not luxuries: they are fundamental to operating fully as a human being.

uation. For example, you can say, "Pirates are frightening, aren't they? I'm happy that in real life there aren't any more pirates, and we can stop playing at pirates whenever we want." Such a discussion helps him manage the experience, feel comfortable in his imagination and play, and trust you as an emotional support and an anchor in reality.

As children become more proficient in understanding emotional expression, they also learn the difference between apparent and actual emotions. By age three or four, a child can hide her disappointment to a certain degree. Adults often coach their children to adopt social rules and polite behavior by, for example, prompting a youngster to smile and say thank you for a present she has received but is not terribly happy with. Although young children become quite able to modify their displays of emotion, they do so at this age simply to conform; they do not intend to mislead anyone.

Nor do they have any idea that people might intentionally mislead one another, and they can easily be deceived or confused when a grown-up displays one emotion while concealing another. Nonetheless, a three-year-old is as skilled at reading body language as he was at reading faces when he was an infant. He often knows when something is bothering the people he loves. He may ask, "What's the matter?" If you smile weakly in response and say that everything is fine, you give him a mixed message, confusing him. Having no idea why you would deny your feelings, he is no longer sure about what he saw. Consistently denying your feelings to your child can seriously impair his own ability to read his and others' emotions throughout his life. You need to give him a simple, understandable version of what is bothering you. As we have said before, the best answers are honest — but, of course, do not tell your child everything. Frame your explanation in language and concepts that he can understand. Openly discussing your feelings and helping your child find words for his emotions will confirm his ability to perceive emotions and thereby enhance his understanding and self-confidence. (See "Self-Esteem and Why It Matters," page 309.)

A Widening Emotional Life: Your School-Age Child

By the time your child is ready for school, more mental and physical transformations have shaped her emotional responses. You can reason and bargain with her (and often have to). She can do much more for herself and is interested in your companionship in a qualitatively different way from wanting to have a caretaker. Her memory capacity has increased; because she now has hindsight and foresight, she can remember and wait and look forward to what is coming. Crucial are her developing skills in expressing and receiving information through language and its associated cognitive abilities. Your child is no longer using language simply to label objects. She is now able to tell stories, to think about how things and people go together, to place events in the past and wishes in the future. She knows that her thoughts are her own and that other people have their own worlds of thoughts and feelings. When she was a toddler, you needed to use actions to help her understand, and she needed to demonstrate things physically in order to express herself to you. Now you can express with words most of what you want her to understand, and so can she.

Each growth spurt and every new experience sets off a flurry of feelings. Some may be familiar, others a little different from what your child knows; a few will be totally new. Some feelings will confuse him, others will be stressful or simply unfamiliar. Each situation evoking these feelings will be occasions for him to reflect on his inner world. As he grows up, your child will depend more and more on language to help him understand these kinds of feelings. And, as we have said, the more able your child is to bring his cognitive self to bear on his inner world, the more effective and confident he will be. A child who lacks the ability to identify, describe, or discuss his feelings will attempt to act out the hard feelings of anger or fear in some inappropriate or hurtful way. (For more on this, see chapter 22.)

Your child's increasing cognitive abilities also allow her to see and empathize with another person's outlook, rather than projecting her own emotional responses onto that person. She can remain somewhat detached, knowing that a situation does not directly involve her, or she can choose to respond. Using the same cognitive skills, she gains more awareness of her own feelings. And around this time your child also comes to appreciate that actions that cause distress to others are wrong, as we discuss further in chapter 27.

As your kindergartner attempts to refine his social skills, he will become more conscious of which behaviors do and do not earn approval from the adults in his life. In the early part of this stage, he longs for adult approval and will often try hard to behave like a grown-up. He will mimic your body language and consciously try to refine his own behavior to match his understanding of what he sees. He will try to help you with your work — hammer nails, write a letter, fix dinner. Your child's games and pretend play will aid her social learning and help her work out her own feelings in the scenarios she chooses. Good guys and bad guys, doctor and patient, teacher and student, waitress and customer — she adopts these roles and others to see how they feel, to control the experience, and to master it. Acting out these pretend stories may help her emotionally process her own experiences and those she may have heard about, witnessed, or simply imagined. (See chapter 16 for more about play.)

Controlling Emotional Expression

The new experience of being in school and interacting with other children and adults transforms a child's consciousness about people, and he becomes very interested in social relationships outside the family. (See pages 351–356 for more on this passage.)

When he was younger, your child thought about and responded to people simply as individuals. Now he can appreciate how people, both in his family and in the larger world, interact and that their actions have consequences. And he realizes that his own actions do as well. To act on this realization, he needs to learn how to control the way he expresses his emotions. Achieving this ability takes a few years.

Starting at about age four, children sense that their very intense feelings will wane in strength over time. That knowledge helps them learn, by about age six, that they can actually manage their emotions, and they also are able to see that the strength of an emotion is connected with how much they continue to think about what precipitated it. So if a child wants to stop feeling sad, he might try to distract himself so as to push away thoughts about what caused his sadness. Furthermore, he learns that choosing to do something that he knows will make him happy can change his mood. Or your child may ask for help, or talk with you about feeling bad, or make up a pretend story. At this age, children have the resources to develop a repertoire of ways to cope with and understand their feelings.

You can encourage your school-age child's interest in practicing socially acceptable behavior by teaching her the rules and conventions for displaying emotion publicly: "I know you're happy you won the race, but it makes the other girls feel bad when you yell, 'I'm number one!' over and over." Thus, around this age, as your child is learning to understand and respect another person's feelings

as well as her own, she can realize that there are public and private feelings and that some social situations require her to hold some feelings to herself and save them for sharing with close friends and relatives.

With your child's recognition that she has a private emotional world, she begins to appreciate its potential. With her new ability to be introspective and to identify her own emotions, she can take a step back and look at herself as if she were an observer. The ability to hold two or more views of herself allows her to decide which picture she would like to display outwardly. In different situations, she may choose to conceal her true response, either to protect her own feelings from the reaction of observers or to protect an observer's feelings. She also learns that the way she exhibits emotions can mislead other people.

The fact that children should learn to limit their display of emotion in certain social situations doesn't mean, of course, that they have to limit their usual feelings. Feelings are internal and unwilled; emotional displays are external and subject to control. Cultures and families differ greatly in how much emotion they consider acceptable for people to exhibit. In some houses, children hear their parents and other relatives laugh loudly, cry easily, and raise their voices in everyday conversation without implying any anger. In others, children grow up learning to keep their feelings to themselves. In both kinds of household, children have strong feelings nonetheless, even as they learn to manage them according to their upbringing and temperament. Although, by tradition, American culture has discouraged one sex or the other from expressing certain emotions, such as vulnerability for boys and competitive pride for girls, the important message is the same for both: While it isn't always easy to learn when it is appropriate to display emotions to the outside world, or how to do so, your child's strong feelings are central to his or her life and should be recognized and respected.

Internalizing Responsibility

Over the next few years of middle childhood, as your child comes to see himself as responsible for gaining or losing a desired outcome, he begins to understand such social emotions as pride, shame, and guilt. Actually, children start to develop the capacity to experience these emotions when they are quite young. For example, a third-grader behaves in a certain way, and his parents approve. He repeats that behavior to test their approval — an important motivation for a child to master new skills. Eventually he may behave in that way primarily to gain parental approval, and his parents may even let him know that they are proud of him. He may anticipate their approval on subsequent occasions and even begin to enjoy his anticipation. But his experience of pride is still, at this point, based upon the approval of people outside himself: he has not yet developed his own standards or his own sense of satisfaction at behaving in a way he feels good about. And he probably does not yet talk about his emotions as pride, shame, or guilt,

but may speak of feeling happy or scared or bad.

Around the age of six or seven, a child begins to feel — and recognizes that she feels — proud or ashamed or guilty only when someone is observing her behavior. The next stage in this emotional understanding comes when, at around eight years old, your child becomes the audience and starts to observe and judge her own actions according to what she believes another person's reaction would be. The technical term for this transition is "internalization," meaning that a child has incorporated into her own mental world the responses of her parents and other important adults. Now, no longer needing to look to others for judgment, she can look inside herself. It may, of course, take many more years before she realizes the satisfaction of doing what she judges to be right for herself and not for anyone else's approval. Indeed, you are never quite free of wondering what important people in your life — even your parents — will think about what you do.

Internalization is a signal that your child has begun to acknowledge some degree of personal responsibility. He has started to feel that reaching his goals is at least partially up to him. Understanding also requires recognition of the importance of normative standards — first and foremost, the standards you set in your family. In school, with friends and in extracurricular activities, he will use and test these standards. (See chapters 24 and 25, respectively.) Gradually, he will incorporate his family's standards with the standards of his community into a profile of his own. (See chapter 26.) Finally, he will put all these together with his own experience to develop a conscience and become a moral person (see chapter 27) — an outcome that will undergird the rest of his life. Before we reach this stage, however, we need to examine hard feelings and violence, and discuss how to help your child to manage one and avoid the other.

CHAPTER 22

Hard Feelings: Helping Your Young Child Cope with Fear, Worry, and Anger

Fear, worry, anger: these feelings can be painful, even frightening in their intensity and persistence. They make you want to lash out and hurt whoever and whatever is (or seems to be) standing in your way, frustrating your wishes, or even attacking you, verbally or physically. And if you can't act on these feelings, either because of circumstances, your own diffidence, or because you don't know how to, they only get worse.

Reflect for a moment on your own experience with these hard feelings: you have had a difficult day at the office — a colleague turned on you angrily and you weren't able to defend yourself. You have come home hoping for relief but, instead, your mind is churning, turning over and over — hours after that scene in the office — your anger at your colleague's behavior, anger at yourself for not adequately responding to her, worry and fear that she may hurt you in some way. Or, it's a snowy night and you're waiting for your best friend to call to say he has arrived home

safely. The longer you wait, the more your fears and worries — even anger (maybe he's gotten home and has forgotten to call) — mount up, crowd in on and overwhelm you. By the time your friend does call, you can hardly speak through the chaos of feeling. Or recall when you have been stalled in a slow checkout line or in traffic and you have wanted to lash out and slap the person who is holding things up. At the same time, you're embarrassed at the force of your own aggressive impulses. You realize, then, how strong your feelings are, how you seem at times in their power rather than being — as you like to think of yourself — master of your feelings and your thoughts.

Keep these moments, and the many others in your life, in mind and don't be surprised the first time your scowling toddler pushes another child out of the way. At this instant, you and your child move from the delicate, baby's world, where the child's every wish has been law, into the social world of other people and their feelings and desires. You may worry that this means that your child is going to grow up to be angry and aggressive, but it is as natural for a young child to grab for what he wants as it is for him to smile when it is given.

Your task is to help your child learn to control her hard feelings: that is (as we said in the last chapter) to recognize them, to put them aside if nothing can be done about them at the moment, and to act on them appropriately without aggression and violence. Thus, in the examples at the beginning of this chapter, you could have eased your hard feelings considerably had you, in the first, been able to address your colleague's concerns without rancor or, in the second, turned your attention to a book or a television program to distract you from your worry and fear. As for the last, you learned long ago not to strike out and know, moreover, how self-destructive doing so would be.

Fear, worry, and anger are not only uncomfortable: they are also unpredictable, going up and down apparently spontaneously. Thus, the kindergartner who has howled through the house all afternoon with a sheet over her shoulders pretending to be a ghost and scaring her little brother insists that evening on having her night-light turned back on in case there really are ghosts. No matter how much her parents reassure her, her fears have taken hold. Or, preoccupied with his father's illness, a middle-school student throws himself into researching a major school report on Russia, then comes down with pneumonia the week it is due. The worry about his father that he has been working hard to push aside has, nonetheless, weakened his body as well as distracted his mind.

In this chapter, we discuss how fear and anxiety arise in infants, toddlers, preschoolers, and older children and how to allay them. We also discuss anger and aggressiveness: that is, all children are aggressive, some more than others. But, with your help, your child can learn to control this tendency. He can learn to be assertive but not destructive, and to speak out effectively for his own needs and wishes without ignoring the needs of other people. Such self-mastery is one of the most important steps in your child's emotional development.

Fear and Anxiety

Fear is a protective emotion telling you to be careful, slow down, limit what you do, even to think twice. Anxiety is also a normal, and inevitable, human condition. No matter how carefully you protect your children or how calm you are in their presence, they will have worries. They have, after all, relatively little control over their safety. They also have fears that they cannot explain and that you cannot brush away for them. Children's fears are different from adult fears and are displayed in different ways, depending on the child's developmental stage. Some children's fears are magnified by their experiences and their environments, while other children's fears come from within themselves: these children may worry even when they are safe and well protected.

The ability to feel fear and sense danger is built into human biology. Sudden fear turns on the more automatic parts of your brain, making you more vigilant and ready to protect yourself if you need to. In this mode, you are ready to respond instantaneously; you don't evaluate your choices, make reasoned decisions, or think reflectively. Even when there is no apparent external danger, you may worry about the possibility of danger, loss, or stress. Your imagination can make you as vigilant as if you were actually alone in a dark alley in the middle of the night. Some people's anxieties can become so debilitating as to prevent them from focusing on or completing any other task.

The same is true for children. A child can move quickly out of danger or become frozen with fear. She can pick up the worries her parents are trying to conceal from her or create new worries entirely out of her own imagination. Some children's brains have a relatively lower threshold for the protective circuits of fear and anxiety; such children are thus more likely to feel fearful and anxious even in ordinary, nonthreatening circumstances. These differences are partly genetic and partly determined by experience. The fact that anxious parents often seem to have anxious children reflects both their common genes and the children's response to growing up in a family permeated by worried tension or concerns about various threats or dangers. The capacity to feel fear and anxiety begins in infancy with the most basic need to feel secure and cared for. Toddlers feel more fears and anxieties about an expanding world they cannot fully comprehend; older children have both the gift and the curse of their imagination to provide them ever more thoughts about unknown possibilities and their attendant worries.

Strangers and Separations: An Infant's Anxieties

A sudden loud noise, a tumble, an unexpected squeeze from a startled parent — experiences like these naturally frighten small babies. They most often burst out crying, sometimes after an initial second of silent shock. Crying is, of course, the most practical way your infant has to express that he really, really does not like something. Fortunately, it is easy for a calm parent to soothe a baby's fearful response to some immediate event. Reassure her that everything is all right, that you are still there, and that the noise or abnormal experience that bothered her is over. Sensing a parent's touch and peaceful voice, an infant usually calms down almost as quickly as she originally became alarmed.

It is much harder for parents to soothe their infant's anxiety about things that are not easy to isolate and identify, such as subtle, ongoing, and hard-to-escape tensions in the home. An infant can usually sense stress in his parents because of changes in the quality of the interactions between himself and one parent or even between both parents.

A baby who suffers from this kind of fear and worry is more likely to express it through fretful behavior or inconsolable crying than by bursting into angry tears. Parents may see a marked change in their infant's usual rhythmic behaviors, such as sleep/wake patterns and eating schedules, or predominant mood. If you recognize this kind of behavior in your baby as fearfulness, take it as a signal that you need to reflect on the problems that are making your family so anxious and to resolve them.

Two specific fears commonly surface in children from six months to a year old: "stranger anxiety" and "separation anxiety." When your baby was younger, she might have looked at a new face with curiosity or even interest, but now she appears puzzled or frightened by a stranger. Within a few seconds, she may turn away and cry. If you are close by, she may seem less fearful, but even in your arms remains more wary than curious.

Stranger anxiety does not necessarily depend on the presence of an actual stranger. Unfamiliar family members may also elicit wariness, even distress, in an eight- or ten-month-old infant, and your baby may even turn away from grandparents whom he has not seen in a few months. (Let these relatives know that such a response is expected at this age so that they won't feel hurt, embarrassed, even rejected.) Around this same age, an infant can even become distressed if you change your appearance in a dramatic way: new glasses, new haircut, shaving off a beard, or wearing a mask (however playful or friendly the intention). Stranger anxiety seems to reflect a baby's increasing attachment to the people he knows as his parents.

He has come to understand that you will take care of him and keep him safe, and he wants only you and no one else to do this.

Around this same age, infants begin to look to their parents for guidance whenever someone new approaches. While your baby has been able to recognize different emotional expressions for several months, only in the second half of his first year has he started to interpret the expressions of your now-familiar faces as clues to how to behave toward a stranger. If you smile or speak warmly to an unfamiliar adult, your baby will respond with less fear and wariness than if you are neutral or hesitant. (The same is true if your baby encounters something new, such as a dog. When you are encouraging, positive, and calm, he will look with interest and may even crawl toward the dog and touch it. But if you are wary or anxious, he will sense your feeling and may begin to cry, even if the dog is across the room.)

Your infant's ability to calibrate and be influenced by other people's emotions, particularly yours, is called "social referencing." This is an important stage in how infants and toddlers learn to manage their own emotions, including fear and worry. When you reassure your young child when a stranger approaches or a new situation arises, she is more likely to internalize your soothing and encouragement. As she grows older, she will make your reassurances part of her own personality and gain the ability to regulate her own feelings. She will, however, continue to use this skill of social referencing throughout her life.

Thus, when she and a friend meet a group of strangers, they will look for social cues from each other; each one's emotional reaction will guide and pace the other's responses. Similarly, as a working adult in a meeting that seems unfocused, confused, or tense, she may look to the most authoritative, articulate, and competent person in the group for guidance.

Separation anxiety occurs when a baby becomes upset when the parent who is his main caregiver leaves his sight, even if only to go into a different room. He becomes fussy, protests loudly, and starts to cry. When the parent returns, the infant may briefly withdraw and be moody. Like stranger anxiety, separation anxiety also begins around the second half of a child's first year. It peaks around an infant's first birthday and gradually declines through her second year. It seems to be universal across cultures, though it varies in intensity and duration. Separation anxiety is not dependent on whether a baby has been left in the care of someone other than his parents or, conversely, has never been out of his parents' sight.

Separation distress may reflect "object permanence," an infant's newly acquired cognitive ability to keep someone (or something) in his mind even when he cannot see the person (or thing). At this age, your baby can think about you even when you are out of sight. On the one hand, this means he can be more easily comforted by the sound of your voices because, we believe, he now can think about you without needing strong visual cues. On the other hand, though he can summon a picture of you, he does not yet know from experience where you have gone and whether you will return and so becomes fearful and anxious. However painful and difficult the crying of separation distress may be, it indicates that your baby knows you and feels especially connected to you. (For practical advice on dealing with separation, see chapter 31.)

So Much to Fear: The Toddler's World

Fears and worries often become dramatically more evident in your child's second and third years, just as separation distress and stranger anxiety are waning. No matter how confident, even bold, your toddler seems, she is almost certain to be timid and anxious at times.

The toddler who is developing well embraces the world with her curiosity. She finds challenges and excitement everywhere: in new people coming and going, cars and trucks making unusual sounds, new foods, new places, other children. The world seems to contain an infinite number of things for her to touch, taste, watch, and try to take apart. But that beckoning world can also be dangerous, and eighteen months is the peak age for injuries because a toddler's curiosity and mobility often outpace her ability to judge danger.

At the same time, a toddler can be fearful and cautious — qualities that keep a very young, very small child from straying too far. Toddlers naturally are fearful of people and experiences they think will harm them, although the reasons for a toddler's fear of specific people and experiences are by no means obvious.

A toddler is able to balance her need to explore with her need to be safe when she knows that she can return to you for protection at the first sign of danger. As your child gets older and is more self-assured and more competent, the balance can shift and she will venture out with more confidence. Thus, we have the paradox in which a child who is well cared for and feels secure in his parents' love is more able to experience normal fear and worry, knowing he can always return to them for comfort and reassurance, while the child who has been neglected and abused is more often heedless of danger, being unable easily to recognize normal feelings of fear and worry as protective signals.

Despite your two- or three-year-old's energy and enormous interest in the world, the world is much bigger than she is. However bold she may be, she has little mastery over her surroundings. Most important, a toddler's comprehension of the world is still limited, and he is still likely to feel apprehensive about new things he encounters as well as about what appears in his thoughts and fantasies. He may feel particularly apprehensive at bedtime when he is about to be left alone. He may want a light to chase the dark away, ask for just one more story to keep you in the room a little bit longer, or gather up his familiar pillow, blanket, pajamas, and stuffed animals. (For helping toddlers go to sleep, see pages 181–184.) Toddlers soothe their

worries through consistency and routine. Indeed, such rituals are the essence of this age. If a child can keep her immediate surroundings unchanging and predictable, the world will seem a little less uncertain and daunting.

In toddlerhood, imagination begins to flower, and what young children imagine usually is far more frightening than their actual experiences. Their bad dreams seem real to them, and there is only a thin line between scary thoughts and actual events. While playing monsters, your child may get scared when she hears a door suddenly open somewhere else in the house: the monsters of her imagination have come to visit! Two- and three-year-olds are certain that just thinking about scary things can make them happen. They are sure that everyone knows about their occasionally angry thoughts and that such anger can actually harm others. Young children thus feel simultaneously powerful and helpless, at the center of their world yet insignificant. They have the power to make things happen and are, at the same time, small in the face of the bad things they can imagine. All this is cause for their normal anxiety.

Unlike older children and adults, toddlers cannot talk explicitly about their worries or try to avoid the thoughts or situations that frighten them. Often, therefore, they show their fears in paradoxical ways. Afraid of the vacuum cleaner, a child actively avoids it or constantly tries to explore and master it. Fearing the dark, another child plays with turning the lights on and off or is frantic whenever he is left alone in his bed at night.

Children may become ever more insistent on certain rituals. Whenever the baby-sitter is coming, Daddy must read this story, Mommy must sing that song, and the toys must be lined up just this way. Some toddlers meet any change in routine with irritability and an insistence that the whole business start again from the beginning. Such rituals are most common around bedtime, but are not confined to it. A young child who is going through a particularly worrisome time may depend on routines about food, clothing, bathing, and going to school because their soothing predictability calms her uncertainty and confusion.

When you reassure your children, don't think that saying, "There's nothing to be afraid of," will sweep away the worries and fears that grow from an active imagination. You also need to communicate in both words and actions that you will be near, that you will keep them safe, and that you understand what it is to feel frightened. You need to be as clear and consistent about daily routines as you can be: be sure your child knows who will pick him up in the afternoon, when Daddy or Mommy will be home for dinner, and why Mommy looks sad one day. Toddlers ask many, many questions, and these indirectly reflect the many other questions they are working on inside. Giving simple, straightforward answers to all of these questions may be tedious, but they allow your toddler to eliminate more easily the much more frightening answers he can come up with on his own. If you respond clearly and comfortably, you also let your child know that

it is all right for him to be curious and that there are answers to his questions — to many of them, at least.

Fantastic Fears: Preschoolers and Older Children

During their preschool years, children's fears become somewhat more realistic. They often express fear about lions, tigers, or sharks, and while most of these fears are far from directly threatening to most Americans who go to nursery school, there is also an element of reality to them. So, for example, while your young child may be eager to swim and look forward to playing in the water, he may still all too easily envision the dangers of deep water, become fearful of oceans and pools, and resist learning how to swim. This developmental shift reflects not only your child's increasing knowledge about the world but also his more sophisticated ability to fantasize about all that he cannot see or understand. As with younger children, an individual's fearfulness depends partly on his genetic endowment and partly on what he has learned from and with his parents.

Often young children show their worry and fear in giddy excitement. The more anxious they are, the more active and uncontrollable they become. Often they are so excited that they cannot heed their parents' or teachers' efforts to help them. Although some adults might interpret this behavior as willful or oppositional, often a child is feeling such internal overstimulation and anxiety that he simply cannot control himself.

Some children can have strong, over-

whelming worries and fears that are not simply responses to developmental pressures or the stresses of day-to-day life. These grow out of proportion to a stressful life event — such as the birth of a new sibling, an illness, a death in the family (for more on these sources of stress, see chapters 30, 32, and 35, respectively), or a family move (see "Johnny's Move," page 323) — and interfere with a child's life at school and at home, with her friendships, and with her pleasure in play. (In respect to such fear, see also "Stress and the Immune System," page 324.)

Parents can feel completely helpless when a very young child is frightened and worried. It is difficult to appreciate the

ERIC AND HIS DINOSAUR

For Eric, a four-year-old boy, play was very exciting. He was fond of pretending to be a strong, invincible character encountering ferocious dinosaurs. Eric was often active, even wild, in this game. But the dinosaurs never seemed to be vanquished. They always returned, even more frightening than before. When Eric was deepest in this play, he would jump at the slightest unexpected sound and anxiously ask his teacher or his mother, "What's that?" Sometimes he would say with fearful certainty, "The dinosaurs are coming."

Eric was well liked by his teachers and the other children at his preschool. His teachers appreciated his verbal skills and vivid imagination, but found his behavior extremely difficult to manage. He was especially disruptive on days when the class's schedule or usual activities did not go as planned. Sometimes, for no apparent reason, Eric would push or even hit another child. At these moments, even his calmest, firmest teacher had trouble helping him settle down. The preschool staff was worried about how Eric was going to do in a larger, more stimulating kindergarten classroom.

As spring came around, they met with Eric's parents and sug-

gested that, despite his obvious intelligence, he was not ready to start school. He was still developing the ability to cope with changes to his routines and to manage his own frightening thoughts. And so Eric spent another year at the preschool, a familiar place he knew and liked. He still played exuberantly, but one day he announced to his teacher that he had tamed the dinosaur: "It's my friend now." Gradually his overall behavior grew calmer. The next September, Eric was ready to enter kindergarten and did very well. (For more on kindergarten readiness, see pages 265–266.)

strength of a child's fear that Daddy won't come home from work or that a monster will destroy the house. Though you know that gremlins do not come out at night and that thinking angry thoughts doesn't make bad things happen, these are natural worries for your child. Children (like adults) need time to think through their most pressing worries

JOHNNY'S MOVE

Johnny was four when he and his parents moved to a new state, away from their extended family. His parents had accepted new jobs with better salaries, but the shift meant a lot of change in Johnny's life. Their old home had been close enough to his grandmother's house that he could run across the backyard and be in her kitchen and was nearby his cousins' houses as well. Johnny's parents missed their relatives, too. His mother, who had always worried a lot, had taken comfort in her older brother and sister's reliable presence and help.

Johnny's parents quickly made all the formal arrangements necessary to settle into their new home. They found a preschool where Johnny could start just after they arrived. But when things settled down after the move and the unpacking, his parents were saddened by the fact that Johnny seemed like a different boy. Once well-behaved and easygoing, he now seemed clingy and irritable. His new teachers reported that he

disrupted nap time, tried to provoke the other children when they sat together in a circle, and seemed generally unhappy and unmanageable. The school warned his parents that unless Johnny's behavior improved, they could not keep him in the class. Yet the more his parents tried to set firm limits at home, the more Johnny seemed out of control. He said repeatedly that he didn't like his new school and didn't want to go. He cried uncontrollably one night after finding that a picture he had drawn of their old house was no longer hanging on the refrigerator door.

Johnny's parents realized that clearly he was upset about moving away from the home and family he loved. He was asking over and over about his grandparents and his parents' new work schedules. Tired and stressed themselves, they were at a loss about what to do. In fact, they were not certain that their son was wrong. Perhaps the move had been a mistake. Johnny's mother talked on the phone to her older sister about bringing him back for an extended visit to cheer him up. "I have a better idea," Johnny's aunt

said. "I'll come visit you." She flew in the next week with her toddler. Johnny got to renew his friendship with his favorite aunt and one of his cousins. He also got to show them his new house and new room and new yard.

As the children played, their mothers talked. It became clear that Johnny's father and mother had always been anxious about the move. And since their arrival, they had made few links to their new community. "You know, Johnny picks up on how you're feeling," said the older sister. "He's always been good at that. When he knows you're not happy, that makes him even sadder." During that visit, Johnny's mother and father decided to commit themselves more fully to their new home. They joined a community group and enrolled Johnny in a new nursery school so he could make a fresh start. With frequent calls home and a new photograph of their extended family on the living room wall, Johnny and his parents all gradually became comfortable in their new home. (For more about helping children adjust to a new house, see pages 456–458.)

STRESS AND THE IMMUNE SYSTEM

The normal human response to stressful events has probably been part of the genetic code for millennia, dating back to when humans had to be constantly on the alert in their daily struggle for survival. When you are frightened or threatened, your adrenal glands release epinephrine (also called adrenaline), a hormone that activates the body's protective functions. The heart begins to race, blood pressure rises, muscles tense, pupils dilate. All of these physical responses focus you on the danger at hand, preparing you either to fight or to escape quickly. Even after the threat is resolved, your body can remain in a state of heightened wariness: tense, jumpy, focused on the immediate. And if the situation is left unresolved — if you do not have a chance to relax — this constant alertness will start to affect your physical and mental functioning.

Not all stressful events are sudden and clearly threatening. Dangers to your well-being in the modern world are usually vastly different from dangers in the wild. Nonetheless, your brain still responds the same way. When a challenge overwhelms you — whether a serious illness, some

difficulty at school, the loss of a friend — it can stress you to the point of physical and psychological dysfunction. Some people are especially vulnerable to stress; even everyday decisions can seem overwhelming to them. Others feel they do their best work under pressure. A few even seek out situations of danger. Children are much the same: many are able to tolerate a lot of upheaval and adventure, while others are upset at any challenge or change in family routine. The differences lie partly in biology and partly in experience.

No matter how well children handle pressure, however, continued stress drains the body's resources and reserves. Often a child will become irritable at the least change in his routine. Stressed children can become overtired or not sleep well; they can lose their appetite or eat too much. A young child may cling to you more than usual or seem despondent. Sometimes a child who is overstressed is also impulsive, overactive, and unusually defiant (just as an adult under pressure may become argumentative and unreasonable).

The feeling of being overwhelmed can disrupt the immune system. Children (and adults) under stress are more vulnerable to colds and other viral infections. Asthma, headaches, indigestion, and dizziness can all be triggered or made worse by stress. Not sur-

prisingly, these are also the symptoms that parents commonly hear a child complain about when he does not want to go to school, music lessons, or some other potentially stressful event. If your child frequently has such symptoms at just those times, his troubles are not necessarily "all in his head." Sometimes children fall seriously ill because of stress and worry, and these illnesses need treatment. But even in this case, the long-term solution for your child lies in addressing the source of the stress and teaching him healthier and happier ways to deal with it. These can include talking about problems with you or a counselor, finding solutions to school challenges, or resolving difficulties in your family's life that you did not realize were so damaging.

Some researchers now believe that chronic stress weakens the ability of a person's immune system to guard against more serious illnesses, such as arthritis or perhaps even some cancers. Unrelieved stress — from real or imagined causes — may bring on high blood pressure, chronic headaches, and other general aches and pains. Children feeling too much pressure also lose the ability to concentrate or perform at their usual level in school and other settings. All these are more reasons to help your child deal positively with the stresses of life.

and fears, and sometimes can work them out in their own ways with imaginative play. (See chapter 16.) Thinking, playing, and talking help, if your child's world is predictably and consistently secure, caring, and accepting. Sometimes it helps to recognize that your child's most excited, out-of-control moments may reflect her own feelings of worry or uncertainty about herself, her parents, or some recent event. Try saying, "You're pretty excited right now. Let's find some way to calm down." Thus you both address her feelings and tell her that there is some possibility of relieving them.

By school age, as your child's cognitive abilities mature, he will begin to fear real, rather than imagined, things. He may worry about failing in school or not making a sports team. He will probably worry about his abilities, whether his peers and teachers like him, and, perhaps, about your health and the health of your marriage or about how much you love him. Adults find the fears and worries of a school-age child more understandable since they usually have some base in reality. While you may not share your child's feeling of life-and-death urgency about buying just the right jacket or getting into a particular club, you can understand that behind these details are worries about being accepted, fitting in, and measuring up.

Anxieties become a problem for your school-age child when they interfere with her ability to function normally. Worry about an upcoming report, test, or class trip can bring on an illness or otherwise affect a student's ability to learn. Anxieties brought from home can show up in school and vice versa. Older children can also mask their fears with aggressive behavior against classmates — boys, in particular, are steered down this path by cultural messages that they should not show fear. When your older school-age child behaves anxiously or aggressively for an extended period without an identifiable cause, acting much like a toddler who throws things wildly because she cannot get her way, she probably has deeper troubles that would benefit from professional consultation. (See chapter 33.)

Aggressiveness and Anger

Aggressiveness and anger are typically thought of as negative emotions. Both suggest contrasts — hate as opposed to love, war against peace, destruction against creativity, hostility instead of affection. Typically, aggressiveness and anger are thought of as going hand in hand: you are angry when you have been injured or wronged and thus feel aggressive toward the cause of that injury. You may visualize aggressiveness and anger as the dark side of your personality, an aspect of yourself likely to spring forth unless you keep it tame and socialized. Marcel Proust expressed most clearly the suspicion that aggressive feelings lie within everyone: "At the heart of our friendly or purely social relations, there lurks a hostility, momentarily cured but recurring by fits and starts." Parents, aware of their aggressive and angry feelings and sometimes fearing them in others, worry that their children may be "too aggressive" or "out of control" — their secret demons let loose.

Aggressiveness is not, however, always related to anger. Sometimes you are aggressive in order to gain what you believe to be rightfully yours. Of course, if the other party disagrees with your sense of ownership, anger soon erupts. Thus, many a playground scuffle begins with one child claiming sole right to the sandbox while another stands by. Aggressiveness is also not always destructive; indeed, it is the core of one's being necessarily and adaptively assertive — a capacity you admire in yourself and in others. Assertiveness serves important social roles. Secretly, you may respect strong, well-honed aggressiveness, especially when it is used to support what you consider to be a good cause. Society celebrates the effectiveness of a well-planned attack, whether verbally in the boardroom, politically on picket lines, or physically on a battlefield. In most cultures, the traits of the warrior have long been synonymous with the qualities of strength, survival, and often maleness. American culture encourages young people to be able to stand up for themselves, to take action against things that upset them, and to mobilize their energies to attain high ambitions. Yet this same culture also wants children to manage their feelings, to play fair, and to love each other. How to instill that balance in a child is a challenge to many parents.

Aggressive behavior in young children has many roots. While some factors in a child's aggression, such as her basic tolerance for frustration, seem to depend in large part on genes, many others are shaped by what she learns from her experiences with parents and teachers. If you react to a mistake by yelling or hitting, or express frustration by kicking a wall or throwing a book, you convey the message that those are acceptable ways of expressing feelings. If you condone or ignore fighting by boys because you expect them to be physically aggressive, you pass on a violent image of masculinity to both your sons and your daughters.

At the very least, aggressive behavior always expresses particular needs and feelings, whether in a child who is extremely anxious on the first day of school or in another who is tired and overwhelmed. Thus, a two-year-old who has only acquired a few words may be more aggressive than his peers because he has no other means to express either his needs or his frustrations. If you can interpret your child's behavior in this light, especially when he is young, you will be better able to help him express his frustration positively without hurting anyone else.

Some children rarely, if ever, express themselves through aggressive behavior, while others find it a ready and comfortable way of communicating. Also, not all thoughts or fantasies lead to aggressive behavior, kicking, biting, and yelling, and not all aggressive behavior is motivated by willful, hateful, or destructive feelings. In infants, aggression is mostly the expression of a need that is not quite satisfied. At first, when your baby is frustrated — by, say, not being able to reach a toy that she wants — she expresses herself by crying inconsolably. As she gets a bit older, she might push you away, hit you, or throw something. Your baby usually does not mean to harm people or things, nor does he even realize he has the power to do so. But even at this age, he can tell when you are upset by his behavior. He must resolve to stop the behavior that upsets you and find other ways to deal with his frustration — as he can do if you help him put it into words.

For very young children, who are becoming eager for freedom, aggressive behavior as in "Mine! Me do. Go away!" is a way of expressing independence. These firm statements, which may be unpleasant, even hurtful, are positive nonetheless. They are your child's adaptive way of asserting his own space and place in the world. Likewise, your toddler's temper tantrums, while tempestuous and surely irritating for you, are strong statements of his desire to be more in control, to be his own boss. This desire is often in conflict with a toddler's feeling of being small, dependent, and powerless. Thus, developmentally, it is no accident that temper tantrums begin as children start to experiment with separation from their parents. The more they move away, the more dependent and little they feel.

Young children do not necessarily act out their aggressive feelings and thoughts, but these are a central part of their fantasy lives. These fantasies are related to your toddler's ever-present feeling of being dependent on a much larger, stronger adult world. As she struggles for independence — to be "grown-up" — she can experiment with the idea of being bigger by pretending to be powerful,

even scary and aggressive. In a way, such fantasies are like whistling through a graveyard — pretending that you're not only not scared, but calm and nonchalant. A young child believes himself to be the center of his parents' world as well as of the world beyond. He feels that everything rotates around him and, like the mouse that roared, a single roar from him would surely make that world notice and tremble.

Aggressive behavior in preschool children has different intents, causes, and outcomes. In trying to figure out why a child is biting or hitting, ask where she directs her violence: toward other people or only toward inanimate objects? In other words, does she kick and break toys or kick and hurt her classmates, siblings, and parents? What typically starts the aggressive behavior? Is she frustrated because she wants a toy she cannot have or because she wants to be hugged by a busy parent or teacher? Is she very tired or very excited — at the end of the day or just after a puppeteer has visited the day care? Is she reacting to another child's teasing about her hair or about falling on the playground or about crying when her father left? Did another child hit or push her? Also, consider the apparent intent of a child's aggressive behavior. Is it a means to an end — to get the desired toy or make a place on the teacher's lap? Is it to create a personal space — a kind of "don't tread on me" signal? Does the goal seem to injure or destroy or is it really to gain another's attention, to win in a game, or to get the best seat in circle time? No child acts aggressively in the same way with the same reasons in every situation. But if you identify what a child really wants, you can tell her not to push or hit while also showing her a better way to achieve her aim. Thus you reduce her frustration and need to act out.

When evaluating a child's aggression, consider how it might be linked to his fears and worries. His behavior may be a way for him to express, without acting fearful, that he is really worried deep down. "Tough guys" are not supposed to be scared, but the combination of fear and shame can trigger frightening violence. Although not all aggressive feelings in children reflect deep-seated fears and anxiety, parents (and teachers) need to be aware of this possibility. In addition, aggressive thoughts worry young children. While it feels exciting and grown-up to imagine yourself the strongest, most ferocious, most powerful lion, tiger, boy, or girl, it's lonely and scary at the top. Who will fix your breakfast, take care of your bruises, put you to bed? That anxiety might, in turn, encourage a child to be even more bold and aggressive.

Remember also that there is little to no separation between thoughts and action in the minds of very young children (before the age of four, sometimes five, and sometimes even in the minds of adults). A three-year-old may declare in swashbuckling pride that he has killed everyone and now owns the whole house, all the food, and the cars: "Even dinosaurs are scared of me!" But if his mother is late coming home from work that evening, he may start to wonder whether he has actu-

ally done what he has imagined. Can he really make someone disappear just by thinking about it? That's scary stuff! Young children also suspect that other people know exactly what they are thinking, including their desires for power and triumph. A child may, therefore, half-expect adults to launch an "advance attack" to punish her for her aggressive thoughts. And she can come to fear that her normal feelings of jealousy toward a new baby sister may bring retaliation from others in her world.

Physically aggressive behavior — hitting, biting, pushing, kicking — begins to subside by the time most children reach their third or, at the latest, their fourth birthday. Verbal aggression, on the other hand — shouting, yelling, and name-calling — all increase between the ages of two and four as children gain more language skills. Most often, all kinds of hostile behavior, whether verbal or physical, diminish in frequency by the time children are five or six years of age and entering the first and second grades. Younger children are most aggressive when they are asserting their territory, their needs, and their wants. Older children, in contrast, focus their aggression on social situations and needs. Indeed, an older child's belligerence is more often related to a perceived hurt or slight. If a particular person has insulted her, she will want to pay back the insult to her self-esteem. Paradoxically, as children get older, they are far less aggressive, but when they do resort to aggression, their actions are most often intended to harm another person.

Efforts to lessen violence among young people often focus on helping them find peaceful ways to deal with perceived insults. (See chapter 23.)

An aggressive, demanding toddler or preschooler is not necessarily destined to be aggressive as a school-age child. Nor, despite parents' and teachers' worries, is the hitting, kicking, biting three-year-old guaranteed to become an angry social outcast as an early teen. What matters most is how you and other adults understand and meet aggressive behavior in younger children. A child whose aggression is met with aggression learns that shouting, name-calling, and physical force are the only acceptable ways of expressing frustration and anger. When, however, you talk to your child about her feelings, you have a good chance of helping her relieve them without hurting anyone. Thus, by finding peaceful methods for your child to strive for mastery, both by asserting herself and protecting herself, you support these developmental tasks without encouraging hostile or violent behavior.

As your child learns to handle aggressive, angry feelings, fears, and worries, she will become better able to tolerate all her emotions, both negative and positive. As she does so, she is developing the ability to love, having learned very young that loving does not cancel out hatred and vice versa. Your behavior toward her will teach her that every human being has feelings — that they love the most important people in their lives for who they are, yet at the same time may get mad at their quirks and disappointing qualities. This knowledge, acquired early in life, will undergird all of your child's relationships with other people. It is the framework for the social tasks ahead, including that most important one of developing a conscience and becoming a moral person. But before turning to these aspects of your social child, we need to address the problem of violence and the child whose aggressive impulses are not easily overcome.

CHAPTER 23

Children and Violence

Like all parents, you want to keep your children safe, but violence — whether through direct experience or indirectly through the media — seems inescapable in today's world. Even though personal crimes may be decreasing in large cities, more and more children are both victims and perpetrators of violence. In this chapter, we will first discuss how children are exposed to violence and then suggest how you can help your children deal with it, whether its source is the world of entertainment or their own experience.

Children's Exposure to Violence Today

Violence, as we have said, affects children's lives both directly and indirectly. Your child may have direct experience with aggression and violence in your neighborhood, such as bullies and fistfights in the streets outside her window, within or around school, or at home. Hunting and other blood sports may also expose a child to violence directly.

Your child also can be indirectly exposed to violence through news coverage of crime, rape, war, and accidents; films and TV; magazines, newspapers, and comic books; video games; and the Internet. Adults are often appalled, yet simultaneously entranced, by horrific depictions of tragic injury and destruction. Psychologists have proposed many theories to explain why so many people are attracted to frightening thrills. Whatever the reason, stories involving a child or children — as victims, witnesses, or perpetrators — can have the greatest morbid attraction. And since such stories are fairly common in print and on television, children have often seen these violent images before their parents even realize it. The exposure may be short — a promotional clip for the late-night news — or ongoing — a video game, for example, that has been altered to include bloody sequences.

Although television networks have started labeling programs that contain violent acts, many children still watch those programs.

Cable-television channels show "slasher films" in the afternoons. Even parents who scrupulously monitor what their children watch cannot shut out promotions for violent shows, and you may not even be aware of some of the video games your child has played or the music she may have heard at a friend's house. Adults often think that news stories from remote areas of the country or the globe do not affect their children or that cartoonish or fantasy violence is harmless. But young children have not yet developed sufficient perspective to distinguish the real from the fictional. Furthermore, studies have shown that watching violent movies or sports produces a measurable short-term rise in a person's aggressive tendencies. All exposures to violence become part of your child's view of the world. Even the violence-prevention programs she participates in at school can cause her to realize that she is not really safe.

Violence among young people seems extremely prevalent these days. Experts estimate that nearly four million American children are exposed to extreme violence each year — a situation the U.S. Centers for Disease Control have called a public health issue. Teenagers and even younger children have shot schoolmates in several states. In some communities, violence and the threat of violence are as severe as if the children were trapped in a war zone. Even though violent crimes by juveniles and at schools appear to be decreasing (in the 1990s, violent crime in general declined across the United States and in most — but not all — of our

larger cities), parents everywhere, even in America's suburban heartland, feel gravely concerned about their children's safety.

For the most part, exposure to violence starts at an early age and increases as children move on to middle and high school. Studies conducted in the late 1990s in Washington, D.C., Boston, Chicago, and New Orleans found that about 20 percent to 50 percent of children in grades one to three reported being directly exposed to violence. The percentage was higher (up to nearly 85 percent) for children in the fifth to tenth grades in cities such as New Haven, New Orleans, and Washington, D.C. Among these children, 30 percent to 50 percent reported that they had been victims of violence. One of the most common effects of such exposure is that a child feels unsafe in his everyday environments of school and home. In one city, nearly three-fourths of the children interviewed reported that they no longer felt secure in these traditional havens.

Parental attitudes toward this situation vary widely. Some parents may not even know about or be able to acknowledge their child's exposure to violence. In one 1997 study of fourth- to sixth-graders in Washington, D.C., more than 75 percent of the children reported witnessing serious violence in their community. When the research team spoke to the parents of these children, almost half either had not known or denied that their child had been exposed to violence. Other studies have also found denial among parents. It may be that parents in these areas were exposed to the same violence at the same time and were thus desensitized to or overwhelmed by it. These parents also may struggle with a sense of helplessness about or guilt for their inability to protect their children adequately.

Other parents react all too strongly to dangers they perceive to be facing their families. They may, for example, keep their child from playing outdoors or with other youngsters. This response can easily go too far. It can discourage a child from becoming independent; it may even deprive her of the important developmental task of socializing with and gaining support from her peers. When parents attempt (consciously or not) to adapt to an environment they perceive as hostile, they may also instill a bleak view of a world in which children cannot trust most people. Of course, some neighborhoods are grim, and protecting your children is important. Nonetheless, lessons in fistfighting, target shooting, or treating strangers as hostile all impart more than a defensive skill. Putting a menacing face on the world your child is entering is likely to make even a resourceful child feel helpless and ready to use violence.

In between these two groups of parents are those who minimize or avoid the impact of violence on their children. They may maintain that hopeful yet erroneous belief that children, especially very young ones, do not notice or remember violent events. Or parents can be so frightened by the threat of crime, for instance, that they don't discuss it with their children. If you are confused about what to do, your young children feel even more vulnerable.

Helping Your Child Deal with Violence

It is not wise to try to keep your child from any exposure to violence — direct or indirect, real or pretend. To do so would, in fact, isolate him drastically and leave him poorly prepared to grow up and help society deal with the problem of violence. Nor would it help him with or protect him from his own naturally aggressive feelings. Thus, you must learn how to help your child cope with having witnessed or been a victim of violence, much as you have learned to help him to cope with disappointments, bumps, bruises, and other developmental challenges. You can do this by talking with your child, by teaching him how to stay safe and how to deal with bullies, and by knowing what to do in the aftermath of violence.

Talking to Your Child

Although the research findings are complex, it seems clear that if a child has at least one close caregiver who understands her needs, accepts them, and responds when she is confused or troubled, she can feel protected and safe. The knowledge that someone is there for her instills resilience in a child. Your support can soften both the immediate experience of violent events and their potential negative social and emotional consequences (anxiety, depression, and so on). Thus, keep in mind that certain events and experiences can scare children (and adolescents) even if they do not scare you and most other adults. Also recognize the different ways that your child may respond to fright. Try as always to imagine how your child is feeling and how she is experiencing a situation given her age and her personality.

Speaking openly with and listening to your young child is, as we have said, probably the best way you can prepare him for later challenges. Most parents are uncertain about when to broach "hot" topics like sex, drugs, and violence with their growing child. You may fear that such well-meaning discussions will cause more harm than good. You worry that somehow you will inspire irresponsible behavior that your child has never previously considered. You may fear that, by letting him know that the world is not as innocent as you believe it has seemed to him, you will frighten or somehow "dirty" him — when actually it is your image of his innocence you fear you will smudge. On the other hand, if violence is a reality in your family environment, not talking about it will make your child wonder why you are denying the obvious. Remember, too, that even if your child is not exposed to violence in her world, she nonetheless needs to learn to manage her own aggressive feelings if, as we said in chapter 22, she is to develop into a mature, responsible adult. Thus, talking about the sensitive issue of violence is more likely to be helpful than harmful to your child.

The following steps can make it easier for you to talk effectively about this issue with your child. First, follow your child's lead. After raising a topic with a simple comment such as, "That was quite a violent show," or "Those people in the paper did some pretty bad things," give your child the time and opportunity to respond. Most parents can read their child's reactions accurately. Tune into that expertise and let your child's responses guide you on what and how much more you need to say.

If during the conversation your remarks get too intense or too complex, your child will look confused or upset, abruptly try to redirect the discussion to other topics, or even walk away to do something new. At the first sign of this discomfort, shift back to simply listening. Ask your child what he is feeling or thinking about. Remember that he will most likely talk to you about difficult issues when he is ready and when he feels that you are able to listen. If this isn't the right moment, be aware that it could come soon. Remember, too, that you have to make an effort to listen. Although many parents find it easier to do the talking, you may know yourself how appealing and reassuring a good listener can be.

After you hear what is on your child's mind, let her know by both your actions and your words that you are open to her concerns. For example, "Yes, when those older boys talk about fighting, that does sound scary. I'm glad you told me about how you feel." In this direct way, you reinforce your child's impulse to think out her concerns with you. It is generally useful to reflect your child's questions back to her and to create an opportunity for further thought and discussion before deluging her with your heartfelt good advice: "Do all the boys want to fight each other?" or "What does hearing them talk like that make you want to do?" This gives your child a chance to take control of her own complex feelings with your support and encouragement. Also, ask your child periodically whether she has ever considered the issues as you describe them: "Have you ever wondered why some kids act that way? Do you think about talking to your teachers when you're worried?" Again, stay tuned to what your child can understand and to what she is interested in; your discussion should clarify rather than muddy the issues.

One guiding principle, which is especially useful in addressing anxiety about violence, is reliability. Trust is a crucial ingredient of family relationships. It is a two-way process: both parties in a relationship learn to trust each other simultaneously over time. The process cannot be rushed.

You start out with an advantage: your baby depends on you and is eager to learn from you. Hence, it is crucial to be honest with your child. He must be able to rely on what you say without worrying about whether it is true. We do not mean, however, that you should tell each child everything; rather, everything you do tell a child should be true. It is honest to say, "I don't feel comfortable sharing that with you because I promised your brother that I'd keep it private." It is just as important to stick to your word about

rewards and privileges: "I said there would be no television if you and your sister started wrestling again, so there will be no television tonight." This is another form of reliability that your children will appreciate deeply — even if they protest at the time. (For more advice on setting and keeping rules, see chapter 27.)

Teaching Your Child to Stay Safe

"Inoculating" children against violence means helping them learn how to keep out of danger and avoid violent acts. It is a long-term effort, starting in the earliest years of life, within the supportive environment of your own home and family. By showing your children how to minimize conflicts and resolve them nonviolently, you help them grow into responsible, critical, independent thinkers.

You must first understand that children naturally feel vulnerable and feel that way even more when their outside world is unsafe. Your job as a parent is not only to keep your children safe but also to help them feel safe. Use the simple notion of "stay safe" to teach a variety of responses that your child can use in a frightening situation. With the goal of safety in mind, a child can learn to control herself, to listen to her parents even when she is highly emotional, and thus to avoid aggressive and angry outbursts. Help your child appreciate the value of safety by talking with her in detail about everyday hazards and telling her that her safety is one of your main concerns. Once aware of safety issues, children can more easily anticipate, avoid, and defuse dangerous situations. Your young child will better understand why he should not run off to play without telling you or whoever is caring for him at a particular time. Your older child will know why she should not drink alcohol or use drugs at parties. Asking a young teen who wants to have her schoolmates over without you around, "Do you think that is a safe plan?" can prompt her to have second thoughts and to see the risk in her proposal without feeling forced on the defensive.

As your child grows up and faces different challenges, he will need different and more sophisticated options for responding to them. Thus, revisit the issues of safety and choice throughout your child's development. If you expect that your child may encounter violent conflicts, try the "What if?" game: you and your child imagine realistic situations involving violence and create scripts for what she should do if something similar happens to her.

You can tell your child about a situation in which you had to handle conflict, and ask her to describe something similar in her experience. You can help her to think through the complexities of her situation and to express how she felt at the time and how she is making sense of it now. Try, also, to detect and respond to incorrect or dangerous assumptions that people advocate, such as "An eye for an eye"; "You should defend your property with your life"; "Having respect is more important than being safe"; or "Someone deserved to be hurt." Teach your child the dangers of false assumptions about other people's motiva-

tions: "She did it deliberately!" And help him recognize the universal tendency to blame others, rather than accept responsibility: "He started it. I had nothing to do with the trouble." By gently questioning these statements with your child, you can demonstrate clearly how conflicts arise. When you provide an opportunity for your child to consider, "How do you think he felt?" you help her develop greater empathy for others.

When you help your child generate and test out solutions to avoid or de-escalate such challenges in the future, do not attempt to solve his problems yourself or lecture him on what to do. Use your experience to help him put words to his strong feelings, to examine the situation fully, and to broaden his array of responses. If he devises a particular strategy himself, he will feel less helpless and better equipped to deal with trouble. Since it takes time for a child to learn to deal with the world this way, start in the early school years, just when your child is able to see situations from different angles. Your child can even formulate a script or set of rules for such moments. The script might go as follows:

- Stop! Think about what you're doing. Think about where you are.
- Come up with more than one solution to this problem and then compare them.
- Don't act without thinking about the possible consequences of doing so.

Remember that the best teaching is by example. Let your standard be, "Do as I say *and* as I do." In the same way that you model good communication and prove your trustworthiness, you also have the power to demonstrate safe choices and nonviolent conflict resolution. Rather than hide from your children all disagreements between you and your partner, let them see Mom and Dad working out some differences through discussion and compromise. If something has made you angry during the day, such as a parking ticket or a rude customer at work, acknowledge your emotion (your children can probably sense the tension already) and say how you will calm yourself or otherwise deal with the issue. Seeing such behavior helps your child realize how she can solve her problems maturely.

An effective antiviolence program includes the message that when you are in trouble, it is good to seek social support and to accept help. Children should neither fear nor

be embarrassed about talking to an adult whose job it is to protect them. Help your child practice how and where to seek help outside the family: from school counselors, teachers, religious leaders, police officers, youth counselors, and other trained adults.

The dangers that can confront a child often overwhelm parents as well. The more real the threat of violence from outside, the more helpless and isolated you can feel. To counter this feeling, take the initiative to talk with other parents who face the same challenges. Create a network to find solutions for the community. By working together, even busy adults can make their neighborhood safer for all the children at once. For instance, parents of younger school-aged children can take turns supervising outdoor activities, and parents of older children can chaperone evening activities. While some children might resist being watched by their own parents, they will more easily accept the establishment of a tradition where parents in general are consistently available.

Violence is not a problem that individual families can eradicate. To be effective, the response must involve the entire community, not simply the police or other authorities. Many cities have set up successful Child Development–Community Policing (CD–CP) programs, which treat the problem of violence on many levels. Neighborhood watch groups and community boards support law-enforcement officials who protect citizens and provide antidrug education and treatment programs that keep down the demand for illegal drugs. Counselors are available twenty-four hours a day to respond when children have suffered or witnessed violent acts. At weekly meetings, senior clinicians and police supervisors discuss the issues and follow up with these children and their families. Some of these programs have expanded to establish violence-prevention programs in the public schools and to try to intervene early in domestic violence.

How to Deal with Bullies

Many parents view violence as a problem that plagues society at large. But while they may readily acknowledge that there are bullies at school, probably even in their child's class, they don't worry about it as a serious issue. Bullying is, however, common, and it is by no means trivial. Indeed, when a child over a certain age (which varies according to the community) physically hurts another, threatens someone, or steals, that is a crime. This kind of behavior often becomes a pattern, as the bully repeatedly seeks out the same victim or victims.

Physical bullying is different from both horseplay and teasing among friends. It is also different from violence between evenly matched individuals or groups. A bully is always stronger than his victim, and that victim is a reluctant participant. Children who suffer from bullying also usually suffer from stress and its effects: headaches and other illnesses, diminished performance in school, reluctance to attend. (See "Stress and the Immune System," page 324.) Sometimes they become so depressed that they attempt suicide. Others learn to bully smaller children. And a few arm themselves, escalating the violence with potentially deadly consequences. Most victims, however, simply carry into adulthood the memory of being bullied and their resentment about it. Physical bullies are usually boys, as are their chosen victims (hence, we refer to them as male in this section). Nonetheless, verbal bullying and social bullying, which are much more common among groups of girls, can generate many of the same feelings among victims.

Most schoolchildren are not involved in serious physical bullying, either as perpetrators or as victims. Rather, a bully chooses his targets, usually in the first weeks or months of school. He seeks out children he can physically dominate, of course. He also looks for those classmates who appear to have low social skills and easily become distraught. If a child quickly ignores or laughs off an initial threat, a bully usually chooses another target. In other words, a bully hones in on those children whose responses best reflect the power he has over them.

Studies of bullies show that many have suffered from indifferent or negative parenting and often have been physically punished at home. Some also have learning disabilities that make school frustrating for them. (See pages 285–294.) They have a great many aggressive feelings and feel little remorse or responsibility for the pain they cause. (Counselors sometimes report, however, that making a bully sit down and talk with his victims in a controlled setting increases his empathy and curbs his abusive behavior.)

Although the common wisdom is that children who become bullies do so because they lack self-esteem, recent surveys have shown that bullies rank above average on standard measures of that quality. (See page 309.) Another typical but unsupportable statement about bullies is that they have no friends. While it is usually true that most students in a class know who the physical bully is and avoid that boy's company, a minority of children are attracted to his power and provide him with a social circle. Only in mid-adolescence does a bully's popularity start to fade. Unless he learns another way of fulfilling his need for dominance, he becomes increasingly challenged by society's expectations for a young man.

In one way, the most common victims of bullying resemble their tormentors: they, too, have a limited array of behavior to choose from. If your child tends to be the victim of a bully, you can help him by teaching him, first, that being bullied does not mean that he is weak or immature. Also, point out to him that he does not have only two choices in dealing with a bully — giving in or fighting back physically. Suggest some of these effective responses:

- Simply walk away, and hide your reactions for the moment.
- Stay with other kids or sit near the teacher. Don't let yourself be put in a vulnerable situation.
- Be assertive. Stand tall, look the bully in the eye, and refuse to do what he says.
- Rather than fight, challenge the bully to talk to you. Persuade him to meet you on your ground.
- Seek help from a teacher, a school counselor, or the principal.

If these responses seem impossibly out of reach to your child who is being bullied, you can help him to practice them at home.

Most children are reluctant to ask adults for help with a bully. Only a small number of bullying incidents are ever brought to a teacher's attention. A child may have internalized the idea that asking for help is a weak response, even if he cannot think of a more effective one. He may either be concerned about losing face with his peers or not trust adults to help him.

Make sure that your child understands that it is not "snitching" or "tattling" to report bullying in order to protect a person's safety (including his own). Telling on someone else is dishonorable only when the primary motive is to get that person in trouble. (See "Tattling," pages 400–401.) You might also suggest that your child take note of other students who witness a bullying incident, especially students who are neither your child's friends nor friends of the bully. Other children know which boys are the bullies and which the victims, and unless there is something seriously wrong in a school's culture and administration, these witnesses are usually willing to answer a principal's questions about what they saw.

Finally, if your child is struggling against being bullied, reassure him that he still has your love and respect. His judgment of himself may be plummeting. He needs to hear that there are things he does right. Once he chooses to speak to his teacher, coach, or principal, be sure to follow through. Make sure that the school is taking steps to stop the problem from recurring. (See pages 278–280 on how parents can work effectively with schools.) Keep your efforts as much behind the scenes as possible for two reasons: to preserve your child's standing among his peers and to prevent the bully from knowing that he has had an effect. A school that truly values respect among its students will prevent further problems between two students and send a message that it will not tolerate bullying.

Signs That a Child Is Struggling with Violence

Child-development experts have tried to identify behavioral signs indicating that a child is struggling with violence issues or has been exposed to violence. The American Academy of Pediatrics and the American Psychological Association have together developed one such list of warning signs:

- Toddlers and preschool children who have been exposed to violence often become more irritable and less consolable. If there is no other explanation for such behavior and your child seems either more distant or more clingy than usual, you may want to have a professional evaluate him.

- Attention problems not previously detected in your school-aged child; disruptive school behavior; oversensitivity; problems relating to classmates; and aggression toward peers, smaller children, and pets.

- Preteens and adolescents who have been exposed to violence may have more difficulty getting along with authority figures and may join an aggressive peer group. Unexcused absences from school and a drop in class performance are always cause for concern, as is the use of illegal drugs or alcohol.

None of these warning signs can ever be definitive, and each can arise from a variety of circumstances. Thus you should always interpret these signs cautiously. Also, keep in mind two things: first, your child is complicated, and second, since you know him better than anyone does, you are in the best position to recognize whether your child's behavior has changed from what is normal for him. If it has, and if any of these signs worry you, consult a professional.

A twelve-year-old boy named John, for example, had been doing quite well in school until, his teacher reported, over a period of only two weeks he became distracted. At the same time, John's parents had noticed how excited he got when he repeated other children's stories about drug deals and guns in the neighborhood. During a parent conference, John's mother asked his teacher for advice, and he suggested that she speak with a professional counselor. After John had completed three sessions with the counselor, he was able to tell his mother that he was upset by recent news on television about extreme violence in other schools. He described how two students at his school had brought in weapons and were threatening other students, trying to extort money for "protection." Clearly, John felt threatened by these students. The news reports about students in other schools who had been victims of terrible violence only magnified his feeling of being in a threatening environment. His violent fantasies, and the talk that had frightened his parents, was his response.

Later, John and his mother met with the counselor together to learn how to talk more openly about his worries. When John's mother spoke with the school authorities, she learned that other parents had similar concerns. She joined the parent association at the school, where she and other families worked with school officials to solve the specific problem with weapons there, and they started to discuss prevention programs. (See pages 278–280 for more on working with schools and other parents to make changes.) As a result, John and his parents felt less isolated and were more confident in their ability to deal with threatening situations in the future. Having learned that he could rely on his parents and his teacher to help him with a seemingly overwhelming problem, John was soon back to performing normally in school.

Help in the Aftermath of Violence

Children who suffer an act of violence, witness someone else suffering, or spend a long time fearing such threats in the neighborhood are inevitably going to feel stressed. They may develop a wide range of difficulties in response. (See "Stress and the Immune System," page 324.) Youngsters exposed to violence have been found to have significantly increased rates of anxiety, depression, low self-esteem, and distractibility. There are also reports of notably higher rates of aggression and acting out with peers, teachers, and parents. In some children, these symptoms are isolated responses to a particular event, but they can grievously affect a child who already has psychological, developmental, educational, or behavioral problems. Post-traumatic stress disorder is common in children who have experienced severe violence; even young children can demonstrate such symptoms as increased irritability, disturbed sleep, heightened fear of being left alone, and regressing from previously mastered skills in toilet training, language, and exploring the world on their own. (For more on post-traumatic stress disorder, see pages 470–472.) This situation becomes even more complex when a child's parents are involved in a violent event — as the victims of an assault, for instance. If the child's parents were themselves physically hurt or emotionally incapacitated, the experience is harder on her than if they were not harmed.

When violence occurs within a child's home, one of the pillars of his world crumbles. When violence occurs within the family itself, the foundation goes as well. Often a child tries to shore up his sense of family by denying to himself that the violence is a problem; even a dangerous and scary family feels safer than no family at all. Or he may tell himself that he was somehow the cause of the violence and thus deserves the suffering. This is one of the most psychologically damaging situations for a child. If you feel your child or children are at risk of abuse, you must get help for them and for yourself right away.

Even when a child's home remains a safe haven for her, you must take immediate action if she is a victim of or a witness to an act of violence. Such a crisis upsets a child's sense of safety and equilibrium in the world, as it does for adults as well, making everyone feel helpless and needy. Response to the crisis requires immediate evaluation of the child's emotional ability to cope with what has happened to her. After ensuring that the child and her whole family are in a safe environment again, parents should take advantage of all available resources — police, social workers or clinicians, and other sources of support, such as clergy and relatives — to regain the family's equilibrium. When adults are feeling safe and supported, they can meet the needs of their children most effectively. Sometimes children are wary of such supporters, especially if they were already shy or distrustful of strangers.

Reassure your child that these people are here to help the whole family and that you will stay nearby.

The next step is for parents and the people supporting them to help the child begin to make sense of the experience, whether an automobile accident or a burglary. The most appropriate and supportive way to talk to your child at this time is to ask nondirective and open-ended questions: "How are you feeling? Do you want to talk about anything that happened?" Let your child share her feelings and seek whatever reassurance she needs. For instance, a child frequently worries about whether her family and other caregivers — the people who are the sources of her security — will be all right. Tell your child about the whereabouts and condition of all her family and friends: "Aunt Jenna is in the hospital, and everyone else is at home." Quite often a child's worries and fantasies are much worse than her immediate reality.

Be aware of your own reactions and how they might influence your child's response to the crisis. If you are still jumpy, she will sense that emotion and become anxious, too — perhaps even protective of you. Be honest about your feelings: "I'm still trying to calm down, because that was scary. I'm glad it's over now, aren't you?" Honesty is also important in explaining what is going on — though, once again, we don't suggest that you tell your child everything: "Yes, the doctors are looking after Aunt Jenna. Now it's time for us to go home, and we'll check on her in the morning." With her trust in the world shaken by the violent event, your child especially needs to be able to trust you.

As soon as you feel ready, you can help your child to label and describe her feelings. Your goal is for your child to feel that you or another caring adult are a safe base or mooring. That allows her to begin to express and organize what has happened. As you help her sort things out, you can try to defuse any disabling thoughts that might emerge in her mind: "It was my fault"; "The bad man will come back to get me." Eventually, with your help, your child can dispose of such destructive thoughts, beliefs, and attributions and reestablish her sense of safety.

A child who is too distraught to talk may find drawing to be a less threatening form of communication. By creating a picture of what he has seen — what he wants to remember about the victim, how he thinks about the other people who were involved, or how the memory makes him feel — he may be able to stabilize his thoughts and organize

them in a positive way. You might keep some form of journal or record of the events and of your child's reactions, so that he can, if he needs to, revisit his memories at a later date.

If you feel that your child's symptoms have persisted too long and that she is not returning to normal functioning, you may want to consult with a professional counselor. Start with your pediatrician, and if he or she agrees that further help is recommended, ask for a referral to a child psychiatrist or psychologist. The simple reassurance from your child's doctor or from a specialist that the child seems to be doing fine, considering what she went through, can help the family. Then everyone can worry less about whether she is recovering properly and get on with their more general recovery. Remember that, however hard you may try, you cannot eradicate violence from your children's world — but you can give them the skills and the strength not only to deal with it successfully, but to grow in understanding through the experience.

CHAPTER 24

Friends: Your Child's Expanding Social World

Look at these snapshots of childhood friendship: two preschoolers bustle around a wooden stove holding plastic utensils and acting out the roles of "Mommy" and "Daddy"; giggling fourth-graders on their first sleepover build a tent out of blankets, then crawl inside and seriously discuss what they will be when they grow up; a chaotic clump of youngsters wrestles over a football, arguing and laughing in equal measure. Similar moments from your own youth may be as clear to you as yesterday. Playing with friends is one of the most intense and pleasurable aspects of being a child. It is also one of the most significant: childhood friendship is the foundation for other close social interactions — the practice ground for dealing with all the emotions of interpersonal relationships. As such, friendships are also, parents know, a potential source of trouble in part because children are just learning to handle their emotions. They also can generate risky and foolish ideas and painful feelings of rejection.

Your child's capacity for friendship has its roots in his relationships with you and with his other caregivers. In many ways, you and these other adults become his first friends as you interact, communicate, and play simple games together in the first weeks and months of his life. If these interactions are not open and happy, your child is more likely to have trouble interpreting other people's wishes and emotional cues as he gets older. You are, however, much more than a friend to your infant. She quickly comes to see you as the provider of everything she needs to live, and you are both protector and disciplinarian. As part of her healthy development, she will begin to form friendships with peers with whom she can build relationships on a more equal basis, since they have not dedicated themselves to being there for her always, loving and caring for her.

If your child has an older sibling or a twin, his first true friendship is most likely to be with that brother or sister. A sibling relationship usually contains a mix of feelings: love, loyalty, pride, jealousy, and rivalry, to name a

ily. But often you have to look further to find potential playmates for them. You probably know other families from among your friends, colleagues, members of hobby groups or congregations, whose children are the same age as yours. Couples who meet in childbirth classes often stay in touch, knowing their babies will be nearly the same age. If your family is new to your community, you may find friends for your children (and, perhaps, for yourself) at the child-care center. If your child's teacher observes

few. It differs from later friendships because the connection between children is involuntary. They share toys and games because they are in the same household; and, while they can stop playing together, they cannot go far apart. (See chapter 30.) Nevertheless, the early experience of being close to a brother or sister is a major influence on your child's relationships with other children. She will, in the future, respond to qualities in others that, consciously or unconsciously, remind her of her siblings or will seek companions who intrigue her for being different from the people she knows at home. For only children, sometimes a cousin is a first friend.

Perhaps your neighbors have small children with whom your children can play eas-

that he seems to play particularly well with another member of the class, invite that child to your home or take him with you on an afternoon outing, and you may create the "beginning of a beautiful friendship."

Do not be surprised when there are moments of friction between young children, rather than hours of unbroken blissful play. Playing with other children, hosting a playmate, or being a guest in someone else's home all are social skills that young children learn over time. Playing with other children contributes to the social development of both your child and her playmates; it reveals the ways of other families and enlarges each child's view of the world. As you watch your child playing with her friends, you may also notice some aspects of her personality you have not had the chance to see before: her ability (or inability) to share toys and precious possessions, her insistence on certain prized roles in pretending, or the ease with which she includes new playmates in her games. In this chapter, we discuss how children make friends in the preschool and school years and how to deal with the problems that may arise from these relationships.

The Preschool Years

In the preschool years, children learn about relationships with persons other than their parents and their close family. A four-year-old's friends may change from week to week, or her cat or a girl she has created in her mind may be her friend. Your preschooler's friendships will often be as turbulent and unpredictable as those you imagined would happen only in adolescence. In these early friendships, your child will not only enjoy the comfort of having playmates but also learn how to deal with the difficult emotions of feeling rejection or anger.

Friends and Companions

Developmental experts once suggested that preschool children are merely companions or play partners for each other. Real friendship comes later, they said, during elementary school. While toddlers do have difficulty sharing toys and fully cooperating with each other's games — two actions that define friendship for older children — this re-stricted definition of friendship was the product of an era when most children under five spent their days at home and thereby had less opportunity or reason to develop close relationships with their young peers. Now that so many children are in day-care programs, the seeds of friendship often sprout between two preschoolers. They also wither in a short time, then blossom again. These short-lived friendships may seem so shallow as not to deserve to be called friendships at all, but each relationship is important to your child as he learns about the world.

A young child usually has an idea of what a "friend" is; the word is in his vocabulary, and he uses it early. Nursery-school teachers often hear, "I'll be your best friend" (and its opposite sentiment, "You can't come to my birthday"). Your preschooler may relate to other children as a partner in play, a trusted companion, or an ally in overcoming obstacles. Some children in child care find security in choosing a particular friend as an anchor within the group. When one child's need for such companionship becomes extreme, she may not be able to function when her chosen friend is absent. The pair may exclude others from their play. They may even pretend to be each other, switching clothing and insisting on each being addressed by the other's name: "I'm not Chris. He is!" Although this behavior may constitute dependency rather than friendship, finding security in a new relationship is one way for a child to adapt to separation from home and to form bonds with others.

In a good day-care program, your child interacts with many other children each day. They move in and out of different areas and forms of play. A well-planned schedule includes activities for small groups, large groups, and individuals. Sometimes an activity (music, building, a field trip) determines which, and how many, children can participate. Teachers may pair children or create groups for various projects, and at certain times of the day each child should also have some choice about how he plays — alone or with others. (For more on developmentally appropriate child care, see chapter 29.)

Ideally, young children will find pleasure in play with other children and discover the ability to be willing partners in a variety of games and activities. As we have said in many other chapters, a child's ability in this area is intertwined with the other skills and traits she is developing. So, for example, speech is important to friendship. If your child can communicate her ideas, she can share playspace and equipment with a

Imaginary Friends

As part of their overall imaginary play (see chapter 16), many preschool children — up to half, according to some surveys — create imaginary companions and insist on their reality. Families often have to pretend to accommodate these invisible creatures, and parents may be in some conflict about whether to humor their child this way. Some parents simply are not comfortable stepping inside their child's fantasies.

More commonly, you may worry that playing along with your child will impede her from learning what is real. But invisible friends should not be a big concern for parents of preschoolers. For children under five, the boundary between fact and fantasy is almost always hazy; in a few years, it will naturally grow clearer. If pressed, most preschoolers would agree that their friends are not really visible, not really hungry, not really sleeping beside them — but they would much prefer for you to play along.

An imaginary playmate often provides a child with companionship when he is alone. (For a discussion of separation issues, see chapter 31.) Invisible friends interact with their creators, tease and are teased, instigate projects or follow along admiringly. A child's imaginary playmate usually has a name, a personality, and a gender that correspond with a child's wishes and even has a life-defining story ("Terry's family used to live in Michigan; his father was a soldier"). The friend can be powerful or aggressive, a monster or a princess or a little boy. Unseen companions tend to maintain these core characteristics; even if, from month to month, your child adds details, his invisible friend's basic features and "history" remain the same, just as those of his real friends do.

Although it isn't always possible to trace the process by which an imaginary friend comes into your child's life, the forms that an imaginary friend takes often reflect your child's concerns and anxieties, as do her games. Thus, a four-year-old whose father is ill names her invisible playmate "Barbara Tall," derived from a medicine she had heard her parents mention. A pair of twins

friend. Her friends, in turn, help her build her language skills. (See chapter 17 for more on language.) And her ability to symbolize — to use blocks, for example, to represent roads and highways and to share this representation coherently — is the foundation for cooperative work in the later preschool years and the early years of elementary school.

In the preschool years, a child moves from solitary play through parallel play (side by side) to associative play. Cooperative play, the fond wish of parents and teachers, is sometimes within reach of older preschoolers and kindergartners, although the child developmentalist Jean Piaget felt that truly cooperative play develops only at seven or eight years of age. This accomplishment depends, in part, on whether your child's environment at home or school fosters and encourages it. We know that games with firm rules and the outcome of winning or losing are often not suitable for children under seven. It may be that cooperative play emerges only when children are mature

---

whose mother is pregnant creates a shared friend they called "Feetis." When a child is worried, her imaginary friend can offer her some psychological protection from her worries by taking on magical powers or even by succumbing to dangers in her place. After being caught in a frightening rainstorm, one three-year-old told her grandmother that her usual friend "was drownded in the big puddle" — but she had a new friend, Frogman, who "is never afraid of puddles."

At times, a child may use an unseen companion as an alibi. One three-year-old with an imaginary friend she called Makid (my kid) would insist, "I didn't spill the water. Makid did it." For other children, however, the invisible friend can constitute an extra conscience, even scolding as adults do. Your child can create an air of secrecy when he decides the companion is lost or hiding. And all of this is unknown to you except when your child "translates."

Indeed, one of the biggest attractions of an imaginary friend is that it is a part of a preschooler's existence that she, and only she, can control. For this reason, wait until your child has invited you to interact with her invisible playmate. Deep down, she knows her friend is not real, and she might be quite disquieted if you take the lead in acting otherwise. Try to discourage your older children from teasing their younger sister about her pretend play, since it is terribly important to her. Remind older children, gently, that not so long ago they had their own imaginary playmates.

Children can create imaginary companions by assigning personalities to a stuffed toy. They may use different modes of speech to express individual desires: a growling tiger, a hungry hippo, a maternal kangaroo. (Or every toy might speak in the same squeaky voice.) You may be more or less comfortable going along with this form of pretend play. If you want to play along, help your child explore different emotions and personality traits through the members of his stuffed menagerie. Improvise scripts about them and take heart from the fact that talking to a stuffed animal will be easier than talking to an imaginary companion. At least you can see when your child's pretend friend is in the room.

enough to tolerate a certain amount of competition.

When Preschool Friendships Make Parents Worry

Strong — and sometimes intractable — feelings will suffuse preschoolers' play. Caregivers hear heated arguments about who will assume what role in games: "But you were the father last time!" "That's not the way I wanted the house to be!" Since toddlers are just learning to see the world through other people's eyes, there is bound to be friction between playmates. At whatever age, two children are unlikely to be evenly matched in thinking ability, temperament, and strength. If they were, they might see themselves as rivals rather than playmates. Also, children who are used to the company of adults may find their peers frustrating: "I want to play by mine self," said Gregor, age four. "It's more peacely."

It is normal for any child to experience occasional difficulties in play: quarrels over

ANIMAL FRIENDS

You must be prepared for the question, "Can we have a dog [cat, fish, horse, turtle, rabbit, gerbil, hamster, parrot, carp, pig, horse, ferret, lizard, snake, or any other creature]?" Everyone has different feelings about pets. Reactions range from seeing these animals as natural family members, and as an essential part of growing up, to feeling unease, anxiety, and avoidance. You may perceive a big, energetic dog as a natural protector for your children or as a danger to them. Pets do not belong in every household; some homes may not be good for animals because of the family's lifestyle, living space, budget, religious beliefs, or medical conditions such as allergies.

On the other hand, if your family has the practical and psychological space to welcome an animal, that pet can provide benefits at different stages of your child's development. Children take memories and lessons from this relationship that stay with them through adulthood. A pet is thus often a "friend for life" — not just for the life span of the animal itself (which, sadly, can be short), but also for the life of your child's imagination.

If a couple owns a pet when they become pregnant, the cat, dog, or other animal has to adjust when the new baby comes home, just as older siblings would. An animal can perceive an infant as invading its turf, changing the relationship it enjoyed with its owners. Some breeds of dog and cat are far more child-friendly than

others; veterinarians often have experience in how different breeds behave around small children. Sometimes couples face the difficult task of parting with a loyal but aggressive guard dog or an aging, temperamental cat just before they bring their baby home. This decision can be especially difficult when the animal has belonged to one partner for a long time, and may heighten his or her tension about becoming a parent.

Fortunately, most pets manage the transition to living in a household with a baby. Cats and dogs are often gentle and forgiving with infants, letting a familiar baby pull their tail, tweak their ears, bury her face in their fur. As a baby becomes mobile, the family dog may be a convenient support for her as she learns to stand or may be willing to be a patient stand-in for a

roles or toys or attention. For the most part, these are situational difficulties to which, usually, you can find a practical solution. For example, your child may be trying to become part of an already established — and heretofore exclusive — twosome. In this case you can give your child a toy with which he can either join the pair's play or start his own game with other children. When a child has persistent difficulties in playing with others, however, parents naturally tend to become concerned. Such trouble might be rooted in

various feelings. A child may be acting too bossy or stubborn, not showing the flexibility and humor that he needs to adapt to others. He may not like the fantasy games others choose, perhaps because he is being overly literal and is unable to pretend, or because he generally finds fantasy threatening, or because he refuses to join in his friends' imaginary worlds. Sometimes a child's ideas are too complex for his peers, and he simply prefers to play alone or with an adult.

Even in the preschool period, you may

---

horse. Preschoolers use pets as vehicles for their imagination, giving the animals roles in their many dramas. For everyone's sake, however, an adult should closely supervise an infant's or a toddler's play with an animal — and be prepared to step in if things get out of hand. Since a young child is still learning that different people view experiences differently, she may not understand that the cat doesn't enjoy dressing up as much as she does.

As children grow, a family pet can be their special companion in ways that adults and even other children cannot. Household animals are steady presences, usually willing to listen and rarely talking back. They accept children as they are and are ever-ready objects for their love and fantasies. Pets also introduce

children to responsibility, particularly if you make the jobs involved in taking care of a pet part of your family routine. These chores may include filling the cat's food and water dishes, walking the dog in the morning or afternoon, cleaning the bird's cage or the fish tank. Since children do not develop a sense of responsibility overnight, it is best to consider any animal to be a family pet until a child reaches the age of ten or twelve. By first participating in a pet's care and then perhaps assuming the major role in it, your child can learn about taking care of someone else and come to know how it feels to have another living thing depend upon her.

Just as valuable as this lesson in responsibility is the lesson that pets teach about the realities

of life. Like the people in a child's life, a pet has its own likes, dislikes, and personality and does not always behave the way the child wants. And, inevitably, a family pet becomes sick, injured, or old and infirm. The experience of watching a kitten or a puppy grow up, saying goodbye when death is near or has occurred, and preserving special memories helps a child learn about life and death, love and loss. Many families are reluctant to expose their child to this kind of sadness, and thus hesitate to take on an animal. Nonetheless, having a pet offers a child the opportunity to focus on these basic and inevitable circumstances of life while she has her parents' guidance and support. (For more on children's reactions to death, see chapter 35.)

feel that a particular playmate is a negative influence on your child, and you may want to discourage the friendship. This is often an overreaction unless your child actually seems to be in danger. First, consider whether your child has spontaneously voiced any regret about the friendship, as in, "I wish Amanda didn't play so rough!" If she has, that is a signal to talk with her about standing up for herself and also with her teacher or day-care provider about steering each child to play with others for a while. If you choose to talk with the other child's parent, describe what you have seen without being judgmental. Even if you are certain your child is not at fault, presenting the problem as a clash of personalities that you two parents together can easily manage will be more effective.

If, however, your child is content with the relationship you find worrisome, consider why your child is drawn to this comrade. Sometimes a shy youngster feels stronger when teaming up with a more active, assertive playmate. A preschooler may be enjoying the chance to be silly or loud — a way of trying on roles, a constant activity at this age. You can still reinforce your values and expectations without dragging your child away from her fun. It may be necessary to watch the pair of friends more closely. Step in when things seem to be getting out of hand, and enforce the rules you have established in your family. Only if the children's behavior becomes dangerous or psychologically destructive should you decide that this is not a suitable alliance and arrange for your child to play with others.

Some parents, thinking that only same-sex, same-age friendships are healthy, may complain if a community or a nursery school does not meet those requirements. In most child-filled neighborhoods, however, youngsters from two to five naturally play with others of either sex and with those who are both slightly younger and somewhat older. Therefore, preschool programs commonly mix three- and four-year-olds, and many schools have combined classes for kindergarten and first grade. This arrangement accommodates the back-and-forth path of most children's early development. If a child is in the same group for two years, she has a chance to be one of the younger children and then one of the big kids. Only when there are more years and wider developmental differences between children should you worry about a child's preference for playmates of a different age.

When children are young, parents usually schedule (and sometimes overschedule) their playdates and other social activities. When you look back on your childhood, you may remember a busy social life: lots of playing, sports, and running around. But sometimes you forget how old you were when you did each of those things. And exciting times with friends are usually more memorable than the many equally important quiet times you enjoyed by yourself. If a young child's life is too programmed or too busy, her resourcefulness and initiative may suffer — and her parents can run themselves ragged. When your child is in day care for much of the day, she needs some opportunity to play alone or with you. Family life can, of course, be shared with relatives and friends, but children and adults need some seemingly empty "hanging out" time at home.

Parents also worry about their children's popularity. No one likes to be rejected by playmates or excluded from a group. This distress was well expressed by a four-year-old who learned that a new friend no longer wanted to play with him: "But we just started loving each other!" Everyone has felt that way at some time. Parents who have acute memories of being excluded from social circles may be anxious about their child's ability to make friends. Is your child spending too much time alone? Should you sign him up for more structured activities where children have to play together? Before you take any action, consider this question: How worried is your young child about friendships? If he plays happily and easily with others but spends more of his time playing alone, that pattern is probably his preference. Sometimes parents project their own hopes for popularity — or worries about being rejected — onto their children. But each person has his or her own level of need for companionship and solitude.

School-Age Children

In the school years, most children progress along the road to greater independence from their parents. Friendships developed during these years may be lifelong and are able to weather far better the emotional storms of anger and hurt. School-aged children also learn about sharing friends with others, working in groups of friends, and even competing to be another child's best friend.

The Best of Friends

A first-grader is away from home for most of the day, perhaps for all of it if he goes to after-school day care. He thus shares most of his experiences not with his parents and siblings, but with his peers in school. During these early school years, his sense of himself largely develops in reaction to, and against the backdrop of, his social group. He learns how to handle strong feelings in resolving conflicts with other children and develops new physical skills based on what his peers value and how much he wants to be like them.

A schoolchild's move away from parents and other adult authority figures does not happen all at once. Six- and seven-year-olds still feel strongly dependent on their parents, but they look to slightly older children as they move into child society. Remember that even as your child is striving for greater independence, her wish is not to take on adult responsibilities but, rather, to immerse herself in childhood and its subculture. This often starts with the children in her neighborhood and then switches to the children in her classes at school.

Toward the later elementary-school grades, a child's affiliation tends to become even more specific. He allies himself with a particular set of buddies in his classes who share his interests or traits. Quiet children typically prefer the company of other quiet children, while all the exuberant students cluster in a noisy mass. For most children, the term "best friend" designates not one particular boon companion but a quality of relationship; your child may have a whole group of "best friends." Some of these groups can be formally defined and organized, as in a chess club, a Scout troop, or a soccer team. But more often children define their set of buddies informally, on the basis of shared interests like hobbies, sports, or favorite video games. (We discuss these activities at more length in chapter 25.) Each of your child's friends also probably has one or two qualities he admires and would like to have himself: loyalty, a sense of humor, intelligence, bravery, and so on.

You may be surprised by how fervently your child values these friendships. A child who has always been eager to do things with her family may suddenly be unwilling to go on outings unless her best friend can come along. She may protest when she has to miss the camaraderie of soccer practice just to visit Grandma: "That would be disloyal to the team!" Your fifth-grader may seem to be spending all her time at her friends' houses, with them in your house, or talking on the phone to arrange one of these visits. Children at this age often form clubs, with varying degrees of formality. Sometimes these groupings actually have a function, such as gathering to build model rockets or to trade stickers. Just as often, however, the only purpose of a club is defining some people as in-side the group and others — either specific individuals or the whole rest of the world — as outside. Among school-age children, inclusion and rejection is more personal and may be felt more acutely than the often temporary "you can't play" announcements of early childhood. Being excluded can be painful for a child because defining oneself as belonging to a particular group is so important in these years.

This need to define a group is one reason popular culture — television shows, pop music, books, video games, and the latest toys — is so much a part of children's interactions at this age. Friends act out Star Wars movies together, trade baseball cards, discuss the previous night's television shows, or learn the latest dance steps. These shared references are another way to confirm what the members of the group have in common. Sometimes groups of friends actually form because of such interests, but just as often the preferences of a group's leaders influence the interests of other children.

Defining groups is crucial to the way most school-age children develop a sense of the larger world and their place in it. Your family provides your child a basic sense of who she is as a person. As she grows, she adds to that sense her place in her neighborhood, her school, and her country. Children go on to learn other forms of identity and ways of belonging: religious affiliation, ethnic and national origin, and so on. With their interest in formulating rules about how people behave, school-age children are vulnerable to stereotypes about other groups, yet are able to appreciate their parents' lesson that intelligent people look beyond surface characteristics to find qualities everyone shares. In chapter 26, we discuss how to help your child develop both pride in your family culture and also respect for the backgrounds of other children.

Similar lessons about the danger of stereotypes based on sex usually do not prevent the separation between boys and girls that sets in by age seven or eight. Sex is simply too convenient a marker for children not to use it in defining their groups and themselves, especially when most of them have only recently resolved their gender identities. (See pages 192–195.) Nevertheless, boys and girls often retain friendships across the gender line and participate happily in activities, such as school chorus or orchestra, where the obvious divisions do not apply. And, in fact, groups of girls and boys do play somewhat differently at this age: boys tend to be more boisterous and girls to cluster in small groups. Each sex tends, however, to have an exaggerated notion of the differences between them.

Groups and their rules are central to the way school-age children play. They often play the sports they see on television, but may also invent their own games. In either case, these sessions often start with a firm announcement of special rules, proceed to picking sides and some actual play, and end with an argument over those rules. Three seven-year-old boys were chasing each other almost aimlessly around a playground, and one stopped to kick off his shoes. As he did, he announced, "New rule! You can go barefoot now." Even what seemed like anarchic play was, to him, tightly governed by rules.

This emphasis on groups and rules does not mean that a school-age child loses a sense of her own mind. As a child progresses through the middle years of childhood, she becomes more able to assert her will with peers and to survive not getting her own way. She has started to internalize a sense of right and wrong and can call on it when she disagrees with the choices others in her group are making. Your child may realize that she can actually apply the lessons she has learned about right and wrong and even persuade her friends not to undertake some risky project. (See chapter 27 for more about moral development.)

In early adolescence, friendships change as children feel much more desire to conform to their friends' tastes and choices. Most children are never again so vulnerable to peer pressure as they are between the ages of eleven and thirteen or so. On the positive side, the friendships of early adolescence often become more intimate and supportive, and less competitive. By about age twelve, it is common for your child to find one or two close friends in addition to all the buddies in her group. (Just as boys typically lag behind girls in entering puberty, so they demonstrate these changes in their friendships a year or two after their female classmates. For more on puberty, see chapter 36.) With tight friendships, children may feel less depen-

dent on the larger group but still can enjoy being part of it. Their increasingly dependable friendships may help them feel secure enough to face the changes ahead. Finding and adjusting the balance between enjoying individual friendships and being an enthusiastic group participant is a constant throughout this stage of childhood.

Problems Making Friends, Problems with Friends

A child's move into the social world outside the family may be rocky. To form a com-

fortable relationship, two or more people must be able to interpret the many signals, nonverbal as well as verbal, that humans use to communicate. Individual children — and adults — differ in the ability to "read" other people. Timidity in venturing forth, a need for continued parental approval, or feelings of insecurity can make it difficult to join the often rough-and-tumble company of other children, and some young children feel more dependent on their home and family. If a child has not developed the skills his peers value — whether they include reading, catching a ball, or telling a joke — he may be embarrassed and worry about being teased.

If your child comes dragging into your house, however, and says, "I don't have any friends," he may not be having really serious difficulties. Few youngsters have immediate confidence in their relationships with others. Your child's sadness may represent his feelings only today or this week. The fact that he has expressed his feelings to you is in itself a sign that he is conscious that friendship is a good part of life.

Your child may tell you about a conflict, a power struggle, a feeling that another child has replaced him as someone's special friend. He may have been teased or bullied, or excluded from a group he was particularly eager to join. Think about ways to help him find the motivation and the energy to try again after a frustrating day. Listen sympathetically. As an adult, you know that all relationships have ups and downs, but children need time to experience this reality. You can probably also remember that, in childhood, alliances often change: you may have had a different best friend in every year of elementary school. Share your experiences if they seem helpful, and try to strengthen your child's own ability to think of ways to resolve his frustration. Do not try to solve the problem by yourself right away; you may not always be able (nor would it always be appropriate) to confer with another child's parents about a conflict. If the problem is bullying, whether verbal or physical, and persists, you may need to help your child figure out a healthy response and, in that case, may decide to speak with your child's teacher. (For more on bullying, see pages 337–339.)

Some parents become concerned if their child does not seem to have a large group of buddies, as her peers do. Despite the typical patterns, there are several children in every class who like to hang out with one close friend to the exclusion of all others. Often this is the case when two children do not share the predominant interest or tastes of their peers in terms of sports, clothes, pop music, and other things. Your child and her friend may simply be less competitive than others of their age. Close friends may also be avid readers or collectors with similar tastes. Their preference may simply represent an earlier maturity and independence from peer pressures. Associating with peer groups before finding a particularly close friend is not a universal sequence, and each child approaches friendship in a slightly different way.

A child with few, rather than many, friends is quite different from a child who truly is an outsider, a loner. There are many questions to ask about such a child. Is he painfully shy or unable to articulate wishes or feelings? Does he lack interest in others or lack simple social skills? Does he actively avoid the company of other children, or is he more comfortable with adults? Does he constantly seek the company of much younger or much older children? An affirmative answer to these questions indicates a need for consultation outside family and school. If your child's relations with peers are few, or if his interest in other children suddenly declines, or if he is so rigid, bossy, or impatient with others that his behavior disrupts his friendships, he may need help. (See chapter 33.) These patterns of friendships and behavior may, however, be relatively normal and understandable in the light of specific circumstances. If so, while they do not require a professional intervention, they do demand casual but sensitive and informed attention from you and other caring adults in your child's life.

Even as your child moves into greater freedom, you continue to play a dominant role in her social life. You should not feel that you have no say over her choice of friends and activities. You need to know where your preteen child is at all times, and to require her still to have your permission before she visits other homes. In most cases, a parent or other responsible adult should be supervising children as they meet outside school. As your child matures (and depending on where you live), he will probably ask for more opportunities to go off on his own for set periods — to a shopping mall, to a park, to the movies. Set rules for these events, and make sure your child sticks to them.

Your child will, of course, test your family's rules about health, safety, and behavior and compare them with what his friends do: "Mom, no one wears a bike helmet!" "How come my friends can stay up until midnight?"

"But everyone goes swimming at the quarry!" Often these complaints are simple pushes for independence. Occasionally, however, they may reflect the rebellious urgings of your child's buddies or a particular friend and thus be cause for worry. A preteen can get into more trouble than a preschooler, and it can be more difficult for parents to intervene. Fortunately, as your child develops, she is more able to tell you *why* she likes or dislikes particular peers. And there is more chance for you to have a dialogue in which you can express why you think some friendships are healthy and ask questions about others, especially those that involve risky or dangerous behavior.

Your child's friendships — whether easygoing or intense, transitory or permanent, strained or relaxed — are part of her life now and will continue to be forever. Seeing your child achieve this closeness with her peers can deepen your pleasure in her life and in your own relationships. With true friends, a child should be able to be her truest self, unburdened by worries about the need to belong, to compete, to achieve, or to pretend. Some close relationships born in childhood may last a lifetime, and close friends may become one's "relatives of choice." But even when childhood friends move or drift apart, the images of those relationships remain part of a child's identity.

CHAPTER 25

Exercises for Life:
Having Fun and Taking Part

Children between five and twelve years of age are involved in an exciting period of discovery and mastery. While this period is conveniently and rightly referred to as the "school years," many of the most important issues your child will deal with and much of her vital development will center on the new responsibilities she assumes in your family and also outside of school. In and out of school, she is exposed to a world of new ideas, activities, people, and influences from beyond the family. Working from the developmental building blocks she attained in infancy and toddlerhood, she extends and consolidates her abilities and knowledge in all domains.

In this chapter, we cover your child's expanding world outside school, including her involvement in sports and other extracurricular activities, as well as the opportunities offered in camps and on the Internet. Your child's new responsibilities at home, including assuming more chores and beginning to manage his own money, expand his world and encourage him to take on new roles in your family. At both school and at home, he is learning skills for life: in the one, having fun while learning to take responsibility for himself and others in sports and other organized activities, and in the other, helping in appropriate ways at home while enjoying more grown-up roles.

Organized Activities Beyond Home and School

Today, schools usually offer lessons and occasionally sponsor clubs or teams devoted to art, music, dance, theater, sports, computers, and perhaps other topics. Yet no school can nourish your child in every area of physical, social, cognitive, and emotional growth especially today, with the increasing pressure on schools to attend more to academic work. For this reason, your role in helping your child develop interests and activities outside school is especially important. If a child shows particular interest in an activity he tried out in a class, such as singing or drawing, look for a program that will help that interest flower and possibly progress to more advanced work.

Most studies of children participating in extracurricular activities show that they also perform better at school and attend school more regularly than those who do not participate in them. In part this is true because participation in extracurricular activities helps children develop persistence, responsibility, and independence. In addition to encouraging your child to develop her skills, extracurricular activities promote resilience and self-esteem. They provide opportunities for social growth: children often make friends and expand their social network by participating in activities with other youngsters who have similar interests. Extracurricular activities also give your child a chance to develop a positive relationship with an adult coach, a Scout leader, or some other mentor — relationships that, as we discuss in chapter 27, can be important for a child's moral development.

While keeping these advantages in mind, you should be aware also of how busy children with multiple commitments can become. Since families are busier and more overextended than ever before, a child can end up with so much on her schedule, or feel so much pressure from all her activities, that she lacks the important time to daydream and just play freely. Sometimes you and your child may need to seriously consider whether a proposed new activity is worth the time and energy it will take. You both must find a balance between passing up opportunities for learning or physical activity and producing a "hurried child" (and family). Most of all, families should not lose track of the most important aspect of any extracurricular activity: having fun.

Throughout the school years, your child becomes better at knowing and letting you know what she likes and dislikes and can voice her preferences with increasing confidence, independence, and self-knowledge. And as she does, she should have more say about which activities she will participate in. Naturally, your family's other commitments, the opportunities that your community has to offer, and the family finances will limit her choices — not everyone can have a pony. Among the realistic possibilities, your child's choice and preferences will depend largely on her abilities and her role models. You are her most important model; but in middle childhood, she will also look for guidance to other adults, teachers, and coaches. And, as she gets older, she will want to do those activities that her peers also find attractive.

Mediating these different influences and facilitating your child's actual participation in an extracurricular activity are among your tasks as a parent. Some children, those who are self-starters, will initiate activities out of school with little hesitation and few requests for help. Children who are temperamentally more quiet or passive may need their parents to be involved in making connections with out-of-school activities.

Particularly in the early school years, children may show enthusiasm for many different things. But by the age of eleven or twelve, most sports or performing arts are fairly structured and require children to commit significant time. By this age, your child can choose what he really likes or is good at, and can balance these internally generated predispositions with the increasing preadolescent pressures to join in activities that are popular. A youngster is very lucky if what he likes to do is also what his friends consider to be cool.

One benefit of organized extracurricular activities is the chance they give a child to develop beyond the shadow of her family, to cultivate a talent that belongs just to her. This testing of independence is a useful developmental step. You may have interests and favorite activities — fishing, golfing, playing in a community orchestra, even reenacting Civil War battles — that you would like to share with your children, but you should also respect your child's choice not to participate on all occasions. She may often enjoy being with you and helping out in what seems to be an adult activity, yet as she grows up and develops her own tastes and priorities, she may want to spend more time with her friends or simply to do something on her own. She is not rejecting you but is, instead, showing that she wants some independence.

When your family moves to a new community, enrolling your children in activities they know and enjoy can help them feel grounded during the transition. (For more on smoothing the adjustment, see pages 456–458.) Children new to a neighborhood can meet children their age with similar interests and also demonstrate and reassure themselves of their own talents. Almost every community offers a broad range of possibilities:

- Scout troops, boys' and girls' clubs, after-school programs, 4-H clubs, and many other organizations provide a varied slate of activities for their members.

- Lessons in such individual sports as tennis, the martial arts, riding, gymnastics, figure skating, and swimming are usually available at local facilities. In addition, children can often make friends through such informal sports as roller blading and skateboarding.

- Leagues for playing baseball, basketball, soccer, hockey, and many more team sports are usually available, and often parents can find groups devoted to other competitive activities, such as chess. If your community does not offer the sport your child is used to — soccer may be popular in one community, softball in another — she may have to take up another team sport. Usually, an energetic and enthusiastic school-age child has little difficulty moving from one sport to another.

- Many towns have arts centers where children can explore their creative talents through painting, writing, sculpting, photography, filmmaking, and other media arts. These centers or other local organizations may sponsor classes devoted to music, dance, drama, magic, and even circus skill. Or your child might pursue these activities privately, on his own or with a few friends.

- People who are interested in hobbies like

coin collecting, studying dinosaurs, trading cards, programming computers, and exploring nature often form groups. Some of these clubs are designed just for children. Others are for all ages and can provide rare opportunities for older school-age children to interact with adults on a somewhat equal basis.

• There may be activities connected to your family's cultural or religious background. Cultural or community centers may offer lessons in languages such as Hebrew or Chinese, or in traditional skills. Churches usually offer religious instruction, social groups, and volunteer activities for children and sometimes provide ways for children to participate in religious ceremonies.

Be aware of the attitudes you bring to your child's activities. As we described earlier, your mental portrait of your child dates back to well before his birth. This portrait might include an image of a child rounding third base, accepting a standing ovation, or writing prize-winning poetry. Yet your child may not necessarily either share this vision for himself or have the talents required to fulfill it. A parent who projects her own aspirations onto her child, hoping he will succeed earlier or do better than she did, can put too much pressure on him. Almost any volunteer coach or official can tell stories of mothers and fathers who become so worked up about their child's games that they embarrass or even worry the child.

Reflect also on what values you attach to different activities. For example, sports are often recommended for teaching children to perform under pressure, to cooperate with others on the team, and to compete fiercely but fairly — and they do teach these skills. But so does putting on a play, as anyone who has followed a production from auditions to opening night can attest. If you argue that only athletics can provide those experiences, you may in fact be valuing sports for other reasons. The choice should be based on your child's own preferences, not on stereotypes. When you choose activities for your young child, start with her strongest interests and talents. Consider all the possibilities we have listed and whatever else your community provides.

Sports

Sports are ubiquitous in the United States and in the lives of its children. Many children participate in organized sports both in and out of school, and others model their informal games after the sports they see on TV — to the point of providing their own play-by-play commentary and rerunning moves in "slow motion." Nonetheless, despite the "sports-obsessed" American culture, each year increasing numbers of children fail to meet minimum standards of fitness on the President's Physical Fitness Examination, and pediatricians report an overall significant increase in childhood obesity. Still, though many children are far too sedentary, many others are involved in extracurricular sports.

The decision about whether to participate

in extracurricular sports, and if so, how much and in which one, probably depends most on individual motivation: how interested your child (as well as your family and his friends) is in a given sport. Successful programs for children are developmentally oriented and focus on participation, building basic physical and mental skills, and cultivating a love for sports that will last for life. Both boys and girls benefit from this type of program. Although many people still think that team sports are most appropriate for boys while dance lessons are best for girls, both activities aid a child's physical development.

While you may want your child to learn teamwork and have the pleasure of feeling part of a close-knit squad and the thrill of rooting for others, do not choose a team sport for her if she is more interested in, for example, karate or swimming. Since children usually learn individual sports in groups and often compete as one club against another, she will gain many of the same benefits from her chosen activity as she would as part of a team.

Successful grade-school-level sports programs are based on a three-part structure of positive relationships between and among players, the coach, and the parent. Emphasizing participation over winning seems to enhance young players' enjoyment and ongoing participation in sports even though that emphasis can, at times, be difficult for both children and parents. At this age, sportsmanship and respect for others should be as much part of the training as physical skill, and highly competitive sports pro-

grams often have high rates of dropout and burnout, leaving gifted young athletes with little inclination to continue playing. When teams, schools, or communities are organized mostly around athletic competitions, children who are less skilled at sports often suffer in self-esteem and peer relations.

Sports programs are often valuable for children with health problems who may have grown to distrust their bodies and physical capacities. Children with asthma, for instance, may shy from running around with their classmates because they fear having an episode of difficult breathing. Yet since this reluctance may erode their self-esteem, they should be encouraged to find activities that don't present the same risk of fear and embarrassment. Swimming is an excellent activity for these children: the humid atmosphere around a pool makes breathing easier, and the exercise itself increases their lung capacity. Young people with asthma have gone on to swim at championship levels. Success in swimming can, in turn, give a child more confidence to play other sports, as most people with asthma can do.

Music, Dance, and Drama

Even as infants, children respond with particular sensitivity to music. By the time they are toddlers, they often enjoy dancing and singing along to favorite songs. For most children, singing is the first form of musical instruction; the voice is an instrument all children can work with. Children usually love singing in groups and choirs since singing in a group is social and, also, individual mistakes are not so easily noticed. On average, children who sing in a choir show improved listening and attention skills in school. Youngsters in any sort of performing group also, out of necessity, attain more cohesion and the experience of working together to accomplish a common goal.

School-age children have the cognitive and fine and gross motor skills they need to begin playing most musical instruments —

SUMMER CAMP

Some of your fondest memories of childhood may be of summer camp. A whiff of pine needles or kerosene can bring back intense experiences you could never have had in your neighborhood. At the same time, summer camp can be a frightening experience for children who have not been away from home before and for whom this is often their first extended separation from their parents. (For more on separation, see chapter 31.)

Choosing your child's camp wisely is the best way to counteract his natural reluctance to be away from home for a week or more. Selecting a program with a sibling or a friend is another way to provide your child with enough close support that he can last the summer happily. You can also choose a camp that holds particular appeal to your child. With the variety of summer camps available today, you are likely to find one that is a good match. There are camps for various sports, computers, theater and music, art, nature exploration, religious activities, and much more. For children who are especially reluctant to leave home, some programs start off as day camps for a week or so, giving a child a chance to make friends and feel secure before she sleeps over.

Nonetheless, parents commonly receive letters, phone calls, and e-mail from their children at camp complaining about being lonely and wanting to come home. Although these pleas may make you feel guilty about having sent your child away in the first place, try to keep the requests in perspective: when your child is having fun at camp, she is too busy to write, so you hear from her only in her quiet or down moments. Keep in touch with your camper, and send gifts or pictures from home to reassure her that you are still connected. Tell her how proud you are that she is taking this step toward independence and how you hope she tries to stay the short time to the end of summer. Before taking your child out of camp, consult with the camp counselors and directors; they will be able to report on your child's behavior and say if they would recommend that step.

although wind instruments generally start later when lung capacity is greater. Young children who show strong musical interests and abilities, however, may choose to learn an instrument even before they start school. Your child's readiness to learn depends on her motivation and emotional maturity, as well as on her musical and motor skills. It is easy to assess these factors through a few trial lessons with a teacher with experience working with young children. The parents of a young preschool to early school-aged child will probably need to be more closely involved in these lessons. Some teachers suggest (or require) that you stay in the room during your child's lesson and even learn the instrument yourself in order to help her practice.

Early in your child's artistic life, she will have the opportunity to share her enjoyment of the art and display examples of her hard work. Preparing for a performance gives her the experience of working toward a shared goal, but for young children, this performance should not be a high-pressure recital. A low-key approach, playing or dancing for small groups of other students and parents, is preferable. As in sports, emphasizing the activity rather than the outcome leads to more enjoyment and continued participation in later years.

While pretend play and dressing up is a nearly universal activity for children in the preschool period, it may develop into an ongoing interest in acting and other performing arts. You can help your child explore all these skills through both lessons and small-scale productions. If you sense early on that your child wants to be in the spotlight, to act silly, or to express himself in other dramatic ways, an after-school drama class might be ideal. Many programs are set up in the manner of the music and dance lessons we just described: sessions consist of exercises and theater games that lead to opportunities for the group to write their own sketches, and culminate in a performance for a relatively small audience. Other programs are more elaborate, with productions performed by a cast of children, usually for young audiences in schools and parks. Occasionally a child is invited to take on a role in a more elaborate production such as a community musical or a television commercial. Performing at this level requires your child to display considerable maturity, energy, and resilience. Often you may have to give him practical support by helping him to memorize lines, driving him to and from rehearsals, and perhaps sitting through each and every performance.

Responsibility at Home

As your child enters middle school, he is ready to take on more responsibility at home.

New chores and learning to manage money are important steps in his feeling more involved in your family and also more mature.

Chores

Once, children's help around the shop or farm was essential for the family to survive, and they routinely did chores. Today, however, parents are more likely to mete out household chores as a sort of punishment. But this need not be the way you understand the notion of chores. It is, in fact, only fair to

CHILDREN ON THE INTERNET

The expansion of the Internet, both in the resources it offers and in the number of homes linked to it, has opened vast new opportunities for children's education and recreation. At the same time, many parents fear that the Internet has made their kids more vulnerable to various threats and temptations. These worries are usually aggravated when parents feel ignorant about computer technology and thus less able to advise and protect their children. (For working with children and computers, see pages 250–251.)

Exploring the Internet has many developmental advantages for children, especially compared with that other tube, the television, which is a much more passive medium. Children actually interact with the computer, choosing what they want to see and when they want to see it. This requires them to practice some valuable skills, among them concentrating on and evaluating information, making choices, and expressing their thoughts. With e-mail, a child can make friends with other young people, explore his interests and hobbies, and keep up with relatives. With your help, he can create his own Web page and let the world know who he is.

Parents worry that their children will stumble onto pornographic Internet sites. It is, in fact, fairly easy to find such sites, but quite difficult to enter them without knowing what they are. Older children who are excited about sexual feelings may well explore these areas, just as an earlier generation used to sneak peeks at books or magazines. Unlike that secret reading material, however, there is a greater chance that pornographic Internet sites will display pictures of unusual and even disturbing practices. There is also the hazard that your child will find sites that espouse various forms of bigotry or teach dangerous skills. To block such information, you can either install software or use an Internet service for the purpose. The shortcoming of such programs is that they often block other, less objectionable material as well.

It is far more positive, however, for you to stay close — physically at first and always psychologically — to your child while she explores the Internet. When she is

involve youngsters in maintaining their — and your — environment. Chores should begin in the toddler years, when basic cleanup — helping to pick up toys and clear the table — becomes part of a child's routine. As he gets older, your child's duties can gradually expand to include more responsibility, such as making his own bed and tidying his own room, and eventually such communal tasks as collecting and taking out the garbage, helping to wash the dishes and clothes, and taking care of the yard. Even if your home management does not depend on your child's help, his involvement helps him feel he is helping you. Indeed, with everyone living such hurried lives, your child's helping may give you some extra time for yourself and for activities with your children. It also gives you time together.

Steve and Joseph, for example, are two young boys who cannot stand to clean the room they share. Instead of turning this reluctance into a power struggle, their parents have made cleanup part of the family's pre-

---

small, you can work the computer together. As she grows, try to remain as aware of what she is doing on the computer as you are of the TV shows she watches. Encourage her to ask questions when she finds something that puzzles her. A child who sees something disturbing on the Internet should be able to talk to her parents without being punished. No software filters can substitute for open communication, shared values, and respect.

In the long run, it may be more important to teach your child how to evaluate what he sees on the Internet as a whole than to shield his eyes from certain sites. Many sites are set up to sell or promote products; others, to promote a point of view. Thus, before a child uses the Internet, he should know how to navigate its seemingly endless, unfiltered, and unorganized facts. Teaching your child how to use the Internet responsibly is just as important as teaching him how to use it effectively. He must first learn both how to define the question or problem he wants to solve and how to determine the necessary tools to reach an answer. Since the Internet offers many opportunities for plagiarism, students also need to know that copying the words of others without attribution is both wrong and detrimental to their learning.

You may find it useful to create a "cyber contract" that lays out the rules for how your older child uses the Internet. This kind of contract may contain such provisions as:

• A child should enter no site that is meant only for people over age eighteen.

• A child should not give out her full name, address, phone number, credit card number, or other personal information without permission from her parents.

• Parents must approve anything on the child's or the family's home page.

• No member of the family should spend more than a certain amount of time on the Internet, both to allow others to log on and to ensure that everyone remains involved in different types of experiences.

By discussing your expectations and listening to your child's interests, you can allay your worries about this networked world and its many temptations.

BUY ME THAT!

Before they enter school, children are usually content with whatever brand of toys, clothes, or snacks you provide. They may ask for an item with their favorite cartoon character on it, but can reconcile themselves with what you choose. After about the age of five, however, children's desires become more specific. You may suddenly learn that the cereal you bought is totally yucky, even if it went down well the month before. The doll you buy for a birthday must be the one that wets, cries, or talks back. The sneaker must be endorsed by a particular athlete or carry the right label.

Parents often blame television advertisements for promoting such brand-name consumerism in their children. Certainly commercials play a role, especially when coupled with TV shows that are basically commercials for their licensed products. Still, some television characters are so ubiquitous that, like a favorite teddy bear, they become sources of stability for young children.

For older children, American society includes so many different cultures, occupations, and habits that television is one of the few experiences they have in common with their friends. No wonder, then, that children often request toys, books, clothes, and less important things branded with names from TV and the movies. When your child requests a licensed toy, consider which appeals to her: the object or the character emblazoned on it. Is the character simply decoration or an essential part of the toy? If your child simply wants something with a familiar face on it, you might satisfy the craving with a better toy that your child is more likely to use.

A force even stronger than television makes older children insist on specific goods and brands: their peers at school. Wishing to be part of the group is a milestone in your child's socialization. No longer content to play by himself, he now wants to play with others, and that means having toys or sports equipment that matches theirs. Since play among schoolchildren is primarily an exercise of social adeptness — competing, cooperating, and sharing with friends — games exercise more than a child's mental skills and imagination alone. Children compare how many stickers they have collected, how high they have scored in video games, and how many books they have read. Yet they are not just competing to be the best or most advanced. Rather, each is trying to make the biggest claim for belonging in the group. Your school-age child does not necessarily want you to buy the latest and most expensive item; she wants the item that most (she would say "all") of her peers have.

The urge to buy may overlap with another impulse of the school-age child: collecting. Kids like to collect things (or facts) as a way to master a particular realm. Whether your child collects the names of dinosaurs, miniature unicorn statues, or trading cards, his collection is a piece of the world that he has mastered, and he may well outdo adults with it. Nothing may bring a child the same feeling of fulfillment as collecting does — not even his artwork or his inventions because they do not conform to an outside yardstick. Your child knows exactly how many baseball cards she has, how valuable her Beanie Babies are (or were), how many more Star Wars action figures she still has to buy. When stores are eager to sell items that have no use but as "collectibles," it is easy for children to start down a big-spending path. If your child does so, try to head her off by engaging her interest in a less consumerist hobby, such as collecting rocks or insects, or in goods that have intrinsic value, like books.

dictable routine and scheduled major room cleanup two days a week: every Friday afternoon and every Tuesday morning. It's not that those hours have miraculously become the boys' favorite parts of the week — they still dislike having to clean their room — but the routine and their parents' regular, predictable attention to their sons are reassuring. This approach provides benefits that outlast the fact that Steve and Joseph can now readily find all their toys. For such routines to be effective, however, you have to stick to them and be consistent in what you schedule and promise.

Children feel more motivated to do chores if they perceive a link between household tasks and growing up; they thrive on gaining this kind of competence. And your primary goal in assigning tasks is to help your child in ways that will help her become independent. Your young child naturally wants to be a helper to you, and most children enjoy "getting to" mow the lawn with a mower or using the dishwasher unassisted. Naturally, your child will appreciate it if you acknowledge his taking on a new responsibility by increasing his independence in some appropriate way. A child who helps with the laundry should have more say in what he wears, and vice versa. When, in the later elementary grades, a child starts to ask for privacy in her bedroom, you can promise to knock before coming into her room if she will be responsible for keeping it clean.

Most important, chores demonstrate to a child that her family members all depend upon one another; that she has a part in that group; and that her jobs, suited to her developmental level, benefit her and her family alike. In this context, chores make sense to children.

Handling Money

As your school-age child gets older, she acquires a sounder sense of numbers and of the concrete value of money in the American exchange economy. She is also learning the psychological value of money, both in your family and in the overall culture. It is appropriate for your school-age child to have some money to spend, and your supervision over how she spends it should diminish over time. Spending money is, in a way, no different from, say, riding a bike. Some children master the mechanics early, some later. Every child needs help in developing good judgment, and you should give your child the level of supervision she seems to require as she moves toward the independent use of money. Learning how to manage one's own money wisely is not an easy task. If your child learns early, she can appreciate how easily money disappears if she doesn't plan ahead or buys impulsively. On the other hand, you want her also to learn that buying something just because it is exciting or pleasurable can be one of life's joys. In learning to manage her own money, your child will learn more about being independent and about balancing plans for the future with living fully and happily in the moment.

Giving your child a small amount of discretionary income can help to teach her to handle money sensibly. You may decide to allow your child to earn some money by doing special jobs for you aside from his regular chores; or her spending money can be her "take" of family income, as one child put it. The choice depends on how your family regards money in general: that is, whether the child as a member of the family is entitled to a portion of its overall income, or whether money must always be earned. Often parents increase the weekly or monthly allotment to a child at each birthday, reflecting her increased maturity (as well as more expensive tastes). Some parents post a chart listing all the extra chores around the house and the payment for doing each of them, so that any child in the family who wants or needs money can choose to take on a job to earn it. This device has the advantage of specifying which tasks earn a financial reward and which are not negotiable, such as regular chores, being polite to company, and doing one's best in school.

In their period of imaginary play, children often pretend to run a grocery store or other shop. At this stage, they are usually content with play money or even invisible cash. (See pages 218–221.) Later, children often want to earn real money by selling lemonade, sodas, or other treats; by walking people's dogs; or by setting up other businesses. Enjoy the opportunity to support these small ventures, but remember that they have the most educational impact when your child gets a sense of the real cost of doing business. If you are baking all the cookies or supplying all the soda for a school-age entrepreneur, she nei-

ther sees her true costs nor has the pleasure of doing the job herself. Oversee these activities, but let your child bear the responsibility she has designed for herself.

Sometimes children solicit or are offered small jobs around the neighborhood: shoveling snow, raking leaves, feeding a neighbor's pet when she is away, perhaps even looking after younger children while a parent is nearby. (Real babysitting, without adult supervision, is too much of a burden for most preadolescents.) These tasks offer valuable practice in taking on and fulfilling responsibility and give children a sense of accomplishment.

You might consider yourself to be the manager of your young worker. While you do not have the responsibility either to supervise the work directly or to do it yourself if he does not follow through, you should provide the time and perhaps any reminders he may need. If your child turns out not to be up to doing a particular job yet, help him to resign fairly and suggest a chore better suited to his capacities.

Naturally, you do not want your child to suppose that the only thing she can do with her money is spend it. Learning how to save money is an even more valuable skill. When your child wants something for which she does not have ready cash, it is a fine opportunity to introduce the concept of saving: "If you save up all your allowance for the next seven weeks and don't use any of it to buy ice cream, then you can buy the computer game you want!" Mark the goal on a calendar, and help your child keep track of her progress. Let older children see you handling the family finances: paying bills each month, choosing investment plans or insurance policies, or debating the pros and cons of whether to buy some expensive item. You do not need to explain all the fine print to them (it is hard enough for adults to understand), but you will demonstrate that managing money thoughtfully is part of being an adult.

You can also help your children develop a sense of conscience about using money for altruistic purposes. Collecting coins for UNICEF at Halloween, giving money at movie theaters for childhood-cancer research, or "adopting" an endangered species by joining a wildlife organization are all ways of engaging your child in the idea that money can work for good as well as be used to buy "stuff." Remember, however, that the essence of volunteerism is that it be voluntary. A child who donates money or performs a community service because you and/or his school require him to do so is not really volunteering. All the benefits of true volunteer work apply but one: the child's motivation to continue on his own. If volunteer work is to become more than an assigned chore, children need to have a choice in it. If your child is particularly interested in animals, he could donate to or work at a wildlife center. If he likes working with computers, he can tutor people in that skill. Only when the task becomes part of how your child sees himself as a maturing person will he find it satisfying.

Inevitably, your child will compare your family's system of dealing with money with the way other families handle it. This concern may appear as a direct challenge: "Bonnie's parents give her two dollars every week." Or your child will make a passing remark about the big-screen TV in the house next door, or ask you directly about your salary. Adults vary greatly in how comfortable they are talking about money: some find it more difficult than talking about sex, while others see their income as the main measure of their success. Similarly, parents differ in how they view money: what levels of savings and debt make them comfortable, whether they prefer to invest in future earnings or buy what they want now, how much pride they feel in how they have provided for their family. Your child is probably more interested in understanding your values in regard to money — its uses and abuses — than in actual figures that only adults, who use and make decisions about them, understand anyway. As it is in other aspects of life, your children will learn the most from what you do, not from what you say. For example, when they see you carefully comparing features and costs for your new family car rather than impulsively buying the most expensive car on the lot, they learn the value of being thoughtful and planning for their financial future. At the same time, when they see you also put into your budget money for something personally pleasurable or for a night out for the family, they also learn that thoughtfully managing money does not mean depriving yourself or others of things that you enjoy or that make your life more pleasant and easier.

These lessons for life learned on the school playing field, theater stage, or music room and in the day-to-day chores of family life are a part of the broader world of family and community culture that encircles and shapes your school-age child's view of the world. We will discuss this culture in the next chapter.

CHAPTER 26

Family Culture:
Passing on Traditions

A community is defined by its traditions — by shared values, beliefs, words and symbols, foods and songs, and the regular activities of its members. Members of a community come together to enact such traditions as holidays, celebrations, and memorials. The community also shapes personal life events: how you welcome a birth, enter marriage, care for others in need, find meaning in growing old, and come individually and communally to accept death. All traditional communities have ways of helping people deal with sadness and loss, and they also sanctify, and thus heighten, personal joys. Among them are a parent's pleasure and pride in launching a vigorous, maturing youngster into adulthood through rituals such as graduation, confirmation, or a bar or bat mitzvah. Through these, you engage in the lifelong process of conveying your spiritual and philosophical values to children.

The United States is made up of an increasing multitude of communities defined by nation of origin, language, religion, and/or class. In one Chicago high school, the student body represents more than sixty languages, with children coming from every populated continent and virtually every major world religion. Immigrant families bring traditions from their native home and transmit them from generation to generation as precious heirlooms. Families established in the United States both hold fast to selected traditions of their forebears and enact new family traditions — everything from a yearly vacation with cousins to a particular way of opening gifts at holidays. Although the differences among these traditions are profound, each serves to provide meaning and emotional support to children's lives.

Today there is much talk about the breakdown of close families, traditions, and shared culture as if it were an inevitable consequence of modern society and globalization. Indeed, many children — perhaps millions of them in this nation — are growing up outside clearly defined traditions. Their parents may not see the importance of defining the family culture or feel they have no rituals and values worth sharing. A mother and a father who come from two very different traditions may opt to carry on neither rather than to risk conflict. Or parents may decide against replicating the family cultures they knew as children, but do not define and ritualize their own beliefs. For such families, discussing community and traditions may seem nostalgic or irrelevant. Since child-care workers and teachers are rightly leery of imposing beliefs on children outside their family circles, those children who lack a family culture will adopt the world promoted by magazines, TV, and movies. They will learn traditions on the street or in the school of hard knocks. On the other hand, even children whose lives seem most hard-pressed have been able to find real comfort and psychological protection in their family's culture and traditions. Children often feel a wish for — indeed, a pull toward — such communities of shared belief and support. Adolescents especially need a stable foundation of values. Those who lack one from childhood may find one in a gang.

We believe that the transmission of traditions is part of parenting, and that a child can become most fully himself when you involve him in your family's culture — whether it centers on a religion, a set of family or community traditions, or individual beliefs and customs of your own. Your children grow up, in turn, either to value the culture you have passed on to them, and thus preserve it — or to challenge and revise it. Passing on your family's culture is a lifelong process, beginning in pregnancy and continuing in your child's infancy, preschool years, and beyond. In this chapter, we discuss how culture creates character in a child, the importance of religion, and the evil of prejudice, which — along with other destructive beliefs — a family's culture may include.

How Culture Creates Character

The word *character* usually denotes the set of values that others see as defining a person's personality and behavior. A person of integrity is known, for example, as having a "good character," while one known as a "bad character" is likely not to be trusted. Your community and family culture contribute significantly to the personal values that will guide your child's behavior and thus form her character.

Children start to experience their family culture from the very first moments of life. Your child is socialized into the community by the way you and his grandparents, aunts, uncles, and friends talk and play with him, and by what he sees in his home. Just as your child learns the accents, inflections, and music of his native language, so he learns the nuances of his culture's style of relating to elders, expressing or holding back anger, sharing feelings, expressing happiness, and responding to pain and disappointment. A baby is made into a particular adult by the ways in which she is cared for, by what she hears and sees in the relations among adults, even by what she smells and tastes.

Most major world cultures have distinct ways of caring for young children and socializing them into the larger tradition. Your manner of child rearing — caring, stimulating, talking, punishing, and praising — shapes your child into the kind of adult your culture values. An Indonesian or a Japanese mother, for example, will hold her baby close to her at all times for the first year or more of life, never leaving him out of sight. In contrast, American mothers often put their infants in day care and return to work six weeks after delivery. Many of your ancestors' habits — or, more likely, your idealized impression of them — have survived your immersion in the overall U.S. culture and affect how you view parental responsibilities. Such culturally based differences are evident among families even within the same big-city apartment house. A few years ago in New York, a Danish mother left her baby in his stroller outside a coffeehouse while she chatted inside with friends. Although this action alarmed several passersby, it is common in Copenhagen, where parents tend to value fresh air and do not share Americans' fear of street crime. On the other hand, Danes often equip their youngsters with safety helmets for climbing on jungle gyms and think Americans are careless about playground dangers. Each culture transmits to its children its own ways of living and showing concern for them.

Early on, a child develops a psychological calendar, recognizing and taking comfort in her parents' regular habits. By the age of eighteen months, she knows the routines of the day (bathing, feeding, playing, going to day care, coming home for dinner) and the bedtime rituals (milk, story, kiss). By age two, she has a sense of the rhythm of the week, including weekends and perhaps a Sabbath

day marked by a family dinner, church, or visits among relatives. By three or four, children start to learn about the predictable patterns of the year: the changing seasons, family birthdays, and such landmark holidays as Yom Kippur, Ramadan, Christmas, Halloween, and the Fourth of July. Holidays such as Mother's Day may be special because your family celebrates them in a particular way. Or your family may have its own special events: a big backyard barbecue once a summer, for instance. Each family ritualizes its life according to its traditional patterns, routines, and rhythms of activity and feeling. These rituals please children by being predictable and because they are easily shared with people they love.

Beyond these regular events, each family makes and transmits its own traditions. On a winter night around the fireplace, Dad may take out his banjo and sing a song he learned as a boy — and his daughters and sons thus learn that custom. Mom may bake a cinnamon torte that came from her Czech great grandmother's recipe book. Aunt Frances may cook a dinner of catfish and greens that once signaled, when she was a little girl in Mississippi, that the whole family would gather for Sunday dinner. As she serves the meal, she tells about the excitement of hearing Grandpa's first car pull up in front of the house. Nephews and nieces hearing the pleasure in their aunt's voice will share some of what she felt as a child, and her stories will be woven into their understanding of their family's past.

Early in life, your child thinks consciously about taking roles in the family culture. Preschool boys and girls play at being mother and father. They envision themselves as grown-ups when they imitate caring for dolls or dress up like firefighters and astronauts. As we noted in chapter 3, children and adolescents think about what kind of parents they will be and how they will do better than their own parents. They are convinced that they will avoid doing terrible things — like scolding, sending a child to his room without dessert, or humiliating a teenager in front of her friends — and that they will succeed where their parents have failed. They surely

will have time to go with their own child to a ball game, to have nothing but fun on holidays, and to be understanding when their child has lost a book or failed a test. As they imagine being a parent, young children also imagine preserving or adding their own traditions: they will be sure that no one in the family works on Christmas Eve, or that everyone gathers to deliver cakes and pies to the church for the community celebration.

Each community tries to teach its children to be fair, kind, honest, and charitable. You want your child to think about other people's feelings (starting with siblings and playmates) and to treat them just as he would like to be treated. And from the moment you started to imagine parenthood and what your child would be like, you had a set of standards and values you wished to communicate to him. Parents usually take pride in teaching their children to show respect by saying "Please," "Thank you," and "May I . . . ?" Parents hand down cherished ideas such as: In order to succeed in life, a child must learn to take responsibility, to accept what cannot be changed, and to work hard to change what can. She should see that cleanliness and promptness are virtues, and be thankful for the thousand good things that come her way (and blame nobody when it rains). These are the ethical and philosophical values of a family culture. In transmitting them, you know that you and your partner are not saints, nor are your children. You accept your own limitations and allow leeway for young minds. And as you do, you will — at some moment when your child has clearly made a basic value his own — feel proud of your efforts to instill values in him.

Valuing Values

How parents convey their values differs dramatically among families, of course. What is most important is not what you preach or say — as we have said in other contexts. What you actually do, and especially what your child experiences in relation to you, is what matters. Jewish and Christian children learn their Bible values not from sermons but from how they themselves are cared for. A child who is treated fairly, kindly, and with thought for his feelings learns the basic values of cooperation and consideration for others. When a child takes pride in his possessions and sees other people treat them with respect, he learns about respecting the property of others. If he sees that his mother and father are faithful to each other and reliable in respect to him, he learns the value of fidelity. Children become considerate, decent, dependable, and warmly affectionate when their parents demonstrate these traits toward them in the daily activities they share. Obviously, these lessons take time. A child must be developmentally ready to grasp them. But that is all the more reason to demonstrate the virtues yourself, so that when your child is ready to take in the whole pattern of your behavior, it will be clear to him.

As we have discussed, toddlers have a hard time seeing the world through anyone's eyes but their own. When your young preschooler is demanding attention just after you come home from a trying workday, it makes no sense to tell her to "think about how Mommy feels." But if you have not shown her that you know how she feels early in the morning, when you are in a rush and she needs you, she will not learn to understand this approach to problems even in her more flexible moments. A father can more convincingly communicate the value of self-restraint if he does not scream at everyone when he does not get his way or has misplaced the keys. A mother who shuts off the TV to hear her child's story about school, however tired she may be (and however long the story), can show how important it is to listen to other people. Thus, a foundation for character is forged in the furnace of daily home life, in its most intimate and intense moments.

We have described how children become avid organizers and collectors during their school years. They like to learn the rules of games (although they may sometimes alter them for their convenience). They collect interesting things like coins, stamps, bottle tops, and baseball cards and try to understand the way things work. Enjoying the predictability of schedule, they are natural ritualizers. At the same time, they are junior scientists, testing their ideas or hypotheses about what makes people act as they do. Their "why" questions express a natural curiosity about rules and sometimes challenge family rules as well: "Why do I have to go to sleep at seven? In Billy's family, they don't." Children notice that their friends' families do not go to the same church, eat different foods, and otherwise have their own ways of doing things. Your child may believe (or try to convince you) that one of her playmates has everything better, or that the family she sees on television is the ideal one for her.

Parents need to know their own standards and feel comfortable asserting, "This is the way we do things." When you set limits, offer explanations in terms that reinforce the child's sense of belonging, rather than dwell on the lack of something other children have. If your family is vegetarian or Hindu or strictly kosher, don't tell your child, "You can't eat at Hamburger Heaven, and that's that!" Instead, you can say, "We don't eat cheeseburgers in this family. If you're interested in going out for dinner sometime, we can start planning a trip to our sort of restaurant. You'll probably find some of your favorites there." Children will grow proud of what is distinctive in their family culture if they sense that it is a gain, not a loss, to be like their parents, older siblings, and respected people in their community. Often linking a tradition to a child's grandparents can be a powerful way of illustrating its value: Grandma and Grandpa usually hold a special place in your child's heart. A young person will be more likely to make family traditions a part of herself if they offer fun and pleasure, as well as order and comfort.

Parents and the Family Culture

Your ease in creating a family culture depends in large part on your memories of and attitudes toward the culture in your own family. If you have come to feel that your family traditions do not reflect the way the world truly is or are inconsistent with your vision of the person you want to be, you may be reluctant to carry them on with your own children. If you also hesitate to create new traditions, you risk depriving your children of the anchor of a clear definition of family life. This approach may also be self-defeating, since parents who do not consciously choose either to behave in a particular way or to create their own family traditions often find themselves replicating their parents' habits, however much they wanted to avoid them.

Nonetheless, it is better to be sincere about the family culture or traditions you adopt than to put on a show because you think it will be good for your children. If you teach your child to follow certain rituals but do not believe in their value or participate in them wholeheartedly, he will be quick to spot the conflict. A young child will be confused by the difference between what Daddy says and does, and an older child might resent what she may see as unfair: "How come we have to go to Hebrew school, but you never go to temple?" Or your child might turn against the notion of family culture, negating the reason for the parent's pretense in the first place and making that pretense doubly hurtful. Again, be honest with your children about your feelings, and respect what they can understand and decide for themselves.

There may be tension in a family in which a father and mother have different values or expectations for their child and their family. Parents usually realize that some issues —

whether they would prefer a boy or a girl, or whether they want their child to play sports, take music lessons, or take up other hobbies — are not wholly under their control. But there are other issues that run deeper. Should we have one or two children, or many? Should we try to conceive soon after we commit to our relationship, or wait until we are financially stable? How will we share the many responsibilities of caring for our babies? Should we live where we see the most exciting career opportunities or near our children's grandparents? While you and your partner can easily talk out certain questions when you foresee them, profound disagreements may surprise you later. The news that your son has bested another child in a fight, for instance, may make one of you feel ashamed and another secretly proud. Although individual couples must come to their own agreements and compromises on these questions, the way you approach them — the answer that you consider to be "normal" — may vary depending on the family culture in which each of you was raised. Be aware, then, of cultural tensions when they arise, and consider how you and your partner have dealt with them in the past.

A couple often first confronts the profound differences between their backgrounds when they marry and decide to participate in a marriage ceremony that reflects ancient rituals but that they wish to refashion to reflect their own personalities, families, ideas, and feelings. A wedding in some ways belongs only to the wedding couple but in other ways is a communal event.

Thus, it brings two families together in a mutual enterprise that may either highlight tensions or reinforce shared traditions. Certainly the couple's parents have a psychological stake in the day: they have imagined it in some way since before the bride and groom were even born. If the couple wish to be wed in a church, its community may also require them to attend classes about what makes a proper marriage — a requirement that either or both of the newlyweds may resent. Society at large also has an interest in the wedding since it signals that groom and bride are changing their status: two people transforming themselves into one family. On top of these deep matters of relationships and faith, engaged couples face vexing, culturally influenced issues of whom to keep on the guest list and what sort of music to play. All these potential stresses aside, tradition plays a large part in making a wedding meaningful to everyone involved and to the wedding couple most of all.

Another event that helps to forge the family culture is the first pregnancy. For some couples, the news poses one of the biggest questions of all: Should we have the baby? If mother and father do not consider themselves ready to commit to parenthood, or if tests show that the fetus is likely to be born with a profound birth defect, the couple may discuss ending the pregnancy. In their private process of deciding on a life together, two people naturally reflect their deepest beliefs and values; they may consult with their religious guides or find one for the first time. After joyfully welcoming the news that they will become parents, most couples will be surprised at the many old cultural traditions that make themselves known during pregnancy. The expectant mother may suddenly learn much more about her own mother's superstitions — that she should recite certain prayers at certain times or avoid walking near a cemetery — and may be surprised to find herself adopting some of them (after all, they can't hurt). The impending arrival of a child may also make the young father alter his behavior, trying to assume the paternal role as he has unconsciously learned it from his family culture. (For more on the psychological experience of pregnancy, see chapter 4.)

As pregnancy develops, a mother may feel that she has unwittingly assumed a special role in her family and her community. Since all cultures highly value a pregnant woman, the life she is nurturing is in some way the community's future. A pregnant woman is also an undeniably powerful symbol of a community's hopes for a better world — as expressed in fertility cults, ancient scripture, and the veneration of the Virgin Mary. Some women enjoy the increasingly public role of being a new mother; others come to resent the attention. The differences in response may reflect how much a mother embraces the community's view of her grander role.

Other cultural rituals surround the arrival of the baby. Each tradition marks a birth in one or more ways — through announcements, pictures, parties, gifts, and religious ceremonies. (See "Circumcision, an Age-Old Ceremony," page 379.) And when you take your first baby home, you may discover that your families and their traditions are valuable to you in a new way. Grandparents bring expertise as well as extra hands. Suddenly they may seem much wiser; maybe your mother-in-law was wrong to suggest that the foods you craved during pregnancy meant you would have a girl — but at least she knows how to bathe your newborn boy in under an hour. Beset with apprehensions about doing something wrong, you can take comfort in the customs you remember from your childhood or hear about from other people. After all, those parenting methods have been tested.

When a baby has health problems, parents need especially to feel grounded, both in their community and in their spiritual traditions. At least 5 percent of newborns have some type of minor oddity, like a birthmark, and some have major problems at birth, such as an extra finger, a cleft palate, or a heart defect. A premature infant must immediately receive vigorous medical care to stay alive. Even with modern methods for prenatal diagnosis, the birth of a child with a serious disorder, such as Down syndrome or a more disabling condition, can surprise physicians. At such times, doctors and nurses try to console the family. But losing a baby, seeing a baby suffer and not being able to help, facing the extra challenge of raising a child with health problems — any of these events can shatter parents' self-confidence and undermine their vision of the world. Their greatest source of strength and comfort is likely to come from their own families and their own traditions. When a grandparent or a close friend lovingly holds your baby in her hands, she shows you that he is beloved and accepted. A minister, by blessing a newborn, can indicate that your child herself is a blessing. When an infant is stillborn or in danger of dying, a priest may offer a final sacrament and give that child a name for her parents to hold on to. With such cultural and psychological support, young families can emerge from such crises feeling stronger and able to go on.

The Importance of Religions

Organized religions are an important part of the American heritage. Native Americans held (and still hold) a deeply spiritual tradition that emphasized the beauty and holiness of the land, the mysteries of nature, the shared vitality of humans and animals, and the importance of mutual support and interdependence. Spanish and Portuguese Catholics were the first to explore and settle in the New World. Many more Europeans sailed to the territories that would become the United

CIRCUMCISION, AN AGE-OLD CEREMONY

Many cultures have elaborate initiation rituals, either at birth or when a child attains adulthood. The physical ritual that has prevailed most in the United States is male circumcision: the surgical removal of the foreskin from the penis. Since the days of the Bible, Jewish boys have been circumcised at the eighth day of life with a celebration. (Today there are corresponding ceremonies for Jewish girls, which, of course, do not involve any surgery.) Circumcision creates a physical sign that the boy is part of the Jewish community. Family, friends, and the rabbi join in reciting a prayer that announces their hope to see the infant later introduced into the world of religious values, marriage, and doing good for others. Thus, during the first week of a child's life, his community already envisions his future development.

In the mid-twentieth century, American physicians began to circumcise all male babies routinely. Doctors thought that an uncircumcised boy was more susceptible to infection, and that newborns did not feel pain from the procedure. More recent findings have shown that the assumption about pain was wrong. Since an uncircumcised boy's slightly increased risk of infection can easily be offset by teaching him to wash his penis carefully, pulling back the foreskin, doctors are less likely to circumcise young boys today. As a result, many of today's fathers are circumcised while their young sons are not. If your uncircumcised boy wishes he were "like Daddy" or, more likely, asks why his penis is slightly different from his father's, answer him straightforwardly.

In the late 1980s, the American Academy of Pediatrics (AAP) stopped recommending circumcision of male infants. Recognizing that some families may feel a strong cultural or religious reason for it, the AAP recommends that whoever performs the procedure, an experienced doctor or mohel (a rabbi trained in circumcision), use a local anesthetic to ensure that it is as safe and painless as possible.

States in order to exercise their various forms of Christian belief. Protestant ministers played key roles in shaping the moral and legal traditions of Great Britain's American colonies. Most of those colonies had established churches: Anglican in the Middle and Southern provinces, Congregational in New England. In the eighteenth century, when colonial leaders gathered for the Continental Congresses, they discovered that their religious differences were a source of tension. Soon they established a new, unifying ideal of respect for others' beliefs and the separation of church and state. This ideal, already practiced in such colonies as Pennsylvania and Rhode Island, quickly spread to the new states.

In part because of that religious tolerance, the United States has been enriched by an influx of people from all over the world. The Protestants, Catholics, and Jews who arrived in the eighteenth and nineteenth centuries have since been followed by virtually every religion on earth. Islam has grown with immigration from the Middle East; Asians have brought Hinduism and Buddhism; and African and Caribbean traditions have arrived from the Atlantic islands. Hispanic Americans have brought their special blend of Catholicism and shaped other faiths. One measure of the vitality of American religion is that sects do not necessarily divide along ethnic lines: a Chinese American, for instance, might be Buddhist or Baptist, Methodist or atheist, or something else. Specifically American churches have thrived, too — among them the Latter-day Saints (Mormons)

and Christian Science. African American churches — Baptist, Methodist, and Pentecostal, among others — which originally formed because of segregation, have become a unique American creation with a theology of hope, powerful preaching, and song.

For millions of Americans, religion plays a central role in their daily and weekly activities and in shaping their values and family life. These families worship, read scripture, pray, donate money and time, and turn to their religious leaders for guidance, counsel, and comfort. For many other families, religion is one of several equal pillars providing structure for their lives; they see their church as one source of tradition and values, but do not necessarily accept all of its teachings. Other American parents, for whom organized religion holds little or no meaning, derive values from their personal spirituality and philosophical contemplation. All of these choices are healthier than no choice — than living an unexamined life without values.

Families teach the scriptures, creeds, and forms of worship of the religion of their choice. They transmit their community's views on the mystery of birth or what happens to the soul of a person after death. Some cultures bring their young people into religious ceremonies early; children are expected to attend funerals and cremations, dress up in special clothes for weddings, and sit quietly for religious ceremonies that may last for hours. Churches that believe that certain rituals will not interest a child, or should be just for adults, usually have special classes or ceremonies that their young members can attend instead. The most confusing religious message you can send your child is to insist that he attend services or follow a particular doctrine that you neither attend nor follow yourself. This attitude implies that religious observance is incidental, something a person can expect to grow out of.

Religion can be an island of quiet and reflection in the life of a busy family. For most of the week, parents are occupied with earning an income, cleaning the house, and perhaps caring for their own parents, while children have school, homework, sports, friends, and other social obligations. The dryer is buzzing, the microwave is beeping, and the telephone is ringing: you may feel that you have a million things to do right now. Worship, however, gives you and your children a chance not only to do, but also to be. And gathering for that purpose at set times each day or each week can provide your busy family with a structure they can be sure of and within which they can find refreshment.

Religious Differences

Seldom do young couples spend time considering their religions until they have children. Then they begin to think about settling down into a community and a rhythm of life. They naturally return to their own religious roots or, if they are not satisfied with them and are adventurous, look around for a form of worship that fits their own ideas of spirituality and community. Often one pleasant discovery is that the major function of a house of worship and its spiritual leader is to help congregants through life. Most ministers, priests, and rabbis are far more ready to console and advise than many doctors, who are not consistently trained in counseling and are increasingly pressed for time. You do not need the approval of a managed-care plan to go to confession, a community supper, or a discussion group about family and stress. In a congregation, you will probably find other young parents with whom you have a lot in common, and many wise older people ready to adore your baby. Best of all, during services, the day care is usually free.

Some couples have difficulty deciding on the religious or philosophical traditions they will share with their children. If they are of the same faith, they may not be equally committed to synagogue, or Sunday school, or fasting. And if they come from different backgrounds, must she convert to his faith, or can he attend her church? While courting, a young woman may have found her boyfriend's atheistic comments an amusing change from her father's preaching. But now that they are bringing up a baby, she wonders, "Will we really never have a Christmas tree?" Some cultural traditions are easier to meld than others. American society happily accepts the notion of a family's having an "Irish side" and an "Italian side," for example, with recipes and songs and customs from both cultures. But it is unwise to commit a child to two different religions that require the acceptance of different ideas. It is better to bring her up in one faith, while explaining the other and emphasizing the concepts the two share. You can offer explanations like, "Daddy goes to his mosque on Friday, and we go to our church on Sunday. If you want to go to the mosque to see what it's like, you can go with Daddy whenever you want to."

Of course, religious differences can also be a source of conflict, especially because there is usually no way for two people to decide whose spiritual values are better. If a mother and father of different faiths divorce, each may want to bring up their child in his or her own faith, and this can become an issue in deciding custody. (See chapter 34.) As in other conflicts, your most important responsibility to your child is to demonstrate a mature approach: that is, to show by your actions that it is possible to hold different beliefs in the same family, and that religious differences do not have to be threatening or dangerous but can peacefully, even respectfully coexist. You and your spouse should work out your reli-

gious differences in your own time together, rather than attempting to solve them first in front of your children.

Religion-based conflict of a different sort arises when a religious majority tries to impose its customs or values on the whole community. American society cherishes the idea that every family should be able to choose which beliefs to practice, as long as these beliefs and practices do not impinge on anyone else's rights. In order to preserve your own religious freedom, refrain from imposing your faith on children from other families.

Religious conflict in families is probably most commonly caused by a growing child's decision to explore other spiritual paths or her explicit choice not to carry on her family's customs. Parents may get confused and feel that their child is rejecting both the faith they hold dear and them as well. Spiritual questing is, however, a common part of forging an independent adult identity. The Amish, for example, who are among the most traditional of the many American religious groups, commonly allow adolescents to try aspects of the non-Amish life before asking them to commit themselves to the church. By encouraging their children to come to their own wholehearted decisions, the Amish strengthen their community. If you raise your children with a solid grounding in your values, they are more likely to continue to embrace them even if they choose to practice another faith.

Your Child's Spiritual Life

Children know that the world is mysterious. Everything is new to them, they are intensely curious, and they are close to nature. It is wonderful to walk through a park in spring with children and watch their excitement at the new buds on bushes, squirrels running up trees, and birds returning from the south. For children, nature and life can be truly awesome — and they can bring that feeling into the lives of busy adults who have scarcely a moment to think and even less time to experience awe themselves.

Through religion, children enter a place within their community that speaks to their feelings of awe and tells them there is a life of spirit. Your child may complain about having to wear fancy clothes, a yarmulke, or a head scarf. He may indeed be bored and squirm around in his seat during a sermon that contains little he understands. During the rest of the week, he may yearn to sample foods that he sees his classmates enjoying, but that are forbidden by your faith's dietary laws. But within your congregation your child will also see that people look at him with love; he will join with others to sing and listen to glorious music and perhaps get to eat cookies at the gathering after the service. Your child can learn the symbolism of a mass, the concentrated force of chanted prayers, the power of spirituals. She can hear inspiring stories about heroes and saints and say prayers that express hope and gratitude. Her

spirituality will take root in her awe, reverence, and comfort — all part of the whole experience of participating in a religious community.

Your child's engagement with religion depends on her developmental stage. Preschoolers are still working to distinguish real from pretend, what is alive and what is not, and how time passes. Believing, as they do, that dogs and even computers think, they are happy to endow these creatures with souls. School-age children may, owing to their interest in understanding rules and belonging to groups, eagerly follow the customs of temple or church and compare how their friends define their religious identity; but doctrine will still be a distant concern. Not until adolescence are children able to do the abstract thinking most spirituality and philosophy demands. Generations of children have grown up envisioning Heaven as in the sky, even though theologians use this image simply as a metaphor for a more ideal level of existence. Even this cloudy representation of a higher existence can, however, comfort and inspire a child.

Most formal religions strive to answer the questions: Why are we born? Why do we die? Why are both good and evil in the world? Through a formal religion, a child can learn that what he does matters to others and to God, just as he has learned at home that what he does matters to his parents and other adults and friends; and that he — and every other human being — is a precious creation. Religion can reassure a child that the universe is fair, or that God cares about her, watching over her when she is asleep and healing her when she is sick. A child faced, for example, with the death of a beloved grandfather can learn that Grandpa is now close to God: God called for him, and now, at special times, he will look down on his family. (See chapter 35 for more on how children deal with death.) Through religion, a child can learn that the spirits of his ancestors live on, and that these spirits delight in being remembered, named, and given special tokens of respect, such as candles or gift offerings. And in religion a child can find both a way to embrace spirituality and mystery, and a source of courage and strength.

Of course, while we stress a belief in God as the root of a spiritual life, not everyone shares this belief, and some people have a spiritual life outside organized religion. It is important nonetheless to convey to your children a belief in values transcending day-to-day living and your immediate needs — whether those beliefs involve helping the needy, preserving a forest or a park, or bringing the beauty of music or poetry to others. In all these activities, you aim to take your children beyond the immediate world of direct experience toward an unseen world of deeper meaning and spirituality.

The Evil of Prejudice

Just as, consciously and unconsciously, parents convey what they think is important, beautiful, and true, so they also may convey ugly ideas, the seeds of hatred, and smoldering antagonisms. Throughout history, religions have battled, each claiming to own God's true word. In recent years, religiously inspired violence has devastated places as diverse as Ireland, the Balkans, the Indian subcontinent, the Middle East, and Indonesia. In America's long conflict over slavery, both sides used theological arguments to justify their positions; some churches split over the issue. Probably no traditional religion is free of prejudice of one type or another. Nor are ethnic groups: pride in one's own heritage too often leads to denigrating other people.

In perpetuating traditions of hatred from generation to generation, a family may pass along prejudgments about race, sex, religion, national origin, or social class; and, indeed, our language is full of slang terms that devalue large groups. The most destructive and long-lasting American tradition is the racism whites express against African Americans. This deep-seated prejudice has infected white Americans whose ancestors arrived in this country long after slavery was abolished. The pervasive cultural bias against Americans of African ancestry has poisoned the relations between blacks and whites and diminished opportunities available to African Americans. Racism is not uniquely American, of course. Rather, it is particularly un-American in its bold defiance of our shared beliefs in equality and tolerance. Intelligent and mutual respect is the primary value you should aim to bequeath to your children.

Children are always curious about people who are different from them or from the people they know. Difference can also make a young child anxious. He may look at a bearded man, turn away, look back, and think about rushing into his mother's arms. He may cry or hesitate before reaching out to see for himself that behind the beard is a smile and a kind person. An older child, though less fearful, can embarrass her parents by making personal comments: "Look at that brown man." "What happened to your other arm?" This frankness or curiosity is different from invidiously characterizing or prejudging a person whose language, color, facial appearance, height, weight, or other outward characteristics are unlike one's own. Whether a young child sees someone who is different as approachable and interesting, or as frightening and dangerous, will depend on the attitude of her parents. The child will look at her mother and father's faces to see what they signal: "This is a nice person," or "Watch out! Danger, dirt, uncertainty." You convey your favor or disfavor nonverbally — but clearly — by facial expression, tone of voice, and body language. When your child is older, he can pick up the attitudes behind your private comments and your use of slang terms, sarcasm, and ethnic humor.

Racism is transmitted at home and in the streets. While you cannot control the larger culture, you can control what your children see and hear within your home. Derisive comments about the intelligence, the lifestyle, and the values of other groups sustain traditions of hatred and pass them on to children who are then likely, in turn, to perpetuate the evil and pass it on to their children. To reverse this hateful tradition, give your children a new tradition to pass on to the next generation. Make a point of expressing your understanding of and respect for people of different races and ethnic backgrounds and try to give your child the opportunity to meet, play with, and become friends with a variety of children. Such cross-cultural experience can happen naturally when children gather, as in a large day care or school. It happens most easily, however, when parents approve and especially when they have a variety of friends and acquaintances of their own. When you open your door to people different from yourself, you offer your child the key to a better and more moral world. And, as we will discuss in the next chapter, that is what a family culture is all about.

CHAPTER 27

Learning Right from Wrong: Your Child's Moral Development

"No hitting."

"Tell Grandma 'thank you' for the sweater she knitted you."

"Don't copy off your neighbor's paper."

"Stick by your friends, and they'll stick by you."

"Thou shalt not kill."

"Judge people by their character, not by their appearance or their background."

"A gentleman never insults anyone unintentionally."

"Subtract line 45b from line 45a. This is your tax due. Send the full amount to the following address: . . ."

These rules apply to nearly every American. They are intended to regulate how people get along with one another, to work out and diminish hostility, and to ensure in other ways that communities function smoothly and continue to benefit people's lives. Moral development is, in part, the process of learning these basic rules; and it is parents, for the most part, who transmit them from the culture at large to their children. This is a responsibility most parents feel keenly as they contemplate their youngster's future. You want to be proud of your child and confident that as an adult she will contribute to her community and to society.

When society was largely organized around isolated villages, children grew up among adults who espoused the same values, followed the same rituals, and worshiped in the same church. This isolation tended to foster the belief that ways of thinking different from one's own were not only false but alarming, even dangerous. But today most communities include people who have different ideas about religion, politics, child-rearing habits, and other aspects of life that involve deeply moral issues. As we discussed in the last chapter, American children are directly exposed to people from many cultures, and television and other media bring even more diverse ways of life into their homes. Obviously, well-meaning, moral people derive their ethics from many different sources.

Teaching this fact to your young child is not necessarily moral relativism; it is common sense. He will still value and follow your family's traditions when you also tell him, "This is how we do things."

For most parents, the ultimate goal of moral education is for their child to develop an inner sense of right and wrong, or what is often called a "conscience." Ideally, one learns to do what's right not out of fear of the consequences of breaking a rule but by taking the rules learned from family and culture and making them one's own. No child is born with a conscience. Every child is born wanting to do whatever occurs to him to want to do. Only gradually does he develop a moral sense through watching and listening — first, to you and other relatives and later, to his peers and adult role models outside the family. While you can teach your child some aspects of morality simply by telling her what to do, you usually teach most powerfully by example. And by observing and absorbing over time, your child will develop her own internal moral standards. She will come to know when to sacrifice for others and when to reward herself; when to adhere to the letter of the law and when to bend rules to obtain a greater good; and when to respect another person's traditions and when to insist on what she thinks is right.

Moral development is also about understanding emotions and their power, and recognizing that anger, fear, and even sadness can motivate you to do things that may not always be kind or fair to another person. In many ways, moral development is mostly about how you learn to behave toward other persons in your lives: how you come to treat them fairly as individuals with rights of their own and also as feeling human beings whom you love and respect, or, at least, whose equality you acknowledge. Understanding moral development as both personal and social in terms of adhering to your community's code of behavior toward other persons is a difficult task. It requires the integration of your cognitive and emotional life and its continual appraisal and adjustment as your world changes and you have more experiences. Perhaps the deepest challenge of moral development is to understand and accept that you will change your mind, have lapses in moral judgment, repair these lapses, learn from your errors, and continue to develop as a moral person. The child who sees a parent openly engaged in this process also sees that living a moral life is not a simple matter of learning a set of rules: it takes work and thought.

For these reasons, you cannot decide every question for your child; you have to let him try to make choices on his own. You are as much his guide as his teacher. In developing physical balance, a toddler learns to stand on her own feet with time and practice; eventually she no longer even has to think about standing. Equally, children learn to balance their principles through practice and thought until they become naturally moral people, considering the ethical ramifications of their daily choices without having to remind themselves each time. As your children pass through the stages of emotional development, helped by your teaching and your example, they achieve the moral independence that is maturity.

Stages in Your Child's Moral Thinking

Just as in other areas of development, a child's ability to understand right and wrong and her moral sense emerges through several distinct phases. The psychologists Jean Piaget and Lawrence Kohlberg have identified stages in moral development through different research methods: Piaget, by observing children from different cultures as they played games; Kohlberg, by telling stories involving ethical issues and noting what children said about them. Other researchers have since discovered that, in respect to moral issues that appear in their own daily lives, children are usually more sophisticated than Piaget and Kohlberg had found. Also, children seem to be less lenient about behavior in hypothetical stories than about the same problems in real life. Nevertheless, thinking about moral development as a series of steps will help you understand your child's actions and what she can and cannot grasp about the morality of a particular situation.

Empathy for other people is one of the roots of morality. Newborns seem to feel an innate emotional response to others' distress: one weeping baby can start a whole nursery crying. In his second year, your child begins to differentiate between his own suffering and other people's and no longer bursts into tears whenever he senses that someone is sad. He will, however, try to offer comfort to another baby in distress. But he is not yet able to understand that different people view the world differently and therefore find comfort in different things. Thus, your toddler might well bring you her own favorite toys to help the crying baby instead of that baby's parent or playthings.

This instinctive response to a nearby person in distress is the start of a moral sense, but only the start. Because no amount of explaining can teach children younger than about three any code of right and wrong, Piaget called them premoral. Thus, a toddler is unlikely to consider how his own choices might cause distress to someone else, especially if those choices will bring him something he wants right now. Although two-year-olds can remember that a certain action makes Daddy say, "No!" they rarely understand why that action is wrong — whether because it is dangerous or it harms someone else — or that it is wrong even when Daddy is not around. This lack of understanding is one reason toddlers need nearly constant supervision.

Even before a child is old enough to understand many rules, his moral development begins as part of his natural inclination to please his parents. A child behaves according to what makes Daddy and Mommy happy because he does not want to lose their approval or their love. He is largely motivated by the wish to be good.

When he sees his parents are displeased,

he feels the beginnings of guilt and tries to win back their affection with better behavior. Since the worry that he might lose your love can hinder your child's healthy development, remember to tell him in words and deeds how much you love him, even though you don't care for his occasional bad behavior. This message helps instill the vital knowledge that it is in your child's power to choose to be either good or bad, to please or not to please. This realization is enhanced by the system of rewards and punishments you have established.

Between three and six, Piaget theorized, children start to understand rules, but in a rudimentary way. They see rules as inflexible, unchanging, ordained by some higher authority. Even the instructions for playing marbles, preschoolers might say, were set down by God. Violating such a code warrants punishment, no matter what a person's intentions; thus, dropping a glass while clearing the dinner table is as bad as willfully throwing that glass to the floor. They also worry when they see someone getting away with a violation of the rules — one reason they tend to tattle. (See "Tattling," pages 400–401.) And, at this age, your child may assume that if someone is unhappy, he — your child — must have done something wrong and thus may feel guilty or confused.

As with so many aspects of life, your child's moral development is intertwined with other strands of her growth. Behaving ethically requires a child to have some ability to empathize with other people's feelings, to anticipate rewards (or penalties) in the future, and to delay gratification of her own feelings and desires. Since these abilities take time to develop, toddlers are not far along the road to acting morally. Young children understand right and wrong, but also tend to see things as black or white.

Not until they are close to school age, around age six or seven, do children begin to develop a nuanced sense of right and wrong and some sophistication in the way they understand rules. As they recognize the difference between morality and conventions, they begin to realize that the rules of the games they play can be changed with their playmates' mutual consent, but they also understand the principle of fair play. They start to factor a person's intentions into their moral judgments. They recognize that not every crime is punished, and that not every distress is punishment for a crime. They start to struggle with telling the truth even if they fear the consequences. (See "When Is a Lie a Lie?" pages 390–391.) But school-age children are very conscious of peer pressure, and it provides a strong motivation to follow rules that preserve the social order.

Next to develop is a sense of internal pride or guilt. Most children under the age of eight have a hard time identifying when another child feels proud or ashamed of her actions. Since happy and sad emotions are revealed by common facial expressions, a younger child recognizes those feelings and therefore might define a proud person as "feeling happy that other people are happy with what he did." Most eight-year-olds, in contrast, have developed a concept of pride that does not depend on an audience. They also understand that a person can feel ashamed of something even if it got her what she wanted, while younger children assume that a person who gets away with an immoral act must be happy. Furthermore, by the age of eight, children tend to be less harsh toward a wrongdoer who feels bad about her actions than toward one who feels no remorse.

Older kids are more able to see gradations in a particular act; they can weigh which of two good outcomes is the greater good, and which of two wrongs is worse. By the time they are adolescents, children are capable of highly abstract reasoning and consequently develop moral principles. They also develop an acute sense for injustice and hypocrisy — usually in others. With a few more years of experience, teenagers are also able to under-

WHEN IS A LIE A LIE?

Before you can help your child learn to tell the truth and play by the rules, you need to know when she actually becomes conscious of whether she is lying or cheating and can understand that it is wrong.

Children under the age of five commonly tell stories that differ from what their parents suspect, or even know, is the truth. We have already discussed preschoolers' active fantasy lives and the imaginary friends they often invent. (See chapters 16 and 24.) Although you can usually distinguish this sort of pretending from an untruth a child tells in order to get what she wants or to keep herself out of trouble, your young child has a hard time with that distinction, just as she has a hard time drawing the line between

real and pretend. Almost everything she says is shaped by her desire to please her parents. She may therefore insist that she did wash her hands before dinner, she didn't take the last cookie, and she certainly didn't push Tommy. For a child of this age, her wish to be loved colors what she feels is true. Will saying a particular thing disappoint Mommy? Would Daddy be happier if she had behaved a certain way? A young child will try to create a pleasing reality with words, even if they aren't true.

Similarly, toddlers see little wrong with doing whatever achieves a desired outcome. When they play, they commonly bend the rules in their favor or take other children's toys. While this behavior may look like cheating to adults, your child's motivations are nothing like that of, say, a poker player who holds a card up his sleeve or a student

who copies test answers off a friend's paper. Preschoolers are still developing their moral sense. It takes time for a child to develop the ability both to cheat knowingly and to resist that temptation.

Your school-age child needs help to acknowledge his occasional errors and to recognize that lying about them only makes the situation worse. In fact, school-age children are often stricter about rules and violations than any NFL referee. They are rule bound, in part because they are trying hard to understand how flexible these social conventions are. You need, then, to teach your child that, while there are consequences for breaking the rules, children who break them are not entirely bad, nor are their relationships with others forever damaged.

Here are some principles for dealing with lying and cheating:

stand the positive necessity of forgiveness as well as of accepting differences in behavior and points of view.

In adolescence, children incorporate the realization that people live their lives according to many different values, based on many types of authority. Teens tend to move toward defining their own independent identities and become more interested in ethical principles separate from their family's or society's conventions. They try to emulate people whom they see as having admirable value systems. At first, young people believe that morality is a sort of legalistic contract, under which people have strict obligations to each other and to society as a whole. When they progress to what Kohlberg identified as the highest level of thinking, they come to believe that morality is based on universal ethical principles and ideally choose to commit

---

- **Pick your issues.** A child's denial that he ate a cookie after you said, "No snacks" is not as serious as his saying that he doesn't know how a toy you know he doesn't own came to be in his backpack.

- Your first step should be to calm down. If you are upset, talking in anger to anyone, child or adult, is seldom constructive and is likely to be counterproductive.

- Address the issue when you and your child are alone, not in front of other children or adults. If your child feels publicly embarrassed during your talk, she is likely to learn that she needs to avoid shame at all costs and might, in the future, seek to come up with a better lie instead of choosing better behavior.

- If you know or suspect a younger child has been involved in lying or cheating, it is better not to box her into a corner and ask her to admit her guilt. State the truth, or as much of it as you have found out, in a matter-of-fact way.

- If part of the consequence you set for your child's infraction is to compensate an adult he has wronged — by, for example, returning a shoplifted item — accompany him when he does so. If he has to do this alone, his anxiety and fear will overshadow the moral lesson, and he will not remember it.

- At the same time that you set the consequence for your child's misbehavior, emphasize that you are also available to help her. If she cheated on homework, ask if she needs more help. If he took a weapon to school because he was afraid, take steps to solve that problem. (See chapter 23.)

Whatever your children do, they should know that you will always be there for them.

If you want to discourage lying and cheating, you must avoid this behavior yourself. Children are exquisitely sensitive both to the nuances of rules and to adults' violations of them. Phrases like "What they don't know won't hurt them" blur the moral line. If you sneak your twelve-year-old into movies for a cheaper price by claiming he is ten, why should that child resist going to a movie for seventeen-year-olds when he is only fourteen? Why is it all right to cheat the IRS but not to cheat on an exam? The more you model responsible behavior and talk to your child calmly and openly about lying and cheating, the more you help him develop strong standards.

themselves to those principles out of a sense of pride and personal identity.

As in other areas of development, children move through each stage of moral development in turn. Researchers almost never see children go backward in their thinking; once they achieve a certain philosophical breakthrough, they continue to apply it, sometimes inflexibly and sometimes creatively. Other investigations have supported the idea that moral development is gradual, that children can make only limited progress in a short time. When older people reason with them about ethical dilemmas, school-age children might advance one stage in their own moral thinking, but they don't advance more than that. Developing sound values takes time, thought, and experience in trying to live by them as one meets the challenges of adult life.

These stages define how children think about moral dilemmas, not the rules and principles they adopt. The rules your family chooses to adopt, whether tolerant or intolerant, fair or unfair, respectful of other people or condescending and resentful, will shape your child's moral reasoning in the future. And as she becomes more sophisticated, the behavior that you both teach and display is her most important guide in life.

As you help your child to develop moral principles, you need to articulate the beliefs that underlie your values. For some families, these beliefs may be a formal religious creed, such as the biblical Ten Commandments or the Buddhist concept of respect for all living things. In other families, moral development may proceed from basic humanistic principles, such as the Golden Rule known best as: "Do unto others as you would have them do unto you." Whatever your family's personal religious or moral beliefs, imparting them to your child at an early age will help her to understand the rules governing daily life and thus, knowing that they are not arbitrary, to trust your discipline. Furthermore, with the family's principles firmly in mind, your child will be able to use them later in determining the right thing to do in unfamiliar and complex situations.

Your Three Rs of Moral Teaching

Just as you help your child with the three Rs at school — reading, 'riting, and 'rithmetic — you should, in respect to moral values, observe another set of three Rs: respect, rules, and role models. Respect your child if you wish to imbue her with the ability both to respect others, whether peers or adults, and to feel good about herself. Enforce rules and be explicit about moral precepts so that your child understands why your rules are important and is willing to obey them. And be a role model for your child in constantly reinforcing the moral guidelines you hope he will adopt as his own.

People tend to parent, as we have said, in ways that echo their own parenting. If you feel good about your upbringing, this is a positive legacy you will want to pass on to

that your child is different, too. Remember, too, your imaginings long before your child was born, when you thought of the ways you would be the same as or different from your parents. You may have been more explicit in your thoughts about how you would respond to your imagined child's bad behavior — whether you would use physical punishment — and how you would teach your children your own moral values.

your child. If not, you may determine to avoid mistakes you think your parents made. Most parents are somewhere between, wanting to repeat the good behavior they recall and to improve on parenting techniques they feel were either not effective or downright bad. It takes hard work and honest thought to avoid parenting in the same way you were parented and unwittingly making some of the same mistakes. Especially when you discipline your children, think about your own childhood and consider how you might do things differently. Choosing a different approach from your parents does not constitute a rejection of them, as you might fear consciously or unconsciously. Instead, you are recognizing that you are a different person from your mother or father, that you live in a different time, and

Respect for Other Human Beings

Children need to feel that their parents respect them. Respect does not mean that you build up your child's sense of herself with constant but not necessarily warranted praise, or that you defer to all her wishes and opinions. Respecting your child means being both fair all the time and reasonable about what you expect of her. After infancy, your child can take on certain responsibilities — to keep herself out of dangerous places, to help to clean up messes she makes, and eventually to look after the house by herself for an evening or a weekend. These responsibilities should develop along with your child's capacities, and your expectations should reflect what he is mentally and physically capable of at each age. So, for example, a younger child should have fewer chores than an older child and may need more help with them. When your child is younger and still learning the difference between real and pretend, her harmless false statements should be treated as such and corrected but not punished. Since older children are able to understand that shoplifting is a crime, it makes sense to treat their thefts more sternly. Small children who do not yet fully understand what belongs to them and what doesn't, or how an object moves from the first group to the second, may grab items off the shelf at the store, but that is hardly the same thing.

By the same principle, be fair both in rewarding your children for appropriate actions and in distributing consequences for misdeeds. A child is often keenly aware of differences in her parents' treatment of her and her siblings. She can understand, even take pleasure in, having greater responsibilities because she is older and more capable. But when all children seem equally culpable, or when two commit similar misdeeds, you should impose equal consequences. (When children start going to school and learn about other families' rules, they may protest, "None of my friends has to do that!" This type of "unfairness" is not as important as fairness within the family. A child understands that his family's rules help maintain the home he loves.)

You also show respect for your child by maintaining self-control when you discipline him: that is, do your best to remain emotionally neutral. Do not scream or yell or hurt him physically. Hitting and spanking are self-defeating for several reasons. First of all, phys-

ical punishment suggests that anger justifies injuring or hurting someone else, and this is not a model of behavior that most parents want to present to their children (see also "Punishment and Family Values," page 395). Why resort to force when as a parent you have so much other leverage over your children, as well as their natural love, admiration, and dependence? Equally important is the realization that spanking a child draws his attention to his pain rather than to his misdeed. He will be more likely to brood about the punishment than to consider the rules he has broken. Lastly, if you spank your child when you are angry, you may injure him: not only is this regrettable, but it is a crime in most states.

Similarly, never humiliate or denigrate children as you discipline them. When a child violates a rule, your response should make her focus on what she did and why it was wrong. Emphasize how the behavior is wrong, not that she is inherently naughty or deficient. When you scream or yell, your child begins to think she is bad, and that worry distracts her from her misdeed. And when your child sees you seemingly out of control, he worries that he has permanently damaged his family. Not only are these the wrong messages to give your child, but they alienate him and make it hard for him to understand your family's rules. Focus on what your child should do better the next time without making her feel she has lost your respect or affection. After all, a child who has come to think that she has completely lost her parents' approval will have lost much of her motivation to follow moral constraints.

Parents want to ensure that their child remembers that certain actions are unsafe, such as running into the street, touching a hot stove, or sticking something into an electric outlet. Calling in a strong warning voice is almost always powerful enough to make him remember the danger. Often such a scolding can reduce a young child to tears, not from pain but from the shock of the noise and the realization that he has upset you.

We basically feel that hitting a child, es-pecially out of anger, is unwise and cruel. When an older sister deliberately dumps her baby brother out of his high chair, you have to let her know, in no uncertain words, that such behavior will never, ever be acceptable. Punishment that requires consideration and discussion of her misdeed is, however, much more effective than yelling, hitting, or belit-tling her. (See "Time Out!" page 398.) Although this kind of punishment is hard work, requiring of you more time, thought, and en-

PUNISHMENT AND FAMILY VALUES

One of the things that defines family culture is the use of physical punishment and scolding in teaching children right from wrong. (For more on cultural values, see chapter 26.) Each tradition has its own ways of dealing with the issue of corporal punishment. Some endorse beatings, believing that "to spare the rod is to spoil the child." Others tolerate only an occasional slap to a child's bottom or a harsh scolding, and still others disapprove of almost any physical punishment. Although family traditions play a vital role in raising a child, and especially in instilling values, we feel that the tradition of corporal punishment damages children's moral development and should be abandoned, not passed on.

There is no doubt that physical punishment can seriously hurt a child's relationships with his parents, his feelings of trust and love, and his ability to learn how to express angry feelings through words. Hitting your child because he hit his baby sister, stole a cookie, or was rude does not teach him not to do any of these things. On the contrary, hitting, especially if you resort to it routinely in punishing him, cruelly teaches him that "might is right" — that hurting another person is acceptable if you are bigger than they are and can get away with it.

Every year in the United States, an enormous number of children — more than 2,300,000 — are reported to child welfare agencies because they have been abused or ne-glected. This horrendous statistic means that millions of children are being deprived of their basic needs for physical safety and human care. Almost all of these children are abused and neglected within their own homes, by their mothers, fathers, stepparents, friends of parents, and other close adults. Although many of these children are surprisingly able to develop into caring adolescents and parents because of their own inner strength and the good fortune of being well cared for by other relatives or foster parents (see pages 30–31 on foster parenting), many are also at high risk for later troubles with delinquency and such psychological difficulties as depression. No amount of preaching to these children about the basic values of compassion and love can make up for what they have learned about the "real world" in their first years of life.

ergy as well as patience and consistency, it is intrinsic to the moral values you want to convey to your children. It is also enormously rewarding.

Writing the Rule Book

The family rules you make and expect your child to adhere to should be clear and specific. The shorter the list, the more easily children can remember and observe them. Start with the moral principles that underlie the behavior you desire. For some parents, family rules will involve participating in formal religious practices. Others will simply choose to express to their children why certain behaviors are desirable and others are not. Most religions help to support and supplement the ethical behavior you hope your child will display, but religious practice is not essential in moral development. It is a matter of individual ethics and can vary from family to family. No matter what the basis of your moral beliefs, you should, as we suggest in chapter 26, start talking to your child when she is young about those beliefs and about the rules you have adopted to support them.

Certain rules in a family are informal and generally understood. These include basic behavior such as not stealing, not hurting, and not lying. They also include tasks you expect every child to perform habitually: taking dinner dishes into the kitchen for washing, for instance, or walking the dog. Other rules are so complex that your family might benefit from making a chart or a list that clearly outlines what you expect of each child. You might draw up a list of cleaning chores or create boxes for your child to check off each time she remembers to do a particular task. Distinguish between rules that affect the whole family, such as the schedule for doing the laundry, and rules that really involve one person, such as a child's steps to avoid wetting the bed. (See page 152.) In the latter case, it may be wiser to post this type of chart or reminder list in that child's bedroom, rather than in a common area. If your child is trying to change a particular behavior — perhaps by adhering to a diet or another health regimen, or by improving her grades on spelling tests, or by doing extra chores to earn more spending money — a chart is especially useful. It can both remind your child of what he needs to do and demonstrate what he has achieved.

Rules, and the way you present them, should be developmentally appropriate to the age of your children. A child who does not know how to read a calendar cannot be expected to figure out which days she should do certain chores. But she can still feel pride in seeing a row of red stars next to her name for every day that she has helped her parents. A child's assignments should become more challenging and important as he grows up and is able to do more. Age is also a factor in the timeliness of your rewards for good deeds or consequences for bad behavior. Most often a preschool-age child requires an immediate reward or penalty if either is to have much real effect on his behavior. An older child might do well with a daily or even a weekly reward.

When a child breaks a rule, there should

be consequences. We prefer this word over "punishment" to emphasize that a consequence should follow directly and clearly from a child's misdeed. For most naughtiness, the consequence should be the loss of some valued privilege. For some potentially harmful behavior, the child might have to do something to make up the damage to others.

As we say often, you know your own child best. You have the best sense of what consequences will matter most to her and how severe a punishment needs to be to have the effect you desire. Either way, the consequence should be relevant to the offense. Match both the nature and the level of the consequence with the child's misdeed. A child who behaves badly at a restaurant, for instance, should be barred from going out to eat with the family for a month; but taking away her television privileges as punishment muddies the connection between misdeed and punishment. If she misbehaves in the house, try to keep the punishment in the house as well; do not add public embarrassment unless she has hurt someone outside the family. If an older child is caught stealing, the most appropriate consequence may be for him to return the item to the store and to write a letter of apology, as well as to explain to you why stealing is wrong.

Do not make the consequences of breaking a rule be something that you would expect of your child in the ordinary course of things. If the consequence is, for example, that he has to take out the garbage this week, by next week he will feel no obligation to remove the garbage unless you catch him doing

something wrong again. Also, reproving a child by insisting he read a book instead of watching television links reading with feeling bad; instead, forbid him to watch television for an evening, and when, ten minutes later, he tells you he's bored, suggest that he read a book. Even though you may feel that you are continually stating, carrying out, and reviewing consequences of your youngster's misbehavior, eventually he will get the message.

When you enforce rules, you must be firm, clear, calm, direct, and consistent. Applying rules inconsistently confuses children. If they always feel in danger of being punished unfairly, they may well lose faith in you and your values. On the other hand, allowing a child to get away with behavior he knows is wrong encourages him to find ways around rules, since he suspects that he may not always be held accountable. He also may put his energy into reading your mood and guessing your likely reaction to an infringement, rather than thinking twice about the rule breaking itself.

Occasionally you may feel that you should make exceptions to rules to avoid being unduly rigid. This is fine, so long as your child does not view such exceptions as chronic inconsistency. You should clearly let her know when you have chosen to overlook a violation of a rule, and why that decision accords with the principle underlying it. For example, if your child has a terrible night at a restaurant but you realize that he is coming down with a cold, you will excuse his behavior and help him feel better. When your child reaches adolescence, her thinking skills and wishes for autonomy are developed enough to warrant your listening to her suggestions about revising a rule or devising a new, more appropriate (that is, less childish) set of consequences. Although you should still make the final decisions, listening, fairly considering her points, and changing a rule when you and she agree it makes sense to do so will make her more likely to follow the family rules. She has, after all, helped to write them.

Being a Role Model for Your Child

Although we have covered many aspects of role modeling in previous sections, your responsibility for your child's moral development is important enough to emphasize it again. You are, whether you want to be or not, a constant role model. Since children learn from what you do more than from what you say, as a role model you need to demonstrate mature behavior and self-discipline. To help

TIME OUT!

Time Out is a useful technique for disciplining your young child. Time Out, which you can start to use when your child is three or four years old, consists of placing him in a nonstimulating environment for one minute per year of age: five minutes by the clock for a five-year-old, ten for a ten-year-old. Thus, you can tell a five-year-old who has just bitten his eight-year-old brother to sit in the downstairs bathroom for five minutes. It is better to put a child in a bathroom or spare bedroom than in his own bedroom, where he could probably entertain himself and would not think about what he has done to warrant a Time Out.

At the beginning of a Time Out, give your child a short, calm explanation of why she needs it, and then, when it is over, briefly discuss the poor behavior that put her there. The point of the Time Out is not to make the child suffer, except in the relative sense of briefly being deprived of some enjoyable activity. Rather, the point is to give her time to calm down so that she can consider her behavior and the rules she has broken.

If you are angry and feeling out of control yourself, you may be tempted to use the Time Out as both punishment and a way of getting your own space and time apart from your child. Either way, you defeat the lesson Time Out is supposed to teach your child. When you are angry, try instead to regain your own composure before you interact with your child. You can even explain to him that you, too, need some time to think and understand your angry, upset feelings.

If your very young child experiences some separation anxiety when removed from you, it may be useful to place him in close proximity to you during the Time Out. If he is in a chair or in the next room, from which he can see or hear you working and moving around, he knows that you are there but that he cannot enjoy your company. This will get his attention without frightening him so much that he cannot think about anything else. Instead, he can respond to the need to change his inappropriate behavior. If, knowing that you are within earshot, your child uses this time to sing or cry or complain loudly for your benefit, ignore her until the end of the Time Out. She'll soon tire of this behavior if you don't respond, and can then think about why she is in Time Out.

your child learn not to hit or threaten or yell at people, you should maintain control of your feelings no matter how angry you may be. Show your child how to refrain from impulsive action when he is upset, and how to take his time in responding. In your actions and the way you explain them, you show your child that you respond rationally as well as emotionally, and that you are concerned above all with what is fair.

When you accept the responsibility of being a role model, you have to act like a grown-up. Do not try to be your child's best friend. In fact, children want their parents to act like grown-ups. Indeed, just as your child does not want you to fall apart like another child, you want your child to learn how to overcome emotional distress without losing control or growing so mad that she might endanger herself or others. Throughout this book, we have spoken about the importance of being emotionally honest with your child: showing her that you can cry and acknowledging that you are scared can help a child deal with her sadness and fear. But losing your temper in front of her does not show her how to deal with anger. When you are truly angry, it is better to say so than to try to deny it. And it is especially important to show that, instead of responding to the situation from that anger, you are relying on your principles and your thoughts to guide you.

As a role model, therefore, be aware of what you teach your child when you honk at the driver who just pulled in front of you, or scream at someone on the phone, or use foul language in speaking to another adult. Until

late adolescence or early adulthood, children see the world in black-and-white. They pay close attention to how adults follow the rules they talk about, and are exquisitely sensitive to people's inconsistencies. Your child notices when you lecture about lying and then leave a voice mail for your boss claiming to be sick when you simply want a day off. But he also notices when you admit to a friend that you made a mistake, forgot to return a book, or unintentionally hurt his feelings. Both sorts of behavior are lessons that influence how your youngster internalizes her notions of right and wrong. Be mindful of the words you use to express your feelings. Teach your child the difference between being assertive and being aggressive: that is, the difference between expressing your feelings and desires in a controlled yet effective manner and losing control of your temper and attacking someone verbally or physically.

Just as you should be your child's first role model of adult behavior, so the family should be her model of society. Since your family is the miniature culture in which your child learns how to deal with competing interests, shared goals, and accepted norms, family members need to treat each other with respect. Of course, a family cannot be perfect, nor does it have to be. But in it your child should be able to learn good behavior. Express affection openly and spontaneously so that your child knows that he is loved and cared for, no matter how many Time Outs or other consequences he incurs in the course of a day.

By showing respect for your children and

for other people, you both teach your children the concept of respect and earn their respect for yourself and your values. The rules you establish and enforce consistently not only become your child's guide to acceptable behavior in the house but are integrated into her own image of herself. Given these guidelines, there may be moments when you feel you are spending your entire time disciplining your child — and a grumpy child may feel the same way. This is why it is also important to spend plenty of one-on-one time with your child, sharing activities that don't involve clear-cut expectations, activities for which there is no right way to do things: taking walks, looking at clouds, or talking about feelings, for instance. Finding this time is difficult in a culture that places great emphasis on children achieving — in classrooms, in sports, in society — but your children should feel that you love and approve of them independent of their achievements in or outside the home. With that feeling as a firm foundation, they can then develop self-discipline and a moral outlook.

Developing a moral sense continues over

TATTLING

Tattling is a difficult issue, even for adults. While most adults value the confidentiality of their conversations with doctors, lawyers, priests, and therapists, they feel some ambivalence about whether news reporters and friends should keep secrets for others. Society praises "whistle-blowers" for their heroism, but treats police informers with contempt.

When one child comes running to complain that another is breaking rules, parents feel similarly conflicted. You do not want to get in the middle of every dispute between siblings or classmates and hope the children will learn to work out minor conflicts on their own. And you worry that a child might become known among his peers as a tattletale.

You should understand the different reasons your child might have for telling on others. As we have said, children are very sensitive to infractions of rules, and a child may tattle to diminish her anxiety at seeing another child doing or getting away with something she thinks is wrong. But children may also tattle to gain favor with their parents or other adults, to exact revenge on a sibling or classmate, or to take heat off themselves. (Indeed, adults do the same to gain favor with a boss or to beat out or take revenge on a competitor.) This mix of possible heartfelt, noble, and devious motivations makes tattling both complex and potentially irritating.

When a young child runs to you accusing a sibling of hitting or taking a toy, what looks like tattling may also be asking for help. If these complaints arrive several times in a day, you can help the complaining child develop strategies for dealing with what has upset him. Early-childhood educators often say, "Learn to use your words," so teach him how to say "no." Help him learn how to take turns sharing toys or to offer his playmate another toy as a compromise in a struggle. With thought, you can lead a younger child away from tattling and toward learning how to mediate aggression and play cooperatively.

In older children, tattling has

a person's life. In America's large, complex society, there are many views — some slightly different and some undeniably at odds — about how to apply moral and ethical codes to everyday behavior. Children learn best about what is right and wrong and how to lead a moral life when the adults around them demonstrate respect for other people's views and conventions. As your child thinks about his personal experiences, whether at home or at school, he learns how to balance society's rules and standards with his own needs and beliefs. And as he sees other people considering moral issues with care and respect, he will develop a conscience that is neither harsh nor easygoing but strong, open-minded, and respectful. Thus, cognitive and social development combine to make the moral child and, ultimately, the moral adult.

all of the potential motivations we have mentioned. Yet, because of their close identification with peers, tattling is far more complex. On the one hand, children's greater independence at this age means that they can cause and get into much more trouble than can preschoolers tussling over a toy, yet school-age children can feel pressure not to tell adults about others' bad behavior. Thus, older children need to learn when it is appropriate to bring adults into a situation and when they can handle it on their own. And you need to learn when your child is telling you about others out of true moral and emotional qualms and when she is trying to manipulate your response.

How you teach your older children to respond to others' behavior should reflect the moral values of your family. But you should not ride forth to punish every wrong your child reports. For instance, it can be very upsetting for a child to see another child take money from a classmate's knapsack, especially if the thief is his friend. If your child tells you about witnessing such behavior, discuss how he might tell his friend that it was wrong. You can explain that he can either remain friends with a person who does things he dislikes, or break off the friendship if he has lost respect for that person, but that in his own conduct he must follow the family's rules. Such a conversation reaffirms your child's moral sense and may help him to decide which course to take. Situations like these present complex moral dilemmas that even adults struggle to work through.

There are, of course, situations in which you as a parent should interfere. If your child is being physically bullied or sees another child being mistreated, you should not only talk out the situation but also take steps to stop it. (See pages 337–339 for more on bullying.) Depending on your values and the support you can expect from your child's teacher and the community, you might take similar action after other reports of bullying. Again, talking over situations with your child as they arise may clarify the moral issues for both of you.

PART VI

Predictable Bumps on the Developmental Path

CHAPTER 28

When Both Parents Work

No child's life unfolds smoothly, however closely it follows the normal progress of development. Everyone is subject to contingency, to "bumps" — the predictable and ordinary events or the extraordinary and unforeseen ones — that lie in the path of development. Impeding this development at times, spurring it on at others, these events always cause anxiety and, thus, stress. The degree of both depends on how you help your child adjust to particular bumps, including the ones we cover in this part: the ordinary eventualities of the birth of a sibling, of caretaking arrangements when both parents work, and of separation. Hard as it may be sometimes to deal with such transitions, through them a child both exercises his or her cognitive, emotional, and social selves and grows, ultimately achieving the ability to negotiate the bumps that bestrew the path of adulthood.

Two eventualities may be in the cards for any child: the arrival of a sibling and separation from parents. Two others are relatively new in American life: the decision for both parents to work outside the home and the re-sulting necessity for their child to be cared for by someone else.

Among the many decisions you will struggle with as a parent, deciding when (or whether) to return to your job may feel particularly difficult. Many parents are surprised at how uncertain they feel about returning to work even if they have agreed upon careful, methodically made plans well before their baby is born. These decisions are sometimes cast in catchphrases, such as "You can't have it all," implying that either staying home with your child or returning to work is a compromise. While surely your decision of how to balance your job and your role as a parent requires thought, blending the two does not have to mean that you lose out in either role — or that your child loses. Indeed, if you take the time to find help and think through the amount and quality of time you spend with your child, then you will realize that being a working parent can offer benefits beyond the usual one of economic stability.

The return to work can be a growth-enhancing experience for both you and your child. It can make parents feel more fulfilled and accomplished in their work. One such parent said to us, "I felt a mixture of anxiety and relief. I was worried about how my baby would be, but I was happy to be back at work and I felt a sense of freedom. I'd enjoyed being home with my baby, but the days had been very long and lonely. I'd been so busy I often didn't have a chance to take a shower until the late afternoon." As for your baby, when you feel more energetic and happy, your interactions with her are more likely to be stimulating and, thus, helpful to her development. And your child's relationships with the persons who help you care for him while you are at work will complement his relationship with you and help form and enhance his personality. Ultimately, after watching his mother and father balance the dual roles of parent and member of the workforce, your child will grow up to be better able to do the same in his own family.

In this chapter, we will discuss the main issues that you as a working mother or father have to face and resolve: designing a compromise that suits your baby, deciding when to return to work, making the transition from home to office and back, and protecting latchkey children. We will also discuss the issues involved in your having a home office.

The Working Parent

"One Sunday morning I found I had some free time," a working mother told us, "so I picked up the Sunday magazine and sat down to relax for a few minutes. I opened it to an ad and began to cry. I don't even remember what the ad was for, but it was a full-page picture with a caption at the top saying, 'You can have it all.' The picture was of a woman with perfect hair in a designer suit, carrying a beautiful leather briefcase (which was not overflowing) and a huge bouquet of flowers in one arm. In the other arm she was carrying a beautiful naked baby. I first wondered how her suit could be so clean, and then thought, 'I never look like that, either going to or coming from work.' I was upset because I was learning quickly that 'having it all' doesn't come that easily."

For most of the twentieth century, American society encouraged mothers to stay home throughout their children's infancy and school years while their husbands worked. This arrangement was the norm for middle-class wives, and most unmarried and working-class women were supposed to aspire to it. Then, around 1970, as women began to enter the workforce in greater numbers, that expectation changed dramatically. This cultural change is reflected in the way the United States has changed the structure of its welfare programs, including Aid to Families with Dependent Children (AFDC) and Women, Infants, and Children (WIC). Originally, as their names imply, these programs were designed to help single parents (usually mothers) stay home to care for their children. Now they are being redesigned to propel those same mothers into the workforce. Single parents thus have little choice but to work unless they are independently wealthy. Even married couples need two incomes simply to survive.

Although today stay-at-home fathers are not rare, most men are still expected back at work several days after their wife has given birth. Most mothers who expect to return to a job are given leaves of various lengths, from a few weeks to several months. Today, well before their first child is born — sometimes even before his or her conception — couples commonly discuss whether they both plan to keep working as parents. Yet although it is now the norm for a mother to return to work, it is not an easy decision either to make or — if both parents return to a job — to stick to. And the experiences of mothers and fathers returning to work are as variable as their personalities. Some parents are relieved to be free for a few hours from the responsibility of looking after a newborn, while others look forward all day to being home with their baby. Some parents are excited at the renewed prospect of rising to the demands of their job, whose frustrations may be more manageable than trying to calm a crying infant. "I knew definitely I wanted to go back to teaching," said one mother, "and I was happy when I returned. I missed my daughter during the day, but I also enjoyed my work and the freedom and separate life I had there. I was happy at the school, and I was also always happy to go home at the end of the day and spend time with my daughter and my husband."

Another parent had a different experience: "All during my pregnancy we discussed how we both wanted to keep working. But in the first months after our baby arrived, I worried more and more about leaving her. She seemed to have a lot of little illnesses. Meanwhile, friends at work told me I was lucky to be missing some major changes. A month before my leave ended, I decided to stay home for another year. Looking back, I don't think my baby was much sicker than anyone else's or the turmoil at my job that unusual. It's just that deep down I really wanted to be a full-time parent and I was lucky enough to be able to do that."

One reason that the decision to return to work is complicated is that becoming a parent changes people. They no longer view the world in the same way they did even a month before their child's arrival. Some of these new parents feel an urgent need to stay with and protect their infant, a need stronger than they may ever have expected. Suddenly, teaching another exercise class or building another office complex does not seem as vital. This is true not only of mothers but of fathers — like one man who spoke of the "strategic plan" he and his wife had worked out for being parents: "I went to my boss and arranged for a three-day-a-week work schedule, and my wife set a date to return to her job. We even chose a day-care program to start six months after our baby arrived! But as that six-month mark got closer, neither of us was prepared for how much we wanted to stay home with our little boy. Then my wife got a terrific job offer. My boss left, and the day care moved to a bigger facility that was farther away. But it all worked out well. My wife loves her new job, I look after the kid and do some consulting from home, and for next year we have our eye on a great nursery school." If you feel like this man, you may decide that you would rather shift your career into lower gear than sacrifice time with your infant. Or you may decide that the best way to provide for your child both economically and psychologically is to keep doing work you love.

To help you make your decision, you should know that there are two constants in the lives of working mothers and fathers. One is that you think about and miss your baby during the workday. These thoughts do not have to be nonstop: a good parent can be fully absorbed in a task for hours and think about her child only when she returns to her office and sees his picture on her desk. Then, envisioning the child at home or in day care can be a natural little pick-me-up and perhaps a reminder of why you are working so hard. Too often, however, parents feel guilt when they think of their absent child. They feel pangs on leaving the house each morning, about working late some evenings, perhaps even about enjoying work. Sometimes a parent may feel simple sadness that he is not home with his child; should this yearning combine with an equal pull not to be at his job, he becomes confused and unhappy about what he really wants.

The second constant is exhaustion. Some working parents find that caring for their baby when they are home leaves them confused, worn out, and unable during the workday to accomplish more than the basic requirements of their job. "Where has all my energy gone?" a working mother may wonder, and then may be doubly overwhelmed with guilt for feeling that she is failing both professionally and as a parent. Such feelings are only exacerbated by the misguided effort to "have it all" — that is, to achieve complete fulfillment at both work and home. Working parents must recognize that they cannot have it all in that sense. They are really working two jobs and, in both, fulfillment will come in time.

Do not, of course, assume that you must choose either full-time parenthood or total devotion to a career. The notion of an either/or choice is as much a myth as "having it all." Today — with the help of a good daycare program, the personal computer, and the telephone — a couple (and a single parent lucky enough to have a high-paying job) can maintain their careers and raise happy children by making a compromise that suits their family's needs. In this chapter, we will discuss making the right compromise, the right time to return to work, the actual return, latchkey children, the alternative of working at home, and the benefits of being a working parent.

The final and primary factor in your decision to return to work involves one individual who cannot participate in your discussions: your baby herself. Although she cannot put together an argument, she can certainly make her likes and dislikes known. Because she is a unique individual, with unique needs for closeness, feeding, medical care, stimulation, and other good things parents provide, you cannot really settle on a plan until you take her needs into account. Later in this chapter, and at more length in chapter 31, we discuss how babies of different ages typically react to separation from their parents. In chapter 29, we discuss various forms of child care and what is appropriate for children of different ages. With all this information in hand, you will be better able to judge what is best for your child and your family.

Designing the Right Compromise for Your Family

As you plan your return to work, take the long view and set realistic goals for yourself. Children are young for a very short time, and they need you to be available to them in a significant way during those years. You do not have to stay with them twenty-four hours a day, but you do need to ensure they are receiving good care when you are away from them. You always need to be nearby and involved in their lives, supporting and, as they grow older, witnessing their development. Of course, this is a large order — one that at times may feel impossible to fill. But, as a parent, you must always strive to fill it even as you remember that nobody does it perfectly.

Parents make different compromises. Some choose to continue working as much as before their baby arrived, and others cut back their hours. Some parents do not have such choices; they have to work to keep strained peas on the table. The important thing to remember is that your choices are your own. Just because your friends, relatives, or parents made different choices does not mean yours are better or worse. They are the choices you think are right for you and your family. The fact that your colleagues all work long hours may be a sign that the organization's culture no longer matches your priorities. Your neighbors may stay home with their children, but you must judge whether such days would be fulfilling for you and significantly benefit your child. Furthermore, you can always change your mind: if you decide to return to work when your child is six months old, you can change your plan a year later if it seems feasible or desirable for either you or your child.

Many factors will affect whatever compromise you work out. The quality of your day care is an important one. Do you feel confident about the child-care professionals you have chosen? Is the facility convenient? And so forth. (For more on this issue, see chapter 29.) Some families find unexpected practical benefits when they enroll in child care. One parent reported: "We lived far away from our families and wished we lived closer. We'd never before felt so overwhelmed and needy. We eventually developed our own support group with other parents from our son's day-care center and the day-care teachers, and these other parents and children became our extended family." Today, since workplaces contain so many mothers and fathers with children of various ages, they, too, can function as an informal group of supporters. As you enlist neighbors to be backup resources for your children, you forge connections within your community, often between generations.

Your support system also drives your decisions about child care. This system includes the relationship between you and your partner — whether it is strong and flexible — as well as with your extended family and your friends. These supporters can help in practical ways (by, for instance, looking after your child for a day in an emergency) and by giving advice and lending a sympathetic ear to your inescapable anxieties and frustrations.

It certainly helps if your workplace is supportive of parents' active involvement in their children's lives. Organizations that offer this kind of flexibility might, for instance, allow an employee to work through lunch for a few days in order to leave early to attend his child's school concert or sporting event. Other employers are not as supportive; you may have the additional job of helping them become more parent- and child-friendly. Although there is much talk in America about children being our most precious possessions, many parents are not supported in the vital task of nurturing those children and are on their own when it comes to balancing that responsibility with a regular job.

New parents are sometimes tempted to compromise by working part-time or at home, or by combining the two, as did the couple we described earlier, where the father stays home and the mother works. But these approaches, too, have drawbacks. Working part-time has been described as doing a complete job but having only half the time to do it in. A parent in a home office can need just as much uninterrupted time as a parent outside the home. And beware of starting a new business soon after becoming a parent: you

may end up feeling as if you have committed to two sixty-hour-a-week jobs instead of one. (For more on these issues, see pages 413–416.)

Most fundamental is the quality of your relationship with your baby before one or both of you return to work. Many variables shape this early relationship, including the difficulty of the pregnancy and delivery. A mother who has a hard time recovering from the birth, or who experiences postpartum depression, is likely to need more time to bond with her child, and thus is slow to return to work. (See pages 69–71.) The health of the newborn is also crucial: a young baby who is often ill needs his parents more; and even after his recovery, they may be reluctant to leave him. Each infant has a unique temperament, as does each parent, and the match among those temperaments affects how easily the grown-ups can go back to work. Both parents and child must be psychologically ready for the separation. You, who have the most experience with your own baby and your own feelings, are the best judge of that readiness (keeping in mind the guidelines in the next section).

A baby brings a lot of extra work into a household. Thus, regardless of what arrangement you choose, you and your partner must support one another, both in your careers and in sharing parenting and housekeeping. The choice to go back to work may bring up other tensions between partners: a husband may worry that he is not being as good a provider as his father; a wife may struggle with fatigue and feel she deserves more help; or each parent may be working under different expectations of how they would raise their child. Work through these disagreements and worries to reach compromises that benefit the whole family.

The "Right" Time to Return to Work

Parents often ask child-development experts, "What is the best age for a baby to be when a parent goes back to work?" Having read that infants experience strong separation anxiety at the ages of nine or eighteen months, some ask whether the return to work would be smoother at six or twelve months after birth. The answers to such questions vary with the child. Naturally, you hope there is an ideal time to go back to work. Change and separation are, however, inevitable in a child's life, and dealing with them is a lifelong process. While there is no perfect age for a baby's parents to return to work, several essential factors can help you determine the best time for your family.

First, the economic reality. The end of parental leave, as mandated by federal law and negotiated with employers, often determines the timing of a parent's return to work. Ideally, the leave should be long enough for the mother to fully recover from childbirth and for both parents to develop close relationships with their newborn.

Both mother and father need to feel ready to go back to work. You must feel your baby's attachment to you is strong enough not to be hurt by your absence, know your baby well enough to be able to help him attach to a substitute caregiver, and feel confident that this person will be able to care for your child. The absence of any of these psychological factors is likely to exacerbate whatever anxiety you may have. And if your child picks up on that worry, the separation will be more difficult for both of you.

Individual psychology also affects a baby's responses, and infants react to their parents' departure for work in a variety of ways. In younger babies (three to six months), there may first be disruptions in their sleep/wake and eating patterns. They may become more irritable and harder to soothe and be unusually exhausted or overstimulated at the end of the day. Unfortunately, this is often just when you are looking forward to interacting with your baby. After an initial period of adjustment, however, most young babies settle into their new routine and begin to make wonderful relationships with their caregivers and other children they see during the day. If a baby does not settle in after about two months, parents and caregivers should work together to determine how to help with her adjustment. (See chapter 31 for more on separation issues.)

Older babies and young toddlers (six to eighteen months) usually have a harder time adjusting after the parent who has been their primary caregiver returns to work. They may cling to you and protest loudly whenever you leave the house. They may be irritable for most of the day and regress in their behavior. Such responses are normal and indicate that your child feels a close and important bond to you. Such reactions lead parents, however, to question whether they are doing the right thing. Separation is never easy, and toddlerhood is an especially difficult period, when your child knows that a person can go away and return but is not yet able to comfort herself through the absence. Nevertheless, toddlers eventually have to learn to separate, and a parent's return to work is an appropriate occasion for that lesson.

The key ingredients to ensuring that a child under two adjusts well to his parents' return to work are loving, sensitive, consistent, and developmentally appropriate child care (see chapter 29) and parents who are emotionally available when they are with him. When you have achieved both of these goals, it will be the right time to return to work.

Making the Transition from Home to Work

Do not expect to enjoy a smooth transition back to work at the end of a long parental leave. If you had been on a vacation for several weeks or even months, coming back to work would be somewhat jarring at first, and you would have a lot of catching up to do. Instead of relaxing on a beach or at a ski resort, however, you have been working hard: caring for and getting to know a small child; arising many times a night; rearranging your home, your schedule, and even your sense of the world around this new person. It takes time to adjust to the sudden shift away from that life. "I went back to work when my baby was four months old," one parent told us. "I seemed okay then, but six weeks later I realized what a fog I'd been in." Eventually you will regain the rhythm of your old job.

Your plan for returning to work should allow for contingencies. A working father reported: "My wife and I were so pleased with the day-care arrangement we made for our daughter. After the first month she seemed to be adjusting very well. Then one morning she woke up with a high fever and a terrible cough, and we realized we hadn't thought to make a backup plan for sick days. The day turned into a juggling act for the two of us as we took turns going to work and taking care of our sick baby. She recovered quickly, but just as she was well enough to return to day care, both my wife and I came down with the same flu." Illness is inevitable, but you also may need to deal with a change in job assignments or travel, a caregiver who is not available every workday, and other unexpected problems.

Try not to let your anxiety or guilt magnify these problems. A mother told us, "I wanted to continue to breast-feed my son after I went back to work. I'd stored up an adequate supply of breast milk in the freezer, and I expressed milk every day at work on my breaks. I'd rush home to nurse him, only to find that often the baby-sitter was giving him a bottle, saying that he just couldn't wait any longer for me." Not only was this mother disappointed to lose the intimate moments with her baby that she had planned on, but seeing another adult feeding her baby in her place may have exacerbated her feelings of guilt and longing. But babies become hungry and meetings run long, and parents have to anticipate that such events may derail their plans. Rather than bemoaning what you have missed, cherish the closeness with your child that you do have.

Latchkey Children

The hard choices for a working parent do not end when your child goes off to school. You still have to deal with the time between the end of school and the time when you and/or your partner get home in the evening. As with the choice of early child care, evaluate your own situation and try to do what both fits your child's developmental age and personality and is possible for you financially and in terms of your support system. Thus, when the mother in "Vanessa's Dilemma" (see page 414) was suddenly left without her eleven-year-old boy's usual sitter, she examined the courses open to her, then chose to give him a key and let him go home and stay there on his own. By establishing routines with her child that he was able to handle, Vanessa achieved peace of mind for both of them.

The Home Office

Affordable fax machines, photocopiers, and networked computers have made it possible for parents in many professions to work predominantly out of their own homes. Although the technology makes the home workplace seem to be a recent invention, the fact is that only in the industrialized world

have people come to expect home and work to be separated. The homes and workplaces of farmers have always been intertwined. Blacksmiths, woodworkers, weavers, and tailors traditionally worked inside, next door to, or at least within sight of their homes. Seamstresses "took work in," and tradesmen lived above their shop. The work of raising children and the work of providing for them were, for centuries, nearly inseparable. The industrial revolution broke that unity apart.

In the nineteenth century, large numbers of parents left home to work on assembly lines and in large stores, construction sites, corporate offices, factories, and malls. That trend spread rapidly after the First World War. Many working parents had to leave their young sons or daughters in someone else's care, and during the Second World War, many mothers joined the workforce. With these transitions, family life for children became distinctly divided between the hours when one or both parents were away at work, the hours when the family was together, and the time fathers (and increasingly, mothers) spent with the children. The departure for work thus became a regular moment of separation. (See chapter 31.) One of the driving forces behind the rediscovery of home offices and businesses is that mothers and fathers want to be available to their children more often during the workday.

On the other hand, many parents worry that setting up a home office will make their children feel even more displaced than when Mommy or Daddy goes away for the day. They realize that while they will be at home, they will not constantly be available to their child. Parents also worry that their children's needs and invitations to play will interrupt work and prevent them from being fully productive at home. Thus, the home office simply relocates the battleground for your conflicting desires about being a parent and wanting to work. While working at home brings you physically closer to your children, it heightens the inevitable tensions of being

Vanessa's Dilemma

Vanessa had been a single mother since her son, Tommy, was three. Having gone to night school for paralegal training, she was working for a local attorney. She and Tommy had moved to a nice apartment, so close to his school that they could walk there together in the mornings before she continued on to her office. Her friend Charlene, who had looked after Tommy in the afternoons for several years, lived just around the corner.

Then, when Tommy was eleven, Charlene had to move away, and the arrangement ended. Eleven-year-old Tommy was already feeling like the "man of the house" and had some household responsibilities he carried out dependably. But Vanessa was not ready to let him stay home by himself until she came home from work. Her employer had been understanding of her needs as a single mother, and at first she had Tommy come to the office every day after school. It soon became clear, however,

that this was not a good solution. The office was very busy, and Vanessa was rarely free; as popular as Tommy was with her colleagues, she knew that letting him hang out there was a special favor to her. Tommy himself said that he preferred to be near his games and television shows once he had finished his homework. Finally, Vanessa decided to let Tommy spend the afternoons alone in their apartment.

Mother and son worked out careful rules for how he would handle the hours until she got home. Tommy carried his own key and let himself in every afternoon. He always locked the door behind him and knew he was not to open it for strangers. As soon as he came in, he called Vanessa to let her know he had arrived safely. Vanessa had spoken to their neighbors on their floor, an elderly man and a retired couple, and they had agreed to be resources in an emergency. Tommy also had their telephone numbers. From time to time, they would call him in the afternoon, and sometimes one or the other would come by to see him.

Tommy, in turn, knew he could visit in their apartments if he first called his mother for permission.

Vanessa did not want to push Tommy to be older than his years. On the other hand, he was growing up, and this solution seemed to be the best of the possible options. Tommy wished he could spend his afternoons going to the arcade or the movies with his friends — he could even, he thought, go out and be home before Vanessa got off work. But since he had promised his mother that he would stay in the apartment and not have any other children over, he contented himself with talking to his friends on the telephone — many of whom were home alone in their own apartments, under similar rules. Occasionally Tommy visited a school friend if a parent was at home and Vanessa had given him permission. Although he felt lonely sometimes and wished his mother could come home early, he accepted the situation until he was old enough to come and go on his own.

both a parent and a working adult. Since these tensions are normal, acknowledge and accept them, and go on from there. They won't go away, however much you try or wherever you locate your office.

When you imagined becoming a parent, you may have envisioned the pleasures of showing your children who you are professionally, perhaps even of having them join in your work and eventually take over the business. But in the actual presence of small children, parents have to adjust such idyllic daydreams. A two-year-old cannot help copy and collate that important report that has to be express-mailed by late afternoon. Nor can a three- or a four-year-old help you write a grant proposal or assemble the fall order for yarns and fabrics. By the time your child is old enough to make significant contributions to the family business, she is usually also independent enough not to want to "help Daddy" just for the pleasure of being close to him.

These basic ground rules will help you run a home office while accommodating your children. Even young children are able to understand and adjust to the compromises necessary if you are to work in your home.

- As with any job outside the home, the more definitely you can structure your day, the better it is for you and your children. Youngsters can feel secure in the knowledge that, for instance, "After breakfast, Mommy will be working in her office until it's time for lunch." You need to decide and clearly state whether cer-

tain times are off-limits to children except in emergencies (and that a sibling's not giving up a toy does not count as one).

- You and your children should also share a basic understanding of boundaries. Some working parents prefer to keep their offspring out of their workspace for a variety of reasons: they need to concentrate, there is dangerous equipment on hand, or a voluble youngster seems to want attention just when the phone rings. Other parents are happy to let their children come into their office and play quietly with crayons or toy animals. You can even set up a space in your office or workshop for your child, with his own supply of paper, pens, paper clips, and even tools and paint. Remember, however, that toddlers and preschoolers are messy and tend to take over whatever space is available.

- If you work at home with a young child, you may want to tackle your tasks in small blocks of time, taking a regular break for cookies or reading or taking a walk together. Adjust these blocks to your own working style. Some people simply cannot work in spurts; they need longer amounts of time to get their thoughts in order. Parents who have the advantages of nearby relatives or paid help can set aside longer uninterrupted time to do their work.

These rules will not, of course, resolve all tensions. If you constantly feel as if you are stealing time from your children in order to work or that at any point in your work you may be interrupted, take some mental steps back. Working at home with such tensions is as psychologically burdensome as if you were away from home for ten hours a day suffering the same worries. Acknowledge and explore your feelings about how to integrate your working self with your parenting self. A home business or an understanding employer can make this challenge easier, but neither can solve the problem for you.

One way to bring those parts of your identity closer together is to include your children in your work. Tell them stories about your day. Show them where you work or something you use in your work. By telling children about what you do, you also model for them how adults bring other people into their lives. You can also include your children in your work by giving them small things to do — opening the box of supplies that just came in, carrying a uniform into the dry cleaner, helping to clean out the delivery truck on a Saturday. Make the tasks small enough so that younger children can succeed at them. For example, if one large box contains several smaller boxes or items, open the large carton and give your preschooler three little things to carry into the house. Naturally, letting a child help this way may take more time. Or the child may not do the task quite as you would. She may drag your shirts on the ground a little, or while sweeping may stir up more dust, or get only half the paper clips into the container. But try to tolerate these drawbacks. Working along with your child is one of the best ways for you two to get to know one another.

CHAPTER 29

Choosing Child Care: Day-Care Programs and Nannies

When, until the last quarter of the twentieth century, most women stayed home with their young children, neighborhoods and extended families were closer, and a mother and her child had more opportunities to meet other mothers. The children played together while the mothers had a chance to talk "adult" or took turns watching each other's offspring. (There were significant exceptions to this pattern, of course; a high percentage of African American mothers worked to support their families in this period.) Today, a mother who stays at home with her children may find it a solitary experience. Her peers are more likely to be at work, and most of the neighborhood children are in day care. In fact, today in America, professionals or other adults, rather than parents, care for the majority of preschool-age children. By the year 2000, over 60 percent of two-year-olds were in some kind of child care.

This cultural shift has naturally affected children. Many American parents feel that their children's day care or nursery program had made them more independent, a trait highly valued in American society. Three-fourths of these parents thought that their children in day care had learned better social skills and were more willing to cooperate and share with other children. Nowadays, a child who has spent her first five years at home will probably have some social catching up to do in kindergarten. (Most children can do this quickly, however, and socialization is not by itself a reason to choose one form of child care above another.)

As positive as you may think child care is going to be for your child, picking a program can be stressful. Most mothers and some fathers harbor some desire to stay home with the baby. Many feel that just as they are starting to know their child, they have to start finding someone to care for her. Even if you feel relieved to get back to your career, you may wonder whether that means you're a bad parent. The child-care decision can loom as weighty as the decision about where an adolescent child will go to college, and the former decision is all on the parents. It would be a lot easier if your infant could just say that she prefers this nanny or this program!

In choosing child care, seek an arrangement that suits your family. You may look for a child-care program close to your work so you can visit during the day and even continue a regular breast-feeding schedule. Or you may be most comfortable having your baby cared for at home by an adult, who either lives in the house or comes every day, or by a relative at his or her home or your own. (See "Keeping Child Care Within the Family," page 419.) If, as your infant gets older, you want him to play with other children, you can enroll him in a nursery school or have your individual caregiver take him to group-play programs. Keep in mind that your needs can change, and your child's needs definitely will.

To get good care for your child, you need to be an active, informed, and discriminating consumer. Thus, in this chapter we address two approaches to child care — full-time care in your home and out-of-home programs — as well as what constitutes a developmentally appropriate curriculum.

One-on-One: A Caregiver in Your Home

In-home care is almost always more expensive than center-based care. Few people can afford the former — and it is not necessarily right for every family. In-home care is one-on-one (unless the caregiver is looking after siblings). For your baby, this arrangement is meant to be as close as possible to having a parent at home. It allows her to stay in a familiar environment with her toys, her bed, her comfortable curling-up spaces. Your baby will not have to get up early to be bundled off to a program, and when he is sick, you will not have to take time off from work because he cannot go to day care (though you may choose to stay home with him).

On the other hand, in-home care has its own uncertainties and disadvantages. If the person coming to your home is sick or snowed in or on vacation, there are no staff members available to take his or her place. Perhaps most significantly, in-home care is not supervised care. In a day-care program, if one person feels too tired to keep up, there is someone else to step in. In your home, you have far less control over whether your child gets attention beyond being fed and kept out of trouble.

In-home care depends on a close working relationship between you and the person you hire. That person must be willing to accept your values and your wishes, as well as your occasional constructive criticism. As the director of a day care for one, you have the responsibilities to compensate your child-care

KEEPING CHILD CARE WITHIN THE FAMILY

Probably the oldest form of child care remains one of the most popular: arranging for a relative to look after your child. Your mother might come to your house to care for her grandchild while you work, or you might drop your child off at your sibling's house to play with his or her child under whatever supervision that family has. If you have a relative who runs a child-care center, you may naturally prefer that facility to others. There are many advantages to such arrangements. The caregiver, being naturally fond of your child, is more likely to remain a presence in her life than a day-care employee. And grandparents often work cheap.

Choosing a blood relative as your child-care provider does not guarantee, however, that you will agree on all the issues of discipline, feeding, and so on. Does your relative have the experience and understanding of child development that a good nanny or nursery-school worker could provide? Does his or her home meet all your standards for safety and learning? Another drawback of family arrangements compared with day-care programs is that in the former your child is less likely to be with several different children at the same developmental level. And money can become a problem unless you establish a clear understanding of how to handle expenses. If your relative makes your child's lunch every day, for example, it is only fair for you to help pay for that food.

Complicating those potential problems is the fact that you usually have less financial leverage and more psychological baggage with a family member. Since you probably would not formally employ your mother or your aunt, you cannot easily insist that she do certain things your way. Even if you do have a formal contract, it is harder to fire someone whom you will still have to see every holiday.

When you have planned to raise your children differently in certain ways from how you were raised, it is difficult to find yourself having to ask your parents to look after them. Furthermore, disagreements about child care are likely to trigger other tensions that may have developed in your family over the years. If you think your mother played favorites between you and your brother, for instance, you may well feel the same resentment if she seems to be treating your children differently from their cousins.

On balance, leaving your child with a competent relative is a good solution for most of the families for whom it is available. A half-day nursery school or other program can provide opportunities for group play and learning social skills as your child grows older. Just be aware of the special tensions that may lurk within this arrangement, and try to work out ways of either avoiding or ameliorating them.

INTERVIEWING A ONE-ON-ONE CAREGIVER

Interview candidates as if they were applying for the most important job you could assign anyone — as they are. Here are some questions parents have found useful in selecting the best in-home caregiver for their children. Make your own list based on your family's particular needs. Have it ready before you place an ad or start sending out feelers, so that you will be prepared for the first calls.

• What kind of training and experience caring for children have you had? Have you ever had sole responsibility for a young child?

• What ages of children have you cared for? Are there ages you like best? (Some individuals prefer to care for infants but cannot rise to managing a toddler. How will the person you're interviewing handle tantrums, biting, and general assertiveness?)

• Why did you choose this line of work? How long do you expect to work in child care? (You do not want to hire someone who has chosen this field because he cannot think of anything else, or who will leave your child after four months if she gets into law school.)

• Do you have references whom we can call? Why did you leave your last job?

• Do you have training in emergency care for children? Are you willing to take emergency-care courses if we pay for them? (If your child has special needs, you will need to explain those needs to your prospects and ask whether they feel capable of fulfilling them.)

• What are your views on early learning? On discipline? (You probably have a feeling, if not a well-thought-out philosophy, of how you want to raise your children. See how compatible and flexible each candidate seems.)

• Do you have a car (if you expect your in-home caregiver to drive your children)? Are you fully insured? Do you own a car seat for children? (You may want to take a test drive with each serious candidate.)

• Do you smoke? (If you do not want anyone to smoke in your house, or if you smoke yourselves, your child-care provider should know.)

• Are there particular times of the upcoming year when you know you will not be available? Are there holidays you want to have off?

If your first contact with candidates is by phone, ask your most important questions in that conversation in order to identify those who seem promising. Schedule an in-person interview in your home with each of those people. The purpose of this interview is threefold: to hear more detailed answers to all your questions, to evaluate the candidates' rapport with your child, and to measure your own comfort with each of them. Even if you feel an instant bond during an interview, take time to interview more than one person, consider your impressions, and ask the most promising candidate for a second interview.

Also, scary as it may sound, you will need to check applicants' driving records and find out whether they have committed crimes or been sued in the past. These are matters of public record, available if you have a person's name, date of birth, and social security number. Let each candidate you interview know that this inquiry is a routine part of your selection process. Notice whether anyone becomes nervous or defensive; if a candidate does, you might want to learn more about this person or search for someone else. Once you go through this process, you can feel much more confident about the caregiver you decide to hire.

worker fairly, to be clear about your expectations, and to provide all the necessary materials.

Some parents hire a mother who brings her own child along to the job. Such an arrangement can give your child a playmate or perhaps an exciting model of older behavior. If you interview a potential caregiver whose older children will come to your house after school, you may want to meet those children and see how they interact with yours.

Live-in or Live-out?

A live-in caregiver both gives you more opportunity to work out a work schedule with him or her and allows you to see how that person interacts with your child in casual moments when you are both at home. On the other hand, a live-in arrangement requires adjustments in your household. A spare bedroom and preferably a spare bathroom, a bit removed from your family quarters, give both you and your in-home help a sense of privacy and independence. Since you are inviting the caregiver into your home, you need to feel that you and your family can be at ease around that person first thing in the morning, late at night, or anytime in between. There may be other things you may want a caregiver to help with: fixing meals, laundry, cleaning. Make these part of your agreement; there should be no unstated assumptions or surprises.

There are many kinds of in-home child-care providers, with a correspondingly wide range of prices. Nannies are professionals.

They may have formal training or bring the experience of having raised their own children, grandchildren, or other youngsters. Au pairs tend to be young people from Europe seeking a cultural experience in America. The term *au pair* is French for "on par with," indicating that this person is to be treated as a member of the family, not as a servant. Good au pair agencies train their young clients in child care, but generally these caregivers are not as mature or experienced as nannies. In making your choice, consider both your budget and how much supervision you expect to give your helper. Spend time carefully studying your options, so that you will feel comfortable and secure about your ultimate decision.

Finding a Modern Mary Poppins

Even if you feel uncomfortable in interviewing candidates for in-home care, as if you were Mr. or Mrs. Banks in Mary Poppins, do not stint on giving time to this effort. After all, you are contracting with a professional and entrusting this person with your most treasured possession. You probably would not undergo major surgery without knowing the credentials of your physician, or choose an attorney randomly off a list to represent you in court. The people who care for your child deserve the same scrutiny, if not more. Referrals from other families, from pediatricians, and even from day-care programs are ways to begin finding candidates. You can follow up personal recommendations, go through agencies, or place a classified ad (in which case, expect to screen a lot of calls).

Whatever route you choose, collecting candidates' names and résumés is just the first step. The interview is crucial if you are to find a caregiver whom you will be comfortable having in your home. (See "Interviewing a One-on-One Caregiver," page 420.)

Using an agency is the most expensive way to find in-home care. Be sure you understand each agency's fee. Some charge a consultation fee plus more on placement — either a flat fee or a percentage of the first year's salary. Not all agencies operate the same way. Many nanny and au pair agencies have high standards for the professionals they list on their rosters, but others take anyone who sends an application. Some provide high-quality training, others none at all. Before you sign up with an agency, ask questions about how each agency screens applicants and what training it supplies. You may even request a copy of its application packet. Ask the agencies for their references. Reputable firms will supply you with a list, sometimes even without your asking.

After you interview a candidate, be sure to check his or her references. Prepare a set of questions for the people each applicant provides. How long did they employ the candidate? Why did she or he leave? How did their children like the candidate? Do they still maintain contact?

Once you have reached a tentative agreement with your preferred candidate, be sure to set it out in writing. Most nanny and au pair agencies have standard contracts for their clients. Since these documents do not cover every family's situation, do not hesitate to add your own clauses or write a separate agreement with your child-care provider to cover issues not mentioned in the standard contract. For instance, you may want your in-home caregiver to attend classes (at your expense, of course) at a nearby child-guidance center or day-care program. Such a side agreement must not, however, be a mechanism either for cutting the agency out of part of its commission or for imposing big new obligations on your helper.

Care Outside Your Home

There are many forms of out-of-home child care — infant care, day care, and nursery-school programs — and all are different. Nursery schools have traditionally been part-time programs where children go two, three, or five half-days per week. Many children who attend nursery school have a parent or a baby-sitter at home for the other half of each day. Day-care programs tend to last for the parents' whole workday and combine educational and basic-care objectives. Some day-care programs also offer infant-care programs for children only a few months old. Most nursery schools and day-care centers have similar curriculums for their children, and these are based on developmental principles.

Many factors influence parents' decision to choose a program, including quality, location, cost, hours, facilities, recommendations, child-care philosophy, and how much help the family needs at home. You know your child best, so pay attention to your intuition about what programs are suitable for him. As with in-home child care, this decision will require several weeks of investigation.

Deciding on Your Needs, Identifying Your Options

The first step in your investigation is to make a list of what you need from a child-care program. Here are some common priorities:

- How important is location to you? Do you want the center closer to your home or your work? That choice depends on whether you might want to visit your child during your workday and on who will most often pick him up in the afternoon.
- How much can you afford? If your entire salary is going toward child care, you may want to reevaluate your needs. While expense is a rough measure of quality, there is absolutely no guarantee that the most expensive day care is the best. Nor is inexpensive day care necessarily terrible.
- Think about your basic needs for the child-care program — structure, educational opportunities, safety, teacher/child ratio, individual attention, special projects, discipline, opportunity for social play with peers. Your list of needs and requirements will help you begin the search.
- Does your child have any special needs? Some programs are organized for children

with particular needs, while others offer opportunities for children of different abilities to play together.

Your next step is to find programs to observe. Your pediatrician and other parents are good sources for suggestions. Some day-care centers are quite visible, with bright signs and playground equipment, so take a drive around to see what facilities are available. Schools, churches, and community centers often host child-care programs for part of the day. Call the programs you are interested in and ask the administrator your most important questions. (See "What You Need to Know about a Child-Care Center," pages 424–425.) Do not hesitate to ask all the questions you need.

In addition to making notes on hours, fees, and other facts, try to gain a feeling for whether a program is receptive to parents who want to be involved in their children's care. If an administrator seems impatient with your questions or does not give what you feel are full answers, think twice about that program. If you have mixed feelings about having someone else care for your child, you may think of day-care providers as doing you a favor. But child-care programs want and need your business. As in all other fields, if the proprietors put short-term profit above long-term growth, they will be less interested in building a mutually satisfactory relationship with your family. You are probably seeking child care for a year or more; if the provider cannot give you fifteen minutes on the phone, he or she may cut corners elsewhere.

Child-care programs must conform to local, state, and national standards for building and fire safety. Either before or after you make your first calls, phone the government office that oversees child-care facilities. (This office has different names in different areas: the Office of Child-Care Services, the Department of Human Resources' licensing department, and so on.) Ask for the history of their review of each of the programs you are

What You Need to Know about a Child-Care Center

Call each child-care program on your list to find out these basic facts:

• hours of the day, days of the week, and times of the year when the facility operates

• number of children and number of staff members on any one day

• openings: a long waiting list may mean that the program is either very popular or lacks adequate staff

• fees

• status of the facility's licensing, including health and safety standards

• staff credentials, including any accreditation by private organizations

• philosophy of helping children to develop and learn

A telephone conversation will not necessarily give you complete answers to all these questions, especially the last three. But it will tell you the basics and give you a sense of whether you wish to visit the facility.

Here is a partial checklist of what to look for and ask when you visit. Add items that are important to you. Before you go, have your principal concerns clearly in mind.

• How clean and attractive is the facility? Is there a clean, designated area for changing diapers? How well are the indoor spaces and the playground maintained? Are staff members supervising all the places where children can go? About half of the injuries children suffer in child-care programs occur outside. The best playgrounds include separate areas for different age groups and age-appropriate play equipment.

• Observe snack- and mealtimes. Does the program allow parents to send special food for children? Does the program charge extra for meals?

• At nap time, does the program allow children to have their own special blankets, pillows, or stuffed toys? Do they limit the number of cribs in a room, so that infants will have a good chance of sleeping undisturbed? Do the teachers pay individual attention to the children as they help them settle down for a nap?

• Do children have individual spaces for their coats and for projects they might be working on?

• Are the children getting more than basic "custodial" care? Is there more planned for each day than meals, naps, and perhaps reading one story? Is the schedule balanced between free and structured play, between group activities and individual projects, and between active and quiet play?

• What is the program's staff turnover? A child-care facility should have little personnel

evaluating, to be sure that each one meets all safety and health standards.

The best day-care programs have a director and a staff of teachers with professional backgrounds in child development or early childhood education. On the phone and in person, you can ask directly about the credentials of the staff. Caregivers should be happy to tell you about their degrees, certifications, or experience. Since there are no na-

change to ensure consistency for the children. If the rate of new hiring seems high, ask what reasons people give for leaving. Programs with high turnover often pay their staff poorly, hire inexperienced people who soon go on to other jobs, or do not follow an integrated staff plan and curriculum set by the director.

• Does the program require all children to have up-to-date immunization records? What is its policy for handling illnesses? Is there a place for children to rest if they are not feeling well? Does the program have a working relationship with a nurse or a pediatrician? Does it have strict rules about keeping sick children home? Ask to see the form the program uses to note children's medical records. Many programs ask for authorizations signed by parents stating which medical facility and physician to contact in an emergency.

• What is the program's system for efficient retrieval of parents' telephone numbers in an emergency? How does the program inform parents about illness or injuries? It should send home written reports about these health issues.

• Do the caregivers appear to enjoy the children? Do the caregivers seem generally happy and relaxed and comfortable working with one another? Do the children look relaxed, involved, and emotionally connected to their individual teachers?

• Do you feel comfortable as a parent in the facility? Can you imagine your child there and feel secure in that thought? Can you daydream and even see yourself playing there as a child?

The success of a preschool depends on the ability of its director and staff to develop close working relationships with parents. Look for a program where you feel comfortable asking for help and letting the teachers know what you have observed about your child's needs and behaviors. The staff, in turn, should have a consistent system of keeping you informed about what goes on during the day. Programs that are developmentally sensitive usually provide regular progress reports summarizing the staff's observations of a child. Along with your daily contact with your child's teachers, these reports allow you to sit with the program director and review your concerns.

Day-care centers should be committed to privacy and confidentiality. You should feel certain that your discussions with the director or your child's teacher will remain confidential. Young children have few inhibitions and will, at the drop of a hat, tell their peers things you did not even think they knew. They talk most about what confuses them — pregnancy, a possible divorce, a serious illness, a parent's job loss. While your child may reveal family information at story time, that is not a license for the day-care staff to talk about what they hear publicly or with other parents.

tional or state minimum standards for the staff of child-care programs, private organizations, such as the National Association for the Education of Young Children (NAEYC), have created accreditation processes. Better child-care programs adhere to such standards or set similar ones for staff training and education. You can ask a program's manager about its training criteria and whether it is accredited by the NAEYC.

Looking Long and Hard

You probably did not think you would be taking school tours with your child until it was time for college, but visits are your next step in choosing a program. After your telephone calls, list your three or four favorite programs. Then schedule times to visit each facility. Visit several times at different hours during the day so that you can see how each program handles lunch- and nap time, outside activities, and other events. Select at least one part of the day that is often stressful for both children and teachers, such as the morning drop-off or evening pick-up, to see how the adults manage the situation.

Use your time at each program not only to observe the staff and children as they interact, but to talk with the caregivers about their goals, philosophy, and curriculum to see whether theirs fit well with your approach to parenting. Find out whether a program provides children of different ages and abilities with activities appropriate to their developmental level. Asking caregivers what they think is important to do for a two- to three-year-old and for a twelve-month-old. Notice

if they adjust their developmental expectations according to the age of the child. (We discuss the needs of different ages in the next section of this chapter.)

Now that you have visited the day-care programs you thought most desirable, and collected as much information about each as you could, you are ready to choose among them. To do this, you may need a quiet period to reflect and talk about what you have seen. Or you may be able to consult with a pediatrician or early childhood educator who is not involved in the programs you are considering; or with other parents who are struggling with the same decision, especially if they have observed the same programs or used one of them for their children.

A Developmentally Appropriate Curriculum

Child-care programs should vary their facilities and activities according to the developmental level and needs of the children they are serving. That means more than providing activities that children usually enjoy or the latest toys or books. It starts with taking into account when babies usually display different skills and how their emotional needs vary. Children at different ages are working on different tasks. For example, very young children do not understand the idea of sharing toys, while this is an appropriate lesson for a four-year-old. If you want more information than appears in this chapter, we recommend the National Association for the Education of Young Children's *Developmen-*

tally Appropriate Practice in Early Childhood Programs.

Infants: Learning to Trust Their Caregivers

As infants come to develop trust in themselves and in others, they form deep and enduring relationships to their parents and to other adults. They start to feel joy in the presence of the people they love and sadness in their absence. In these first months and year, infants' ability to take in the world through their senses is also developing rapidly. (For more details on infant learning, see chapter 15.) They grow almost day by day not only in size and motor coordination, but also in their ability to understand the complexities of social interaction.

With these developmental tasks in mind, a program for infants must first and foremost fill a baby's need for consistent attachment to the person caring for him. The necessary tasks of feeding, cleaning, clothing, and bathing a baby are opportunities for rich social interaction. A program that sees these activities as simply jobs for anyone on the staff to perform does not understand their developmental importance. Infant-care programs need to assign one or two people to an infant. If a caregiver is temporarily unavailable, the person in his or her place should also be consistent and not just anyone (except, of course, in an emergency). A program for infants should be small and intimate, with a stress on continuity and consistency of care.

The program should appreciate each infant's individuality. Since babies have, as do adults, particular sleep/wake rhythms, they should not all be expected to nap and eat at the same time. The staff should also be large enough to cover all the infants if they all need attention at once. If your baby is hungry or wet, she should be learning to tolerate these discomforts temporarily and to anticipate that someone will come to comfort her. But being among many babies crying at the same time makes it hard for a child to master those basic lessons.

The playspace in an infant day-care program should be clean and safe. All child-care spaces should be, of course, but infant spaces have special requirements. Developmentally appropriate toys, such as rattles, teething toys, swings, mobiles, and bouncy chairs, should be within easy reach of the staff and, when appropriate, of the babies. The infants should be able to play in different areas: lying on the floor on a blanket, sitting in a bouncy chair, curled up in a caregiver's arms, looking around from a stroller. They should have lots of social stimulation, toys to look at and manipulate, and many opportunities to hear adults speaking to them.

Your baby should sometimes be with other babies, sometimes alone with her caregiver, and sometimes quietly in her bed or stroller. The need for "downtime" begins early. Environments that are too stimulating (e.g., too many toys, too much noise, packed spaces) may quickly overwhelm an infant, and she will either retreat into fussing or go to sleep to shut out the outside world. If, on your visit to an infant-care program, infants are sleeping in the midst of chaos (as opposed to during nap time), you should see this as being as ominous as if they were all crying at once.

Toddlers: Standing on Their Own

Toddlers are rapidly developing their ability to coordinate their body movements and their language and imagination. They can drink from a cup; say, "I drink juice"; and pretend to help a toy bear drink — all impressive achievements. Toddlers begin to assert themselves; they say "no" often and with great energy. They declare their own territory with a lusty "Me" or "Mine." Children in these years display wonderful enthusiasm and irascible stubbornness. They love to be on the move and to explore their worlds. They are their own biggest fans, in love with their bodies and their newfound abilities. At the same time, they are easily upset and maddeningly controlling. Whether curling up in her parents' arms or struggling to pull on her own clothes, a toddler feels the world to the depths of her soul. Happy is flying high, and sad is down in the dumps. Toddlers make great demands on a day-care staff, not only because of their energy but also because of their emotional intensity.

The main task toddlers need to work on — at least, in American culture — is to develop a sense of independence. A day-care program for this age group must be prepared for the intense separation worries your child may have as she tries to leave you but fears that she will never see you again. A develop-mentally appropriate curriculum for your toddler will help her make a gradual transition into the program. The staff may allow time and space for you to stay and help your child adjust, and teachers can find many ways to help your toddler keep his family in mind after you leave. Pictures of parents, brothers, and sisters are good reminders of home. Special blankets or stuffed toys also help children hold on to their connection to home while they are away at school. A school routine that is consistent, predictable, and flexible offers reassurance that the final event on the schedule — Daddy or Mommy coming to pick me up — will also take place. (For more on separation issues, see chapter 31.)

Toddlers should play in small groups. Some children this age have not yet learned to pay attention to the needs of other children, and while they play side by side, they are not yet really sharing or cooperating. The day-care program must have enough toys of each kind that several toddlers can play together without being expected to share. Since toddlers also need many opportunities for active play and learning social skills, teachers should help them use words to express their feelings and needs, even when those feelings are extreme.

Preschoolers: Developing Discipline

Independence and dependence continue to be major themes for preschoolers. Preschool programs should acknowledge that separation is a lifelong process, and that children make a healthier transition to school if

preschool program is how it sets limits. Appropriate discipline acknowledges that young children are beginning to develop inner controls over their emotions and actions. They learn best how to deal with their feelings and desires when they trust the adults who care for them. Children need to know the rules of the school. They need help from the teachers to follow these rules, help that differs from child to child and from moment to moment during the school day. At times a gentle reminder prompts a child to follow a rule; at other times a teacher needs to say something like, "You can't hit the other children! I'll help you stop now because you are having a hard time being a good boss for yourself."

A preschool program's curriculum should show that teachers understand what children of this age need to master. Preschoolers have many more language skills and are becoming better and better storytellers. Their playroom should include areas for blocks, books, playing house, science exploration, and dramatic play. It should also include areas where children can be active (often called a "gross motor" play area) and tables for art. Optimally, the staff creates a balanced program of activities: child- and teacher-directed, group and individual, indoor and outdoor, structured and unstructured, active and quiet. When you are observing the program, watch how involved the children are in the activities. Can they choose what they want to do? Do they receive help in completing projects and interacting with others? Are the teachers not only aiding the children in an activity but also

they have made a comfortable and supported adjustment to their day care. When a preschooler leaves his parents each morning for school but consistently returns home in the afternoon, he learns to master such coming and going. Ideally, parents and teachers should work as partners to ease the transitions. A day-care program that requires children to be dropped off at the front door on the first day of school because the staff believes, "If parents stay any length of time, the children cry and cling," does not understand a child's need to figure out separations. It would be safe to assume that the staff would probably overlook your child's other needs as well.

Another important thing to look for in a

offering ways to extend or elaborate on their work? Is the children's art displayed?

Difference Makes the World Go Round

Day-care programs often have remarkable cultural diversity, particularly in cities with colleges or large employers. A good day-care program makes use of every bit of cultural difference. Teachers ask parents to bring in foods or special garments. They mark many holidays, display pictures of other countries, post signs with words for an object in different languages, read stories from a range of cultures. Just as travel lets adults see the diversity of the world and at the same time appreciate how much people have in common, day care is one way young children can experience this diversity — in language, food, holidays, music, art, games, even styles of parenting — early enough to allow them to accept and be interested in people different from themselves.

The same point applies to children with physical or mental disabilities. Many day-care programs have special-education certification and trained teachers. More and more programs are designed to mix children with special needs and those without, and when they work, all the children benefit. A child with special needs can play and develop with a range of other kids. A child without visible special needs has an opportunity to understand and not be afraid of differences. Most young children are fearful or worried when they meet another child who has a physical handicap or does not seem to think the way

they do. (Adults worry, too, but have been socialized not to comment most of the time.) Young children are especially concerned about their bodies: Is everything working right? Will I get bigger? If I scratch my leg, will it fall off? Preschool-age children revel in stories about the grotesque — the two-headed baby, the cow that is half human. Thus, a preschooler meeting a child with a physical or mental disability may (to her parents' horror) ask direct questions: "What happened to your legs?" "Why don't you walk like we do?" "Are you stupid?" These queries reveal both fear and curiosity.

Not only should the staff in such programs be properly trained in special-education needs, they must also be able to help the children understand disabilities without increasing their worries. Preschoolers are concrete. A preschooler who hears someone say, "Jamie was very sick and now he can't see," may worry about the next time he is "very sick" with a cold. Teachers and parents need to reassure him. "Jamie wasn't sick the same way as when you have a cold or an earache. It's not the kind of sickness you can catch from Jamie, either."

Dealing with Your Anxiety about Day Care

You surely feel, in your heart of hearts, that no one, not even your own parents, can care for your baby as well as you can. So asking somebody else to do it can, as we noted in the last chapter, make you feel guilty and anxious. But remember that no matter what kind of care you have chosen and how old your child is, you have not given up your role as a parent. While you have allowed other people to share the responsibility, they are only sharing it, and to do so is a privilege. You are still your child's mother or father.

Still, even with caregivers who share your values and purpose, and with whom you feel comfortable working, anticipate some worries. The first minor accident when you are away, the first illness your child brings home from nursery school, the first fight on the playground — these unhappy incidents are bound to make you wonder about your choice. But they are unavoidable on the road to growing up, whether your child is at home with you full time or at a day-care center. Since they occur at all day-care programs, your most useful response is to focus on how the staff responds to them.

At work there will be moments when your mind is really at home — wondering how lunchtime is going, wishing it was you spreading jam on your child's bread. Any mixed feelings you may have about leaving your child are ready to swirl up in you the first time your child skins a knee without your being there to catch her. And your baby may well take his first steps in day care or with his nanny, and then, for several days, demurely decline to show his parents this skill.

It can be emotionally difficult to realize how very attached your baby becomes to a teacher or nanny, particularly if you have chosen the person well. Caregivers take a prominent place in a child's gallery of mental portraits. Children talk about them, want to take them special gifts, and mourn their departure. Your child may adopt some of her teacher's likes or dislikes or even mannerisms. You may feel that a bit of the love meant for you is now spread more thinly among strangers, and resent the caregivers a little or lament moments you miss. You may even question your parenting values.

Yet, to succeed in life, children must separate from their parents. At an early age — in day care, kindergarten, or first grade — your child will inevitably begin to spend greater and greater amounts of time in the care of other adults. Sharing your children is never easy. But your child's ability to love and accept many other people, to give of himself to teachers and friends, ultimately depends on your own acceptance of and love for him. Your aim must be for your child to go out into the world — whether to day care or to college — confident that you are, and will remain, with him.

CHAPTER 30

Why Do We Need a New Baby?
A Sibling Joins the Family

After your first child, you know all about the sleepless nights and the dirty diapers that come with raising a newborn. You know how that little, helpless child monopolizes your time and attention. But you also know the wonderful feeling of falling in love with an infant, the peacefulness of a sleeping baby in your arms, and the thrill of your child smiling directly at you. If some years have passed, that tiny bundle you brought home from the hospital is now a walking, talking, thinking child. You may feel, now that your baby is a toddler or older, that you have to be even more watchful than before. Yet you've decided to do it again — to have another baby.

Like your first romantic love, falling in love with your first baby is an extraordinary experience, unforgettable. Parents sometimes worry that they will never be able to fall in love so entirely and so intensely again. Fortunately, love is not finite. While the second time you fall in love may be less thrilling than the first, it is no less passionate and deep. Parents of a second newborn are usually relieved and pleased to find that their new baby

reawakens strong and marvelous feelings. They may have less exclusive time for each successive child, but none receives less affection.

Yet you are inevitably different with your later-born children than with your firstborn. For one thing, you are busier: being a parent, as you now well know, is an extremely time-consuming activity, which sometimes leaves little emotional or physical space for other endeavors. So it is not unusual for parents, even when they wanted and completely adore their later-born child, to take somewhat fewer pictures, to be slower to send out birth announcements, or to be less enthralled with the physical details of their new baby — his soft skin, his tiny fingers and toes. This change reflects the hectic pace and fullness of life, not a lack of love.

In addition to being busier, however, parents of later-born children are more experienced and often calmer than they were as neophyte parents. Even though you will still have several weeks of preoccupation and adjustment — just as with your first baby —

you now know that colic really will end, that your baby will not break when you pick her up, and that children make their wishes known. You are an expert diaperer. Your more self-assured stance translates into calmer and more easygoing interaction with your new child. Observers can usually spot how experienced parents hold and play with their babies (you may have seen that yourself with friends and envied their ease). Furthermore, just as you are different, your later-born child is different. He is a unique individual and will act and react in significantly different ways from his older sibling.

The relationship between siblings is usually a concern for parents as they care for their second newborn. How will their older child react to the new baby? For a firstborn child, especially if she is very young (see "Birth Order and Only Children," pages 434–435), even the news of her mother's pregnancy is a startling, life-changing event — almost impossible to comprehend. Your child may seem not to respond to this news right away. She may try to change the subject or go back to playing in order to give herself time to process it. Many questions will go through her mind, but from the beginning, she understands that the only family she has ever known will change. In this chapter, we discuss when to tell your child about the baby to come and how to handle sibling rivalry.

What to Say When

You may worry that your new baby will change your firstborn's life forever, but the change need not necessarily be for the worst. Still, the fact that you feel ready to hear the happy babble of a newborn does not mean that your toddler is eager to share her parents, her playthings, and what she has come to think of as her spotlight.

Thus, the best way to tell a first child that a new sibling is on the way is a major issue for concerned and psychologically aware parents. As in most parenting issues, the solution to this one depends on understanding your child's developmental level and finding a style that feels comfortable for you. It is probably not wise to tell a child before the pregnancy that you and your spouse are trying to have a baby, even if he asks if he can have a little playmate. You can say that Mommy and Daddy would like to have another baby, without implying any promise. A child cannot understand the time involved in the effort to conceive, or its potential frustration, not to mention the confusing details of the actual process. Such an early announcement could also cause prolonged inner conflict in a child who is ambivalent about having a sibling. It is wiser to present the coming of a new family member as a near certainty, not an option the child may think he can talk you out of.

Many parents choose to tell their children about the impending arrival sometime in the first trimester — often after the doctor has detected a heartbeat and just as the mother is beginning to show. Parents who plan amniocentesis may want to wait until they have received and responded to the results —

usually in the fifteenth to eighteenth week. Often parents find it hard to wait that long. You may be very excited and want to share the wonderful news with everyone you love. Furthermore, your child may have guessed or at least suspected something important was happening.

Children, even very young children, are often extremely perceptive about detecting small changes in the people whom they care about most. Although they may not articulate their suspicions, they will often notice changes in their mother's energy level or wonder about meaningful glances they see their parents exchanging. A child may actually worry that his mother is sick ("Why so

BIRTH ORDER AND ONLY CHILDREN

Birth order has long been debated as an important factor in how children approach the world and succeed in it. In many cultures, a firstborn son was treated differently from his siblings and stood to inherit most of his parents' land, wealth, and political power. In the late nineteenth century, the English scientist Francis Galton pointed out that most of the scientists in Great Britain were firstborn children (he was a third son). Recently some researchers have argued that later-born children tend to support revolutionary scientific ideas, while firstborn children defend more traditional ones. On a more mundane level, television comedies have publicized "middle-child syndrome," where one character is trapped between attention-getting siblings. And in everyday life, parents watching youngsters on a playground may decide that a little boy who plays by himself and demands a lot of attention from his father is "a classic only child" — only to discard this diagnosis when his siblings arrive.

How much influence does birth order have on a child's behavior and development? In the past, researchers have attributed a wide range of advantages to being the first (or only) child in a family. These have included more rapid language development in the first years, higher scores on tests of intellectual capacity, better academic performance, greater motivation and curiosity, and even more likelihood of going to college. Later studies that involved large numbers of children and took social customs into account have not confirmed that firstborn and only children have an inherent advantage in IQ or academic achievement. The one area in which being a firstborn child seems to have a regular effect is language development, and this is easily explained.

The firstborn does have a spe-

many visits to the doctor?") or suspect that he has done something to influence her mood or to cause her exhaustion. Toddlers and younger preschoolers believe everything is about them — the same quality that makes the news tough to break. If you sense that your child might be worrying about you, it is probably best to tell him that you are pregnant, since his theories about what is happening are likely to be much more distressing than the reality.

The words you use to actually break the news are not as important as the tone in which you speak them. Your child wants to know that you love her and that your feeling will not change — that she can still be Mommy or Daddy's baby and continue to bask in the warm glow of that unconditional love. Telling a two-year-old, who is struggling with the issue of being a big girl or staying a baby, how great she will feel about becoming a big sister is only going to incite her oppositional feelings. This message may actually spur her into regressing to more infantile behavior. A four-year-old who is off in nursery school, and beginning to establish a world for himself with peers, may love the idea of becoming a big brother, but may falsely assume that you are about to provide a ready-made ball-playing partner. Without preparation, he may well be disappointed with the dependent, time-consuming infant you produce instead.

cial position in a family, with unique privileges and benefits, as well as responsibilities and burdens. A firstborn or an only child has a closer relationship with her parents than a younger sibling simply because no other child is around to demand attention and care. When a family already has children, they compete with a newborn for their parent's energy and time — resources that are inevitably limited. The parents of a firstborn (and her other caregivers as well) naturally have more time to talk to her, and their conversational attention fosters her early language skills. (For more on this process, see chapter 17.) Having an older sibling gives a newborn a different language environment from a firstborn's. A three-year-old sister's conversation is a less sophisticated model than an adult's.

The other benefits some researchers have attributed to being born first may, in fact, derive from family size and other related variables. The shapes and habits of individual families can also increase or work against these effects. Often large families follow cultural traditions of having many relatives help look after the children and encouraging cousins to play together like siblings. A very late child may actually benefit from having much older siblings, who provide both attention and examples of the use of language. It will be interesting to see whether any perceived advantage for a firstborn or an only child changes as patterns of child-care change; as we noted in chapter 29, toddlers who spend time in day care with other children of the same age often achieve social skills earlier than children who spend those years at home.

A child also, of course, responds to his birth order in accordance with his individual temperament. Indeed, the traits we have come to associate with an only child, a firstborn, a middle child, and the baby in the family probably arise from a complex arrangement of factors and certainly do not hold in every case.

The following often-quoted exercise may help mothers (or, if slightly rewritten, fathers) understand how their children might perceive the news of a new addition to the family: Imagine that your husband comes to you and announces he loves you very much and, because of that affection, has decided to get another wife to make the family complete. She will come home soon to live in your room and eat at your table, and he hopes you will understand that he may be a little busier at first. He wants you to welcome her into the family and share your things with her. Of course, this doesn't diminish any of the love he feels for you.

Presented with such a scenario, you — and most people — would be jealous, angry, perhaps go on a rampage. You can't expect your child to react differently.

Instead of this approach to telling your firstborn about a new sibling, try to speak to him directly and calmly about the psychological truths as you know them to be:

- "We love you very much, and we always will."
- "We've decided to have another child."
- "When that little baby comes, we'll all need to change how we do some things in our family."
- "But we'll try to keep as much the same for you as we can, because we love you as much as ever."

Figure out what you will be able to keep the same in your firstborn's life so as to cause as little disruption in important routines and things as possible. Focus your discussion on how the new baby will directly affect your older child's life, rather than on how wonderful it will be to have a baby in the house or how much she will enjoy becoming an older sibling. If your firstborn is excited about the idea of a new baby, that's wonderful. Nevertheless, it is certainly consistent with the egocentrism of young children, and therefore something for you to anticipate, that her main concern will be, "How is this going to affect me?"

Preparing Your Child During the Pregnancy

As the pregnancy progresses, there will be many opportunities to prepare your child for a sibling. During an obstetric visit, he may see an ultrasound image of the fetus or hear a Doppler heartbeat. You can prepare for such a visit by talking over what you will see at the doctor's office. Consider what about the office might seem frightening to a small child, and ask her what she expects and wants to see there. Experiences such as these, provided that they are not done in a frightening medical context, can help your child to understand your rapidly changing body. He can watch your abdominal wall as the baby kicks and moves — again, you may want to assure your child that this action is not mean-spirited or painful. The older child can sing quietly to the baby in the womb. These activities can both give your child a more concrete image of the baby and begin to promote a positive relationship between the siblings.

If your hospitalization for the delivery and postpartum recovery is your first overnight separation from your child, it might elicit strong feelings in her, independent of her sibling's arrival. Many hospitals offer sibling programs in which, as your due date approaches, your older child can tour the maternity floor and peer into the nursery to see actual newborn babies. By seeing the room where you will stay, your child may be able to create a mental image of what is happening to you when labor begins and you suddenly disappear to have the baby. Such experiences also help him to begin working through some of his feelings before the actual birth, when you are available to provide him with love and support.

You can also read some of the many thoughtful books for children that either describe pregnancy or tell about life with a newborn. Reading these books together with your child will give her a chance to ask questions or consider the events ahead. Such closeness is also comforting and pleasant. (For more on the importance of reading to a child, see chapter 18.) Do not, of course, push your child. He will absorb all the information he can process at his own pace. Some children will want to read a "babies book" all the time, and others may firmly fling it into a corner but return to it later. Give your child opportunities to express his feelings or concerns, but do not force him to share his thoughts if he does not want to.

During the later phases of your pregnancy, your child may become a little more clingy, demanding, or needy. She may be letting you know that she is anxious about how family life will be after the new baby comes (just as you may be wrestling with your own questions). Sometimes it helps to talk together about where the baby will sleep and what newborns are like, as well as to review the many things in your child's life that will not be changing. Make a plan for the delivery that covers who will take care of her and where she will go when you go to the hospital, and tell her about that plan. Some families like to have an older child or children prepare small presents for the new baby: cards, "baby-sized" stuffed toys, little T-shirts, and so on. Many parents wrap a few extra presents for the baby to "give" to the older child when he comes to the hospital to visit you and his new sibling. You might want to pack a framed picture of your older child to take with you to the hospital and prop beside your bed — not only for your enjoyment but to further reassure her about her special place in your heart.

Even though you would like to have only one baby in diapers, the months right before a sibling's arrival are probably not a good time to encourage the older child to use the toilet or take other major developmental steps. If your toddler suddenly wants to be toilet trained, or to give up his crib or bottle, that is terrific. You should certainly support him in his efforts. On the other hand, pressuring your child to make these leaps might make any success short-lived; some regressive behavior after a new baby is born is fairly common.

When an older sibling does begin to act

like a baby, it is a sign that she is feeling anxious. She will likely respond well to continued reassurance and attention. Tell her that she's your "big baby" and the newborn is your "little baby," and that you love them both. You might remind your older child about how much the two of you love reading together or playing games or doing all the other grown-up activities that only a big girl can do. In so doing, you give her a chance to retain her role as your beloved baby but also to differentiate herself and explore her life as the more competent and older child. While she may have less of your attention now, she gets to engage you and her other parent in exciting and meaningful ways. As she realizes this, she will likely soon feel ready to give up the beloved bottle or crib in favor of the grown-up cup or bed.

The New Arrival

After months of planning and worry about jealous feelings, many families are pleasantly surprised when the new baby arrives and their older child does just fine. Thoughtful friends and relatives who bring a present for the new baby sometimes also provide one for the older child as well. And older children are usually pleased and excited when beloved relatives come to spend time and help in the days following the birth, and celebrations are usually happy. Remember, however, that young children usually thrive on a consistent routine. Allow your older child to continue going to school and carry on with her usual activities, despite the new excitement at home.

Sometimes an older child, though apparently doing well with the baby, seems angry or distant with his parents. If your older child generously bestows kisses on the newborn and seems eager to amuse her, but approaches you with some anger and resentment, he may be jealous and is displacing the emotion onto you. This behavior is highly adaptive and, surely, protective of the little newborn, who could not defend herself if the older child turned his anger on her.

In some families, the newborn arrives home to no sibling difficulties and only adoring glances, but jealousy and resentment arise during the latter part of the infant's first year as she becomes active, learns to crawl, and gets into the older child's things. For other children, the immediate postpartum period is the most stressful, and they do much better as the baby matures into being a playmate.

The jealous feelings your older child may experience often vary in intensity throughout the years. There may be days or minutes when your two children seem to adore one another, and others when the fervor of their rage astounds you. Such emotional intensity is common in love relationships. It probably reflects more how much your children care about one another than anything sinister. An experience that may draw first and second children together is the arrival of a third. Your oldest will have been through this before, but now your second child will be reacting to the news that she will no longer be the baby in the family. One small advantage you have at this juncture is that your second child was born a sibling and knows that parents can

have more than one child and love them both. (See "When the New Sibling Is Adopted," pages 440–441.) On the other hand, sometimes the oldest child and the newcomer develop a close bond that squeezes out the middle child.

Sibling Rivalry

Relationships between siblings are often unique and powerful. Only with a sibling do you share a particular family history and a particular genetic endowment. (See chapter 8.) Nonetheless, when you exchange tales about your childhood with your siblings, you may sometimes feel as if each of you had grown up in a different family. Although sisters and brothers live in the same house with the same parents, each sibling's experiences and relationships in that environment are individual, unique to him or her. Age, gender, birth order, spacing, and personality style all influence how family members connect with one another.

Competition among siblings takes different forms at different ages. When children are young, they may fight over particular playthings or their parents' time and attention. As they enter school, children begin to compete over grades, sports, social life, or other measurable indices of success. Siblings who are close in age, or whose interests are similar, may compete with one another more than those who choose different activities or are far apart in age. Similarly, competition between same-sex siblings may be more intense than between a brother and a sister, who know they each have a special, separate identity.

Some children will purposefully focus on different areas to distinguish themselves or to avoid competing, or may discover differences in native ability or interest. Encourage each child's interest, but try not to classify either one by it. For example, when early on one child excels in sports and another shows great academic potential, it is easy to refer to "our little athlete" and "our little student." This kind of labeling can become a self-fulfilling prophecy that discourages each child from fully exploring her own potential in areas designated as her sibling's. Depending on how her peers value such designations, a child may also come to resent or rebel against it.

At times, despite your best efforts to serve as diplomat and peacekeeper, your children will probably seem to be fighting and arguing more often than not. Sibling rivalry, and the squabbles that accompany it, are a normal part of growing up in a family with more than one child. At times a child may seem to go out of his way to tease his brothers or sisters, or to feel they are teasing him. An older child can complain, "He's copying me!" as resent-

When the New Sibling Is Adopted

A great deal has been written about talking with adopted children about their situation and otherwise helping them adjust to their new families and bridge cultures where necessary. It is equally important to talk with other children in the family about the newcomer. If your older children are adopted themselves, they may understand and accept the process relatively easily. In other cases, however, parents must prepare their biological children to deal with and accept a new adoptive sibling.

Of course, every time a new child comes into a family, all members must adjust. Older siblings have to adapt to the baby as a rival for attention, and parents have to learn how to divide their time among all their children. Bringing an adoptee into a family with other children raises the same sibling-adjustment issues — as well as special ones.

Have open discussions with your existing children about the meaning of family and the choice to care for a new child. There are many reasons parents with one or more children may decide to adopt another: they may no longer be able to have another child, yet feel they have not had all the children they hoped for, or they may decide to adopt a child with special needs or a child orphaned by the deaths of relatives or friends. While parents usually make a decision about having any new baby, biological or adopted, the choice to "go and get another child" through adoption can seem especially willful, particularly to younger children. Furthermore, an adopted child is often not a newborn, tiny and helpless and asleep most of the day. The new child may be six or twelve months, or even six years old, mobile and with a clear personality, habits, and desires.

Explaining to your children why you would like to bring such a child into your family requires thought. Talk through all their con-

fully as if it were a felony. Imitation is flattery but does not always feel that way. To this older child, her sibling's mimicry robs her of her individuality and uniqueness. Try to soothe her by telling her that her younger brother is copying her only because he thinks she's "so cool."

Your children's fights, however upsetting to you, provide them with opportunities to learn about getting along with each other. Working out peaceful relations with someone as annoying and inescapable as a sibling will be an invaluable skill as a child grows older and has to get along with other people out-side the family. Set down general rules for everyone in the family: no hitting, no taking or breaking other people's things, and so on. Enforce these rules fairly (see "It's Not Fair!" page 442), live by them yourself, and be ready nevertheless to field complaints. (See chapter 27 on how to encourage children's moral development.)

Your response to squabbles should be guided by your knowledge of each child's de-velopmental abilities as well as by how much dissension you can stand. When preschool children argue over a beloved toy, they can learn a lesson about sharing, but they will

---

cerns. Younger children may be cu-rious about why this baby does not have parents to take him home and perhaps why he looks differ-ent. Older children may worry about how they will explain the change to their friends. Let them be part of the decision to adopt or, at least, have some role in the sec-ondary choices — preparing the new sibling's room, shopping for what he or she will need. As with any new baby, it is important both to reassure your older children that you still love them, and to dis-play your love to them as they con-sider how their lives may change. Feeling confident in their existing family relationships makes it eas-ier for children to welcome a new sibling.

Your adopted child may have special needs that you cannot fully anticipate; and every child is, of course, special. Therefore, even after everyone in the family has embarked on this new ven-ture, the going can get rough. Your biological child may voice doubts or resentments about the new adopted sibling that are sim-ilar to the doubts he might have about a biological sibling. In adoption, however, children of-ten want you to "take the baby back" since, after all, you went somewhere to get their new sis-ter or brother. It is unwise to deny or squelch these sentiments; in fact, you may be feeling similar doubts, but are unwilling to put them into words. Instead, tell your child you understand her feelings, but that the family has a responsibility to help their newest member.

Indeed, adopting a child is a commitment for a family in the same way that giving birth is: each carries its own special chal-lenges, and the members of a family have a commitment to one another to work these challenges out together. Every time a new child enters a family, you need to think carefully about how to wel-come him or her. Adoption simply calls for a more explicit recogni-tion of these tasks and, in so do-ing, may give all your children a deeper understanding of what it means to take care of and love someone.

probably need your help in negotiating a way to split the toy or to take turns with it. Older children can often find a peaceful resolution if you leave them to their own devices, although you may need to suggest ways to talk about a conflict or to set up rules about how to disagree while still coexisting peacefully. If you saw the start of a dispute and feel that one child has acted maliciously, say so. Otherwise, resist taking sides in siblings' conflicts: in part, because you rarely see enough of an argument to know who is truly in the right; and, in part, because siding with one child removes the opportunity for the two to learn how to settle disagreements themselves. With older children, you can explain that since they created their conflict, you want them to solve it. Of course, you must intervene if you see a threat of damage or violence. Family meetings, where children and

"It's Not Fair!"

"It's not fair!" seems to be a recurrent refrain of childhood. Although you know that life isn't always fair (as much as you still wish it were), you can try to be consistent and fair in your dealings with your different children.

Being fair rarely means treating all siblings identically, however. Tell your children that you will be fair, but that fairness does not necessarily mean they will get the exact same privileges or responsibilities. You will consider each child's own needs, interests, and developmental level when making decisions that will affect him or her. For example, if your children have different bedtimes or allowances or chores, try to be consistent. As your younger child matures, see that she attains the same freedoms and responsibilities as her older sibling, neither significantly later nor significantly earlier. (For some children, one day's difference is significant.)

On the other hand, if your younger child is very musical, it makes no sense to keep him away from music lessons until age ten because that is when your older child started. To avoid resentment on the part of the older child, you may want to grant him a new privilege around the same time that his younger sibling begins something new "ahead of schedule." But, again, that will depend on the interests — and best interests — of the older sibling. By responding to the desires and talents of each child, you may treat them all differently but still fairly.

Sometimes parents worry about "playing favorites," unconsciously giving one child more attention or opportunities or deference than the other. You may catch yourself comparing one child's behavior or talents unfavorably with another's. Although you should refrain from voicing such comparisons directly in front of your children, it is perfectly natural for you to notice differences between them.

It is also not uncommon for one child to spend more time with her parents than her sibling does, especially when they are at different ages and different stages of development. One child's personality may simply lead her to enjoy the company of grown-ups, while the other prefers to play with her friends or by herself. You are not necessarily, in this situation, pushing one child away. Here, as in all parenting, recognize the special bonds you share with each child. Focus on how each brings you joy in her or his own way. By appreciating the particular abilities and personal strengths of each of your children, you affirm the uniqueness of each.

adults each have a chance to voice concerns and resolve them together, can be useful both to address immediate problems and to demonstrate how people should behave when conflicts arise.

Having a child is an act of faith: you and your partner create out of yourselves another being who will, you hope, both delight and enrich your lives and contribute to society. In bringing into the world more than one child, you have the added opportunity to help two human beings turn their special bond into a lasting friendship and thus contribute to the web of loving relationships within that larger society. It is a matchless gift.

CHAPTER 31

Anxious Moments:
Helping Children and Parents Handle Separations

A toddler cries inconsolably as his father carefully hands him to Grandpa so Mommy and Daddy may enjoy a long-awaited evening out. At day care, a three-year-old holds tenaciously to the few threads of a tattered blanket. A school-aged child on the eve of her first sleepover comes to her parents' room and wants to crawl into bed af-

LINDA'S LOSS

A young mother named Linda came to a child-development clinic because she felt her three-year-old daughter, Emily, was having increasing difficulty making the transition to day care. Each morning as Linda and Emily approached the nursery school, the little girl would begin to look worried and sad. By the time they opened the door, she was clutching her mother's hand. And even when Emily's favorite teacher came to greet her, the little girl would be sobbing quietly. Since Linda could not bear to leave her daughter in this state, the teacher had made a place for her to sit in the classroom. Gradually, Emily would leave her mother's side and join the other children. After a time, Linda could stand up and quietly tell Emily good-bye. But sometimes, even with this careful preparation, Emily would stand at a window and tearfully watch her mother drive away. Yet Linda knew from Emily's teacher that after she had driven out of sight, Emily would eagerly join the circle of other three-year-olds. In the afternoon, Linda often had a hard time pulling an energetic and gleeful Emily away from the playgroup. And over supper, Emily talked about her friends and her teacher and what she would take to school the next day.

These morning scenes haunted Linda. She found herself preoccupied at work and worried about Emily in a way she had not done with her six-year-old son. He had adjusted quickly to the same day care. He seemed as bold as Emily was cautious. Clearly, Linda told the psychologist she was consulting, her children had very different personalities. Emily seemed much more like her, while her son took after his father. Linda had always met change with a mix of sadness, dread, and excitement; she usually enjoyed the challenge, but was relieved when the stress was over. She said she probably worried more about Emily because she understood how anxious her daughter

ter a frightening dream. An adolescent going off to college shyly packs her old stuffed bear; another gruffly asks his father if he needs help cleaning out the garage. All these children are facing, in their own ways, the challenge of separation.

Separations are an inevitable part of living. Rarely do you spend your entire life in the place you call home, within one circle of friends and relatives, or remain at the same stage in your personal development. Even those of you who live in the community where you grew up have watched that community change as friends and relatives come and go. A woman doing the dishes far from her childhood home may suddenly realize she is following the same wash-and-dry routine as her mother, with even the same hand motions. She could sit for hours in the warmth of her mother's kitchen, she remembers, and wishes she might have that experience one more time. That longing grows from the same instinct for closeness that your children show.

Early mapmakers marked the edges of their charts with the phrase, "Beyond this point lie dragons." So it is with separation and your anxiety about losing someone or something important, moving to a new job or home, or meeting new people. You do not know all that lurks off the map of your familiar life. Separation inevitably makes a person

---

felt. Separations had always been difficult for her, too.

When she was a little older than Emily, Linda explained, her mother had gone to the hospital to have a baby. She remembered being awakened in the night and carried, wrapped in her blanket, across the street to a neighbor. She did not clearly understand what was happening. She recalled her mother coming home many days later, looking tired and perhaps sick and smelling funny. For many weeks after that, the neighbor helped take care of her and her new little brother. It seemed like a long time before Linda and her mother were able to be together again, just the two of them. In Linda's mind — though she was never sure why she felt that way — her mother was never quite the same after that departure. (The consulting clinician wondered whether Linda's mother may have suffered a postpartum depression.) Linda truly felt that she herself was never quite the same either and wondered whether day care was a similar kind of experience for Emily.

Although Emily surely brought her own personality to the unavoidable stress of separation from her mother, the child's worries were amplified in Linda's mind by memories of her own loss. Each of them was working through the challenge of a separation. Each sensed the other's tension and responded to it by becoming more anxious. The clinician discussed with Linda how Emily and she were probably responding to each other's anxieties.

At the recommendation of the clinician, Linda screwed up her courage and left Emily at the nursery school more quickly. Though this change was difficult at first for both mother and daughter, Linda could soon see that Emily benefited from having more hours of play, and that she was much less anxious at work. Tensions may resurface when Emily goes to first grade, to high school, and to college, but when they resolve them, mother and daughter will have the confidence of having achieved one more successful separation.

both excited and worried, happy and sad, for all separation implicitly involves change, loss as well as gain. Memories of separations that have worked out well help adults take on new adventures. Recalling how much fun you had at summer camp can make going far away to college more exciting. Enjoying a friendship that continues even across thousands of miles may embolden you to accept a job in a new city. But no one ever escapes a twinge of uneasiness that maybe this time things won't work out so well.

How you manage beginnings and endings reflects a mixture of three things: your past experiences, your genetically based sensitivity to stress and change, and the strength of the network of friends and family who support you. This network includes people you know, people you remember, and (especially for children) people you imagine. Your observation as a child of your parents' presences and absences, their stability and moments of faltering, shaped your own ability to cope with anxiety about change and loss. And your confidence in that ability is rooted in how your family helped you with the inevitable losses and separation of childhood. For nearly everyone, current separations bring to mind past transitions. Good-byes not completed, close friends left behind, departures before you were quite ready — all of these feelings have a way of coming back, especially when you, like the mother in "Linda's Loss" (pages 444–445), try to help as your child struggles with separation.

With their parents' consistent presence, children build up memories of when they felt distressed and then comforted, afraid but then reassured. You, like everyone else, draw on this bank of emotional memories when undergoing stress in your life, and if you understand this process in yourself, you can better help your child weather separation.

The Vital Link Between Parents and Children

For parents and their children, beginnings and endings occur most often in human relationships. Until the middle of the twentieth century, psychologists did not recognize that infants and very young children could have deeply adverse reactions to changing caregivers. Losing a parent or another important family member was not thought to be as traumatic for a young child as for a young adult. It was a groundbreaking observation that many infants in hospitals and orphanages, even when physically well cared for, did not thrive. Deprived of a consistent, stable adult who cared for them emotionally as well as physically, many orphaned infants not only failed to grow but sometimes succumbed to severe weight loss and even died. Today we take for granted that human relationships are critically important for the development of infants.

A young child's first explorations of the world away from his parents are cautious and safe. A quick crawl to the hall outside the kitchen can take him out of Mommy's sight but still within hearing range and easy rescue. As your child becomes more confident and bold, the new frontier is the next room,

the upstairs bedroom, the backyard. For him each step seems as momentous as America's first ventures into outer space. As the earliest probes beyond the atmosphere were made with small, unmanned rockets and test animals, so a toddler may throw a favorite stuffed toy out the door ahead of him just to see if it will be safe. The first manned space flights were quick trips up and back to test systems. The toddler's version is apparent in her love of peekaboo and disappearing/reappearing games. With enough practice in these games, a child gains confidence that the person he is playing with will indeed reappear. Eventually, with great boldness, space explorers traveled to the moon and lived in orbit for many months. It is no less a triumph for a toddler to fall asleep without her parents in the house. Such graduated

steps toward separateness and independence appear at all stages of development.

All children — both the one-year-old toddler and the eighteen-year-old college freshman — need loving, consistent, and predictable adults in order to develop self-reliance and to learn to trust themselves and their world. Going to sleep, to school, to college — all these ventures happen only in the presence of supportive people in one's life and memory. Even the "self-made individual" triumphs because of an instilled faith that she has the ability to succeed and will be safe however far she travels. Indeed, the more a child feels secure and comfortable and loved within his family, the more able he will be to leave — and the more he will want to. Through their parents' love, children gain confidence in their ability to take care of themselves and to take on the world on their own, even when that love is not immediately near.

Centuries ago, the majority of people lived their entire lives in one village or region. While such societies may have had as many problems as benefits, an individual could be reasonably certain that most of his relatives and friends would be living nearby for most of his life. In today's culture and economy, transition is a part of life. Adults face frequent disruptions in the relationships that sustain them: people change jobs, employers reorganize operations, and families move across the country. Seldom do high-school and college friends all remain near each other as they build careers and families. Your parents and elderly relatives are usually no longer living nearby and may well be thousands of miles away. Having thus learned how to handle these kinds of disruptions in your own life, you have a good chance of passing that knowledge on to your child.

How Children Deal with Loss and Separation

Researchers who have studied attachment and separation have found that a normal human reaction to loss is protest and anger, mixed with anxiety about having been left alone. Children of all ages feel real pain at being separated from their parents: when a toddler gets a new baby-sitter and says good-bye (however fleetingly) to a familiar one; a three-year-old goes to nursery school for the first time; a busy, preoccupied, or sad mother goes into another room to do some work without telling her preschooler where she will be; a beloved schoolteacher goes on maternity leave; or an adolescent goes off to college. Your child's protests at your leaving may shock you, because you are confident that you will always be there for him; he, however, has not yet had time to build up that assurance.

What defines a separation experience, how your child deals with it, and how much help he needs vary according to his developmental stage and personality. Similarly, the ability to cope with the fear of future separation is influenced by many things, including the qualities of a child's relationship with parents and extended family, her develop-

mental level, her previous separation experiences, and the qualities of the day care or school or whatever new experience she is embarking on. One important measure of that quality is how well adults help the child remember home and family while she is away from either. The goal, in guiding children through separation and related anxieties, is to help them remember your love for them and feel the strength of their tie to you. With this goal in mind, we discuss in this chapter how children are affected by loss and separation at various ages and also how to help them adjust when your family moves from one home to another.

Infants: Who Will Be There for the Baby?

In the first months of life, an infant depends on his parents for the most basic survival. You keep your baby fed, clean, warm, and safe. In those weeks, your baby "knows" your presence by your actions, by how you satisfy and comfort him. In thousands of basic acts — feeding, holding, bathing, rocking — your baby begins to recognize the sound of your and your partner's voices, the quality of your touch, your smiles and smells. These basic sensations become the stuff of his earliest emotional memories. (See also chapter 21.) Within a few months, a hungry baby can be comforted, if only briefly, by just the sound of his mother's voice. As young babies develop unique relationships to the people who love and care for them most often, they will respond fretfully and change their sleep and eating habits if those people disappear.

As we described in chapter 5, in the days after bringing your new baby home from the hospital, you rarely leave her. Yet, in the first months after delivery, many families decide to bring additional people into their lives to care for the baby. Infant day care meets an important need for a family in which both parents are working or in which there is a single parent. A baby is able to adapt to being cared for by different people — two parents, a grandparent, and an every-other-day baby-sitter, for example — as long as this larger group of caregivers remains consistently present and available. (For specific advice on choosing a day-care provider, see chapter 29.)

Toddlers: Will You Be Here When I Wake Up?

Late in their first year and early in the second, children start to show their acute awareness of their special tie to their parents by reacting warily to strangers. A baby who heretofore has smiled broadly to any friendly adult now looks cautiously, if not fearfully and tearfully, at a new face. He may even be cautious when he greets his grandparents, whom he has not seen for a while, and look quickly back to Mommy or Daddy for reassurance. While you may feel this change as a step backward from the sociable infant you knew, it actually marks a critical developmental shift in the child's relationship to you. The toddler now trusts that Daddy and Mommy know all about the world and every-

one in it, that they are the key to interpreting any new situation — a response called "social referencing." Thus, a two-year-old feels that it is not safe to go too far out of her parents' sight, however curious and excited she may feel about what's around the next corner.

Toddlers, therefore, need a great deal of reassurance that, even when absent, their parents are still their parents. Children of this age can tolerate separations for much shorter periods than infants can, and need more comforting reminders of their parents' existence. They may carry pictures of Mommy and Daddy or a special blanket or teddy bear as concrete reminders of their familiar world. Adults use the same trick to ease changes. Even as you move to a new home, you take your old dishes, towels, even that old couch you probably should have thrown out years ago. Many an adult only reluctantly gives up a comfortable pair of pajamas or a threadbare sweater. Astronauts always pack some personal mementos of home into the small living quarters of their spacecraft. Knowing that you have familiarity to return to lets you move ahead into the unknown, whether into nursery school or a new job, a house, even outer space.

You can also help toddlers by putting their worries about separation into words: "You wish I could stay with you." "I know you don't like it when I go to work." Reassure your child that everything will be okay: "You will go to school this morning, I will give you a peanut butter sandwich in your special lunch box, and just as I always do, I'll pick you up in our red car and we'll come home." "I know you'll have a good time with your teachers and friends today." "I will think about you when I'm at work today." "Daddy and Mommy miss you, too." Repeat these reassurances almost ritualistically, like the refrain of a song, to show that you understand your toddler's strong feelings. As they become a comforting piece of your parting routine, you will be giving your child a model of how to express his feelings once his language abilities mature.

Toddlers work out much of their anxiety not through words but through play. The games they love — hiding and finding things, filling up and dumping out — are practice in controlling comings and goings. Toddlers can play as often as they want and, at least on

TATTERED TEDDY BEARS AND OTHER TRANSITIONAL OBJECTS

Even as an adult, you hold on to things that remind you of people you love: the birthday card a child drew, the ring Grandma used to wear, the shirt worn on a first date. Such objects allow you to keep the people you associate with them in your thoughts and your life, even if they have grown up, moved away, or died. On some level, the reality of the object makes the person seem more real and present.

The same is true — much more urgently — for young children. Infants and toddlers reach a stage in which they remember people they love just long enough to miss them, but not strongly enough to be certain they are still around and will return. One way young children deal with this frightening period is through what we call "transitional objects." When an infant or a toddler begins to display a fondness for one special blanket — or pillow, stuffed animal, pacifier, or other item — this is more than his "favorite blankie." The blanket helps him endure those times when his mother or father is absent or out of reach. The familiarity of the blanket, which he can touch, smell, and see, reassures him that the people he cannot sense nearby are still real, too. The term "transitional" refers to how these objects help children through the passage in life when they learn to tolerate worry and sadness about being away from their parents. Children need time to mature from wanting always to be with particular people to being able to hold those people in their minds. The psychological space a child creates during this transition remains with him always. His ability to live within it, enjoying the mental company of those he loves, means that he can tolerate being alone.

Commonly children choose transitional objects that carry smells, textures, and even colors that recall the important times they share with their parents — bedtime, breast-feeding, cuddling. Thus, the blanket that a mother wrapped her baby in as he fell asleep is often popular. A toy tiger or bear may become a little girl's favorite because it was her companion through a long night's separation. The softness of most transitional objects is a reminder of being held close and rocked to sleep. Hence, children are unlikely to pick a truck or other hard toy as their transitional object — unless that toy was a part of a very special routine with a parent.

Whatever object a toddler chooses, all of its smells, stains, and textural qualities are as im-

some level, know that the game's outcome is in their hands. Things always reappear — just as they hope their parents will. A toddler who is worried about, for example, a grandparent's departure after a holiday visit gets his parents repeatedly to play a game of hide-and-seek. For days, he cannot get enough of this game. Every time he is found or he finds the hidden person, he tumbles on the floor in excitement. Although you may tire of it pretty quickly, it is psychologically important for your toddler. He is, in this, like an adult who pores over old letters or photographs of an absent loved one.

Early in their second year, children who have been sleeping through the night may begin to wake up again. And when they do, they are alone — and it's dark. For some chil-

portant as the object itself. These aromas, rough spots, tears, and blemishes are "memory traces" that help her feel comfortable. Though in the interest of health and cleanliness, you may want to wash that smelly, tattered, dusty blanket, those disreputable qualities are often what the child most values, and she may cry if you put it in the laundry. She dislikes not just being separated temporarily from her favorite object but also the change in its familiar, comforting smells and textures. So powerful are transitional objects that sometimes any part of one will do — an old blanket worn down to a little square of trim or a bear that has lost half its stuffing, one leg, and an ear. (Similarly, you may be keeping in your closet a favorite old sweater — even though one elbow has a hole, the cuffs are stained with paint from a first apartment, or it's really uncomfortably snug.)

As children develop a more elaborate mental world, they have less need for their transitional objects and typically give them up around time for kindergarten or even a year or two earlier. Do not be surprised, however, if your school-age child suddenly asks for that old bear or blanket again when he is ill or when there is a big change in your household. A very competent eight-year-old may desperately cling to his teddy bear as his family packs up to move to another city, for instance. (For more on such moves, see pages 456–458.) Even college students often pack a special toy or other object from home (rarely, you'll be happy to know, the same tattered object he or she clung to as a toddler). The desire for concrete reminders of absent people never goes away.

Some children, however, never have a transitional object. Such children may not have enjoyed a secure, loving home — through having moved many times in foster care, for example. Despite this apparent paradox (Shouldn't children without a home have greater need for comfort?), the ability to invest an inanimate object with memories and reminders of a parent's love arises only in the context of a loving relationship. Without even a brief experience of such ties, a child has no way of knowing how to invest part of her imagination into loving a favored toy. On the other hand, some children who grow up in stable, secure, and loving homes never seem to have a transitional object — or, at least, not one their parents can identify. Some of these children may suck their thumb as a kind of "transitional behavior," but others may not need even that. They seem to get along without any special object to help them keep in mind persons who have loved or cared for them.

dren of this age, sleep is the first time they truly perceive separation. How can they be sure that their parents are still there? Many bedtime rituals spring up around this age: books that have to be read every night, toys that belong on the bed (see "Tattered Teddy Bears and Other Transitional Objects," pages 450–451), favorite blankets, special pajamas, pillows that must be fluffed just so, and sheets that must be tucked in tight. All of these serve to reassure your child that there is a predictable sameness in the world; the people she most wants to stay around will be there the next day, just like her blanket. At the same time, these rituals also effectively postpone sleep and keep parents close by. (For much more advice on getting toddlers to sleep, see chapter 13.)

Preschoolers: I'm Grown-Up, But Don't Go Far

A preschool-aged child (three and older) wants you to see her as totally grown-up and as a baby at the same time. Since you can never know which wish is uppermost in her mind, you will often err by expecting too much or too little independence. Preschoolers can be most unpredictable around separations and transitions. They can swagger into day care without a look back one day and the next day tearfully hang onto your hand as if you were saying good-bye for ten years. The preschooler has a mantra — "Me do myself" — that she tries to apply to everything. Working on such independence and practicing being "grown-up" always brings

worries about a safety net: What if I fall or I get lonely? Who will be there? If I say I can do this myself, will they be willing to help me the next time?

An outside stress, such as the birth of a new baby, may make separation more difficult. Your child may feel an intruder has arrived to take his place, so it seems like a good idea to hang close and protect his turf. (For more advice on smoothing sibling relationships, see chapter 30.)

Many preschoolers have had some successful experiences with separation: going to day care, staying with a baby-sitter while parents go out. Each successfully weathered separation bolsters a child's ability to withstand the next. But preschool children have to work extra hard to comfort themselves because their repertoire of coping abilities is still limited. Tending to live from day to day, preschool children can neither easily recall previous transitions nor think of ways to assure themselves that everything will be all right.

This is the reason a preschool child often questions her parents over and over, even about daily experiences such as day care. "Where will you be? When will you come back? Are you picking me up today? Do you have to go to work? I don't like it when you go to work." This litany of questions may confuse and frustrate you and make you feel guilty, but your preschooler is not trying to distress you. Nor do these repeated questions indicate poor learning skills: your child probably does remember your answers from yesterday and the day before. Preschool children ask because they are using their new-found language skills to deal with uncertainty. Just as you recite a telephone number to yourself when you cannot find a piece of paper to write on, young children ask the same question over and over to hear the same answer and feel comforted in that sameness. A preschooler's saying, "I don't like day care," or "I hate school," is not a solid indication that she really is miserable after you leave; she may be seeking your verbal reassurance that all will be well. If you see her enjoying the program, offer the comfort she is really seeking: "You will have fun at day care. Yesterday you told me what you're going to draw today. I'm looking forward to seeing that when I pick you up tonight."

Preschool children are also just gaining the ability to think symbolically: to let one thing stand for other things or for people. A stuffed bear can thus become a stand-in for you. Or something that belongs to you, such as your scarf or an old cap, reminds your pre-schooler that you are still around. The ability to think symbolically also helps adults maintain strong mental images of the important people in their lives. You may plant a tree at a beloved friend's death; that tree, though looking nothing like that person, makes you think of him or her each day. Preschoolers' use of symbolic possessions shows their new-found capacity for "object constancy," or the knowledge that something can be out of sight but nonetheless continue to exist. Preschool children are just beginning to grasp this idea as it pertains to people. They are starting to create mental images of their absent parents and to ask questions like "What is Mom doing right now?" and "Is Dad thinking about me as I'm thinking about him?"

You may be surprised at how hard it is for your preschooler to say good-bye to a favorite teacher at the end of the year. Children of this age also mourn the loss of a regular baby-sitter or nanny. They do not easily replace someone with whom they may have spent hours each week. Thus, a preschooler needs help in mastering partings from people outside the family. She needs to be reassured that her caregiver did not leave because of her. Visits with an old nanny or teacher after the farewell are helpful, as are pictures, letters, and phone calls. Although you may think that continued contact will make it harder for your child to get used to a new teacher or nanny, cutting off contact rarely helps a preschooler. Even years later, your child may mention an early teacher or baby-sitter you have long forgotten. Time and

PRACTICAL WAYS TO DEAL WITH CLINGING

Nearly every young child worries about being left alone or separated from his parents. This is true no matter how thoughtful or careful you are and even if you have not, so far, been away from your baby. Children especially need their parents close when they are afraid, feeling sick, going through important changes such as moving, starting a new school, or sensing something wrong with Mom or Dad. A small child can be so worried that he is not only tearful but holds tight to a parent's body as if he'll never let go. Such clinging often seems to happen at a most public place or a most untimely moment — in front of other families at day care or just as you and your spouse are about to leave for a long-awaited special evening. How can you anticipate and respond to this behavior?

When your child grabs your leg and holds on for dear life, that is first and foremost an act of communication. She is telling you in the most dramatic way that she is frightened and worried and feeling out of control. She is also telling you that she needs your help (even though you may be feeling fairly helpless or quite exasperated yourself).

Clinging is hard to deal with when it happens. You can, however, do some things in advance if you know that your small child is especially sensitive to your comings and goings. The more concrete, specific details you can give your child about what to expect, the more he can feel reassured. For example, you can explain to your young son that you are going to take him to visit his grandmother, and that you and Daddy will go to dinner together while he is with Grandma. Let him know that you will come back very soon to bring him home and tuck him into bed just as you always do. Routine is also very helpful with preschoolers who cling. Remind your child how every morning when you go to day care, you walk to her classroom, help her put her snack in the refrigerator, and kiss her good-bye. Promise to wave to her as you walk to your bus stop and, as you do every day, to come back to fetch her at the end of school. Tell her also that you will think about her all day, and that she can think about Mommy and Daddy while they are at work. As we have said before, you can also give your child something to remind him of home while he is at school or at a baby-sitter's — a picture, a scarf, an old billfold.

Even with all this preparation, some children will still at moments become upset and hold on tight to their parents. What can you do in the midst of such urgent crying and clinging? First, put your arm around your child, speak calmly, and say you know he is very upset and doesn't want you to go. Reassure him that you will not leave him while he is upset, but that he is going to be all right and does not need to cling. Talk about all the familiar things around him: his school, his teachers, his grandmother. Tell him that you know he is worried or scared, but you will still be around to keep him safe. However difficult, try to stay calm but firm in these moments. If you know that your child is likely to respond to your imminent departure this way, you may want to leave extra time so as not to feel rushed while you help her to calm down.

again, a child will return to rework the separation and think about what that person meant in her life.

Schoolchildren: Not Too Close

By second or third grade, children are separation veterans. They have gotten used to the morning routine, and school offers the broader world of friends. Your school-age child may even suggest that while it's nice to see you, you should not stand too close to her when you pick her up in the afternoon. And hugs in the morning — how embarrassing! Not only can your schoolchild remember you clearly while you are away, but her language abilities let her tell others about her home, parents, and what she likes and dislikes. School-age children spend hours comparing notes on each other's home life — what their parents do, what the household rules are, who is invited to whose party. Your child's social world is now an extended network of friends and those friends' parents and families.

On the other hand, children of this age are still learning how to manage separations. They suffer when their social networks are disrupted. They miss favorite teachers or wonder about baby-sitters who have gone off to college. Some of their school friends may well have moved away; a parent changing jobs or a family buying a house in a new neighborhood are common events for American children of this age. Divorce and parental separation are another reason that families move. These disruptions are even harder for schoolchildren to deal with be-

cause they undermine the central pillar of their established and supportive friendships. As we explain in chapter 34, during a divorce you need to offer your children verbal reassurances and physical proof that you and your former partner will both remain in their lives even if the two of you no longer live in the same home.

How well schoolchildren deal with major upheavals depends in large part on their history of earlier separations and on how well their parents have helped them feel safe and secure. Children whose earlier separation experiences have been traumatic will continue to struggle even in primary and secondary school. They may find many reasons not to go to school, including physical complaints such as repeated headaches or just feeling too tired. Pediatricians often see such problems, but the solution really lies within the family. Avoiding school is one way of staying close to home and not leaving a parent whom the child is worried about.

Adolescents know they have to separate from their parents psychologically and sometimes physically. By this age, they have rich and evocative memories of their families, dreams for themselves, and more control over their own lives. Leaving the family for college or work or marriage is still a separation, however. Older adolescents may make many calls or trips back home, feel hurt at any change in their old room, and move back in for a period. Generally, however, they accept that now is the time for them to begin living their own lives. This final successful transition allows them more easily to help their own children start the same process anew.

Moving Away from Your Old Home

Sooner or later, most American families will move from one house to another. They may be following a parent's new career opportunity or switching to a larger or smaller home as their economic circumstances change. Children experience these moves as a separation of sorts. Departing from a familiar home, sights, and even objects stirs up feelings of loss, just as leaving favorite people does — in large part because one connects such things to those people. While a move to a new home and new neighborhood may be positive over all, it still can stress both adults and children. The upheaval in familiar routines leaves everyone feeling unsettled and uprooted, even sad and confused for a while. Some researchers have found that children whose families moved many times showed more difficulties later in life. The real problems in these children's development may, however, have been the reasons behind the moves — if they reflected family strife or economic deprivation, for example. But many children whose families move frequently — because of their parents' military assignments, for instance — prove to be resilient and practiced at making new acquaintances and strong family ties.

If you are about to move to a new house or a new town, you can smooth the transition by viewing it from your children's perspectives. Young children in particular may have trouble leaving the only home and neighborhood they know. They depend on their parents for a consistent, predictable daily pattern. Moving, especially the days before and after the actual moving day, surely disrupts that routine. Home is also like a young child's comforting teddy bear, favorite pillow, and worn blanket: it brings comfort simply by being familiar. This attachment is further strengthened if the neighborhood is filled with extended family members or friends who have played central roles in the child's life but whom the move will leave behind. Try to preserve and restore as much as you can of a young child's former routine and surroundings in the new place.

A school-age child's strong attachment to friends and peer groups means that each move to a new neighborhood brings a new and vital challenge: How will I find friends and fit into the established groups at school? Parents usually ask Realtors if a prospective home is in a neighborhood with other youngsters and what the nearby schools are like.

Your school-age child is also curious about this information. When you visit the neighborhood before moving or shortly after you arrive, explore the parks, playing fields, and shopping areas with your child. Be sure to invite young neighbors over to play — they are probably just as curious about the new arrivals as your child is about them. Children should be prepared for some changes: for instance, they might move from a town where everyone plays soccer to one in which baseball rules. Reassure your child that what is fundamental — friends, classes, and family — does not change. Since older children also enjoy acting as competent members of the family, include them in discussions of the new house, their new bedrooms, and at least some of the practical aspects of the move. In this way, they feel part of the decision to move, rather than as if they were passive victims.

For both older and younger children, saying good-bye to your old home is essential to helping them with the separation. Children say good-bye in very different ways: some quietly and even casually, others with drama and fanfare. Whatever your child's style, you may want to set aside some time in the hubbub of moving for a "remember when" discussion about the old house and what you did there as a family. Children, like adults, orient their lives around such landmarks as birthdays, Hanukkah, and Christmas. Thus, you can tell them such things as, "When you were a tiny baby, we brought you home to this house. It was winter, but the sun was very bright in the windows in your room. We sat in the sun holding you and just admiring how beautiful you were." Or, "When you had your third birthday, we had all your friends over to a party in our backyard. Billy brought his new puppy for you to see — you didn't know that we had a puppy for you, too." Take pictures of your soon-to-be-old home. These will be important reminders for your child (and, at some point, for you). You and your child may want also to bring some mementos with you: a rock from the garden, an old bird's nest, even a cutting from a plant that you will grow in your new yard. The message for the child is, "You don't have to erase from your mind this place you love. You can hold it in your memory."

All children benefit from having a definite time frame for an upcoming transition. Make a calendar for the move, as specifically as you can. Help a younger child mark off each day: "Only three more days until the movers help us go to our new home." This will give him an anchor in an inevitably chaotic time. Try to help your children pack up their rooms, or at least their special things, and be sure you either move these yourself or let them see "their boxes" go onto the moving truck. For a long move, a child can draw or write her name on her box so she can see her things safely away. On the actual moving day, if you are busy supervising the move, you will have little time or patience for helping your children and may want a relative or baby-sitter to help take care of them, depending on their ages. Nevertheless, it is good for children to watch at least a part of the move. If they see it in action, they are spared the shock of leaving their old house full of furniture and then finding it empty, without understanding how that change came about. Older children are usually able to stay for the whole packing process and even help. Some young children — entranced by the big truck, the big movers, and all the excitement — may want to help, too. Giving each child responsibility for his own small box can fulfill that desire without putting him in harm's way. Other young children, however, may not tolerate the chaos for long.

In the new house, you may ask your children's help to unpack some boxes, particularly those containing their things. Try to arrange the furniture in a child's room as much as possible the way it was in the old house. Don't talk about redecorating those rooms until the family has settled in. Make sure children's beds, night clothes, and bathroom linen are in place by the end of the first day. As fun as it can be for children to tear around a big empty living room with no sofa in it yet, they still value having a comfortable and familiar place to sleep as night falls.

Just as you enjoy revisiting old friends and loved ones, you may need to revisit a former home. If it is impractical to drive through your old neighborhood — you could be hundreds of miles away — you can still revisit through photographs, letters from old neighbors, and conversations. Your children may well ask questions about the home they remember, such as "Are those new people happy in our old house?" "Do they have a dog like we did?" "Do they know about the hole in the old tree in the backyard?" They may also draw pictures. These queries and activities indicate that they are thinking about the old place and settling it in memory. These are moments for talking again about what you all remember — both good and not so good memories.

The saying "Home is where you make it" means that you bring yourself to wherever you live. Your feelings and fantasies become woven into the structure of all your houses, apartments, and neighborhoods. Similarly, your family remains part of you even when individuals are far away. After leaving beloved people and places, you and your children need time both to adjust to the new, separate existence — whether it lasts a day or a lifetime — and to preserve a place in memory for what you have left behind. This is the process of separation.

PART VII

The Unpredictable Troubles in a Child's Life

CHAPTER 32

Children's Physical Troubles: Facing Illness, Injury, and Hospitalization

You hope always that your child's life will be happy, fulfilling, and free of trouble and that he or she will be always growing, going forward, and learning. But contingency is the essence of life. And just as good things can happen to good people — and good children — so can bad. Out of the blue, seemingly, trouble can come: illness or injury, emotional distress that may blow up into a mental problem, family turmoil ending in separation of the parents and divorce, or death. Even the troubles of adolescence, with its many changes and significance for the future, can catch both child and parent unawares. Neither you nor we can predict whether any of these mischances will occur in your family. Nor can any of us predict how, if one does occur, it will affect your child. But we do know that any of these circumstances will affect your child's feelings, behavior, and development. They will also drastically affect your imagining of your child and his or her future, and require you to give extra attention and care to him or her. Ado-

lescence is, of course, in store for every child. Here as with the blows of chance you will again — as before your child was born — have to balance your imagining with strenuous practical measures. The first rule in all of these cases is "Don't panic." The second, "Be patient" — with yourself and with your child.

In this chapter, we will discuss illness in children: the ordinary illnesses of childhood, going to the hospital, serious injury, and chronic illness. Your response to illnesses and injuries will, as with many other aspects of caring for a child, reflect your own parents' treatment of you when you were young and how they understood your problems. Because your understanding of disease may stem from experiences a generation old, you are likely to have some outdated notions. The medical profession's ability to manage most diseases has improved enormously in recent years, making illness much less fearful than it used to be. There is also much better treatment of various injuries, from scrapes to broken limbs.

Ordinary Illnesses in Childhood

One of the scariest moments in your life as a new parent is the first time your baby runs a high fever. Even if you know that young children run high fevers with even the mildest illness, you cannot help but be anxious. You worry that what appears to be a simple sniffle is the start of something worse. Such anxiety is a normal part of being a parent. You worry similarly about the possibility of your child tumbling downstairs, coming home from school with the flu, being bitten by an infected tick. Like all parents, you want to protect your baby from every threat, including microscopic germs. Nevertheless, your child will get sick. She may have any of various gastrointestinal ailments, the common cold and other viruses, ear infections, throat infections, bronchitis or pneumonia, and other illnesses. She will suffer some injuries as she runs and plays and will be emotionally distressed by any injury to or illness of other people in her family. In all cases, you will need to attend to her emotional as well as her physical needs.

The seriousness of fever in a child varies with age. If she is only a few months old, your pediatrician is likely to want to see her in a hospital emergency room, where he will have the appropriate equipment for tests to rule out serious illnesses. For older infants and children, there is less concern. The height of a fever does not necessarily indicate the seriousness of a disease, nor does it dictate the type of treatment your child should receive. It is not at all uncommon for children to have temperatures as high as 104°F or 105°F (40°C) and behave almost normally, especially with viral illnesses such as flu, roseola, or Coxsackie disease. Because children have small bodies, some symptoms — the dehydration produced by vomiting, diarrhea, and sweating, for example — do produce serious problems more quickly for infants and young children than they do for adults. But after the newborn period, fever alone is rarely a major problem.

For most viral illnesses, over-the-counter fever medications such as acetaminophen or ibuprofen, along with fluids and rest, may be all the treatment a child requires. (At one time, aspirin was the drug of choice, but since we now know that it can cause rare but serious complications in combination with certain viral infections, you should no longer give it to your child to treat a fever.) Since we do not, in fact, have drugs for most diseases caused by a virus, we can treat only their symptoms — something your child's own immune system does quite well by itself. If your pediatrician feels the infection is caused by a bacteria instead of a virus, he or she will want to see you and your child so as to identify the bacteria involved and pick the correct antibiotic, if he or she decides to prescribe one. Most illnesses that give a child a fever will dissipate quickly, without consequences, under the appropriate treatment.

Since discussing all the other types of illness children regularly develop, even with the many immunizations available today (see pages 79–81), is beyond the scope of this book, you should buy or consult in the library one of the several fine reference guides to children's symptoms and diseases. With the information in one of these, you can avoid worrying about minor symptoms and feel more confident about responding when major ones appear. In turn, your confidence will help your child feel less anxious about being sick and allow him to attend to how he is getting better.

Children's View of Their Illnesses

A child reacts emotionally to an illness according to her understanding of it at a particular age and through the way you and other concerned adults behave toward her and speak of it. At some ages, your child's reactions to being ill may be more disturbing to you than his physical symptoms.

Infants and toddlers, with their limited ability to understand cause and effect, are likely to be frightened and irritable about their physical state. Your presence and reassurance — both physical and verbal — will help to control this reaction. Slightly older children, with their strongly self-centered view of the world, often believe that an illness is punishment for something they have done wrong, either real or imagined. Although they do not necessarily say this, they do think it. You and your pediatrician or any physician should, therefore, reassure your child repeatedly that the illness is not her fault and that it is not a retribution for either bad thoughts or bad behavior.

Some parents are much more anxious than others about diseases and much more active in trying various remedies. Consider how your child might read your response when he becomes ill. If seeing him sick worries you a lot, he is likely to worry as well. If at every sniffle you go to the drugstore for a new medicine, he will come to associate all his healing with medication and may not learn to trust the healing powers of his own body. Often a minor scrape heals more quickly if you gently wash it and give your child a big hug than if you apply an ointment and a bandage (however much young children enjoy wearing today's multicolored bandages). If people in the family regularly take any pills or other medicines, be sure to tell your child that each is for a specific person and a specific purpose; none of these is a magical potion that will cure anyone and anything. (Since toddlers are too young to remember this lesson, treat medications like all other potential household poisons; keep them out of your growing child's reach.)

By school age, sick children begin to overhear bits of what their parents, nurses, and physicians are saying about their condition. Sometimes, based on inadequate information and insufficient knowledge, they misconstrue what they hear. Fitting together their limited understanding of their bodies and their concrete sense of cause and effect, they form elaborate fantasies about the nature or cause of their illness. These fantasies can be terrifying and lead a child to react in bizarre ways that affect his health or long-term pleasure: being overly concerned about hygiene, for instance, or refusing to swim in a lake ever again. To avoid this reaction, you need to explain illness to your child in language and concepts he can understand. Since you know your child best, including her usual speaking and learning styles, take the lead in translating her doctor's assessments. After explaining, ask your child to express back to you her understanding of the situation so that you can correct any misconceptions. Especially if a child's disease is serious, you need to give her a reasonably realistic and accurate understanding of what is going on. For you and everyone, adults as well as children, the devil you know is less frightening than the devil you don't.

Even with careful explanations, the symptoms of a child's disease may acquire a symbolic importance to him. Conditions that affect important bodily functions are more likely than others to permanently affect a child's behavior and fears. For instance, a disease that interferes with breathing, such as asthma, frightens parents and child alike. It is alarming for anyone to have to labor to get air in and out of the lungs, and the effort can leave a child feeling fragile and helpless. Seizures are similarly nerve-wracking. Watching your child struggle with these problems can severely tax your resolve to be steadfast and supportive. Nonetheless, remaining calm at such times can be profoundly therapeutic for both the physical and the psychological course of your child's disease. If the problem is part of a chronic condition, your child must learn to manage it for years to come — a task

that is much easier in a composed, reassuring atmosphere. By learning to manage difficult symptoms, your child may well start to feel capable in other areas as well.

Some diseases, such as urinary tract infections, require doctors to use instruments or otherwise manipulate a child's genital area. This, too, can be upsetting. Since children learn early in life that this is an important part of their body, the prospect of a doctor working down there can make a child very anxious. Tell your child ahead of time, if possible, and reassure her that what the doctor is doing is necessary to help her get better. In these difficult moments, stay with your child to provide comfort, allay her fears, and hold her hand.

School Phobia

Once in school, your child may begin to wake up every morning complaining of a stomachache, a headache, dizziness, or other symptoms, which only appear on weekdays and often disappear soon after the school bus has passed by. When these complaints start, they will usually seem real and serious to you. Over time, as they are repeated and the child misses more and more days of school, you and your physician should consider the possibility that these complaints really stem from his wish to avoid school.

In younger children, "school phobia" is generally a specialized form of separation difficulty: your child fears that something will happen to you while he is away. (See chapter 31.) Often parents inadvertently collude in the problem by not being firm and direct when insisting that their child go to school. You need not only consult your pediatrician about this problem, but also to participate actively in resolving it.

For older children, school phobia usually has its roots in academic problems, social challenges, or bullying. (See chapter 23.) Should serious and long-lasting symptoms arise from these anxieties, you must address both the symptoms and their underlying cause. (For more on such stress, see page 324.)

Illness in the Family

The illness or sudden disability of a close family member may seriously upset a physically healthy child. Seeing a parent become ill is very frightening for a child even up to adolescence: it means that an adult on whom he has depended all his life so far for support, nurture, and protection has lost the power to provide for him. This is especially so for a young, and thus more dependent, child, and even a minor illness such as a cold may worry her. She may repeatedly ask her ailing parent whether he or she is all right or feeling well yet. The child's behavior may change radically — often for the better — as though she feels that her actions or thoughts have somehow caused the parent's illness. When a major illness — cancer or a heart attack, say — throws off a family's routines and relationships, the child may become depressed and regress in key areas, such as sleeping, eating, or toilet training.

Do your best to be honest with your children about your condition. Before you sit down to explain an illness, consider what each child has proven developmentally able to understand and what concerns he or she is likely to have. Not simply whether Daddy might die, but who will coach the soccer team next fall? And is the disease catching? And why can't the doctor fix it? It helps children to include them in activities relating to the parent's health when they are able to understand and cope with them. In addition, the well parent — though already stressed to the maximum — should give each child as much attention as possible.

A child's reaction is more complicated when a sibling is the ill or disabled person. In most families, the sick child will get more attention — perhaps for just a while, perhaps for life. The well child may become jealous. Once again, a child's behavior may alter, but now with negative acting-out. The child may declare that she is angry at or jealous of the ill child and may even wish that she were the sick one. If this makes you angry, try not to express your feeling or punish her. Try instead to understand where this child's feelings are coming from, and find a way to sympathize with her and yet move her away from her anger to some positive attitude toward her sister or brother. (For more on sibling relationships, see chapter 30.)

Going to the Hospital

The prospect of going to a hospital and staying there as a patient can make a child, as it does adults, very anxious. In the first place, it separates the child from her parents for long and critical periods — sometimes the first such separation in her young life. Before the 1950s, this separation was even more profound. Young patients in hospitals were allowed visits from their parents for only brief periods each day or, in some places, only once a week. The fact that children often cried after their parents' visit was cited as evidence that such visits were hard on them and should remain limited. Also, the system benefited the hospital staff, since many children became so depressed that they caused little trouble on the wards, and nurses and physicians seldom had to deal with worried and inquisitive parents. The system was, however, terrible for children. Studies showed that it not only severely compromised the long-term psychological health of young patients but also slowed their physical recovery from illness or accident.

Today all major children's hospitals and hospital units provide for constant parent attendance, including facilities for family members to sleep over. They also have playrooms with child-care personnel who try to accommodate each child's age-appropriate needs. Despite these improvements, it is critical for you to arrange to be at the bedside of your hospitalized child as much as possible. The stress of whatever illness or accident sends your child to the hospital increases his need for physical and emotional caring. The technology of an intensive care unit — beeping, buzzing, and blinking — can make him even more anxious. And sometimes encountering other youngsters who are very sick is even more disturbing to a child than his own physical condition. As for a toddler, who is already struggling with the issue of separation at home, being apart from her parents in a hospital only enhances her normal separation fears. Since this situation can create permanent psychological problems, it is vital for at least one parent to stay with the young child in the hospital.

A different kind of separation problem arises when parents withdraw from a child because of guilt, stress, or the seriousness of her condition. Such withdrawal is easier when a child is in the hospital, away from home and under the care of other people. Although a parent may not even pull away consciously, the child is nevertheless very sensitive to such changes. Even if the parent remains by her side, the child may well perceive the emotional distancing as more painful than physical separation. Parents also change their parenting styles when a child becomes ill — as often they must, in order to look after one child in the hospital and other children at home, or because of some other necessity. One or the other parent is home more often or at unusual times, or the parents may change or relax the usual household routines and rules. Since such changes can upset the sick child returning home from the hospital, you should acknowledge them and explain why things have to be different for a while.

One aspect of life in a hospital that children find difficult is the forced inactivity. For toddlers and preschoolers to be confined to bed can be extremely frustrating, especially if they are in traction or another restraint or forbidden to touch stitches. Try to distract your child by reading stories, playing video games or cards, watching television together, and so on. Also, being pushed back into a state of dependency can be frustrating for a child who is old enough to be working on being independent of his parents and other caregivers. Here again, by providing intellectual and social stimulation, you can help your physically restrained child feel better about himself.

Several anxieties usually beset the child who is about to undergo surgery or another hospital procedure. A child under the age of five usually worries the most about being separated from her family and in a strange environment. The older a child is, the more he will worry about being anesthetized and the operation itself. Young patients also worry about pain and "needles" in general. In children from four to six years old, these anxieties often produce physical symptoms: nausea, dizziness, having to go to the bathroom frequently, and so on. While you and your child may both connect such difficulties to the problem that brought her to the hospital and thus think it is getting worse, this is not necessarily so. You will find that calming your child's worry about the surgery will usually relieve the symptoms. A child from about six to ten years old is less likely to show her anxieties physically. She may deny the extent of the problem she faces as a way to maintain her sense of control and express her fears through fantasies of death and mutilation. However disturbing to you, these are not abnormal when a child is under such stress.

Most pediatricians and hospitals try to minimize the anxiety a child feels before surgery. If she trusts her parents and pediatrician enough to agree with their decision about an operation, the procedure usually goes more smoothly and successfully. Often, therefore, the doctor tries to explain the procedure, including what parts of her body (if any) will hurt. A nurse can describe everything the child will experience: the food (or lack of it) that day, what the anesthesia will feel like, when she will probably go to sleep, where she will wake up, and so on. Tell your child about a prospective surgery as close to its date as possible to minimize the time he has to wait for it and worry. Also, arrange for your child to return quickly to surroundings he finds familiar and the toys and people he likes to play with. A child who is not overanxious about an operation will need less medication before it and usually enjoys a smoother recovery afterwards.

Serious Injury

While not as common as a cold, significant injury — cuts, sprains, burns, head injuries, and more — is also a hazard you should be prepared for. In one study of nearly 5,000 infants, almost 9 percent of them suffered an injury that required medical care in their first year, usually while they were learning to walk. Other researchers who followed all children born in a certain period have consistently found that about half of this random sample has a memorable accident before they are five. At every age, boys are more likely to be injured than girls and more likely to suffer serious injuries. A child who is aggressive or very active also seems more likely to be injured. Fortunately, few childhood injuries have long-lasting physical effects. Children who do, however, suffer serious injury — broken bones, burns, and concussions, for instance — can have difficult physical and psychological problems. Accidents are, in fact, the biggest cause of disability and death for children in this country — far more destructive than diseases.

A child is as anxious about going to the hospital for an injury as for an illness. Although dealing with your child's emotions as she recovers may seem like just one more thing to worry about in a difficult time, the benefits of this attention and care go beyond simply making your child more comfortable. As doctors consistently see, they actually speed up the healing process and make for a more successful outcome.

Sometimes, as in an automobile accident or house fire, one or both parents are injured at the same time as their child. At other times, parents are physically well but depressed and perhaps mourning other losses. It only adds to your family's difficulties if you feel guilty about your child's injuries, thinking that you could or should have prevented them — especially when the child is very young. If you act ashamed or defensive, or try to deny the seriousness of the problem, you may unintentionally — as we noted earlier — distance yourself from your child. Not only does this not comfort him, but it may add to his desolation. In such a difficult period, you and other adults close to you must often make a superhuman effort to maintain a calm, giving attitude and stay close to everyone in the family.

After an accident, both an injured child and his family pass through several familiar psychological stages. The initial shock gives way to feelings of denial and panic. Often anger, resentment, and protest follow. The child may regress to a less mature state and refuse to cooperate with the doctor's treatment. After a period of mourning for what they have lost, the child and family usually manage to adjust to the new reality and move on. (If the accident has actually taken someone's life, the mourning and adjustment are likely to take longer or to be more widespread, as we discuss in chapter 35.) You and other adults in the family need to keep these stages in mind during what can be a difficult and frustrating recovery.

Although a child may not be able to express all her thoughts and questions about an injury, she usually understands how serious it is for her and its likely consequences. She knows very well that she cannot move her arms without pain or cannot see or that she feels dizzy all the time. And she knows how such conditions are impairing her regular activities. She worries about what she will be able to do in the future and, after peer relationships become important, about how her friends will react to her new condition. After a serious injury, as with illness, be honest with your child and tell her as much about it as she is developmentally ready to understand. Help her to talk through her concerns.

Use your knowledge of how your child thinks and expresses herself to help her communicate with her doctors.

A child who has suffered an injury often regresses to an earlier phase of development, to when he was cared for more closely, to when he wasn't hurt. For example, after an accident or a serious illness, a young child who is becoming or has just become toilet trained may well lose that skill. He may also regress in his eating habits. Though regression is in some ways self-protective, a child does not really like to lose any of her hard-earned control over her body. Even a small child fears and mistrusts events that turn him back into a helpless baby. Having already lost control of some part of his body or life because of the accident, such a child now sees something else "going wrong." Regression becomes another thing to worry about. Assure your child that the loss of skill is temporary and that he is still a big boy and will be able to keep growing and maturing as the crisis passes.

Pain is often a difficult issue for injured children because they cannot objectively understand its causes as well as adults sometimes can. Children often perceive pain as punishment for having done something wrong. This perception is only exacerbated if a child already feels guilty, rightly or wrongly, about having somehow caused her injury. Often, as in surgery, doctors must provoke discomfort in order to relieve worse pain. To a child, both types of pain feel the same. She is not likely to understand why either is occurring, and usually her parents — not she —

make the decision to go ahead with the procedure. Thus, remain aware of your child's possible psychological reactions to the pain of an injury or treatment, and comfort her both physically and emotionally.

The Special Problems of Burns and Head Injuries

Children have special psychological problems after burns and head injuries. In respect to the first, many children who suffer a serious burn do so through their own actions: one started the fire, accidentally or on purpose, or went too near something dangerously hot. The child may have known he was taking an unwarranted risk, or may have been injured in a brief moment when his parent was not close by. Even if a burn is entirely accidental, young children may feel guilty about it. This perception of deserving the burn can affect how much a child feels he deserves to recover from it. Parents can also be wrestling with guilt after a child is burned, because they feel either negligent or that they deliberately caused the burn, as is the case with a minority of children's burns.

One unusual aspect of a burn injury is that, since the burned person's nerve endings are often destroyed, he feels less pain or discomfort at first. The family can thus easily underestimate the damage a child has suffered until sensation returns, as it soon does, and, with it, pain. Also, when the child's dressings are removed, the damage and scarring can be a great shock. All these factors: pain, the trauma of the fire, the shock of seeing the damage, and the child's feeling of guilt can drain a child's energy. A child who has suffered a burn often becomes irritable, panicky, and uncooperative, dreading and resisting each change of bandages. In this situation, try hard to remain close to your child and to encourage him to let the doctors and nurses give him the best possible care.

Injuries and burns to the face can leave prominent scars. Other accidents can produce damage to or even loss of a limb, or cause a person to lose control of parts of her body. Scars, and these drastic injuries and their effects, can give a child a troubling body image of herself. After all, it was not long ago that, as an infant, she realized how all her body parts fit together and belonged to her. Generally, the success of a child's psychological recovery from such an injury depends not so much on the severity of her burn or wound as on the visibility of its effects and how well her friends and classmates support her return to their regular play and schoolwork.

Head injuries that result in a concussion are all too common among children, especially those who ride bicycles or roller skate without a helmet. Like adults, they often suffer a headache after such an injury. But children seem more likely also to have psychological symptoms, including anxiety, disturbed sleep, irritability, withdrawal, overactivity, and impaired attention. Researchers debate whether people who suffer a serious head injury in childhood are at an increased risk of psychiatric symptoms later in life. The evidence is ambiguous because children who come from an unstable family situation are more likely to suffer from all kinds of injury, to have trouble recovering after one, and to display symptoms. Whatever the connection, avoid the chance of such difficulties by making sure your child's head is well protected.

Post-Traumatic Stress Disorder in Children

Although you try to keep your children safe, to protect them from overwhelming trauma, bad luck may in a moment cancel out your efforts. A child may be in an automobile crash or other accident, for instance, or — in rare cases — witness violent or otherwise disturbing acts. Such an experience can traumatize a child, destroying many of her assumptions about the safety of her world. As a result, a child may come to view herself as less capable, to fear her environment, and to fear the future. She may feel depressed and behave in disturbing ways. And, like an adult, a child may reexperience such a stressful event for weeks, months, and even years afterward. This psychological aftermath, which goes beyond a person's usual reactions to normal stress (see page 324), is called post-traumatic stress disorder (PTSD).

Our understanding of the biology of PTSD in children is still being refined. Nonetheless, we know that in some ways the mechanisms are similar to those in adults whose normal stress response systems, which alert you to danger and help you respond quickly, are overwhelmed by emotional trauma. In essence, the trauma has lowered an individual's "danger threshold," so that the person fears many more experiences than before and is constantly on the alert. With sufficiently early and careful help, children (and adults) can recover from PTSD, but the recovery process can be long. They are helped by a mental-health clinician who can provide psychotherapy, sometimes combined with medication.

A child with PTSD may become hypervigilant about the possibility of something bad happening to her or her family. She may thus seem excessively irritable and respond with exaggerated fear to loud noises, shouts, or other startling sounds. After the trauma, a child may have difficulty going to sleep, wake at night with bad dreams, or be unable to sleep in his own bed. He may develop partial memory loss. He may regress to an earlier developmental stage: for instance, a preschooler can, long after having been toilet trained, begin to wet the bed or lose bladder control during the day. A child need not develop all of these responses, however, to be classified as having PTSD.

Other responses to trauma differ according to a child's age and personality. Preschoolers cling to their parents, afraid to let either one go out of sight. A joyful, carefree three-year-old may suddenly become somber or irritable and out of control. A previously imaginative young child may play over and over in an urgent, joyless way some aspect of the traumatic event. While you may worry that such dwelling on something frightening will only make your young child feel worse, play is (as we discuss in chapter 16) one avenue children have for working out what is bothering them. They need to play their game — however hearing it over and over may trouble you — about crashing cars or bad robbers or when the policemen came.

An early school-age child who has developed PTSD may start to act helpless, casting his fear onto people and events unrelated to the traumatic event. He may not be able to speak directly about what is bothering him; indeed, some children stop speaking altogether. Like an adult with PTSD, a child may feel the whole emotional experience return when something reminds her of it: for example, getting back into the car after an accident, passing the place it occurred, or even hearing a siren. School-age children may also have trouble concentrating on their class work. Some may even feel guilty about their continuing emotional distress. A child can also feel guilty for what he perceives as his role in the incident or even for the fact that, while friends or relatives were hurt, he was not.

Not all children exposed to severe trauma develop PTSD. The likelihood of this complication varies not only with a child's age but also with many other factors in one's life. For example, a child is at much greater risk when his parents were also involved in the traumatic event and were themselves overwhelmed and, at least temporarily, unable to help him. Conversely, a youngster is less vulnerable and often does not develop PTSD when her parents were able to protect her or, at least, remained in control during the emergency. A child who has usually been relatively anxious or sensitive about unsettling events is more likely than another to be overwhelmed by trauma. Children whose earlier experiences have been very stressful — as in abuse, neglect, or long and chronic illness with hospitalizations — are also more vulnerable.

Chronic Conditions

Some children are born with a physically disabling condition such as cerebral palsy, blindness, hearing deficit, and so on. Others may develop any of many genetically determined chronic diseases, such as diabetes and cystic fibrosis, at any time during childhood. Unlike other illnesses, where you have an acute crisis to deal with and then dismiss once it is over, these go on for the child's entire life. Any of them is a blow to your hopes for a completely normal child, as you gradually understand that she will have to spend her life using extra energies and strategies to get around the effects of her condition. While the specifics of these diseases and the remedies involved are beyond the province of this book, we can point out the issues that are common to all of them and that parents of such a child must deal with.

As we said in chapter 5, the arrival of a child with a birth defect is likely to be a blow to a parent's own ego and self-image. Many such parents will go into psychological mourning for the loss of their "other child," the normal one who was never born. This can lead to depression and even, in some cases, to rejection of the actual child. Some parents will struggle with these feelings at different levels of awareness for the rest of their lives. But most parents will, with or without help, fight through the depression and come to value their new child for his or her own unique qualities. Sorting out these feelings as early as possible is essential if you are to make sound judgments and plans to meet your child's needs. For almost any congenital or genetic condition, the earlier the appropriate treatment begins, the more effective it is in easing the long-term complications of the condition.

Once you have recovered from the initial impact of learning that your baby has a disability, you can begin to make effective plans with your doctors for her immediate and long-term care. Parents are often valuable advocates for their child's special needs. Adjusting to the new reality will not be instantaneous. It takes time — days, weeks, months — depending on the individual parents and the kind of help and advice they receive from physicians, nurses, and other health-care providers. The support that a mother and father can give each other and receive from their extended families is crucial. The birth of such a special child can put an enormous strain on the relationship between husband and wife, and you need to acknowledge and address this as openly as possible. Raising such a child actually brings some couples closer together.

When a child develops a chronic disease after infancy, she and her family face a somewhat different set of issues. In this case, the parents must bid farewell not to an imaginary child, but to the perfection and good health of the child they know and love. Of course, by that age the child has developed her own personality. Her parents know that she is more than perfect: she is herself. Their sadness focuses on the fact that the health of someone they love deeply is going to be severely compromised for the rest of her life. Fortunately, a child past infancy has usually developed both a web of relationships with family members and perhaps friends and some psychological resilience. However much her chronic condition may force her to readjust her daily habits and her image of herself, that adjustment has the best chance of success if you and your partner continue to treat her as the same person you have always loved.

If your child develops a chronic condition, join the appropriate group and take advantage of the resources it offers. Work with your schools and community programs to find the widest range of opportunities for your child, just as you would for a child without a chronic condition. American culture tends to treat children struggling with chronic health problems as noble and heroic. But sickness does not automatically confer either quality on parent or child. There will be many times when you and your child will be far from being either heroic or noble. But if you are patient and caring, you will find that both you and your child have real strengths. These not only help him cope with the disability but expand your own appreciation of one another.

CHAPTER 33

Children's Mental Health Problems

A child's mental disturbance is probably one of the most painful experiences any parent can have. Here, the discrepancy between what you have imagined for your child and her actuality is profound. It strikes at all your daydreams for her and may destroy them all. Moreover, all the fine things you have imagined for your child can make it hard for you to absorb this disturbing new reality. And, even once you recognize it, it is still a mystery — one with no ready solution and one that carries a social stigma.

Most parents have a vision in which their child starts out healthy and then glides blithely through childhood. But such a child is rare. Just as your child will have colds, growing pains, accidents, and other physical problems, so too will he have emotional or behavioral ones: some mild and transient; some painful, even frightening.

That this is so is not really surprising. A child's mind and body are among the most complex phenomena in the universe. And there are bound to be small, and sometimes large, glitches in the way they work: in the basic equipment, in the hardwiring of circuits in the brain, in the programming and unfolding of behavior during the first years of life. Likewise, no matter how hard you may try to avoid them, there will be mishaps, large and small, in your child's environment: the death or serious illness of a close family member, divorce, the birth of a sibling, family strife, or the abrasiveness of peers. These situations, and other disruptions in a child's life, can be the source of trauma, causing varying degrees of anxiety and fear.

Children differ greatly in their resilience, in the ability to deal with stress and to integrate and "bounce back" from anxiety and fear. This inborn ability is enhanced if a child has good intellectual abilities, physical health, artistic and athletic talents, religious beliefs, and the help of consistent and thoughtful parents and of other protective adults.

It is also enhanced by the many psychological and often unconscious methods that the average youngster has, even from the first months of life, for defending himself against anxiety. An infant who is frightened by a scary face will defend himself by looking away. An older child may simply pretend a frightening person is not there or will distract herself with happier thoughts. A child who is homesick at camp may daydream about being at Sunday brunch with his parents or playing cards with his brother. A twelve-year-old who is anxious about an upcoming surgical operation may simply refuse to talk about it and try to fool herself that the day will not come. A fourteen-year-old who is anxious about sexual feelings may become preoccupied with religion — going to confession, praying, and being overscrupulous about small sins — to avoid thinking about these new temptations.

Psychological defenses are useful and necessary. Just as the immune system protects both adults and children from harmful bacteria, psychological defenses allow them to deal with the inevitable small setbacks in life (hurt feelings, fright, disappointment, and rejection) and to recover from major trauma (such as accident or divorce). Psychological defenses include exercising imagination and humor, taking some kind of action instead of remaining passive, denying danger, intellectualizing, ritualizing, and diverting one's thoughts. Thus, when a child seems to be so overwhelmed by worry — say, by the illness of his grandmother — as to be unable to function properly (for example, he is unable to do schoolwork or sleep at night), you might enlist one of these psychological processes to help him cope. Thus, for instance, offer him the chance to divert his

thoughts by taking him out to a movie. Just as one's immune system can go out of control, however, a child's defenses, especially denial or intellectualizing, may do so, too. These may become so entrenched that they prevent her from confronting and dealing with real problems. A child facing an intimidating examination, for example, may, instead of preparing for it, pretend that she has mastered the subject and that everything is fine. It will take all your tact and skill to help her to see reality, and you may even need to call in a therapist.

Emotional and behavioral problems have recognizable patterns, but each child's difficulties are unique. They reflect his own life story — his strengths and vulnerabilities, his history of burdens and gifts. Thus, children respond to similar traumas in very different ways. For one child, the birth of a sibling is a mild annoyance or even an exciting opportunity. For another, it is a moment of crisis during which he starts to feel betrayed and angry. (See chapter 30.) During divorce, some children and adolescents find a way of navigating between their two parents and are able to sustain their relationships with both. For others, the marital stresses and arguments that precede divorce and the final breakup are an overwhelming betrayal of their trust in one or both parents. They may become angry, depressed, and inattentive. They may fail in school or take risky, destructive actions outside it. (See chapter 34.)

Part of healthy development is a child's growing ability to understand what upsets her — to recognize her internal anxieties and stresses and to use this information to guide her thoughts and behavior. And helping your child understand normal difficulties and the occasional serious upsets; understand that painful feelings are part of life; and see their connection with events, hopes, desires, and relationships is an important part of parenting. Remember that even children who seem remarkably blessed, the "golden boys and girls," may be worried under the surface. At times they may feel more threatened and bothered than they would like others to know, even more than they know themselves. When a real crisis occurs for such a child, his facade may crumble quickly. Children who are more secure allow others to see that they are upset. They can reach out for help and can cope with their problems; they don't feel it is necessary to push them aside.

During the school years, about one child in eight or ten will have a behavioral, psychiatric, or developmental difficulty. These include learning problems, overactivity, depression, phobias, eating difficulties, and a host of other types of worries and dysfunctions. These problems may last a short time, fading as quickly as they emerged, or they may interfere with learning, friendships, and personal happiness. They can erode self-esteem, undermine a child's ability to achieve, and may ultimately require psychiatric help.

For a child whose troubles are not lasting or debilitating, consistent, thoughtful, calm care will help her develop the emotional skills to move through these and other, future difficulties. For others whose problems are

more troubling, however, loving care and time are not enough. Their emotional problems persist for months or years, interfering with life at home or in school. This is mental illness — and it is an illness. It causes pain and suffering to both child and family and can threaten a child's life as severely as some medical conditions. And as with some medical conditions, people in the various generations of a family seem to be vulnerable to certain mental illnesses — schizophrenia, autism, attentional problems, depression, tic syndromes — and much research on the genetic factor in mental illness is now going on. The current consensus is that a disorder probably arises when a child with a specific genetic vulnerability is so seriously disturbed by either ongoing events or by a particular one that occurs that she is unable to integrate them. As a result, her emotional control becomes seriously disorganized: she loses the ability to regulate her behavior appropriately and her parents are not able to handle her without psychiatric help.

Mental illness is not a parent's fault, but parents can alleviate or exacerbate it depending on their response to their child. When a child's behavior changes sharply, parents often do not know what to do: whether to ignore it, to care for the child in a special way, or to scold him or her. They wonder whether the behavior is a symptom of a serious problem. If they suspect that it may be due to a mental illness or disorder, they may feel that shows that they are bad parents. Because of this feeling, which is enhanced by the undeserved stigma attached to mental illness, they may hesitate to acknowledge the problem and get help for their child.

Since mental disturbances, both great and small, are still something of a mystery, having a child with one is not only distressing but frustrating to parents. In this chapter we aim to give you some insight into children's mental problems. We will talk about how to recognize the symptoms of developmental disorders that your child may develop in preschool and in school, how to find help for your child, and how to deal with your own feelings.

Recognizing Symptoms of Disturbance

You should expect some common problems as your children grow: temper tantrums for two-year-olds, separation worries on entering day care, a period of bed-wetting after an upsetting event like a bad accident, sassy arguments when there is a lot of pressure at school, or preoccupation with appearance in adolescence. Several factors make it hard to know whether these problems are symptoms of serious disturbance. For example, about 25 percent of all mothers of a four-year-old boy will think that he is overly active. But we must ask, overly active compared with what group? And when? Preschoolers do present a tiring combination of energy, mobility, and verbosity. Almost every child will become annoyingly overactive on a long car ride. Since some families are much more tolerant than

others of an ebullient child's incessant questioning, chatter, and fidgeting, it is not possible to zero in on exactly how much activity in a four-year-old is too much and how much may reflect a real disturbance.

Another factor that makes it difficult to judge a child's mental health is her parents' expectations of what she should be like. A suddenly rambunctious daughter may not match the quiet, introspective girl you have lived with for years. Common quirks and difficulties may appear ominous because they seem to spoil your hopes for perfect offspring.

Some symptoms reflect mild interferences with your child's healthy functioning and adaptation to stress, and often he can right himself with the help of his parent's patience. When a problem arises gradually and fades over a week or two, most parents recognize that it is similar to the nervous stomachaches and moods of their own childhood (and those they may still have, from time to time). Children have a right to their symptoms and bad periods. Pediatricians often prescribe "tincture of time" for minor illnesses, giving a child a day or two for his physical resiliency and immune system to bring him back to health. Similarly, by remaining calm, affectionate, and engaged, without too much personal distress, you can give your child time for her emotions to settle down. For a beloved parent to make a big deal about something can reinforce its seriousness in a child's mind, thus increasing his anxiety level.

Most problems that children experience are transient: they reflect a period of transition or increased stress or are just part of the normal difficulties of life. For example, about 10 percent of all children exhibit some sort of nervous habit (tics, nail biting, nose picking) at some point in the first years of school. A child can have trouble falling asleep, get up during the night, wake too early and get into his parents' bed, then resist getting out of his own bed — all of these problems are common. Everyone has good and bad days, good and bad periods. A child can become clingy and immature for no apparent reason, and then a surge in maturation will make him seem much better put together. Children become picky eaters and then start eating well. A sweet boy may start to lie about things in the first grade, covering up mistakes with wild excuses. For several nights a girl may awaken with nightmares and then become a good sleeper, or the other way around. Experienced parents, who are not likely to feel particularly worried by such a symptom, provide normal, affectionate care. They try to resist making too much of a child's bad behavior or getting too worked up when he is anxious. Often this continuity of thoughtful, calm care is exactly the medicine the child needs to develop the skills to move through a difficult period.

Symptoms of children's mental illness are as varied and complex as is their normal development. (For more on understanding development, see chapter 7.) Some symptoms show up, in fact, in delayed development. For example, a child may speak much later than normal or be slower in her intellectual development. Other symptoms are reflected in patterns of regulation or organization, such as when a child has trouble staying still, paying attention, or achieving normal sleep patterns. Difficulty in the normal unfolding of a basic competence, such as the ability to form loving, reciprocal social relations, is another type of indicator.

As we discussed earlier, lines of development are useful in charting how a child is doing compared with other children. They also suggest the many different, concurrent processes that take place within a child as she grows and the range of psychiatric, developmental, and emotional problems she may face. We think that there are inborn forces, both biological and neurological, that help keep developmental lines in motion. When a child seems stuck or derailed, or when development slows down or becomes distorted, therapists can work with him and his parents to identify what may be impeding or interfering with his functioning. They will do a "developmental diagnosis" to help a family understand when and why a problem may emerge and to learn how to help a child regain the momentum he needs to move ahead along a pathway. For most children, once these impediments are recognized and dealt with, the child's normal, inborn maturational forces will help him move back into a healthier course of development.

For young children, periods of stress and symptoms tend to affect many areas of functioning, and the developmental difficulties of very young children are often global. They may have physical problems (lack of growth, diarrhea, stomach pains) alongside emotional difficulties (irritability, anxiety, temper outbursts). As children grow older, their problems usually become specifically localized to one area: bodily functions, emotions, behavior, or thinking. An older child may become depressed or overly excitable; steal, lie, and disobey authority; or be frightened by new situations, avoid groups, and generally feel overwhelmed. A child may have trouble with reading or math, or simply dawdle, unable to attend to schoolwork or homework.

Some children's emotional problems are mostly inwardly focused: they are sad, moody, anxious, and unable to enjoy life's pleasures. Others are mostly outward: they disrupt family life by being overactive, impulsive, and disobedient. Or a child's problems cut across their inner and outer worlds, including feelings and thoughts as well as behavior: they feel terrible and are confused about what they are doing and thinking, and as a result, they create terror in those around them.

When parents recognize that their child's symptoms are serious and suspect that she has crossed the line from transient upset to persistent distress, they usually begin to worry. Although their pediatrician may reassure them that everything is fine, parents may remain troubled by what they see in their child at home. They may even feel panic and dread and may not know where to turn. They may hesitate for months or years before they find suitable help to diagnose and suggest treatment for their child. If your child's problems seem serious and are protracted, listen to your worries and seek help as soon as possible from a mental health professional.

Major disturbances include serious attention deficit hyperactivity disorder (ADHD), autism, Tourette's syndrome, obsessive-compulsive disorder, and depression, all of which we discuss later. In the course of evaluating an individual child's problems, those of us who treat children do not like to use diagnostic labels too early, but prefer to wait and see how things unfold. There comes a moment, however, when a child's difficulties crystallize in a persistent pattern of symptoms, and a specific diagnosis can help guide treatment. At such times, the use of a diagnostic term is not labeling a child invidiously, but is a way to help explain his troubles to him, his family, teachers, and other people. Some children even find comfort in knowing that there is a name for what is bothering them and that other people have undergone and survived the same difficulties.

Developmental Disturbances

Small problems are commonly part of normal physical and behavioral development. At least 5 percent of children are born with some physical birth defect, usually quite mild, such as a birthmark, an extra nipple, or a skin tab on an ear or finger. There may also be small anomalies in the development of a baby's nervous system, anomalies that can place a child at risk for common behavioral, learning, or emotional difficulties. The major disorders of development result from impairment in the unfolding of such basic competencies as social relations, language, and intellectual skills.

When things go well, a baby naturally smiles and looks at her mother and father. She seems to be prewired to be socially engaged and engaging. But there are babies who, from the first months of life, seem apathetic and hard to engage, turn away or look through their parents, and fail to warm up. These babies become a greater worry for parents if they reach nine or twelve months and clearly seem to lag behind more outgoing children. You may worry that your child is deaf and ask your pediatrician whether something is wrong. Sometimes a baby may indeed have trouble with her hearing, other children may just be normally quiet, and still others may already be showing a major developmental disorder.

Children with mental retardation — or, as we now also call it, intellectual disability — are sometimes identified at birth because of associated physical problems or signs. For instance, in the newborn nursery, you can recognize the distinctive facial appearance of babies with Down syndrome; their condition is then confirmed by chromosome tests. Other intellectual disabilities are diagnosed by laboratory tests performed on tissues from all newborns, such as PKU (an inborn error of metabolism that can be mitigated by a special diet) or hypothyroidism (low levels of thyroid hormone). Children who are born very premature and quite small are at high risk for neurological problems in their first months; they may have bleeding in

the brain because of their fragile blood vessels or may develop breathing problems. These medical problems also place a child at risk later for intellectual disability; but many very small infants, even with such difficulties, go on to develop well — especially if they go home to well-functioning and facilitating families. Yet other forms of intellectual disability become apparent to families only during the first months or years of life, as a child shows delays in achieving such skills as walking and speaking.

The majority of children with intellectual disabilities are only mildly slower than typical children in their language, abstract thinking, and motor skills. If an average IQ is about 100, these children may have IQs in the 60s and similarly slow development in adaptive skills (self-care, communication, socialization). Only a small percentage of children with mental retardation have clearly defined biological or organic causes for their problems and function in the more severely retarded range with IQs in the 30s and 40s. (For more on intelligence tests, see chapter 20.)

The ultimate level of independence and adaptation that any child with retardation achieves depends a great deal on the child's experience, not just on inborn brain capacity. Loving acceptance in the family, engagement with peers and others in the community, suitable education, and opportunities for recreation and achievement make enormous differences in their lives. Indeed, the quality of an intellectually disabled child's social life, motivation, and self-esteem may make as much or more difference in life than would ten or fifteen points on an IQ test.

The most serious disorder of development is autism, a condition that was identified more than fifty years ago and that has since been seen throughout the world in every racial group and social class. Autistic children have pervasive difficulties in every sphere of development, particularly in social relations and communication. Many autistic children are also intellectually handicapped. About half never speak. These children have a range of unusual behaviors, such as a stereotypic flapping motion, and they find it difficult to play imaginatively. (See "Understanding Autism," pages 126–127.) In its full-blown form, autism is relatively uncommon, affecting perhaps one child in a thousand. But milder developmental disorders produce some of the same types of dysfunction in social relations and language; and perhaps one child in two hundred may have autistic-like problems. Autism is a biologically based developmental disorder; it is not caused by a child's upbringing. Nonetheless, a child's experiences in her family, special education, and therapeutic treatments may, as with intellectual disabilities, make a great difference in the outcome.

The most frequent developmental disorders are probably those of language and communication. Some children speak earlier than others, and some speak abnormally late. Children who are still not speaking by the age of two and a half deserve thorough evaluation and treatment. At times, such slow development of speech is the result of a sensory problem, such as deafness or recurrent middle ear infections, or being deprived of opportunities to engage in talking. For most children, the cause of delayed speech is not known.

Problems of the Preschool and School Years

Three-year-old children are imaginative, outgoing, and ebullient; they are fun to watch at play and eager to have you join as a partner in the game. They like snacks, horseback rides, swinging, balloons, and running in the park. They help plant flowers in the spring and wrap presents at Christmas. They cuddle at bedtime and look at the pictures as you read a story. At this age, they remember what they did yesterday and look forward to tomorrow's trip to the bakery or the zoo. They understand, or at least seem to, virtually everything you say to them, and they talk about life in sentences and short paragraphs.

But there can be problems in each of these areas of emotional, intellectual, and physical achievement. A three-year-old can worry constantly. Or a child can be overactive, inattentive, and disruptive. Another can resist playing with other children or not be able to make friends. Sometimes a child may have trouble recounting her experiences, planning, or waiting. There are many different diagnostic labels for these troubles. A child with the diagnosis of attention deficit hyperactivity disorder (ADHD) is overactive, inattentive, and impulsive. A child with an anxiety disorder is, beyond the ordinary fears of this age (see pages 321–325), excessively frightened of animals, spiders, new situations, new people, trying things out, being on his own, and possibly much more. A child who is diagnosed as having oppositional disorder disagrees with his parents about everything, fights back, and resists accepting the normal rules of social life.

The behavioral signs of emotional or psychological difficulty in an older child include severe temper tantrums, severe aggressiveness or hyperactivity, the inability to make friends, fire setting, lying and stealing, inappropriate sexual activity, poor school behavior and/or achievement, substance abuse, withdrawn or isolated behavior, excessive preoccupation with fantasy to the exclusion of normal social behavior, refusal to go to school, excessive fears, lack of motivation or decreased enjoyment of activities, self-mutilation, and suicidal ideas or suicide attempts. In the school years, emotional problems may manifest themselves as academic difficulties. Sometimes, for example, a student who has learning disabilities in the areas of reading (dyslexia), spelling, or arithmetic has other symptoms as well, such as ADHD.

When a child has trouble in school and fails to keep up with his peers, he becomes at risk for developing other behavioral or emotional problems. He may come to suffer from low self-esteem, feeling worthless and dumb, or depression and continual worrying. He may avoid school or act out to mask or distract himself from his troubles. (For more on how schools treat learning disabilities, see pages 285–294.) If a child's behavior changes sharply, or you wonder whether her development is normal, consult your pediatrician. If your doctor identifies a problem, he may recommend further evaluation with a mental health professional to clarify its nature and severity and decide whether the child needs psychological or educational help.

Tics

Tics are common in childhood, especially in the second and third grades. A tic can be eye blinking, nose puckering, grimacing, or other small, fast muscular contractions. A tic

seems to a young child to just pop out of his body without his being aware of or willing it. Although older children grow aware of these movements, they do not know why they happen. A child will describe a funny feeling, like an itch, in a part of her body — for example, tension in the stomach muscles — that she can ease by making a tic movement. Tics generally come and go over a period of weeks to months, and a new tic may replace an old one. For most people, simple childhood tics go away, leaving no trace.

Some children, however, develop many tics of the face and body and may, in addition, start to make little noises or sounds (phonic or vocal tics). These can disturb other students in school and their family at home. Children with the most severe tic problems may have six or ten different types of muscle and vocal tics and emit them many times a minute for most of the day. A child can have a range of ever-changing tics that last for many months — a condition known as Tourette's syndrome. Children diagnosed with this disorder often report that a funny feeling in a part of their body tells them that a tic is about to occur and that the tic then lessens that feeling. Although Tourette's syndrome is visible, and vocal tics can be especially disruptive and embarrassing, some people have managed to do quite well in life with the support of understanding families, teachers, and friends.

Obsessions and Compulsions

Around the age of ten or eleven, children normally enjoy hobbies, collecting, and learning the rules of games. For some children, however, their patterns of organizing ideas and things become excessive and develop into a behavioral, or obsessive-compulsive, disorder. A child with this disorder may compulsively do the same thing over and over, such as washing her hands, lining up toys in her room, or checking to be sure that she has not broken something. The child also begins to display irrational fears, believing, for example, that she will catch AIDS from touching a doorknob. She may spend hours in the shower using up bars of soap, be unable to move through a doorway because she cannot step over the threshold, or be afraid that if she steps on a crack she truly will hurt her mother. She may hoard unnecessary string or paper or feel too worried to throw something away. Eventually this disorder comes to control a child's life. Parents may be forced to help with their child's rituals to keep him from feeling too scared. For example, you may have to wash the silverware over and over to convince your child that it is clean or flush the toilet after he has defecated so that he will not have to touch the handle.

Many children with Tourette's syndrome also have obsessive-compulsive disorder. Both conditions seem to reflect a genetic vulnerability that is transmitted within a family. Although a good deal is known about the interaction between genetic vulnerability and environment that can lead to disorders such as Tourette's or debilitating obsessions and compulsions, we still do not know why some children succumb to them.

Anorexia nervosa is another condition often associated with obsessive-compulsive disorder. Around age fourteen, many girls start to diet because they think they are not as thin or as attractive as they would like to be. Most girls stop dieting when they have lost a few pounds or even before. For a few girls (and, much less often, boys), however, dieting takes over their lives. A girl who develops anorexia is in pursuit of an ideal thinness that makes her starve herself,

THE GENETIC ROLE IN PSYCHIATRIC DISORDERS

For many decades, scientists have known that certain types of medical conditions run in families: arthritis, hypertension, coronary artery disease, baldness, and colon cancer, among others. While being born into such a family — even inheriting some of the specific genes — does not automatically lead to heart disease or cancer, it does increase a person's risks. The search for specific genetic factors that make one vulnerable to a particular illness has been very successful for medical conditions, where new genes are being discovered almost every day. Similarly, the genetic factors have been detected in literally thousands of types of physical birth defects and forms of mental retardation.

Recent international scientific research has also shown familial patterns in some forms of mental illness, such as schizophrenia, autism, attentional problems, depression, and tic syndromes. The study of identical and fraternal twins, for example, has pointed to a genetic factor in certain disorders when it can be shown that identical twins are much more likely to share that disorder than are fraternal twins. Although the search for genes for specific psychiatric problems has not been as successful as that for medical ones, some of the genetic contributions will be likely found within a few years. Most scientists believe that these complex conditions will turn out to result from many different genes.

Because genes do not operate in a vacuum but are expressed in specific environments, another major area of research focuses on the ways in which genetic vulnerability interacts with environmental risks at different periods of development. A disorder probably arises in a child whose specific vulnerability makes him unable to respond normally to a particular environment — or to an event in that environment — at a particular moment in his maturation. Today the most advanced theories for understanding why a child develops a particular mental illness draw upon these ideas of biological and environmental risk as they relate to the strengths and sources of resilience in a particular child and family.

Unfortunately many parents feel excessive worry or guilt about acknowledging that their family is transmitting a particular type of medical or psychiatric problem. Neither feeling is justified. And, however distressing the knowledge, it has several advantages. For one, it may help in family planning. Prospective parents whose families show certain types of physical and medical illness, including forms of mental retardation, can know the risks for some difficulties and even use prenatal diagnosis to find out whether a fetus carries the vulnerability. You can use genetic information to predict the likelihood of your family having a second child with autism or a tic syndrome. There is as yet no type of prenatal diagnosis for a psychiatric disorder, but genetic prenatal tests are likely in the not-too-distant future.

overexercise, or use laxatives to keep her weight down. Sometimes, her restricted eating oscillates with periods in which she overeats and then vomits from anxiety — a related disorder called bulimia. Once a girl develops anorexia, worrisome changes occur in her endocrine system: for example, her menstrual periods stop. Conditions like anorexia and bulimia are complex, and we do not know why the common fad dieting of adolescence becomes, for a few children, a life-threatening illness.

Depression

Since the 1970s, psychologists have recognized that both children and adolescents become depressed. A child feels blue, cannot enjoy normal pleasures like parties and friendships, is tearful, loses weight because he finds no pleasure in eating, has trouble falling or staying asleep, and may think about suicide. During adolescence, perhaps one-quarter of all girls and almost that many boys suffer some depression for periods that usually last a few weeks or months. Depression can, however, become more serious and sustained and lead to a range of other problems: social withdrawal, school failure, and real attempts at suicide. Depression is a painful illness, and suicide may seem to be a way to reduce the suffering.

Surprisingly, even adolescents who are not depressed have thoughts about suicide or actually try to hurt themselves. Thus, depression in adolescence, when a child may be naturally disposed to suicidal thoughts, is especially serious. Sometimes a depressed adolescent will make a serious suicide attempt, especially if he is using alcohol and is impulsive. It is especially serious when a child has access to guns or other means, such as poison, of hurting himself. An adolescent may exhibit no signs of depression, drug abuse, or psychosis, yet try to kill herself because of some trivial misstep or loss, such as getting a grade that does not match her perfectionist standards. Although such a suicide seems like a "death without warning" rather than a consequence of serious mental illness, hidden depression probably plays a role.

Some situations make it more likely that a child will develop a particular type of disturbance. For example, when a child is exposed to violence at home or is abused or neglected, she is likely both to feel anxious and depressed and to be inattentive and impulsive. Children raised in families where there is drug or alcohol abuse, or whose parents are involved in crime, are also at high risk of substance abuse, disruptive behavior, and later crime. Exposure to violence in war and crime-plagued areas may lead children to develop post-traumatic stress disorder (see pages 470–472), in which they become highly sensitive to danger, startle easily, have flashbacks to the violent situation, feel somewhat numb to normal experiences, and are generally distracted and less able to engage in school. (For advice on helping children deal with violence, see chapter 23.)

Seeking Help for Your Child

Your next step, after you have recognized problematic behaviors in your child, is to find help. You need to seek out professionals who are qualified to evaluate your child's behavior and development and to help you assess her need for different forms of therapy, psy-

ANXIOUS LISA

As an infant and toddler, Lisa was so lovely that people stopped on the street to smile at her. She spoke in charming phrases by eighteen months and was a sweet young lady at two years. When her baby brother, Jason, was born, she seemed thrilled and told all her friends about "my baby." She would run to console Jason when he cried and bring a clean diaper when their mother was caring for him. Lisa was especially helpful when Jason had to have minor surgery on his ear for a birth defect. She liked to bring him things to cheer him up but would get very worried whenever she saw a bloody discharge on the bandage that covered his ear for a few weeks.

Lisa was such a competent child that everyone was surprised when, at age three, she became miserable on the first day of nursery school. She clung to her mother, begged to go home, and wept until her eyes were red. Both Mom and Dad accompanied Lisa to nursery school

during the first days, taking turns at being with her, but to no avail. After a few weeks, she had her first toilet accident and wet her pants. Then her parents realized that Lisa was holding back her stools. Her stomach began to hurt, and every two or even three days, she would have a painful bowel movement and so began to fear these events even more.

During the next six months, Lisa's whole personality seemed to shift. Her smile dimmed, and she would grimace or hold her lips tight together. She no longer enjoyed her dollhouse or dressing up in her mother's costume jewelry. She seemed distant and preoccupied. On some nights, she would awaken with a nightmare. Her parents talked with their pediatrician, who found nothing physically wrong and suggested they consult with a child psychiatrist. Dr. Matthews first met Lisa's parents for an extended discussion of her development, current problems, and family. They described Jason's high energy and how he had taken over the family with his tricks and enthusiasm — a dynamo of a boy who looked just like Dad.

Dr. Matthews then spent several sessions with Lisa, who had just turned four. During their first meeting, Lisa's mother stayed and watched quietly, helping to make her daughter feel more comfortable in the doctor's office. At the next sessions, Lisa was able to be alone with Dr. Matthews, but she checked the waiting room a few times to be sure Mom was still there. Dr. Matthews allowed Lisa to take the lead in talking and playing. She spoke softly about being worried. "I have thoughts on my mind" was the longest explanation she offered for her sadness. Among his questions, Dr. Matthews asked about her stomachaches. Lisa said that they were "all better," but the doctor could see her wince with some spasm in her colon. Lisa gravitated to a box of toy figures and cars, then to a dollhouse in which she placed various family members. She worked calmly in her play, bringing Dr. Matthews into the narrative she was creating about a tense moment as mother is making supper and the baby throws up.

Over the next few sessions, Lisa played out various scenarios

chotropic medications, or even hospitalization.

The first step in seeking help for a child is to recognize that she is suffering — that her development has gone off track. Sometimes this is apparent by the end of her first year, but often the earliest symptoms become clear only in retrospect. When a child devel-

---

about family life, the arrival of a new baby, trips to the country, and airplane rides. Often, the "nice family" would have a sudden change of fortune. Someone would get very sick and have to be rushed to the hospital, or a car would crash into the family standing at the side of the road. The little girl in the family — clearly a stand-in for Lisa herself — was sometimes angry and even "wicked." She would throw stuff from the top of the dollhouse. At times, she got hurt: her finger or head was cut, and she was badly injured by a "dynamite bomb." Dr. Matthews would play alongside Lisa and gently ask questions or elaborate the dialogue. Mostly, he wished to convey that she could explore her own feelings and tell the story on her mind in her own way.

After two months, Dr. Matthews felt that he was better able to understand Lisa's inner world and the transformation that occurred in her with the birth of Jason and his surgery. With her effort to be a very good girl, she had covered over her natural angry feelings about sensing she had been displaced in her par-

ents' life. Inside, though, she felt furious, especially with her father, who was thrilled at having a son. "They play basketball," Lisa would say about Jason, both directly and in playing with the toy figures. "They are just alike." When Jason got his "ear cut" — actually, the ear was only slightly reshaped — Lisa thought that maybe her thoughts about hurting him had caused the injury. This thought scared her, though part of her felt that he got what he deserved for displacing her.

Dr. Matthews could appreciate the rage underlying Lisa's depression and anxiety. He felt that she was worried that her anger would hurt her mother, just as it had hurt Jason. Her inside world — her mind and then her body — became filled with frightening fantasies. In simple language, Dr. Matthews shared some of his thoughts through the play. He would comment on the angry feelings in the girl figure and on the fears that Mommy and Daddy would be furious if they knew what she was thinking. He helped Lisa to express her own worries more openly and then actually to share her conviction that

she had to be very good because being angry was so dangerous. They discussed her jealousy and her well-justified annoyance at her father for making such a big deal about Jason.

During these months, Dr. Matthews also met with Lisa's mother and father every other week to talk about their feelings and thoughts. Slowly, they were able to discuss Lisa's experiences in the family. Dad appreciated that he was too interested in Jason and "boy stuff" and that this must have hurt Lisa, whom he adored (as annoying as he had found her during the last months). As the family became more aware of Lisa's feelings, and as she was able to express her needs, anger, and confusion more clearly, they rediscovered their old pleasures in being together. Dad and Lisa went for long walks in the nearby park, talked about the flowers, and had a nice time buying jelly doughnuts. Ten months after she had first played at Dr. Matthews's office, Lisa simply sat down on the toilet one day and had a bowel movement, without thinking much in advance about pain.

ops dramatic symptoms — seeing things that do not exist or hearing voices yelling at her — a family knows, within a few days or weeks, that something is frightfully wrong. At other times, a child's illness is recognized more slowly. A sad, withdrawn child may strike her parents as just quiet, even refreshingly undemanding, until they realize that she is failing in school, tearful, and without friends.

Generally, you can find counselors or psychologists in your child's school who can provide an evaluation. You can also consult your pediatrician, who is medically trained to understand each child as a whole person. When symptoms persist or are impairing a child's behavior, try to get a more specialized evaluation from a child psychologist (a nonmedical specialist in child development and treatment) or a child and adolescent psychiatrist (a medical specialist in the area of children's emotional and psychiatric problems). These professionals have advanced training both in the assessment of normal development and in conducting diagnostic assessments.

A psychiatrist may need a few hours of discussion with you and then with your child, will gather information from his school and his pediatrician, and will conduct specialized psychological and medical tests to carefully evaluate a complicated problem. Understanding a child's difficulties requires a full understanding of his strengths and competencies, as well as the specific symptoms. It means knowing the child's whole life history and current situation at home and in school.

The process of evaluation and discussion is in itself sometimes therapeutic. It may help both your child and your family to understand better what is happening, when problems really arose, and how each family member is reacting. This insight sometimes leads to changes in a child's world: for example, when parents who have been having marital problems realize how their actions — their criticism, scolding, or preoccupation with their own lives — are affecting their child.

Therapy for Children

For children with serious problems, there are many approaches to treatment and care. In psychotherapy, a child can explore his feelings. Other professionals, such as social workers or child psychologists, may offer specific guidance to parents and teachers or teach a child more effective behaviors, such as alternatives to throwing a temper tantrum, or ways to resist a compulsion. Special education can help children with reading and other school problems. (See chapter 20.) Some children can benefit from group therapy, and others may need to be in a special class or school.

Child psychiatrists and psychologists working with a very young child often encourage her to draw pictures of what is on her mind or to play with dolls and other toys they keep in the office. Because of their limited capacity for introspection, the elementary level of their language skills, and their likely inhibitions, children often express themselves more elaborately and ultimately more effectively through nonverbal means than through speaking. In this way, a child like Lisa (see "Anxious Lisa," pages 486–487) can successfully work through potentially destructive symptoms.

Psychotropic Medication

Today, medications are formulated to help children with specific types of psychiatric or behavioral problems. The most widely used are called stimulants, which improve a child's attention and reduce impulsivity in ADHD. Ritalin is the best-known stimulant; one study found that it is being prescribed to 1.5 million American children between the ages of five and eighteen — almost 3 percent of all school-age children. Other medications have proven effective in reducing tics, helping with obsessions and compulsions, reducing anxiety, and alleviating depression. Children with the most severe disorders, such as psychosis or autism, may need to take highly potent medications for years; these drugs can make the conditions more manageable, but do not remove them. Some people, unfortunately, receive no benefit from the medications that are currently available.

Any decision to use medication must be made on the basis of a thorough evaluation of all the factors that may have led to a child's problems and of their possible remedy. If you decide to use medication, you, your child, and your physician (usually a child psychiatrist) need to review the drug's potential benefits and short- and long-term side effects. These will vary according to the age of your child. You should know how long the doctor expects to prescribe the drug for your child.

You should feel comfortable calling that doctor with questions or after-hour emergencies. The decisions to start a medication and to stop it must be based on a child's overall development, not just on the presence of a symptom. In the case of a second-grader named Brad, medication proved to be an effective part of treatment. (See "Impulsive Brad," page 490.)

Today, medication may be used too often for certain kinds of problems — especially when ADHD is suspected — before other approaches have been tried. At the same time, some children who might benefit from a judicious use of medication are not receiving it because specialists have not recognized or carefully evaluated their problems. In any case, for children and adolescents, medication is almost always best used as part of a general therapeutic approach and only at the lowest doses and for the shortest periods possible. There is no perfect medication, but by and large, the side effects of psychotropic drugs are mild and tolerable.

A school-age child who has to take a medication may feel that it means he is "bad" or defective. This impression may be reinforced if his siblings and friends do not take medications or if he must take a dose in school, as is often the case with stimulants. Alternatively, some children assume that medication will take care of all their problems and lapse into a passive attitude, blaming any further behavioral difficulties on an unhelpful drug. A child who feels "trapped" into taking a pill she never asked for can refuse to take it, avoid her doses, or merely pretend to take the pill and then spit it out. The more your child is engaged in the process of choosing his treatment, the more likely he will be to follow it. It often helps a school-age child to be in the office while his doctors and parents consult and then to have an opportunity to talk privately to the doctor. A child who gains a sense of safety, care, and openness is more likely to participate whole-heartedly in her treatment.

Impulsive Brad

As a baby, Brad ran before he walked, and after his first step, never stopped. In day care, he took what he wanted and bumped into the other children on the way. At home, he had one accident after another. One day his parents were terrified to see him run into the street and be thrown into the air by an oncoming car. The screeching brakes were engraved in their memories for years, and any time they heard a car squeal, they would recall their panic. Brad suffered a concussion and a fractured arm. He left the hospital bruised and with a cast and was — for a short while — less impulsive and quieter than before.

Soon after Brad started in school, his teachers complained that he kept popping in and out of his seat — he could not control his behavior. His handwriting was poor, and he daydreamed while the other children read aloud. He, in turn, felt annoyed to be always the object of their criticism. The school psychologist tested Brad as he entered second grade. The results were encouraging. His intellectual abilities were solidly above average, although his academic skills were lagging behind. The psychologist documented his distractibility, impulsivity, and tendency to blurt out answers before thinking. She felt these findings were consistent with the clinical observation of attention deficit hyperactivity disorder.

The school psychologist and special-resource teacher worked out an educational program for Brad to help him focus on work, learn to plan ahead, and develop more internal controls over his activity. (For more on this special education process, see pages 285–294.) By teaching Brad verbally and rewarding him for success, they showed him that he was more able than he or others thought he was both to persevere and to organize himself.

Around this time, Brad's pediatrician met with his parents to discuss other ways of helping him. The doctor suggested that it might be worthwhile to try a stimulant medication. She asked the boy's teachers to use a scale to rate Brad's behavior in school, and the parents did the same thing about their observations at home. She then started Brad on medication at a low dose to lessen the chance of a poor reaction. During the next several weeks, the dose of medication was slowly moved up to a usual therapeutic range.

The pediatrician, the parents, and the teachers followed Brad's behavior and also watched for side effects. The results of the medication, in combination with the behavioral and educational interventions, were impressive. Brad was far more cooperative with the resource teacher, began to take pride in his work, and was able to settle down for longer periods at home. His teachers scolded him less, and his parents were not yelling at him as much. The house was so quiet one afternoon that Brad's mother, feeling that something was wrong, went looking for her son. He was in his room quietly absorbed in a picture book.

Residential Treatment

Occasionally a child is unable to make developmental progress because of severe and unremitting emotional and behavioral difficulties his family cannot adequately address at home. He might also be in danger of hurting himself through attempting suicide, self-destructive behaviors such as cutting himself or hitting his head on a wall, or behaving without regard for his safety. Such a suffering child might also endanger his family, attacking them or setting fires in the house. These children need an intensive, long-term therapeutic environment, which keeps them safe and gives them intensive twenty-four-hour-a-day treatment.

Residential treatment is like a boarding school with considerable therapeutic intervention, programming, and expertise. The staff's goal is to help children with emotional problems gain the coping skills needed to live safely at home. A child may stay in residential treatment from a few months to a few years, depending upon the extent of her difficulties and her response to treatment. Family participation or an intensive long-term placement plan are required to help the child make the transition back into the home setting when she is judged ready to return there. Many residential placements are expensive, and parents whose insurance coverage is not adequate may need to seek other sources of financial assistance, such as state agencies.

Dealing with Your Own Feelings

Parents who are told that their child has a serious emotional, behavioral, or psychiatric disorder usually feel a mix of emotions. On one side, they are relieved to learn that the behavior that has troubled them and possibly frightened their child fits into a pattern or diagnosis and is treatable. On the other hand, the gravity of the news — that their child's problems will not blow over, as they were probably still hoping — may fill them with despair and disappointment. They may wish to ignore the severity of the diagnosis as a way of protecting themselves from both. Or the diagnosis can re-ignite parents' worries about whether they are in any way to blame for their child's difficulties. Did we not provide enough care in the early months? Did we pass on a bad gene? In this case, you need to recognize the sadly counterintuitive fact that not even the advantages of an intact family, good schooling, and robust genetic background can fully immunize a child against certain kinds of serious trouble.

Any parent of a child with a serious psychiatric disorder finds it extremely difficult to adjust his or her imaginings and expectations. It is a task demanding strength, compassion, and sacrifice from every member of a family — parents, siblings, grandparents. Marriages are strained; siblings are emotionally stressed. Sometimes the adjustment is so difficult that families come apart; at other times, families come together closer than before.

Good care is essential, of course, to allow

a child more easily to express his needs when he is upset and to show his symptoms. Good care for your child is also essential for you; it enables you to address your child's needs head on and to adjust to the changing needs of his illness. Try to see your child as a whole person, not just a set of behavioral or emotional symptoms. And understand these symptoms in the context of his strengths and how he is functioning in all spheres of life, as well as in relation to the supports and stresses in his family, school, and community.

Thoughtful developmental diagnosis is not a matter of finding a single label, such as "obsessive-compulsive disorder (OCD)" or "Tourette's," but is instead a short story about a child with many facets. Labels often carry a stigma that does not help parents live with the complexity and ups and downs of mental illness. Accepting the seriousness of mental illness and understanding the deep impact mental problems have on you and on your family is a long process. Trying to see your child's problems as not just a diagnosis but a part of the person he is becomes an important step in your child's and your family's pathway to adaptation and recovery.

CHAPTER 34

Family Troubles: The Impact of Divorce and Remarriage

From your child's earliest months, you are the center of his world, providing food, protection, and love. Your young child feels likewise that he is the central preoccupation of your and your partner's lives. To a young child, divorce is unthinkable. It is world shaking, then, to discover that Mommy and Daddy have sides that he knows nothing about, that his parents cannot find all their happiness within the family they all share. Although older children are, today, usually familiar with the concept of divorce, the prospect of a break in their own family deeply troubles them. If most children had their way, their mothers and fathers would never separate, no matter how tumultuous or unhappy their lives.

Nevertheless, parents do separate. They have done so throughout history; virtually all cultures have divorce customs. In the industrialized world, there is a high rate of separation; currently in the United States, between divorce and other types of breakup, two of every three first marriages fail. Fortunately, not all of those breakups involve children, but each year divorce affects approximately one million children. Of these, many become stepchildren when their parents remarry and acquire stepsiblings when a parent's new husband or wife brings children to the new family.

One hundred years ago, we might have discussed remarriage in a chapter on death, because that was the most common way for children to lose one parent. Today, however, a parent is far more likely to drop out of the family through divorce than death. In this chapter, we discuss issues not only of divorce and separation but also of life as a single parent, new relationships, and stepfamilies. Much of the advice in this last section applies equally to the situation of both a widowed parent ready to marry again or to a single parent preparing to marry for the first time.

Issues of Separation and Divorce

When a family breaks up and the parents decide to live apart, their children inevitably experience a series of losses — to their familiar routine, seeing one or another parent regularly, perhaps their room, school, and friends. And when these parents are absorbed in their own conflicts as they move toward separation or divorce, their children are often caught in the middle.

What Separation Means to Children

To a child, her family is a stable haven, a shelter from which she can explore the world and her own abilities. When a little girl has trouble learning a new game at nursery school, she can retreat to her home and find sympathy, encouragement, and familiar surroundings. When your school-age child faces the shock of being ostracized, he knows that his family will always love him. This ideal of the family as a guaranteed source for safe and trusting relationships stays with a child throughout childhood and probably throughout life as, indeed, you may yourself still believe it to be true. What children learn about divorce from television programs, news stories, and their playmates does not weaken this faith or the desire of each child that his or her own family will stay together. Even when there is severe conflict, the separation is a painful shock for young children.

If the family ideal doesn't prove to be possible, parental separation threatens a child's overall security, pulling down a central pillar of her view of the world. Thus, during a separation of any kind, your primary goal should

ABUSE AND SAFETY

Although it is important for children to maintain close relationships with both their parents during and after a divorce, that concern must take second place when the child's safety is clearly in danger. If one parent or stepparent has abused a child, physically or sexually, the other parent and the community have a responsibility to protect that child.

Look in the phone book for the numbers of hot lines set up to prevent or respond to abuse and domestic violence. Parental stress lines provide someone to listen to you if you feel in danger of losing control with your children. Child-abuse lines connect callers to child-welfare authorities. Many cities have hot lines for women who are being physically abused by their partners (a wife, being smaller and weaker, usually suffers the most from violence). Battered women's shelters can provide emergency housing for you and your children; they have systems to hide families from people who have histories of violence or are making threats to their safety.

A child who has suffered abuse and has seen her family break up over it — or even over unrelated problems — may feel guilty, believing that she has done something to cause the trouble. The people who care for her must reassure her many times and in many ways that she is not responsible for what happened to her or her parents. Two major blows — learning that her family is neither safe nor stable — have blasted this child's conceptions of the world. Rebuilding her sense of trust so that she can form close emotional bonds with her remaining family and new people usually requires professional counseling, patience, and love. (See chapter 33 for more on children's mental health needs.)

be to restore or maintain your child's sense that, despite your marital difficulties, she is still safe and loved. A child needs at least one loving adult to be a constant in his life. Even a child who has experienced great stress in growing up is likely to become a successful adult if he maintains his ties to his family or other caregivers. For a child, a constant, loving adult presence is all important. Other important rules for divorcing parents to follow for their children's well-being are: minimize conflict, avoid litigation, and form a cooperative parenting arrangement.

Deciding to Divorce

Couples have many reasons for splitting up. Sometimes, unable to resolve their conflicts, they find living together has become intolerable. At other times, personal changes may motivate them to seek other relationships. It is sometimes a shock to one partner when the other asks for a separation, but usually this moment arrives after a long period of tension.

What does such tension mean for children? Obviously, they hear loud arguments, discussions full of tears, and chilly silences. Also, just as they can feel loved and secure without being told, they can sense trouble between parents who argue privately. Some pediatricians have noted a higher rate of asthma attacks, sore throats, and ear infections in children whose parents turn out to be heading for a separation. Even a newborn can pick up tension when, for instance, her mother has a harder time producing milk. In these circumstances, a child may become

fearful that something bad will happen. He may be weepier than usual, wary of new experiences outside the home, or eager to be especially good. Parents often find it harder to soothe their children's anxieties when they themselves are at a high emotional pitch. The whole family may thus be caught in a spiral of tensions.

Some experts say that children become acclimated to the tension within their families. They don't like to hear their parents' angry voices, they don't like to see their parents unhappy — but they can tolerate and become accustomed to those things. As long as the family stays together, this view holds, the child feels more secure than otherwise. As long as both Mom and Dad are still around, children may tell themselves those conflicts can't be too bad. If the parents do separate, children may even express longing for the old storm and stress because they have come to associate that atmosphere with the family itself.

Other experts, however, argue that children raised by two parents who no longer enjoy each other's company — who are remaining married "just for the sake of the children" — are, in fact, doing them a disservice. The children would learn better how to enjoy relationships with other people if their parents were happier and more relaxed, freer with their own emotions and able to express real love for their partners. From this perspective, a child is better off living with one tranquil parent than with two tense ones.

Studies have found that children whose parents divorced are more likely to show developmental or emotional damage later in life. But since all those children also lived through their parents' predivorce tension, it is unclear whether the divorce itself was the problem. The fact that in American culture more couples are choosing divorce does not mean that tense marriages of earlier generations that were maintained for the sake of the children were any healthier.

In fact, as Tolstoy wrote, ". . . each unhappy family is unhappy in its own way." No formula will work for all families. The best advice we can give you if you are having trouble in your marriage is to consider all your options. Have you and your partner tried counseling to work out your differences? What help can you call on from your families and your community? Do you have the financial resources to maintain two homes? Can you ensure continuity of care for your children? Just as families come in many shapes today, so there is a range of solutions: reconciliation with new understandings, separation within the same household, temporary separation, and divorce.

Telling the Children You Will Separate

Divorce is usually an extended process, but for a child, the major disruption comes when his parents start to live apart or announce their decision to do so. Children do not care about the legal status of the marriage: whether their parents separate without divorcing or whether they have ever been married. They just know that Mom or Dad is not at home anymore. If the parents have

separated before or if they have not made clear the permanence of their new living arrangements, the children may need more time to absorb the reality of the change. The realization will still be painful, but is often more so if they have cause to think that either parent has not been truthful.

Thus, it is very important not to lie to your children both while you are discussing any marital difficulties and after you have come to a decision about them. As we noted earlier, children can sense tension in the family, and older ones know that divorce is a real possibility. If you give your child misleading or inconsistent answers, he can lose faith in you or in his own senses. A child who feels she cannot trust her observations will become even more apprehensive or cut off from her emotions. Do not put off telling a child about a divorce by claiming that, for instance, Mommy is going on a long business trip or Dad is going to live closer to Grandma because she is lonely.

Being honest does not mean that you should reveal everything to your children. Answer the questions they ask. Your children are not interested in all that has led up to your decision; they do not care about midlife crises or affairs. (See "Sexual Issues in Separations," page 500.) Do not press information that they have not shown an interest in knowing. Consider how your children will understand what you say. Telling an eight-year-old, "We don't love each other anymore," can be even more shocking to his worldview than saying, "Living in the same house is making us unhappy." And never say in front of your child — the product of your relationship with your partner — that you made a mistake in getting married.

Explaining the Decision to Separate

It is best to break the news to your offspring together. As bewildered and upset as children may be at this moment, they will nevertheless have the reassuring sight of their mother and father working together as parents. This is true even for an infant who cannot understand words: feeling both parents hug and kiss him before one of them departs is better than a sudden disappearance. Similarly, siblings will benefit from hearing the news together, even though children of different ages will understand and be concerned about different things. If the tension between you and your spouse makes a joint session impossible, it is still useful for the two of you to plan what you are going to say. Consistency is important. It confuses a child to hear Dad say, "Our marriage just isn't working out," and then hear Mom say, "I've fallen in love with someone else."

Try to go into this discussion thinking of yourself as, above all, your child's mother or father, not as a person who has been hurt in a relationship. Try to avoid showing anger toward your spouse. Do not discuss blame, even if one of you is clearly at fault. Blaming one another can only push your child into taking sides, and this increases her anguish over the separation. Your child should be able to continue to love both of you and receive love from both of you without feeling she is hurting either of you. Do not, on the other hand, deny anything your child has seen or heard.

When children learn that their parents are separating, what they most need is solid evidence that Mom and Dad are still looking after them. Even if they cannot maintain their belief that their parents will always be together, they at least need to hear that you tried to resolve your problems but could not and that after thinking long and carefully, you have chosen to divorce in order to create a better future for everyone involved. Children also want reassurance about their near future. Express this in concrete terms, appropriate for the age of each child. Reassure a three-year-old that Daddy will read him a story each evening just as Mommy does. Promise a fourteen-year-old that one parent will still pick her up after hockey practice next week. It is often difficult in a separation to look far ahead. If you can promise not to move in the immediate future or allay other common worries, do so, but do not make a promise you know you cannot keep.

A child who has heard her parents quarrel about anything related to her — discipline, expenses, schedules — may wonder if she is to blame for the divorce. Even if she does not ask about this, you may wish to repeat that you and your spouse are separating because you are not happy with each other, that many couples divorce and their choice to do so is based on adult issues. Be sure to tell all your children how proud you both are to be their parents.

Tailor your explanation of the breakup to what you know each child can understand.

For instance, when speaking to a five-year-old, you might use concrete terms: "Daddy is not going to live in this apartment anymore. You and I will stay here, and Daddy will come to visit you every week." For a child of ten who is able to think in more abstract terms, you might say something like, "Your mother and I haven't been getting along. We think we'll all be happier if we don't live together anymore. We both love you just as much as ever. That's why I want you to visit me at my new place." Since a fifteen-year-old has probably sensed more of the trouble and wants to participate in decisions that concern her, you might tell her, "You may have seen how things haven't been right between us for a while. We've decided to live in separate houses, and we'll probably get divorced. Both of us still want to look after you, of course. We want to work out a way to do that while you live in this house, and we want you to be a part of that discussion." Try not to tell different children contradictory stories; they will discuss their new life among themselves and will compare notes.

These examples are meant simply to show how you address children of different ages. Each parent has a unique way of communicating with each child. Consider what is important to your own child as you know him, what he understands, what he might worry about. Be prepared both to answer questions and to anticipate that your child will ask questions you are not ready to answer. Any query, whether it is about your plans to remarry or your plans for the dog, is important to your child when she asks it. Do not give a dishonest answer or brush her off. Instead, ask why that issue is important. You may find you can dispel the real worry more easily: "No, Daddy is not planning to move to Alaska with a masseuse like Jamie's father."

This first discussion of the separation will be the start of an ongoing process of reassuring your child about the family's new shape. Young children, especially, will have concerns that they cannot articulate quickly and easily, but that may bubble up later. Meanwhile, you will be finding out more about the legal situation, living arrangements, and other matters. Maintain a flow of honest reassurance and love.

Children's Typical Reactions to the News

After you tell your children that you plan to separate, expect different reactions according to their ages and personalities. Infants and preschoolers usually start to feel a nameless, shapeless dread. Even though you describe your reasons for separating in words preschoolers understand, they still will not be able to grasp how those reasons can possibly outweigh what matters to them. "Who knows what will happen next?" a preschooler might wonder. "Maybe Mommy will send me away, too." That loss of security may show up in disturbed sleep or feeding, as infantile behavior, or even as slower physical development. Show your young child in the most concrete ways that you will still be there to care for him: hugging, chatting, reassuring him about his fears, continuing to be present in his life.

School-age children feel the same anxiety about what might come next. Often, however, they attach that fear to the concrete things they know a family provides: food, clothing, shelter. An eight-year-old may suddenly become concerned with the family bank account or grocery bill, or seem overly preoccupied with her health. It is not unusual for children to have trouble in school while sorting out their new family status. A child might also benefit from your talking with her about what to tell her friends, teachers, neighbors, and other family members; fortunately, people no longer whisper about divorce or conceal it as a shameful secret. Again, be sure to give your child the real reassurance she needs with hugs and time together.

Adolescents respond to the news of a breakup in a different way. Already in the process of separating themselves socially from their families, they may feel that their haven of retreat has suddenly been cut off. Even the teenager who seems to spend all his time with friends wants to have a loving family as well. And the young adult off at college and planning a long trip next summer wants to have a stable home as a base. The psychological process of becoming independent from one's family involves choosing when and how to separate. The breakup of his family may cause an adolescent to miss this step. With the extreme thinking typical of his age, he may decide that his future is ruined. Do your best to reassure him about the stability that remains in his life. Do not try to probe his feelings or interpret his behavior, but remain available to talk about anything that bothers him.

In many ways, experiencing the end of a nuclear family is like watching the end of a life: a period of mourning is natural even though divorced parents may also feel relieved or liberated. Remember that your children do not share this joy. Do not ask them to. Let them know that, despite your mixed emotions, they can mourn for the family they knew. For the same reason, do not hide any sadness you feel over the separation; talking about your feelings can validate your children's grief and help them through the transition.

Children also feel angry when their parents separate. A girl may be bitter both at her mother for having left the household and at her father for having let her mother go. Some adolescents act out by staying out late with their friends, committing crimes, or engaging in risky sexual behavior. When confronted, a bitter teen might tell his parents, "Oh, I didn't think you cared." Although that statement is an expression of his anger, it does not reflect the full range of feelings he has for you. In that respect, it is no more realistic than an eight-year-old's assurance, "I'll look after you now, Mommy." Both children are attempting to express their complex feelings toward their parents and about the breakup. They also need to reassure themselves that they will survive just fine.

Children can direct this anger at themselves in the form of guilt. Your child wants to feel that she lives not only in a stable home, but in a world where good things happen to good people. One way she can restore that faith is to convince herself that the separation happened because someone was bad. Children also wish to feel that they are not helpless. By deciding that *she* was the bad person, a child can reassure herself that she actually brought about the change, that she is not simply caught up in the turbulence of her parents' relationship. Did the breakup come because she once wished something awful would happen to Mommy? Was it because of all the times she didn't clean her room? This sort of thinking prompts a child to promise to be better if only her parents will reunite.

Almost all children going through a divorce fantasize that their parents will come back together. One important difference between death and divorce is that there are no rituals for divorce, such as a memorial service or visits to a grave. A young child can find little meaning in a court decision. Furthermore, in a child's mind, a parent who moves out can always come back, and children will keep their fantasy of reunification alive as long as they can.

SEXUAL ISSUES IN SEPARATION

Sometimes separation forces parents to openly confront sexual issues long before they expected to. A child may want to know why his parents are no longer getting along. If one parent is departing to live with another person, the child may wonder about the attraction — an even more awkward question if the new partner is the same sex as the parent. Furthermore, children ask such questions just when the parents are probably themselves resentful and confused.

Remember that children who have not reached adolescence are more interested in love than in sex. They want to know whether Daddy and Mommy still love each other. Even more important, they want reassurance that both parents still love them. Explain that there are different kinds of love, some more breakable than others, but that yours for your child is strong and lasting; you don't have to explain other facts of life.

Remember that, whatever the prejudices in some segments of American society, a person's sex life has no bearing on whether he or she is a good parent. Someone who has had an affair can be a good parent. Someone who is living with a lover, of the same or opposite sex, can be a good parent. What your child needs is to feel continuing and consistent affection and care from both parents.

A school-age child may feel embarrassed about the facts behind a divorce: Will my friends laugh at me because my Mom is gay or because my Dad had an affair with our neighbor? For teens, these questions are sharpened by their belief that people are watching them and also by their explorations of their own sexual identity. They wonder: Am I gay, too? Will I have stable relationships? (For a brief discussion of sexuality in adolescence, see pages 529–535.) Remind your children that in this society most people keep their sex lives private; those outside a family rarely know, and even more rarely deserve to know, the reasons behind a separation.

The Question of Custody: Where Will I Sleep Now?

From a child's point of view, custody — the decision about which parent he or she will live with — is the most important outcome of a divorce. In the American legal system, there are two sorts of arrangements: one in which one parent receives sole custody of a child, the other in which the parents share joint (or "divided" or "alternating") custody. A parent with sole custody not only provides a home for and looks after the child most of the time, but also makes the decisions about that child's schooling, religion, health care, and so on. The other parent may pay child support, but does not necessarily have a legal right to be involved in these choices. Parents with joint custody, in contrast, share the decision making.

Within sole or joint custody there are, however, other possible arrangements. Sometimes (too often) one parent raises the child, and the other vanishes from the child's life. In other cases, couples manage to continue a close parenting partnership even as they pursue otherwise separate lives. Under joint custody, children may live almost all the time with one parent or half the time with each. A child may move from house to house,

or stay in one house while the parents move in and out. Or children may alternate between their parents every day, every week, or every year, or spend some parts of each year with one parent and the rest with the other, depending on what works best.

The legal standard for deciding which parent receives custody in a disputed case is "the best interests of the child." That is also the best guide for you and your spouse as you discuss custody. Recall the ancient story of Solomon, who is asked to decide a custody dispute between two women, each of whom claims to be the mother of the same infant. "Bring me a sword," the king, according to the Bible, commands. "Divide the living child in two, and give half to one woman, and half to the other." One claimant agrees to this

division; the other immediately offers to give up her claim if only the baby is spared from death. Solomon then awards custody to the latter woman, saying that, in wishing to save the child, she has shown true maternal love. The lesson here is not that you should give up your claim for custody to keep your child out of a legal battle. Rather, you must never forget to put your child's best interests first.

Deciding on Custody Together

You and your spouse should decide on long-term custody arrangements together if you can. Eventually, however, you should retain separate lawyers to help you in court. Divorce has as many pitfalls as any legal procedure. Choose an attorney with whom you feel comfortable, lay out what you have agreed on, and make sure your lawyer follows your wishes. Never use custody of your child or visitation arrangements as a bargaining chip for other issues between you and your partner. Clearly, neither would be in the child's best interest.

Consider each of these questions about custody carefully from your own perspective, and then from that of your children as you know them:

- Do both of you *want* responsibility for your child? Some divorcing parents seek custody because they fear that someone — their child, their family, or society — will think less of them if they do not. You do not have to fight for joint custody to remain a helpful, influential, loving parent. In other

cases, parents are so angry about the breakup that they want to punish their spouses through the custody judgment. Remember, custody is not about your interests: it is about the interests of your child. Depriving a parent of seeing a child is also depriving the child — who has done nothing to cause the divorce — from seeing the parent.

- Which of you would find it easier to be a single parent, without the other person's daily support? If there are no compelling financial and psychological reasons for both of you to work, which of you is in the position to earn more income for the two households by working?

- Has one parent provided most of the child's day-to-day care? Which of you usually feeds the baby or changes her diapers? The younger the child, the more valuable it is for that parent to continue caring for her; infants can tolerate changes in their surroundings much more easily than changes in their caregivers.

- If you have more than one child, what is the best way to keep all your children together until adulthood? Even if they seem to fight all the time, in a crisis they will almost always comfort and support each other.

- If you have a school-age child, which of you is more likely to remain in the neighborhood? School-age children are attached to their surroundings and friends and benefit from attending one school consistently. A child should live in what he considers his home; he must not go through life feeling like a guest in "Daddy's home" and "Mommy's home."

- If you want to maintain joint parenting responsibility, is it likely that you will be able to put aside the differences that have led to this divorce? Did you argue often over parenting decisions? Do you share the same attitudes toward health care, school, money, television, and bedtimes? Can you avoid competing for your child's loyalty? For a child to be caught between her parents in conflict makes the situation even worse for her.

- If you and your spouse want to share your child's time, can you devise a practical arrangement for doing that? At what times will she be with her father and at what times with her mother? Will she move from house to house, or will you move? Children of different ages respond differently to such shifting.

- How will you handle any accidental disruption to your custody arrangement, such as when one parent moves or remarries? What will you do if your child is consistently unhappy? Will you adjust your custody schedule when your preschooler starts going to school five days a week?

Children in Divorce Court

In most divorces, the parents agree on custody arrangements; the court reviews their plan and usually approves it. When parents cannot agree on custody, or their arrangements strike the judge as not protect-ing the best interests of the child, the court steps in. To reach a decision, the judge may investigate the mother's and father's characters and parenting styles. Expert witnesses may testify. The court may feel the need to appoint an independent advocate for the child. If this process takes a long time, the child can end up feeling in danger of being cut apart, like the baby in the story of King Solomon. It is usually better for custody to be decided quickly; long deliberation seldom produces a clearer answer and is likely to make your child more insecure.

In some states, a judge is bound by law to consider the preference of children of a certain age. The best way for a judge to do so is to ask the advice of the child's advocate or another professional who is expert in speaking and listening to children. Many psychologists feel that it is harmful to ask a child to express a direct preference between parents, either in open court or in a judge's chambers, and there is no evidence that such questioning produces a better decision. It is very hard for a child to have to openly state a wish to live with one parent over the other; doing so may make a child feel disloyal toward one of his parents. Testifying in court is daunting at any age, and judges are rarely trained to interpret a child's responses. You should, therefore, do all you can to protect your offspring from being used in this way. But if your divorce proceeds to court testimony, be sure your children understand that they can speak freely about their experience and their wishes, that both parents will continue to love them, and that the judge will be responsible for the final decision.

Life as a Single Parent

Once separation and divorce are final, parents live in separate households — one belongs to the primary caregiver with whom the child lives, and the other belongs to the parent who does not have custody. Each parent now has different responsibilities in regard to the child, and each has different constraints and problems to contend with.

The Primary Caregiver

If you are your child's primary caregiver, you may feel tempted to be a "superparent" to make up for her loss or to prove that you can make it on your own. Be realistic. You, too, are coming out of a wrenching transition. More changes and adjustments probably lie ahead. You may be facing the necessity of going back to work, which means, in turn, that your child may have to get used to day care. (See chapters 28–29.) Your child may sting you with her complaints about the new household arrangement. But her love for or loyalty to you has not lessened. It is simply that she is likely to feel more secure in her relationship with the parent with whom she is living and thus finds it easier to express her resentment about the whole situation to you.

As a single parent, money is likely to be a big constraint. Elementary math shows that a couple paying for two homes will have less money to go around than when they were paying for one — and the standard of living of the household with children is usually the one that falls further. You may end up moving into a smaller home. You may need to watch expenses more closely. Depending on your child's age, you may wish to explain your general financial situation to him and that this will mean fewer flashy new clothes and less expensive meals. Do not feel that because your child has suffered through a divorce it means he deserves to have everything he wants. If you are working longer hours, he may have to do laundry or look after the smaller children or pack his own lunch for school. Accepting such financial realities is an important step in growing up. At the same time, your child still needs his childhood. Do not burden him with every fiscal detail or make him a full partner in all household decisions.

Try not to spoil your child when it comes to discipline. Rules are important, and children know that. Even though an older child often presses for greater freedom, she also values knowing where her boundaries are. Indeed, the disintegration of her family may make those boundaries more important as a sign that her parents will still be parents. (See chapter 27.) Make an effort to be consistent about discipline in each household; custodial parents often complain that they have to provide *all* the discipline and that the other parent always gets to show the children a good time.

Even after a difficult breakup, try to help your child maintain contact with his other parent and that parent's family. Children who do not know their absent parents often fantasize about them, making them out to be more appealing than they really are. If your child perceives you to be blocking his visits to his other family, he may project more of his bitterness about the divorce onto you.

The Noncustodial Parent

As a parent without custody, you probably love your children as much as ever, but see them only a fraction as often. The divorce has irrevocably altered your relationship with your child, who probably feels resentment as well as love and questions where she stands in your affection. The best response, if possible and reasonable, is to try to continue working with your former spouse in raising your child. If your child feels that she still has two parents who love and care for her, each parent should have the chance to provide that love and care. If a child's parents undercut each other or provide inconsistent guidance, she may end up feeling she has two "half-parents" instead.

Do not try to bribe your way back into your child's heart with gifts, lax discipline, and exciting experiences. You have probably never left your child's heart, and spoiling her will make her think more of your wallet than of your time. That does not provide for the consistent child-rearing children need to

HOW TO HANDLE VISITS

Here are a few guidelines to make your visits work out for both you and your child:

On a visit, you are supposed to be with your child in fact and in spirit. Avoid asking your child to relay messages to your ex-spouse: a message (written or remembered) can distract from that time together. When you have something to say to your ex-spouse: use the telephone or e-mail or write a letter — methods that are more reliable than an eight-year-old, anyway.

Remember that time with your children is not a zero-sum game: every minute with Daddy does not mean another minute that Mommy "loses," and vice versa. Use the time when your former spouse is looking after your child to look after yourself: see a movie for grown-ups, visit friends, work out. Be flexible if schedules have to change. On the other hand, when you are scheduled to pick up your child, *never be late*.

Noncustodial parents should look for activities that both they and their children enjoy. Do not feel obligated to go to the zoo or some other "special" place each weekend. Conversely, do not expect your child to enjoy coloring while you catch up on work during what is supposed to be your time together. Your child needs to interact with you. Find activities that you can share happily. Do not be afraid to experiment — not every visit has to be perfect. Discuss what happens and how you feel, even if you feel bored. When you and your child are truly sharing, that will make your visits enjoyable for both of you, rather than a stiff ritual to be endured.

Some children balk at visiting the parent they do not live with. Unless there is evidence of abuse, court decisions give noncustodial parents the right to see their children. Explain this reality to your child, try to discover what is really bothering him about the visits (Is he feeling disloyal to you? Is he upset at not being able to go out for soccer?), and work with your former spouse to resolve the problem.

grow into responsible and healthy adults. In both sole and joint custody arrangements, the children often live with one parent and visit the other for a night, a vacation, or just a few hours each week. Owing to their comparative rarity, a child can invest these visits with a great deal of emotion — both positive and negative. Since these visits are also the most common occasion for former spouses to interact, they need to be negotiated carefully and without recrimination. (See "How to Handle Visits," page 505.)

New Relationships for Ex-Spouses

It is likely that one, if not both, former spouses will form a new relationship after the divorce. Children respond to these new relationships, as they do after the death of a parent, with mixed emotions. In the first place, in at least a small way, the children often wish to see their parents back together. The new relationship reminds them of what they have lost and may shred their fantasy of reunification. A child may fear that by showing too much affection for the new partner, she will upset her other parent. Yet your children also want to live with two loving parents again, and (especially as they grow older) they want to see you happy, too.

Be alert to these conflicting impulses in your child. A mother just starting to go out with men again — nothing serious, just a date — may be flustered to find her two-year-old wrapping herself around the gentle-

man's knee and asking to call him Daddy. In the same situation, a usually polite ten-year-old might be embarrassingly rude. Head off such problems by explaining to your child what you are and are not planning. To an older child, a father can say, "On Friday I'm going out to dinner with Helen. I'm not looking to get married again now, and I don't think she is, either." To avoid confusing young children, do not hug and kiss your date in their presence. When you consider bringing a lover into your household, remember that your young children are likely to become attached to that person. Even if you do not consider the relationship permanent, it will be confusing and difficult for them if he or she eventually leaves.

Remarriage

In 1990, over seven million American children, or 11 percent of the young population, lived in stepfamilies. In previous centuries, this proportion was probably even greater because mothers' life expectancy was low and fathers quickly remarried. Despite the frequency of this experience, no one has ever come up with a never-fail recipe for happiness in stepfamilies, as the old tales about evil stepparents show.

When a parent remarries after being divorced or widowed, the household must go through a second transition. Some of these changes are for the better: the child has another adult to care for her and presumably sees her parent happier. On the other hand, she has to give up some monopoly on that parent's time. There may also be the disruptions of a move, of new siblings, of new customs. If the stepparent is not loving or the new marriage turns sour, the child suffers a second loss.

When a parent remarries after a divorce, not only does a child undergo all the changes in his daily life we just described, but he is also giving up part of his fantasy life: the hope that his parents will reunite. Even a child who has been friendly to his parent's boyfriend or girlfriend may act coldly when talk of marriage comes up. News of the betrothal might also ignite tensions in the child's other parent — tensions which he would respond to. If you remarry and cut down on visits with your child to spend more time with your new spouse (and perhaps your new stepchildren), that change amplifies your child's initial loss.

Sometimes all the awkwardness and potential conflict in a new stepfamily comes to focus on one issue: how children address a stepparent. A child may feel that calling his stepmother "Mom" implies disloyalty to his absent mother, another may feel that calling her stepfather "Dad" means she is neglecting the memory of her father. Reluctance to use these names for the new spouse does not imply hostility or disrespect. To avoid such potholes, many stepparents invite children to call them by their first name. Some kids eventually work out different labels for their different caregivers: "Daddy," "Poppa." To a child, caring and affection by any name smell just as sweet.

If, when you remarry, you also move to a new house or a new neighborhood, keep in mind your child's need for continuity. Arrange her room as it was before; do not use this occasion to throw out old toys. (For more advice on moving to a new house, see pages 456–458.) Work with your former spouse to ensure that visits and shared custody continue. If possible, arrange for your child to visit her friends from the old neighborhood. Spend time with her alone, as well as together with your new spouse.

Blending Families

Sometimes a stepparent brings more children into the family as well. Stepsiblings are rivals for both parents' attention. An only child might suddenly be one of five. A son might see his mother giving time — perhaps even extra time at the start — to children she didn't even give birth to! Or a daughter may have to adjust not only to a new adult living in her house, but to a new child from that adult's first marriage who arrives every weekend. And then there is the potential sibling rivalry between two ten-year-olds who have each been used to being the eldest.

In these circumstances, a child may feel like an outsider and become depressed. He may start to act more possessive of his own parent or move closer to his other parent, if he has one. In time, however, the blended family will develop its own comforting rituals and structure. In the meantime, try to reassure your child that the new family takes nothing away from him (certainly not your love) and that it may even have gained him something. A child who once resented a stepsibling will probably grow to rely on that brother or sister for support as much as on a natural sibling.

Similar issues can arise when a new baby is born to the new couple. (For normal sibling responses to a new baby, see chapter 30.) Emotions seem even more acute in the case of a half sibling, regardless of whether the baby will be part of the child's household. A child who has seemed to adjust well to her new stepparent may suddenly start to behave badly, show resentment, or withdraw. An older sibling may fear that the baby will supplant her in her parent's heart: "If Mommy loves me, why is she starting a new family? Isn't it natural for my stepfather to love the new baby more?" And after a divorce, a half sibling is another blow to the child's fantasy of reuniting her parents.

As with all the challenges involved in blending new families, do all you can to provide continuity in your child's life. You cannot remove his new siblings or even ensure his own room, but you can reserve time for him. You can stay alert to his needs and wishes. You can work with your former spouse and your new spouse to reassure him that you will always be there to love him. And in any separation, divorce, or remarriage, that is what children want most.

CHAPTER 35

A Death in the Family: Helping Your Children Through a Final Loss

Discovering the inevitable and irreversible fact of death is a crucial part of growing up into a full human being. Its truth takes both adults and children time to realize, and its unpredictability is part of that hard lesson. For both parents and children, watching someone die or having to respond to sudden death can be frustrating, confusing, and frightening. Although you may hope that your child will never experience the death of someone whom she loves and who loves her — whether relative, teacher, or playmate — many children do suffer that tragedy. Some parents try to shield their offspring from an older relative's ill health or to hide their own sadness after the death of a close friend. Such attempts are usually unsuccessful. As in dealing with other painful issues, you should use your energy to answer your child's questions, acknowledge his emotions, and reassure him that the loss has not diminished the love you and others have for him.

In this chapter, we will discuss several issues connected with helping your child deal with final loss: how to think about death in general, how to respond to specific deaths, how to deal with a dying child, and memories and grieving.

Thinking about Death

When, you may wonder, does a child begin to understand that life ends? Many children grasp this concept at a relatively early age, observing dead insects, goldfish, gerbils, birds, and other animals. Rather than ignoring these experiences, you can use them to help your young child begin to understand what it means to be *alive* and to be *dead*. Introducing these concepts to your child well before someone whom he loves dies will ease the shock of that death and help him both accept and mourn.

Schools often call in pediatricians and psychiatrists to counsel classes that have suddenly been forced to deal with death. Several years ago, one doctor visited a group of nursery-school children gathered on the day after their teacher had found their pet guinea pig dead in his cage. The animal, embalmed by a kindly veterinarian, lay on a colorful blanket on a small table in the center of the room. The children stood quietly, gazing at the lifeless body of their pet. A four-year-old reached out and stroked the animal, commenting in a soft voice, "What's in him can't come out anymore." This boy had a clear, simple understanding of what it means to die.

Other such visits bring more awkward moments. The same pediatrician accepted the invitation of an elementary-school principal to meet with a first-grade class the day after their teacher, Mrs. Chan, had suffered a fatal heart attack in the school hallway. The children begged the doctor to take them to see their teacher. As he struggled to think of an appropriate response, a seven-year-old girl raised her hand and said, "My dog was hit by a car last month. I found him lying in the snow. When I petted him, he was stiff. He didn't know I was there. If we went to see Mrs. Chan now, I don't think she'd know we were there either." Having experienced the sad but edifying loss of a pet she loved, this girl was able to share some of what she had learned with her classmates.

The death of an animal is, of course, a vastly different experience from the death of a significant person in a child's life. Having experienced the death of a pet does, however, help children to comprehend that death means no eating, no sleeping, no movement, and no pain. Living through the death of an animal and being able to remember the happy times when it was alive also help a child who is grappling with the loss of a beloved family member or friend. Teachers often use the death of a classroom pet as a lesson in what it means to die: indeed, some have to address that question at length so young students can console themselves.

Children learn about death in other ways as well. Until medical care in this country dramatically reduced childhood mortality and extended adults' life expectancy, almost all children had witnessed the death of a sibling, a grandparent, or a parent before they reached their teens. Today, in our media-saturated culture, children often receive their first exposure to dying people from news reports about politicians or entertainment figures; occasionally they will have become quite fond of these people and may feel truly saddened by their departure from life's stage. While these experiences may prompt your child to ask you what happens when people die, watching television is not really a good way to grasp the full meaning of death. The flurries of news reports about the life of a celebrity who has just died, which make him or her seem even more visible and active, do little or nothing to show a child why people are sad.

Even young children who understand what it means not to be alive have difficulty grasping the *permanence* of death. Toddlers are, after all, still working on the notion of time. While they may see a dead fish in the aquarium and dead birds and animals on the ground outside, a few days later these same children may see seemingly identical fish, birds, and animals alive and moving around. Similarly, beloved performers in the movies live on in reruns on television or the VCR. Thus, the ongoing reality of death may not make an impression on them. Never again seeing a real person you have come to love is one of the hardest lessons for anyone to assimilate. It is especially hard for young children.

A child who suffers the death of a pet, sees newspaper stories about the death of a public figure, or witnesses a funeral procession may well wonder whether someone in her family will die soon: her parents, other family members, even herself. She is most concerned, of course, about the grown-ups who care for her. Young children are acutely aware of how much they depend on their parents. If your child asks whether you are going to die, you can respond, "Not for a long time, I hope." It may reassure your child if, at this moment, you mention relatives or friends who would care for her if you ever do get sick or meet with an accident. Once you have made formal arrangements, you can say

something like: "I don't expect to die for a long, long time. But if anything ever happens to me, Grandma and Grandpa will come to take care of you."

You may be reluctant to talk about such contingency plans because you wish not to worry your child or you think she is too young to benefit from the discussion. These rationales may mask your own fear of dying — a fear that is eminently human and completely natural. While any conversation about death will force you to acknowledge your fear and uncertainty about the subject, doing that is healthier than implying to your child that death is unspeakably horrible. You cannot, of course, prevent your child from thinking that you and your partner may die at some point. But it is better to make her feel both secure about the future and free to ask important questions than to let her worry alone.

When a relative is very ill and close to death, explain what is happening to your young child with words like: "All the grown-

PLAY IT SAFE AND MAKE A WILL

Couples are often advised to make their wills as soon as they have children, usually to be sure that most of their estate goes to the benefit of those children or other heirs. Even more important than your material possessions, however, is the part of a will that states who will have custody of your children in the event of your death. The last thing a child needs after such a trauma is a period of uncertainty when she does not know who will look after her or when she is caught in a conflict between relatives.

The best "backup parents" to choose are adults the child already loves and he feels love him. That is, usually close relatives or sometimes nearby friends. Choosing a household in the same community is not as important as choosing a household where you think your child will feel most comfortable; going to a new school is much less daunting to a child than coming home after school to people who feel like strangers. Naturally, you should discuss your plans with the people you have chosen, and make sure they feel up to the responsibility of raising your children.

ups in the family are feeling very sad because Grandpa is so sick." An older child can often handle more details of a loved one's condition and prognosis, and may already suspect the truth. Although discussing such a serious matter with your child is difficult, he needs to understand why you and other adults in his family are preoccupied. Children can adapt to difficult experiences with far more equanimity if they know why their caregivers are acting oddly. Failing to share the reason for your unusual behavior and emotions leaves them feeling confused and deserted.

Expect your child to ask different questions, according to her age. A young child may ask when the other people in her life may die. Or she may wonder, "If Grandpa is sick, why can't the doctor make him better?" or "Will I catch what he has if I go visit him?" An adolescent also may wonder about this but in more sophisticated terms: "Does Grandpa's disease run in the family?" Or he may wonder about his own health or ability to be independent. Answer his questions to the best of your ability. Express your answers in ways your child can understand: a toddler, for instance, will not be able to comprehend the idea of someone's chances of surviving or the number of weeks they have left, but she will be able to understand the importance of her telling Grandpa she loves him every time she visits. (For more about illness, see chapter 32.)

When a family member is dying, you may want to spare your youngster the confusion and tension at home and consider sending her to stay with relatives or neighbors. Here,

as in many other situations, your own wishes probably play a role: hoping not to experience the loss yourself, you try to shield your children from it. It is better, however, for children to remain in their customary surroundings. They will find support in their own rooms, beds, toys, books, and play areas. If you feel so busy or preoccupied that you cannot tend to your child, ask a familiar relative, friend, or baby-sitter to assume some of this responsibility. Do not let your circumstances completely wear you out.

Helping Your Child Respond to Death

When a family member or friend dies, it is wise for you to sit down quietly with your young child and explain the situation. If the person has been ill and the death expected, you can say something like: "Remember how I told you a few weeks ago that Grandpa was very sick? I'm sad to say that he died yesterday." Choose your words carefully. Children do not know how to interpret the euphemisms people often use for death, such as "passed away." The statement, "We just lost Grandpa," will confuse a young child; one five-year-old boy responded to it by asking, "Why don't you go look for him?" Describing death as "going to sleep" might make a young child worry whether she will wake up the next time she goes to sleep.

A death that comes as a surprise is often harder for parents to explain because they may still be struggling with the shock themselves. But a child who has not experienced the loss of a loved one will probably not be so rocked by it as you are. In fact, it can be easier for little children to understand an automobile accident than a wasting disease. What will upset them, however, is to see you upset. Older children and adolescents, in contrast, are able both to recognize that death is possible and even to understand death is inevitable in their distant future. Your child may well react to this news with the customary complaint, "It's not fair." And indeed, death is not fair. If you are involved in an accident or other cause of sudden death, do your best to keep your children together; to reassure them that the foundation of their lives — the family — is still functioning. If you cannot all be together, do all you can to remain in contact by telephone. (For advice on dealing with the aftermath of violence, see pages 340–342.)

Parents are especially challenged by what to say when a loved one has taken her own life. On top of the emotional turmoil that comes with any sudden death, they wonder whether to tell their children about suicide, which is both perplexing and, in some families, still taboo. This concern is well placed; studies have shown that children have trouble understanding suicide. You need to consider your child's developmental age, the circumstances of the death, the closeness of the person, and other factors. In general, honesty is better than deception or complete silence. You can tell a young child, "Martha got sick and died," without going on to say that the illness was depression and that she took her own life. You might tell a somewhat older child something like: "Martha took too many pills at once, which was poison. We don't know why she did that. She was very sad — probably so sad that her brain wouldn't let her feel happy again. I wish Martha could have remembered the times when she was happy with us." While there is no need to relate details, simply mentioning in this fashion that someone has committed suicide will not "give your children ideas." It may make adolescents more concerned about their own mood swings, but by that age they have already learned that some people kill themselves.

A young child's sadness at the news of a death outside the immediate family often appears short-lived. Soon after being told, he may ask to go outside and return to playing as if nothing has happened, as if he did not understand that an important person in his life was gone forever. Many experts believe, however, that this behavior really suggests that the child is so upset at the idea of losing a person she loved, and perhaps relied on, that she chooses not to think about the event. Like a baby shutting down when she becomes overstimulated, going back to familiar play may be your child's way of giving her mind time to process the new information. You can be certain that, in the days ahead, the child's sad feelings and questions will surface repeatedly.

If your family frequently used to see the person who has died — at dinner every week, for instance — your children will have regular reminders of the loss. Otherwise, it is easy for a young child to forget or put aside the news that she will not see that person again. A few days after being told of the death of her grandmother, a preschooler may ask, "Will Grandma be back for my birthday? She always comes to my party!" One five-year-old even said with great seriousness a few days after a funeral: "Grandma called today. She said she'll be here Sunday for dinner just like always." Such comments suggest that a child is not yet able to accept the reality of the family's loss.

You may find it difficult to respond to such denial. On the one hand, you, too, may wish Grandma would come back. On the other, you probably worked hard to find the right words to explain death to your child, and they do not seem to have penetrated. But respond matter-of-factly: "You remember that Grandma died last week. She can't come to visit us anymore. It would be nice if she could, but we will have to remember all the good times we had with her when she was alive."

At whatever point your child accepts the reality of a person's death, he may well start crying. Give him a firm hug. Some parents try to hold back their own tears at these moments, fearing that they will further upset a child. Crying yourself is not necessarily harmful. Your sadness may encourage your child to express his feelings. You can even say things like, "I wish I could make Auntie Ito come back," acknowledging a desire the child probably also feels. In many families, people let out their emotions only in isolation. Many adults remember, as children, weeping at night in bed under the covers after a loved one had died. One woman recalled how, at the age of ten, she felt overcome by the death of her grandmother and was crying alone. Tiptoeing down the hall to her parents' room, she discovered that her mother was also crying in bed. Mother and daughter found relief in being sad together as they let loose their grief at losing someone both of them had loved.

Sharing Your Beliefs

Though a constant in human existence, death remains one of our deepest human mysteries. Over the centuries, people have come up with many ways to find meaning in it. Usually adults formulate beliefs that work for them, relying on family traditions, spiritual and philosophical credos, and gut feelings. (See chapter 26 for more discussion of family cultures.) Children do not have a library of life experience to mull over, nor are they sophisticated thinkers yet. Just as they turn to you for answers about many parts of life, they will also look to you for answers about death. They may ask tough questions during a moment of crisis — soon after they hear that a person has died — or their questions may arise later as they try to figure out the world.

Describe your beliefs in terms your child will understand. If, for example, you believe in a heavenly afterlife, you may say, "The *body* of a person who dies rests in a special box in a cemetery. I believe the *spirit* of that person goes to a special place called Heaven, where there's no sadness, no hunger, no poverty, and no war or other bad things." If you do not feel certain about what happens after death, you can describe concepts from different traditions: "Some people think that a dead person's soul goes to live in Heaven. Other people think it comes back in another person's body, or in the body of an animal or in a plant." Mentioning the idea of life hereafter, even if you do not believe in it, prepares your child for conversations with friends whose families do firmly believe in an afterlife.

Do not feel, however, that you have to misrepresent your beliefs to comfort your child. Children, even at a young age, are quick to sense insincerity. If, in the hope that it will somehow help your child, you present a picture of an afterlife you do not believe in, you are likely only to confuse her. It is better to be honest. Do not attack other beliefs, but describe your convictions in a positive way: "I think that dying is like resting forever." If you have no convictions about the nature of death, you can be honest about that as well, and focus on concrete aspects of your child's life: "I'm not sure what I believe about dying. Nobody knows for sure what happens. I do know that Grandma won't be able to visit us anymore, and that we'll all miss her very much."

Preparing for the Funeral

Memorial services serve many functions for the family of a person who has died. They are, usually, religious ceremonies that impart spiritual and psychological comfort, allowing individuals to say good-bye to the deceased for a final time. And they provide occasions for people to gather and show solidarity and respect for the family. Children can benefit from all these functions, as well as from seeing how grown-ups act on such important days. Yet funerals and similar events can be strange and frightening, especially when young children notice that all the adults involved are sad or solemn.

With the best of intentions, therefore, some parents send their young children to live with relatives or friends during the mourning period. As we discussed earlier in regard to a home in which someone is dying, a child experiences less disruption if he remains in his own house, with his own room and his own bed, even if the house is much busier or sadder than before. Try to anticipate your child's particular needs at this special time. A shy girl, for instance, may become extra anxious at meeting many relatives and strangers and prefer more quiet time in her room; her siblings may find the arrival of far-flung family members to be so exciting they wear themselves out and need to be put to bed. Take advantage of offers from your relatives to look after the children in your home.

Parents often wonder whether it is appropriate for a child to attend a funeral of a family member or friend. Every youngster is different; some will not be able to sit still, no matter how much they loved and respected the deceased, and others will feel left out if they cannot go. We believe that children as young as four should be allowed to decide for themselves if they wish to attend a funeral. Describe what will take place and what polite behavior you expect. Consider ways your children may be able to display their special love and respect for the deceased: for instance, by drawing a special good-bye card. (Discourage young children from donating a favorite object to go into the coffin; if they want it back later, it will be hard to make them understand why that is impossible.)

Before attending any memorial service, describe to your children the procedures the deceased's family has chosen — a wake with open or closed casket, a funeral service with eulogies, cremation, and so on. Think about the concerns your children might have. Be ready to explain, for instance, that cremation does not hurt; tell them how the ashes might be stored and treasured, or scattered in a place important to the person who died. Explain that a body, after embalming, may not look exactly like the person they remember. Prepare your children for as many details of the event as you know, as in: "It will be a very quiet time. The rabbi will talk for a while about Uncle David. His body will be lying in a special box called a casket. Many of the grown-ups might cry. That's how we'll say good-bye."

You may still be concerned about whether your young child will find the ceremony too long and stressful. You may also have important responsibilities at the event or know that you will need to mourn without having, at the same time, to keep an eye on your child. In these cases, consider asking a family member or friend to come along and look after your child. If the child becomes upset, that person should feel free to take him home. In any event, after the ceremony, share with your child the different parts of the service you

and she found meaningful. You may be surprised at how much your child remembers and values as well.

If a child chooses not to attend the memorial service, she should remain at home with a close family friend or baby-sitter she knows and trusts. Her familiar bedroom and play areas are comforting at this sorrowful and mysterious time. Be sure to tell her when you will be home from the ceremony. After you return, even though you may still be grief stricken, try to spend a few minutes sitting and talking quietly with your child. She needs to know that you are still part of her life and concerned about her feelings, too. Some children who choose not to attend the memorial service nevertheless ask to visit the deceased's grave the next day, or later. One little boy would even invite his friends: "Would you like to go see where my grandfather's buried?" If a child chooses not to attend a service, you can still refer to it later as "the time we said good-bye," and include your child by adding, "You stayed home, but we said good-bye for you."

When Another Child Dies

Children most commonly experience death through the loss of an older relative or a close family friend, but they may also experience the loss of another child — a sibling, a young relative or neighbor, a classmate. Even news reports about the death of a child due to crime, accident, or war can upset young viewers deeply because they so easily identify with other youngsters. Sometimes, depending on the circumstances, parents' sadness at the death of a baby may profoundly trouble a surviving sibling. In other cases, you may not recognize how deeply the death of a baby sibling has affected your other children. Try hard to see the situation through your child's eyes and understand the fears she is suddenly experiencing.

Miscarriage, stillbirth, or a major health problem in the first months of life are the most common way for a family to lose a child. Such a misfortune is painful for all members of the family. Adults must abandon their hopes and wishes for the baby; it is particularly difficult for parents to grieve such a loss because they have little to remember about the infant other than their fantasies. Some doctors and hospitals encourage parents to hold their stillborn baby at least for a few moments so as to experience the baby's reality. Other children in the family have also had expectations for the new sibling, but their fantasies and biological adjustments are not as elaborate as their parents'.

Nevertheless, there is no doubt that beyond infancy, children both feel real loss on these occasions and are acutely aware of their parents' reactions. All children worry when they see their mother and father feeling sad, and that sadness may especially trouble a surviving sibling, making him hesitate to express his own sorrow. Meanwhile, the parents may not want to burden their living child with grief for a child he never knew. Together, child and parent unwittingly enter into a conspiracy of silence. As a result, you may not recognize how deeply a death has affected your child, and your child may become bewildered and wonder if he has caused your distress. Always remember that your child had his own expectations about the child who died and that he is sad at the loss and needs your support to cope with his feelings. Again, you will find it easier to give this comfort if you explain why you are upset.

A healthy child may die suddenly because of an accident, homicide, sudden infant death syndrome (see page 177), or some other cause. If the death is immediate or occurs in a hospital shortly after the incident, the family has no time to say good-bye to their child. In such cases, despite the potential turmoil, keep your surviving children together with an adult family member. The children can offer each other support and reassurance that the family will go on. Later, after the public funeral, on some occasion such as the anniversary of the funeral, organize a private, informal family ceremony in which each child and parent offers a favorite memory of the dead child as a form of farewell. This will symbolize the special bond that brothers, sisters, mother, and father will always have with the departed.

When an older child contracts a disease and dies over a number of months or years, the family experiences a long decline instead of a shock. The illness often gets better and then worse, and some treatments bring troubling side effects, putting the whole family on a roller coaster of emotions. Although the other children in the family are usually very sad about what their sibling is going through, they may also secretly resent all the parental time and attention the sick child gets. This feeling in turn leads to some guilt, which may make the period after the sibling's death especially hard. Losing a sibling can feel like losing part of yourself, especially for a younger child who was born being "Sadie's little sister" or "Jack's brother."

Some families who have lost a child find solace in joining a support group of other people who have suffered comparable losses. Parents who have helped children through the same diseases and treatments, children who have lost brothers and sisters — these people know best what your family has endured and continues to go through. In many children's hospitals and hospices there are bereavement groups in which parents and siblings can participate. Other families, however, prefer to find comfort within their religious communities or by other means.

When a child dies, especially suddenly, schools often try to help the surviving classmates deal with their feelings of loss or fright. Sometimes grief counselors come to speak to these students, but it is usually wiser for these professionals to share advice with the school's teachers, administrators, and other personnel — adults whom the children already know, trust, and listen to. After a death in the school community, students are sometimes prompted to write letters to the deceased to be posted on a bulletin board or "sent" in another symbolic way. They can also donate a little money to a charity, plant a flowering bush or tree, or dedicate a publication or performance to the memory of their friend. Such actions help youngsters express their feelings and demonstrate that death does not mean the person is forgotten. After such a loss, be sure to offer your child closeness and reassurance at home.

Avoiding Adverse Reactions

Many parents who lost a beloved friend or relative during their childhood report that they felt deserted owing to their parents' preoccupation with their own grief. One parent, who was eight when her grandmother died, recalled, "I just wanted to be alone with my mother instead of being in a crowd of crying relatives." Make time for your children during this mourning period, however busy it is. Do not be afraid to display and discuss your own sadness.

When children experience the loss of a loved one, they often suffer — as adults do — exhaustion, headaches, episodes of asthma, digestive disturbances, and muscle and joint pains. People under this type of psychological stress of mourning also have less resistance to viral ailments: colds and other respiratory illnesses, gastrointestinal problems. Research has found that bereaved children even suffer a higher rate of ulcers than children who have had surgery for appendicitis — a different, but significant, kind of stress. Children and adolescents may become frightened by such symptoms, fearing that they may be dying as well. You need to acknowledge these fears, while reassuring your youngster that the problem is almost certainly not fatal.

If your child shows symptoms of an illness at this time, call your pediatrician or family physician. Indeed, children and adolescents often spontaneously ask to see their doctor or nurse practitioner for a checkup after a death in the family. Visiting a familiar doctor is reassuring to a child. It indicates that his doctor is still present to take care of him, even though one beloved adult has departed and others may be preoccupied. It is always possible, too, that he does have a significant illness that happened to appear at this sad moment. Phone the doctor before such a visit to let her know your child has suffered the loss of an important person in his life. It also helps a child deal with his feelings about a death to let his school know what has happened. (See "Letting the School Know" below.)

Helping a Dying Child

For parents and pediatricians, nothing is sadder than trying to help a dying child. Watching a young life end feels deeply unfair. This feeling is heightened with each advance in medicine; since researchers have found cures or inoculations for many of the diseases that carried off children in previous centuries, every case that does not respond to treatment is all the more frustrating. Unfortunately for some children, facing premature death becomes part of their life.

Often children diagnosed with a serious

LETTING THE SCHOOL KNOW

After his father died, a high-school boy spoke of feeling bitter about how his classmates had reacted — or did not react: "After all I did for the basketball team, none of the guys or the coach or my teachers ever told me they were sorry about Dad dying."

It is important to notify your child's teacher about the death of a close family member or friend. Children who have experienced such a loss appreciate sympathy from their teacher and classmates. Some children will want the teacher to share this news with the whole class, perhaps on a day when the child is absent if she is feeling especially self-conscious. Others might like the news to be spread without an announcement. Knowing that a student has experienced the death of a loved one also helps a teacher understand why she suddenly seems sad or distracted in class.

Encourage your school-age and adolescent children not to fear talking to friends and classmates who have recently lost someone they love. School-age children tend to be straightforward, even blunt, with their feelings and questions, so such discussions are probably less of a challenge for them than for adolescents. Self-consciousness can tie up an adolescent's tongue in his desperate attempts to avoid saying the wrong thing. A bereaved family is likely to remember not so much what people said, but who took the trouble to say something comforting. So reassure your teenager that it is more important to express sincere sympathy to a friend than to say anything profound or original. Simple statements like: "I was sorry to hear about your Dad," or "I know that must be hard," can ease a grieving classmate.

disease respond positively to the initial treatment. Many return to school. If these children suffer repeated relapses, however, they come to realize that they may not recover after all. Moments of improvement are followed by episodes of feeling worse, and some treatments are uncomfortable or even painful. Children with serious diseases are aware that they may die. They notice when a fellow patient in their hospital ward, perhaps with the same illness, is quietly rolled away. They know when their cycles of relapse and improvement grow shorter. As time passes, many of them sense that they are entering a terminal phase of their illness.

This realization can be much more difficult for parents than for their dying child. A sick child has already confronted the discomforts and frustration of being ill. (See chapter 32.) In acknowledging the likelihood of death, she may be giving up her hopes for the future, but she is not as aware as her parents of all that she will miss. In contrast, when parents realize that medical treatment offers little further hope for their child, they may become depressed and overwhelmed. Unable to safeguard their offspring's life, they may in some way believe that they have failed as parents. They must give up their aspirations for and dreams of their child as an adult. Instead of protecting, nurturing, and teaching her, they are reduced to standing by, feeling helpless. Doctors are equally frustrated when their best treatments are not working; some are much better than others at offering families emotional support at this period.

Often the parents of a child who acknowledges to them that he is dying become very upset. They may stop talking to and listening to him or may even cut short their visits to the hospital. In response, he may avoid discussing what he knows about the course of his disease with his parents, but will talk freely about it with nurses, medical students, social workers, and physicians. Yet hospital professionals cannot offer all the closeness parents can. And in this situation, when there is less time for the family to be together, closeness is even more valuable than usual. If it hurts too much to talk about the course of your child's disease with him, talk about something else. A child would rather have his parents present and silent than not with him at all.

Even when her medical prognosis is poor, you can do many things for your dying child. One of the most helpful is to listen to his wishes about the treatment he wants. Try to ensure his comfort, and consider that trying painful treatments may not make sense eventually. Most important, remember that this is a time to be close to your child. You may well find it difficult to hear him expressing sad feelings about dying, anger, or fear. You may hate to witness what looks like giving up. Nevertheless, you cannot protect your child from these natural emotions; that he can share them with you is a tribute to your successful nurturing of him and your relationship. Reassure and support your child, and be honest about your own feelings. Reminisce about happy times you have had together. Read books, play cards, or watch something on TV that you both enjoy. Show your love.

Doctors who counsel dying patients often report that children approach dying more peacefully than adults do. One twelve-year-old boy, a baseball enthusiast, was nearing the end of his life after a long illness. Noting that his TV set was turned so that he could not see the game being played, his doctor offered to adjust it. The boy answered, "It doesn't matter anymore." He extended his frail hand to the doctor and said softly, "Thanks for everything." He died the same day. Another boy of the same age took off the prized watch his friends had given to him when he became ill and handed it to his younger brother, saying, "I want you to have it." He died a few days later. Many adults would be grateful to depart life so peacefully.

Memories and Grieving

Grieving in childhood and adolescence is, as in adulthood, a long process. It is often episodic: you can unexpectedly feel a surge of sorrow after dreaming about the deceased, coming across his old letters, or even spotting a figure on the street who resembles him. Children and adolescents often break into tears as they remember a dead relative or friend. Rather than crying alone, a child benefits from being able to express these feelings in the presence of caring adults. The urge to weep may especially trouble children who feel they should avoid such displays of emotion — because they are males, or they want to avoid worrying others, or the dead person is supposed to be in "a better place." You may wonder how long children normally mourn before achieving what some people call "closure." Children are as variable in how they grieve as in everything else they do: there is no clear answer — nor does anyone ever "close the book" on deep feelings of loss. On average, it takes about a year for a person to regain full equilibrium after losing a close friend or relation. For some people, the process takes longer. In both cases, one's inner world is never the same.

Losing a Parent

The loss of a father or a mother places a dual burden on the surviving parent. A child will experience sad moments repeatedly, particularly at birthdays, holidays, and special events such as graduation. Seeing other families gather around their children may remind your child of the absence of her own parent. The surviving parent, who may be feeling the same pain, should nonetheless tell a child things like: "Daddy would have been proud of you today." Although the comment may stir up the child emotionally, particularly soon after the death, it will help her to preserve the image of her deceased parent and will foster her healthy development.

Losing a parent during adolescence has unique meaning. It is during adolescence that your child develops a separate, adult identity. This phase of growth is, as parents know well, characterized by bursts of independence as a teenager tries to make his own way in the world. Yet that same adolescent, particularly during a time of physical or psychological stress, may return to a less mature phase, seeking parental care, sympathy, and advice. This comforting option is difficult to achieve after a mother or a father's death: half the team is gone. And the surviving parent is likely to be distraught and perhaps not up to comforting the child. He will miss the particular qualities he had come to expect from the deceased parent. At the very least, he cannot feel the love of both parents as he did when he was younger. (Although a stepparent may eventually provide some of this support, his or her arrival is complicated by the child's attachment to his original parent. (See pages 506–508 for more discussion of remarriage.)

After a death, a teenager may report rela-tively minor symptoms and seek an appointment with her doctor on her own. These health concerns are often a reaction to the very real pain and anguish of mourning, which medical care cannot prevent. Although a physician cannot become a substitute parent, his interest in and long relationship with the teenager will help during this difficult time. But the psychological discomfort of mourning will continue for some time.

Teenagers often ask their doctors whether their symptoms indicate they may have the same disease as the person who died. This is a common concern, particularly in a family where adults have died from cancer or heart disease. Shortly after her grandfather suffered a fatal heart attack, a fifteen-year-old girl complaining of chest pain sought an appointment with the physician who had known her since birth. After the doctor's examination found her completely normal, she commented, "Good! I know there's nothing wrong with me. I wanted to see you and have you listen to my heart and tell me that I did *not* have heart trouble."

A Year Later, and Beyond

Many families recall their sorrow about a death at particular moments: on the anniversaries of the loved one's birth and death or on holidays they would otherwise have spent together. Some follow formal traditions of memorializing the deceased ones. Even if you decide against such rituals, you may well feel sad as these dates approach. One fourteen-year-old girl reported that her mother acted "berserk" each year around the anniversary of her father's death. Children and adolescents experience such emotions just as adults do. It is important to acknowledge these occasions of remembrance. You may tell your young children, "This is a sad day for all of us. We all will be remembering those happy times when Judy was alive and was so much a part of our family." If you are feeling sadness about a person your children are too young to have known, tell them why you are upset so they do not worry about you.

As children grow up, these anniversaries may bring up questions they were not developmentally or psychologically ready to ask before. They may ask about how the person died, or what happened to her spirit, or what was the meaning of some part of the ceremony they remember as mysterious. Children may develop new interest in hearing old stories, looking at family photographs, or visiting a loved one's grave. After learning about genetics in biology class, an older child may ask whether her relatives died of some hereditary disease. Be prepared to help your children deal with their memories and feelings of loss.

Whatever you may choose to do on these significant dates, include your children. On anniversaries, many families visit a grave site and bring flowers or arrange a special service in church or synagogue. Hospice nurses report that many relatives return to the facility on the anniversary of someone's death in order to reestablish a link to the staff or seek mementos, such as drawings or poems, from the final phase of their loved one's life. Sometimes families create new traditions for sig-

nificant days. Some parents present their child with a book or other gift, saying, "I'm sure your grandfather would have wanted you to have this." A relative or a friend of the family may offer to do something special with the child. One friend of a father who died takes the children to the state fair each year, commenting, "I know your dad would have taken you if he were here." Again, this acknowledges the child's love for the deceased and keeps her memory of that person alive.

Even years after a death of a close friend and companion, the loss can bring on depression. You or your child may try to return to normal activities, but be unable to. If members of the family are showing signs of depression — difficulty sleeping, disconcerting dreams, problems in school or work, or trouble leaving home — there are many people you can turn to for advice and support. Your doctor and pediatrician will be able to recognize the signs of clinical depression or perhaps refer you to counseling. You can also discuss your feelings with your minister or rabbi, or a clinical social worker at a family counseling agency or child guidance clinic. (See chapter 33 for more on children's mental health problems.)

As with the other hard chances of life, however, keeping the lines of communication open by answering questions and validating emotions is the most important action you can take to help your child. While you can never protect your children from all the troubling effects of a death, you can comfort and support them as life goes on.

CHAPTER 36

On the Threshold:
The Flowering of Sexuality

Suddenly your twelve-year-old turns surly, moody, and ready to argue about everything from the dinner menu to foreign policy. Or your fifteen-year-old comes home and cheerfully announces that he's gotten a job at the mall and will need a ride there every afternoon. Or, waiting for your child to return from her first date, you anxiously watch the clock tick half an hour past the time you and your spouse told her to return.

Children usually look forward to the developmental stage of adolescence much more than their parents do. Depending on how you remember your own teenage years, you may look forward to revisiting those events with your children, as if going back to the good old times, or you may worry about the impending earthquake. Some parents begin to dread adolescence as early as their toddler or preschooler's first signs of stubborn independence. Others view the changes wistfully as their children lose their childlike faces and bodies and become, almost overnight, beset with adult worries.

You may understand that this is a passage everyone must weather in life, or you may wish to protect your child from the storminess of adolescence as you remember it. Your anxieties may have been influenced by the portrayal of the difficult teenage years that prevailed in the mid-twentieth century. Studies during the 1980s and 1990s have shown, however, that adolescence is by no means a universally troubling time for teens and parents. While a full discussion of adolescence is beyond the scope of this book, we anticipate it here to emphasize how this transition is both about one's coming of age as an adult and about reviewing childhood.

It is also about sex. Indeed, "sex" is the word that parents first think of in association with "adolescent." (Most school-age children say, however, that what they anticipate most about adolescence is "driving.") And sexual awakening is surely central to this transition in a child's life. In this chapter, we provide an overview of adolescence, puberty, and sexual development, along with some guidance on being a parent to a teenager. Your child may want to read this chapter, too, and you can discuss your reactions to it together. It is especially vital that both you and your child understand sexuality. The consequences of unguided or misguided sexual exploration are, as everyone knows, potentially dangerous. Through ignorance or misunderstanding, an adolescent can all too easily run two serious risks: of becoming a parent well before she is psychologically and economically ready and, as a result, hindering her development and perhaps that of her children; or of developing a sexually transmitted disease that could threaten not only his health but even his life.

Remember as you read that — contrary to what some parents and teens like to believe — sex is not an issue just for adolescents. Sex is also crucially important before and after the teen years. (See chapter 14.) Keep in mind as well that in normal sexual development in adolescence, as with many other aspects of growing up, children vary widely in when they feel the onset of certain significant changes and in how they express these feelings.

Defining Adolescence

Until the twentieth century, there was no adolescence. The passage from childhood to adulthood was a single physical event. For boys, this was a puberty rite. For example, a boy took on heavier work in the fields or a regular job, and with that transition, he became a man. A solitary religious event was also capable of changing a boy to a man in a single day. In some cultures, circumcision was the marker that set off young men from older boys, symbolically focusing the passage on a sexual organ. Girls also often became women in a single day — the day of their first menstrual flow. For both sexes, puberty defined adulthood. Today, however, adolescence begins with puberty and is a developmental phase that includes the transition from childhood's relatively complete reliance on parents to adulthood's relatively complete reliance on oneself for managing one's own life. However vague that repetition of "relatively" may be, adolescence cannot be defined more narrowly.

Traditionally, the body changes of puberty denote the onset of adolescence. The end of adolescence is not, however, biological. It is social. Society decides what defines an adult, and this definition varies drastically from country to country and from era to era. Furthermore, adolescence has a psychological or mental dimension defined by how adolescents feel about themselves and their larger bodies, new capacities, greater expectations, and higher status in society. These feelings are greatly influenced by their biological maturity and by social demands. Adolescence is thus most accurately described as a "biopsychosocial developmental stage."

American society defines adulthood by a variety of legal and personal landmarks: an adult can vote, work, drive, marry, have sex, have children, drink alcohol, go to court, go to war, go to college, and do many other activities. The ages at which young people reach these milestones have changed significantly over the years. At the beginning of the twentieth century, many more children worked much of the day, often starting before their teens. Women commonly married and bore children in their teens or early twenties. In recent decades, the legal age for obtaining a driver's license has risen, and the age for buying alcohol has gone up even higher, while the national voting age and, most recently, the age at which a teen can be tried in an adult court have dropped. Some communities and cultures perceive adolescence as arriving earlier or ending later than others do, or define the transition differently for boys and for girls. All these shifts show how difficult it is to draw clear lines around adolescence, especially for a particular individual.

The Arrival of Puberty

Puberty is the name for the biological changes that eventually allow a person to reproduce. It is a landmark on a child's way to adulthood. Although there is great variation in when puberty begins for individuals, it generally begins for girls about two years before boys, typically toward the end of grade school or the beginning of middle or junior high school. A year or so before sexual body changes occur, children experience a spurt in height. Because of this head start into puberty, many eleven- or twelve-year-old girls are, at least for a while, taller than the boys in their classes. Following a child's growth spurt, body hair begins to grow. Hands and feet get bigger. Girls' breasts develop, and boys' genitals grow larger. A boy's voice lowers and his muscle mass increases, and a girl begins menstruation.

A girl's first menstrual period, or menarche, occurs approximately two years following the start of her breast development. Menarche is likely to occur during a girl's twelfth year, but two or three years before or after age twelve can still be considered normal. We know that hereditary factors help determine the age of menarche: for example, girls with African ancestry traditionally go through it earlier than girls with European ancestry. Obesity can speed up the onset of menarche, while vigorous exercise, stress, and malnutrition can delay it. Because of the improved nutrition in this country, menarche on average now occurs more than a year earlier than it did for girls in mid-nineteenth-century America.

An Emotional Storm

Children in early adolescence, typically toward the end of grade school or the beginning of middle or junior high school, work on separating themselves more from their parents and family and on becoming closer to their friends. You may notice changes in hairstyles, clothing, and attitude that stand outside the traditions of your family. You may find this early stage of adolescence bewildering, and so may your child. Each of you may feel at moments as though you don't know who you really are.

To adolescent children, the normal changes in their bodies, thoughts, and behavior may seem abnormal. You may worry about these same events and wonder, too, whether they are normal. Because so many changes take place during early adolescence, your child may appear anxious, vague, or argumentative. Sexual thoughts become more common and explicit at this age. (See "Talking to Your Young Teenager about Sex," pages 530–531.) For both sexes, masturbation begins or becomes more frequent. Although young adolescents may develop strong romantic crushes on an older and unobtainable person — such as a teacher, a movie star, or a high-school senior — for most preteens sexuality remains more mental than physical.

Many children are as dumbfounded as their parents by how enraged they can be at one moment and how happy-go-lucky at another. In early adolescence, many children feel that they are always on the edge of getting out of control; sometimes this is exciting, often it is frightening. A young teen feels that he is no longer on firm ground, that the old rules and understandings don't work anymore, but nothing new seems to have taken their place. He is alive to his parents' inconsistencies and vulnerabilities and sometimes provokes them in an effort to gain or prove his independence. Your child may display a wish to return to his past comforting and predictable relationship with you, but then will quickly seem to drive you away, insisting, "I'm not a baby." Common sentiments in this

period include "I can *so* do it!" and "Everybody else's parents let them do it!" ("It" means going to R-rated movies, wearing certain styles of clothing or makeup, listening to certain kinds of music, and so forth.)

The dreaminess of children of this age can also drive parents and teachers to distraction. Your child is likely to sit staring off into space, "doing nothing," for long stretches of time. She may seem more disorganized, less attentive, and in many ways something of a mess. Not only is a child self-preoccupied and uninterested in obeying family rules or meeting obligations, but his heightened interest in his peers is often manifested in endless telephone conversations. Your child may try to tie up the phone with his friends for hours, sometimes watching television simultaneously.

A mindless, peer-driven, crabby person seems to have replaced the child you thought you knew so well. Your little darling may suddenly seem secretive, uncooperative, even disrespectful. It is easy for parents to attribute this change to the undue influence of peers, television, or pop music — all of these factors, and others, certainly influence children and should be monitored. Nonetheless, your growing child is attempting, through these new ways of being, to find some foothold in what appears to be a shaky universe. He may, indeed, be seeking a way to bypass this whole rough passage and leap into the seemingly firmer world of midadolescence. Young adolescents will sometimes attempt to block their anxiety by masking it with outward certainty. They will uncompromisingly criticize other people or groups, such as parents, homosexuals, disabled people, or adults in general. When confused, an adolescent may think that offense is the best defense. As a couple of years pass and they become more settled in their own bodies, teenagers typically become more calm and forgiving toward others.

Calming Down Again

Midadolescence typically occurs during the early to midteen years. Again, there is wide variation among children in the timing of adolescent development. In a large eighth-grade class, there can be girls who appear to be sexually mature adults and boys who display few, if any, adult sexual characteristics. Fortunately, the biopsychosexual changes slow down during midadolescence, allowing some teens to "catch up" to their peers. More important, this slowing down generally lessens

their "Who am I?" fears. With a somewhat more consolidated and sure sense of "I am me," midadolescents who were formerly shrill in their rebellion can become less harsh. They now feel less need to attack lifestyles — yours or other teens' — that appear different, competitive, or otherwise threatening.

During midadolescence, children's sexual experimentation is likely to move from the mental to the physical realm. This shift brings up the question whether the midadolescent is heterosexual, homosexual, or bisexual. Homosexual experimentation is more common at this age than at any other; it may be less frightening for a child to explore sexual feelings and touching with someone whose body is similar to his or hers than with someone whose body seems foreign.

As a social transition into adulthood, adolescence continues through the late teens and into the early twenties. Generally we agree that the endpoints for adolescence include attaining a steady job or preparing for a career, being able to form a stable and long-term personal and sexual relationship, and separating from parents enough to be able to decide, with good judgment, the course of one's own life. These are ambitious accomplishments that many chronological adults never attain, acting somewhat like adolescents for much or all of their lives. Nonetheless, to be an adult developmentally, a person should at least be aware of the importance of these attainments and strive to accomplish them. It is generally not good for one to grow up too soon, suddenly leaping into adulthood as a parent or full-time worker in one's midteens. Young people still have important developmental tasks to complete as they enter the stream of adult development. In earlier generations, marriage was a common end-mark for adolescence, but now people frequently do not marry until after their midtwenties. Late adolescence in American society, however, requires decisions about whether to continue schooling, get a job, take chances with crime, leave home, have a baby, live with someone romantically, or get married. It is helpful to your child, and will relieve your anxieties, if you can discuss her options together.

Your Child's Sexuality

Around 1900, Sigmund Freud noted that human sexuality does not begin during the teenage years, but is noticeable from the preschool years onward. This declaration shocked much of middle-class society, but not experienced governesses who had noted young children's sex play for years. A younger child's sexuality usually focuses on discovering features of one's own body, occasionally touching the genitals of other children, and daydreams about marrying one's mother, father, or some other close or powerful adult. The surge of gender-specific sex hormones during early puberty, however, brings a definitive change in the quality and quantity of a child's sexual life.

Adolescents' daydreams are more explicit in expressing their sexual impulses. Unlike the toddler or grade-schooler, the pubertal girl or boy is now becoming physically capable of being a sexual partner. Fantasies about parents or older siblings are now frankly incestuous and therefore taboo, to be avoided at all costs. This taboo is influential in initiating the way many young teenage boys avoid, if not scorn, their mother. On the other hand, the father of a sexually developing girl may become more distant emotionally and physically as he adjusts to his daughter's new sexual maturity and seeks to avoid the same incest taboo. An unfortunate side effect of adolescents' emotional withdrawal from their parents is that your child may, at the same time, withdraw from your values. Thus, though this distancing may help your family avoid the incest taboo, it may also separate your child from your moral underpinnings just when her new sexual urges and fantasies are at the greatest intensity and when she most needs that stability.

Another crucial aspect of sexuality concerns whether an individual is heterosexual, bisexual, or homosexual. With so many body changes occurring in early adolescence, children commonly wonder whether they are gay or straight. Society's judgments again influence how these terms are defined. Today most people readily accept "tomboy" girls but many adults have a negative reaction toward boys they perceive as effeminate in looks, interests, or behavior. But, of course, despite the stereotypes, sexuality and gender are different qualities. Effeminate boys will not necessarily become gay, but their peers and perhaps adults are more likely to assume they are and to treat them as such. Adolescents typically explore bisexual behavior more than adults do. The vast majority of adolescents who have same-sex sexual experiences, however, do not continue them as adults. (See also pages 192–195.)

More important than your adolescent's physical features or hobbies or even sexual exploration in determining adult sexual orientation are the nature of his sexual fantasies and earlier childhood play preferences. Adolescents whose sexual fantasies are pretty much exclusively gay are likely to be gay, while those whose fantasies are typically het-

erosexual are likely to become heterosexual adults, regardless of any gay experimentation. A son who, as a younger child, avoided rough-and-tumble play, cross-dressed as a girl, and preferred to play with girls is more likely than another boy to become gay as an adult, but that is not a sure thing. Why people become heterosexual or homosexual is still not known, but seems largely influenced by as-yet-unidentified biological givens. Although heterosexual parents often prefer that their offspring be heterosexual

TALKING TO YOUR YOUNG TEENAGER ABOUT SEX

A healthy, effective dialogue about sexual issues should begin when a young child first has questions. (See pages 189–192.) Trying to start that conversation when your child is already an early adolescent is far more difficult. Teenagers feel uncomfortable about the changes they experience during puberty. And they want to act, at least some of the time, as if they no longer need your advice. Meanwhile, you may now often notice that age has started to affect your own appearance and endurance. All of these factors make it awkward to begin a dialogue about sexuality. If, on the other hand, you have been answering your child's questions

since toddlerhood and, as appropriate to her age, sharing your view of ethical sexuality through your words and behavior, continuing that dialogue will seem natural and relatively easy.

You may have forgotten, or wish to deny, the bewildering intensity of sexual urges that pubertal children experience. You may want to leave your child's sex education to schoolteachers and hope his classmates will fill in the gaps. Both these approaches are a mistake. A young person's sexual ability precedes, sometimes by many years, good sexual judgment. Sex-education classes stress facts and schoolmates stress thrills, but as a parent you have the responsibility to link your moral beliefs to the facts and feelings of sex. Ignorance leads young people to rely on pseudo facts and pseudo feelings, and

these are likely to lead to heartache, pregnancy, infection, or all three. Individuals are always going to make more responsible choices about their lives when they consider those choices from a solid intellectual, emotional, and moral foundation.

Your child's most powerful sex education comes from how you express your own sexuality. Your child absorbs this by witnessing your actions, remarks, jokes, and judgments. Whether you have displayed consideration, affection, tenderness, and constancy; or disrespect, violence, and inconsistency; or a mixture of positive and negative behaviors, that pattern is your child's fundamental sex education.

If you do not have a history of discussing sexual issues with your child, he is not likely to bring up the topic first. If he

like themselves, the gender direction of a child's sexual desire does not lend itself to being easily taught or redirected.

In regard to the surge of sexual impulses, people often speak of "hormones." Although hormones are most important in initiating puberty, studies comparing the number of sexual hormones in adolescents' bodies during midadolescence with their sexual behavior have shown little or no correlation between the two. Thus, an adolescent's aggressive or sexual actions, or lack of action, cannot surely be traced either to "raging hormones" or to "lazy hormones."

The timing of puberty in a child influences how strongly various psychological and social forces also shape her development. There is a broad span of ages during which physical sexual changes begin. Your daughter may begin to develop breasts when she is ten or eleven, for example, while your son's voice may not start to change until his midteens. Psychosocial conventions favor girls who develop relatively late and boys who develop relatively early.

---

does, however, gently inquire about the specific question or area he wishes to discuss. An adolescent usually is looking not to learn everything, but has a particular and (for him) urgent inquiry. For instance, he may want to know what a slang term means in order to decipher his classmates' conversation, but has no wish to know how to perform the act the term refers to. To avoid giving the wrong answer, get the question right. You can say, "I want to be sure I'm answering the question you're interested in." If you reply to your child's initial question in a reasonable manner, it is likely that he will feel comfortable moving on, then or later, to other areas of concern.

If you do not have a history of discussing sex with your child and she does not bring up the topic, get a hold of the sex-education curriculum that her school follows, and use it as a basis for initiating a conversation about sexuality. You should have no trouble discovering areas in the lesson plan that you would like to discuss, emphasize, or question. You can also ask your child how she thinks the teacher is doing and which parts of the course seem easy, wrong, or difficult to understand. If your answers make sense or are helpful, your child will probably come to you on her own the next time or, at least, be receptive if you propose further discussions.

Here are more general tips that might ease the conversation:

• Since you and your child will probably both be nervous, you may ease the awkwardness of your conversation by first commenting on it.

• Listen as well as talk. Discussions work; lectures do not.

• If you do not know an answer, do not fake it. Work together to find an answer.

• Do not make your questions so intrusive that they drive your child away.

• Do not be afraid to set reasonable rules to protect your child. On the other hand, if you had bad sexual experiences as an adolescent, do not let your personal history distort your response to her.

Finally, remember that sexuality is the only force that creates human life. In speaking to your child, you are helping her to take part in that creation in the best way possible.

Most early-developing girls feel awkward about their breasts. Older males may equate a girl's physical development with sexual readiness and make advances to her. Since such a girl is not psychologically ready, these advances may lead her to feel ashamed and to want to hide or downplay her changing body. Early-developing boys, on the other hand, usually revel in their advanced height and body mass. They are picked first for athletic teams and are tall enough to dance with the average-developing-age girls in their grades. A boy who develops later than his classmates may feel shy around girls who seem to be forever taller. He may be picked toward the end of the line for sports teams and as a dance partner. Adults might mistake him for a younger child, an acute embarrassment when emotionally he is striving to become more adult. Fortunately, by the early twenties, the psychosexual advantages and disadvantages of early or late sexual development have usually disappeared.

Dating

Dating is the relatively formal way for males and females to get to know one another romantically. As a practice, it is most ritualized in middle-class social groups. There are customs, even among the most iconoclastic teenagers, about how two people set up a date, what constitutes a normal date, and when a relationship becomes "serious." Paradoxically, dating may actually lengthen the time between when a couple meets and when they engage in real sexual activity. Young people who date are, after all, abiding by some conventional standards. The custom of dating may not, however, lessen the tendency of your son and his male friends to tell each other stories of dates filled with imagined or exaggerated sexual exploits. These conversations make boys feel successful and grown-up. Such talk tends to focus almost exclusively on girls' physical characteristics and sexual availability. While your daughter may talk to her girlfriends about a boy's looks, she is also likely to comment on his personality and attitude toward caring — characteristics seldom mentioned in boy-to-boy sex talk.

Dating in early adolescence is at least as important socially as it is sexually. Whether one is dating and whom one is dating are important and sometimes crucial in determining a teenager's popularity. Writing notes and telephoning are common ways for early teens to ease into actual dating. The phone lets your adolescent negotiate an important task of growing up without ever having to leave your home or — with e-mail or a cell phone — never actually having to meet someone face-to-face. (Seldom after adolescence do most people hope that all telephone calls are for them.) A major reason for the popularity of the telephone or e-mail is that your teen can speak semianonymously, concealing body language (blushing, smiling, erections). E-mail and Internet chat rooms provide even more anonymity, and you may, therefore, want to monitor such online activities. (See pages 364–365.) When young teens get around to dating, they often go out in groups that provide protection for girls who may not want to be approached sexually and for boys who fear they may not be able to perform well sexually.

By the middle teens, however, group outings and double dates may seem immature. A driver's license allows your adolescent greater privacy for sexual intimacies, whether in a place away from home or in the car itself. Kissing and sexual fondling usually precede intercourse, although in surveys a majority of teenagers comment that their first intercourse "just happened." According to Planned Parenthood surveys, one-half of women and two-thirds of men report that their first intercourse occurred before their seventeenth birthday. Often teens say the first time is not enjoyable. One recent survey found that over 80 percent of sexually active teenagers recommended having first intercourse at an age *older* than their own first experience. Although the age of first intercourse in this country dropped precipitately in the 1970s, with the emergence in the 1980s of HIV, teenagers now view the decision whether to have intercourse not as only moral, but also as self-preservative and medical.

Sexual Opportunities and Experiences

Regardless of race, religion, or stage of adolescent development, males are more likely than females of the same age to report that they have begun sexual activity. Unfortunately, neither males nor females show much correlation between attaining the ability to have intercourse and conceive a child with the maturity to care for and raise that child.

Surveys show that the age of onset of sexual experiences is associated with a teen's social and ethnic background. Your family values are the first and foremost influence on the timing of your child's sexual behavior, but religious and neighborhood values are also important. Sometimes biological and social factors coincide. For example, African American children begin puberty earlier than white children, whether Hispanic or non-Hispanic. African American teenagers also tend to report early sex as relatively positive. For a teenager who subscribes to such beliefs, early sexual intercourse will make him feel better about himself, and holding back will lower his self-esteem. As a result of this combination of biological and social factors, African American adolescents have intercourse earlier, on average, than whites do. To a lesser extent, economic factors seem to be also associated with an adolescent's choice about sex: teenagers living in poverty generally have sex earlier. Adolescents from any background who do not view early sex as desirable, or whose self-esteem does not depend on their sexual experience, begin intercourse later.

Early sexual experience is not only a social issue, but is a serious health issue as well. Teens who begin their sexual activity young are much more likely to catch sexually transmitted diseases. For example, the human immunodeficiency virus (HIV) infec-

tion rate for African American adolescent females is almost fifteen times that for non-Hispanic white females of the same age range. Other factors also put young adolescents at particular risk for sexually transmitted diseases. Young adolescents are much less likely than older teens to use condoms. Drinking alcohol and using drugs are associated both with early sexual activity and with not using condoms. Teenagers from lower socioeconomic backgrounds are more likely not only to start sexual activity younger, but also to begin adolescence with poorer health and poorer overall health habits; thus, they are likely to be more vulnerable to any disease.

THE DANGER OF DEPRESSION AND SUICIDE

Depression is relatively common during a child's prepubertal and pubertal periods. For most children, this state is simply a downhearted mood that lasts no longer than one or two days. You should, however, be attuned to the possibility of depressions that are longer and more severe. In addition to such common warning signs as difficulty sleeping, lower spirits, weepiness, and lack of appetite, your child may try to deal with or hide the problem through intensely defiant behavior, in-

creased aggression, and clinging to her peer group. In this phase, professional consultation may be particularly helpful in averting a deepening of the depression.

As we say in chapter 33, depression can be lethal in an adolescent child who may already be having suicidal thoughts. Sometimes depressed adolescents will make a serious suicide attempt, especially if they are using alcohol or drugs and are impulsive. The danger is even more serious, and the attempts more likely to be successful, when an adolescent has access to guns, poison, or other effective means of hurting herself. Guns run far ahead of all the others as the tool for an adolescent's suicide.

Your child's questions about his sexual orientation or prowess can initiate an internal struggle that may bring on or coincide with depression, preventing him from recognizing less drastic ways to resolve the conflict. Especially when a parent is hostile toward homosexuality, a child with such feelings may perceive that he has nowhere safe to turn; he cannot escape his sexual feelings, which for him have developed normally, nor can he feel sure of his parent's love. This is yet another reason for you to understand the range of normal sexual development and to be sure your children know you love them unconditionally.

Finally, pregnancy is a major risk of early and unprotected sexual activity. Having a child forces a teenager to assume adult responsibilities before she or he is able to fulfill them adequately. The teenage parent may have to pass up educational or career opportunities and also risks long-term poverty for his or her family.

Your Duties as a Teenager's Parent

You probably remember your own adolescent sexual awakening with a mix of nostalgia and relief that it is long over — and, thus, feel uneasy as your child enters this period of life. Do not, however, let the attitudes, joys, and anguish you remember become burdens on or expectations for your children. Instead, by modeling healthy sexual behavior and by listening to your teenager's concerns while providing clear expectations for safe and moral conduct, you will help both yourself and your child to weather and learn from the ups and downs of adolescence. You will also be able not only to enjoy your teenager's growth and development in these years, but to look forward to an even closer relationship afterward when you are both adults.

Your influence on your child, especially in respect to sexual behavior, came into play before any of the child-parent tensions of adolescence. Even if you do not believe in "sex education" as something that can be formally taught, your family — whether single parent, couple, or extended group of parental figures — has been a significant model in the tenderness and affection your child has or has not felt growing up with you. How you and your partner act toward one another — whether you respect one another sexually and as separate individuals — is powerful, and its effect only accumulates over the years. Remember the danger of preaching one type of behavior but living another: your teenager will model herself on the behavior she has observed over the years, not on how you tell her to behave now.

You should neither hurry your offspring's sexuality in order to experience vicarious thrills, nor prohibit all romantic activities in a futile effort to protect your child from temptation or exploitation. And between these extremes there are other, more common pitfalls you should avoid. While it is important and proper to know who your children's friends are and where they go together, your adolescent will usually be less inclined to share aspects of his "private" life than he was previously. This is part of his normal adolescent separation from his parents (in a turning of the tables from when you tried to keep your sex life secret from your young child). It is best not to pry into your adolescent's secrets unless you have a sound reason to believe that either a strong moral issue or his health is at stake. Be careful before making a strong negative judgment about your teenager's close friend. At times, expressing disapproval is warranted and necessary, but if you do it too often, your criticism may only enhance that friend's allure.

Finally, you should have rules about how often your adolescent child goes out, how late she stays out, and whether you must meet her dates beforehand. There are, alas, no universal rules for rule making. Your ongoing relationship with your child, her age, her track record for good or bad judgment, and your family's and community's expectations for teenagers are important factors. You and your spouse should discuss together and agree on guidelines before presenting them to your child. Both of you need to value and enforce a rule if your adolescent is to take it seriously. A relatively small number of rules strictly enforced works best. Your teenager should have the opportunity to make a case for modifying any of the rules you present. When her case is convincing, changing one rule will actually improve your child's compliance with all of them. You must make clear to your child that breaking a rule will mean certain consequences for her. Be sure to stick to this promise.

As we said at the opening of this chapter,

JASON: MOVING ON WHILE STILL IN SIGHT OF HOME

Lynn's son, Jason, was getting ready to go to college. August had always been vacation time in her family. From the time Jason was a baby, Lynn and her husband, Frank, had packed up and driven to a beach house that belonged to Lynn's parents. But this summer, for the first time, Jason talked about staying behind, spending one last month with his high-school friends, perhaps moving onto campus as soon as the dorms opened. He ended up deciding to come to the shore as usual. "I can't let you guys go without me," he said sheepishly. But Lynn could still feel the shock of hearing that he might not come.

Every so often Lynn found herself gazing across a room at her son's stubbled cheeks as if she were trying to memorize every feature of his face. Sometimes he would catch her at it, and once or twice had exclaimed, "Mom!" half exasperated, half concerned. She had excused herself with some practical question: "I was wondering, do you need new shoes?" But she knew she had left out the really important words: ". . . for college?" And even as she asked, her mind was filled with the image of Jason when he was five years old and first going off to school.

Lynn and her family set off for the shore on schedule. Jason, having been out late the night before with his buddies, slept in the backseat almost the whole way. "Like the first times," Lynn whispered to her husband.

"He always fell asleep on long trips."

"I don't think you need to whisper," Frank replied with a smile. "We could be driving past a jackhammer, and he wouldn't wake up." But Lynn noticed he was keeping his voice low, too.

In the house, Lynn unexpectedly came across a picture album her mother had assembled. It held Jason's portraits from each year in school and, several pages earlier, photographs of her and her sisters, too. She was leafing through the album when Jason ran downstairs in his bathing suit. "Aren't you coming to the beach?" he called. Looking over her shoulder, he spotted a snapshot of himself at age four, dressed as a clown. "Aw, Mom, don't get all sentimental. I'm not a kid anymore."

"I'll be down in a few minutes," Lynn promised. But she

in many ways, but in a new guise, adolescence involves a replay of your child's early developmental phases. Teenagers leap forward and look backward. You and your adolescent child will revisit many of the developmental issues we have talked about in this book: controlling one's emotions, caring for one's own body, making friends, being independent while maintaining ties to the people one loves, managing sexuality and sexual curiosity, and of course, separating from parents and leaving home. Reviewing and revisiting happens as much for you as for your adolescent son or daughter. And, of course, for you it may be a kind of time-warp trip, where — as for Lynn in "Jason: Moving On While Still in Sight of Home" on pages 536–537 — you replay both your own adolescence and your child's early years.

Thus, development and parenting come full circle, back to where they began. Nearly eighteen years ago, you were imagining your-

---

spent an hour with the picture album before she left for the beach.

As usual on the first night, the family ordered pizza for dinner. But this was the first year that Jason was the one who drove into town to pick it up. When he came back into the kitchen, arms full, his parents cleared the table.

"What's this?" Frank asked, picking up the picture album.

"Don't put that away!" Jason said.

Lynn looked at him. The teenager shrugged, may even have blushed under his late summer tan. "Mom was looking at it," he said, turning away.

After dinner, Lynn sat on the porch with a novel, the album lying beside her on the wicker couch. Jason came outside after washing the dishes. Seeing him glance at her, she picked up the album and opened it at random.

A bit awkwardly, Jason sat beside her and asked, "Who's that you're looking at?"

"This? This is a photo of your grandfather at my college graduation. You know, you're starting to take after him."

"Really?" Jason gazed at the photograph. Lynn tried to imagine him old enough to have a child in college. He did have the same quiet style as his grandfather. "What else is in here?"

Lynn turned to another page and talked about the picture that appeared there. The day when she and Frank had brought their baby home to a little duplex apartment. How Jason had dressed up as a clown for his fourth birthday. He had always come to find her during a thunderstorm, "So you won't be scared," he would explain. Lynn told Jason some things about his growing up that she had never

told him before and some she was sure she had, but he did not seem to mind. The album fell open to one of the early pages, and Lynn saw her own high-school prom picture. They laughed at the dress she was wearing, and Lynn talked about how her sisters had debated which college would be right for each of them.

Memories of that year flooded her mind, and she recognized the mix of feelings Jason must be dealing with — to move on, to figure out his roots, to be on his own, yet not to lose sight of home.

The sun had gone down. Lynn closed the album. "Thanks, Mom," Jason said. "That was cool." He stood up. Lynn thought she saw his eyes shine a little in the twilight as he went inside the house. She wiped away her own tears and followed him.

self as the parent of a child — long before you actually held a baby of your own in your arms. You, too, have grown with your child and are not the same person you were when you first began to imagine being a parent and thinking about your baby. Now that baby is a young adult, a stage when he or she, too, will imagine and perhaps create a family. She is an amalgam of the qualities you imagined and recognize in yourself and others in your family and of traits only she possesses. Even when that child is a parent, you will still from time to time see in him the small child whose development you shepherded for so long. Thus, the circle of your life links with that of your child — as your child's will with his child's — and on and on in a chain that is ever changing, ever the same.

Index